Working From Home

Other Books by Paul and Sarah Edwards

Best Home Businesses for the 90s
Getting Business to Come to You
Making It on Your Own
Making Money with Your Computer at Home

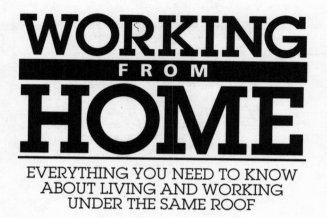

WORKING FROM HOME

EVERYTHING YOU NEED TO KNOW ABOUT LIVING AND WORKING UNDER THE SAME ROOF

PAUL and SARAH EDWARDS

A Jeremy P. Tarcher/Putnam Book
published by
G. P. Putnam's Sons
New York

Most Tarcher/Putnam books are available at special quantity discounts for
bulk purchases for sales promotions, premiums, fund-raising, and educational needs. Special books, or book excerpts, can also be created to fit
specific needs.
For details, write or telephone Special Markets, Putnam Publishing Group,
200 Madison Avenue, New York, NY 10016. (212) 951-8891.

A Jeremy P. Tarcher/Putnam Book
Published by G. P. Putnam's Sons
Publishers Since 1838
200 Madison Avenue
New York, NY 10016

Published simultaneously in Canada

Library of Congress Cataloging-in-Publication Data

Edwards, Paul, date
Working from home : everything you need to know about living and
working under the same roof / Paul and Sarah Edwards.—4th ed.
p.   cm.
Includes bibliographical references and index.
ISBN 0-87477-764-X
1. Home-based businesses.   2. Self-employed.   I. Edwards, Sarah
(Sarah A.)   II. Title
HD62.5.E39   1994   94-10999 CIP
658'.041—dc20

Cover design by Susan Shankin

Design by Robert Tinnon
Illustrations by Mike Cressy and Martin Elkost

Printed in the United States of America

9 10

Fourth Edition

C O N T E N T S
....

INTRODUCTION
■■■■■■■■■■■■■■■■■■■■■■■■■■■■■

This book is about living life to its fullest. It's about having your cake and eating it too, about having the best of all possible worlds.

It's a book for everyone who's tired of the daily commute and the pressures of the nine-to-five routine. It's for everyone who dreams of economic security, more free time, a healthier or more productive lifestyle, and a chance to be closer to family and friends. It's for people who want to take charge of their day-to-day lives and their futures.

This book took root at a time in our lives when our days were full and exciting. Paul was a chief executive officer for a corporation. Sarah was an administrator for a government agency. We both spent too many hours flying across the country, keeping tight schedules, and waving goodbye to each other in airports. We were smoking too much, sleeping too little, and leading the ulcer-prone lives that have come to characterize what our society calls success.

Sarah

In the late 1960s I didn't feel I had many choices as a working mother. Juggling a successful career and motherhood meant being dead tired most of the time and not being able to do either job with the dedication I wanted. I was determined, however, to have both a career and a family, so I did my best in a difficult situation.

Then, one day in the early 1970s, I visited the home of two consultants I worked with. They were doing what, at the time, seemed an unusual thing: operating their business from home. I took one look at their arrangement and knew with certainty, "This is for me!"

My parents grew up during the Great Depression, so I had been raised to think that nothing in the world was better than the security of a government job. Still, two years, one master's degree, and a first-time-ever home mortgage later, I left my secure government position and opened a psychotherapy practice in our new house.

Most people I knew predicted I would miss the benefits of a government career and regret my decision. But they were wrong. I haven't regretted my decision for one day in the sixteen years since I left the hallowed gray halls of the Federal Building.

Working at home was like having flowers delivered to me every day. I felt healthier immediately. For the first time in my son's young life, I could be a real mother and still pursue my career. I was more relaxed, and I relished working in an environment with windows and trees and the out-of-doors just a few steps away.

Paul

Initially I was hesitant about working from home. I had concerns about the image it might create and worried that I wouldn't get my work done. So when I started my own consulting firm, I opened a downtown office and hired a secretary.

I found I'd start working at home in the morning and go into the office later and later in the day. Many days I'd see no reason to drive in at all. Eventually I closed that downtown office and set up a work space in our basement recreation room for my secretary. At first she was a bit uncomfortable with the idea of working in someone's home. But after thinking about it, she decided it was a wonderful opportunity. She could work within two miles of her own house and be closer to her children.

To me, working at home meant having all my files and books in one place. It meant saving a lot of time that used to be wasted commuting and a great deal of money that used to be spent in overhead. It meant being free to put those resources into making my home as pleasant as I wanted it to be. After all, I was working there! Most important, the saving on overhead has meant I can afford to pursue the kind of work I want to do instead of taking business just to pay the overhead.

A Joint Effort

When we were first married, we were both in college and spent most of every day together. On graduating, we discovered that "growing up" and going out into the world meant seeing very little of the ones we loved. How nice to find there's another way! We've been working from home for sixteen years and we see more of each other than ever before.

When we first began working from home it seemed somewhat unusual to our friends and neighbors. But soon the novelty aroused curiosity. People asked us many questions about how we did it and how they might do it too.

As the tempo of the questions intensified, curiosity about working from home has turned into a major social trend. Through this book, our column in *Home Office Computing* magazine, our radio shows, tapes, seminars and speeches, and The Working From Home Forum on the CompuServe Information Service, we've been able to reach hundreds of thousands of people from all over the country with our message: working from home is a good life, and you can do it too.

A Reference Book for People Working from Home

With this in mind we've created a reference book to help you at every stage of working from home—from the time you first begin considering it to the day you wonder if maybe you're outgrowing your home office. It's intended as a basic reference you can turn to any time a question arises or a problem develops.

If you're trying to decide whether working at home is for you, Part 1 should be helpful. In it we address the questions of who's doing it and why, what work is being done at home, the benefits and problems you can anticipate, and how you can tell whether it will be difficult or easy for you. If you think you'd like to work at home but need to figure out how you can earn a living doing it, you will find that in Part 1 we also provide concrete ideas for setting up your own home business or finding a job that enables you to work at home.

If you already know what you're going to do and are ready to set up your work at home, or if you are already in business from home, turn to Part 2. In it we give detailed suggestions about where to put your office, how to keep your work and personal life separate, what equipment you'll need, and how to arrange the most efficient work space.

Another aspect of getting under way, but one we find many new or established home business people also need guidance on, is protecting yourself from legal regulators, tax authorities, and calamities. So in Part 3, we cover legal issues, tax matters, and insurance.

With the ever-increasing amount of paper in our lives and demands on our time, working efficiently and keeping clear of all kinds of clutter are challenges. In Part 4 we provide specific guidelines for such practical matters as managing your time, your money, and your paperwork.

Dealing with people and personnel is the subject of Part 5. Since you'll be your sole supervisor, solutions are given for problems like loneliness and staying out of the refrigerator. You'll discover strategies for dealing with children and family, and making sure your marriage survives. You'll also learn how to find employees and support services.

For home business people, pricing your services and finding customers or clients are important issues. That, together with what you can do if you find yourself outgrowing your home office and want to retain the benefits of working from home while you expand or move up the professional ladder, are covered in Part 6.

You'll find some of the topics we cover, such as interior design, time management, and computer technology, have been the subject of entire books that go beyond the scope of issues directly related to working from home. Throughout the book, we make mention of such resources and have included a Resource List at the end of each chapter so you can read further about those areas you would like to know more about.

Working *From* Home

You'll notice that our book is called **Working *From* Home**—not working *at* home. We chose to use the preposition *from* for two important reasons.

First, because "from" embraces not only those whose workplace is their home but also those for whom home is mainly a base of operations because much of their work is performed on others' premises. For example, home-based salespeople, contractors, consultants, and trainers do most of their actual work away from home.

The second reason we chose this broader definition is to communicate the importance of going out and reaching out to get business, of participating in the broader professional and business community. Having your office in your home doesn't mean withdrawing from life. On the contrary, it's a way to become more involved in living because you're in charge of your life, released from the fatigue of being trapped for hours in a car or bus. Freed of the limits placed on your entrepreneurial spirit by traditional office structures, you become the creator of each and every day of your work life, shaping it instead of reacting to it. You can have a fuller sense of being your own person.

Sometimes we look at the days in our lives and marvel that we are living them. They are rich and varied and always full. For many years they were brightened by the sound of our son's feet as he ran in the door after school around four o'clock. Some afternoons were punctuated with a family trip to watch him play soccer. Last year he graduated from college and we're thankful our working lives were flexible enough to let us enjoy his growing up.

For us, that flexibility and variety is what makes life interesting and keeps us feeling young and vital. Yesterday was a typical day. We got up at 6:15 A.M. for a telephone interview on a radio show in Abilene, Texas. After the interview, we made long-distance calls to the East Coast, read the paper, fed and exercised the dogs, and then headed off for a half-hour bike ride.

We had breakfast, got dressed and, at 9:00, Paul began making myriad phone calls while Sarah began planning an upcoming speech. We had lunch together and drove over to the outdoor farmer's market held each Wednesday here in Santa Monica to get in our produce for the week. We also dropped off the outgoing mail, made a bank deposit, and picked up some printing.

For Paul the rest of the afternoon was filled with rewriting segments of this book and responding to incoming calls. Sarah met with a client about setting up his home-based business, and taped an interview with an author for an upcoming radio show. Later, she edited that tape and wrote an introduction for it.

Because work ran into the evening, we went out for a dinner of what we call Westside soul food—sushi. Later we watched television, read, answered electronic mail, and got ready for bed. We were tired, but content. The day hadn't been perfect; there had been the ordinary mishaps. Answering the messages on CompuServe had taken longer than expected. Sarah hadn't finished as much of the speech as she'd wanted to. Paul couldn't find something he'd been looking for in the files. Still, the day was a good one. It ended with the satisfied feeling that comes from thinking about what you've accomplished, along with a twinge of excitement about all the next morning might bring.

Our goal in *Working From Home* is to have you feel like this too when the day is done. Whatever your ideal workday would be like, this book is designed to help you create it.

PART 1

∙∙∙∙∙∙∙∙∙∙∙∙∙∙∙∙∙∙∙∙∙∙∙∙∙∙∙∙∙

New Freedom, New Choices:
Living and Working under One Roof

CHAPTER
ONE

■■■■■■■■■■■■■■■■■■■■■■■■■■■■

Putting an End to Nine-to-Five

For most of us, going to work from nine to five, or a version thereof, has been the story of our lives. For some, it's no longer a very satisfying way to live. For others, like the handicapped, the elderly, or parents with small children, working away from home isn't always feasible. But until recently there haven't been many other choices.

Since the early 1980s, people have begun to explore new options for living and working. Today we can say goodbye to the daily commute, the dead-end job, the office politics, and the feeling that everyone else is in charge of our lives. Today we can work from home and shorten our commutes to a minute or less.

Your workday can begin with a brisk walk from the breakfast table to the den. The extra time you save every day by not commuting to work can be used doing whatever you want—sleeping late, jogging, taking care of your children, gardening, or getting a head start on the job that needs to be done. Think of it. Even if you only have a twenty-minute commute each way, working from home is like getting an additional four-week vacation every year.

Interested? You're not alone. According to repeated surveys, one in three American workers would prefer to earn their livelihoods at home. Today many of them have the choice, and more and more are exercising the option. Growing from six million home offices reported in the October 27, 1980, issue of *Business Week*, nearly 32 million people were found to be working from home in Link Resources' annual 1993 National Work-at-Home survey. That's more people than live in either California or Canada. By the end of the 90s, perhaps as many as one of every two workers will be engaged in a full-time or part-time home-based business or doing salaried work at home during normal working hours.

The New Dreams

Although our society has made strides in material well-being in the past fifty years, the fast pace of the modern industrial world has not been kind to our personal lives. Work life and personal life have generally become two isolated worlds, separated in time and space by the daily commute.

Often people have to struggle to squeeze in a little "quality time" by themselves or with their loved ones—catching a few free moments between the late shuttle and the eleven o'clock news, between the extra load of laundry and the early-morning meeting. Divorce rates have soared. Stress-related illnesses like high blood pressure, chronic headaches, back pain, alcoholism, drug abuse, heart disease, and even cancer are taking a heavy toll. In short, many workers need a change.

From this perspective, working from home holds the promise of a new American dream, opening the door to a better way of life while maintaining or even expanding our standard of living. Of course there are problems and adjustments to contend with, but in most cases they're outweighed by basic advantages.

We call today's home-based people "open-collar workers" because the comfort of being able to dress casually symbolizes the freedom, the convenience, and the flexibility of earning your living in your own home. This is in contrast to a Robert Half International survey that showed the vast majority of business establishments expect male employees to show up wearing neckties. Women's equivalents to neckties are, of course, high heels. Today's new open-collar workers, however, often can wear what we've been tempted to designate as the official work-from-home uniform—sweat suits, athletic shoes, and jeans.

Options for Earning a Living at Home

Working from home is actually not a modern invention. In the Middle Ages and Renaissance, European merchants located their shops and artisans their work areas on the main floors of their homes. Family living was done in a single shared room upstairs.

The mixture of work and home migrated to America. Paul Revere, like many of his time, did his silversmithing in the front of his home in Boston. You can see that on the Freedom Trail today. Some of you may have had grandparents who operated mom-and-pop businesses, living either upstairs or in the back of their store.

In the late 1800s, however, the Industrial Revolution's demand for workers drew people from their homes and farms to staff factories and offices. The advent of the automobile helped make work at home unfashionable except for writers, artists, and some salespeople. However, history has a way of repeating itself. So by 1980 when we began writing *Working From Home*, Alvin Toffler was predicting in his book *The Third Wave* an upsurge in what he called "electronic cottagers," people who would be working from home in a computerized information age. And indeed, today's information-centered society has opened many opportunities for people to work at home, with or without a computer.

After-Hours Work

The largest number of people with home offices are being called after-hours workers because these corporate employees bring their work home after normal working hours. It's no wonder their numbers are swelling. A recent *Fortune* magazine poll of five hundred chief executive officers revealed that the majority expects their subordinates to put in more hours than they did ten years ago. Fifty- and sixty-hour weeks are common. The result is legions of overstressed survivors of downsized corporations are thinking about another way of living and working.

Once someone starts taking work home and has set up a working office, it becomes tempting to spend more and more time there. So we find after-hours work often leads to taking office work home during the daylight hours as well, and, even more frequently, it leads to a growing number of sideline home businesses.

Ken Camp, a systems consultant for AT&T, is an example of this process. He began taking after-hours work home when AT&T offered substantial discounts on personal computers to its employees. He bought a computer and found he could leave the office around 5:00 P.M., have dinner with his family, and put in a couple of hours of work before his favorite prime-time television shows. He found he had fewer interruptions at home than at the office, so eventually he talked his supervisor into letting him work from home two days a week.

Before long he began moonlighting. For the past two years he has made a modest profit from a part-time consulting business helping small businesses on office automation. He envisions that one day he'll leave his job and run his consulting business full-time.

Working a Salaried Job at Home

Nearly eight million employees now work at home during normal business hours, according to Link Resources. This fastest-growing part of the working-from-home population is made up of salaried workers, called "telecommuters" or "teleworkers," who spend some portion of every workweek at home. This has many advantages for both employees and employers.

Jane Minogue, a technical writer for CompuCorp, is such a person. She began telecommuting when she was expecting her first child. "I didn't want the stress of driving to and from work every day while I was pregnant, and I wanted to be with my baby after he was born. My boss didn't want to lose me, so when I suggested working at home, he said okay."

Like many telecommuters, Jane works at home most of each week, at the office for the remainder.

You don't have to use a computer or work in a high-tech field, however, to work a job at home. "Low-tech" organizations are using the new work options as well. Pet Organics, which manufactures and distributes natural health products for pets, is entirely home-based. Founder Bob Baxter runs the company from his home, and his six sales representatives work from their homes too. "It's the most practical solution economically," Bob says. "Some of my people work full-time, others work part-time. Why pay for an office when you can just as easily get the job done from home?"

The future is bright for more such opportunities. The number of tele-commuters or teleworkers grew by one million people from 1992 to 1993, reflecting an annual rate of increase of over 18 percent over the past three years. In chapter 4, "Working for Someone Else," we describe the best routes for taking your job home or, alternatively, finding a new job that lets you work from home.

Full- and Part-Time Home Businesses

The research firm of BIS Strategy Decisions finds that 23 million of America's 96 million households—nearly 25 percent—now have income-producing home offices. That number is growing too. You may be surprised to learn that 8,493 new home businesses begin every day—that's one every ten seconds! How many new home businesses have begun somewhere since you began reading this book? Equally important, three out of four will still be in business five years from now.

Home-based business owners refer to themselves in a variety of ways: as small businesses, home businesses, self-employed, independent contractors, entrepreneurs, freelancers, or consultants.

Bill Spees of South Bend, Indiana, and Nancy and Mark Porter of Los Angeles are examples of this growing trend to strike out on your own.

A licensed professional engineer, Spees and four colleagues created Legendary Systems, Inc., a successful engineering consulting firm. "We started this business after we were forced into early retirement by the recent economic unpleasantness. Except when we're traveling to consult on site with clients, we all work at home," he reports.

The Porters' business, the Susquehanna Hat Company, imports Chinese sun hats. Nancy transforms the hats into brightly colored designer sunwear by dying them in her bathtub. Then she and Mark market them to department stores all over the country. Nancy sees this as just the beginning. "I was a starving artist struggling to feed two kids when I started this company," she says. "Now I'm doing so well, I plan to start manufacturing a second product, a rain hat."

In chapter 3, "Working for Yourself," you'll meet others like Bill, and Nancy and Mark, who have started their own businesses. You'll find out how they developed the ideas for their businesses and what they do to keep them going and growing.

Why It's Possible Now

If you're already working from home or seriously thinking about it, you're definitely in the right place at the right time. That much is clear. But, you may be wondering, What happened? Why, all of a sudden, are there so many opportunities to work at home? Several factors account for the new options and suggest that working from home is not only here to stay, it's the wave of the future.

Restructuring of the Economy

The United States has changed from a society based on an industrial economy to one based on an information and service economy. By 1980, over half of U.S. workers held information- and service-related positions, employed as bank tellers, clerks, librarians, systems analysts, programmers, accountants, lawyers, therapists, managers, secretaries, doctors, nurses, journalists, trainers, salespersons, or advertising and public relations specialists. With the proper equipment, much of their work is done as easily in a spare bedroom as in an office.

This transformation has brought about significant changes in the way we work. Increasingly, well-educated managers and professionals seeking to climb the corporate pyramid have found mid-level positions disappearing as the corporate hierarchy begins looking less like a pyramid and more like a pancake.

Many find not only no upward mobility but also no opportunity to stay put. White-collar workers are being made jobless at about the same rate as blue-collar workers. Most people know formerly high-paid managers and technical and professional workers let go from companies with whom they thought they had secure futures. Many of this number are unable to replace their old jobs with work at equivalent pay or stature. Some settle for very significantly lower wages. Still others have no luck at all and report sending out hundreds of résumés. One frustrated job searcher reported he was told everything—that he was too old, too young, too technical, too general, too specialized, in the wrong industry, obsolete, too focused, had too-diverse a background, from too small a company, from too big a company, and on and on.

While the *Fortune* 500 companies have laid off 4.4 million workers since 1980, all companies with more than 20 employees have been reducing the number of people they employ. In the early 80s *Fortune* 500 companies accounted for more than 20 percent of the workforce; today just 10.9 percent work for the *Fortune* 500. In 1993, the paring of people took place at the rate of 2,200 jobs a day and appears to be continuing. Further, workers are not being *laid off* today. In prior economic downturns, 44 percent of workers were expected to return to their old jobs; today only 15 percent are temporary layoffs.

Industrial and clerical workers are also feeling the squeeze. In the 1980s, over ten million factory workers lost their jobs. Only three out of five of them found other work. Given frequent plant closings, layoffs, and automation, the specter of unemployment looms over many heads. Workers who are repeatedly downsized, reorganized, purged, and merged are eager to find ways to take control of their careers.

As a result, starting a part- or full-time home business, or having a spouse start one, begins to look very attractive. And while economic restructuring is causing problems of dislocation and dissatisfaction, it's also creating the solutions. As industries consolidate into a few large corporations on the one hand and splinter into a multitude of smaller companies on the other, the mass market is narrowing into definable niche markets that can be easily served by small companies and even by self-employed individuals. One result is that one out of three new businesses today is started at home.

Geologist Thomas Ballard was working for the Burlington Northern Railroad in Northglenn, Colorado, when the minerals industry took a downturn. Suddenly he had to fend for himself. Having what he calls a prospector's spirit, Ballard decided to stay in the mining business by creating a limited partnership that acquires properties and then leases them to large mining companies.

Lila Hexner was a manager for Northern Energy Corporation in Cambridge, Massachusetts, when the company's business outlook turned sour. She decided to explore an idea she had. Using the managerial skills she'd acquired, she began lining up experts in many fields and assembling a computer database of their names. She then approached corporations she thought would be interested in using their services and The Consulting Exchange was born. She's been in her home business seven years and earns over $50,000 a year.

Landscaping architect C. Thomas Fitzwilliam has a similar story. He was working for a large landscaping company that went under when the Texas economy took a downturn. He had always wanted to have his own business and being out of work provided the impetus to start. He now operates Fitzwilliam Landscaping and Irrigation from his home in Arlington, Texas.

Changing Demographics

As the bulk of today's population is entering its thirties and forties, these babyboomers have reached the age when people seek autonomy and promotion to higher levels of responsibility. But with American corporations cutting back and flattening out, advancement opportunities are shrinking. So achievement-minded babyboomers are striking out into their own business ventures.

Harry Brawley had been an electrical engineer for twenty-five years when he decided his future could be brighter if he were on his own. His eight-year-old home-based company, Sigea Systems, produces software that automates electronic mail.

As Don Crescimanno neared forty, he began to feel tied down by corporate life. So he left it behind to start a clearinghouse that informs subscribers about upcoming events in Honolulu.

Like many women, market researcher Elizabeth Donovan bumped into the corporate "glass ceiling" in her early thirties. When she asked for a raise she was told she was earning enough for a woman of her age. At the encouragement of her accountant, she left her job to start her own market research firm. Over the past seven years she's turned her home-based business into a $600,000-a-year income working all by herself.

We also believe the generation following the boomers, now being called the "X," "13er," and "lost" generation, can be anticipated to contribute to the home business landscape. Historically this type of generation has had a strong entrepreneurial talent, producing people like Andrew Carnegie, John D. Rockefeller, J. P. Morgan, Levi Strauss, and Dale Carnegie and innovations like cafeterias, chain letters, comic books, frozen foods, plastics factories, shopping centers, and supermarkets. Today's milieu is computers and communications media—businesses that can be developed at home.

Sophisticated Information Technology

The availability and ever-decreasing cost of compact electronic office equipment in the form of computers and high-speed communications have made it possible to conduct business as easily from home as anywhere. When we began working from home, the most advanced equipment suitable for a home office was an IBM Selectric typewriter and an answering machine that half the callers hung up on. Since that time, personal computers, modems, fax machines, laser printers, and briefcase-sized copy machines make working from home as productive, efficient, and competitive as it is in any office. Many companies like AT&T, Avery Brother, Canon, Fuji, Herman Miller, IBM, Leading Edge, Panasonic, and Smith Corona are designing products specifically for home offices. It's hard to walk into an electronics store or mass merchandiser that doesn't have a home-office section.

People can literally live anywhere and transact their business in style.

The owner of a skip-tracing agency does business from his home in the Virgin Islands, communicating daily by computer with his main office in Washington, D.C.

Steven Roberts, inventor, author, and computer specialist, has made his home on an "electronic bicycle." He bicycles across the country with two computers he uses to write and transmit his work to book and magazine publishers.

Thanks to a computer, Rohn Engh left the hassles of life in a large metropolitan area. Behind his barn in rural Osceola, Wisconsin, he now publishes *Photoletter,* an electronic newsletter that pairs photographers with photo editors of magazines and other publications. The personal computer creates hundreds of business opportunities like Engh's that can easily be started and operated at home. With small computers, home businesses like these have many of the capabilities once reserved only for organizations with many employees or large mainframe computers.

Larry Nickel, director of data processing for a publishing company, offers an example of how a computer can give birth to a home business. He says, "I started writing programs for myself for fun, but then someone at a computer club offered to hire me to help write a program. I did the job, and when I wanted to get a more powerful computer I decided I could make it pay for itself." He started moonlighting at home by creating N2 Data Serv, a company providing data-processing services. His wife, Nancy, saw potential for a full-scale operation and quit her job in real estate to manage the company. They now have their new computer *and* what has become a thriving home business.

The computer and improving communications technology also offer job and business opportunities to those who cannot work outside the home because of physical or family limitations. Georgia Griffith, who is blind and deaf, uses her computer and a machine that prints computer Braille to work from her home in Lancaster, Ohio, as a music proofreader for the Library of Congress. Doing word processing for American Express, through the company's Project Homebound in New York, Joseph Wynn is able to make more than three times the money he received from Social Security disability. In tiny Reardan, Washington, Bruce Johnson produces computer graphics at home on his Apple computer. Confined to a wheelchair by a high school football injury, he finds this a feasible and satisfying way for him to work.

Workforce Trends

Another result of corporate mergers and downsizing is an increasing demand for part-time or freelance consultants, researchers, and designers. This demand has created a new category of employees collectively referred to as the "contingent workforce."

Loosely defined, the contingent workforce includes part-timers, independent contractors, freelancers, leased employees, temporary workers, business services employees, and the self-employed. Contingent workers have grown from 20 percent of the workforce in the early eighties to 25 percent today. Charles Handy, author of *The Age of Unreason*, states contingent workers comprise 50 percent of the British workforce. The U.S. is following behind and Manpower, Inc., is now the nation's largest employer.

For some like Wendy Perkins, author of *Temporarily Yours*, "temping" has become a way of life, and a route to self-sufficiency. Wendy, who left her job as a stockbroker to seek greater self-expression, considers herself to be an independent contractor and has worked for over two hundred and fifty companies.

Beleaguered by the high cost of doing business, some corporations have actively helped the entrepreneurial exodus along. Rank Xerox, a London-based subsidiary of the Xerox Corporation, and Connecticut Mutual Life Insurance Company have developed programs to encourage middle managers in areas such as purchasing, personnel, and planning to quit their jobs and sign on as part-time outside contractors. A number of occupations such as medical transcription, instructional design, and notereader/scopist work are becoming largely cottage industries.

New Pressures/New Values

With growing numbers of two-career couples, singles, and single-parent families, both men and women are feeling the pressure of having to juggle many conflicting demands on their personal and professional lives. Almost a third of Americans say they feel rushed and two-thirds suffer from frequent stress. Many burn out on their jobs and on their lifestyles. And it's no wonder. Even weekends seem to be shrinking as job responsibilities, errands, and housekeeping all get squeezed into the two days that were once reserved for recreation and relaxation.

As a result of these pressures, people are looking for greater control over their time and more flexible work arrangements. Nearly eight out of ten American men and women would sacrifice rapid career advancement in order to spend more time with their families. A recent survey reported in *USA Today* showed that the love of one's family has become the value Americans cherish most. So they're opting for home and hearth—family, health, and personal satisfaction.

Today's workers are also looking for new rewards from their work. They want more meaningful, satisfying work and they want to work with people they respect. These priorities have come to matter more than money or opportunities to advance.

In search of a more rewarding lifestyle, increasing numbers of people are determined to become their own boss or to work more independently. Repeatedly as we travel across the country, we hear people saying things like: "I've been told 'It's none of your business' so often that I've decided to start my own business." Or "I want to set my own hours and keep what I earn for myself. I'm tired of the rat race. I'm fed up with nine-to-five." Or "I want to succeed and excel in whatever I do. I want to work for myself even if it kills me. I am determined to work to live, not live to work!"

Gil Gordon's experience is not uncommon. After nine years, he left his position as a personnel manager to start his own management consulting firm; he had become disillusioned with corporate life. "The jobs I could be promoted to didn't look that attractive. They all involved managing rather than doing. Now I'm not working any less, but my attitude is different. I'm happy. The biggest satisfaction is knowing I'm doing something important."

New Locations

Middle-class Americans are choosing to leave the crowded urban centers and suburbs, particularly those on the coasts, and make new lives for themselves in small towns and rural areas. This has given rise to books and consultancies to help people relocate. We find in traveling to places like Salt Lake and Boise new vitality brought about by newcomers who take their skills and their expectations for culture and conveniences with them. In smaller towns in which there are few industries and fewer jobs, they must also bring their means for earning a livelihood. In chapter 3, we describe some ways newcomers are creating livelihoods in small towns and rural areas.

Working from home holds the promise for having it all—meaningful work and more time to be with family and loved ones. The potential rewards are great, but what is it really like and would it be right for you? In the next chapter, we'll explore these issues and suggest ways to prepare yourself to work successfully from home.

Resources

Books

The Age of Unreason. Charles Handy. Boston: Harvard Business School Press, 1989.

Career Shifting. William A. Charland. Holbrook, Mass.: Bob Adams, Inc., 1993.

Country Bound! Marilyn and Tom Ross. Buena Vista, Colo.: Communications Creativity, 1992.

FutureScope. Joe Cappo. Chicago: Dearborn Financial Publishing, Inc., 1989.

Generations: The Future of America's Future 1584 to 2069. William Strauss and Neil Howe. New York: Morrow, 1991.

Greener Pastures Gazette, a quarterly newsletter, Greener Pastures Institute, P.O. Box 2190, Pahrump, NV 89041; (702) 382-4847 or (800) 688-6352.

Ideas and Information: Managing in a High Tech World. Arnold Penzias. New York: Simon & Schuster, 1989.

Information Payoff: The Transformation of Work in the Electronic Age. Paul A. Strassman. New York: The Free Press, 1985.

Managing the Future. Robert B. Tucker. New York: Putnam, 1991.

Megatrends 2000: Ten New Directions for the 1990s. John Naisbitt. New York: William Morrow and Company, 1990.

Penturbia. Jack Lessinger. Seattle: Socio-Economics, Inc., 1991. The author identifies emerging counties as part of an overall population shift in the United States.

The Popcorn Report. Faith Popcorn. New York: Doubleday Currency, 1991.

2020 Vision, Transform Your Business Today to Succeed in Tomorrow's Economy. Stan Davis and Bill Davidson. New York: Simon & Schuster, 1991.

The Virtual Corporation, Structuring and Revitalizing the Corporation in the 21st Century. William H. Davidow and Michael S. Malone. New York: Harper Business, 1992.

CHAPTER
TWO

■■■■■■■■■■■■■■■■■■■■■■■■■■■■■

Is Working from Home
for You?

"It's the only way to go! I'd never go back!" That's the spontaneous reaction many have to working from home. But others can't wait to get back; they miss the office. Are such different reactions surprising? Hardly. We've all been groomed to work in an office setting, from the first day we started school. You got up, got dressed, ate breakfast, and went to class. You sat at a desk all day long and worked at various tasks and projects with others around you. When the bell rang you packed up your things and went home. Without the bell, this description could fit any day at the office.

When you venture into working from home, these familiar routines go the way of the coal chute and the hitching post. You get up in the morning, and you don't have to be anywhere. Do you get dressed? When do you start working? Do you work at your desk or on the couch? There may be no one there but you, unless your kids pop in or a neighbor drops by, and then what do you do? In every case, it's up to you. No wonder people have such diverse reactions! The whole experience is different from everything we're used to.

Some people flourish with the freedom from old structures, and other people flounder. Some handle the change matter-of-factly, while others find it profoundly upsetting. Tina Lenert took to working from home like a fish returned to water. "I loved it from the moment I started. I never missed my old job for a minute. And honestly, I can't think of any real problems I've had working here."

Reporter Duane Tompkins's experience was quite different. "When the

17

editor told us we could work from home and send in our copy by computer, I was excited. It sounded great. But it wasn't what I expected. I became disillusioned right away. I missed the hustle and bustle of the pressroom and everyone being up against the deadline together. Without anyone else around I found myself goofing off, and I was always at the refrigerator. I think I gained twenty pounds before I finally decided to move back downtown."

Carlin Stevenson had a similar experience when she left a real estate agency to create her own company at home. Her reaction was different, however. "I didn't want to go back. I really wanted to work at home. I just hung in there. It was a difficult year, but after a while I made the adjustment. Now I have many professional friends, and I certainly have accomplished more than I would have staying where I was. I had to learn a whole new way of operating, though, and it took some time."

What You Can Expect

For those with creative business minds, working from home can be the ticket to realizing their potential. For single parents and many women, working at home facilitates juggling family and career. For fathers, it can lead to more time and involvement with their children. For others, it's a step toward goals like gaining financial independence, or moving to a rural area, or simply escaping from the exhaust fumes, crowded trains, and crime-filled streets that bedevil the urban commuter.

Working from home can provide the means for stretching a tight budget or maintaining an accustomed lifestyle in the face of inflation. Couples who have invested time, energy, and money in building meaningful relationships find that when they work from home they see more of each other. For the retired, or the increasing number of people considering early retirement, working from home becomes a way of contributing, of staying alive and vibrant. And for many with handicaps or disabilities, it's the door to self-sufficiency and a productive future.

Working from home can be the answer to many dreams. But what can you really expect? What are the actual benefits you may enjoy and what problems might you encounter?

Most People Love It

While working from home is not for everyone, most people doing it are quick to recommend their lifestyles. Tom Miller of Link Resources, who has been conducting the National Work-at-Home survey for years, finds that about one out of five people has a "complaint"; the rest are happy. *Home Office Computing* readers are even happier. Of 4,200 readers responding to a 1992 survey, 96 percent said they would recommend working from home to others, and 98 percent of the home-based business owners said they were happier at home than in a corporate office.

After giving a speech in Washington, D.C., we met a woman in the audience who does data entry at home. She told us enthusiastically, "It's the best thing that ever happened in my life." A man in the same audience piped in that after being self-employed for several years, "I'm unfit for employment now. I could never work for someone else again." These comments form a familiar refrain.

You Have Greater Freedom, Flexibility, and Control

When we ask people what they like about working from home, over and over again they tell us it's the freedom. They cherish the flexibility, convenience, and control it gives them over their lives. As Ann McIndoo of Computer Training Services says, "The bottom line is freedom. The side effect is I'm well paid."

Freedom means different things to different people, however. To Javier Ferrier, who transcribes court reporters' notes in Garden Grove, California, it means "the freedom to set my own hours. I work the hours I want." For Lewis Mann, a life- and health-insurance broker, freedom means "to work as hard or smart or casually as I want." Phoenix scriptwriter and audio/video producer Bill Burkett finds the freedom of working from home means "I can do it on my own terms." Or as Ivan Misner, founder of The Business Network Associates, says, it's "the freedom to make my own decisions and be in control of my professional destiny."

For designer Sandra Stratton of Kahului, Hawaii, and Robert F. Dobnick of Chicago, who does space planning for wholesale showrooms, it's the creative freedom they love about working from home. To David Chazin, who operates a Las Vegas laser cartridge remanufacturing company, it's freedom from the corporate world, "freedom to set my own direction." Washington, D.C., housing consultant David Freed prizes the "freedom, to be able to do socially meaningful work." And to Edward L. Svadlenka, who operates a carpet-cleaning and window-washing service in Hometown, Illinois, it "gives me the freedom to take time off."

Your control extends to when you work and to what you put first in importance. You no longer need to react to a boss's urgency like a fire department responding to an alarm. You can create an office with the lighting, colors, furnishings, music, sound, or silence you desire. You're not a captive of modular office systems that provide minimal privacy and require you to converse in hushed tones. And even though there are family and household distractions, for almost everyone there are many fewer interruptions than at an office. You're away from office politics, backbiting, and those disagreeable people you would never invite into your home.

You Get More Done:
Productivity Increases an Average of 20 Percent

Speaking of the growing trend of working from home, former President George Bush observed, "Millions have already found their productivity actually increases when they work nearer the people they're really working for—their families at home." Indeed, research consistently indicates productivity rises 15 to 25 percent when work is done at home in telecommuting programs, according to telecommuting consultant Gil Gordon.

It's well established that the self-employed are the most productive people in the economy. With fewer interruptions, meetings, and office politics, it's not surprising that both the employed and the self-employed get more done at home. A study of 90,000 managers by Booz, Allen and Hamilton found that managers waste 25 percent of their time. Another study by Accountemps found 34 percent of the average employee's day was frittered away. Still another study indicated that employers lose no less than four and a half hours a week per employee as a result of lateness, long lunch hours, and working another job or business during office hours.

Psychological factors contribute to the productivity gains of working from home. People experience more of a sense of ownership of their work, gaining a new feeling of pride in accomplishment. They work at their own pace. If you're an early-bird person, because of the flexible hours, you can begin your work early in the morning during your hours of peak performance. But if your body functions best after midnight, it's your choice to work then. When you feel better, you do better.

Lucy and Frank Knights, who both work from home for an eastern utility company, agree with those findings: "We're surprised more companies aren't letting their people work at home. This is like owning your own business. You get more done. We're working harder than we did at the office, but we're enjoying it more."

When San Francisco computer consultant William Slavin started his business at home, he explained the gain this way: "The idea of being an entrepreneur is a real thrill to me. I really like it. I work more and I get more done. But instead of it being drudgery, I'm driven by pure joy."

Costs Go Down

At the same time that productivity goes up, costs go down. Think what you save if you don't drive to an office every day. You save wear and tear on your car, and you probably save on auto insurance. If you're putting 20,000 miles a year on your car, your mileage might drop to 12,000. Assuming the cost of driving 20,000 miles a year to be 29 cents a mile, which is what the IRS is allowing as a deduction in 1994, you'd be saving $2,320 a year, or almost $200 a month.

Pete Silver, a marketing consultant in Miami, Florida, told us he got a note from his dry cleaner asking, "Where are you?" As people go from white collars to open collars, the washing machine takes over for the dry cleaner.

If you operate your business from home you can usually keep your overhead down so you can break even more quickly in starting up. Some businesspeople use what they save on office rent to buy a house or an apartment building.

Working from home is also a legitimate way to keep more of the money you earn from the tax collector. You can also save money on the obligatory office collections, luncheons, and the purchase of candies and cookies from other people's children. Some people miss these social functions. For them, this is a trade-off. It's a matter of whether you think of them with fondness or as a pain in the neck.

Even when they cover equipment costs, companies usually save money by allowing employees to work at home. And for the self-employed it means only one monthly rent or mortgage payment. In cities, a cost of $12,000 a year for office space is not uncommon. Particularly when you're first starting, that expense can mean the difference between making a profit or closing the business.

Income Can Go Up

People who work from home on their own feel a sense of financial independence. They can say goodbye to what Mark Malone of the American Business Management Association calls the "40-40 plan"—forty minutes in traffic for forty hours a week. To that we add a third "40"—doing it for forty years. Joyce Brooks-Wiley, a computer graphics consultant and systems analyst, says, "My business has been good enough to allow me to improve my standard of living about threefold and meet lots of interesting people at the same time. I can run my office the way I like, hire and fire, and wine and dine, as well as be wined and dined." Greg Souser, who operates Tri-State Mobile Power Wash Company from his home in Grand Prairie, Texas, says, "I like the personal and financial freedom to have fun while I work and there's no ceiling on my income."

The sky's the limit when you're in a business from your home. How much you make depends on your own ingenuity, determination, and willingness to work at it. When Lynie Arden was doing research for a cover story for *Home Office Computing* on home-based millionaires, she found more home-based million-dollar businesses than she could include in the article.

While most home-based businesses don't reach six-figure incomes, the financial gains can nevertheless be substantial. When the White House asked us to talk about the issues concerning people who work from home, we asked members of the Working From Home Forum on CompuServe for their comments. This message from freelance writer David Palmer gives a perspective on the importance to many people of what could be considered even modest income gains.

"I hope you can enlighten the folks on the Hill that self-employment is no longer synonymous with doctor, lawyer, or accountant. It also includes a growing number of displaced homemakers, single parents, factory workers, miners, and others whose skills are either no longer marketable in industry or who live in an area where self-employment is the only alternative to a service job stocking shelves in a chain drug store or flipping hamburgers. To a single parent with two or three kids, being self-employed and making $20,000 to $30,000 a year looks a whole lot better than being "employed" at $4.50 an hour."

You Save Time

How much time do you spend commuting to work every day? Look at the chart on the next page to see how much of your irreplaceable time is spent driving in rush-hour traffic. The average commute in the United States is still about twenty minutes each way. That amounts to four forty-hour weeks a year! Many people in large cities and even those in small communities commute far greater distances. It's no longer unusual for people to tell us about one- to two-hour commutes each way. (In speaking recently to an audience of Los Angeles County employees, Paul cited a *Los Angeles Times* study that found the average commute in Los Angeles was twenty-two minutes. He never imagined that would be one of his bigger laugh lines.)

Then there's the time you spend getting dressed to go to work. It may add another five or ten hours a week to get dressed up so you can go sit in traffic. What would you do with the extra ten or fifteen hours a week you spend dressing and driving that no one is paying you for now?

What do people who work from home do with all this time they save? *Home Office Computing* found that two out of three people use it to get more work done. Three out of five spend it on exercising more. And, of course, many spend more time with their families.

And what do people do on their breaks at an office? Have a cigarette, a cup of coffee, eat a snack, go to the restroom. Taking a break at home means you can pet your dog, change the kitty litter box, water your plants, wash your hair, toss a load of laundry into the washing machine, exercise, have your lunch by the pool, start your dinner, watch part of a talk show or a soap, or read a paper or business magazine.

Stress Goes Down, Health and Lifestyle Get Better

Would you like to feel more relaxed, eat a healthier diet, have more time off, exercise more, and have a better sex life? That's what the top five positive effects of working from home were in 1992, according to 4,100 *Home Office Computing* readers.

In contrast, nearly half of American workers worry about their jobs and feel pressure. Two in every five workers find their jobs to be "very" or "extremely" stressful and 35 percent are thinking about quitting. *Prevention* magazine finds that the percentage of Americans who say they are under a "great deal" of stress once a week or more has risen from 55 percent in 1983 to 64 percent in 1993.

What's the cause of this stress? According to one relatively recent study, heavy traffic is the number-one cause of stress in daily life. Number two is

How Much of Your Life Do You Spend Commuting

Daily One-Way Trip in Minutes	Round Trip	Hours Each Year	Equivalent Number of Forty-Hour Weeks
5	10	40	1
10	20	80	2
15	30	120	3
20	40	160	4
25	50	200	5
30	60	240	6
35	70	280	7
40	80	320	8
45	90	360	9
50	100	400	10
55	110	440	11
60	120	480	12

frustration from interruptions at the office. Another survey indicated that the most frequent work-related stress for women is having to balance work and family demands. Work from home reduces or eliminates all these major causes of stress.

Research also indicates the more control we feel over our lives, the less stress we experience. Perhaps that's the reason the one quality people want most in a manager is someone who allows them autonomy. Being your own boss is the ultimate in autonomy. Despite working harder and longer hours, most people report their stress level goes down once they are in charge.

Recent medical studies confirm these reports. Despite the hard work and increased productivity involved, working at home produces less stress than working at similar tasks in the office. For example, Nancy Nickel finds that having the flexibility to adjust her hours and her work pace is relaxing. "It's almost like magic. I can tailor my work to what I want to do. I can stop and take a TV break and still get more done. I feel great at the end of the day."

As Jeremy Joan Hewes, author of *Worksteads,* has described, "If you have the safety valve of a walk around the block or a cup of hot homemade soup, you may not feel the pressure of deadlines as strongly as if you were in an office where the people and the energy level are often frantic."

You also avoid common office stress factors like fluorescent lights, ringing telephones, clattering equipment, buzzing conversation, and fighting rush-hour traffic. Financial consultant Michael Fey explains how the difference has affected him: "When I was commuting to and from work, I had to have a glass of wine when I got home to unwind." Now that he works from home he rarely has a drink outside social occasions.

Often it's small things that make big differences in reducing stress. Open-collar workers appreciate not having to put up with other people's smoking. Or, if they smoke, they enjoy the freedom to do so at home. People are glad to be rid of the negative attitudes of co-workers, the gossip, and the office politics that interfere with getting work done, not to mention the frequent meetings that consume a reported 45 percent of managerial and professional time.

It's well established that lower stress means better health. Stress lowers the white blood cell count and the immune system's resistance to disease. Heart disease and high blood pressure, which affect one in four Americans, are acknowledged to be stress-caused diseases. Not only do people working from home experience fewer of the major causes of stress, they also have more time to exercise and more control over what they eat. So better health is another benefit of working from home.

Family Members See More of One Another

According to recent studies the average father spends only eight minutes a day in meaningful conversation with his children, whereas the average couple has only four minutes of closeness. While you can expect to work more at home, you can also expect to see more of the people you love. Many mothers want to raise their children themselves. By scheduling their work when the children are at school or when they're sleeping, about 50 percent are able to be full-time parents.

The alternative in the workaday world is day care. Good day-care centers are in short supply and day care is expensive. Working from home may not completely eliminate child-care costs, but it can cut down on day-care costs that often run as much as $500 a month for each child. Because medical research finds toddlers are more at risk of getting serious infections in day-care centers, many parents feel safer having their young children at home.

Graphics designer Mary Stoddard finds having her studio at home makes playing two roles in life more manageable. "I used to have my business downtown, and the children would come there after school, but this is easier. I can stop and talk with them when they come home, and then they can go out to play with their friends. By being here where everything's in one central location, I save on baby-sitting costs and get work done in the time I used to spend driving my kids here and there."

Medical transcriptionist Glenda Noble loves being there when her children get home after school. "It may sound silly but I like being able to give them a snack and be there to answer their questions. Plus, I didn't miss all those 'firsts' that all of us mothers like to see."

For fathers, working at home means more time with family and loved ones. One parent jokingly told us he'd discovered children he'd forgotten he had. Gil Gordon says, "I feel closer to my children. Yes, it's a hassle sometimes, but I'm able to get involved with things other fathers can't."

With growing concerns about street gangs, teen suicide, drugs, and alcoholism, parents of teenagers are also finding working at home helps put their minds at ease. Tax specialist Alsey Graham of Kansas City had worked for the IRS while her daughter was in grade school, but she felt that the teen years were an important time to be there for her daughter. So she left her job to open a tax and bookkeeping service from her home. "If it weren't for my daughter I wouldn't be in business. But I'm glad I did it. You only get one chance with a child. I wanted to do it right." Sales trainer Ray Dunlop of Indianapolis would agree. He found running his business from home "made being a single parent of teenagers a lot easier."

Community Assumes New Importance

The rise of home offices makes a reemergence of community life possible. Three out of five *Home Office Computing* readers report they participate more in community activities as a result of working at home.

As Bob and Stephanie Wilson have found, the neighborhood takes on a new significance when you work at home. "The focus of our friendships and activities used to be in town. Now the focus has shifted. We find our friends and involvements right here in the neighborhood."

Working at home, you experience the events of life in the community. With someone on the block at home every day, the neighborhood becomes a safer place to live. It becomes a friendlier place, too. Not having colleagues down the hall to meet at the coffee machine, you may find yourself talking over the back fence to somebody with whom you once had only a nodding acquaintance.

Suddenly, the neighborhood is no longer just a place to come and go from. It's now the center of your daily activities. Clients and customers, perhaps employers and co-workers, pass through it when they visit your office. You patronize nearby businesses like the post office, the print shop, the office-supply store. Perhaps you have business lunches or meetings in the area. As the condition of your community becomes more important to you, you may even find yourself becoming involved in civic activities.

And working from home is helping communities in a number of other ways. It becomes easier for them to tackle air pollution and, in the process, forgo the impending gridlock on freeways and streets.

It's 100 Percent What You Make It

As you can see, working from home, whether you're salaried or self-employed, means more control over your schedule and your environment than ever before. You are in charge. There is no boss standing over your shoulder. There is no time clock to punch, no bell to tell you when to start and when to stop. There is no procedures manual for working at home—it's up to you. It can be either a dream come true or a nightmare, depending on what you do. It's 100 percent up to you!

Common Problems

Even with these many advantages, working from home is not without its challenges, at least initially. Below is a list of the most common problems of working from home, drawn from a number of studies and surveys, including ones done by the Roper Organization, *Home Office Computing* magazine, and us. Superseding these, however, the top two problems for home-based businesses are the business challenges of getting enough customers and managing money and finances, subjects of later chapters.

Expectations and Reality May Vary

Often the problems people anticipate they will have in working from home are not the same as those they actually encounter. But the good news is that all types of problems occur much less frequently than people fear. For example, whereas the largest concern expressed in one study was not having necessary office supplies and equipment, this was not reported to be a problem for any of those who actually work from home. And the other anticipated problems that were reported were far less significant than expected.

Overall, the most common problems were these: distractions from family and friends, not being taken seriously, feeling lonely or isolated, separating work and personal life, and self-management. Other problems included space limitations, lack of privacy, lack of time, missing support personnel, child care, and staying out of the refrigerator. You'll notice that many of these common problems arise from the freedom, flexibility, and autonomy working from home provides.

Being Taken Seriously

In our survey, slightly fewer than one in five home-business people reported a problem with being taken seriously by customers, clients, supervisors, co-workers, colleagues, family, or friends. To some, working from home raises the fear of missing out on promotions, losing touch with the grapevine, and being forgotten when it comes to special projects that could advance a career. Entrepreneurs worry about their professional image and whether their clients will consider a home-based business a substantial one.

Top Ten Problems of Working from Home

1. Distractions from family and friends
2. Being taken seriously
3. Working too much
4. Separating work and personal life
5. Lack of support services
6. Not enough space
7. Feeling isolated
8. Lack of privacy
9. Self-discipline and self-management
10. Zoning

Although a few horror stories of lost clients and missed promotions are enough to panic anyone, concerns over credibility are usually much more of a problem initially than in the long run. If you take yourself seriously and project a professional business image, others will take you seriously too. Many home-based businesses work successfully with *Fortune* 500 clients. Employees at home, like technical writer Jane Minogue, are usually pleasantly surprised to find that they continue to advance in their careers. Jane, who initially began working from home to care for her newborn baby, was promoted to a supervisory position while working from home.

In chapter 3, "Working for Yourself," you'll find a list of specific steps you can take to create a substantial business image. In chapter 4, "Working for Someone Else," we talk about how to keep a high profile in your organization.

Separating Work from Personal Life

Since the whole day is spent under one roof, one to two out of ten people report they have a difficult time juggling the demands of both home and business. They're bothered by family interruptions, housework that needs doing, deliveries and service calls, friends who drop by, barking dogs, and not having a transition period between work and play. They find it hard to switch gears from the computer to Cuisinart and back again.

Although this may sound potentially chaotic, there are many creative solutions presented throughout this book for keeping your personal and professional lives in perspective. Setting up a schedule, finding the right place for your office, getting an answering machine, and arranging for proper child care are just a few you will learn about.

Self-Management

Although research consistently indicates that productivity goes up when people work from home, without the structure of a formal office routine about one in ten people in our survey has a hard time with self-discipline. They report problems with getting out of bed, getting to work, and sticking to business. Some find themselves sneaking in too much TV and taking too many trips to the refrigerator. At the other extreme, an HOCM survey shows that 15 percent have difficulty closing the door on work and leaving it behind at the end of the day. They find work becomes all-consuming because it's always there.

You'll be delighted to find many creative solutions throughout this book that people have developed to help them learn how to manage themselves successfully. We call it developing the "self-management muscle." It means learning to work on a schedule of your own making, putting personal time on your calendar, and having a separate office space that is out of sight and therefore out of mind.

Feeling Isolated

While nearly a third were *concerned* about isolation in the Roper study, only 10 to 12 percent of those in the other surveys actually reported feeling isolated and lonely. They said they missed the social contacts of an office setting. We've found problems with feeling lonely are more likely to occur under three circumstances:

1. A shaky start. Problems with isolation are more common initially, when new open-collar workers aren't fully clear about the direction they're going in with their work. They don't know whether their business or job at home will work out, and there's an initial lack of structure. Once business routines get going and they begin working with clients and colleagues, this problem disappears.

2. Solitary work. Sometimes problems of isolation are related to the fact that the nature of the work involves virtually no personal contact. Nancy Rabbitt, who operates Keyline Graphics, an electronic typesetting and graphic-design service, finds that "sometimes I may not leave the house all day. I mean, literally. If it's a really busy day I may not get out the door, even to get the mail. It can reach a point where grocery shopping is an adventure."

When your work demands long hours alone, however, feelings of isolation can arise whether you are working from home or in an outside office. As writer Marsha Seligson and career counselor Naomi Stephan found, moving into an office building didn't solve this problem. They both tried renting office space but eventually moved back home. The benefits in terms of contact in an impersonal building weren't sufficient to offset the added costs and commuting time.

When working from home, it's important to have this kind of "people break" even if there are not lots of friends or acquaintances right outside the door or down the hall. You need to replace these office contacts with routine phone calls and personal visits that you initiate yourself. Like many people working from home, both Marsha and Naomi created a support network of friends and colleagues they can call on. You'll find more information about how to create such a network in chapter 17.

3. A social personality. About one-sixth of the American population is primarily motivated by the social interaction of their work. For these individuals, talking and dealing with others is the central focus and highlight of their day and working from home can become a problem indeed. Knowing this, few such people are attracted to working from home. They're only tempted to do so when illness, child-care needs, or some other necessity requires them to consider becoming home based. If you fall into this category, we recommend that you do whatever you can to stay in an office setting or, when that is not possible, arrange to have partners or employees who work with you at home.

Ten Tips for Avoiding the Common Problems of Working from Home

1. **Be sure all your printed material communicates that you're a serious business or professional.** This includes using professionally designed business cards, letterheads, and stationery.
2. **Have a separate business telephone line.** Keep your residential line for your personal use and for your family. Don't allow children to answer your business line.
3. **Answer the telephone with a pleasant, businesslike greeting** that communicates you're delighted to hear every caller.
4. **Have a physically separate space for your office**—a separate room if possible. Don't try to make the most intimate room in your home—your bedroom—also your office.
5. **Give yourself permission to treat household interruptions as if you were at the office.** If you need child-care help, arrange it, particularly for children under five.
6. **Establish a work schedule.** You may work more hours at home than you would at an office, but don't work morning, noon, *and* night. Establish time for yourself and your family.
7. **Develop your self-management muscle by setting goals for every day.** Work on those goals first since there is never enough time to do everything. Don't get bogged down reacting to interruptions and demands. Think about what it means to separate the *important* from the *urgent.*
8. **Don't allow paperwork and office equipment to take over your home.** Use space-saving storage systems; if you need help, consult with a professional organizer.
9. **Have the attitude that you work *from* home, not *at* home.** Get out of the house at least once a day. Remember, your home is a base, not a prison.
10. **Get the support** of family members, clients, and, if you're employed, coworkers and your management.

Deciding Whether Working from Home Is for You

Despite facing these problems, experience clearly shows that the difficulties you may encounter need not be roadblocks if you are sufficiently motivated to find a way over, under, or around them.

So how will you know if working from home is for you? Who is suited to work from home? We've talked in depth with hundreds of individuals to determine the answer to this question, and what we discovered surprised us.

Indeed there are certain personal qualities that seem to make working from home easier, particularly at first. As a general rule, those who are most successful are self-starters who like the line of work they're in, know what they want, and are determined to achieve it. They enjoy working independently and are comfortable with minimal structure and ambiguity. They are capable of establishing and following their own schedules and deadlines.

Surprisingly, however, we find that while these attributes make it easier and less stressful to begin working from home, they are not prerequisites for success. Many people working from home successfully and with great satisfaction did not initially have these attributes. Apparently the ability to work from home and to find it rewarding is not primarily a matter of being "suited" for it. It's more a matter of wanting to do it enough to find ways to make it work.

Like many others, home-based producer Ellie Kahn is not particularly well suited for working from home. She says, "Actually I would rather be employed and work in an office. I'm more suited for an office structure and a boss directing me and setting priorities, but my work as an oral historian is very important to me and I have yet to find anyone who will hire me to do it. So I'm learning how to be my own boss and it's worth it, because I love what I do." Had Ellie listened to conventional wisdom she might have decided she would be unable to work from home before giving herself a chance to see what she could do.

Actually, most of us do not initially have the *mind set, skill set,* or *knowledge set* to work successfully on our own because we've had so little opportunity to acquire them. But research indicates that achievement is one human quality that's not determined by innate capacities. It's something we can learn from the experience of doing.

Since it's obvious that you too have some desire to work from your home or you wouldn't be reading this book, we suggest that instead of asking yourself whether you are already suited for work from home, ask how much you want to work from home and to what extent you are willing to learn how to do what it takes.

What Does It Take?

In addition to being a producer of a good product or a provider of a good service, working from home requires that you wear many other hats, some of which may be unfamiliar to you. Whether you are self-employed or working from home on a salary, you will undoubtedly need to carry out all the following roles at one time or another.

- **The Executive.** Plans for the future, defines and schedules what you will be doing, determines how and when you will do it, and monitors to see that you are doing it adequately.
- **The Supervisor.** Makes sure you get to work, stick to business, and don't burn yourself out overworking.
- **The Administrator and Purchasing Agent.** Equips and supplies your office, handles correspondence, answers the phone, schedules repairs, runs errands, files and manages financial record-keeping, obtains insurance, and so on.
- **The Security Guard.** Establishes clear boundaries between work and home so that family and friends don't interfere with your work and work doesn't interfere with your personal life.
- **Public Relations, Marketing, and Sales Manager.** Gets the word out about what you do, why people need you, and promotes you so your business thrives or your career advances.

And you may have to be the janitor too!

How Motivated Are You?

Since motivation and a willingness to learn seem to be the most important variables for success at working from home, first ask yourself on a scale of 1 to 10 (with 1 being "not at all" and 10 being "more than anything in the world"), "How much do I want to work from home?" The greater your desire above a 7, the more likely you will be motivated to do whatever it takes to master the many required roles mentioned above to succeed at working from home. The lower your score is below 7, the more important it will be that you already have the attitudes, skills, aptitudes, and knowledge you need before you start.

If you seriously want to work from home, you will probably be able to find a way to make it work for you. In fact, many people tell us that one of the greatest joys of having decided to go off on their own and work from home has been the satisfaction that comes from meeting new challenges and accomplishing things they never imagined they could do.

Assessing Your Potential for
Working Happily from Home

Here's a brief survey to help you identify what you could encounter, and some clues for minimizing problems, before you go to the trouble and expense of actually moving your office home. If you're already working at home, the survey will provide some insight into problems or ambivalent feelings you may be having and what you might need to do to improve the situation.

The survey takes only a few minutes to complete. Read the directions, make your choices, and then read on to interpret the results.

A Working-from-Home Suitability Survey

Below are descriptions of five offices. Choose the office you would most like to work in. Mark that office with the number 1. Then rank the other offices from 2 to 5 in order of their interest to you. Just be sure to include all the offices as you rank your preferences.

____ **Office A:** Walking into this warm, comfortable environment, you feel right at home. This office has a friendly, lived-in feeling. Cushioned chairs and couches are gathered around a casual seating area. The hum of conversation fills the air.

____ **Office B:** Everything about this office is unexpected. It's not like any workplace you've seen before. There's a sense of surprise and drama that makes just being here an adventure. The hustle and bustle of excitement fills the air.

____ **Office C:** The first thing you notice about this office is that there's a place for everything, and everything is in its place. There is a sense of history and tradition about it. Everything down to the last detail is as it should be and exactly as you would expect it.

____ **Office D:** This office is first-class. There has been no compromise in quality. Excellence is clearly the standard, and from the awards tastefully displayed around the room, you know it has been achieved. Whatever is done here is done extraordinarily well.

____ **Office E:** This commanding office communicates a forcefulness that gets your attention. When you walk in the door you straighten up and take notice. It conveys a no-nonsense approach that demands results. The feeling of power in the office leaves a lasting impression.

Adapted from the *PSE Preference Survey and Motivation Profile,* © 1982, Paul and Sarah Edwards

Interpreting Your Score

Each of the offices described in the survey represents one of the basic needs people seek to fill through work. By listing them in order of preference, you are indicating which needs are more important to you at this time in your life. Your choices provide some hints about how you're likely to respond to the most common concerns people have about working from home.

	If Your Rating Was:	
	1 or 2	4 or 5
Office A: *Will You Be Lonely?*	You may miss working with other people at an office. You'll probably like working from home better if your work brings people into your home or takes you out to work with others. You can create your own opportunities to get together with people. Schedule frequent meetings with customers and colleagues at meal times or get active in various organizations and associations. *See chapter 17.*	You are probably well suited for working at home. Relating to others is not the most important part of your work. You will probably not be unduly stressed by leaving the social interaction of an office setting. But to maintain your social skills and to prevent becoming isolated from people in your field, you need to schedule face-to-face contacts with other people.
Office B: *Will You Be Bored?*	Your work itself had better be exciting and stimulating. Otherwise, you'll find working at home could be too dull. Running your own business, however, with the challenges and risks of entrepreneuring could keep you sufficiently stimulated. *See chapter 3.*	You may enjoy escaping office pressures and hubbub by retreating to work in the quiet of a home office. The demands and uncertainties of running your own business could be more stimulating than you want, however, so perhaps you'd be more comfortable working from home on a salary or a long-term contract. *See chapter 4.*

	If Your Rating Was: 1 or 2	4 or 5
Office C: *Will You Be Disorganized?*	You probably like a well-organized environment and value the order that comes from attention to detail. If you're able to create and stick to your own schedules and organization, you may well enjoy working from home, where how you organize things is completely your responsibility. All the filing, scheduling, mailing, and cleaning will be up to . . . guess who?	You may enjoy the freedom from imposed schedules and rules that working from home offers. At home you can work anytime, day or night; the work's always there. You can leave things messy or organize them as you wish. Left entirely on your own, however, you may find your desire for order will increase somewhat, and you will need to motivate yourself to be sufficiently organized to get your work done. *See chapters 12 through 16.*
Office D: *Will You Goof Off?*	You may be well suited for working from home because you're motivated to work hard and set high standards for yourself. You probably won't need a supervisor to keep you working all day. You may actually accomplish more with the independence of doing it all your own way. You could have a tendency to overwork, however, and if your other top choice was Office A, you may need to find a way to get recognition from others for doing a good job. *See chapters 12 and 17.*	You may find it difficult to work at home. You may start working later in the morning and stop earlier in the afternoon. Your attention may drift away from your work to nearby attractions like the refrigerator, the garden, or the TV. You may not be as productive as you would be with the structure and supervision of an office setting. *See chapter 12.*

| | If Your Rating Was: | |
	1 or 2	4 or 5
Office E: *Will You Feel Less Important?*	You could enjoy being in command of your work and your destiny without the encumbrances of an outside organization. But you might miss motivating and directing others to action and feel limited by the confines of a spare bedroom. If so, you may want to consider building a full-fledged organization that you can run from your own home. *See chapter 15.*	You may feel relief from the power games and maneuvers of office politics and enjoy the freedom to work on your own.

As you can see, whether you'll find working at home a pain or a pleasure will depend primarily on you. While the survey may not determine whether working at home is right or wrong for you, it highlights some of the issues you may encounter and gives some direction on what to do about them.

Other Considerations

Here are some other questions to answer in deciding to make the move home:

Do you enjoy spending time in your home?
Is there adequate space for your work?
Do you like your neighborhood?
Do you get along with your neighbors?
Are the business resources you need available within a reasonable distance?
How will others you live with react to your working from home?
Will you enjoy being around them more often?
How will your customers or clients, your boss or co-workers feel about your
    working from home?

A strong negative response to any of these questions could mean that you may have serious adjustments to make. Fortunately, however, working from home affords great flexibility, so if you want to make the move, the chances are you will be able to find some way to accommodate your particular needs and circumstances.

A trial week or even a weekend of working at home can help you discover what you need to do to make it practical for you. Once you start experimenting, you may find you'd rather fight than switch back to an outside office. The rest of this book will help you deal with the problems that can arise and with how to make the necessary adjustments for success in working from home.

C H A P T E R
T H R E E

■ ■

Working for Yourself:
Full-Time and Part-Time

Estimates are that for every person who actually starts a business, three to ten more are thinking about it. Perhaps we all have a little bit of the entrepreneur in us, a secret wish tucked away somewhere to become a consultant, write a book, open a little shop, sell our prize spaghetti sauce, or invent a better mousetrap.

In the comfort of your living space, you can now take your ideas and desires out of the back rooms of your mind and start your own business. Actually, this is the easiest route to working from home, and the business advantages are encouraging:

- **The sky's the limit on your potential income** when you're your own boss. Your business can be anything from a part-time sideline effort that brings in several extra thousand dollars a year to a multimillion-dollar enterprise like Hewlett-Packard, a company that began at home in a garage.

- **Starting a business at home keeps the initial costs down** so you can get established more easily, turn a profit sooner, and increase your chances of success.

- **You can save $7,000 to $20,000 a year** on office rental at current rental rates.

- **You can turn personal expenses like rent, furniture, and telephone costs into tax-deductible items** if you meet IRS requirements (see chapter 10).

- **You can test a new business idea,** or see whether you like running your own business, without much risk. In fact, by trying out the idea from home, you can tailor the amount of risk to your financial circumstances.

- **You keep more of what you earn.** Both from people moving from an office to home and from their home to an office, we often hear that it takes 2.5 to 3 times the gross income to produce the same net income when you work from an outside office.

Going Out on Your Own: What It Takes

You've probably heard it said that entrepreneurs are a special breed. Some observers, like psychologist Alan Jacobwitz, have even gone so far as to say that entrepreneurs are born and not made, or at least that their early environment predisposes them to business success.

We agree that to succeed in your own business, you have to have the "right stuff." But today we live in an age of information, and almost anyone can acquire the knowledge and skills of a successful entrepreneur. All you need is to be sufficiently committed to start and run a profitable business from home. Men and women of all ages and backgrounds have done it.

Some were successful corporate professionals before they started their businesses. They had confidence, and skills in selling, marketing, and managing a business when they began. But others were total novices, fearful of business basics like selling and negotiating.

So what was the "right stuff" for them? What did it take to achieve business success? We've met many people who found an answer, but there wasn't any one way. However, our interviews do indicate that by the time entrepreneurs achieve success, they have several things in common:

- They enjoy what they're doing enough to keep going when times are rough.
- They are good at what they do.
- They specialize, providing a product or service that a particular group of people wants or needs.
- They have learned how to sell themselves and their businesses. They know how they measure up to their competition, why their prospective customers should come to them, and how to let people know what they have to offer.
- They stay in charge of their money.
- They are flexible enough to adapt to unforeseen circumstances and adjust their workday to the demands of the business.
- They believe in themselves and are sufficiently committed to their work to persist until they get the job done right.

Success depends on finding the right combination of your personal preferences, talents, and skills to meet the needs of the marketplace, and then having clearly defined business goals and an effective plan for reaching them. It's like putting together the pieces of a puzzle, starting with selecting the right business for you.

Will you succeed? That, of course, depends on you, but the odds are surprisingly in your favor. Contrary to the myth that nine out of ten new businesses fail within five years, home businesses do much better. Analysis of data from Link Resources, which does an annual survey of the work-at-home population, indicates that on average only 5 percent of home-based businesses go out of business each year. This means that over a five-year period, three out of four home-based businesses are still in business. Beth Terranova, who annually updates her mailing list data for all small businesses in Pittsburgh and surrounding counties, finds similar results for home-based businesses whose names she obtains from newly issued city business licenses.

Why do home businesses do better than office and store-based businesses? Probably because the risks of loss are fewer. There's no lease, and probably no employees, so the cost of staying in business is less. Add to this the fact that if you choose a business that you like doing, you're more apt to persist at it even with a lower return. We think, too, that while there may be many who might say, "I tried a home business," like business opportunity buyers who never open their business-in-a-box, these are people who don't do enough to be counted in a survey, such as getting a business license, a Yellow Page listing or joining a trade or professional association.

Virtually any of hundreds of businesses can be started from home. In fact, a list of over five hundred of them appears in the Appendix. The only limitations are the space you have available and any legal restrictions that may apply. So the question is not so much "What's possible?" as "How do I select a business that has success potential and is right for me?" To answer this challenging question, here are four different roads you can take: starting a business on your own; buying a franchise you can start at home; joining a direct sales organization; or buying a business opportunity. Let's consider each in more detail.

Starting a Business on Your Own

By far the majority of people who have a home business start their business from scratch. They select a business idea based on their unique interests, talents, contacts, and expertise and set out to serve customers and clients with their services or products.

We like to say that selecting a successful business requires that you tune in to the two most popular radio stations in the world: WPWPF ("What People Will Pay For") and WIIFM ("What's In It For Me?"). In selecting a business, you need to determine what you will enjoy and profit from as well as what people need and will pay you money for.

Market research will help you tune in to WPWPF. It doesn't need to be complicated or expensive. Your market research can be as simple as asking prospective customers what they need and investigating what the competition is like. Find out what people are paying now and what advantages you can offer over the competition. Can you compete on price, service, quality, variety, or

Honor Roll of Home-Originated Companies

Amway
Apple Computer
Avon
Baskin-Robbins ice cream
Ben & Jerry's ice cream
Bonne Bell cosmetics
Borland International
Brookstone Company
Cape Cod potato chips
Celestial Seasonings
Day Runner
Domino's Pizza
Electronic Data Systems
Estée Lauder cosmetics
Ford Motor Company
Gateway 2000
Gillette razor
Hallmark Cards
Hershey Foods
Hewlett-Packard
Johnson's Wax
King World Productions
Lane Bryant

Lillian Vernon catalog
Liquid Paper
Marion Laboratories
Mary Kay
Microsoft
Mrs. Fields Cookies
Nike
Pepperidge Farms
Phonemate
Playboy
ProComm
Purex
Reader's Digest
Redken
Russell Stover Chocolate
Sierra On-Line
Smith Brothers cough drops
SOS scouring pads
StairMaster
Steinway pianos
T. J. Cinnamon
Walt Disney
Welch's grape juice

ease of use? You may also find your competition even needs you to help cover their overload.

To tune in to WIIFM, consider these factors:

- How much do you want to be involved with people? All the time? Some of the time? From a distance? Not at all?
- Do you want it to be a full-time or part-time business? Hobbies are more apt to become part-time or sideline businesses and some people report that by making their hobby their work, they kill it as a diversion or a source of entertainment.
- How many hours a week are you willing to invest in your business?
- How important are prestige and image to you? For example, will your self-esteem remain intact as "Grunt and Dump Hauling" even if you are making good money?
- How much money do you need to make? How much money do you want to make? Each week? Each month? Each year?
- What resources do you have available in terms of money, equipment, and know-how?

- How much risk do you want to take? How much money can you afford to lose—or write off as "an educational experience"—if the business is not successful?

- Do you prefer a proven type of business or are you willing to take the chances of a pioneer?

- Do you want to start a business from scratch or would you prefer to buy an existing business or franchise? A business that's been franchised is ten times more likely to succeed than one that's started from scratch, but most franchises require a larger investment because you're buying other people's experience, and many can't be operated from home.

- Will you and can you get help from other people, including your family?

- Who do you know or where can you find people who will help you?

- How big is your market? Are there enough buyers that you can reach to support the level of income you desire or need?

- Do you need any special licensing or training? For example, tax preparers, private investigators, and investment advisers often do.

With these considerations in mind, here are six possibilities for finding the ideal business for you:

Turn What You Most Enjoy into a Business

If possible, turn your favorite hobby or interest into a business. There's nothing better than getting paid to do what you most enjoy.

When teacher John Lewis neared retirement, he became interested in how people could remain vibrant and active after they retired. He found that knowing what to do was a problem for many retired people, so instead of retiring, he began doing retirement counseling.

Every free moment script supervisor Maureen Bender had away from her job she spent at an exercise salon. "Since I love exercising so much, I figured, why

---

Options for Turning a Hobby or Interest into a Business

- Creating arts and crafts
- Becoming a travel guide
- Selling antiques or collectibles
- Selling cosmetics
- Doing interior decorating
- Teaching dance and exercise classes
- Offering tennis lessons
- Breeding, training, and grooming dogs
- Giving singing lessons
- Appraising collections (stamps, coins, art)
- Running a recording studio

not share it with others? Instead of paying to exercise, why not get paid for it?" She set up her own exercise classes and was in business.

For years Clyde Glandon performed as an amateur magician while employed as a corporate executive. An unexpected illness woke him up to how important it is to do what you want to do while you have the chance. He became "Colonel Boone," a professional magician.

Here are some questions to help identify what you enjoy most:

- What do you get so involved in and intrigued with that you lose track of time?
- What do you do first when you get to a new city you've never been to before?
- What are you doing when you feel most like yourself?
- What are you doing when you like yourself the most?
- What are you doing when you feel most alive and energized?
- What do you like to talk about? What are other people talking about that draws you into the conversation?
- What do you take immediate action on? What do you delay?
- What do you do during your time off? When you're on vacation?
- What do you read? What newspaper or magazine headlines catch your eye?
- What do you collect? What mementos and photographs do you keep around your home and office?

Turn Your Existing Job Skills into a Business

Accountants, engineers, graphic artists, health-care personnel, lawyers, programmers, sales and marketing professionals, scientists, secretaries, teachers— people from all walks of life—are turning their salaried jobs into profitable independent businesses. So whatever job you're doing now, consider how you could turn it into an entrepreneurial venture.

Gil Gordon was a personnel director. He became a telecommuting consultant. Larry Nickel is a director of data processing. He started a sideline business handling data-processing overload. Karen Youngblood was a full-time mother. She runs a day nursery. Peggy Glenn was a secretary. She started a secretarial service, wrote a book about how others could do it, and is now a nationally known speaker, writer, and publisher.

Sometimes losing your job, or the threat of losing it, creates the momentum to start a home business.

Rob White worked for the Insurance Commissioner of the State of Georgia and was stymied for months about how he could turn his skills into another job that was not to be found. He decided to create his own work and became what he calls a managed health-care consultant, serving as a "marriage broker" between health-care providers (doctors, hospitals, and other health services) and health-care payers—insurance companies and health-maintenance and preferred-provider organizations.

George Eagan had been with the auto workers' union for fifteen years when the layoffs began. At first he spent many a depressing day hoping he'd be called back. Finally he took charge of his life by setting up his own business custom-painting automobiles.

Sue Rugge started the highly successful research service, Information on Demand, after losing her job as a librarian owing to heavy cutbacks in the aerospace industry. In seven years, she and her partner turned the $250 they used to start the business into over half a million dollars' worth of sales. Reflecting back on the day she was laid off, Sue remembers, "I felt strongly that the only way I would ever have the job security and salary level I wanted was to work for myself. In other words, if you can't get a job, create one!"

Solve a Problem

Problems and complaints hold the seeds for many new businesses. People will pay to have someone do tasks they either hate or need help with. Career counselor Lynne Frances had been teaching this philosophy to her students at the center where she worked. When she decided to take her own advice, she opened a home-based cleaning service.

Actress Dorene Ludwig, of Los Angeles, took her career in a new direction after the Clarence Thomas Senate hearings catapulted concerns about sexual harassment onto the corporate agenda. Utilizing her acting background and political savvy, Ludwig created a sexual harassment training program for companies to educate employees and discourage sexual harassment in the workplace.

Chef Don Silvers couldn't get a kitchen designed to meet his needs, so he decided to design his own. That led to his new career designing kitchens for people who love to cook. His L.A.-based business is called Kitchens by Design.

While Marsha Zlotnick was fighting to survive a life-threatening disease, she discovered that recovering involved many changes in what she could eat and other daily habits, but there were few places for people like herself to turn to for information, support, and assistance in making those changes. When she recovered, she turned her kitchen, dining room, and living room into a center for helping others conquer illnesses. She teaches cooking classes, offers courses in relaxation, acupressure, and massage, provides counseling, and has an extensive bookstore where people can get current information about getting and staying healthy.

Use a Hidden or Latent Talent

Sometimes the most obvious business to pursue is right under your nose, but too obvious to notice. Karen Nestler had always given outstanding parties. She never thought of being a party planner until a friend asked her to plan a party for a family occasion. She gladly agreed and loved doing it, but still didn't think of it as a business opportunity until her friend said, "That was so great I would have paid for it." Then the light went on, and her business was born.

Start a Business Doing Things Other People Hate to Do

- Income tax service
- Investment counseling
- Estate planning
- Real estate management
- Inventory or mailing-list management
- Selling (as an independent rep)
- Cleaning service
- Window washing
- Van and RV washing
- Shopping and gift-buying service
- Equipment repair and fix-it service
- Pickup and delivery service

Writing computer programs had been only a pastime for engineer Earl Patterson until someone in a local computer club hired him to write a program for a print shop. His sideline business, writing custom software, had begun.

Jill Connors thought of her cartoons as doodles until friends asked if she would decorate the wall of their nursery with her drawings. Seeing the finished nursery, another friend asked for her services, and then another. By the time she finished the third nursery, she had decided to start a business. Now in addition to custom-decorating nurseries, she is planning commercial lines of wallpaper, drapes, and toys that feature her designs.

Use Technology and Resources You Have around the House

What you have lying around the house can become a business. Raymond Clark turned his VCR and video camera into a business taping weddings and other memorable events. Teacher Linda Hutton turned her 35-millimeter camera into a sideline photography business. Bonnie Moodyman used her typewriter to start first a part-time and then a full-time typing service. Ray Jones's pickup truck became We'll Haul, a pickup and delivery service. A van or pickup truck, in fact, can be used to start a number of home businesses.

Beverly Matthews is one of hundreds of people who have turned their spare bedrooms into bed-and-breakfast inns. Two women in Texas even use their washing machines to supplement the family budget. They created a business called Washer Women, a laundry service for the crews of ships that dock in the local harbor. Your kitchen is another room that can be transformed into a wide variety of businesses.

Because of their versatility, personal computers can literally become any one of hundreds of new businesses, from writing software or keeping mailing lists to helping people design personalized nutrition or exercise programs.

Dorothy Baranski used her computer to start an executive service providing word processing, accounting, and bookkeeping for small businesses. Others have used their computers to start electronic shopping or referral services.

Use Your Van or Pickup to Start a Business

- Gardening or yard service
- Carpentry or house painting
- Swimming-pool maintenance
- Home maintenance and repair
- Mobile lunch wagon
- Party-plan sales (clothing, cosmetics, computers, housewares)
- Plant-care service
- Hauling or moving service
- Mobile computer-repair service
- Mobile auto-repair service

Many people are using their mailboxes to start profitable businesses. Opening the mail each day to find a stack of cash orders feels great, and selling products through mail order is a growing business opportunity. Bud Weckesser actually turned a home beer-making guide he wrote into a $700,000 mail-order enterprise. People spend over $350 billion a year on mail-order items, everything from books, clothing, and candy to housewares, plants, and sporting equipment.

Use Your Kitchen to Start a Business

- Catering services
- Homemade cakes and cookies
- Pet-food products
- Cooking service for specialized diets (macrobiotic, Pritikin)
- Cooking school
- Herb and spice packages
- Specialized candy
- Healthy snack food
- Canning gourmet fruits, jellies, and preserves

Put What You Know to Work

Since this is an information age, you can turn virtually anything you know into a business if enough people want to know it too. Sandra Canter sold her recipes in a booket, *101+ Instant Hamburger Dishes*. It was the first item in what became a profitable mail-order business.

Having taken singing lessons all her life, Marie Moran knew how to use her voice effectively. Noticing that a major problem people have is not projecting their voices adequately, she started a speaker's training program teaching executives how to give dynamic presentations.

Having worked in a computer store, McCallister Merchant knew how to operate different kinds of computers. Noticing that new computer owners often had difficulty learning how to use their equipment, he offered his services as a consultant and was excited by the response. "I found many people will gladly pay me $40 an hour to come to their homes and show them what I know." So consider your particular expertise and the number of ways you can capitalize on it.

Other Ideas for Putting Things Around the House to Work

- Use your piano for lessons, or rent practice time on it.
- Give swimming lessons in your pool.
- Turn a family room into a day-care center.
- Convert a side porch into a hothouse and sell exotic plants.
- Turn your yard into an organic vegetable garden and sell the produce.
- Dry the flowers growing in your yard and create gift sachets.

For more than five hundred business ideas, see the list of "Home Businesses from A to Z" in the Appendix.

If after reviewing so many business possibilities, you're still wondering just what would be the best business to pursue, here's a simple procedure developed by Mark Kleinschmidt, a Maine computer consultant, for narrowing down your choices:

"Sit down and *honestly* write down what you can and can't do. Put down everything. Then write a letter to yourself really bragging up your strong points.

Most Popular Home-Based Occupations

Farming 5%
Manufacturing/Crafts 7%
Insurance/Real Estate 4%
Finance 4%
Wholesale Trade 5%
Retail 5%
Others 19%
Daycare 4%
Education 2%
Health Services 2%
Professional Services 8%
Engineering/Computers 3%
Consultants 3%
Construction & Trades 29%

Source: BIS Strategic Decisions 1994

There is no room for modesty in this step. Then start looking around your area and see what people are buying that you are able to provide. This will greatly cut down the list of options. If you are lucky, you will only have two or three choices. Then ask yourself if you can run one of these businesses professionally. If you think you can, sit down and draft a plan for how you'll proceed. Show your plan to colleagues and professionals, and get ready to make some changes in it. Once you have gotten this far, you will definitely know whether or not you want to follow through."

When you get to the stage of writing up your business plan, there are computer programs to help you do it, such as *B-Tools for Windows* (Star Software), *Success, Inc.* (Dynamic Pathways), and for Macintosh owners, *Tim Berry's Business Plan Toolkit* (Palo Alto Software). See the Resources list at the end of this chapter.

On the next page is a list of start-up steps you need to take once you make a decision to proceed with a home business. In the upcoming chapters of this book you will find the details of how to carry out each step.

Turn What You Know into a Business

- Plan parties and weddings.
- Become a consultant (management consulting, wardrobe or color consulting, interior decorating, home and office organization consulting).
- Write and sell "how-to" books (how to find a job, how to grow prize-winning azaleas, how to coach Little League soccer).
- Produce "how-to" tapes or video cassettes (how to buy investment property, how to sell your own home).
- Publish a specialty newsletter (backpacking news, organic gardening tips, guide to summer camps).
- Teach classes, give seminars, or tutor in your areas of expertise.

Buying a Franchise

If the idea of starting a business of your own from scratch feels too risky for you, one way to reduce your risk is to purchase a franchise from a company that has already established a track record of success and will teach you how to use their proven methods. There are more than 3,600 franchises available today and, since the fastest-growing number of them are service oriented, many of them can be easily run from home. In fact, the lower overhead of working from home makes starting a franchise even easier.

Examples of the types of service-business franchises that can be run from home include General Business Services, which provides financial support services to small businesses, including bookkeeping, tax preparation, and financial planning; Sandler Systems, whose franchisees teach sales through seminars and workshops; Computertot franchisees, operating from their homes, who teach computer classes at day-care centers, nursery schools, and community facilities;

Car Checkers of America, whose franchisees provide used-car buyers evaluations of a car they are considering buying; cleaning services like TGIF domestic help; home-inspection services like Housemasters; direct-mail advertising like Money Mailer; and directory publishing like Finderbinder.

Start-up Steps for a Home Business

- Select a business that meets the WIIFM and WPWPF tests. Expect to spend 6 to 9 months researching and testing.
- Develop a business and marketing plan.
- Deal with the legalities—zoning, form of business, licensing, name registration, trademarks, permits, tax requirements.
- Create a financial structure—business bank account, bookkeeping system, credit, insurance, pricing.
- Set up your office—select an adequate location in your home; get needed equipment, furniture and supplies; establish telephone service; arrange for a separate mailing address if necessary.
- Develop marketing materials—business cards, stationery, samples—and join associations.
- Establish a schedule and go to work getting business.

When purchasing a franchise, you pay the franchiser for the right to use his or her trademark, trade name, products, and business system in exchange for an initial fee and ongoing royalties on your earnings.

In order to avoid the high costs of complying with franchising registration laws, small businesses will sometimes offer a license instead of a franchise. A license gives the start-up business person permission to use trademarks, proprietary methods, materials, or know-how and may also include training in using them in exchange for a fee and other ongoing costs of goods or materials.

The major advantage of buying a franchise is that you should be buying a tested and proven business for which you receive training and support from the franchiser and other franchisees. In turn, this should reduce your learning curve, shortening the time before you are making a profit and increasing your chances of growing a successful business.

Although you are on your own, you're not alone. With a good franchise, you get the benefit of valuable business training and support. You have access to manuals with step-by-step instructions on procedures that have worked again and again. Some franchisers even offer financing for start-up fees and costs, specialized equipment and customized software, promotional materials, and the benefit of a national advertising campaign. Then, if you do well in your business, you can often sell it easily because the new owner will have not only your ongoing experience but the franchise name to help him or her get started.

In fact, buying a successful established business from an existing franchisee has several added advantages. You have an existing cash flow. How much you can make from the business is not at question because you can look directly at the books and see just how supportive the franchiser has been. In other words, even more of the guesswork is removed from starting a business.

Whether you buy a new or existing franchise, the expertise and support you receive can dramatically reduce the learning time involved in getting a business up and running. Walter Heidig of Binex Automated Business Systems, Inc., estimates that his franchisees are a full year ahead of consultants who try to run a computerized accounting and financial planning service on their own.

Starting a home-based franchise, however, is not always peaches and cream. It usually means acquiring a debt, and sometimes the franchise royalty is too high to justify the amount of money you can earn from running a one- or two-person business. You may find you're paying too much for a name that few people know. Low start-up fees that make entry easy may mean the parent company doesn't have the resources to provide you with as much support and training as you need. Lawsuits by franchisees against their franchisers for not delivering promised advertising and support are not uncommon. And if you're an independent-minded "my way" type of person, you may find the policies and procedures prescribed by the franchiser too restrictive and limiting to your creativity.

How to Determine Whether Franchising Is for You

Basically in buying a franchise you are buying a successful format and the assistance to use it effectively. So in deciding whether you are interested in owning a franchise, ask yourself:

■ **How much structure do I need?** Are you already proficient at most aspects of running the type of business you are considering? Do you prefer to operate with a lot of flexibility and few rules? Do you work best when you make your own rules? Or are you new to this business and uncertain how you should proceed? Do you like to rely on the guidelines, policies, and procedures of someone with greater experience than you?

■ **How much am I willing to pay for the support?** Could you almost as easily learn what you need to run the business from books, seminars, college programs, or consultants? Or does the franchise offer a superior or proprietary method of doing business that will give you a clear-cut advantage in attracting and satisfying your future customers and clients?

■ **Do I have enough working capital to make the business work?** Generally you need at least three to six months to generate a profit. Could you start such a business for less than what the franchiser wants as a down payment? Many franchisers offer financing for a portion of the fee and the start-up costs. Others will provide you with assistance in developing a loan package. Would you be able to arrange for such financial backing if you were on your own? Franchise attorney Ira Nottonson of Sherman Oaks, California, advises that a good business opportunity should buy itself. In other words, after an initial down payment, the operating profit of the franchise should be enough to cover the payments on the balance of your loan.

For Herb and Linda Schulze, purchasing a home-based Chem-Dry franchise has worked well. Linda had been a nurse for twenty-five years; Herb a clergyman for twenty-three years. They were both feeling "burned out" when they met at a personal-growth seminar. They fell in love, married, and began dreaming about expanding their lives in a business together. Since neither had any business background, a franchise made sense to them and they borrowed the $4,000 they needed for fees and start-up costs from Linda's parents.

More than three years later, they're happy with their business. Looking back, Herb says, "A franchise means people who have never been in business can just follow the book and set up their business. We like the independence. The money is good. We made a profit immediately and paid back the loan within the first year. Best of all, we like to be of service to people."

66 Types of Franchises You Can Run from Home (from No Fee to $50,000)

Alarm and security service
Answering service
Balloon delivery
Bingo publications
Bookkeeping service
Business consulting
Business networking organizations
Carpet cleaning and dyeing
Carpet restoration
Catering service
Ceiling cleaning
Chimney sweeping
Cleaning service
Companion service
Computer classes for children
Computer consulting
Computerized accounting
Dance classes for preschoolers
Direct mail advertising
Drapery cleaning service
Education for children
Elder care
Environmental safety
Executive search
Financial planning
First-aid training
Handyman service
Holiday lighting and decoration
Home inspection service
House-sitting
Interior decorating
Kitchen remodeling
Laminated child ID tags
Lawncare service

Leak detection
Loan brokering
Management training
Medical claims processing
Mobile disk jockey
Newborn announcements
Parent education
Party planning
Payroll services
Pet-sitting
Photo IDs for children
Prenatal education
Publishing local resource
  directories
Real estate advertising
Refinishing and restoring
Sales training
Screen repair
Securities and commodities
  brokering
Sewer cleaning
Skin-care products
Sports team photography
Tax preparation
Upholstery cleaning
Used-car evaluations
Wedding planning
Window cleaning service
Windshield repair
Venetian blind installation
Video photography service
Video repair
Waterproofing

He believes those interested in a franchise should talk with other franchisees about their experiences. For him the most important factors have been the integrity of the franchiser to follow through on promises; to provide strong initial training; and to supply immediate technical assistance when there's a problem.

Picking a Franchise

The criteria you apply when picking a franchise should be similar to those you'd use to select any business. Ask yourself the following:

■ **Is this business something I enjoy?** Just because someone else has made a franchise into a successful business doesn't mean you would enjoy doing it. Because you'll be trained, however, a franchise is an excellent way of making a career change into a field that's more to your liking. Over 75 percent of people who do it go into new fields.

■ **Am I knowledgeable or interested in learning more about this field?** Just because the franchise will train you to apply its methods doesn't mean you won't need to have a proclivity for the business and the type of work involved. As more than one franchiser has said, "We provide support, but we don't run the business."

■ **Is this a business that people in my community need and will pay for?** While the franchise may have worked elsewhere, it may not work in your area. There are strong differences in what people buy from region to region, even including such everyday items as mayonnaise and catsup. Also, a community may already have enough of one type of franchise—instant print shops, for example—so explore whether there are already more than enough businesses providing the service you're considering investing in.

■ **Is the franchiser reliable, reputable, and financially solid?** We advise that you thoroughly investigate any franchise you are considering. Federal law requires all franchises to provide all prospective franchisees with a Uniform Franchise Offering Circular, or UFOC. This disclosure document will provide the basis for your investigation. Don't just talk with the franchisees the franchiser recommends; for a full picture that includes the good, the bad, and the ugly, talk with a number of other franchisees. Also, do talk with other franchisees and franchisers in the same field. Here are the kinds of questions you need to be able to answer:

1. How long has the company been in business?
2. How many franchisees does it have?
3. What is its cash position or credit rating? You can do a computer search yourself or hire an information broker to gather this information.
4. Are there any lawsuits pending from customers or franchisees?
5. Is the product or service guaranteed? Can it be sold all year long? Does the U.S. Bureau of Labor Statistics indicate that this is a growing industry?
6. Will you have an exclusive territory? Is the demand in that territory adequate to support another business?

7. Can your contract be renewed, sold, transferred, or terminated?
8. Does the company offer financing or assistance with developing a loan package?
9. What training does the franchiser provide? Is it ongoing? Can you call for help and expect to get it?
10. Does the franchise company have standards for screening applicants? If it is too eager to take anyone, makes big promises, and puts on the pressure for a quick decision, it's a bad sign.
11. Is the franchiser registered in your state?

Since there are so many franchise opportunities today, you will undoubtedly be able to find one you can run from home in a field that's suitable for you. In the Resources list at the end of the chapter, you'll find resources for learning more about franchising.

Joining a Direct-Selling Organization

For 5.5 million people in the United States and 12 million worldwide, working from home means being associated with companies like Avon, Discovery Toys, Fuller Brush, Mary Kay, Nu Skin, Quorum, Rexall, Shaklee, Tupperware, Vaxa, Watkins, and, of course, the largest and most controversial multilevel company, Amway. These companies sell products such as cleaning supplies, cosmetics, foods, vitamins, security devices, and long-distance telephone service directly to consumers. Direct selling—about $14 billion in the U.S. and $62 billion worldwide in 1992—makes up somewhat less than 1 percent of retail sales in the United States. Direct selling includes door-to-door sales, home-party sales, and multilevel marketing (MLM) or what is now popularly being called "network marketing."

Direct selling has advantages. It's a way of getting into your own business with little capital or sales experience. A number of companies provide extensive sales training and motivational support. And there have been enough cases of people with little education becoming wealthy through building multilevel marketing organizations to make many others see their opportunity in direct selling.

From the perspective of product manufacturers, direct selling, and MLM in particular, is a relatively low-cost way of bringing products to market. They avoid the high cost of establishing store distribution systems and national advertising. Because it costs a company less to establish an MLM organization, many companies that are longer on hope than capital come into existence. An estimated 90 to 95 percent of them, however, are out of business within two years.

So before investing your time and money in a direct-selling organization, it's important to make sure the company you're joining is worth investing your time and your priceless energy in. This means being able to distinguish a sound business from an undercapitalized company or from an illegal pyramid scheme.

An illegal pyramid scheme exists if your profits are to come from signing people up rather than from product sales. An indicator that your profit comes from signing people up is that there is a cost, usually over $500, for obtaining the *right* to sell the product. If you have doubts about whether a plan is a pyramid scheme or you have questions about the soundness of the company, check out the company with the Better Business Bureau in your community or in the headquarters city of the company. You can also check with local and state consumer protection agencies, the assistant attorneys general responsible for consumer protection both in your state and in the headquarters state of the company, the regional office of the Federal Trade Commission, the U.S. Postal Inspection Service, and the Direct Selling Association in Washington, D.C. Be aware, however, that not finding a complaint does not mean the offer is legiti- mate. It may be new or people who have paid money for it may feel too embarrassed to complain.

Be skeptical of companies that promise you lifelong riches for a few hours of work a week in ads that feature well-dressed people standing in front of a Rolls- Royce, parked in front of a mansion with an Olympic-sized swimming pool. Neil Offen, president of the Direct Selling Association, says, "The opportunity in direct sales is real but it's hard, hard work to be successful. It takes forty to seventy hours a week." Recruiting other people into an organization takes endless meetings, phone calls, cajoling, counseling, and training.

If direct selling interests you, here are some questions to ask to help you find the right opportunity.

1. *Would you buy what this company is selling if it was not also a business opportunity?* You will find your own enthusiasm for and evaluation of the product or service more important than anything you are apt to gain from a motivational tape or sales seminar.

2. *Is the company selling consumable products that appeal to most peo- ple?* Because it takes many contacts to make sales, you want a product that large numbers of people desire and use often. Products should have some advantage, such as good price or high quality, over products available in stores or by mail or people will turn to established brands or discounted prices in stores. Quality products encourage repeat sales. That's important because it's easier to resell to people you've already sold to than to find new customers.

3. *How long has the company been in business?* Companies that have been in business for several years are better risks. Eldon Beard, who has been in- volved with MLM companies for a number of years, advises, "While 'ground- floor' and 'start-up' opportunities can be good, there is a much greater risk involved."

4. *Do you stand to lose much money?* Beard says, "Most legitimate MLM companies only require you to pay a small fee for a distributor kit; initial purchase of a volume of product is not a requirement for getting started in the business." If you actually stock and deliver products, does the company have a buy-back policy for the products you stock? Beard says, "A good company should offer to buy back unsold inventory for at least 80 percent of what you paid. If the company has no such policy, you could be stuck with a lot of unsold inventory should you decide to quit selling the product." In fact, you may want to select a company that requires little stocking of products. Products consume your capital, take up space, and force you to keep records and inventory.

5. *Is the sales and marketing plan easy to understand?* A complex plan with a hard-to-explain commission structure will make it difficult for many people to do well with it.

6. If success in the company you're considering depends on recruiting other people, do you have the ability to inspire other people's efforts and the stamina to deal with people's problems and long hours? The skills of a sales professional are less important than those of a sales manager, and it's been found that traditional sales skills do not translate into success in multilevel marketing. This is because most people who are *sold* on a business opportunity drop out as distributors within sixty days.

Direct sales is not for everyone. Common complaints are:

- Depending on your personality, it can be discouraging to encounter negativity from people who don't like direct sales or have themselves been involved with a failed MLM effort of one kind or another.
- With the exception of major companies that have lasted for decades, most companies and their products have short life spans. Fewer than two hundred companies account for 90 percent of the sales volume in direct sales.
- With mature companies, finding potential customers can be difficult.
- The constant emphasis on recruiting new people can be disconcerting.
- Contact with sales "evangelists" who prod and spur, and classify those who do not perform as "losers," is offensive.
- Some companies restrict advertising and limit the way products can be sold, such as not permitting their sale in retail stores even if the distributor is the store owner.
- Having to attend many evening and weekend meetings and rallies can mean sacrificing home life and relations with friends and family members who, as a result, may not look favorably on your enterprise.
- Most people don't make much money. According to The Amway Business Review for 1992 (SA4400), the average monthly gross income for "active" distributors was $65. From gross income must come all marketing expenses, travel, rallies, tapes, etc. Only 46 percent of distributors had active status. Similarly the average monthly income for Nu Skin distributors has been reported at $67 a month. On the high end of the industry, according to data compiled by the Direct Selling Association, only 1 in 1,000 MLM distributors (.1 percent) earned $150,000 or more in 1992.

Buying a Business Opportunity

Working from home has become so popular that today thousands of companies are selling *businesses-in-a-box* or what we sometimes call *just-add-water* or *mix-and-stir* businesses. Usually sold through television infomercials, magazine ads, or seminars attended by tens of thousands a week, these businesses generally are easy to understand and explain and place a premium on your ability to sell a product or service. Popular ones include 900 numbers, personalized children's books, scholarship matching, various services employing voice mail, and bi-monthly mortgage payments. However, others are actually in established fields or actual careers such as medical billing, and some may involve months of training. For example, At-Home Professions of Ft. Collins, Colorado, offers in-home training with award-winning course materials for people to become home-based medical transcriptionists, who turn doctors' taped patient notes into medical transcripts; and notereader/scopists, who convert and edit the stenotype produced by court reporters into fully written transcripts. Parent Effectiveness Training licenses people to teach its parent-education courses.

So while some business opportunities are of legitimate value, many of those sold through ads demand that you proceed with caution if you don't want to be disappointed. Lee Graham, who has analyzed hundreds of such business opportunities, says, "Eighty-five to ninety percent of what is advertised has no business value. Typically they're cheaply produced booklets eight to ten pages long containing little information of real value." Business opportunities sold through seminars may pump you up and create group feeding frenzies with $50,000 changing hands in minutes.

Business opportunities are not franchises. Although they may promise the buyer will make money from the business activity, they usually cost less, don't require payment of ongoing fees, and offer far less training, legal protection, and use of exclusive trademarks and procedures for operating the business.

We do meet people and hear about people on the Working From Home Forum on CompuServe who have made money at business opportunities. Because the price is generally under $500, buying a business opportunity can be an economical way to get a business. You can think of the investment as similar to one you would make in buying an expensive workbook or training program. However, we offer several cautions. Just as with a business you would start from scratch, make sure a business that sounds simple and easy is also one you will enjoy doing. Chances are good that much more hard work is involved than you might imagine or are led to believe. Few businesses prosper just by placing ads in newspapers and magazines. And because business opportunities are being sold by the thousands each week, you can expect plenty of competition from other people offering the same product or service in your area. So chances are your ad will be alongside a number of others offering the same thing. Remember you're not buying a business, you're buying an opportunity.

States are increasingly passing laws that provide consumer protection for buyers of business opportunities, generally for those costing more than $500. These require vendors to register with the state and disclose information to prospective buyers. Alabama, California, Connecticut, Florida, Georgia, Indiana, Iowa, Kentucky, Louisiana, Maine, Maryland, Michigan, Minnesota, Nebraska, North Carolina, Ohio, Oklahoma, South Carolina, South Dakota, Texas, Virginia, and Washington already have laws regulating business opportunity vendors, and other states will be joining them as more and more people battle to keep their middle-class standard of living in the 90s.

It only makes sense that the more money and time you will be asked to invest in a business opportunity, the more you owe it to yourself to check out its validity. Some ways to check out the value of a business opportunity are:

■ *Determine if the company has had complaints filed with the agencies listed on pages 54–55 and the state attorney general's office of your own state and the state in which the company is based.* If so, has the company satisfactorily resolved all or most complaints?

■ *Ask for the names and phone numbers of people who have bought this opportunity.* Call them. Check to see how long they have been in business. You want to talk with people who have been at the business for at least a year. Often the most enthusiastic people are those who are new to the business and still filled with high expectations. If there has been a training class, ask for the names and numbers of other people who were also in the class and talk with them. Check out the people you talk with to see if they have become "official" businesses, that is, have they obtained a business license or a business telephone line. Statistically at least one in ten will have.

■ *Ask the people you are talking to if they are being paid to talk with you.* Some unscrupulous companies use "singers"—people who are not actually doing the business but are paid to say they recommend it.

■ *Know what you are buying.* Are you buying a booklet, a training program, a business plan, a software package, ongoing support, special equipment, the right to sell the company's products retail or wholesale, or a license that allows you to use the company's business name? Different business opportunities may offer any one of these or any combination thereof. Assure yourself that what you receive is what you were told you would and is commensurate with what you're paying.

Common Work-at-Home Schemes, Scams, and Rip-offs

- Stuffing envelopes. This scheme involves nothing more than selling instructions and sample ads directing you to use them to get people to pay you to find out how they can stuff envelopes.
- Simple tasks like clipping newspaper coupons, keeping a diary based on watching TV or listening to the radio, reading books, taking photos, making videos and renting time on your computer that require you to send money to register or enroll.
- Lists or directories of work-at-home jobs.
- Any business plan that represents that you can easily make thousands of dollars by placing similar ads yourself.
- Plans that promise that many people will send you money and instruct you to send money to the top few names on a list, removing the first name and adding your name to the bottom of the list. Beware that the scheme may be called a mailing list or mail-order business and claim to be legal.

Resources for Identifying, Reporting, and Getting Help with Work-at-Home Schemes

Better Business Bureaus are located in about two hundred communities. The Council of Better Business Bureaus, Inc., 4200 Wilson Boulevard, Ste. 800, Arlington, VA 22203 publishes pamphlets entitled *Tips on Multi-Level Marketing (How to Tell a Legitimate Opportunity from a Pyramid Scheme)* and *Tips on Work-at-Home Schemes.* (703) 276-0100. Send a self-addressed envelope; include $2.00 for postage and handling.

Call for Action is an organization of volunteers based in Washington, D.C., that works with radio and television stations to help people get money back for victims and publishes a booklet *Scams, Schemes, and Deceptive Offers: How Small Businesses Can Survive the Great American Rip-Offs.* (202) 537-0585.

Consumer's Resource Handbook from the United States Office of Consumer Affairs is the most comprehensive listing of state, local, trade associations, and other sources of finding help on work-at-home scams and other consumer issues. It is available free by writing Handbook, Consumer Information Center, Pueblo, CO 81009. (719) 948-3334.

Federal Trade Commission, Division of Marketing Practices, Sixth Street and Pennsylvania Avenue, N.W., Room 200, Washington, DC 20580. (202) 326-3128.

National Business Opportunity Services, P.O. Box 6271, Washington, DC 20015 sells an explanatory guide covering many types of business opportunities and a summary of federal and state laws that protect business opportunity buyers.

National Fraud Information Center, Consumer Assistance Hotline. (800) 876-7060. 9:00 A.M.–5:30 P.M. Eastern Standard Time weekdays.

U.S. Postal Inspection Service, Fraud Branch, Room 3147, 475 L'Enfant Plaza, Washington, DC 20260 or contact your local postmaster for the number of the nearest Postal Inspection office. We recommend making a habit of sending the postal inspector chain letters, underpayment of first-class postage schemes, and other questionable offers you receive in the mail or that instruct you to use the mail.

Royal Canadian Mounted Police, 225 Jarvis Street, Toronto, Ontario, M5C 2M3 Canada

---

Making Sure You Don't Get Suckered

When we decide to pursue our dreams, to go for what we truly want instead of settling for whatever comes along, we automatically become vulnerable to being suckered. Dreams are often so fragile and yet so formidable that they're easily trampled on or abandoned. So whenever someone comes along who tells us what we so much want and need to hear, we can be like putty in their hands.

Following a dream can blind us to what would otherwise be the most obvious of hucksters. We've met countless people who purchased business opportunities or signed up for multilevel programs they had no business getting involved in because "it sounded so good." Even worse are the many painful stories we've heard from people who were taken in by unscrupulous partners, investors, agents, or reps who seemed to be the "answer to all their prayers." If you're a stay-at-home mother, a senior citizen, someone with a disability, unemployed, seeking a second income, or a college student, you are even more likely to be victimized, according to the Council of Better Business Bureaus.

Make sure you don't get taken. Whenever you hear someone saying the things you've been yearning to hear or things that sound so good you never dreamed you'd hear anything like them, let it be a warning signal that sets off an alarm in your head with bells, whistles, and bright shiny lights saying "Proceed with Caution." The minute you hear that alarm, immediately start to think of yourself as two distinct people traveling in a foreign country:

- A small child who's so thirsty and hungry that he would eat and drink anything he could get his hands on. That's the part of you that's pursuing your dream and believes it will happen despite the lack of support and negative messages you've encountered.
- The parent of that child who wants to make sure whatever his or her child eats and drinks won't poison him or make him ill. That's the part of you that cares enough to objectively protect you from getting suckered.

With this image in mind, here are some guidelines the parent part of you can use to protect your eager and hungry child from the tempting sights and smells of opportunity knocking.

1. Don't make decisions about opportunities from your heart alone.   Run all such "offers" through careful, objective scrutiny.

2. Always arrange to take the time you need to make an objective, informed decision.   Do not let yourself be pressured into acting immediately.

In fact, the more someone pressures you to act this very minute, the more suspicious you should be. We once had a salesperson tell us, for example, that we had to sign a contract that very day after a thirty-minute phone conversation or they could not proceed. We ran like a couple of rabbits. What kind of company would want to do business with someone who would make a decision like that on the spot?

3. Don't be tempted by special offers that prevent you from making an objective, informed decision;   i.e., "My prices go up tomorrow. This discount only applies today." Fine. Find out what the price will be once you've had the time you need to make an informed decision and consider that paying the difference will be well worth the investment. If the cost at that time will be prohibitive, look elsewhere.

4. Do not do business with any company or individual that refuses to give you the names, addresses, and telephone numbers of other people they have worked with.

5. Never, never ignore that little voice in your head or that little twinge in your stomach that's telling you to proceed with caution.   That's your intuition and if you don't listen to it, later you'll be saying, "Something told me this was too good to be true. Why didn't I listen!" If you have any doubts, wait. Gather more information. Give your doubts time to surface so you can either dismiss or address them with confidence.

6. Ask yourself, what's the worst thing that could happen?   Sometimes an offer sounds so good, you just want to throw caution to the wind and go for it. Before you do, however, make sure you're willing to live with the worst thing that could happen.

For example, if you impulsively send off $100 for a guidebook, the worst thing that could happen might be that it would sit on your bookshelf unused.

But if you buy a $10,000 business opportunity at an expo, that could set your family finances back more than you can afford.

If someone requires you to sign a two-year exclusive distribution contract, you're giving up all other opportunities during that period.

These guidelines and the ones in chapter 4 should help you protect the tender, but challenging, dreams you're raising into a healthy, strapping business that will provide ample sustenance for you and your family.

Roadblocks: Six Problems to Avoid

Our favorite questions to ask successful home business people are: "What surprises did you have? Did you encounter any detours? Were there any land mines hiding along your path?" And, indeed, whether they start a business from scratch, buy a franchise, or join a direct-sales organization, their answers indicate common surprises, detours, and roadblocks. Here are six of the most common problems and some ideas on how to avoid them.

Never Getting Started

Many who hope to start a business never get beyond the wishful-thinking stage. In the press of our day-to-day responsibilities, some brilliant ideas and good intentions get put on the back burner and remain a matter of "Someday I'm going to . . ." Some ideas, of course, are best forgotten, but unless you give them a chance, you'll never know which ones would have worked—until one day you read in the paper or hear on TV about someone else who beat you to it by turning your idea into a success story.

To avoid the death of a good idea, plan to research and test yours as soon as you get it. Begin by reading up on the subject and talking with others who know about what you want to do. Find out who's already working in the field. Tell other people about your idea and get their reactions. If the idea still seems good, set out a step-by-step plan to test it, and establish target dates to complete each step. Then put your plan into action.

The Capital Squeeze and Money Mismanagement

Lack of capital and proper financial management are the most common reasons small businesses fail. Some of the typical financial problems home businesses encounter are: not enough money to cover start-up and operating expenses; not enough money to grow; too much debt; cash-flow problems; inadequate financial planning; not charging enough to make a profit; poor credit and collection practices; inadequate bookkeeping. Here are some rules of thumb for avoiding these problems.

Start small. Unless you have extensive experience in running a business like the one you plan to start and have contracts in hand, we advise that you keep your start-up expenses low. Peggy Glenn started a successful typing service in her kitchen with $65. She rented a typewriter, bought a few supplies, and advertised by placing index cards on college bulletin boards. Within three months, she was earning a profit.

Your business may demand more of an initial investment. But try at least to keep it under $10,000, or preferably under $5,000. Many businesses can be started for under $1,000, particularly if you already have an answering machine, computer, and printer so that most of your money goes into marketing materials (business cards, stationery, association dues, samples, fliers and newsletters) and software to operate your business.

If your resources are limited, start gradually. Use your brains instead of your checkbook. Find a college art class to design your logo, cards, and stationery. Have your business cards printed one month, your stationery the next. Even if you're unemployed and have little savings, you may be able to use unemployment insurance funds to start your business. Based on successful pilot programs in Massachusetts and Washington, Congress as part of the North American Free Trade Act authorized the states to in turn pass legislation that will allow up to 5 percent of people receiving unemployment insurance to start businesses. The Washington and Massachusetts programs found that people starting businesses were able to get off unemployment more quickly than those who were looking for jobs.

Go easy on loans and investors. Finance start-up yourself, if possible. There is no single way to finance a business. You can use your own funds, find investors, or borrow. Although it's very tempting to try to find investors or to get a loan, we advise planning to finance your business yourself to the extent possible until you see that it will be a winner. Often it's difficult to get loans or investors for a start-up home business anyway unless you are beginning with lucrative contracts or purchase orders in hand, have an outstanding reputation in your field, or are buying a franchise or existing business that backs you up with a known name. And borrowing, even from friends or relatives, puts your new business under the additional financial pressure of having to pay back the loan.

Fortunately, however, most home businesses do not involve extensive start-up costs. As a result most people can "bootstrap" their business. That is, they can get under way using financial resources they have on hand such as existing earnings, savings, investment income, retirement funds, or insurance loans to start the business. Many people finance limited start-up costs on credit cards. Here is a list of possible sources of bootstrap funding:

Five Sources of Bootstrap Financing

- **W-4 adjustment:** Since you will become eligible for some business and home office tax deductions, reduce your W-4 withholding on your existing job and use the additional income you will get in your paycheck to cover your business start-up costs.
- **Credit cards:** You can put many business expenses such as printing or even postage on a credit card. We recommend having two credit cards: one for your personal expenses, one for your business expenses. To avoid building up

a large debt at credit card interest rates, however, limit credit card charges to smaller costs or costs for items like a computer, laser printer, or goods that will pay for themselves relatively quickly by generating immediate income.

■ **Personal loans:** If you or a spouse has an existing job and a good credit record, banks will sometimes make a personal loan more quickly than they would make a business loan to someone who has no business track record. Credit unions are another possible route to get a personal loan.

■ **Home equity loans:** Some people who own their own home are able to refinance their home loan as a route to obtaining a reservoir of start-up capital. If you have a good credit history, you may be able to get a "line of credit" on your home loan that you can draw upon as needed.

■ **Character-based microloans:** The Small Business Administration and a variety of private foundations are creating a growing number of microloan programs that make small loans, i.e., from under $100 to $25,000, to very small businesses, including home businesses. Under the federal program, money can be used to buy machinery and equipment, furniture and fixtures, inventory, supplies, and for working capital. It may not be used to pay existing debts. The money must be repaid in no longer than six years.

These loans are based, not upon your credit history or collateral, but on good character, sufficient management ability, and commitment to making your plan successful. The Small Business Administration funds local nonprofit organizations to process microloan applications. Call or visit the nearest office of the Small Business Administration to find the agencies processing these loans in your area.

Develop an entry plan. Depending on the business you're in, it can take from six months to a year to get under way, a year to three years to turn a profit, and three to five years to become self-sustaining. How to cover your costs of living and doing business until you're turning a profit is one of the biggest challenges a home entrepreneur faces.

If you have a job, keep it. Meanwhile, find out whether the business is viable. Do your homework. Figure out the bare minimum you need for living expenses and business expenses. Then establish an entry plan, a way to cover that minimum until your business is going.

Using the moonlighting plan, Sandra Oker started doing career counseling in the evenings and on weekends. When she had enough clients to pay for her rent, food, and gasoline, she quit her job. On the part-time plan, John Eldridge worked part-time in a health-food store for several hours a week while building a community theater into a viable business. Market researcher Ken Sobel lined up six months' worth of work from his employer in exchange for a six-month noncompete agreement in which a dozen key clients were named whose business he agreed not to solicit. On the cushion plan, James Milburn used his personal savings to support himself after leaving his position as an accountant to become a computer programmer.

Examples of Home Businesses Receiving Microloans

Accounting
Air-conditioning
Baked goods
Beauty shop
Bedspreads
Bookkeeping
Business services
Cash register sales
Catering
Children's books
Christmas wreaths
Cleaning services
Clothing design and creation
Computer services
Computer training
Computerized embroidery
Contract estimating
Dance studio
Data processing
Day care
Designer watchbands
Desktop publishing
Dog sleds
Eldercare
Exotic birds
Financial services
Fishing lures
Fitness trainer
Forestry consulting
Fuel additives
Graphic arts
Greeting cards
Gun bluing
Image consulting
Income tax preparation

Interior design
Inventing
Jewelry
Laundry/video arcade
Lawn care
Legal firm
Limo services
Maple products
Marketing firm
Metal manufacturing
Model soldiers
Motor repair
Musical entertainer
Organic gardening and vinegar
   production
Patio furniture
Pet-sitting
Pig farm
Renovation
Seamstress
Security services
Seminar leader
Signs in Braille
Signs and banners
Soap manufacturing
Software sales
Sporting goods
Tour guide
Transporting handicapped
Making truck liners
Trucking company
Utility auditing
Video documentary
Word processing

Six Plans for Starting a Home Business

1. **The Moonlighting Plan.** Keep your full-time job and develop your business as a sideline. When it takes off, you can go full-time. Be sure to work at least eight hours a week on a sideline business.
2. **The Part-time Plan.** Work a part-time job to provide a base income while you're building up the business. When your business equals the base income, drop the part-time job.
3. **The Spin-off Plan.** Turn your previous employer into your first major customer or, when ethically possible, take a major client with you from your previous job.
4. **The Cushion Plan.** Find a financial resource to support yourself with while you start your business. Your cushion should be large enough to cover your base expenses for at least six to twelve months. Time can be another cushion. You might start a business while on sabbatical or leave.
5. **The Piggyback Plan.** If you have a working spouse or partner, cut back your expenses so you can live on one salary until your business gets going.
6. **The Have-Your-Clients-Finance-You Plan.** If you have sufficient stature in your field, you might obtain retainer contracts with clients for the first year that provide you with assured revenue in exchange for offering them services at 25 percent less than the billing rate you establish.

Manage your cash flow. In a new home business you often must pay cash up front while waiting for your own customers to pay for your products or services. Covering expenses while waiting for income is the bane of small businesses.

Here are three basic strategies you can use for managing cash flow wisely:

1. Minimize what others owe you. Get deposits, retainers, and partial or progress payments. Take bank cards instead of giving credit. Ask for cash at the time of the sale.
2. Get maximum benefit from cash on hand. For example, deposit cash in interest-bearing accounts and use cash-management programs.
3. Hold on to what you've got. Ask for interest-free credit from suppliers. Charge your expenses on bank cards. Make timely, not immediate, payment of bills. Lease your car or truck instead of buying it.

Inexperience

The second most common reason small businesses fail is their owners' lack of experience and knowledge. In the past this was often an unalterable limitation. Our knowledge was restricted to what we could learn at home, school, or work. But not today. Today information is available on virtually everything you might want to know.

If you're weak on sales skills, you can take courses, read books, or get private consultation on how to sell. If you're timid in negotiating contracts, you can use assertiveness-training courses, personal-growth seminars, or private counseling to improve your skills.

A recent survey of new businesses found that after three years of being in business, successful entrepreneurs had:

1. Taken six to ten months to research and to prepare for their business ventures.
2. Used professional advisers in setting up the business.
3. Taken business-related courses and read regularly about business management.

You can also learn a field by working as an apprentice. Apprenticing is a very old practice deserving a new look for those starting a new life. Apprenticing yourself can range from taking a job that will also qualify you for a license, like a private detective, to paying someone already in the business of your choice to follow him around, accompanying him for a week or longer. You may avoid paying for this real-world training by exchanging your being a free assistant in return for experience and the ability to ask questions. It may even be worth your while to pay for the experience.

To increase your odds for success, become an information consumer in your field and in the general area of business. Read books, magazines, and newsletters. Attend seminars, conventions, and classes. Buy and listen to tapes by experts who have the skills you need. Talk with those who can advise you in business matters.

For specific information about your business area, contact professional or trade associations. Ask your local reference librarian to recommend a reading list. You can start with the resources listed at the end of this chapter.

Marketing Misconceptions

Accountant Susan Gwenn made the mistake so many people with new businesses make. After completing long and arduous training, she sent out announcements that she was opening her practice. Then she sat back, waiting in vain for the phone to ring. Similarly, potter Gloria Greene displayed her wares in one art fair after another only to carry most of her pots home again, wondering if she were as talented as she had thought.

The problem in both cases was marketing, or the lack of it. Thinking a good product or service will sell itself is the most common marketing misconception of new entrepreneurs. Often artists, writers, professionals, technicians, information specialists, and consultants start their businesses with little knowledge, interest, or skill in marketing and selling. Without it, you have no business and, let's face it, you aren't a business until you've got business.

As researcher Sue Rugge found in starting Information on Demand, "Marketing is the key to everything. Doing your work is the easy part. It's the selling that's the hard part. You can never sit back. Every day you have to sell yourself again." Starting with this philosophy, Sue made "house calls." She sold her research services door to door. She gave her card to everyone she knew. It was this effort that turned the $250 she and her partner started with into sales of half a million dollars.

Since most home businesses can't hire a marketing agency in the beginning, selling yourself and your product or service will probably become *your* task. Consequently, you'll need to develop what we call a "marketing mind-set," a way of thinking about business from a marketing viewpoint. This doesn't mean you have to take on a phony sales personality, but you do have to become good at letting the people who need your business know about it in a way that will convince them to buy. And you can. To learn the marketing mind-set and the skills you'll need, start with the books, tapes, and newsletters in the Resources list at the end of this chapter, and refer to chapter 23: "Successfully Marketing Your Home Business."

A Marginal Business Image

Think about the businesses you patronize. What do you expect from them? Of course, you want a good price, but people also want to feel confident that the business they're buying from is substantial, that it will be here tomorrow. They want to believe they can count on buying a quality product or service that delivers what it offers.

How do you know whether a company has those qualities? Until you've bought from a business and tested it, all you have to go on is image. Image is where some home businesses fall down, however. Started on too tight a budget or operated too casually, a home business can look like an amateur effort.

Unfortunately, such a marginal business image creates a negative image for all home businesses and leaves the impression that a home business is not a real business. So in setting up your enterprise, pay attention to creating a professional image. It doesn't take a big budget. It only requires attention to detail. Avoid such indicators of an amateur operation as letters printed on a dot matrix printer, no one (or children) answering the phone during business hours, dirty clothes and dishes in business areas, irregular hours, unclear fee schedules, and a backlog of unpaid bills. Take conscious steps to make a professional impression.

Giving Up

Like the "golden hour" in emergency medical care, the first year is the most critical year for business survival. It can get long and lonely. But you need to experiment, adjust, and test. As Thomas J. Watson, the founder of IBM, ironically advised, "The way to succeed is to double your failure rate." Persist until you find what works. In the meantime, make friends, and join relevant groups and organizations for support and encouragement through the rough spots. Listen to the advice of people who have been there and can make your way smoother. And always conduct your business in accord with the highest ethical standards.

Proposed Home-Business Code of Ethics

Because being taken seriously remains one of the top concerns of home business owners, we recommend that all home businesses consider subscribing to the following code of ethics as a way to build the credibility and image of their own business and home business throughout their community and nationwide.

1. Conduct your business in an above-board professional manner, operating within local, state, and federal laws.
2. Accurately and realistically represent what you do in all marketing, advertising, and promotional activities.
3. Undertake only that work which you are qualified for and capable of providing within the time frame and price agreed to.
4. Communicate all fees or the basis for fees in advance of providing your service or product.
5. Obtain clear, up-front agreements of precisely what you will be providing.
6. Notify clients or customers immediately if, for any reason, you cannot complete the work you have undertaken within the agreed-upon time frame.
7. When necessary, contact clients about any changes in what you will be providing them, prior to proceeding.
8. Stand behind your product or service.
9. Operate within the same professional standards and practices that you would expect from a business located outside the home.
10. Keep all proprietary information obtained from clients and customers confidential, and refrain from using such information for personal or financial gain.
11. Avoid all conflicts of interests in serving your clients or customers.
12. Work within your community and field to enhance the image and reputation of your home business.

Tips from Successful Entrepreneurs

In the long run, the successful entrepreneurs we talked with managed to avoid these problems and learn, not always the easy way, how to survive and grow. Here are a few of their conclusions:

■ **"You have to be the best at what you do.** You can't fake it. Even then, the phone doesn't always ring on the first day. You're always three months away from a new client. You have to develop your marketing plan to ensure that the phone does ring. You have to set aside time each week for PR. I try never to have lunch alone, for example. If I'm going to eat lunch, I eat with a business contact. I never know who a prospective client will be, so I treat everyone like a prospective client."—William Slavin, consultant, William Slavin and Associates.

■ **"A satisfied customer is always your best source of business.** When you advertise, though, you don't have to buy a big ad. In fact, the small ads I run regularly draw more business than the several-hundred-dollar ads I ran only once. I find running an ad regularly that has some kind of logo and catchy copy draws best."—Barbara Elman, writer.

■ **"Everything in business is a result of networking.** Whether it's getting an article published or finding a distributor, I keep in contact with old friends, past co-workers, and sales reps who used to call on me. I can't stress it

---

Twelve Money-Saving Ways to Give Your Home Business a *Fortune* 500 Image

1. **Spring for a business telephone line.** An effective name doesn't help you a whole lot if people can't find it in the phone book or when calling for information.
2. **Answer the phone with finesse.** Answer after two rings with a positive professional greeting using your name or the name of your business. Have an answering service or answering machine take calls when you're not there. Call yourself to listen for the impression your answering machine recording or voice mail makes.
3. **Communicate quality with a custom-designed logo.** Use your own unique custom-designed logo on business cards, letterheads, envelopes, and invoices. Do not select a logo from among the standard designs offered by your printer. To keep your costs down, arrange to have a college class design your logo as a class project.
4. **Show substance with a federal ID number.** If you have an employee or are a partnership, use a Federal Identification number for business purposes in place of your Social Security number. It's a no-cost way to dress your business for success. To obtain a Federal ID number, simply apply at the nearest Internal Revenue Service office.
5. **Select a strategic location for your office.** If you have business guests coming to your home, consider locating your office so you can have a separate business entrance, or locate your office near the front or side door so business guests don't have to walk through or past personal areas of the household. Make sure that any areas business guests must pass en route to your office are neat, clean, and clear of overly personal items like toiletries, children's toys, photographs, and household items. Use tasteful screens, drapes, or dividers if necessary to separate personal areas from business areas of the house.
6. **Let your checks speak for you.** Use full-sized checks on business stock with your business name printed on them. They cost no more than the smaller decorated personal checks. Use a check protector for entering the amount in large raised numerals, or use a computer with software to print your checks.

7. **Use only top-quality paper.** Choose paper that looks and feels top grade for your letterhead, envelopes, and business cards. Fine paper doesn't cost that much more. We recommend 70-lb. bond for letterhead and envelopes. Buy the paper at a printer's supply house or directly from a paper company. You then supply it to your printer as "customer stock."

8. **Equip your office professionally.** The cost and size of electronic office equipment today makes it possible to equip your home office with the kind and quality of equipment you'd expect to find in any top-notch office in your field. Equipment that will enhance your image includes a photocopier that makes quality plain-paper copies, a letter-quality printer (preferably a laser printer), and a fax. Here's an added tip: Next time you reprint your business cards, include your fax number.

9. **Polish your correspondence.** A recent nationwide survey of executives by Communispond, Inc., showed that four out of five executives listed the ability to write as the most neglected skill in business. Even if your words don't flow magically from your fingers to your screen, your correspondence can be grammatically and stylistically correct using grammar-checking software.

10. **Incorporate for image.** Although there are several other reasons for incorporating, think about adding *Corporation* or *Inc.* to your company name to enhance your business image. Before making such a change, however, consult with a knowledgeable tax professional and an attorney to determine whether this would be a wise business decision. If you decide it is, have these professionals help you select one of several options for the way your corporation will be taxed.

11. **Dress for success.** Although the sweat suit may be the official uniform of the open-collar worker, dress like a successful person at the top of your field when meeting with customers, clients, and suppliers.

12. **Project a positive attitude.** Share good news. Radiate confidence. Remember, self-assurance attracts, self-doubt repels.

---

enough—your friends and contacts are your best assets."—Gil Gordon, management consultant, Gil Gordon and Associates.

■ **"You have to really care about what you're doing.** Everything takes three times longer and costs five times more than you think it will. We wouldn't have kept going if we hadn't had a strong commitment to what we are doing."—Elizabeth Scott, developer and co-founder of Rhiannon, a software company.

■ **"As you travel down this path, discomfort is sometimes a companion,** though seldom for extensive periods. And on the other side of discomfort you will discover a new high that comes with a deeper sense of your own worth. To me that is the bottom line."—Sue Rugge, co-founder of Information on Demand.

Resources

Books

The Best Home-Based Franchises. Gregory Matusky and The Phillip Lief Group. New York: Doubleday, 1992.

Being the Best You Can Be in MLM: How to Train Your Way to the Top in Multi-Level Marketing. John Kalench. San Diego: Millionaires Press, 1990.

Best Home Businesses for the 90s. Paul and Sarah Edwards. New York: Tarcher/Putnam, 1991.

Career Shifting. William A. Charland, Jr.. Holbrook, Mass.: Bob Adams, Inc., 1993.

The Complete Handbook for the Entrepreneur. Gary Brenner, MBA, JD; Joel Ewan, MBA; and Henry Chuster, Ph.D., CPA. Englewood Cliffs, N.J.: Prentice-Hall, 1990.

The Complete Work-at-Home Companion. Herman Holtz. Rocklin, Calif.: Prima Pub Communications, 1990.

Entrepreneurial PC series of books on specific home-based businesses. Edited by Paul and Sarah Edwards. For list, write Windcrest/McGraw-Hill, Inc., Blue Ridge Summit, PA 17294.

Creative Cash: How to Sell Crafts, Needlework, Designs and Know-How. Barbara Brabec. Huntington Beach, Calif.: Aames-Allen Publishing, 1986.

Encyclopedia of Associations. Detroit: Gale Research Company. Published annually.

Government Assistance Almanac: The Guide to All Federal Financial and Other Domestic Programs. J. Robert Dumouchel. Detroit: Omni-graphics. Annual.

Government Giveaways for Entrepreneurs. Matthew Lesko. Information USA, 10335 Kensington Pkwy., Kensington, MD 20895.

Growing a Business. Paul Hawken. New York: Simon & Schuster, 1987.

Home Inc.: the Canadian Home-Based Business Guide. Douglas A. Gray and Diana Lynn. Toronto: McGraw-Hill Ryerson, Ltd., 1989.

Homemade Business. Donna Partow. Colorado Springs, Co.: Focus on the Family, 1992.

Homemade Money. Barbara Brabec. White Hall, Va.: Betterway Publications, 1994.

The Home Office Book. Mark Alvarez. Woodbury, Conn.: Goodwood Press, 1990.

Info-Power II. Matthew Lesko. Detroit: Visible Ink Press, 1994.

Making It on Your Own. Sarah and Paul Edwards. New York: Tarcher/Putnam, 1991.

Making Money with Your Computer at Home. Paul and Sarah Edwards. New York: Tarcher/Putnam, 1993.

Multi-level Marketing. The Summit Group, Ft. Worth, Texas, 1994.

Running a One-Person Business. Claude Whitmyer, Salli Rasberry, and Michael Phillips. Berkeley, Calif.: Ten Speed Press, 1989.

Self-Made in America. John McCormack with David R. Legge. Reading, Mass.: Addison-Wesley, 1990.

Schemes and Scams. Douglas P. Shadel and John T., North Hollywood, Calif.: Newcastle Publishing, 1994.

Succeeding in Business, Jane Applegate. New York: Plume, 1992.

Thomas' Register of Manufacturers. Thomas Publishing Co., One Penn Plaza, New York, NY 10119; (212) 695-0500. A multivolume affair listing the makers of many industrial products. Some companies have their product catalogs included. Useful in locating sources of supply, either for your own use, or for resale. Available at most libraries.

A Whack on the Side of the Head—How to Unlock Your Mind for Innovation. Roger von Oech. New York: Warner, 1988.

Periodicals

Entrepreneur. 2392 Morse Ave., Irvine, CA 92714. **Entrepreneur** also periodically publishes **Entrepreneur Magazine's Guide to Home-Based Business.**

Head Office at Home: The Canadian Magazine for People Who Work at Home. Abasco Communications, Ltd., 145 Royal Crest Court, Unit 2, Markham, ON L3R 924.

Home Office Computing. Scholastic, Inc., 730 Broadway, New York, NY 10003.

In Business. Magna Publications, Inc., 2718 Dryden Dr., Madison, WI 53704. Focuses on environmentally oriented businesses.

Small Business Opportunities. Harris Publications, 1115 Broadway, New York, NY 10010.

The Whole Work Catalog. The New Careers Center, P.O. Box 2193, Boulder, CO 80306.

Courses

Hire Yourself and Work From Home. Eight-week course created by Sarah and Paul Edwards, Home Business Services, 1873 South Bellaire Street, Ste. 1110, Denver, CO 80222; (303) 758-9005.

Government and Community Resources

Small Business Administration:
The Small Business Administration offers a variety of services that although primarily focused on larger small businesses can also benefit home-based businesses. These include:

■ Advice and technical assistance through Small Business Centers operated by universities and chambers of commerce, the Service Corps of Retired Executives (SCORE), and Small Business Information Centers in major cities. To contact the Small Business Administration for the locations of these services in your area, look in your telephone directory under U.S. Government for your local SBA office or call the Small Business Answer Desk at (800) 8-ASK-SBA ([800] 827-5722).

■ Publications. To determine current publications and prices, write for order forms 115A and 115B, Small Business Administration, P.O. Box 15434, Ft. Worth, TX 76119.

■ Microloans processed by local nonprofit organizations. See page 59.

■ SBA Online is available using your modem by phoning (800) 859-INFO for 2400 baud access; (800) 697-INFO for 9600. Some parts of this service are free, some are not.

Department of Defense:
The Department of Defense has a Small Business Innovation Grant program. To get information, call the Defense Technical Information Center at (800) 225-3842.

Internal Revenue Service:
New Business Tax Kit. Available in local IRS offices or phone (800) 424-3676 for further information.

State and Local Sources

Most parts of the United States and Canada provide some assistance to small business. These include:

■ state and provincial economic development agencies
■ local colleges
■ public libraries
■ chambers of commerce

Radio and Television

Home Business Show on some local cable stations and available with a satellite dish on Galaxy 7, Transponder 20V.
Working From Home with Paul and Sarah Edwards. On the Home and Garden Cable Network (fall 1994).
Working From Home Show. Hosted by Paul and Sarah Edwards (Sundays at 10 P.M. Eastern, 7 P.M. Pacific) on the Business Radio Network and available with a satellite dish on Digital: Satcom C-5, Transponder 15 and Analog: Satcom C-5, Transponder 3.

Software

B-Tools. Star Software Systems, 363 Van Ness Way, Torrance, CA 90501; (310) 533-1190.
IdeaFisher. Idea Fisher System, Inc., 2222 Martin Street, Ste. 110, Irvine, CA 92715; (800)289-4332, (714)474-8111.
Success, Inc. Dynamic Pathways, 180 Newport Center Drive, Ste. 180, Newport Beach, CA; (714) 720-8462.
Tim Berry's Business Plan Toolkit. Palo Alto Software, Inc., 144 E. 14th Street, Eugene, OR 94301; (800)229-7526, (503)683-6162.

CHAPTER
FOUR

■■■■■■■■■■■■■■■■■■■■■■■■■■■■■

Working for Someone Else:
Paychecks and Other Possibilities

Every three hours every day of the year, someone uses the Working From Home Forum on CompuServe to seek information about how to find a job they can do at home. Still others seek advice on how to get their management to let them take their job home. They want to combine the security and benefits of a job—health insurance, a pension plan, sick leave, paid holidays and, above all, a paycheck—with working from home. They tell us:

"I like my job, but with all the interruptions at the office it's hard to get anything done. I'd like to convince my supervisor we would all benefit if I could work at home part of every week."

"I'm the sole supporter of my kids. I need a steady income I can count on every week, but I'd sure like to be there when they get home from school."

"I've thought of starting my own business, but I think I would have a hard time getting customers. With my disability it's hard for me to get out of the house. I'm trained in keypunch, though, and if an employer could get the work to me I'd be in business."

"I'm in a bind. Next year my husband will be transferred to a city three hundred miles away. I'm going with him, but I hate to leave my job. I could do almost everything it calls for with a telephone and a computer terminal. Maybe I can arrange to stay on and work long distance."

"I hate losing one to two hours commuting in traffic and another hour getting dressed up every day. And I cannot say enough bad things about having to wear high heels to work."

Fortunately, there is a trend in many companies and government agencies to allow employees to work from home. Since 1992, more than 40 percent of corporations with more than 5,000 employees have established formal telecommuting programs. At one point, AT&T and IBM were even making work from home mandatory for thousands of salespeople. This trend is a phenomenon in search of a name. Variously called telecommuting (substituting *commuting* for *communications*), teleworking (working from a distance), flexiplace (flexible workplace), each expression has its champions. Whatever you choose to call it, let's take a look at some of the many jobs being done from home.

Salaried Jobs You Can Hold at Home

Accountant
Actuary
Advertising copy writer
Advertising sales representative
Answering service operator
Architect
Assembly worker
Auditor
Booking agent
Bookkeeper
Budget analyst
Buyer
Computer programmer
Computer systems analyst
Computer technician
Cost estimator
Customer service representative
Data entry clerk
Database administrator
Desktop publisher
Economist
Editor
Environmental analyst
Financial analyst
Graphic designer
Illustrator
Indexer
Instructional designer
Insurance agent
Insurance claims adjuster
Interpreter
Interviewer
Inventory control clerk
Lawyer

Market research analyst
Marketing planner
Medical records technician
Medical reviewer
Medical transcriptionist
News reporter
Operations research analyst
Paralegal
Patent searcher
Personnel analyst
Pollster
Probation or parole officer
Public relations professional
Purchasing agent
Real estate agent
Records manager
Researcher
Reservation agent
Sales representative
Secretary
Social worker
Software engineer
Speechwriter
Stockbroker
Technical writer
Telemarketer
Telephone order taker
Transcriber
Translator
Travel agent
Typesetter
Urban planner
Utility rate forecaster
Word processor

The opportunity to work at home spans all levels of the office hierarchy, from vice-presidents to data-entry workers. Writers, artists, accountants, researchers, lawyers, and computer programmers can easily work from home. So can many clerical, data-processing, and communications personnel. Technical jobs that require a lot of reading and report writing are well suited for work at home, as are jobs that require large amounts of travel or fieldwork. Even many managerial or supervisory positions in areas such as purchasing, pensions, sales, and planning can be done at home.

Although there are an ample number of jobs that can be done at home, finding one that is right for you is not necessarily easy. There are two primary routes to finding a job at home. You can convince your present employer to allow you to start working from home. Or, when that's not possible, you can start from scratch and find a new job as a work-at-homer.

Bringing Your Current Job Home

Senior Editor Nick Sullivan of *Home Office Computing* magazine, himself a teleworker, says, "In general, I think it's easier to get a job and *then* talk about doing it at home." And we agree. Although it's still not the norm, more companies are allowing employees to work at least part-time from home.

Salaried work at home grew at an estimated 20 to 30 percent a year during the 1980s. In a recent study of corporate plans for the nineties by the Conference Board, a business research firm, it was reported that 56 percent of corporations plan to allow home-based work in the future. Increasingly, companies are finding it makes more sense to move the work than to move people. Some companies institute formal work-at-home programs for which you apply in order to work at home. However, more than three out of four companies that allow employees to work at home do so on an informal basis.

The extent to which you can work from home without a formal program depends on what arrangement you can make with your supervisor. Whether done on a formal or an informal basis, being able to work at home means first proving that you are a capable and reliable self-starter. Even then, you can still expect to have some convincing to do.

Convincing Your Employer to Let You Work at Home

Even if your job can be done at home, why should your company allow you to work from home? What motivates a company to step outside convention and try something this new and revolutionary? Obviously companies need to see that the benefits will be worth the risks. Here are several of the primary reasons companies are having employees work from home. Think about which of the following will motivate your management.

■ Increase productivity. After studying over two hundred companies with work-at-home projects, telecommuting consultant Gil Gordon reports that "company productivity rises from 15 to 25 percent when people work at home." These gains are possible because employees can work at their own pace and at their peak energy hours. They can work longer because of time saved commuting. Also, work gets done more quickly without office interruptions and socializing. Instead of taking "work breaks," as they might at the office, they take "rest breaks."

■ Overcome staff shortages. Whenever the demand for workers exceeds the supply, as is currently the case with secretaries, medical transcriptionists, engineers, and software engineers, the alternative of working at home can become a way for companies to attract prospective employees not available for office work. Employees working at home can also reduce the cost of temporaries.

■ Reduce turnover. Because of high job satisfaction, salaried at-home workers rarely quit their jobs. And by allowing valued employees to work at home, companies don't lose them if they move (or the company relocates), or if they decide to start a family, or need to care for someone who becomes ill. Not having to train new employees can result in considerable savings for a company.

■ Decrease absenteeism. Employees can work at home despite illness, bad weather, sick children, waiting for home deliveries, or service calls that would otherwise cause them to miss work.

■ Lower costs. Companies can save on space and parking. Savings of $5,000 or more per employee are not unusual. Growing companies do not need to have their growth limited by the cost and lost time involved in finding additional office and parking facilities. Companies with their own buildings can even consider leasing the space made available by employees who are working at home, and the rental income can increase profits.

■ Use as an incentive. Allowing people to work at home is an alternative to promotion in companies where reorganization or downsizing provides fewer management positions. It can also be used to acknowledge and reward valued employees.

Once you are aware of what factors may motivate your company to let you work from home, your next step is to consider carefully the feasibility of doing your job at home. What tasks can be done at home? Which ones require you to be in the office? What difficulties might develop and how would you handle situations such as suddenly needing information that's only available at the office?

For most managers to consider having employees work at home, the work must be easily measured. You and the manager need to know without a doubt when the work you do has been completed. It should have a precise beginning and end and require minimal face-to-face contact with co-workers. Before proposing a permanent plan to work at home, build a track record of working from home informally. Occasionally ask to take your work home for the afternoon. Then try proposing to work at home on a specific project for a day or two.

Only take work home when you feel confident you can do an outstanding job. Keep in touch by phoning in each day to find out if anything has arisen that you need to handle. Follow up on all messages immediately, so no one will feel you are inaccessible.

Consultant Gil Gordon suggests that even after doing your homework and building a track record, "don't go for broke all at once. Approach management with the idea that you'll work at home on a small scale—perhaps starting one or two days a week at most—for the first two to three months."

Finding a New Job to Work at Home

Although taking your existing job home is your best chance of working from home on a salary, there are several ways to find a job to work at home.

Long-standing home-based jobs. Salespeople and repair and customer service personnel in some industries, such as publishing and pharmaceuticals, have long used their homes as their work headquarters. But these are generally work-*from*-home jobs as distinct from work-*at*-home jobs.

How to Determine Whether Your Job Can Be Done at Home

☐ Does your job require little face-to-face contact?
☐ Can needed face-to-face contact be scheduled into a weekly time at the office?
☐ Are the expectations for what you produce and when you produce it clear?
☐ Is your performance easily measurable?
☐ Can you work without physical access to resources and materials at the office?
☐ Can needed access to resources and materials be scheduled into a weekly time at the office?
☐ Does the job require a great deal of concentration without interruptions?
☐ Is there adequate security at your home for your work?

Each yes answer you can give increases the likelihood that your job can be done at home.

Personal contacts. Your most likely way to get a new job to work at home is through people you know or meet. Nearly two out of three people hired to work at home are employed by firms with fewer than a hundred employees. Your best chance to work at home, therefore, is with a small company in your hometown. Such a job might be doing word processing, typesetting, desktop publishing, billing for a doctor's office, taking telephone calls, or doing bookkeeping.

You find these jobs the same way you find any other kind of job. Research by the National Center for Career Strategies indicates that fully 70 percent of all jobs are obtained through personal contacts, or what is called "networking." As one employer who hires people to work at home told us, "The only way to get work is to ask for it." Networking is a way to make contact with the people you need to ask.

To locate the likely companies and get the interviews you need, tell everyone that you're looking for a job you can do at home and tell them the type of work you can do. Attend professional and trade association meetings in your field. Ask for ideas and suggestions. Follow up on any leads you get until you are successful.

To land the position you want, you might offer to work at home under contract on a specific project, or to provide overload services during emergencies. Do outstanding work and the company may call on you again and again, or even put you on salary.

Make your work at home a bargain. One of the most creative ways of getting to work at home was accomplished by a Los Angeles writer. In negotiating a job offer, her soon-to-be employer asked her how much she expected to earn. She gave him two figures. The first was what she needed to earn to work at the company office. The second, although still a good salary, was $10,000 less— provided she could work at home. Her new employer developed a brand-new attitude about the benefits of employees working at home.

Classified ads in newspapers. Newspapers regularly have ads for telemarketers in the "Help Wanted" section. Telemarketing includes selling by telephone as well as taking incoming phone calls. Many of the "800" numbers you see used for ordering products, making reservations, and contacting customer service are phoned into people's home offices. Even if the ad doesn't say so, you may be able to persuade the prospective employer in some fields to let you work from home.

Home assembly. Despite many sham offers of this type, there are some home-assembly companies that do provide income-producing work, according to Ruth M. Howard, who has made a study of home-assembly opportunities. She publishes a booklet, video, and newsletter naming and evaluating the companies that deliver what they promise. Potential earnings from legitimate companies doing piece-rate work range between $100 to $400–$500 a month. To earn $500 a month, one can expect to work full-time with good manual skills. Remember this is work in which the earnings are below minimum wage and is without employee benefits—and there are sharks that do not deliver on their promises.

Lists of work-at-home jobs. Many ads labeled "Apply Now" are simply selling lists of companies that will supposedly hire people to work at home. Some urge you to mail money, others to call a "900" number. The lists virtually always prove disappointing. First, companies that are hiring almost always want people in their local area. Second, once a company's name appears, so many people contact the company that even if there were some jobs, they're quickly gone and subsequent applicants either find their calls answered angrily or their letters ignored.

Companies that market homeworkers' services. Still there are companies that seek to match the needs of companies that want work done with home-based people. Home Business Services of Denver is marketing and operating several innovative programs to assist home-based workers. One refers home-based people to businesses seeking help and collects a fee from the company. Another contracts with companies for market-research work and in turn subcontracts with home-based workers to do the job. The company is extending its programs throughout the country.

Virtual corporations. Business Week was among the first to describe a change in American business when it did a cover story called the "Hollow Corporation." A similar concept is the *virtual corporation,* described in a book by that name by William Davidow and Michael Malone (New York: Harper Business, 1992). A virtual corporation, unlike traditional heirarchical organizations, has a small core of permanent employees and uses independent workers who may never see the inside of the corporate office or meet face-to-face with co-workers. Work is more project oriented than permanent. Debbie Dewey, who herself has operated from her home serving a number of companies, defines a virtual corporation as ". . . a group of people with different areas of expertise working together as a team, remotely or locally, to provide a service/ product to meet a business need with specific predefined goals."

For the past year, we have had a message section and library of the Working From Home Forum on CompuServe titled "Virtual Corporation." We have seen independent workers struggle to create them successfully for themselves, guests who operate them, and occasional calls for people to be employed by them. The idea of a virtual corporation is just over a decade old and very much still in the process of developing with a great deal of promise for home-based workers with technical and analytical capabilities.

Work-at-Home Employment Schemes

Some ads are outright schemes to take your money. A typical one might read: "COMPUTER—do you own or have access to a personal computer? Up to $35/ hour. Full/part-time, starting immediately." It sounds like a job but asks you to send money for what turns out to be worthless information. Other types of work that have proved to be scams are clipping coupons and newspapers, data entry, envelope stuffing, listening to the radio making neckties and sewing, typing and watching TV. Envelope stuffing is the most common of these schemes. Stuffing envelopes sounds like easy work, but in actuality it is always a pyramid-like sales scheme in which you get a set of instructions telling you "to place ads similar to the one to which you responded."

How to Spot Work-at-Home Schemes

First, work-at-home schemes require you to send money before explaining how you are going to make money. An ad for a real job opening will not ask for money before you learn the details. Second, if an opportunity sounds too good to be true, it probably is. If you suspect a scheme, check it out with the Better Business Bureau, local consumer protection offices, state consumer protection and attorney generals' offices, the Federal Trade Commission, and the U.S. Postal Inspection Service. Addresses and phone numbers for a number of these can be found in chapter 3.

If you feel the urge to send in your money, follow the advice of Sidney Schwartz, who has made a study of these schemes. Here are his suggestions:

1. Keep copies of all ads, claims, and guarantees. If the only guarantee is on the order form, photocopy it before sending it in.
2. Pay with a charge card instead of by check or with cash. You can dispute the charge if you feel you've been taken.
3. Save the envelope or package the merchandise is shipped in so you will have a dated postmark.
4. Send all correspondence by certified mail. Should you return the merchandise, always get a signed return receipt as proof of delivery.

5. Remember, when you respond to one of these ads, you're gambling. So don't bet more than you can afford to lose.

What Kinds of Companies Have At-Home Employees?

Companies with fewer than one hundred employees and *Fortune* 500 corporations are the ones employing the most home-based workers. The reasons for this are that large companies and agencies are able to accommodate specialized work arrangements; and small companies are willing to be flexible in order to compete for qualified personnel and to save money.

Assuming your skills enable you to work in a job that can be done at home, let's consider the characteristics of the companies that are most likely to allow people to work at home.

Information-Intensive Organizations

Often, but not always, jobs in these information-intensive companies are computer or communications oriented and involve data entry, word processing, telemarketing, or teleordering. Representative industries and companies with employees working from home include:

- *Banks and financial institutions:* American Express, Citibank, First Chicago Corporation, Mellon Bank.
- *High-technology companies:* Control Data, Data General, Digital Equipment Corporation, DuPont, Hewlett-Packard, Honeywell, Hughes, IBM, Lanier Business Products, Xerox.
- *Governments:* City of Los Angeles, County of Los Angeles, states of California, Hawaii, and Washington, and various federal agencies.
- *Insurance companies:* Allstate, Blue Cross/Blue Shield of South Carolina, Blue Cross/Blue Shield of Maryland, Equitable Life Assurance, Hartford Insurance Group, John Hancock Mutual Life, New York Life, Travelers.
- *News organizations:* Time-Warner, Gannet, United Press International.
- *Retailers:* JCPenney (customer service), Bell Atlantic, Montgomery Ward, Sears.
- *Telephone companies:* AT&T, Bell Atlantic, GTE, New England Telephone, New York Telephone, Pacific Bell, US WEST.
- *Translation and transcription:* Berlitz Translation Services, Globalink Language Services, Journal Graphics.

Sales Organizations

Sales organizations have customarily allowed, or sometimes required, representatives to work from home. Businesses making extensive use of sales reps include insurance, publishing, real estate, printing, pharmaceuticals, and other product manufacturers.

Fast-Growing Small Businesses

Instead of renting office space or having employees come into the founder's home, growing businesses like Escrow Overload of Los Angeles and Letter Perfect of Baltimore, both of which began as home-based businesses, prefer to hire employees who will work from their homes. Such small businesses need employees to do secretarial jobs, sales, bookkeeping, product assembly and shipping, art, public relations, and computer programming.

Special Advice for the Disabled

The disabled are a minority group, now numbering 43 million Americans, that anyone can join at any time. But being or becoming disabled does not extinguish the need or the desire to work. We have heard from dispirited and sometimes angry disabled people who, despite repeated attempts, have been unable to find work. And this, when they know that, thanks to personal computers and adaptation devices developed by companies like IBM and Apple, they can now work from anywhere. This could be discouraging for anyone. But the road to finding a job demands persistence. You have to become a "squeaky wheel." As Brian Wettlaufer, who operates a consulting practice in Miami called Handicap Placement Services, Inc., advises, "Don't give up. There are opportunities."

If you have a rehabilitation counselor, consider working with him or her to develop a "rehab" plan. Such plans may be funded by federal, state, and local resources and may allow you to work at home either as an off-site worker, as an employee, or being self-employed. Plans may include training to enable you to develop new skills. Though funds are limited, occupational and vocational rehabilitation agencies have provided equipment.

Once someone has identified a work possibility, the Job Accommodation Network, funded by the President's Committee on Employment of People with Disabilities, provides consulting on methods and devices directed to working out problems necessary to make the situation work. The network may be contacted by phone at (800)ADA-WORK; it also has a computer bulletin board at (800)342-5526.

An important resource for the disabled is the Handicapped Users Database on the CompuServe Information Service. Created and managed by Georgia Griffith, herself blind and deaf, this immense collection contains resources for employment arranged by state, and a list of local bulletin-board systems that enable local networking.

Problems You May Encounter as a Home-Based Employee

Aside from the general problems work-at-homers encounter, being a home-based employee introduces some other considerations.

Negotiating Satisfactory Compensation

Some critics, primarily from labor unions, fear that "electronic cottages" could become the sweatshops of the future, with low-paid employees slaving over computer terminals and being paid on a monitored piece-rate basis. Electronic Services Unlimited, which conducted a study to explore the potential of telecommuting, did not find this fear to be a reality, however.

In speaking across the United States we've met a wide variety of employees working from home, but never one who complained of abuse. To avoid problems with compensation and benefits, however, get a clear agreement about your employment status.

Among salaried positions at home there are differences in benefits, support services, and equipment and supplies provided by the employer. Let's discuss a variety of possible arrangements.

Teleworkers

Teleworkers/telecommuters are salaried employees who do part of their work at home during normal working hours. Teleworking has been growing at an annual rate of 15 percent a year, reaching 7.6 million American workers in 1993, according to Link Resources. However, the vast majority of these telecommuters are doing so informally. For example, someone taking work home an afternoon or two a week is considered a telecommuter, but the worker's company does not have a formal policy covering working at home. Formal teleworking is also growing and has been stimulated by a landmark teleworking pilot program and evaluation in California that took place in 1988 and 1989.

The State of California program involved 150 people and used outside researchers who found that:

- Productivity increased from 9 to 10 percent from the standpoint of supervisors and from 20 to 30 percent from the standpoint of employees. State offices that did the best job of supporting and managing telecommuters showed productivity gains double that of other offices.

- The program paid for itself in thirteen months, and at the end of two years the benefit-to-cost ratio was twenty to one.

- Only 40 percent of teleworkers needed personal computers for their work, but 64 percent used them.

- Thirty percent of the work done by California state employees can be done at home.

The research on California government employees was followed by a study by the University of San Francisco's Institute of Distributed Work of office workers employed by private companies who telecommuted one to two days a week. These workers increased their productivity by an average of 16.8 percent.

The 1994 Los Angeles earthquake has jolted traditional managers in Southern California into rethinking their opposition to allowing employees to work at home. The underlying opposition managers have to working at home is based on:

(1) losing the feeling of control over employees they think they have when they can see the employees and (2) the often-mistaken belief that they can adequately monitor only employees in their sight. For most, it takes something as powerful as a major earthquake to change.

What are the ingredients for successful telecommuting? The two most important are self-motivation on the part of employees and supportive management support on the part of employers. There is little doubt that increasing amounts of the work of salaried people will be done in their homes.

Commissioned Positions

Gilda Silvani works from home, overlooking the blue Pacific at Laguna Beach, California. As an employment counselor for Escrow Overload, she specializes in providing temporary personnel to savings and loans, banks, and real estate companies.

Gilda interviews prospective overload personnel, checks out their backgrounds, and follows up on marketing done by the company's corporate office in Los Angeles County. As companies call her with needs for temporary workers, she matches the people from her files with the requirements of the job. She's one of the home-based workers paid on a commission.

When working on commission, alternative arrangements are possible. On straight commission, you simply receive a percentage of every sale you make. Sometimes you can get hired into a position that provides salary plus commission and fringe benefits. And some companies offer an advance, or "draw," against your future commissions so you will have some income while you are getting started or when business is slow. Ken Wasil, for example, works as a salesman for a wholesaler of housewares, hardware, and sporting goods. He receives a $1,800 draw each month toward his sales commission, which is 3 percent of the profits on what he sells, or 15 to 17 percent of the selling price.

The percentage of commission varies depending on the price of the product or service you are selling and your employment arrangement. Generally, when you are an independent contractor representing a company, the percentage of commission will be higher than if you work for a company that offers salary plus commission and fringe benefits. Bob Baxter of Pet Organics pays his independent sales reps a 20 to 25 percent commission plus an incentive if they reach their dollar sales goals. He says his commission is higher than most.

Owing to savings on overhead, some employers pay substantially more to commissioned employees who work at home. Escrow Overload, for example, can pay their employment counselors four to eight times the commission of their competitors because of the savings in overhead they realize by having the staff work at home. Customarily, temporary-help agencies pay commissions of 25 cents to 50 cents per hour of employment booked. Escrow Overload is able to pay $2 per hour booked, enabling some workers to make as much as $1,000 per week.

Benefits and support services also vary from employer to employer. Most certainly the company should provide you with a territory, sales leads, or a route to cover, as well as promotional materials, samples, and any backup information you need in order to sell the product or service adequately. Although benefits often are not included, the better-commissioned position will include group insurance coverage, a car, or travel expenses.

Negotiating a Work-from-Home Agreement

Whichever payment arrangement you negotiate, make sure to confirm such points as:

- The hours you will work, and how often you are expected in the office.
- The method of payment: salary, hourly wage, piece rate, commission.
- What fringe benefits are included, such as health insurance and employer's share of Social Security.
- Whether you are covered under workers' compensation.
- What liability insurance you'll need on your home and who will pay for it.
- The process used to determine when work is completed.
- The amount of work expected.
- What equipment and supplies you'll need and who will pay for them.
- Method and degree of supervision and performance evaluation.
- The training available to you.
- Opportunities for wage increases and career advancement.
- Requirements and opportunities to return to work at the office.

On the question of whether the employer or the employee provides computers and other equipment needed to work at home, better than three out of five companies with official telecommuting policies surveyed in 1993 by the Business Research Group of Newton, Massachusetts, provided either a portable or desktop computer to their at-home workers.

Keeping in Contact

Feelings of isolation can be more of a problem for home-based employees than for home-based entrepreneurs. Those whose work requires them to sit at home and work alone all day at a computer terminal or typewriter are the most susceptible. Anyone, however, who is away from the office long enough can start to feel like an outsider. As time passes, company shop talk can begin to sound like a foreign language and you may discover you've missed out on special projects because no one thought of you when assignments were handed out. After all, out of sight, out of mind.

There are several solutions to this problem. Some lie with the employee, some with the organization and the supervisor.

To maintain contact, spend at least a part of each week in the office. Sharon Miller, who telecommuted for Northwest Computer Systems in Minneapolis, found that she "felt like I was in a vacuum all by myself. I had to use the manuals and the telephone instead of personal contact." She was concerned about being uninformed about company developments.

By going into the office once a week, however, and spending time on personal contacts, Sharon was able to maintain her work relationships. She did no work in the office that she could have done at home, but instead had her secretary fill up her time with appointments and meetings. She told us, "Not only did I enjoy talking with people when I went into the office, I enjoyed getting out of the house for a while."

Anyone working at home who wants to maintain contact needs to let people know it. Sharon Miller found that some people "had reservations about calling me at home." At the other extreme, employees like Gilda Salvini find that "when people know you're at home, they call early or late, any time of day or night."

Arranging Office Support

Working from home can feel like living on an island. Office support that used to be outside your door—supplies, secretaries, copy facilities, special equipment—is now ten to thirty minutes away. You end up missing a copy machine when you need one, handling all your appointments and phone calls yourself, and being your own file clerk.

Some of the support you need can be provided on your day in the office or perhaps by an expense allowance to cover the cost of buying stamps or having copies made in your neighborhood.

Getting Appropriate Supervision

Management consultant Marilyn Miller points out that in many offices, "You can be in the upper 50 percent of your field if you just show up at work, the upper 30 percent if you show up on time, and the upper 10 percent if you show up on time with your eyes open." Obviously, managing home-based workers requires something besides seeing them in the flesh.

Like other employees, work-at-homers need information, guidance, feedback, and support from their supervisors. Sometimes, however, since the supervisor can't see them in the hall or hear about it when they run into difficulty, at-home workers have to take a more active role by asking for the information and direction they need.

Being Aware of Possible Family Conflict

One survey showed that family conflict is more often a problem with those employed at home than with those who work for themselves. While the self-employed are more likely to list family closeness as one of the chief benefits of working from home, those on jobs at home are more likely to list it as a problem.

We suspect this may occur because more people working at home on a job are doing so out of necessity, while most people who start a business do so because they want to. Family conflicts are also more prevalent when the kind of work you do keeps you from getting out of the house, as is more usually the case if you're employed than if you work for yourself.

The best safeguard against family conflict is to be aware of how working at home will affect those you live with. Then set up your office and workday in the manner described in the subsequent chapters of this book to minimize or avoid problems.

If you plan your office space and work schedule with your family in mind and have honest family relationships, the period of adjustment can be brief and manageable. For example, the biggest problem telecommuter Sharon Miller faced was having to work when her family didn't want her to. But her husband would help out by fixing dinner or taking the family out to eat. Specific suggestions for easing family tensions when working at home are discussed in chapters 19 and 20.

Certainly, working from home is not for every employee. There are workers like Sophie Wojicik, who tried working for a bank from home but eventually went back to the main office because she missed a traditional office environment. But there are also employees like Sharon Miller, who will change jobs to spend more time working from home, and like Gilda Silvani, who describes her situation as "heaven on earth."

So while securing a job at home may be an uphill battle, if you think you're suited for it, persist in your efforts. Aside from the other advantages, the satisfaction of strolling from your desk out to your own mailbox where your paycheck lies waiting will make the effort worthwhile.

Resources

Books

The Age of Unreason. Charles Handy. Boston: Harvard Business School Press, 1989.

Making Telecommuting Happen. Jack M. Nilles. New York: Van Nostrand, Reinhold, 1994.

The Telecommuter's Handbook: How to Work for a Salary Without Ever Leaving the House. Brad Schepp. New York: Pharos Books, 1990.

Teleworking Explained. Mike Gray, Noel Hodson, and Gil Gordon. Chichester, West Sussex, England: John Wiley and Sons, Ltd., 1993.

The Virtual Corporation. William H. Davidow and Michael S. Malone. New York: Harper Business, 1992.

Report

California Telecommuting Pilot Project Final Report. Stock No. 7540-930-0400-6, State of California, Department of General Services, Publications Unit, P.O. Box 1015, North Highlands, CA 95660. $10.90. (Provide a street address as this comes via UPS.)

Newsletters

Telecommuting Review: The Gordon Report. Gil Gordon Associates, 10 Donner Court, Monmouth Junction, NJ 08852.

Telecommuting Times. P.O. Box 143, Cheltenham, PA 19012.

Organizations

American Telecommuting Association. 1220 L Street N.W., Ste. 100, Washington, DC 20005.

The European Community Telework Forum. 12 Castle Street, Totness, Devon, TQ9 5NU, United Kingdom.

National Telecommuting and Telework Association. Ste. 200, 1650 Tysons Boulevard, McClean, VA 22102.

Telecommuting Advisory Council, c/o Law Offices of Joseph C. Luman, 1030 15th Street N.W., Ste. 410, Washington, DC 20005.

The Telecommuting Powerhouse. 27 Gloucester Street, London WC1N 3XX, United Kingdom.

Information about Home Assembly Companies

Dollars at Home Directory, Ruth M. Howard (800) 786-2985.

PART 2

....

Making Your Home Office Convenient,
Functional, and Professional

CHAPTER
FIVE

■■■■■■■■■■■■■■■■■■■■■■■■■■

Keeping Your Work and Personal Life Separate

A peaceful marriage of home and office depends on establishing effective boundaries. The office, with its phone calls, mail, paperwork, noisy equipment, and business visitors, can invade the sanctity of the home. In the same way, the friends, neighbors, kids, barking dogs, soap operas, and peanut butter sandwiches of home can clutter up the halls of business. Creating boundaries, however, preserves the character of each.

Fortunately, the boundaries you set up to maintain the privacy of your home will also help create a professional business atmosphere. And, as you'll see in chapter 10, may help you qualify for valuable tax deductions. But recognizing the boundaries you need to create is a first step in making practical decisions that will ultimately affect the success of your home office.

Keeping Your Home a Home and Your Office an Office

There are many tools and techniques for setting boundaries between your home and your work. Walls, doors, windows, lighting, furniture, and clothing are all material means you can use to define the boundaries you want to create. The way you use time and space—your office location, work schedules, and household rules—are other more subtle means you have at your disposal.

There are some general guidelines for using these tools and techniques. But obviously you'll be adapting the guidelines to your individual circumstances.

Financial consultant George Gaines separates work and home by a single door. He lives alone and detests housework. "My kitchen may be stacked with dishes and the bedroom a shambles. But that's okay. That's 'my' space. I keep it any way I want. On the other side of the living-room door, it's a different world. It's always neat as a pin, because that's where I meet with my clients. That's my office."

87

Programmer William Keen keeps work in bounds with a basement telephone. "I could work in the middle of a tornado. Nothing bothers me. I just tune it all out. Actually, I work best if two or three things are going on at a time. But if my boss or a business contact calls, they don't think so highly of the stereo blaring or the kids yelling in the background, so I have a little office in the basement for my business phone."

Joan Cullen creatively defines the boundaries between her work and home with a bedsheet. As an editor who works several days each week at home, she keeps her office on the dining-room table, which she has covered with a king-size sheet. The table is piled with manuscripts in various stages of editing. When she's ready to put the work away and claim her apartment for herself again, she stacks all her materials in the center of the table, carefully marking off each project with a rubber band or colored paper, folds and ties the four corners of the sheet over the pile, and puts her whole "office" in a closet.

We use these examples because they illustrate how personal and how simple establishing useful boundaries can be. Whether you prefer the peace and harmony of a monastic retreat, the intensity and excitement of a politician's campaign office, or something in between, the essential task is to define bound-

---

Tips for Keeping Your Home and Office Space Separate

1. **Clearly demarcate your work space** by using a separate room, partition, bookcase, screen, or room divider so you and everyone else will know precisely where the home stops and the office begins. Make sure you can close your office off when you're working.
2. **Set definite work hours** and let everyone know precisely when you will be available for business and when for personal activities.
3. **Have a signal** that makes it clear when you do not want to be disturbed; for example, when the office door is closed or when you put up a Do Not Disturb sign.
4. **Learn how to say "No, I'm working now"** firmly, but politely, and stick to it so everyone will know you mean what you say.
5. **Use a separate business telephone line** and have an answering machine or answering service to screen calls or record messages when you are not available.
6. **Soundproof your office** by using a solid-core door and other materials and equipment that reduce noise.
7. **Dress in a particular way** when you're at work. You need not resort to coat and tie or hose and heels, but wearing work attire can help you and others know it's time for business if doing so becomes a problem.
8. **Organize your office** so you can keep work materials, paper, and equipment in clearly defined office spaces.
9. **Have a separate outside office entrance** for the ultimate in privacy or locate your office in a converted portion of a garage, in a guest house, or in a separate building.

---

aries that can keep both your household and work space the way you want them.

Let's consider some of the basic decisions you need to make about the boundaries of your home office. As you make these decisions, what becomes clear are the boundaries you need to set for yourself and others.

How Much Privacy Do You Need to Work Productively?

We all need some degree of privacy to think, to concentrate, or to discuss sensitive material. But how much and what type of privacy do you need to get your work done? This privacy questionnaire has been adapted for the home-based worker from Franklin Becker's *The Successful Office*. We've designed it to help you identify the kinds of boundaries you need to create the right amount of privacy.

1. Do you close the door when you work?
2. Does the sound of music, television, or people talking in the background distract you from your work?
3. Do you prefer to work independently and autonomously?
4. While you're working, would you prefer not to see what's going on outside your office?
5. When you're concentrating on a particular task, do you ask people not to disturb you?
6. Do you have phone conversations or business meetings that should not be overheard by others in the house?
7. Do you have information in your files or records that must be kept confidential?
8. Is it important to your business visitors that they not be seen or overheard by one another while they are in your home?

If you answered "yes" to seven or eight of these questions, you'll want an office that is as separate as possible from the rest of your household. If it's feasible, you may wish to consider a separate structure or at least a separate entrance for business guests, or soundproofing your office in one of the ways suggested in chapter 7. If you live with others, establish clear rules as to when they can and cannot interrupt you.

If you answered "yes" to just four to six of these questions, you'll probably want to have a separate work space, but involvement with people and other activities is important to you. So you'll likely want a door to your office, but you'll also want ready access to what's going on outside the door at different times during the day. If you work alone at home, arrange at least weekly contact with colleagues, co-workers, friends, or clients.

If you answered "yes" to only one to three of the questions, you'll probably perfer your office in the midst of plenty of activity. In fact, you may prefer open office space in the heart of the household. If you work alone at home, occasionally try to take your work out to a public place like a restaurant, library, or hotel lobby, and try to have contact each day with customers, clients, co-workers, family, or neighbors. If there's nothing going on at home, you may even want to create some noise and activity there by turning on music or the TV.

If you answered "yes" to question 7, have locks put on your files and your office door. If you answered "yes" to question 8, arrange to have a double entrance into your office or schedule your appointments carefully.

Now let's consider the other basic decisions you'll need to make in setting up boundaries between your home and office.

Do You Let People Know You Work at Home?

Eighty percent of the people we've talked with say, "Sure, why not?" Essentially we agree that you needn't feel any stigma about working from home. It's growing in popularity, and today most people would respond with friendly curiosity and even a bit of envy.

But for some, not letting people know they're working at home can help solve problems. For example, when Jean Hilman first began doing calligraphy, some of her customers were hesitant to phone her at home. So, since she gets her work through local print shops, she just doesn't mention that her studio is at home until after customers know her better.

One consultant expressed his decision this way: "I work with *Fortune* 500 companies. They're used to working with consultants who have Madison Avenue addresses. I don't actually know what they would think if they knew I was talking with them in my bathrobe, but I'd just as soon not find out."

Jack Gibbs intermittently works at home so he can get away from office interruptions at the public relations firm that employs him. "The last thing I want is for people to know where I am. My secretary is the only one who knows—and my supervisor, of course."

If for these or any other reasons you feel at all uncomfortable with people knowing you work from home, usually there's no need to tell them. By arranging outside business meetings, having a business phone and special mail service, you can just as easily appear to be working in a regular office setting.

Theresa Arnerich works with her husband, providing seminars and speeches for large business organizations. "We had an office before, but we find working from home much more enjoyable. As far as our clients know, we're still in an office. In fact most of them don't know I'm his wife. They know me by phone and by mail. I'm the business manager."

Do You Want Business Visitors Coming to Your Home?

Sooner or later most people who work from home are confronted with this decision. There are several points to consider in making the choice.

Security. Will you and your premises be safe if your business brings strangers into your home? Nancy Rabbitt decided that instead of having strangers deliver artwork to her design studio, she would offer early-morning pickup at her customers' locations. Instead of having new psychotherapy clients come to her home office, Cheryl Smith arranged to do her initial interviews at a nearby clinic.

Privacy. Will you feel as though your inalienable right to privacy has been taken away or that your home is being invaded by strangers? How much space you have and how you arrange it will probably determine whether business visitors seem like an intrusion. For Kitty Friedman, who lives and writes in a one-room guest house, there is no way to close off her personal space from business guests. She makes most of her business contacts by phone or meets clients at a publisher's office.

When you have a little more space than Kitty does, closed doors or separate business entrances work to retain your privacy. Graphics designer Mary Stoddard didn't like having customers come into her office when it was in the living room. She felt her home had become too public. So she converted her garage into a studio/office and had a separate entrance installed. This created the boundaries she needed to keep business from invading her home.

Image. Is your office space appropriate for business meetings, and do you want to keep it looking presentable for clients or customers? Thomas Kerr thought not. He didn't feel his small apartment would convey the image he wanted to establish as a management consultant. His solution was to join a private club where he could hold business meetings. Some people join airline clubs for this purpose.

Word processor operator Barbara Bickford has her own prohibitive factors to contend with: five children from three to ten years old. "I couldn't have my customers in here. It's a three-ring circus! Sometimes I pick up and deliver, but whenever I can, I have them mail me their manuscripts or send them electronically."

Jeanett Eastman solved a similar problem when she had a photography studio in a small apartment. "There really wasn't room for guests, with all my equipment and my daughters' toys cluttering the living room. But the apartment building had a lovely porch that looked onto a garden, and, depending on the weather, I either met my customers on the porch or in the garden. It worked well. In fact, they told me they enjoyed it."

Another option should you decide your home office doesn't convey the right image for business meetings and appointments is to rent an office suite on a part-time basis from an organization like HQ, which provides all the professional office services you need, including conference facilities and office space, at a cost lower than renting an office full-time. You use the facilities only when you need them. These office-rental organizations can also provide secretarial services, take phone calls, and receive mail for you.

Before jumping to obtain outside space because a client requests a site visit, however, marketing consultant Laura Douglas suggests exploring why clients want to come to your office. If they want to make sure you're a real business, she advises, "Don't try to mislead them. Be straightforward. Tell them that your business is home based." On the other hand, Douglas points out, "it's possible that the reason clients want to come to your office is simply to get out of theirs. They could want to feel free to discuss something with you they don't feel comfortable discussing in their own office or they might just want an excuse to get out of their cubbyhole for a while. If that's the case, figure out somewhere you can meet like a restaurant, hotel, or airline club where you can get together without setting up a separate office facility."

But should the time come when you definitely need more space, you still have a variety of choices of how to expand without losing the benefits of working from home (see chapter 24).

How Do You Handle Business Phone Calls?

According to freelance cameraman Steve Haines, the best thing about working from home is that he never misses a phone call. "Crews are notorious for calling at all times of day and night. Many times I've gotten the job because I was there to answer the phone no matter what time it was."

Not everyone is as willing as Steve to be available for business calls. Lynne Frances, for example, felt differently about taking customer calls for her cleaning service. "When you have your business at home, there's no respect for your personal life. People knew I would be at home, so they disregarded my business hours and called me anytime they wanted. For my own peace of mind, I had to find a way to limit business calls to business hours." She got a private line and hired an answering service for her business number.

As Lynne found out, the dilemma in setting up home-office phone service is how to make sure you don't miss important business calls without becoming a slave to the telephone twenty-four hours a day. The following is what we recommend.

1. Have a separate telephone line for business. We recommend this second line be a business line rather than a residential line so that:

- People who call Directory Assistance to ask for you by your business name will get your number.
- You will have a listing in the Yellow Pages; sometimes two listings.
- You can avoid having to take personal phone calls during business hours.

What to Do When You Don't Want to Meet Business Visitors in Your Home

1. Offer pickup and delivery services.
2. Meet at the customer's, client's, or employer's location.
3. Transact business by mail or telephone.
4. Meet on neutral territory, such as a restaurant, hotel lobby, or club.
5. Communicate electronically by computer.
6. Rent a hotel suite or conference room.
7. Rent an executive office suite by the hour, day, or month. Such services provide office space, conference or meetings facilities, as well as mail, phone, and secretarial services.
8. Use a fax machine.

- You can choose whether to take business calls after business hours, thereby protecting your private life.
- You can leave your residential line free for other family members to use without interfering with your business.
- Facilitates claiming business telephone costs as a tax deduction.

Switching a residential line to a business line usually costs about half of what it costs to install a new business line. Some people use one line for incoming calls and the other line for outgoing calls and, increasingly, people are installing separate lines for their fax and modem use. This keeps voice calls separate from "machine calls."

2. Locate your business phone away from household noise. Unless you're providing child care, pet care, or cleaning services, household noises that can be picked up over the receiver are a disaster during business conversations. Since you can't always predict when the neighbor's dog will bark or the kids will turn on the stereo, your best bet is locating the business phone away from such activity and using good sound-control techniques.

3. Answer your business phone in a formal manner. Use either your own name or your company name. The way you answer your business phone will often determine whether or not the caller perceives you as a professional who is at work.

If you don't have a secretary answering your phone, *you* will be the one to create the proper impression. To create a positive professional image, we greet callers with "Good morning" or "Good afternoon," followed by our name. It also works to our advantage to put a "smile" in our voices when we answer.

Do not have young children answer your business phone. If you want other adults in the household to answer business calls, instruct them to use the same professional procedure as you do.

4. Use an answering machine, answering service, or voice mail. Whether your goal is to free yourself of constant business calls or to be sure you don't miss any, your home business needs to use these resources to preserve your peace of mind.

You can think of voice mail as an electronic substitute for a secretary. It operates like the systems used by large corporations. It turns your phone into a sophisticated answering machine that gives callers choices. Callers can select a number on their phone pad that instructs the computer to take a message, another number to obtain information you've recorded for them, or a third number to have the computer forward their call to you or someone else. Voice mail can also tell callers that all lines are currently busy and ask them to stay on the line until you're free.

If you use a service, check to be sure it is courteous, prompt in answering, and accurate in taking messages. We suggest periodically calling the service yourself, as if you were an unknown customer or client, to see how you are treated.

If you use an answering machine or voice mail, create a polite and business-like message. Avoid the temptation to record anything "cutesy." And don't start an answering-machine message with "Hello," followed by a pause. This leaves callers feeling foolish when they realize they've responded to a greeting from a machine. An answering machine or voice-mail message should:

- Begin by giving the name of your business (e.g., "You have reached . . .").
- State that you're away from the phone right now.
- Ask that the caller leave a name, number, and the time of the call.
- Assure the caller that you will return the call as soon as possible.
- Keep voice-mail choices simple, offer no more than four, and make instructions easy enough for any seventh-grader to follow.

In chapter 8, we'll examine these and other new telephone features that can facilitate your work.

Do You Use Your Home Address for Business Purposes?

The majority of people who work from home use their home address for both personal and business mail. There are no special arrangements you need to make, nor should you encounter any difficulties with the post office regardless of how much business mail you receive.

However, if you're concerned about giving your home address to strangers or if you have an address on "Easy Street" or "Sleepy Hollow Lane" and don't like the business image it conveys, you can make other arrangements for mail delivery. If you're employed, use your employer's address and have your mail forwarded. If you're self-employed, rent a post office box or an address from an office-suite service like HQ, or use a mail-receiving service, such as Mail Boxes, Etc. Mail-receiving services provide you with a street address and a suite number instead of a post office box number. This removes the doubt created in many people's minds when they see a post office box as a business address. The cost is usually less than twenty dollars a month.

However, if you decide to use a private mail-receiving service, keep in mind that if you move, the post office will not accept a mail-forwarding order on a private post office box and often the private post office will forward for only thirty days and will charge you the postage to forward mail to you.

An advantage of a post office box for businesses that receive a high volume of mail is that mail is sorted and placed in postal boxes several times a day. However, courier services, such as Federal Express, will not deliver to a post office box. To get the advantage of a post office box and still get courier deliveries, include both your street address and post office box as follows:

> Your business name
> Your street address
> P.O. Box 415
> Anytown, NY 10222-0909

Using this format, approved by the U.S. Postal Service, your regular mail will be sent to the post office box, but your street address directs courier deliveries to your home address and shows you are not just a mail drop.

Private firms like Airborne, DHL, Federal Express, or United Parcel Service will, of course, provide door-to-door delivery to your residence. For a modest fee, they will also pick up outgoing mail from your home office.

How to Help Business Visitors Locate Your Home and Feel Welcome

1. If your residence is at all difficult to find, send directions by mail in advance describing how to get there. If possible, use a separate entrance for business visitors.
2. If you live in a multifamily dwelling, cut out the typeset name from your card or stationery; have it laminated and post it on your own door or on the building directory. If you live in a single-family home, hang a simple sign by your front walk displaying your name and address. Although business signs are usually prohibited in residential areas, signs like the one shown in Figure 5-1 should pose no problem and can greatly assist visitors.
3. Arrange for a convenient and easy-to-remember place to put guests' coats, hats, and packages. Since people are often unaccustomed to business meetings in the more relaxed atmosphere of a home office, be sure they've retrieved their belongings before they leave or you'll soon have a closetful of assorted wraps and umbrellas to return.
4. Have coffee, tea, or water available as you would in a traditional office, and offer it to guests when they arrive.
5. Keep bathroom facilities fresh and supplies available.
6. Keep the areas where your business visitors come clear of personal items like children's toys, family photographs, and clothing so that visitors don't feel they're intruding on your personal life.

Setting Boundaries for Other People

When you're working in a traditional office, the assumption is that while you're there, work has priority. This assumption generally defines how, when, and in what way people interact with you. When you're working at home, however, there is no single assumption about what you're there for. After all, it's a place where you play many roles: worker, neighbor, friend, mate, parent, citizen.

Under these circumstances, it isn't always easy for others to know how to interact with you. Therefore you need to set limits and define boundaries so they will know when you're working and when you're not. It's up to you to let them know what you expect and to help them feel comfortable with an unfamiliar situation. Here are some tips to help you accomplish this with various kinds of people.

Business Visitors

Let colleagues, co-workers, customers, and clients know specifically when they can call you. For example: "Call me on weekdays between nine and five." "Please call me after twelve o'clock." "Call me anytime and leave a message with my service. I check in every hour, and I'll call you back." To reinforce this boundary, do not answer your business phone after work hours. If you wish, you can put your answering machine or service on your business phone so you can return any calls you receive after hours.

If customers come to your home, clearly define business hours. We suggest having customers call before coming. Set a time to meet with them and give them an idea of how long the meeting should last. "We can meet from nine to ten tomorrow morning." "If you could simply drop the papers by, I would certainly appreciate it. I don't have much time right now." Again, to reinforce your limits, avoid making too many exceptions to transacting business before or after the hours you've set.

A study at the University of Southern California found that when you have regular business visitors, a separate outside entrance works best. Of course, a building will further separate your home life from your business life. For example, David Palmer erected a prefab building in his backyard for about one-fifth the cost of adding on to his home.

When having business visitors come to your home, be prepared for them. Once they arrive, make them feel welcome and comfortable. If family members are present when business visitors arrive or while you're meeting, take the initiative in introducing them briefly to your guests, and let them know you will be working and wish not to be disturbed.

Since you're not in a traditional office setting, cueing guests that it's time to

Figure 5-1.

leave can be an awkward moment. Sometimes they wonder whether to stay and chat after the meeting. To ease the situation, stand up, or move toward the door to let visitors know it's time to leave. Thank them for coming and, when necessary, tactfully remind them you have more work to do.

Neighbors and Friends

As Mary Smith, a production manager for a telecommunications project, has found, "Sometimes it's hard to go into the study and shut the neighbors out."

Let friends and neighbors know your work hours and when you are available. "Come by after five," for example, or "Let's visit over lunch. I'll come over at noon." Tell them when they can call. If they call while you're working, politely say you'll call them back when you're finished. Do not start a conversation. If you wish, you can put your answering machine or service on your personal line while you work.

Of course, you don't want to antagonize people in the process of getting them to respect your work boundaries, but as writer David Goodfellow found, you do have to be hard-nosed about it. "My family and friends know that during business hours my office is strictly private, but I had to get downright unfriendly to make that happen. It worked, though, and with no lasting hard feelings."

To keep bad feelings from building up, and still be firm about boundaries, psychotherapist Ellen Barker uses the "not now, but when" approach to telling people not to bother her while she's working. Instead of just turning people away, she tells them exactly when she will be available.

Family

Plan your work schedule and go over it with your family to show them when you will and will not be available. Do not assume anything. Let them know at what times and for what reasons you can be interrupted.

Introducing Business Visitors to Family Members

Men are introduced to women. For example, introducing a male visitor to your wife you would say, "Margery, I'd like you to meet Jim Evans. Jim, this is my wife, Margery."

Or, introducing your female visitor to your husband, you would say, "Jill, this is my husband, George. George, this is my client, Jill Rose."

Younger persons are introduced to older persons. For example, you would introduce your son to a business visitor with "Jim, this is my son John. John, this is Mr. Evans."

People with less status are introduced to people with more status. For example, you introduce the vice-president of a company to your secretary like this: "Georgia, I would like you to meet my secretary, Susan Scott. Susan, this is Georgia McGuire of Holt Advertising."

Set rules for your family about your business telephone and your equipment. Let them know what help or support you need and expect. Discuss what noise you can and cannot tolerate, what areas must be left neat and tidy, and what they are to do when you have business guests.

Employees

If you have workers coming into your home, help them feel comfortable in what may be an unfamiliar arrangement by explaining exactly what you expect. Because working from home may feel much more informal than working in an office setting, it is particularly important to establish a businesslike manner.

Set clear hours. Define when employees can take breaks. Show them what areas of the house are open, and which bathroom to use. Make it clear whether or not they can use your business phone, your dishes, your refrigerator, or your food. Chapters 19–21 go into more detail about working at home successfully with family members and employees.

Special Considerations Regarding Pets

Managing pets while working from home can be a problem. First, if you have customers or clients coming to your home, a small but significant number of people are allergic to dogs and cats, and some people are afraid of dogs. In fact, a survey of three thousand Americans found that dogs were the tenth most common fear. So keeping your pets in a yard or a part of the house away from your business visitors makes good sense, even if your animals "wouldn't hurt a soul."

Another problem faced by dog owners who work at home is when the dog begins barking loudly right in the middle of an important phone conversation. So much for the professional business image!

Short of keeping your dog away from the work area, you can solve this problem by having a mute button or a hold button on your telephone, preferably both. The mute button allows you to hear the person you're talking with but prevents him or her from hearing you as long as you're holding the button down. The hold button keeps the caller on hold and frees you to leave the phone and take care of the disturbance. With these features, simply say, "Just a moment. There's a dog barking outside my window. Let me close it." They're also ideal for unexpected disruptions from children or other household emergencies.

Veterinarian Roger Kuperways points out to home-based pet owners that pets will raise a fuss when you change the rules on them. He recommends that when you start working from home, sit down with your family and decide what the rules will be for your pet now that you're working from home. Make a definite list of what your pet can and cannot do: i.e., be in the house during working hours, get on the office couch, come in your office, sleep under your desk, jump up on guests, sit on your lap while working. Then get agreement that everyone will stick to these rules.

Whenever you set new rules for your pets, be ready for a month or two of whining, barking, and other forms of protest. They will want to do what they've been used to doing, but if you and everyone else are consistent during this period, they will get used to the new rules and settle down.

Keeping Your Office Space in Bounds

By necessity, most home offices are confined to a relatively small space. But work projects don't always fit neatly in small spaces, especially as your business activities at home grow. Defining the boundaries helps you maintain the best aspects of a home and an office. Fortunately, as we'll discuss in the next chapter, you have options as to where you locate your office. And entire industries of products, supplies, and consultants are now available to help you keep your office space sufficiently organized to prevent its overtaking the rest of your home.

Resource

Healing Environments, Your Guide to Indoor Well-Being. Carol Venolia. Berkeley, Calif.: Celestial Arts, 1994.

CHAPTER
SIX

■ ■

Finding the Right Office Space

You can put a home office almost anywhere—on a boat, in an RV, on the dining-room table, or in a converted basement. The critical question is, which place will maximize your potential for success and help you remove any obstacles to working from home?

In actuality, most home offices start out in the first place that comes to mind, and end up somewhere else.

Lynne Frances's cleaning service started out in her bedroom, but ended up in the living room. She didn't like waking up in the middle of the night and being reminded of the work she had to do.

Gary Eckart's stained-glass factory started out in the den and ended up in an RV parked beside his house. His toddlers were too interested in his tools and the brightly colored glass.

Mary Stoddard's graphics studio started out in the living room and ended up in the garage. She found she didn't like strangers entering the privacy of her home.

Tom Girard began his translation service on the kitchen table and ended up converting the basement into an office. He didn't like the breakfast table piled with his papers or his papers adorned with telltale jelly stains.

In fact, almost every problem people have in working from home—whether it's overeating, too many interruptions, or not getting enough work done—is either aggravated or alleviated by where they put their offices. The location of your office can even be the solution to problems that seem to have no relation to office location. The McNaughtons are a case in point.

Bill McNaughton is a professor and has worked at home part-time for many years. As a high-school teacher, his wife, Bonnie, had always worked away from the house. But when she left teaching, she completed a degree in instructional design and opened a business at home writing technical manuals.

She set up her office at the top of the stairs in a bedroom left vacant when the

100

kids moved out. But from the very beginning, this arrangement didn't work. Two, three, or maybe four times a morning her husband would come into her office to ask a question, share some news, or just say hello. She kept urging him not to interrupt her, to please wait until lunch to talk. He would apologize and agree to leave her alone, but then interrupt again. She tried being tolerant, but once distracted from her work she would lose her momentum and find it hard to get started again.

On the verge of renting an office, she decided to have one last talk with her husband. The more they talked, the clearer the problem became. Because her office was right at the top of the stairs, he had to walk by it as he went to and from his office in the den. This happened quite often since he was used to pacing while thinking. Seeing her office, even with the door closed, was too much of a temptation for him. He couldn't resist dropping in to visit.

They solved the problem by trading offices. From the bedroom office, he could walk up and down the stairs freely, as many times as he wished. With his wife's office out of sight down the hall, it was also out of mind. She got her work done and they chatted over lunch.

Like so many of us, Bonnie hadn't really given much thought to where she'd put her office. The spare bedroom at the top of the stairs had seemed only natural. Yet this location created unnecessary problems, as unplanned office sites often do.

Finding the right space for your office is a matter of putting together several factors and coming up with the best possible location. The right space meets the demands of your particular job. It matches your personal work style and budget and qualifies you for tax benefits you're entitled to. And it fits in with your household environment. The object of this chapter is to help you identify the office location that will work best in your situation.

Minimum Home Office Space Requirements

To work effectively at home, most people need these basic work areas:

1. Space for a desk and chair, where you can do paperwork and make phone calls.
2. Space where you can work with a computer, typewriter, calculator, or other equipment.
3. Contemplation or conversation space with chairs or a couch, where you can collect your thoughts or hold business meetings.
4. Storage space for filing cabinets, books, and reference materials.
5. Shelf space for storing supplies and infrequently used equipment.
6. Large work space for activities like assembling or producing materials and doing mailings or shipping.

In addition to these basic work areas, consider your needs for specialized space. Do you need room for particular equipment? Work space for employees? A waiting area for customers or clients?

All of these work areas needn't be in the same room. Attics, basements, garages, or an enclosed back porch are good for storage space. Closets will hold filing cabinets, and linen cabinets are adaptable for supplies. The living room makes a good meeting room. The dining room can serve as a conference room.

Plan, however, to choose areas that are arranged so you can use them conveniently. Everyday supplies should be as near as possible to your work space, while less frequently used equipment and files can be kept in more remote areas.

Finding a Place for Everything

Since everything obviously can't be kept in your immediate desk area, use this formula adopted from Stephanie Winston's book *Getting Organized* to decide where to keep what. On a scale of 1 to 7, rate the item you're storing or filing in terms of how frequently you use it. Give items you use every day a 1; those you use once a year, a 7. Place the items in the following locations according to how you rate them:

> 1—place all items you rate as a 1 within arm's reach of your desk area.
>
> 2–3—keep items you rate as a 2 or 3 within your immediate office space in files or cabinets, on countertops or shelves.
>
> 4–5—store items you rate as a 4 or 5 in nearby cabinets or closets, or shelves outside your office space.
>
> 6–7—store those items you use only once or twice a year in remote locations like attic, basement, or garage.

From our experience, here's a final tip. Plan to add at least 10 percent of whatever office space you think you need for storage space. There are a number of places other than available closets and drawers for storing office supplies, equipment, and files.

Matching Your Work Style

It's very tempting to recommend locating your home office in a separate room with a sturdy door. This does seem to be the best and most obvious solution for many people. A separate office, however, is not always possible, and since we've found so many successful home offices that break this standard mold, we've come to another conclusion.

You've heard the saying "Home is where the heart is." It applies equally to home offices. The best office space will be a space where you want to work. We all have our idiosyncrasies and preferences, and the right place for one person can be a disaster for another. Elizabeth Forsythe Hailey, Noel Cavanaugh, and Marcia Seligson, for example, are all writers who work at home, but each prefers writing under quite different circumstances.

Elizabeth likes to write in the kitchen so she "can keep an eye on things." Noel locks himself away in a basement hideaway. "Everyone knows if I'm downstairs they'd better not interrupt me unless a new baby or a million-dollar check has just arrived. When I'm writing, I can stay down there for twenty-four hours at a time." Marcia Seligson likes to move around when she writes. She may type at her desk for a while in the sunny office she had built over her garage. Then she may get up and stroll outside to think and jot down some notes, and afterward resume writing in the comfort of the living room.

So how can you know the best place for you? Here are several decisions you can make to help you match your office space to your personal preferences and work style. Mark where you fall on each of the folowing continua.

Private?_____or_____Public?

This is probably your most important space decision. Do you like or need to work in an exclusive private space away from all other noise and activity? Or do you like to work in the midst of it all? The privacy questionnaire in chapter 5 should give you a good idea of where you are on this continuum.

At one extreme is Dr. Richard Ricardi, whose office is located in a separate building behind his garage. As a psychiatrist, he finds that "a separate location helps my clients feel this is definitely a professional office and not a social setting. I also find by walking back to the office in the morning I 'go to work' and then at night I close the door and I 'go home.' "

At the other extreme is Brenda Rosetta, who runs her cookie company entirely from her spacious kitchen. She says of her kitchen office, "I'm always at the heart of the action and never miss out on a thing that's going on."

Shared?_____or_____Exclusive?

Can your office space serve other household purposes when you're not using it for business? Too often we don't have a choice about this one. The question often becomes which room can be used both for an office and for household purposes, without totally disrupting the operations of either.

At one extreme is Mary Stoddard, who sets up and takes down her graphic-design studio every workday. Each morning she moves the cars out of the garage, pulls down tables that are hinged to the walls, and starts working. Every evening she puts her work away, folds the tables up, and drives the cars back into the garage. For her, sharing this space on a daily basis works out fine.

At the other extreme is William Lecker, who will not share office space with other household activities even on an infrequent basis. When he started creating handmade jewelry, he thought the guest room could easily serve as his workshop, since guests used it only once or twice a year. He found instead that his metals and stones could neither be put away nor moved without considerable difficulty, even for a weekend. He decided to move his workshop into an unused breakfast room where he could work and visit with his wife when she was in the kitchen.

Windows?_____or_____No Windows?

Some people find windows distracting. They can't keep their eyes and their minds on their work. Others feel almost claustrophobic in windowless rooms.

As a data-entry clerk, Helen Gilles sits at the computer most of the day. To minimize glare problems, she likes an interior room without windows.

Jack Gates works in sales so he's on the road most of the week. He doesn't look forward to the reports and other paperwork awaiting him on the weekend, but it becomes almost enjoyable as he does it near the large sliding glass door in his office, which looks out onto the backyard. "We have one of the most beautiful jacaranda trees I've ever seen. I like to look at that tree and see the sunlight flooding through it into the office. It relaxes me. I even enjoy watching the kids play out there with the dog."

Compact?_____**or**_____**Spacious?**

You may like a lot of elbow room, space to spread out your things while you work. Or you may prefer keeping everything close at hand.

When Sharon Kirkpatrick started working as a seamstress, she set up a sewing room on an enclosed porch off her living room. It was a big, open space and seemed ideal. She could spread out her patterns and tackle many projects at once. But she ended up feeling as if she were working in a giant wastebasket. Thread and scraps, patterns and half-cut garments, pins and tape were everywhere. She was embarrassed to bring people in there for a fitting.

So she decided to set up her sewing room in a large walk-in closet, where she sews on one piece of work at a time. The porch, which she put back into order, is a space she now uses to store her material, cut her patterns, hang finished garments, and have fittings.

Fitting into Your Household

Once you have a picture of the type of office most suitable for you, you can match your needs with what goes on in your household.

Engineer Jeff Knoghton set up his office in the den off the family room. The den was a natural place. In fact, one reason he bought the house was that he saw the den as the place he would use one day to start a consulting practice. When that day finally arrived, he proudly set up his desk, files, and comfortable chair and went to work.

Everything was fine until 3:00 P.M. when the kids came home. From that hour on, the television was playing almost continuously, with the children laughing and carrying on nearby. At Jeff's request, they became pretty good about keeping the set turned down, but every once in a while, usually just as he was on an important call or in the midst of a crucial thought, he would be bombarded with the sounds of a high-speed chase, with police sirens and screeching brakes. Despite efforts at restricting viewing hours and other creative "solutions," household tensions increased until he finally moved his office to an upstairs bedroom.

A careful review of household activity patterns *before* deciding on his office location would have helped Jeff avoid the problem in the first place. Spend a day or even a week noticing what goes on in your home. Keep notes as to who does what during which hours.

Is the living room the most likely place for a romantic evening with a date? Would the answering machine and computer equipment interrupt the mood there? When and where do family members or roommates use noisy equipment like power tools, the lawn mower, the dishwasher, or the vacuum cleaner? What room do other people gravitate to when they come over? Where do the kids play? What are the traffic patterns through your home and the noise patterns outside your home? Does someone in the neighborhood practice the piano? Or even worse, the drums? Will the kids run down the hall past your office on the way from the living room to their bedrooms? Do you have to walk past your office on the way to your bedroom? With this kind of information, you're in a good position to decide what will be the best use of the space you have.

Making the Most of Your Available Space

We've known a few people who've moved to a new home just to have one that's better suited for a home office. But most of us are limited to what we've got. The space you have, however, is probably not as limiting as you think. As we've said, you can consider working in almost any part of your home. You can convert or remodel your space into something more suitable. And if all else fails, you may be able to expand or add on. Let's review some of these options, beginning with the most commonly used rooms.

The Spare Bedroom

The spare bedroom is the most popular candidate for a home office. Since it is a spare room, the work space can generally be used without sacrificing a great deal of living area. In fact, you may find it possible to continue using the room for other purposes when you want to. If there's a sofa bed in the room, it can still be a guest room or, if it has ample bookshelves, it can serve as a library. Using the room for nonbusiness purposes, however, jeopardizes your home office tax deduction, as you will see in chapter 10.

Spare bedrooms are often far enough away from the mainstream of household activities to offer some kind of privacy, yet accessible enough to make having business guests or running out for occasional household chores convenient. Most important, however, a spare bedroom is usually large enough to feel like a real office and not like a makeshift work space.

The Living Room

Many executive offices today have been carefully designed and decorated to look like living rooms. Bookcases, casual conference tables, comfortable chairs and couches are standard office furnishings. So why not have a living room that's an office?

For the right business, a living-room office has many advantages. As long as you keep your desk neat, the living room can serve as your home office by day and return to its role as a living room after working hours.

The living room is usually the most spacious area of the home, making it more easily divisible into a separate office space with partitions, bookcases, screens, or furniture. It is almost always near the front entrance, which makes it accessible to business visitors. It is usually designed as the public part of the home, so personal areas are located away from it. It is often the most formal part of the home and as such is suitable for creating a business image. In addition, closets and guest bathrooms are usually found nearby.

In some homes with a family room or den, the living room is actually anything but a "living" room. It's reserved for holidays or the arrival of special guests. If this is your situation and you don't need a more isolated office area, the living room can be an excellent choice.

The Family Room

If you have both a family room and a living room, you can use the family room for your office, and move activities that used to take place there into the living room.

Family rooms are generally located near the kitchen and back entrances and therefore make good workshops, studios, or labs. They're somewhat removed from the sound of street traffic. But often they open onto other living areas. This can be an advantage if you like to be in the center of activity, but a disadvantage if you're seeking a more secluded work space.

The Kitchen

Since the kitchen is such a central part of any home, locating your office there usually puts you in the heart of household activity. And since the kitchen probably has to be used, water, food, and cooking grease may gum up your office space. But if you need access to plumbing, electricity, or of course cooking equipment, this may be the right location.

A breakfast nook can often be turned into an office (see figure 6-1). Sometimes the kitchen itself can be divided to create a separate office area.

Beware, though, of the temptation to snack your way through the day, and of a possible negative effect on your business image. A professional atmosphere in the kitchen is possible, but often difficult.

The Dining Room

Many people get along quite well without ever using their dining rooms, preferring to eat in the kitchen, family room, or breakfast nook. This infrequent use, along with the size and location of most dining rooms, makes them excellent candidates for home offices.

Sometimes the dining area is an alcove off the living room. For a business like consulting, this can be a particularly attractive setting, with the living room serving as a meeting room or waiting room for the office beyond. Or the dining room can become a second office for employees you hire, with your primary office located in the living room.

Figure 6-1. Breakfast room converted into an office.

Closets, Dressing Rooms, and Storage Spaces

An area twenty-four to twenty-seven inches deep and five feet wide allows enough room for work or filing space. Therefore, walk-in closets, long closets with sliding or louvered doors, storage rooms, nurseries, guest bathrooms, or spaces beneath and along stairways are areas that can be transformed into home offices.

The advantages of these tiny, hidden areas are that they create a compact, self-contained work space, and one that is out of the way when not in use. The disadvantages, of course, are that such work areas may be too small and outgrown too quickly.

The Bedroom

Sometimes bedrooms are large enough to be divided, partitioned, or screened off for separate office space (see Figure 6-2).

Generally, however, we discourage people from using their bedroom as a home office. Your bedroom is probably your most private and personal space, a place of retreat. Working in your bedroom, you may find you can't ever get away from business. Setting up an office in a bedroom you share may present even more problems, since your work is invading somebody else's private space as well. Some couples we interviewed had declared the bedroom off limits for business, to preserve this one area of their home for intimacy and relaxation.

Converting or Remodeling

When existing space doesn't lend itself to a home office, you may be able to transform it into space that does. This transformation can be as simple as using screens, partitions, shuttered folding doors, furniture, or wall units, or as complex as putting up or tearing down doorways and turning a dusty attic into a skylit studio. The costs can range from a $50 screen to thousands of dollars for a major renovation.

New Space-Making/Space-Saving Resources

Products to help you organize your home office. Manufacturers such as Rubbermaid and Rolodex are creating a rich array of clever products for the home office that provide innovative ways of organizing lots of material into cramped or underfurnished space. For example, the Design-a-Space helps you customize a system for handling mail, disks, files, business cards, etc., to suit your needs. Shelves and wall units like the Office Tower by Alumax Corp., or Basket Systems by Sculte, feature variable-sized floor-to-ceiling shelves. These products are available at office superstores, hardware stores, home center stores, and specialty stores like Containers & More, Function Junction, Hold It!, the Container Store, and Placewares.

Integrated equipment. The trend in consumer electronics is toward combining functions once done by many pieces of equipment into one space-saving unit. Manufacturers like Canon and Panasonic are creating fax-phones, fax-copiers, answering machine-telephones and many other functional combinations. Alacrity's *E-Quip Office in a Box* serves as a copier, modem, fax, and scanner all in one ([908] 813-2400). (800) 252-2748.

Professional organizers. Over the past fifteen years a brand-new consulting specialty has emerged—the professional organizer. These information-age specialists offer space planning and design, paper management, storage systems, and general office organization. Often they specialize in home offices and they have access to many creative ideas and products that enable the person cramped for space to use every square inch to its maximum advantage. They charge from $50 to $125 an hour to help you set up your office in a way that maximizes your space.

Voice and communication coach Sandra McKnight, for example, hired a professional organizer when she found her growing business was taking over her one-bedroom apartment. She found the $475 she paid organizer Susan Rich to be worth every penny. Six hours and sixteen trash bags after Rich arrived Sandra discovered she actually had plenty of space. She just hadn't been using it well. She describes the process as follows: "Susan rearranged my desk, phone, and filing cabinets so I have easy access to everything. Then she turned some of my kitchen cabinets into an office supply area. Most importantly, however, she created a system for me to get my desk cleared off and keep it that way. Now I can immediately process the endless amounts of paper that come across my desk and quickly access what I need when I need it."

To locate professional organizers in your area, write to the National Association of Professional Organizers, 3824 Ocean View Blvd., Montrose, CA 91020, or consult your Yellow Pages.

Decorative screens like these available through The Bombay Company mail-order catalog, (800) 829-7789, are attractive, affordable, and practical. Smith Corona has an acoustical screen for separating home and office use ([203] 972-1471). And for maximum flexibility, Herman Miller has an expandable home-office screen in three heights, which diffuses glare and can extend up to six feet or fold back when you want the space open ([616] 654-3000).

Another option is to use one of the open-plan modular systems popular in today's offices. In the past, most of these systems were too cumbersome and expensive to use at home, but today manufacturers like National Origami, National Steppes, and Kimball Footprint are designing modular office systems for the home office (see Figures 6-3 and 6-4). These units include desktop, file drawers, shelves, and space for a computer and printer all built in. They can be assembled in various floor plans. Some can be assembled yourself; others must be assembled by a professional upon delivery.

Or you might even explore movable walls available from companies like Clestra Hauserman, (216) 498-5000; The Mills Company, (216) 442-2900; and USG Corp., (312) 606-4000. These walls go up quickly; can be taken down, moved, and reused; come in various sizes, fabrics, or finishes; and fall into the same tax category as furniture and equipment.

When ideas like these don't meet your needs, you might consider some of the more expensive remodeling options described below.

Converting a Garage

To completely transform a garage into an office, you'll usually need to remove the garage door, build a new wall with a standard door installed, upgrade the floor, and put in the necessary insulation and waterproofing. Then you'll need to refinish the interior and exterior and add any necessary utilities. If the weather in your area is particularly severe and your garage is detached from the house, you may want to add a breezeway or covered walkway between your home and garage/office.

Usually, garage conversions mean giving up car space. However, converting only part of the garage or using an attached garage storage area instead may save enough space for a daytime office and a nighttime garage.

If all this sounds like a big job, it is. When you're finished, however, you'll

Figure 6-2. Sometimes bedrooms are large enough to divide or partition off. A storage wall can create office space without distrupting the room.

have a spacious home office that provides ample privacy and a separate entrance for business visitors.

Converting an Attic

If you haven't used your attic in a while or removed the inevitable cobwebs, its initial appearance may put you off. But don't let appearances stop you from considering this space option. An attic/office is removed from the rest of the house, can provide a large work and storage area, and may even offer a view.

If you're interested in remodeling your attic, take a look at the current design of the room. Generally, building codes will allow you to convert your attic to living space if the ridgepole (the horizontal timber at the top of your roof to which the rafters are attached) is at least seven feet above the subfloor (the rough, unfinished floor of your attic).

The higher the ridgepole, the more comfortable your space will be. As a rule of thumb, at least one-half of the usable space needs to be seven feet high in order for the attic to be considered a viable home office option. The remaining less high areas can be used to create efficient storage space.

A frequent problem with attic conversions is access to the office. To build a stairway leading there, you need to have two feet by ten feet of space on the floor below and in the attic itself. A longer space would be needed if your ceiling is higher than eight feet. If you don't have this much space, you can consider a spiral staircase, which usually requires an area of four to five square feet. Remember, though, it may be difficult to get equipment up to the office on a spiral staircase.

Since the attic is subject to extreme temperatures in summer and winter, working conditions in an attic/office will be intolerable without proper insulation and an efficient means of heating and cooling. For both floor and ceiling, using fiberglass insulation batts, packed between the structural supports, is reported to be one of the most effective ways of controlling the room temperature. You can also use portable heaters and fans, but take safety into consideration before you purchase any portable appliance.

Converting a Basement

If you have a basement, that too can be turned into an office. Again, don't be put off by appearances. Clear it out, clean it up, and then look at the possibilities. Like attics, basements are removed from the flow of household activities and can offer you a quiet, private place to work. However, in addition to the inconvenience of stairs, the image of going "down" to see you could be less than desirable for business visitors.

The biggest problems in remodeling a basement are water leakage and humidity. You can waterproof the walls with commercial water sealants painted onto the inside of each exterior wall. Wood-textured board can then be placed between the exterior walls and a final covering of wall paneling or plasterboard.

If you decide to paint the walls, make sure you use waterproof paint and add a mildew retardant to the paint. If the room continues to feel damp, you may want to install one or two air vents that lead outside or to the house. Heaters, of course, will greatly help reduce the damp feeling, since the heat will cause the moisture to evaporate.

Since most basements have concrete floors, you may want to install a warmer-looking surface like a wood floor or carpeting. With proper padding and insulation, a carpet can enhance the atmosphere and provide further protection against cold and dampness.

Basements are notorious for exposed pipes, unconcealed wiring, and conspicuous utility meters. You can turn these eyesores into "architectural elements" using some bright paint over pipes, ducts, or other outcroppings to make them match the background or to create a colorfully pleasing design. Ceiling tiles, plasterboard, or textured wallboard can also be used. Make sure, however, that all the ducts and pipes are properly sealed and leakproof before you cover them.

You might set up a useful partition in front of the harder-to-hide heaters, meters, or wire boxes. Cabinets and freestanding closets can be cleverly placed to conceal a number of these unsightly objects, as can room dividers.

Wall units

Modular panel systems

CLIENT APPT—
10 A.M. — THURS
BRING FILES

Bookshelf dividers

Screens

Accordion doors

Room dividers

Bookshelves

Divider

Desk

Living room

Divider

Entryway

Figure 6-3.

Figure 6-4. Three modular home-office system layouts, available through Desks Incorporated, Commercial Furnishings and Systems, 1385 South Santa Fe Drive, Denver, CO 80223; (303) 777-8880.

Making Space When You're Renting or Can't Add On*

1. **Use your imagination.** If you start with the assumption that there's always more room somewhere, our experience is you'll find it.
2. **Convert dead space into office space.** The space under stairwells can make an excellent storage and supply closet. Unused space between wall supports can be carved out for built-in storage units. Space above filing cabinets also makes a great location for storage. A forty-eight-inch round table tucked into a corner can become a conference table.
3. **Use wall units and bookshelves to quadruple your storage area.** All walls in your office can be turned into usable space by lining them with floor-to-ceiling shelving. This shelving doesn't need to be expensive. Avatar makes reasonably priced ready-to-assemble units, and there are retail stores that specialize in creative and inexpensive wall unit arrangements.
4. **Convert closet space.** A whole office can be tucked into a walk-in closet. Linen closets make ideal supply cabinets. Open up more space in the center of the office by taking the doors off the closets and using them as a recessed area for your or your employee's desk. Conceal file cabinets in closets by building a frame around the space and closing it off with sliding doors.
5. **Divide an existing room with a room divider or screen.** Custom shutter and blind companies can build a custom-designed wood divider with shutters that can be opened for light and visibility or closed to put your home office completely out of sight.
6. **Turn any existing room into an instant office with a folding desk unit,** like Origami, a desk unit designed especially for home offices by National Office Furniture (see Figure 6-5). Or use Herman Miller's Scooter, a tiny movable stand that can be tucked under any surface and pulled out to be used as a keyboard holder, writing surface, or laptop computer stand. Small when folded, when opened it becomes a full-blown sixty-four-inch desk with lots of storage and filing space. A folding desk can also be built to fold down from a small closet with ample storage built in along the back wall of the closet.
7. **Make furniture serve multiple purposes.** Recognizing that home-office space can be tight, manufacturers are developing multiple-use furniture. Herman Miller, for example, has filing cabinets that can serve as nightstands, a table desk that can become a buffet service, and drop-leaf desktops that expand or fold down as needed.

* If you rent, remember to check your lease and talk with your landlord about any physical alterations.

Converting a Patio or Porch

Patios and porches can become functional, attractive, and airy offices. These areas have the advantage of providing an exterior entrance and are usually set off from household activity. As with an attic, an enclosed porch or a patio requires insulation, heating, and cooling.

Figure 6-5.

Adding On

When your home simply isn't big enough, you may have the option of adding on to what you've got. When adding on, you have three choices. You can build up, out, or down. The first step is to begin mentally breaking down walls, imagining rooms where there are none, figuratively digging out new foundations, and filling the yard or sky with a bigger house or perhaps separate structures.

You can begin by drawing a map of your house and the surrounding property, experimenting with different additions. Let your imagination go. Don't limit your ideas to office space. Consider adding on other areas that will free your existing space for office use. A master bedroom off the living room, for example, can become an ideal office when you've built a new (and improved, of course) bedroom in another part of the house.

To help plan changes in the layout of your home and office, you can use computer software like Design Your Own Home by Abracadata, Ltd., or Floor-plan Plus by ComputerEasy, to try out various space-making alternatives.

After you've generated as many ideas as you can, check how feasible they are with more than one construction professional. Talk over your ideas with friends, relatives, or others who have added on.

When we realized we would have to add on, or move at least one of our offices out of the house, we began analyzing every possibility. We thought of building a second story over the garage, adding space off the living room, or constructing a separate building in back of the house. We weren't satisfied with anything until Sarah's mother suggestsed an ideal alternative we never would have thought of—leveling the redwood cathedral ceiling in our family room and building a second story over it.

A Dormer

If you have a steep roof, you can add work space to existing rooms or create new rooms by building single, double, or full dormers (windowed projections built into the roof).

Raising the Roof

You can expand your available space by raising one or both sides of your roof. A small attic space can become a loft/office or a second floor over one or several rooms.

A Loft

A loft can make an ideal office space because it is usually removed from the mainstream of household activity. Since lofts typically involve raising the roof above existing space or opening ceiling space from rooms below, they do not afford privacy. Doors can be fashioned, however, to slide over a loft opening to solve this problem.

A Second Story

You can have a second story constructed over all or only a part of a single-level home. Of course, building a second story is a major project that is both costly and time-consuming. Also, the living space below the new story will be out of use while building is going on. This can create considerable disruption to both your household and your work. So we recommend moving out of the house during construction, if possible.

Despite these drawbacks, adding a second story can double your space. When we built a second story over our family room, we created a bedroom and private bath for our teenage son, as well as a storage room. This addition freed our son's old bedroom, which was ideal for Sarah's office because it was right off the living room.

A Basement

If you have a partial basement, or a crawl space under your home, you can convert this area into a full basement and a viable home office. If you have no basement, you can create one under all or part of your house.

Creating a basement is another complicated and expensive option, but it *is* possible. It requires specialized knowledge of construction, so when considering this option locate a general contractor with previous experience and a proven track record doing such excavation.

A daylight basement can become a pleasant alternative to a damp and dingy underground basement/office. A daylight basement has all or part of one wall open to ground level, with windows that allow substantial light to enter into the office area. This windowed wall, which can be made of double-insulated glass, may also create an interesting entry. With sliding glass doors, it can even provide a patio extension to your office in warmer months.

The only requirement for a daylight basement is that there be a full-height foundation wall that is large enough for a door or at least a good-sized window at ground level. The amount of excavation and reconstruction of your foundation depends on the slope of your yard. Most homes can have at least a partial daylight basement built into the foundation.

A Separate Building

If you do not have the extra space, you can build or buy a separate structure. This structure can be attached to your house by a covered walkway or breezeway if you desire.

Because you're starting from scratch, building a separate structure can be more expensive than adding on. For some people, the advantages of adding a new, separate home office may be worth the investment, however. Construction doesn't disrupt the household, and when the building is finished you can have business visitors without their intruding into the privacy of your home. Your office will be completely self-contained.

If building a separate structure is outside your budget, you might consider prefabricated or precut construction kits. These kits cost anywhere from 20 to 40 percent less than comparable custom-built units—and they serve the purpose just as well. The sizes vary according to style and manufacturer, but most lines include models that are at least nine feet by twelve feet. To locate them, refer to the "Building" listings in your local Yellow Pages.

Mobile homes or recreational structures can also be relatively affordable office sites. Public relations consultant Jennifer Ash came up with one of the more creative office-space solutions we encountered. She occupies a two-room cottage with a large decked terrace off the living room. When she couldn't find a workable space for her desk in either room, she literally pitched a tent on the deck.

Her canvas gazebo, manufactured by Moss Tent Works, is totally self-contained and waterproof. By day it provides adequate work space for her and one associate. At night, Jennifer merely zips up the tent and "comes home for the evening," carrying her phone along with her.

Another choice is a yurt, a freestanding structure by Pacific Yurts, Inc., that also can make a self-contained external home office (see Figure 6-6).

Getting a Professional Opinion

If your budget allows, consider getting advice from professional builders, designers, and architects. Lloyd and Suzanne Faulkner of Encino, California, are examples of designers who specialize in creating attractive and workable home-office spaces. They've helped clients with such innovative solutions as turning a pool table into a desk and finding a coffee table that can be raised, when needed, to desk level. They've even designed rolling desks for those who are confined to their beds. Aside from specialists like the Faulkners, various other professionals can be helpful.

Depending on your eye for design and the extent of your skills, you may be able to implement many of the ideas in this chapter yourself. Whenever remodeling or adding on to your home, however, contact your local city or county government to determine the permits and specifications required, and call on a licensed contractor of good reputation to carry out any extensive work. Also, recognize that finding the right office space may become an ongoing process, as it was for author-photographer David Goodfellow.

"Ten years ago I divided a twelve-by-twelve-foot spare bedroom in half and turned one half into an office for technical writing and the other half into a darkroom, but both areas soon became too small.

"Five years ago I sealed in our carport, the top of which doubled as a patio deck. It became a twelve-by-eighteen-foot office, a twelve-by-six darkroom, and a twelve-by-twelve junk room.

"To keep water from dripping down my neck when it rains, I had to have a composition roof put on the deck. Then our central heating didn't have enough selectivity to keep the office warm. So I bought a space heater.

"The advantages of the new arrangement are many, however. First, a nice percentage of my house is a tax write-off. Second, the new office is far enough away from the kitchen to make munching a real effort. Third, the office is bright and comfortable, which makes working there a joy."

A Guide to Professional Help
When Remodeling or Adding On

Architects
- Prepare detailed plans and specifications for bids on the work to be done.
- Draw up all plans in accordance with local health, safety, and engineering codes.

Figure 6-6.

Side porch became this sunny office.

Back porch off kitchen became this handy office.

Patio converted into studio

Loft office

Dormers

Raising the roof

Adding a wing

Installing a yurt

- Provide workable plans to contractors.
- Supervise all construction work.
- Inspect the completed work.

Draftsmen or building designers
- Draw up plans for straightforward and fairly simple remodeling.

General contractors
- Work with the architect, designer, or owner in meeting all specifications for materials and construction of the work to be done.
- Hire subcontractors to handle specific phases of the job and ensure that each phase is completed.
- Set up all work schedules.
- Secure all building permits and arrange for all necessary inspections.
- Purchase all materials and supplies.
- Furnish all tools and equipment required.

Interior designers or decorators
- Assist you in utilizing your existing space more creatively or efficiently.
- Assist you in furnishing and decorating the space.
- Purchase furniture and decorator items at a discount.

So whether you find the right space for your home office immediately or, like David, create it over time, finding an arrangement that suits you can make a positive difference in your feeling about work. And remember, the costs involved in creating your office space are deductible, so keep your receipts. The next challenge becomes setting it up in the best way possible for your business.

Resources

Books

Healing Environments, Your Guide to Indoor Well-Being. Carol Venolia (See Chapter 5 Resources for full citation).

Home Remodeling Illustrated. Menlo Park, Calif.: Sunset Publishing Co., 1988.

Home Storage: Projects For Every Room. David H. Jacobs. New York: McGraw, 1994.

Sunset Complete Home Storage. Menlo Park, Calif.: Sunset Publishing Co., 1989.

Sunset Home Offices & Workspaces. Menlo Park, Calif.: Sunset Publishing Co., 1986.

Software

Design Your Own Home. Abracadata, P.O. Box 2440, Eugene, OR 97402; (503) 342-3030.

Floorplan Plus. ComputerEasy, 414 E. Southern Ave., Tempe, AZ 85282; (800) 522-3279.

My House. Design Ware, 17 Main Street, Watertown, MA 02172; (617) 924-1699.

Other Resources

The American Society of Interior Designers. 608 Massachusetts Ave. NE, Washington, DC 20002; (202) 546-3480.

Pacific Yurts, Inc. 77456 Highway 99 South, Cottage Grove, OR 97424; (503) 942-9435.

CHAPTER
SEVEN

■■■■■■■■■■■■■■■■■■■■■■■■■■

Outfitting Your Home Office
with Furnishings and Supplies

In the not-too-distant future, we'll live in smart houses that will monitor and manage the lighting, temperature, humidity, telephone system, security, air, and all other aspects of our household environment. A handful of demonstration smart homes already exist. It's only a step beyond that when our furniture and equipment will adjust immediately to our touch or command. At this moment, however, these are still things we must attend to.

Mistakenly most people often take a "ready, fire, aim" approach to setting up their home office. Eager to get under way and keep costs down, some just "make do" with whatever's around the house. Others go after "bargains" that don't hold up to day-in, day-out use and end up costing more because they need to be replaced within no time at all. Still others spend a lot of time and energy trying to set up a professional office only to find when the furniture and equipment they selected arrives, it doesn't fit their home-office-sized space.

Too often, open-collar workers put up with the mistakes or oversights they make when first setting up their offices and suffer through bothersome backaches, headaches, eyestrain, and other irritations and inconveniences. But having the wrong office setup can be even more serious. Dramatic increases in the use of personal computers with their keyboard, mice, and VDTs can result in cumulative trauma disorders like carpal tunnel syndrome, bursitis, ganglion cysts, tendinitis, epcondylitis, thoracic outlet compression, tenosynovitis, myositis, and other virtually unpronounceable disorders. At their worst, these illnesses can incapacitate someone to the point of paralysis.

Aesthetician Lori Tabak discovered this the hard way. Several months after obtaining new facial equipment for her home-based salon, she strained her back muscles so severely that she was unable to work for over a month. Only gradually with careful attention to ergonomics and the help of medical professionals was she able to build back to a regular work week. Such ailments have become a common occupational hazard for home businesses like medical transcriptions and writers.

At the other extreme, however, research by Dr. Mark Peltier and Dr. Robert Baron has shown that an ideal home office environment can have the invigorating effect of stepping outside on a beautiful morning after a good rain. Working in an optimal environment has been proven to result in a more positive mood, greater efficiency, a better memory, greater willingness to cooperate, higher goals, and a pattern of appropriate risk taking!

Fortunately office furniture and equipment manufacturers are responding to the needs of home office workers. Many manufacturers are designing furniture, supplies, and equipment just for the home office, with ergonomics among their top considerations. But if we are to benefit from these many new resources, we must stop settling for a "make do" office and outfit our office as effectively as we can. In this chapter we'll provide some guidelines for cost-effectively creating a productive, safe, and healthful office.

Of course, setting up a home office that works is not just a matter of avoiding problems. To establish what matters most to people about their home offices, we interviewed both veteran homeworkers and professional organizers, who get called in to help when a home office isn't working. Again and again, the veterans and experts listed four bottom-line criteria for making a home office work:

- Convenience—the setup needs to save you time and simplify your work; you should be able to come in and just start working.
- Comfort—the office needs to satisfy you physically and emotionally, and cause you no pain or strain while you're working.
- Functionality—work needs to flow smoothly, with items used every day within arm's reach.
- Privacy—the office space needs to be free of intrusions and disturbances.

With these standards in mind, we organized this chapter like a department store, to offer as much variety as possible for addressing these major considerations, while taking into account both appearance and finding bargains in the process. We'll begin with the furniture department.

Choosing Your Furniture

Furniture is one of the things that home office workers tend to over-economize on, at least at first. Marge Abrams, who calls herself a Paper, Space, Possession, and Time Management Consultant, says, "Until people are 'successful' in a home business, they don't spend a lot of money on furniture. They use what's in the house. I've done the same thing."

If you're like over half the office workers surveyed in a Louis Harris poll, however, you spend over 75 percent of your day sitting at your desk. This means there are some very good reasons not to use just any desk and chair. The wrong desk and chair, more than any other item in your office, can set you up for the whole array of ailments mentioned above. And the effects are not always physical. Fatigue, loss of concentration, and irritability are some of the more subtle problems traced to the wrong furniture. On the other hand, productivity gains of up to 40 percent have been made once the right office furniture was found. More specifically, one-third of workers interviewed listed a comfortable chair as one of the top two contributors to their productivity. Designer William Strumpf suggests approaching chairs, desks, and other important office furniture as if the piece were a garment: "It should be proportioned to fit the person who's using it."

Not all designers are like Strumpf, however. According to a survey reported in *Interior Design* magazine, interior designers rank aesthetics over comfort in selecting office furniture (77% to 45%), so if you use a designer to help you select your office furniture, be sure you choose one who believes in safety and comfort first. Here are the kind of things you should consider.

The Desk

Desk surfaces need to be different heights for different tasks. While writing surfaces should generally be 30″ off the ground, typing or computing surfaces are usually 26″ high. Of course, you can have both a writing desk and a separate typing or computer table, but today some desks are designed to include

---

Furniture Checklist: What Do You Need?

- ☐ Desk
  - ☐ Different heights for different tasks
  - ☐ Appropriate width and depth
  - ☐ Suitable style
    - ☐ Solid
    - ☐ Cube
    - ☐ Open table

- ☐ Chairs
  - ☐ Desk Chair
    - ☐ Supportive back
    - ☐ Firm seat
    - ☐ Breathable material
    - ☐ Firm armrests
    - ☐ Adjustable height
    - ☐ Footrests
    - ☐ Tilt mechanism
    - ☐ Rollers
  - ☐ Easy chair

- ☐ Side or conference table chairs
- ☐ Filing Cabinets
  - ☐ Legal size
  - ☐ Standard size
  - ☐ Vertical cabinets
  - ☐ Lateral cabinets
  - ☐ Hanging files
  - ☐ Nonhanging files

- ☐ Tables
  - ☐ Worktable
  - ☐ Conference table
  - ☐ End or coffee table
  - ☐ Other:

- ☐ Couch

- ☐ Bookcases

- ☐ Storage racks

- ☐ Lamps

---

surfaces of more than one height. Others can be adjusted up and down or tilted to the position you desire as you change tasks. For example, MicroCentre has an ergonomic workstation designed to fit into a corner with various surface levels ([800] 966-5511). And Winners Only has *The Power Desk* that is designed to hold just about every piece of equipment a home office could need at varied heights and angles ([619] 941-9559). Haworth has created the *Tracker Adjustable Table*, which tracks the amount of time you work in a certain position and then beeps to alert you to adjust your position. The table can move to as many as 19 different heights at regular intervals throughout the day! Call (800) 344-2600 (see Figure 7-1). Herman Miller's *TD Collection* desks, designed specifically for the home office, combine ergonomic principles like a retractable, adjustable keyboard tray

Figure 7-1. The LapTop Desk, by American Business Concepts, perhaps the smallest ergonomically designed desk, can fit almost anywhere.

The Tracker Adjustable Table by Haworth moves to change heights.

3 Way Adjustable Document Holder

Keyboard/Telephone Cord Grommet

Adjustable Monitor Rack 360° Turn, 15° Tilt

Power Director with Power Surge Protection

Left Handed Mouse Pad

Wrist Support System

Scanner Placement or Extra Work Surface

Right Handed Mouse Pad

Fax Machine Area

Pencil Drawer

Diskette Drawers

Portable Notebook Drawer with Pull-Out Mouse Pad

Peripheral Equipment Storage

Power Center Panel

Laser/Dot Matrix Printer Storage

Pencil Drawer

Box Drawer

CPU Storage

Legal/Letter File Drawer

The Power Desk by Winners Only fits just about everything you would need to operate a home office in an ergonomically designed corner desk.

Input-Ez's tabletop retractable unit sits on a desk or table to hold computer, monitor, document holder, and keyboard.

and fold-up display shelf for document viewing in tight residential spaces and a distinctly residential-decor look ([800] 897-8719).

Besides height, other features to be tailored to you and your home office are width and style. Unless the office is 20 feet or more across, choose a desk no wider than 7 feet. Larger desks will overpower and crowd the room. Even the style of your desk affects how large it will seem. Available choices are solid, cube, or open-style desks. In smaller offices, a table desk will appear to take less space than a cube desk of the same size.

And if you're thinking you need to have a lot of space to have an ergonomically designed office, think again. *The Laptop Desk* is possibly the smallest ergonomic desk unit in existence (see Figure 7-1). This ergonomically adjustable desk is designed for a laptop computer and although it could fit in the tiniest of closets or corners, has room not only for your computer but also your mouse, copyholder, task lamp, printer, diskettes, documentation manuals, pencils and pens, coffee cup, surge protector, and more (American Business Concepts, [800] 877-4797).

The Desk Chair

A fully adjustable ergonomically designed chair can help avoid just about every problem we've discussed. On the other hand, an improper chair can not only aggravate these problems, it will cause muscle strain, swelling of lower legs, reduced blood circulation (which in turn diminishes your ability to think), and varicose veins. According to William C. Isenberg, furniture industry analyst, many desk chairs are imitations of the good ones and most manufacturers claim to have an ergonomic chair, but they're designed to keep their price down. So it's essential that we educate ourselves as to what to look for in a truly ergonomic chair and vital that we sit in any chair we're considering to personally evaluate the back, seat, arms, and optional features.

The back of the chair should provide support for the base of the spine, helping it hold a slight forward curve. The backrest should be high enough to allow you to relax against it, coming to at least the lower part of your shoulder blades.

Chairs with tilt mechanisms work with the seat and back fixed or with a separately adjustable seat and back. A five-pointed base to the chair, rather than the customary four legs, will help avoid tipping over if you lean back too far.

The seat of the chair should be rounded so it won't dig into your thighs and restrict blood flow in the legs. The seat should also be adjustable up and down over a range of six to nine inches, so you can adapt it to different work tasks. Preferably, you will be able to adjust the chair by gently pressing a button or lever under the seat from a sitting position.

When your chair is properly adjusted, your feet should be flat on the floor and the seat should be parallel to the floor. If you are short, you may need a footrest to keep your legs from dangling.

Often people assume that a soft seat is the most comfortable. Actually, this is only true for a short time, since too soft a seat limits the natural **S** curve of your spine. The seat material should be a rough, porous fabric that lets body heat dissipate.

The arms should have a hard surface that wears well and resists soiling, but preferably should not be made of metal, which feels cold and slick. As far as height goes, the arms should be low enough not to rub the underside of the desk or hit other furniture.

A chair with rollers will enable you to move from one work area to another. Make sure, however, that the rollers have self-locking casters that travel smoothly over carpeting but not too quickly over wood or linoleum. "Dual-wheel" casters are preferable to the "ball" type because they move more smoothly, distribute weight more evenly, and don't cut into the flooring.

How a Bad Chair Can Cut Your Earnings

If you're using an uncomfortable or ill-fitting chair, it can easily cost you 5 minutes an hour in lost productivity. Here's what that costs you a year, based on a range of hourly rates you might earn or pay an assistant working 2,000 hours (8 hours a day, 5 days a week, 50 weeks a year).

Hourly Rate	Annual Cost
$10.00	$1666.66
$15.00	$2499.99
$20.00	$3333.32
$25.00	$4166.65
$30.00	$4999.98
$35.00	$5833.31
$40.00	$6666.64
$50.00	$8333.30
$75.00	$12499.95
$100.00	$16666.66

Industry analyst Isenberg considers Herman Miller's Equa, Steelcase's Sensor, and various model Harter chairs to be examples of good ergonomic desk chairs. Equa was designed by William Strumpf, one of the leading designers in this field. Ergomax from American Ergonomics offers chairs that permit users to assume the posture they like best from reclining to kneeling, leaning forward to upright without losing proper support. But these chairs are generally priced above what most home offices can afford. He recommends HON of Muscatine, Iowa, as providing lower priced chairs that have many features of the more expensive ones. *Managing Office Technology* magazine recommends The Anthology II Advanced Task Chair by Rosemount for its eight directional movements and five ergonomic stress relief and relaxation functions. Most people find that spending from $400 to $1,000 on a good chair is worth the investment. Fortunately more and more manufacturers are creating high-quality furniture scaled to the size and the budgets of the home office. For example, Haworth, a leader in top-of-the-line office chairs, has introduced the new Accolade line of ergonomic chairs with home office budgets and needs in mind.

But keep in mind, the higher the cost of the chair does not necessarily mean the better the chair will be for you. One person, for example, who has been experiencing a lot of lower back pain, traded in his expensive designer chair for a $135 chair and the back pain went away. There's perhaps nothing more individual than a chair. Case in point, a lawyer took his entire office staff in to select new desk chairs. Each person chose a different chair!

Finally, whatever combination of features you choose, even the best chair isn't designed for long-term sitting, so get up and move around every twenty minutes or so while working!

Choosing an Ergonomic Chair

The best way to know if you're getting the ergonomic chair you think you're buying is to talk over your needs with the vendor, and try it out, of course. Here's a glossary of terms provided by Dr. Leonard Kruk of Westinghouse Furniture Systems to help you talk about the ergonomic features you want:

- **Static ergonomic chair**—a chair without controls to adjust back, seat, and arms that has been designed ergonomically to fit the dimensions of the average body type. Poor choice for anyone who doesn't fit the norm.
- **Active ergonomic chair**—has controls for manually changing the positions of the back, seat, and arms precisely to each individual. Good for everyone who will take the time to fiddle with the controls to get them just right. Studies show most people don't.
- **Passive ergonomic chair**—automatically adjusts ergonomically to the body of the person who sits in it. Especially good if anyone else uses your desk chair.
- **Posture back chair**—has an adjustable back and a stationary seat.
- **Posture-tilt chair**—has a back that tilts back twice as far as the seat, reducing pressure at the back of the knees when tilting.
- **Swivel-tilt chair**—has back and seat that tilt and swivel together.
- **Pivot-tilt chair**—prevents the front of the seat from rising when the chair tilts back, keeping the feet on the floor and reducing pressure on the back of the knees for better circulation.
- **Forward-tilt locking chair**—the chair can be locked so it won't tilt, keeping the sitter in a forward position. Good for keyboard-intensive work.
- **Pneumatic chair**—has a gas cylinder you can control by a button or lever that will lower or raise the chair while you are sitting on it.

Remember, the more adjustments a chair has the more closely it can be customized to your body; but the more complex it is, the less likely most people are to use them. Unfortunately most people don't take advantage of the ergonomic features of their chairs. To address this problem, Haworth has developed an Electronic Hang Tag that accompanies all the chairs in its line of Accolade desk chairs. The Electronic Hang Tag is a software program that shows you how to make the proper adjustments on your Accolade chair.

Filing Cabinets

Just as you can never be too rich or too thin, you can also never have too many filing cabinets. Whether you need two file drawers or a bank of cabinets, you have several basic choices to make:

Size. Because of Paul's law background, our files are legal-size, but the more convenient option is the standard letter-size.

Shape. Although lateral files have gained in popularity, they can take up a substantial amount of floor space and we find them less convenient to use than vertical cabinets. A lateral cabinet can, however, be functional as a room divider as well as a spacious storage unit.

Filing features. Hanging files fit on racks in a standard file drawer. While they make your folders easy to see and manipulate in the file drawer, the folders are clumsy to handle when removed from the cabinet.

Locking. If you have confidential material, locks are a requirement for your cabinets. In fact, you may want to get even stronger file cabinets that are burglar- and fireproof as well.

Quality. Whatever kind of file cabinet you buy, stick with recognized brands such as Shaw-Walker, Steelcase, and Litton. As Stephanie Winston points out in *The Organized Executive,* cheap cabinets jam easily. Their drawers may slip off the tracks or fall out completely, and their tendency to tip over makes them dangerous.

Isenberg points out that a five-drawer vertical file is not very accessible to a short person. He recommends mobile files mounted on casters that can move from place to place.

Ergonomic Tips to Save Your Body: You Can't Work without It

When you're working from home on your own, there's no one looking after office safety but you. But if you can't work, you won't get paid. So here's a list of tips other home office workers have passed along for setting up their offices in a way that keeps their body parts in running order. Because everyone's body is different, not every tip may be helpful to you. Products like those mentioned are available through office supply stores and catalogs unless otherwise indicated. Catalogs featuring ergonomic products include Action Computer Supplies ([800] 822-3132) and Ergonix ([800] 328-ERGO).

1. Use a visorlike hood over the top of your monitor or a glare screen to reduce glare. Some screens like NoRad ultraglass form fit shields ([800] 262-3260) or a plug-in device like Clarus VDT Clear System ([800] 425-2787) also screen out electric field radiation. NoRad ELF Pro Tech bands wrap around your monitor to reduce electric field radiation emitted from the back, sides, and top of your monitor.

2. Try out an ergonomic keyboard like the MiniErgo by Marquardt Switches ([315] 655-8050) that allows the elbows to rest at shoulder width, taking pressure off wrists, elbows, and shoulders (see Figure 7-1). A study by office manufacturer Haworth, Inc., found using an ergonomically designed keyboard increased keystrokes by 25 percent and reduced typing errors by 50 percent.

3. Build up the strength and dexterity of your fingers, hands, wrists, and forearms with a kneading ball like Eggercizer by ACCO.

4. Place your monitor 16 to 28 inches from your face, and position it so that the top of the monitor is at eye level or slightly lower. To get your monitor in the right place, you can place it on an adjustable monitor arm. To get your monitor at the right height you can use an adjustable VDT stand, or simply place books underneath it. Input-Ez has created a compact retractable tabletop unit that sits on a standard desk or table and houses your computer, monitor document tray, and keyboard at a proper angle. Call (800) 227-0810 (see figure 7-1).

5. Use a copyholder to save crooking your neck when entering data from another document. Position it as closely to the screen as possible within the same arch of vision as the monitor and keyboard. PerfectData has six models from monitor side mounted to easel based (805) 581-4000. The Input-Ez desktop unit described above (figure 7-1) has a built-in document tray.

6. Make sure your feet are on the floor while working at your desk and that your elbows are at a 90-degree angle to your keyboard. If necessary use a footrest like the ComfortTread Footrest by MicroComputer Systems Accessories ([800] 521-8270), which keeps your feet flat and eases strain on the legs, feet, and lower back.

7. Equip your phone with a headset so you can write or keyboard while talking on the phone. Plantronics ([800] 544-4660) has a variety of models including ones with a microphone that filter out noise. Or Bell Atlantic offers the Earphone, a hands-free Touch-Tone phone with an ultralight one-ear earpiece that you can use alone, with your own phone or a 15' cord to talk on the phone while you compute, write, file, cook, etc.

8. Use a wrist rest like one by MicroComputer Accessories ([800] 521-8270), which sits under your keyboard and keeps your hands/wrists/arms in a straight line up to the elbows instead of bent while you keyboard. Or use a lap keyboard pillow with a built-in wrist rest, which allows you to rest your keyboard on your lap. One worker created his own rest using a $1 piece of tubular foam pipe insulation held in place with a rubber band.

9. Take frequent breaks, blink, and fidget. Various studies show that short, regular rest breaks alone can increase productivity from 7 to 10 percent. And according to the *New England Journal of Medicine*, computer users blink less and keep their eyes open wider when looking at the screen, which results in eyestrain.

10. Try cushions or foam padding to support your back. The Adjustable Back Cushion, for example, inflates at the touch of a button to conform to the contour of your back (MicroComputer Accessories [800] 521-8270).

11. Protect your wrist from mouse stress with an ergonomically designed mouse like Microsoft's J-Mouse, or a wrist protector like the MouseMitt ([408]

335-9599). American Packaging Corp. has wrist rests for mice, keyboards, and calculators ([503] 852-5577). You might also do as Paul did and switch to using your other hand. When Paul, who is right-handed, started using his left hand to work the mouse, all the strain problems he'd been having disappeared.

12. If a mouse gives you too many aches and pains, try a track ball. Kensington Turbo Mouse is a track ball with customizing software ([800] 535-4242). Or Keytronics has a track ball built into the keyboard ([800] 262-6006).

13. Wear a wrist splint while keyboarding. Many people do this routinely to prevent problems.

14. Since working at a VDT can be hard on your eyes, uncorrected or improperly corrected vision can result in fatigue and other problems. So talk to your eye specialist about whether you would benefit from special glasses or lenses. Reading glasses are not always appropriate for computer work, but special glasses just for working at the computer or monofocal, full-width bifocal, flat-top, or progressive additional lenses may be of value.

15. Consult with a chiropractor or other specialist familiar with ergonomics. Our chiropractor corrected many posture and seating problems we would never have recognized. One man was able to stop wearing a splint at the keyboard within a month of implementing his chiropractor's advice.

Often it's a combination of several things that will make working painless. For example, to reduce eyestrain one person replaced his desktop and CRT with a laptop and a well-lit supertwist LCSD VGA screen. Then he got rid of neck and shoulder aches by replacing his old desk chair with one that would adjust to only 1.5 inches higher.

Noise Control

Noise, among all environmental factors, has the strongest correlation to job stress and dissatisfaction in an office, according to a Columbia University study. Even moderately high noise levels cause increased blood pressure, faster heartbeat, and other symptoms of stress, while excessive noise causes fatigue, distraction, and errors in work. Actually, noise may have consciously or unconsciously played a role in your choosing to work from home.

While too much noise certainly interferes with work, a total absence of sound is also stressful. As one person who moved his office home says, "The first thing I noticed was the silence. I never realized how much I appreciated the sounds of the office."

Just how much sound do you need to stay mentally alert? Probably not more than thirty decibels, about the sound of a normal air conditioner. Even better would be twenty decibels of sound, about equivalent to leaves rustling in the breeze.

The average office has a noise level of about fifty decibels. The sound of an average conversation is about sixty decibels, while the vacuum cleaner in your home runs at about eighty decibels. Prolonged exposure to over seventy decibels may result in hearing impairment.

To keep the sound levels in your office down to a comfortable level, you can simply increase the distance between your office and outside activity. Doubling the distance between your office and outside activity will decrease the noise that travels between the two points by six decibels. If this is impossible, you can use one or more of these sound-control techniques.

1. Draperies over windows. For maximum effectiveness, these need to be floor length and lined.
2. Ceiling treatments that don't reflect noise, such as acoustical tile or commercially applied sound-absorbent material.
3. A thick pile carpet with an underpad to absorb noise in the room.
4. Weather stripping on doors and windows to keep unwanted street noise out and prevent noises that might bother neighbors from traveling.
5. Relocate noisy equipment to a separate room or closet.
6. Use flashing lights or a soft ring setting on telephones.
7. In-room barriers such as a room divider or an acoustical screen like Workroom, available from Smith Corona ([203] 972-1471).
8. Outdoor barriers like a concrete block wall over five feet high, shrubs, and foliage.
9. Solid-core doors in place of hollow-core ones.
10. Double-glazed windows.
11. Wall coverings such as fabric or cork. Armstrong Soundsoak is a fabric over acoustical fiberboard that will absorb 60 percent of noise.
12. Acoustical drywall and paneling on top of your existing walls, with thick insulation placed between the studs of the new wall.

Of course, you can always use earplugs or a headset like NoiseBuster by Noise Cancellation Technologies ([800] 278-3526 [203] 961-0500) if you're unduly distracted by household or outside noise. Also before you spend a lot of money or time on any sound-control measures, find out if the undesired noise is coming through a heat or air vent. If it is, using one of the sound "masking" techniques described below will be more effective. Because these sounds are rhythmical, they will also help mask noise you can't screen out by other measures.

These methods can also be used to produce enough sound to keep yourself alert when working from home alone:

1. A stereo playing low.
2. A gurgling fish tank with a water filter and air pump.
3. A cage of songbirds, such as canaries.
4. A "white noise" generator like those available from Sharper Image ([800] 344-5555) or Hammacher Schlemmer ([800] 233-4800). These machines, about the size of a portable radio, play restful countryside and seaside sounds as well as pure white noise.

5. An endless-loop audiotape cassette that plays office sounds. One such tape is listed in the Resources list, or you can make your own. Also available are audiotapes of music designed specifically to relax or boost productivity.

If you're having problems with bothersome or inappropriate noise while talking on the phone (i.e., barking dogs, rattling dishes, giggling children), try one of the following solutions:

1. A mute button on your telephone will block out a temporary disruption like reprimanding a barking dog or telling a child to turn down the television. With the button down, you can hear the other party on the line, but they can't hear you.

2. For continual noise from equipment, conversations, nearby children playing, etc., you might consider a product like The Confidencer, by Roanwell Corporation ([212] 989-1090), which fits into the mouthpiece of your telephone handset and cancels 80 percent of the background noise normally picked up through the telephone. Not only can you be heard better, you can also hear better.

3. Some headphone models like those from Plantronics include a microphone that filters out background noise ([800] 544-4660).

Tudor Barker of Dorset, England, made soundproofing his home office into a low-cost do-it-yourself project. He began with the floor by laying ½-inch-thick polystyrene tiles along the floor and covering them with hardboard and sealing the gap between the floor and the walls with silicone. Then, to soundproof the windows, he bought the thickest glass panes he could afford, triple-glazed each frame at a slight angle, and once again sealed the edges with silicone.

Lighting Your Home Office

According to a Harris poll for Steelcase, lighting is the number-one contributor to productivity. The amount and type of light you need depends on your age, the kind of work you do, and your preferences.

Generally, the more detailed your work, the more light you need. So if you're a cartographer making maps, you'll need more light than someone taking notes while on the telephone. Also, as you age you need more light. A person over fifty may need 50 percent more light than a younger person, and a person over sixty may need 100 percent more light.

In using a computer at any age, however, you may need less light, not more, in order to avoid glare on your computer screen, because readability of a computer screen depends on the contrast between onscreen characters and the screen background.

Here are some general guidelines to follow when considering the best lighting for your office.

Use Natural Light When Possible

The best light for your office is also the cheapest—daylight. Daylight provides the truest color and is the least tiring and puts the least strain on your eyes of all light sources. This means you will be more productive in natural light. The quality of daylight, however, is affected by a number of factors: direction of exposure; the color and texture of your walls, ceiling, and furnishings; the arrangement of your work space; and, of course, the time of day and the weather.

Daylight entering from the north is usually a soft, indirect light, shining steadily most of the day. Artists and craftspeople prefer this type of natural light, especially if it hits pale-colored interiors. Because of its lack of glare, northern light is best for operating a computer too. More direct light enters from an eastern or western source and, to a lesser degree, from the south, and will not only cause more glare but also an imbalanced illumination.

One way of getting nonglare daylight is to add clerestories, or windows that are installed high up on a wall. Clerestories throw diffused light into the center of a room, providing balanced illumination without glare, and because of their height they also provide privacy. Installing clerestories in an existing building, however, is likely to be expensive. Skylights are another attractive way of bringing additional daylight into offices where it is blocked or nonexistent. Various skylight styles enable you to direct light to a work area or diffuse light evenly throughout your office.

Supplement with Artificial Lighting

Of course, it's impossible to work by daylight all the time, even in an ideal room. At night or on gray days you have to turn on the lights. The most common types of artificial light are incandescent and fluorescent lighting. Both have their advantages and disadvantages.

Incandescent lights are usually small and have a high degree of intensity, so they can be used for task lighting—that is, supplementary lighting focused directly on your work. A desk lamp provides task lighting, as do track lights. Used in conjunction with ceiling fixtures, a desk light can eliminate shadows on your work.

The color emitted by an incandescent bulb is warm-toned. It is softer, reflects better on the skin, and is gentler on the eyes than fluorescent light, although newer types of fluorescent lighting provide as good or better color rendition as incandescents. Incandescent light is also the most expensive form of lighting available, consuming the most electricity for the light produced, and it converts much of this energy into unwanted heat.

Fluorescent lighting is diffused, produces little heat, and provides a steady,

Comparison of Incandescent and Fluorescent Lighting

Light Source	Power Required	Light Output (Lumens)	Approximate Lifespan
Incandescent	150 watts	2,880 foot-candles	750 hours
Fluorescent	50 watts	3,200 foot-candles	12,000–20,000 hours

highly efficient light source. It generally requires large, relatively expensive fixtures, however, and cannot easily be used to spotlight specific areas. Fluorescent lights also blink, and if you're near enough to the light source to notice the blinking, you're apt to experience eyestrain and fatigue.

Because incandescent and fluorescent lighting both have advantages, you may want a balance between the two. If you use fluorescent lighting, the most desirable kinds of bulbs for a home office are full-spectrum bulbs, which are most like natural daylight. One source of such bulbs is Consumer Lighting Concepts in Tampa, Florida; (800) 842-0052.

New products offer exciting solutions for home office lighting problems. Compact fluorescent bulbs are now being made that fit into standard lamps. These bulbs offer long life (approximately 7,000 hours) and use only about one-fourth the energy of a conventional incandescent bulb. Though compact by fluorescent standards, these bulbs are still more than twice the size of an incandescent bulb and may not fit within enclosed fixtures. Another innovation, halogen bulbs provide a white light, last about 2,000 hours, and use about 10 percent less electricity.

We are making use of Chromalux bulbs made with neodymium. These bulbs produce the color rendition of natural sunlight with a 99.6 percent rating. The bulbs fit standard lamps and last about 3,000 hours. You may be able to find these new bulbs only at stores specializing in lighting fixtures.

Use Light to the Best Advantage

Making the eye adjust to varying levels of light in a room is one cause of eye fatigue. Therefore, to avoid eyestrain, have the general level of light in the room as near as possible to the level of light on your work.

One option for keeping this balance is to use dimmer-switches to adjust the level of light in the room. They also save on your electricity bill and can change the mood from a bright work setting to a softer conference-room atmosphere. Installing a dimmer-switch for incandescent lighting is simple and inexpensive, but for fluorescents it is costly. It's more economical to install a dimmer-switch on fluorescents when they are first put in, instead of at a later date.

Another cause of eyestrain is glare. The more illumination you have in an office, the greater the risk of glare. Therefore you need to find a balance between having too little light and too much. You can reduce glare by making sure

---

Best Ways to Deal with Static Electricity

1. Antistatic mats
2. Aerosol spray
3. Humidifier
4. Plants in your office
5. Uncarpeted floors

---

lightbulbs are not in your line of sight and by avoiding light that reflects off shiny surfaces such as picture glass, mirrors, and the like. Another simple way of reducing glare is to have several small light sources rather than one bright light. A Cornell University study found that indirect light bounced off the ceiling is better than fluorescent lighting for working at your computer. Workers with standard overhead lighting experience greater lethargy.

A simple way to enhance lighting in your office is using color to your advantage. Dark colors absorb light; light colors reflect it back into the room. One of Paul's previous offices had redwood paneling on about half of the wall area, while the other half was white. At night, there was a noticeable difference in the level of light needed in each area. Where the wall was darker, we had to increase the amount of electricity we used. So one way of cutting down your electric bill is to have light-colored walls and ceilings.

The Environmentally Conscious Home Office

We believe every open-collar worker is entitled to a bumper sticker that reads "I save air, water, and energy—I work from home."

By not commuting to a job, you are not contributing to air pollution. As former President George Bush pointed out to the California Chamber of Commerce, in the first speech in which a president endorsed working from home, ". . . if only 5 percent of the commuters in Los Angeles County telecommuted one day each week, they'd . . . keep 47,000 tons of pollutants from entering the atmosphere." By working at home, you're probably using less water than if you were at an office.

People working from home can also conveniently practice additional conservation measures. Here are eighteen things you can do:

1. Use halogen and compact fluorescent bulbs that produce more light, last longer than ordinary incandescent bulbs, and use less energy.

2. Install low-flush toilets. They use only one-third to one-fourth as much water as standard toilets.

3. Use word processing and desktop publishing software that previews what your printed page will look like. This will reduce the number of test copies you need to make.

4. Use personal information management software instead of making notes on paper.

5. Fax information instead of hand delivering it or using a messenger service or an air freight company. You'll save on fuel and energy. Choose plain paper fax machines instead of those that rely on nonrecyclable, chemically treated thermal paper.

6. Make use of an internal fax in your computer. You can send and receive faxed messages without having to produce printed pages.

7. Store information and documents on computer disks instead of in paper files.

8. Use outdated stationery to make notepads instead of throwing it away.

9. Buy products made from recycled paper.

10. When it will not create confusion, use the back sides of paper for lists and scratch paper.

11. Save for reuse shipping boxes, plastic foam balls, and other plastic packaging materials to avoid generating nonbiodegradable trash. Or create your own packing material by buying a paper shredder designed for the home office. The Hunt Boston shredder, for example, is just 18⅛ inches wide by 12 inches deep and 19½ inches high. It can shred up to five sheets at a time and shred card stock, plastic credit cards, and film. The cost is under $200.

12. Consolidate as many errands as possible into one trip. Use your own shopping bags, rather than plastic bags.

13. Be environmentally conscious about the office products you use. Use paper, for example, made from 100 percent postconsumer waste recycled, never-bleached.

14. Without decreasing your productivity, reduce air-conditioning by scheduling your work for other than the hottest hours of the day, using attic fans and skylights that open. Heat only the rooms you need to use in winter.

15. Recycle everything from your PC to your toner cartridges. Hewlett Packard's Toner Cartridge Recycling Program provides all its buyers with cartridge return instructions and will donate money to the National Wildlife Federation and the Nature Conservancy for each cartridge received. For more information, call (800) 752-0900, extension 1872. For other cartridge manufacturers, check the materials that come with the product or call their customer service lines.

16. Use mugs rather than plastic foam cups.

17. Retro-fit lights with fixtures that use much less energy. Generally, such lighting increases lighting quality and yields a 20 to 30 percent annual return. Turn off lights whenever you leave a room. EPA says it's a myth that turning lights on and off wastes energy.

18. Use environmentally friendly materials like cleansers, paints, glues, furniture, carpets that can be found in environmental directories like *Enviro Clean: Sourcebook of Environmentally Responsible Cleaning Products* ([800] 466-1425) or in many natural food stores.

     For more information on creating an eco-friendly household, MicroBase Publishing has created *Green Explorer*, a software program that shows you how to build and remodel your home eco-consciously. Or you can subscribe to *In Business, the Magazine for Ecological Entrepreneuring*.

Providing Security and Fire Protection

Having a home office both increases and decreases your security risks. On the one hand, you have added equipment and material to protect while you may be bringing strangers into your home. On the other hand, you are at home more often or at least away at irregular times. Either way, you reduce your chances of being burglarized, because thieves avoid houses where someone might be home.

Here are thirteen ways to further protect yourself from theft and to safeguard confidential materials.

1. **Secure your doors and windows.** The more difficult you make entry into your home, the less chance there is someone will go to the trouble of breaking in. In addition, since thieves have often been in a house as visitors before they burglarize it, you can substantially reduce your risk by having prominent safety features like dead bolts and good locks. Even if potential burglars figure they can get into your home, getting things out will appear difficult.

2. **Light your premises well,** both inside and outside. Special motion-activated superbright halogen lights, for example, will flood outdoor areas at night if intruders enter your property, startling them and alerting you without running up your electricity bill ([800] 999-3030).

3. **Have a dog that barks at strangers.** Convicted burglars who were surveyed rate a dog as the most effective deterrent.

4. **When you're away from home, give the appearance that someone is there.** For example, arrange to have someone take in your newspaper and mail, use timers to turn sprinklers on and off during the day and to turn lights on and off automatically in different rooms at night, store garbage cans out of sight, set your phone on a low ring, and if you'll be gone for a considerable time have the lawn mowed while you're gone.

5. **Hire a housesitter** when you're going out of town. At least be certain the newspaper and mail are picked up every day. Students at theological seminaries are reliable housesitters.

6. **Create environmental barriers around your home.** Research at the University of Utah has shown that creating a sense of privacy around your home is as important in preventing burglaries as the locks you use. Hedges, fences, shrubs, and trees act as psychological barriers to would-be burglars because your home looks less exposed. (The research has also shown that chances of burglaries are less if your home is on a cul-de-sac instead of a through street, in a suburb instead of a business area, and on a street without traffic signs.)

7. **Have a security inspection.** Some police departments offer free security inspections, or you can hire a security consultant.

8. **Hire a private patrol service,** or participate in a Neighborhood Watch program on your block. These operations have cut the crime in some areas by as much as 40 percent.

9. **Purchase a safe** like one of the many Sentry Fire-Safe Security Safes, for important papers, money, valuable tools, photographic plates, computer disks, and so on. Just having a safe may prevent theft, because the police estimate that most burglars are in and out of the house in six minutes, and breaking into a safe takes time. Safes can be fireproof, waterproof, and even explosion-proof.

10. **Install a burglar alarm system.** To protect a 2,000-square-foot home, you can get a reasonable measure of security for as little as a few hundred dollars. For example, infrared sensors that detect intruders by sensing changes in infrared radiation or heat cost from $25 to $125 each. One device can cover several rooms. Because they don't emit sound or light waves, they are less apt to trigger false alarms and they're fairly easy to install. Also easy to install is a wireless system using sound and motion detectors with a remote control. Other devices are sensitive to changes in air pressure. Some people use an inexpensive computer to create a sophisticated alarm system for themselves. If you have pets, you can get motion detectors with a "pet alley" that scans only above the height of your pet. If you need to protect only one door or a specific object like a safe or filing cabinet, you can get a self-contained alarm for under $50.

    Instead of doing it yourself, you can also get your house wired by companies like ADT, Brinks, Sears (which uses local contractors) or by a local independent firm. Charges vary dramatically for basically the same work from installer to installer so it's wise to get several bids. Often companies will offer a lower price if you sign up for a monitoring contract. Keep in mind that the monitoring station is in a distant city so you cannot inspect its operation. It's also a good idea to check with the Better Business Bureau or other consumer agencies because some alarm services use outdated equipment that is easily set off by a dog's bark and that triggers false alarms that can lead to your being fined.

11. **Place a pair of size 16 work boots outside your door.**

12. **Install smoke detectors** and make sure to have your electrical service checked routinely to protect your home office against fire damage. When we moved into our first house and needed additional wiring for the porch we were enclosing, our horrified electrician discovered we had a slow fire in our fuse box.

13. **Install a surveillance camera** so you can see who's at the door or elsewhere on your premises. The DAK catalog offers several "micro-sized" systems that range in price from $200 to $300; (800)325-0800. Even a nonworking camera like the Fake CCTV Camera they sell may discourage a would-be intruder.

Aside from these common precautions, you can also keep small fire extinguishers on hand and buy fireproof files. However, they are seven or eight times as expensive as conventional office files.

Creating the Image and Decor You Want

The way your office looks can make the difference between feeling productive and motivated or disorganized and demoralized while working. If employees, customers, co-workers, or clients come to the office, appearances can also be important for gaining their respect and trust. This is especially true in a home office, where establishing a professional atmosphere is more of a challenge than in a building full of other offices. A Herman Miller study of home offices found, however, that trying to mix home and office decor was often a visually jarring experience as fine wood family antiques mingled in the same room with steel filing cabinets and metal printer stands. With a little thought and planning, however, this need not be the case, especially now that manufacturers are designing furniture and accessories especially for the home office. Here are five basic steps you can take to achieve the image you want:

1. Take a fresh look at your office space. Imagine you're starting a new job and seeing your new office for the first time. Ask yourself if this is a place where you would feel like working and could be productive. Decide if it looks too homey or too stark.

Rooms that look fine in a home may be too "busy" for an office, because of too many bright colors, too much clutter, or too little space. On the other hand, if you've cleared everything out of a room, attic, or basement, and all you have is a desk and a chair in an empty room, the space may be too large, drab, or cheerless for productive work.

Take a look at your office from the viewpoint of the people who will be

---

Wall and Floor Coverings: What Are Your Options?

Wall Coverings
Paint. Quickest and cheapest way to change a color scheme. Quality of appearance depends on surface beneath the paint.

Wallpaper. Colors, textures, and patterns offer wide variety of looks; covers blemishes.

Foil. Shiny, bold, distinctive appearance, but possible glare problem.

Sheet vinyl. Durable and easily maintained.

Textured coverings (grasscloth, linen, wool, jute, felt, carpet, and other fabrics by the yard). Coverings give plush and homey look and disguise rough wall surfaces.

Wood paneling and boarding. Warm, durable, and insulating.

Cork. Warm, handsome, good noise absorption. Comes in tiles or paper-backed cork. Walls can double as bulletin boards.

Brick. Looks warm and solid.

Mirror paneling (glass, plastic, or acrylic). Creates the illusion of space, but possible noise and glare problems.

Murals. Photo wall-murals reproduce actual scenic photographs. Give life to a room without windows but may become tiring.

---

coming there as clients, customers, employees, or business associates. Consider their expectations and the statement your office makes about you and your business. If you're an accountant, for example, does your office convey the attention to order and detail that suggests you give careful advice about money? If you're an artist, does your office look like a creative place?

2. Decide on the look you want. Choose the tone or overall impression you want to impart:

Practical	Elegant	Creative	Homespun
Classic	Casual	Contemporary	High-tech

If you aren't sure about the look you want, think about the offices of people you respect and admire in your field. How do their offices look? Go through some decorating magazines and clip out photos you like. Remember offices you've worked in before and what you liked or disliked about them.

3. Coordinate your office. The furniture, the wall covering, the floor covering, the colors you use, the lamps, the ceiling, the window treatments, any wall decorations, and even the equipment and supplies should all work together to send the same message.

Color will have a particularly strong influence on the overall effect of your office. The colors you choose will affect you and those who come into your office both physiologically and psychologically. Color helps determine whether people feel their surroundings are cramped or spacious, and how hot or cool the

---

Floor Coverings

Hardwood. Looks good if in condition; warm; wears well; improves with age; can be refinished. Can be covered with polyurethane finish or treated with acrylic solution for greater wear. Dry heat may cause shrinking; dampness causes swelling; expensive.

Vinyl. Comes in both tiles and sheeting; waterproof; resistant to staining; cushioned vinyl is quiet and resilient underfoot; variety of colors and patterns; no-wax vinyls require less care. More casual than hardwood or carpeting.

Reinforced vinyl or vinyl-asbestos. Much like vinyl but less expensive.

Rubber tile. Doesn't conduct static electricity, wears well, quiet, waterproof, and soft. Recovers well from indentation but rubber heels make black marks and it stains easily.

Concrete, masonry, ceramic tiles. Tough, hard-wearing, can be washed or hosed down. Cold, hard, noisy, tiring to the feet.

Carpeting. Comfortable, and quiet. Available in wide variety of colors and textures. Wool carpet is longest wearing, but most expensive and builds static electrical charges. Nylon carpet is most popular, and least expensive, but even worse for static electricity unless blended or treated. Industrial carpeting with tight weave doesn't get as dirty and is very durable.

---

room feels. For a sense of excitement, cheer, and relief from boredom, use warm colors. Reds, oranges, yellows, and browns increase heart rate and respiration. There are indications that yellow also results in higher productivity in the workplace, while reds contribute to tension.

If you want to create a calmer, more serene and restful environment, use cool colors. Blues, greens, and grays slow down bodily responses. There is evidence that natural wood reduces stress while the color gray is experienced as depressing. Gray carpeting, however, will hide dirt, lint, and spills better than other colors, so if you want to take advantage of gray carpeting, balance it by using warm colors elsewhere in your office.

4. Decide what has to go and what can stay. You don't have to start from scratch. Decide what present furnishings are consistent with the image you want. Often you can re-cover, refinish, repair, or repaint what you now have. Or you can leave it all as is and purchase items consistent with your new look piece by piece as your budget allows.

5. Consider consulting an interior decorator or designer. These professionals can not only help you select a new decor but can also show you how to make the most of what you have. In fact, they often will save you money by suggesting a few inexpensive accessories to tie in what you have available with the look you want. Of course, they can also guide you through the labyrinth of decorating options for major decisions like new floor and wall coverings.

Maintaining Adequate Temperature, Humidity, and Air Quality

Studies show that people work better when temperature and humidity are at comfortable levels and the air is clear and fresh. You can usually maintain these optimal working conditions without much effort.

While climate is a matter of individual preference, people are most comfort-

---

How to Make a Small Room Look Larger

- Use one light color, such as an off-white or pastel, for walls as well as for drapes or curtains.
- Cover the floors with bright wall-to-wall carpeting.
- Keep the furnishings simple and uncluttered.
- Use mirrors (but remember they reflect light).

How to Make a Large Room Look Smaller

- Use bold colors and contrasting wall and floor coverings and furniture.
- Use large, heavy furniture.
- Use area rugs to define one or more sections of the room.

---

able and productive in temperatures between 68 and 75 degrees, with the humidity between 40 and 50 percent. In other words, if you're sweating it out without an air conditioner during the summer, buying one can be good for your productivity as well as your comfort. Studies have shown that when the office temperature rises to the mid-eighties, mental performance becomes impaired.

If you have a problem room that's always too hot or too cold, there are a number of possible solutions.

The human brain works in such a way that even though the temperature remains constant, we can use color to make ourselves feel cooler or warmer. You'll feel cooler in a room decorated with blues, greens, and grays, but warmer in a room decorated with pinks, reds, oranges, yellows, and browns. To get the effect you want, you needn't paint or paper your entire office with these colors. Use them in accessories like large wall-hangings, graphics, or pillows and even change them with the temperature of the season.

To keep the air in your office clean and fresh, you can install an electrostatic air filter, also called an electronic air cleaner. Adding these devices to most heating and air-conditioning systems costs approximately $500. Buying a portable air cleaner for the room will cost less. The Enviracaire portable air cleaner, for example, comes in light- ($169.95) and heavy-duty models ($245.95); (800)

To Warm Up a Home Office

1. Add solar panels to capture heat from the southern and/or western walls.
2. Install skylights and arrange your work area in their light path.
3. Carpet the home office and use ⅝-inch padding.
4. Plant deciduous trees outside windows for sunlight in the winter and shade in the summer.
5. Draw curtains, drapes, or blinds to retain heat when there is no direct sunlight.
6. Use insulated glass and make sure walls as well as ceilings are properly insulated to a standard of R-19.
7. Install a room heater.
8. Add a room humidifier to make the existing temperature seem warmer.

To Cool Off a Home Office

1. Place bookcases on all southern and western walls.
2. Use fluorescent lights.
3. Shut off appliances and lights when room is not in use.
4. Plant evergreens outside walls and windows with southern or western exposures.
5. Use indoor plants to shade direct sunlight.
6. Install a window air conditioner.
7. Use roof ventilating fans.
8. Arrange work areas in the direct path of circulating air.
9. Use blinds or curtains to block out direct sunlight.
10. Tint windows that receive the full glare of the sun.
11. Install heat-absorbing double windows.

869-6000. Either option removes smoke and cleans your air of microscopic particles that create a film on surfaces. The operating cost of an air cleaner is about the same as the cost of using a 60-watt light bulb.

According to research findings at the National Aeronautics and Space Administration, common houseplants can also help purify the air. Not only do plants such as English ivy, dracaenas, and palms freshen stale air, they also remove toxins such as benzene, formaldehyde, and carbon monoxide that can build up in any home office from the use of paper products, cigarette smoke, cleaning and office supplies, natural gas, and so forth. NASA researcher B. C. Wolverton recommends that plants be included in your operating expenses, like pencils and fax machines. Although any plant will help, research has shown that Gerbera daisy, mother-in-law's tongue, pothos, and spider plant absorb the most toxins. Wolverton claims that eight to fifteen plants will "significantly improve" the air quality in the average home. That's about one plant per 100 square feet.

An ionizing air filter can also improve air quality. These filters are useful in rooms without access to outside air, in areas where smog is a problem, or in rooms with electronic equipment such as office machines, television sets, and computers. Quantum Electronics manufactures such ionizers.

Finally, the odor of a work environment is normally overlooked unless fumes become consciously unpleasant or obnoxious. Research is pouring in, however, that fragrance can have a significant effect on the workplace, affecting alertness, performance, stress levels, and even heart rate, muscle tension and blood pressure. The Japanese are already using scents in the workplace, and in one experiment keypunch worker errors dropped 21 percent when the air was scented with lavender, 33 percent when jasmine was added to the air, and 54 percent when a lemon aroma was used. Here's how research is showing that you can assist your performance by adding scents to the air:

- **Improved work efficiency:** lavender, jasmine, and lemon
- **Learning aids:** basil, rose, bergamot, and cardamon
- **Reduce anxiety:** basil, bergamot, cedarwood, and hyssop
- **Reduce stress:** rose and tangerine
- **Relaxing:** lavender, chamomile, apple, and spice
- **Stimulating and invigorating:** lemon, jasmine, pine, eucalyptus, and rosemary

You can create these effects with potpourris; also, the Origins stores ([800] 723-7310) sell a line of essential oils aromas called Sensory Therapy along with diffusers for subtly filling the air with positive fragrances, and Aroma Véra offers a line of essential oils and diffusers in room or whole house models (800) 677-2368.

At the other extreme, to rid your home of unpleasant, embarrassing, or unprofessional household odors you can use a line of products called NonScents ([800] 942-8565) to control any odor, including those from pet accidents, lodged in carpets, furniture, floors, air vents, cars, laundry hampers, ashtrays, etc. These products have no fragrance. They absorb the undesirable odors. To freshen the air, research suggests using basil or peppermint.

Dust Busters

1. Dust your office regularly.
2. Use tacky dust cloths available at drugstores.
3. Spray your monitor with an antistatic spray like STAX made especially for electronic equipment.
4. Use an air filter. They range from $16 to $299 for ones that trap particles by charging them electronically so they stick to the filter.
5. Have a service come in to clean your air conditioning and heating ducts and vents annually.

Purchasing Office Supplies and Small Equipment

When you first set up your office, we suggest you generate a list of the minimum equipment and supplies you'll need. A good way to start, if you're currently working at a job, is to go through your office and list what you find on top of your desk, in your drawers, and in your cabinets. If you have a secretary, find out and list the common supplies he or she keeps on hand. Otherwise, review the equipment and supplies listed below.

Supplies and Small Equipment Checklist: The Basics

Supplies
☐ Accordion files
☐ Business cards
☐ Business envelopes
☐ Calendar or calendar software
☐ Computer diskettes
☐ Cleaning kit for disk drives
☐ Cartridges or ribbons
☐ Correction fluid
☐ Dust-Off air-spray cannister
☐ Envelopes and shipping boxes for air-express companies you use
☐ File folders
☐ File labels, tabs
☐ Glue, rubber cement
☐ Index cards
☐ Jiffy padded mailing bags
☐ Mailing labels
☐ Paper, laser and copier

☐ Paper clips, fasteners
☐ Pens, pencils, erasers, markers
☐ Postage stamps
☐ Priority mail and overnight mailing envelopes
☐ Ring binders
☐ Rubber bands
☐ Rubber stamps
☐ Staples
☐ Stationery: letterhead, billhead
☐ Tape: cellophane, packaging
☐ Tavek mailing envelopes

Small Equipment
☐ Calculator
☐ Check protector (businesslike and inexpensive)
☐ Flip chart (for brainstorming and planning)
☐ In and out boxes
☐ Letter opener
☐ Letter tray
☐ Mousepad
☐ Paper cutter
☐ Paperweight
☐ Pencil holder
☐ Postage affixer or a digital postage meter (saves time)
☐ Postage scale (improves accuracy and saves money)
☐ Pencil sharpener
☐ Ruler
☐ Scissors
☐ Staple remover
☐ Stapler

For special time-saving supplies, accessories, and equipment for organizing and running your home office, see chapters 13 and 15. For special supplies and materials for marketing your business, see chapter 23.

With the growth of the small office/home office (SOHO) market, you have more choices than ever before for where and how to buy office furniture, supplies, and equipment. You can roam the aisles of office superstores like Office Depot, Office Max and Staples, computer megastores like Computer City and CompUSA, specialty stores like Crate and Barrel and Hold Everything and specialty departments in larger stores like the Office Center at Sears. And while local stationery and office-supply stores are giving way to the "power retailers," you may still be able to get a discount as well as personal service by dropping in to your local mom-and-pop or independent store. But you don't even need to leave your home office to get nearly everything you need. You can also get good service buying by mail and by computer.

We recommend taking a tour through office-supply mail-order catalogs and also specialty paper house catalogs where you'll find everything from preprinted four-color designed papers for letterheads, envelopes, presentation folders, and business cards to papers for postcards, coupons, news releases, newsletters, gift certificates, presentation folders—all of which you can color coordinate and customize with your computer and printer and top off with iridescent laser color foils. You'll find lists of these various catalogs among the resources at the end of this chapter.

At one time mail-order catalogs were thought to offer your best price, and sometimes they still do. But there are many times when you just can't beat office superstore prices. And if you live in a city large enough, walk-in paper dealers, such as Kelly Paper and Kirk Paper in Arizona, California, and Nevada, may offer a larger variety of papers at better prices than you'll find in office-supply stores. Of course, price isn't the only factor to consider in deciding where to shop. Convenience, variety, availability, and service count too. Let's look at some of the factors to consider in deciding where to shop.

No matter where you buy your furniture, equipment, and supplies, there are some cautions you should always exercise. For instance, don't buy anything in broken or torn packages unless you have a chance to inspect the product or the opportunity to return it. Sometimes you can save money buying seconds or damaged merchandise, but be certain that the product is still usable. Since such items are generally sold as is, you probably won't be able to get a refund or make an exchange.

Buying by Mail

If you buy from a mail-order catalog, you may find some products at bargain prices. Keep in mind, however, that you will also have to pay for shipping and, often, insurance. When these costs are added to the order, you may not save much money, particularly when compared with prices at office superstores.

Features to Look For: Buying from Office Supply and Office Superstores

- Variety and quality of products offered.
- Availability. Is merchandise on hand or must it be special-ordered from a catalog?
- Delivery. Is it offered? Free or for a charge? Is it same day, twenty-four hour or less?
- Convenience of store location and of merchandise in the store.
- Toll free 800 number to place phone orders.
- Offer to match or beat lowest advertised price.
- Membership required for best prices? Membership free or for a charge?
- Helpfulness and knowledgeability of store personnel.
- Return policies: no return, money back, or store credit?
- Truth in advertising. Do you often go in to buy highly desirable advertised items which are sold out by the time you get there?

Moreover, shipping can be delayed, especially during the holidays. If you have to return an item, it may take as long as two weeks before the return is processed. Finally, judging a product from a photograph is not quite the same as seeing it in person. Unless you're already familiar with the product, you may find it smaller, clumsier, or not quite the same color you had in mind. That's why it's important to read product descriptions, including measurements, and to check model numbers carefully before ordering.

Most catalog companies offer liberal return policies and will refund or exchange products to the customer's satisfaction. This, however, is not always the case, so review the return policy before buying. In other words, read the fine print, which should state the return policy next to, or on, the order form. When you have to pay return or exchange expenses, an item can end up costing more than if you had bought it locally.

Because of a lack of local suppliers or the specialized nature of an item, the only way to get some supplies may be through a catalog. Even in Los Angeles, we've found it easier to order some things by mail than to find a local supplier. In ordering such items, we suggest you keep a three months' supply on hand at all times and order quarterly.

For quick service, make sure to place your orders either before or considerably after a holiday rush. Actually, mail-order firms report that their busiest times are January 1–15, April 1–15, September 1–15, and the entire month of December.

Ordering by mail is a common cause of complaints to consumer agencies. To guard against having a problem yourself, order from a known firm with a good reputation. Before ordering, check out who's responsible for damage during shipment.

If you're responding to an advertisement, phone or write the magazine in which the advertisement appeared to find out if the mail-order business has a record of complaints. Other excellent places to check on a company as well as on a product you're considering buying are on the forums on an information service like CompuServe and on computer bulletin boards.

Unless the company has stated a specific time for delivery, it must ship within thirty days of receiving your order. If the company fails to do so, it must notify you and give you the choice of receiving a refund or agreeing to a new shipment date. You automatically have the right to cancel and get a refund if you don't receive your order within the required time. On the other hand, by ignoring the first notice of a delay, you imply that you are willing to accept later delivery. You must be notified of any further delays, however, and you must specifically agree to them.

To protect yourself from problems when returning unsatisfactory products, pay by credit card rather than by cash or check. Then should you have a problem, you can often get the charge reversed. Sometimes when you can't get sellers to respond to your concerns, simply advising them that you will be asking their bank to credit your bill will spur them to action. While banks do not usually advertise this service, it is one which was brought about by the federal Fair Billing law, and the wise buyer takes advantage of it. The ability to protect yourself against problems of nondelivery or defective merchandise is reason enough to have at least one credit card.

One further tip: if the problem with a product is its quality, keep in mind that

What to Look For: Buying from Mail-Order Vendors*

- Toll-free order number.
- Shipping costs.
- Other handling fees.
- Always offer their lowest prices.
- Next-day delivery.
- No quibbles on money-back guarantee.
- Shipping paid on returns.
- One-year or lifetime guarantee on all items.

* According to *What to Buy for Business*

quality is always arguable and somewhat subjective. You will have more success by describing your problem as "not having been delivered in accordance with the agreement." Calling a problem a "billing error" rather than a "dispute" also increases the likelihood you'll get the charges reversed. And when the goods you've ordered by mail arrive, watch for any labels or stickers on the boxes that read Warranty Void. You may be wise to return the package unopened.

How to Handle a Problem with a Mail-Order Company

Here are some agencies you can turn to with a complaint:

The Postal Inspection Service. You can locate the postal inspector in the seller's area by contacting your local postmaster or postal inspector. The post office has a mediation service for settling disputes.

Better Business Bureau. To find out the address and phone number of the bureau in the seller's area, contact the Council of Better Business Bureaus, Inc., 4200 Wilson Boulevard, Ste. 800, Arlington, VA 22203.

Direct Mail/Marketing Association, Mail Order Action Line. This is the trade association of the mail-order business. It provides for self-policing of the industry and can be contacted at 6 East Forty-third Street, New York, NY 10017.

In California, the agency responsible for consumer complaints is the Department of Consumer Affairs, Complaint Assistance Unit, 1020 N Street, Sacramento, CA 95814.

In New York City, contact the Complaints Division, Department of Consumer Affairs, 42 Broadway, New York, NY 10006.

If you charged your purchase on a credit card, contact the issuer of the card in writing to get a credit on your account. You're entitled to withhold payment. Federal law and regulations provide extensive procedures for resolving disputes, and you will receive this information once you have notified the credit card issuer.

Mail-order companies that have the best reputations for prompt delivery and customer satisfaction appear under Resources at the end of this chapter.

Buying by Computer

Buying by computer has become big business. The major electronic services—America Online, CompuServe, Delphi, GEnie and Prodigy—offer electronic shopping. For example, the Electronic Mall® on CompuServe offers goods and services in fifteen departments such as Computer Hardware, Computer Software, and Office Supplies/Business Services. Well over a hundred different merchants sell through the Mall. These include large companies like AT&T and Sears selling home-office products to Hammacher Schlemmer selling its selection of innovative products. Smaller merchants sell through the Mall as well. One of them is Computer Express, a home-based company operated by Phillip and Leslie Schier. The Schiers sell over $2 million worth of computers and computer accessories a year at 30 to 40 percent off list price. Other merchants, like Jeff Freeman of Front Porch Computers ([800] GO PORCH), frequent the on-line networks offering advice to users that often enough results in sales. Jeff says he's on "CompuServe and the Internet twenty-five hours a day."

Avoiding Office-Supply Telephone Scams

Watch out for office-supply telemarketing scams. These solicitors try to get you to buy common items of poor quality at high prices by confusing you into thinking that they are your usual supplier or that you or someone else in your office already placed an order with them. Sometimes they will send you the items and bill you for them later, so you just routinely pay the invoice. We have made it a policy never to order from a telephone solicitor. We always ask them to send a catalog or written material for us to consider. That usually takes care of it; they don't have one. But we would also immediately return anything neither of us ordered marked *Return to Sender.*

Buying Bargains

1. Ask for a business discount. Usually you will need no more identification than a business card. Ask for discounts for cash or early payment.
2. Use recycled products. Companies like Computer Recyclers, (800) 635-2816, Media Value, (800) 845-3472, and Direct Micro, (800) 288-2887, sell high-quality recycled computer disks. Recycled toner cartridges for both printers and copiers can save 25 to 40 percent of the cost of new ones. They're available from companies like Data Products, (800) 232-2141; HP, (800) 752-0900; Nashua, (800) 258-1724; and Nu-Kote Holding, (800) 448-1422.
3. Shop at business liquidation sales advertised in the classified section of most newspapers.
4. Shop at estate sales.
5. Go to police auctions.

6. Buy checks directly instead of from your bank. They can cost 50 percent less from companies like Checks-in-the-Mail, (800) 733-4443; Current, (800) 533-3973; and Image Checks, (800) 562-8768.
7. Look for moving sales when large companies change locations; shop at garage sales and bazaars or at secondhand stores, including veterans' rebuilt-merchandise shops.
8. Use erasable products like Multi Comp's Label Once erasable labels you can use again and again, (800) 354-1213.
9. Shop at discount retail warehouse clubs that offer 25 to 30 percent discounts to members. Membership fees for clubs like Costco, Pace, and Sam's cost about $25–$35.
10. Buy unfinished furniture, unassembled furniture, or furniture kits.
11. Build your own furniture with basic carpentry tools, using patterns or suggestions in popular "do-it-yourself" books and magazines.
12. Find out if you can buy slightly damaged furniture from shipping companies.
13. Investigate buying furniture that has been abandoned at storage companies.
14. Shop in rural or out-of-the-way sections of the country.
15. Buy seconds or furniture with manufacturers' errors.
16. Look for discontinued styles, specials, clearance sales, inventory sales, and "loss leaders" used to draw people into a store.
17. Shop in the want ads or in "bargain" newsletters for items being sold because a company is remodeling or redecorating.
18. Look for floor samples or demonstrator models sold at reduced prices.
19. Look for mill ends and remnants at carpet and flooring stores.
20. The federal government regularly auctions off surplus equipment and supplies. To learn about bidding on these items, write to the Federal Supply Service, General Services Administration, Washington, DC 20406, and to the Department of Defense Surplus Sales, P.O. Box 1370, Federal Center, Battle Creek, MI 49016.

For more ideas on saving money, subscribe to *The Banker's Secret* ([914] 758-1400 [800] 255-0899) or *The Tightwad Gazette* ([207] 524-7962), the bible for dedicated penny-pinchers.

Resources

Books

Getting Organized. Stephanie Winston. New York: Warner, 1991.
The Green PC, Making Choices That Make a Difference. Steven Anzovin. New York: Wincrest/McGraw-Hill, 1993.
Healing Environments, Your Guide to Indoor Well-Being. Carol Venolia (see chapter 5 Resources for full citation).
Making Your Office Work for You. Jan Yager. New York: Doubleday, 1989.
Nontoxic, Natural and Earthwise. Debra Lynn Dadd. Los Angeles: Tarcher/ Perigee, 1990.

Organized to Be Your Best. Susan Silver. Los Angeles: Adams Hall, 1991.
The Light Book: How Natural and Artificial Light Affect Our Health, Mood and Behavior. Jane W. Hyman. New York: Ballantine, 1991.
Save Your Business a Bundle: 202 Ways to Cut Costs and Boost Profits Now. Daniel Kehrer. New York: Simon & Schuster, 1994.

Magazines

Consumer Reports (monthly) and **Consumer Reports Buying Guide Issue** (annual). Consumers Union, 256 Washington St., Mount Vernon, NY 10553.

Newsletters

Beyond Scents, The Quarterly Journal of Aromatherapy. 1830 South Robertson Blvd., #203, Los Angeles, CA 90035 (800) 677-2368. $20/yr.
Enviro Clean: Sourcebook of Environmentally Responsible Cleaning Products. (800) 466-1425.
Ergonix. 2515 San Fernando Rd., Los Angeles, CA 90065; (800) 328-ERGO.

Ergonomic Product and Supply Catalogs

Action Computer Supplies. 6100 Stewart Ave., Fremont, CA 94538; (800) 822-3132.
In Business, The Magazine for Ecological Entrepreneuring. 2718 Dryden Drive, Madison, WI 53704-3086; (608)246-3584.

Tapes

Sound Legit: Office Sounds on Endless Loop Tape, Here's How, P.O. Box 5191, Santa Monica, CA 90409.
Sound RX. P.O. Box 1726, Novato, CA 94948; (415) 453-9800.

Software

Green Explorer. Micro Base, Inc., 3923 S. McClintock Ave., #402, Tempe, AZ 85282; (602) 897-7800. (800) 897-3637.

The Smart House

Smart House, 400 Prince George's Boulevard, Upper Marlboro, MD 20772; (301) 249-6000.

Mail Order Office and Computer Supplies

Hello Direct. 5884 Eden Park Place, San Jose, CA 95138; (800) 444-3556 (telephone products).

Inmac PC Select. 2300 Valley View Lane, Irving, TX 75062; (800) 547-5444.

Lewis & Lewis. 1600 Callens Road, Ventura, CA 93003; (800) 342-3607 (Hewlett-Packard printer supplies).

MacWarehouse. (800) 255-6227; and MicroWarehouse; 800/367-7080, 1720 Oak Street, Lakewood, NJ 08701.

PC Connection. 6 Mill Street, Marlow, NH 03456; (800) 800-0004; and Mac Connection, 14 Mill Street, Marlow, NH 03456; (800) 800-0002.

Penny Wise. 4350 Kenilworth Avenue, Edmonston, MD 20781; (800) 942-3311.

Quill. 100 South Schelter Road, Lincolnshire, IL 60069; (708) 634-4800 or (909) 988-3200.

Reliable Home Office. P.O. Box 1501, Ottawa, IL 61350; (800) 869-6000.

Viking Office Products. 13809 South Figuroa, P.O. Box 61144, Los Angeles, CA 90061; (800) 248-6111 and (800) 421-1222.

Wholesale Supply Company. P.O. Box 23437, Nashville, TN 37202; (800) 962-9162.

Specialty Paper Sources

BeaverPrints. Main Street, Bellwood, PA 16617; (800) 9BEAVER.

Idea Art. P.O. Box 291505, Nashville, TN 37229; (800) 433-2278.

Laser Label Technologies. 1333 South Jefferson Street, Chicago, IL 60607; (800) 882-4050.

Paper Direct. 205 Chubb Avenue, Lyndhurst, NJ 07071; (1-800) A-PAPERS.

Queblo. 1000 Florida Avenue, Hagerstown, MD 21741; (800) 523-9080.

CHAPTER
EIGHT

■■■■■■■■■■■■■■■■■■■■■■■■■■■

Equipping and Computerizing
the Up-to-Date Home Office

Hundreds of thousands of people have started home offices with nothing more than a desk, a telephone extension, and a filing cabinet. Some people begin with even less. When we began working from home in 1974, very little real office equipment was available or affordable for a home office. So we began operations with two desks, an answering machine, and an IBM Selectric typewriter. Consequently, we depended on outside services for photocopies and for turning our rough manuscripts into copy we could submit to clients and publishers. Now these are all things we routinely do ourselves because of the wealth of equipment that has become the heart of our home office.

The typical home office today has at least one personal computer, a printer, an answering machine, and a variety of special telephone features. Many home offices also have a copy machine, a fax machine, and a modem as well (see figure 8-1).

Why this high-tech transformation in home offices? First, the prices of electronic equipment have come way down. By shopping carefully, you can now get all the equipment mentioned above for under $3,000. Second, equipment is increasingly more compact so it fits in small office spaces. Third, to be competitive today, a home business needs to use as much of the latest equipment as possible. In fact, the growth of personal computers has gone hand in hand with the growth of working from home, as you can see in figure 8-2.

So what equipment do you need? You need enough to do business efficiently and remain competitive. But you don't need to get everything at once. Most people start with the items that will make the biggest difference in terms of getting ample business, doing their work more effectively, and projecting the

The Technology in Home Offices

Answering Machines

Personal Computers

Cordless Phones

Pocket Electronics

Cellular Phones

Fax

Copiers

0   20   40   60   80

Percentage of Homes Having

Source: 1993 Link Resources Work-at-Home Study

Figure 8-1.

most professional image. Then, as those items pay for themselves by assisting your business to grow, you can add the next most useful item and so forth until you have everything you need to be most efficient and effective.

In this chapter, we're going to take you on a verbal tour of the well-equipped home office and prepare you to shop confidently for your own home-office equipment. You can actually take the Features-to-Look-For checklists you'll find in this chapter with you when you shop to make the selection process easier.

We consider the items that appear on the checklists in **boldface type** to be important features of equipment that will be used at home for business purposes. Items in *regular* typeface are "nice to have," but not vital. We must caution you that the features and models of products for the home office change rapidly—faster even than those for automobiles or stereos! So keep in mind that the checklists are constructed as of this writing for 1994 models.

To get up-to-the-moment information and reviews of specific equipment, you need to check recent issues of magazines that conscientiously evaluate new products. These magazines are on the Resources list at the end of the chapter. Let's now imagine we're going shopping to equip your home office. We'll be taking a tour of the kind of equipment that you'll find either in successful people's home offices or on their wish lists. Let's start with the telephone: the lifeline of most home offices.

Personal Computers in U.S. Households Compared to People Working From Home

Figure 8-2.

Note: All prices, standards, features, models, and brands described in this chapter are as of this writing.

Costs, models, features and even manufacturers of home-office equipment change almost daily.

Generally speaking, prices and sizes are going down, and quality and the number of features available are going up.

The Well-Equipped Home Office

— Two-line cordless telephone
— Answering machine or service
— Voice mail
— Pager or cellular phone
— Fax or fax/modem
— Computer: desktop and portable
— Laser or ink-jet printer
— Modem
— Copier
— Scanner

Even what we describe as state-of-the-art may well be surpassed by the time you read this book.

So, something you think is unaffordable as you read this chapter may actually become a bargain. And features you want that aren't mentioned or are said to be unavailable may be awaiting you. In fact, unless something unforeseen intervenes, all these goodies are the very least you can get!

Telephones

Research (ours and others) shows that people working from home spend more time on the telephone than on any other single activity. In fact, the telephone is usually the lifeline for anyone working from home. More often than not, it's the way customers and clients reach us in the first place. It's the vehicle through which much of our paid work gets done, from setting up appointments to tracking down past-due invoices.

When we started working from home, the world of telephone services was not particularly friendly to home business. Phone services to homes were limited. We had an answering machine that about half the people hung up on and that was state-of-the-art. But worst of all, phone companies did not look with favor upon using a residential phone for business purposes. Today, however, is a whole new world—a world in which telephone companies coast to coast are eager to serve the home-office needs of their customers, and they have a vast array of products and services to prove it!

Today your primary challenge will most likely be choosing from among your many options. We suggest that the quickest way to do that is to start by identifying your needs and then review and arrange for the services that will most cost effectively meet them. Ask yourself the following questions to set up your optimal telephone system:

1. How often do your work or personal activities take you out of your home office during times when clients and customers will be calling you? How will you make sure you don't miss those calls?

2. Do you want certain callers to be able to reach you while you are at locations other than your home office? How will they reach you without disrupting your activities at these other locations?

3. How much time do you spend talking on the phone each day? How frequently will other calls be coming in while you are on the phone? What will you do to be sure that important business callers don't get repeated busy signals?

4. Will there be times during the workday when you will be working in your home office but don't want to be interrupted by phone calls? How will you screen and record these calls?

5. What personal telephone needs do you have going on in your home? Will family members or roommates be making and receiving calls? How will you separate these other household telephone needs from your business phone needs? Is there more than one location in your home where you will need to pick up your incoming business calls?

6. Do you use or will you be using a fax and/or a modem? How will you make sure you can send and receive such transmissions without interfering with your voice calls?

With your answers to these questions in mind, review the following service and equipment options and contact your local telephone company to find out how they can best meet your needs.

Why You Should Have a Separate Telephone Line for Your Business

Whether you are self-employed or telecommuting, if you are working from your home on a regular basis full-time or part-time, we believe you should have a separate line for your business activity. It's true many people who work from home do not. Many people, at least in the beginning, rely on their one residential line for their business phone, but here's why we believe that, *as soon as possible*, you should have a separate line.

▪ *A separate line will help you better manage your personal and business life.* For example, your children can let your business line ring through to a service, voice mail, or an answering machine. Your family can use the personal line while leaving the business line free for incoming business calls. You can put an answering machine, service, or voice mail on either line when you want to be free to work or enjoy your personal life uninterrupted.

▪ *A separate business line will provide you with a more professional business image.* For all the reasons just mentioned above, a separate business line will convey that you are a "real" business. With a business line, you can answer your calls with a professional greeting and have a service, answering machine, or voice mail respond appropriately when you cannot answer personally.

▪ *A separate business line will help your clients and customers reach you.* A separate business line will enable you to have a yellow page listing and to be listed in the business white pages. So when someone looks your business up in the phone book or calls the information operator, your business will be listed. Home businesses that do not get a separate business line lose out on an undeterminable amount of business when people cannot locate them through the phone company.

Although at one time phone companies were intent upon not mixing business and residential lines in a home, today they are usually no longer interested in playing "telephone cop" or "tariff sheriff." Most companies today are eager to help you find the best solution for your needs. Some companies like Bell Atlantic offer a Home Business Line, which includes many business services and a yellow page listing for less cost than a traditional business line. For options on how to cost effectively have sufficient phone lines, see #5: Not Enough Telephone Lines in the box "Popular Solutions to the Top Five Home-Office Phone Needs" on page 164, and talk with your phone company representative. Many phone companies, like Bell Atlantic, Pacific Bell, Nynex, and US WEST, now have Home Office Consultants who are specially trained to understand and work with your needs.

Choosing Telephone Services

Having recognized the rapid growth of the home office, telephone companies and others now offer a rich array of services and products to address most of our work-from-home telephone needs. The following box lists the rich variety of solutions now available to address the five most frequently mentioned telephone needs. Each of these services is explained below.

Not all these services are available through all telephone companies at this time, however, most have them on the drawing board. The names of these

---

Popular Solutions to the Top Five Home-Office Phone Needs

1. Taking messages when you're busy or out of the office
- Answering machine
- Answering service
- Voice mail—from the phone company
                —private voice mail services
                —voice mail on your computer
- Call forwarding
- Fax in or fax back
- Caller ID

2. Receiving calls when you're out of the office
- Call forwarding—delayed call forwarding
                —remote call forwarding
                —priority call forwarding
- Cellular phone
- 700 number
- Paging system

3. Handling incoming calls while you're on the phone
- Voice mail
- Call waiting with call cancel and three-way calling
- Call return
- Busy call forwarding
- Call forwarding of call waiting
- Call hunting

4. Screening your calls while you're working
- Answering machine
- Special call acceptance
- VIP alert

5. Not enough telephone lines
- Distinctive ringing
- Fax/phone/answering machines
- Fax/modem switches
- Call pickup
- Integrated equipment
- House-wide systems

---

services vary from one phone company to another. So describe what you need to your phone company, and they will tell you about the services they have.

Leading-Edge Options for Optimal Telephone Service

- **Caller ID.** If you have too high a percentage of hangups when callers get your recorded message, Caller ID is an ideal service, because by obtaining a simple device like Deluxe Caller I.D. by US WEST, (800) 229-2901, or Call Display by AT&T, (800) 222-0300, that records the phone numbers of callers (even those who have hung up), you can call these individuals back to ascertain interest in your service. For example, if you are a computer repair service, you can call back your hangups and ask if they ever have a need for computer repair services.
- **Call forwarding.** Call forwarding sends your calls to another telephone number. So, for example, you can have your calls forwarded to a meeting you're attending, to a client site where you're working, or to a cellular phone you carry with you. A number of other options may also be available if you subscribe to call forwarding, for example:

- **Busy call forwarding.** If you don't want to use call waiting, you can use *busy call forwarding* to forward your incoming calls to a second phone line when you are on the phone. For example, you can send incoming calls to your residential line or to a second business line. If you place an answering machine on your residential line during working hours, your business callers will never get a busy signal. Not all phone companies provide busy call forwarding to a residential line, however.
- **Delayed call forwarding.** This service will automatically forward your calls to another number after four rings so that you don't need to take the time to program your phone for call forwarding each time you leave the office.
- **Remote call forwarding.** This is an added feature offered by some phone companies that allows you to program call forwarding remotely from one location to another so that you do not need to be in your office to direct your calls elsewhere.
- **Priority call forwarding.** Offered by some phone companies, priority call forwarding allows you to program your phone to forward calls only from specific phone numbers that you designate. In other words, you may not want to have all your incoming calls forwarded, but you can give priority to particular calls you don't want to miss. For example, you might forward a particular call you've been waiting for, calls from your partner, or calls from key clients, but not others.
- **Call forwarding of call waiting.** If you want to use **call waiting** under some circumstances, but not others, **call forwarding of call waiting** will forward your call waiting callers to a second line when you don't pick up on the call waiting signal.
- **Call forwarding to a homebound assistant.** Another option for taking your phone messages while you're away is to have your calls forwarded to

a reliable individual who will take your messages for a reasonable charge. By responding to distinctive ringing, this person can answer your calls with your company name.

■ **Call hunting.** If you have more than two lines, you may be interested in call hunting, a service that will seek out or hunt for the free line when an incoming line is busy. By having voice mail or an answering machine on these lines, you can avoid missing incoming calls. This hunting feature is not always available for crossing over to a residential line, however.

■ **Call pickup.** This service ties two or more lines together, enabling you to answer an incoming business call at the closest residential phone by entering *8. Some companies like Pacific Bell offer this service along with the ability to transfer calls between your residential and business lines should, for example, your children's friends call in on your business line. And your phone line can also be used as an intercom between the various phones in the home.

■ **Call return.** Like caller ID, call return enables you to call back the last caller immediately. This can be useful, for example, if you have call waiting and decide not to pick up the incoming call when you're talking to someone else. After you complete your call, call return will call back the number that you missed.

■ **Call waiting, cancel call waiting. Call waiting** allows you to hear when another call is coming in so that you can interrupt the call you're on to answer an incoming one. Essentially, you are putting your first caller on hold while you find out who is calling. You can then either handle that call or put the second caller on hold while you wrap up your initial call.

Some people find taking another call in the midst of a phone conversation to be rude and disruptive, but if you generally like call waiting except under certain circumstances, you might want to use a feature called **cancel call waiting.** It enables you to punch in a code that will cancel call waiting prior to placing a call or while you are in the midst of an important phone call.

■ **Three-way calling** enables you to talk to two people in different locations at the same time—no matter who placed the call. For example, you might be on the phone with a client and realize that you'd like to include another party in the conversation. You simply place the first call on hold, dial the other person, and then depress the hook switch or Flash button to connect all parties.

Using these three features together gives you the equivalent of having two incoming lines and two outgoing lines all with one telephone line, and the monthly charges for these services are minimal.

■ **Cellular phone.** If you routinely work at various client sites during the day, travel a lot in your work, or spend considerable time making deliveries or sales calls, a cellular phone is practically a necessity for conducting business. The prices for cellular equipment are declining rapidly. By having your calls forwarded to your cellular phone, you won't need to give people two phone numbers: one for your office and one for your cellular. If you do this, however, you may want to use **priority call forwarding** (described above) to keep your cellular costs down.

If you think you will be spending a lot of time talking on your cellular phone, you may want to check whether **call waiting** is available for your cellular phone service so you won't miss incoming forwarded calls while you're talking to someone else. You may even find that by having your calls forwarded to you while you are out of town and using your cellular's ability to "roam," you can get calls forwarded without an additional long-distance charge either to you or your caller. For more information on selecting and using a cellular phone, see pages 177–178.

▪ **Distinctive ringing.** Although different companies call this service by different names, distinctive ringing enables you to use one line for up to three different incoming phone numbers, each with a different ring. For example, if you have only one phone line coming into your home, your family might use one phone number, while your business line uses another. This way, your teenager will know not to pick up your business calls when he or she hears the distinctive ring. Or if you and your partner have separate businesses, you can give each one a separate number and a distinctive ring. You could also use a separate number for different aspects of your business, as larger companies do; i.e., there would be one number to reach your "order line," another to get your "business office."

Of course, because you still have only one physical line coming into your house with this arrangement, distinctive ringing still has a drawback: you can't do two things on the one line at once. So, for example, you can't send a fax while you're talking on the phone. And callers to one of the numbers will still get a busy signal whenever the other line is being used, unless you have call waiting on both phone numbers—in which case, each of your numbers has a distinctive call-waiting beep, so you will be able to tell which number has a call.

Although distinctive ringing can be a good stop gap measure, getting a separate business line is still truly the best arrangement for most home-based businesses because having a separate line assures your business callers privacy and also makes it easier to track phone expenses for tax purposes. But if you do decide to use this option, talk to your phone company about how you could make sure that the distinctive ring number you're using for your business could be transferred to a business line in the future if need be.

You might use one distinctive ring for your voice calls and the other ring for fax calls. This is especially helpful when your phone setup requires that your fax machine be answered manually. To make distinctive ringing even more valuable, and to take care of your phone and fax needs when you are out of the office, you can add a device such as **Ring Director** by Lynx, **Ring Decipher** by Command, or **Fone Filter** by South Tech Instruments, which allows several different phone devices to share one line. For example, you would hook the **Ring Director** to your phone wall jack, then hook your phone and fax/modem or fax machine individually to the **Ring Director.** Then when the phone rings, the Ring Director automatically directs the call to the appropriate device ([206] 744-1582).

▪ **Fax in or fax back.** Because callers often want either to leave or obtain information of some kind, you might want to consider using your fax to respond to certain calls when you can't or would rather not answer the phone. For example, your voice mail or answering machine message can inform callers that they can fax certain information to you that you can respond to upon your return. Or by using a fax-back service, also called fax-on-demand, your callers can select an option to have information like a price list or service descriptions faxed to them automatically.

There are two types of fax-back systems—one- or two-call. Using one-call fax back, the least expensive, a caller pays for the incoming call and the outgoing fax he receives. The caller calls your fax using the handset of her own fax, listens to the voice prompts, and presses her machine's Start button to receive the desired material. Using two-call fax back, the caller uses any Touch-Tone phone to call your voice/fax system and selects the desired information, enters his fax number, and your system then automatically faxes back the requested document. In this case, you are paying for the outgoing fax.

You can get a one-call system fax back for as little as $495 from RoboFax-EZ by Fax Quest ([800] 995-9141 [408] 736-1485), but this system requires that you dedicate a separate computer just for this use that has a fax card and a voice board, and at least a 40MB hard drive. You also need two phone lines. Ricoh (800/524-1801) sells a system that doesn't require a separate computer as long as yours has a fax card, voice board and a 100 MB hard drive. Although setting up fax-on-demand software is not difficult, you might want the assistance of a computer consultant to get up and running. Alternatively, you can work with a service bureau such as SprintFAX ([800] 366-3297).

▪ **Fax/modem switches.** If you already own a fax machine or are using an internal fax/modem board inside your computer, buying a fax/modem switch will enable you to use the same phone line for both voice and fax/modem transmissions. There are three types of these switches:

Voice priority, which sits in waiting, listening to hear if a fax or modem call is coming in. The incoming caller doesn't have to key in or otherwise notify your system which type of call is coming in.

Machine priority, which requires that the incoming caller instruct the switch as to which type of call is coming in. If you've ever called someone and had her answering machine message tell you either to leave a voice message or punch in a number if you are sending a fax, then you've encountered one of these devices.

Answer-and-detect devices, which cannot detect manual-dialing fax machines or automatic machines used in manual mode.

Having tried multiple fax/modem switches that have not worked consistently with our manual fax, we believe that voice priority is the best system. Fax/modem switches do have two drawbacks, however, compared to having two separate lines for voice and fax/modem: (1) You cannot send or receive a fax *and* talk on the phone at the same time because you have only one line; and (2) we have never heard of a fax/modem switch that functions with 100 percent accuracy. Some calls or faxes will be lost, but the more expensive switches do offer greater reliability.

▪ **House-wide phone system.** Few home offices want the expense or complication of having the entire house wired for a phone system like those used in most office buildings. Who wants fat gray wires protruding throughout her home, and who has an extra closet or small room just to house the "brain" that such a system requires? But once you've grown to the point of needing multiple phones with three or more lines, you may well yearn for the convenience of a system that links all your phones. When you get to that point, a system like the AT&T Partner offers an all-modular alternative, without the unwanted drawbacks.

The Partner can link all the phones and all the lines (up to four) in your home without requiring a special closet or room for the "brain." The control unit can be desk mounted or wall mounted, and you add lines simply by adding cards. It can usually be run off regular home wiring. (There's also The Partner Plus, which can be expanded up to eight lines.)

The Partner has a speaker phone and a hands-free intercom system that enables you to call a room and overhear what's happening in that room without anyone answering. This can be a valuable feature for a working parent who wants to monitor a child's or baby's room. An added feature for anyone who has employees coming into his home is that the Partner can be programmed to restrict the use of personnel making outgoing calls on your phone (long-distance calls, 976 calls, etc.).

▪ **Paging system.** Another alternative for remaining accessible to your clients and customers is to use a paging service that takes your calls and then pages you through a remote-control unit that you carry with you. The pager service provides you with a telephone number for your pager that you can give out to your clients and put on your business cards so they can call your pager directly. When they reach the pager, they enter their phone number; then you can see the number on the pager screen and can call them immediately without having to call the service.

▪ **700 number.** A 700 number is an AT&T service that enables you to remotely forward calls made to you on your 700 number to virtually any phone you're near. It can be a cellular phone or a pay phone. You can make this a toll-free call for your clients and customers, be selective about whom you give your 700 number to, or have it printed on your business card.

▪ **Special call acceptance.** Some phone companies offer this service as a way to screen calls. To use this service, you enter a list of selected numbers that you want to have reach you even when you're not taking other calls. When you receive a call from these numbers, the call will ring through to you while other calls will hear a recording which requests that they leave a message.

▪ **VIP alert.** This service alerts you to special incoming calls. In other words, if you're busy and only want to take certain calls, or you would rather not pick up call waiting unless it is from a special caller, VIP Alert will announce calls from special numbers you have identified.

▪ **Voice mail.** Voice mail answers your calls and takes messages like a sophisticated answering machine, but it offers additional advantages. First, because most large companies are using voice mail now, a home business with voice mail becomes virtually indistinguishable to callers from a *Fortune* 500 company. And in many ways voice mail is like having a receptionist because it can carry out so many of the tasks a receptionist would provide. For example, in addition to simply leaving a message, callers can choose from among a variety of options. They can listen for a list of your services, get directions for getting to your office, or obtain instructions for ordering a product. Having such information available on a prerecorded message saves you the time of taking or returning such calls and provides your callers with immediate access to frequently requested information.

Also, voice mail systems usually offer the ability to set up different outgoing messages that can be programmed to run at various times of the day. In addition, voice mail enables you to set up individual "mailboxes" where you can leave private messages for different people in addition to your generic greeting. Each mailbox has its own ID-coded extension which you can assign to those people you want to stay in touch with. The value of mailboxes is that you can leave detailed messages for any individual with whom you may need to communicate and thereby avoid playing phone tag with hard-to-reach people. It's like an answering machine; you can pick up your voice mail messages from wherever you are by dialing your own number.

One of the best features of voice mail is that it will pick up incoming calls while you are on the phone, so your callers will never get a busy signal. The only limitation, however, is that you won't know you had a second call coming in until you complete your call and check to see if there were any calls while you were on the phone. Here are three different ways you can set up a voice mail system for your business:

Voice Mail Answering Machines. Newer, more sophisticated digital answering machines have been introduced that offer many voice mail–like features such as voice mail boxes, selected outgoing messages, call-forward capability, and much greater voice recording time. Bogen Communication, for example, has introduced "Friday," its personal receptionist, in both one- and two-line versions.

Voice Mail through Your Phone Company. Most local telephone companies are now offering voice mail service for a modest monthly charge through your existing phone and phone number. For example, Bell Atlantic has Answer Call, which for under $10 a month provides the ability to record thirty to forty-five minutes of voice messages. As with an answering machine, you can access your messages from a remote location, save some of the messages to replay at a later time, and erase others. A similar service is GTE's voice mail, Personal Secretary; US WEST offers Voice Messaging; Pacific Bell's service is called Message Center; Ameritech's is Call Minder; and Bell South's is Memory Call. Note, though, that the voice mail systems offered through specific phone companies may not have all the features described above.

Private Voice Mail Services. If a voice mail–like answering machine or voice mail through your phone company don't meet your needs, another choice is to sign up with a private voice mail service. In the short term, using one of these two methods is probably the most simple, effective, and least expensive option for most home businesses. You will pay from around $5 to $20 a month, depending on the number of mailboxes and other options you select.

Voice Mail on Your Computer. A more versatile and cost-effective solution over the long haul might be to set up a voice mail system on your own computer using specialized software and a voice mail card that you install in your computer. The voice mail card digitizes voice so that it can be stored on your hard drive just as if it were computer data. When a call comes in, it is picked up by the voice mail card, the caller hears your greeting, and the person's message is recorded on your hard disk.

You can set up your own voice mail system using a reasonably priced system like Talking Technology's *BigMouth* or The Complete PC's *Complete Communicator*, which are currently selling for as little as a hundred dollars. These systems handle only one line and have more limited features, however, so you might want to select a more capable voice mail. Eden Technology's *Office Phone*, which has 999 mailboxes, will page you when a message comes in, provide fax back to callers, and can hook up to music on hold for from $495 to $695 ([510] 526-7733). Because, like an answering machine, your voice mail system will need several seconds to reset between incoming calls, a system that will handle two lines is an advantage for people receiving a heavy volume of incoming calls.

To accommodate any of these systems, you will need a large-capacity hard drive, because the outgoing greeting or messages you leave combined with any incoming messages from callers require about ten megabytes per hour of high-quality speech. While some voice mail systems offer a low-quality recording speed that doesn't take as much disk space, if you will want to be using voice mail while you are working at your office, you will probably want to buy a computer that you can dedicate to your voice mail system.

Features to Look for: Voice Mail Boards

- **Voice mail boxes.** The heart of most systems, allows personalized messages; number and features of mailboxes vary.
- **Automatic attendant.** Allows callers to route themselves through the system; i.e., "push 1 for . . . push 2 for . . ."
- *Audiotext.* Allows callers to hear recorded information of their choice.
- **Capacity required.** Will the voice mail system run in the background so you can use your computer at the same time voice mail is operating, or will you need a dedicated computer? Most more fully featured systems require so much memory that you should have a separate dedicated computer handling voice mail. Otherwise, it slows down and may conflict with other operations.
- *Fax capability.* Allows users to receive faxes into the same mailbox as their voice messages.
- *Fax-on-demand.* Allows people calling in to request that specific information be faxed to them automatically; i.e., price sheets, newsletters.
- *Message-waiting indicator.* A flash or tone that lets you know you have a message waiting.
- *Single phone line/double phone line:* The more effective, but more costly, systems require two phone lines.
- *Modem capability.* Serves as a modem as well.
- *Forwards to phone or beeper.*
- *Announces call for call screening.*

Using an Answering Service

Answering services provide a person to take your calls and, according to some surveys, most people prefer a warm body on the other end of their telephone call. Nevertheless, we find most home-based businesspeople do not use answering services. The cost is one factor. An answering machine or voice mail is a one-time cost instead of a monthly fee that adds to your overhead each month. In addition, answering service personnel are sometimes rude and abrupt. Some people contend this is particularly true of services that handle doctors' offices, probably because doctors' offices are busier and their services put callers on hold longer.

If you decide to use an answering service, locate a good one. Start with those you've enjoyed speaking to when you've called others. Here are a few ways to do some comparison shopping. Visit the answering service's office without an appointment. Notice how many times the phones ring before they're answered. Are the operators courteous? Do they personalize their conversations around their customers' businesses? Most services have many switchboards with different operators. Insist on an operator whose manner you like and be specific about how you want your phone answered. Many are now actually automated voice mail and pager services. So find out if real people are taking messages or if it is a voice mail/pager service.

Ask for the names of three or four of the service's customers, preferably people with businesses similar to yours. Call to find out if these customers are satisfied. Ask if they receive their messages reliably. Find out if their customers complain about the service and how well the service handles urgent phone calls.

Once you've started with the service, occasionally call your number to be certain your customers are receiving the treatment you want them to have. Stop by the service once a week and get to know your operator. And remember him or her on birthdays, Christmas, and other occasions. You'll be a sharp contrast to customers whose only contact with the service is to complain. The quality of your service should reflect this difference.

What to Do about Telephone Tag

Two out of three business calls aren't completed on the first try. One party calls the other, who is not available; the second party returns the call, and the first party is not there; and so on. This back-and-forth calling has been calculated to amount to two years over a lifetime. To avoid playing telephone tag:

- Set up a telephone appointment, and agree on a specific time to call.
- Determine when the person you're calling will be in the office. State that you will call again at that time.
- Use a voice mail box, fax-in, and fax-back to take care of communication that doesn't actually require you to talk person-to-person to confirm a meeting, provide directions, get a price list, etc.
- Use E-Mail through on-line services like CompuServe, the Internet, Prodigy, or America Online.

Naturally, you can combine a variety of these many telephone products and services to arrive at the best solution for your business. Your telephone company can help you find creative combinations that will meet your personalized needs for a top-notch home-office phone system.

Ten Ways to Save Money and Time on Your Telephone Bill

1. Dial direct. This can save you 60 percent of the costs of operator-assisted calls.
2. Place long-distance calls during off-hours whenever possible. The rates are lower when you call before 8 A.M. or after 5 P.M. on weekdays. Take advantage of time differences in placing calls to people in other areas. Remember, if your call extends beyond the off-hours, you pay the full day rate.
3. If your long-distance calls amount to more than $10 a month, use a discount calling plan, such as AT&T's Reach Out America, MCI's Prime Time, or Sprint's Sprint Plus. Also carriers frequently offer special discount programs as part of new promotions.
4. To find out the current best rates for the major long-distance carriers, obtain the research of organizations like the Telecommunications Research and Action Center or *Consumer Reports,* which do impartial cost comparisons. Factor into your decision additional benefits like sign-up bonuses and getting frequent-flyer miles for using particular services.
5. To keep track of different types of calls, use more than one long-distance carrier. Then you can differentiate personal from business calls, one client from another, or one business from another. To gain access to the three major long-distance carriers, use these codes prior to dialing the long-distance number: AT&T, 10288; MCI, 10222; US Sprint, 10333. Calls will be listed by company on your telephone bill.
6. Use "800" numbers whenever possible. When you're calling an out-of-town business, it's a good idea to check an 800 directory or call information: 1 (800) 555-1212.
7. Check your telephone bills for errors. If you find them, call and get credit.
8. Use Touch-Tone phones. It takes four times as long to dial a number using a rotary dial.
9. If you spend more than six hours a week making phone calls, use an automatic phone dialer in the form of hardware or software.
10. While your business is first getting under way, use only one telephone line with distinctive ringing for both your business and personal telephone line. Most companies will allow you to turn your distinctive-ringing number into a separate business line at any time without changing the number.

Choosing Telephone Hardware

Telephone equipment is keeping pace with all the new telephone services and offering myriad phone configurations with useful styles and features for complementing the many new phone services. You can buy a telephone with a variety of combinations of the following features:

Features to Look for: Telephones

- **Mute button** turns off your microphone to screen out sounds, like a dog's barking, while your caller continues talking.
- **Adjustable ring volume**
- **Automatic redial** calls back the last number you called.
- *Recall* calls back the last number that called you. Important if you let a call go by during call waiting or didn't make it to the phone for some reason before the party hung up.
- **Hold button** puts your caller on hold.
- *Call on hold indicator* reminds you that you have a caller holding.
- **Message-waiting indicator** tells you that you have a voice mail message, a must if you have voice mail that picks up your incoming calls while you're on the phone.
- *Programmable memory keys* provide one-touch dialing to frequently called numbers or immediate access to phone features like *Call Forwarding*, *Three-Way Calling* or *Call Waiting*.
- *Speakerphone* lets you talk on the phone without using the handset.
- *Call forward indicator* reminds you that your calls will be forwarded to another number.
- *Call I.D. display* shows the phone number of your caller (not allowed in all states, however).
- *Call log* stores incoming phone numbers so you have access to the numbers of people who have called you.

And, of course, you can get two-line phones, cellular phones, cordless phones, and two-line cordless phones. And if you don't like using a speaker phone, you can get a telephone headset.

Two-Line Telephones

We strongly recommend getting one or more two-line telephones: one line for your business number and one line for your personal number. With two-line phones you will be able more easily to answer each line appropriately no matter where you are in your home, without the added clutter of having two separate phone sets. Who wants to be running from room to room to answer calls on your various lines, especially if your house has several floors? We have a two-line phone in our office, which is on the third floor of our town house, another in the kitchen, which is centrally located on the second floor, and a third in the bedroom, which is on the first floor. Two-line phones are available in both corded and cordless models.

Cordless Telephones

We also highly recommend a cordless telephone for the home office because you can take it with you anywhere, indoors or out. This comes in especially handy when a delivery arrives in the middle of an important call, an important file you want to attend to is out of reach of your desk phone, or other personal matters need attending to during the business day. It's not uncommon, for example, for the phone to ring while we're outside getting the mail or taking the dogs for a walk. But we can stick the cordless in our pocket and not miss the call.

A cordless phone is almost an essential for parents working with children at home, according to home-based writer Rosalind Resnick. Her three-year-old is at that age where she has just discovered how to climb out of her playpen. With a cordless phone, Resnick can trail her toddler from room to room, safeguarding not only her daughter but her own peace of mind as well. Using the intercom on his cordless phone, computer consultant David Moskowitz has been able to work in his office downstairs and still take care of his daughter when she's home sick from school. Whenever she needs anything from Dad, she just "beeps."

Be aware, however, that if the electricity goes out, your phone service on a cordless phone will go out too. So always have at least one corded phone for both your personal and business lines.

Features to Look for: Cordless Phones

- **Transmits your voice clearly,** so people won't guess that you're using a cordless phone.
- **Range of quality transmission** is wide enough to cover your home and yard. Some models also have an out-of-range tone feature to alert you that you're going out of range.
- **Ten or more multiple-secured channels,** to offer you the best chance that other types of signals won't interfere with your phone. Some models will automatically select a clear channel each time you use the phone.
- **Light handset,** for convenience in carrying around.
- **Mute button** enables you to handle office or household activities without letting the person on the line hear what's going on.
- **Flexible handset antenna,** a shorter, flexible antenna like the one on the Panasonic two-line Easa-Phone is less likely to break than metal telescopic antennas.
- *Speakerphone* provides you with a microphone and speaker so you can answer the phone and talk at the base if the handset is elsewhere.
- *Ringer in the base* let's you know the phone is ringing even if the handset is elsewhere.
- *Two-way paging,* to enable someone at the base set to beep the handset, and vice versa.
- *Intercom capability* between base set and handset.
- *Automatic standby,* to avoid having to flip a switch from Standby to Talk.

Cellular Phones

A cellular phone is becoming a staple for the four out of five people who work most of their time from home, as opposed to at home. Fortunately, prices on cellular phones continue to drop as does their size. You can have calls forwarded to your cellular, or with the newer digital phones or those with "DTMF"—tone-dialing sound—you can pick up your answering machine or voice mail messages. You can even receive faxes over your cellular phone.

A cellular phone also makes working from home easier for parents who want to remain in touch with clients while chauffeuring kids to and from school, watching a daughter's soccer games, or waiting at the tennis court while a son trains for an upcoming competition.

The cost of the phones runs around $200 to $700, with options like spare batteries, recharger, and car kit added on. You can get the best deals on phones when you sign up for a cellular service. If you want to buy a new phone after you've signed up, you can pay as much as several hundred dollars more. So when you're ready for a new phone, cancel your existing service and start a new one. You might have to change carriers to do this.

The price of cellular calls, both incoming and outgoing, is still high—around 25 to 45 cents per minute, up to 90 cents in some areas, in addition to your monthly access charge and an initial setup fee. To keep costs down, you can be selective in giving out your car phone number. Or, instead of giving out your cellular number at all, you can use a service like Priority Call Forwarding to forward to cellular only those calls you urgently want to receive.

To make using your cellular phone more convenient Ora Electronics has a recharger that restores power to your phone in minutes. Called the Quick Charger, it also refreshes and recycles your phone's battery, restoring it to full capacity. It comes with an AC adaptor or vehicle adaptor ([818] 772-9977). ([800] 423-5336).

Features to Look for: Portable Cellular Phones

- **Size and weight.** The smaller and lighter, the better, of course. But often smaller and lighter means more costly. The heavier and bulkier, the more wattage and therefore the range.
- **Portability.** Select a model that matches how and where you'll be carrying your phone.
- **Durability and ease of use.** The sturdier, the better. Some cellular phones come with a carrying case. Consider the vulnerability of the antenna, flip hinges, keypad. Do they fit your fingers, face, and hands?
- **Wattage.** 0.6 watts is adequate in major metropolitan areas but can be a problem in outlying regions. Blaupunkt has a portable that has 1.2-watt output. Car kits can be equipped with 3-watt boosters.
- **Battery power.** Most are NiCad batteries, although some use a newer, more desirable battery called NiMH. It typically takes 8-10 hours to recharge, but you can buy a rapid-recharge accessory that can do it in under two hours.

- **Battery life.** Typically you can expect about 60 minutes of talk time and about 12 hours in standby, but this varies. Some vendors offer longer-life batteries, but they are heavier.

- **Fuel gauge.** If possible get a phone that will show you how much battery power is left, because if you recharge before the battery runs down, you reduce the battery's life. An indicator that shows exactly how much power remains is better than a low-battery light.

- **Retractable antenna.** Some phones have fixed antennas longer than the phone itself. If you plan to be carrying your cellular into meetings in your pocket or purse, a retractable is a must.

- **Call timers.** Most cellulars display how many minutes you've been talking, but you can also get a one-minute alarm beeper inaudible to the other party to alert you to wrap up before starting another minute of costly air time.

- *Call-in-absence indicator.* This feature lets you know if someone tried to call while you were away from the phone. Some indicate how many calls. But most phones don't know who called, so a few phones let the caller leave a phone number, like a display pager. Muratec has a model that has a built-in voice messaging capability, like an answering machine. You leave a message, and the caller can leave a very short message on a voice chip in the phone.

- *Alphanumeric memory dialing and displays.* Almost all cellulars have a memory dialing feature that allows you to store commonly called numbers (100 is typical), but who can remember what numbers go with what codes? Alphanumeric memory stores the names of the people so you can scroll down and pick the one you want to dial.

- *Scratchpad.* This handy feature lets you enter a phone number someone gives you during a phone conversation into a "holding pattern," without any sound to the caller. Then you can dial that number by pressing a single key once you've finished with the first call.

- *Auto credit card dialing.* If you make long-distance calls on your cellular, you may want to charge them to your long-distance carrier instead of to your cellular bill. This feature automates entering the long-distance carrier access numbers and account data. This feature can also be used for checking your voice mail.

- *Data link.* This allows you to link your PC with your cellular so you can send or receive data or faxes. However, according to *What to Buy for Business*, this feature isn't always reliable as yet and digital cellular will do better. If you want this option they recommend looking at Motorola, Nokia, OKI, and Fujitsu.

- *Car kits.* Although not necessary, car kits give you several valuable features: you can talk without holding the handset, some have a hands-free dialing feature, automatic answer, better reception, wattage booster, and some have a feature that will honk your horn if you have a call coming in while you're out of the car!

Telephone Headsets

A headset frees both your hands for writing, using your computer, or carrying out other activities while you talk. Of course, a speaker phone accomplishes the same task, but many people hate talking to someone on a speaker phone. The room noise gets carried along with your voice and, of course, there's a loss of privacy. A headset, on the other hand, provides both the voice privacy and quality of your handset.

Plantronics has been a leader in telephone headsets since 1961, and they have a wide variety of models ranging from $99 to $240 ([800] 544-4660). Recently they've introduced their StarBase 2000 telephone with a built-in headset which saves desk space and reduces cord clutter in an already-crowded home office. It comes with many of the state-of-the-art telephone features we've mentioned like automatic redial and speed dialing.

Plantronics also has a modem headset called CompuSet which connects your telephone and your headset to your computer, so you can dial outgoing calls directly from your contact or information management software by just pressing a key. It can also be used with laptops while you're away from the office.

And if you want to use a headset with a cordless phone, Tropez Digital has created a cordless/headset combo, so you can clip your phone to your waistband and walk about the house talking with your hands free ([800] 444-3556).

Answering Machines

At one time, an answering machine was just about the only cost-effective way for many people working from home to make sure they didn't miss important calls. Today, having an answering machine remains a popular and economical solution, although using one these days can identify you as a small operation. Larger companies have a live operator or, more frequently now, voice mail. To overcome this limitation, some newer lines of answering machines have added multiple message capability and voice mail boxes that enable them to resemble voice mail. Still, if a "corporate" image is vital to your business, an answering machine may no longer be the best solution. Certainly it is no longer your only option.

The good news about answering machines is that fewer people hang up on them now than in the past. In fact, in some parts of the country it's considered rude not to have an answering machine. And some people prefer an answering machine to an endless litany of voice mail selections.

As the prices of answering machines have come down, our experience is that they have become more prone to mechanical failure. An answering machine that's used for business has to perform day in and day out. It can't lose messages. It can't be temperamental. It has to be there when you're not. So, if you decide to use an answering machine, don't buy a flimsy one just to save money! Consulting magazines like *Consumer Reports Buying Guide*, *Home Office Computing*, and *What to Buy for Business* can help narrow your search for a reliable machine that meets your needs. Once you have your machine, it's a good idea to call home periodically to make sure the machine is working properly and messages are being recorded.

Here are some things to watch out for that might not be that much of a problem when using an answering machine for family and friends but just won't do for a business:

- Message recording delayed in starting after the greeting.
- Pause by speaker halts recording or hangs up line.
- Machine stops recording if speaker's voice is too soft.
- Outgoing message slurs or speeds up your voice.
- Extended delay before resetting to answer after a previous call.
- A complex sequence of commands to retrieve messages remotely.
- Messages automatically erased upon rewind.

Features to Look for: Answering Machines

Many of these features have become standard on most machines, but don't assume a machine has the ones that are important to you. Most don't have everything listed here.

- **Reputation for reliable performance.** Ask clerks how often a machine you're considering is returned.
- **Obvious, easy-to-reach and -use controls.**
- **Clarity of outgoing message.** Your voice should be recognizable and clear, not scratchy or distorted.
- **Incoming message length.** For business purposes a caller's message should never be cut off in midstream. This can be accomplished with a "voice-activated" or VOX setting.
- **Ring selector.** Lets you select the number of rings before the phone answers. Two rings is best.
- **Ample total incoming and outgoing message capacity.** Some outgoing messages are limited to 60 seconds or under. Total incoming message capacity can be as low as six minutes, which is insufficient for most businesses, particularly if you're away from the office for more than a few hours at a time and can't pick up your messages. Having up to 30 minutes is preferable. Some models let the caller know when the machine is full. This is great, because otherwise the phone goes unanswered altogether.
- **Easy fast-forward and rewind to specific messages,** as well as the ability to play back new and old messages separately and rewind without erasing the messages.
- **Turn on, retrieve, and record new outgoing message from remote location** lets you turn on the machine if you forgot to, get your messages while you're out, and change your message as circumstances arise.
- **Call counter** tells you how many calls you have waiting.
- **Time date** tells you when each call was made.
- **Pause and skip** lets you stop, play back, and skip messages. This can be important in a home office when you receive a call while taking your messages off the machine.
- **Power backup** stores your messages even if there is a power outage.

- *Voice mail–like capabilities*, i.e., multiple mailboxes; ability to leave personalized message retrievable with a special remote code.
- *Call screening* lets you monitor calls and automatically stops recording if you decide to pick up the phone.
- *Security codes.*
- *Announcement only* without message recording.
- *Bypass greeting* lets callers skip directly to their message and lets you retrieve your messages without listening to your greeting.
- *Programmable remote controls* make retrieving messages quicker and easier.
- *Second greeting.*
- *Answers a two-line phone.*
- *Room monitor* feature.
- *Skips hangups.*

Fax Machines

When the desktop or personal fax machine was first introduced in the late 1980s, we attended a focus group of home-based professionals from management consultants to public relations specialists to react to the idea of using a personal fax. One by one they told the group they couldn't imagine what they would need a fax for! Now, of course, many professionals can't imagine operating without one.

A fax, short for *facsimile,* allows you to transmit information over the phone lines instantly to another fax machine or to a computer that's capable of receiving faxes. Using a fax saves time over conventional mail, costs a fraction of what messenger and overnight delivery services cost, and is easier to use than a computer plus modem. It takes less than twenty seconds to fax a page of text, so a three-page fax will require only a one-minute phone call even if sent to the other side of the world. From coast to coast, sending a short document by fax costs less than sending it by U.S. Mail for 29 cents. After a computer and a

"Live" Operator in a Box

If you would like your calls to sound as if they are being answered by a live operator, consider using the ImageVox. For under $300, the ImageVox Response Unit answers your calls courteously and promptly using your business name, asks who's calling, and places your caller on hold with music playing in the background. Then you pick up the call to carry on a live conversation. To the caller, it sounds as though your secretary has transferred the call to your extension. Additional features include voice mail, transfer to answering machine, and after-hours operation. For additional information, call (800) 578-8424.

telephone, a fax is probably the next most important piece of equipment to have in terms of enabling people to work effectively from home.

Fax technology comes in several forms—as a self-standing machine or as a board or card that's placed inside a personal computer. The advantage to a fax that's mounted on a computer board is that it takes up no additional desk space, generally costs less, enables you to transmit documents created in your computer without first printing them out in hard copy and, because a document sent by your computer doesn't need to be scanned, the document received by the person you send it to looks better. However, you cannot transmit a document not stored inside your computer through a fax board. So if you want to fax a receipt or a copy of a magazine or newspaper article, you must use someone else's fax or a separate scanner. A self-standing fax can also be used as a backup photocopier.

Devotees of each method feel strongly about their choice. One person told us that he thought using a stand-alone fax was the equivalent of using a typewriter instead of a computer. He especially values his ability to compose a document in his computer and, with his internal fax, automatically send it to 1,000 people simultaneously. He likes being able to convert and edit faxes he receives and return them to the sender. He likes having a fax board in his laptop so that he has fax capability on the road.

On the other hand, we know people who feel equally strongly about their stand-alone fax. They don't want to leave their computer on in order to get faxes while they're gone. They don't like faxes clogging up their disk space, which can become full while they're away from the office and cause them to miss incoming faxes. They don't like not being able to send off a clipping or memo that's not stored in their computer. Obviously, there are pros and cons of each and the choice is highly personal, depending on your needs. An increasing number of people are solving the problem by having both. That's what we do. Paul prefers an internal fax; Sarah prefers the external; but we each use both, depending on the circumstances.

An internal fax like Intel's *Satisfaction Card* or Practical Peripherals' *FaxModem* that you install in your computer and use with fax software like Delrina's *WinFax* certainly costs less, currently only a couple of hundred dollars. If you decide on a freestanding fax, you'll find many choices including models from Canon, Hewlett-Packard, Panasonic, Sharp, and Xerox. The cheaper models (as low as $200 at this time) are thermal printer faxes, which use rolls of slippery chemically coated paper. Models that come with a page cutter to separate incoming pages are slightly more expensive. Plain paper faxes print on ordinary paper, which is far superior because no special paper is required but most importantly because thermal faxes fade and become illegible over time. Plain paper faxes have come down dramatically in price, currently available for as low as $500.

If you decide to go with a freestanding fax machine, here are other features to consider:

Features to Look for: Fax Machines

Paper type. Thermal or plain paper.

Resolution quality. Sufficient to your needs. A graphic designer will need higher resolution than most businesses do. Measured in dots per inch, popular models range from 200 to 400 dpi. Measured in gray scales, 16 is typical; 64 is quality, permitting transmission of photos, illustrations, and graphics.

Image enhancement. Resolution relates to the image of your outgoing faxes. Image enhancement, also called image smoothing, enables your machine to improve the quality of incoming faxes.

Document size. Thermal faxes can receive a document of any length. Most plain paper faxes receive only letter-sized paper. If you receive a legal-size document, the machine will either reduce it to letter size or carry the extra copy over to a second page. If you want to receive on different paper sizes, you can select a model with a dual on-line cassette. The machine will automatically select the appropriate page size for the incoming fax. Some models will also take documents 11 inches wide for ledger sheets.

Document feeder and handling. On low-end models document feeders range from manual, which you must feed in page by page, to up to 20 pages that the machine automatically feeds. Some higher-end models go up to 50 sheets. If you send multiple-page documents, feeding them by hand or cluster by cluster is very time-consuming. In poorer models multiple sheets may feed through together, and so you need to refax pages. In fact, misfeeding is the number-one gripe *What to Buy for Business* hears from owners of low-cost fax machines.

Paper supply. Trays for receiving plain paper faxes typically hold a 200-to-250-sheet capacity; some go up to 500. If you travel or are out of the office, you will miss faxes once your paper supply runs out. If the fax has sufficient memory, however, your machine can store incoming faxes when the fax runs out of paper. Memory in typical budget faxes stores 7 to 20 pages.

Footprint. Personal faxes range in size from 13 to 30 inches wide, 4.5 to 14 inches high, and 7 to 20 inches deep, so in some cases your choice will be limited by the space you have available. Canon has an upright fax, for example, that's perfect for a narrow shelf, ledge, or credenza. It stands upright and is only 8 inches deep and 9 inches tall. Lanier, on the other hand, has a model that's 4.5 inches high but 12 inches deep, perfect for fitting under a low shelf or even stacking on a rack. Others are nearly the size of a personal copier.

Dialing:

Automatic redialing: Also called auto-retry, with this feature, the fax will keep dialing a busy number at intervals of two or three minutes until it answers.

Speed dialing: As on the telephone, speed dialing lets you program frequently used numbers so you can send them with the touch of one or two keys.

Voice request: If you want to talk to the person after faxing, this feature will not hang up immediately.

Memory:

Size of memory. Usually 7 to 20 pages, but you can upgrade to 100 to 200 pages. This is important for storing incoming faxes when paper runs out and for broadcasting.

Fast scan. If memory is sufficient the fax can scan in documents in as quickly as two seconds; more commonly it's five to six seconds. This is important when sending multiple pages or for broadcasting.

Broadcasting. This is a real time saver if you will be faxing the same document to several people. The fax stores the document in memory and you tell it all the numbers you want it sent to.

Dual access. Also called transmission reservation, this feature lets you do more than one thing at a time on your fax. You can copy something while dialing an outgoing fax while receiving and then walk away. Once the line is free, the outgoing fax will be sent.

Other features:

Header/date/time stamp. When you set up your fax, you can enter a heading that will appear on all documents you send listing your name, business name, phone number, even a logo. Also, like a VCR, most faxes have an electronic clock so you know exactly when each fax you receive arrived.

Data compression. Reduces telephone time if you send documents at fine resolution or internationally.

Automatic cover sheet. Few machines have this feature, but it lets you customize an automatic fax transmittal cover sheet from information stored in the auto dialer. This feature can be a real time saver!

Restricted access. Enables you to program your fax to block calls from certain phone numbers.

Fax/phone and handset/answering machine combinations. Most models of fax do double duty as a fax and voice phone, but some also route calls to or include an answering machine.

Using One Piece of Equipment to Do the Work of Many

Between business and personal lines, fax modem lines, answering machines and fax machines, your home office could start looking more like an electronics store than a residence. But today's phone equipment is getting smaller and smaller and one piece of equipment may do what once took two, three, or more pieces to do. Using such integrated equipment can save you money as well as desk space.

While integrated equipment doesn't always save you the cost of installing a second or third phone number, it does reduce clutter on your desk, improve your efficiency, and save you the cost of buying multiple pieces of equipment. You have a growing selection of space-saving integrated telephone equipment like two-line cordless phones, speakerphones, and single- or two-line telephone/ answering machines and combinations. With a fax/phone/answering machine, you can have one line serving three purposes. By having all three of these devices in one, when you are not available or in your office, the machine answers incoming calls and detects if it's a fax to receive or a voice call. Voice calls trigger the answering machine, and of course, if it's a fax, the fax machine will receive it. The Canon Fax Phone B150 and 140 are two such machines.

To date, people who try to combine voice and fax on one line report that they do miss some faxes and, of course, call waiting will interrupt fax transmission although some machines let you program in a dialing prefix to deactivate call waiting before sending a fax.

Shopping through catalogs, computer stores, office superstores, and other sources of home/office electronics, you'll find a rich array of space-saving integrated products. Alacrity Systems has created what they call *E-Quip Office in a Box*, which they claim can serve as a copier, plain paper fax, full-page sheet-fed scanner, modem, and optical character reader all in one. ([800] 252-2748). It's important to think about your needs in advance of buying, though, as the variety of options is almost overwhelming, and each choice has its own advantages and disadvantages. To benefit most from one device or another, you may also need to use other options we've discussed in this section.

Computers

As you can see from the chart in figure 8-2, well over half of all home offices now have a personal computer. You can think of a computer as your staff-in-a-box, the equivalent of having two or three people working for you, enabling you to perform many of the tasks a secretary, bookkeeper, receptionist, marketing manager, business planner, and tax advisor would do for you. Peter McWilliams, author of *The Personal Computer Book*, claims the right computer and software can keep your overhead down and your profits up in the following ways:

- If you're working alone, add a computer and you can double or even triple business without hiring staff.
- If you're working with a secretary as your only employee, add a computer and you may never need to hire additional staff.
- If you're working with a secretary and a bookkeeper, add a computer and your staff of two can do the work of three.

In the early eighties, when we first wrote about computerizing home offices, one of the reasons we gave for doing so was to gain credibility with clients and be able to compete better with larger, more established businesses. Today, the reasons for computerizing are even more compelling. Businesses without computers or those needing to upgrade older home computers run a serious risk of lagging behind their competition in terms of sheer productivity, capability, and professional image. Computers have become like telephones, a staple of office life.

Your choices today for finding a computer or constellation of computers that meet your needs are more abundant than ever before. Your choices today include not only a variety of standard desktop models but also a rich array of notebook computers, many of which are sufficiently powerful to run your business, as well as subnotebooks, palmtops, and personal organizers.

Features to Look for: Computer Hardware

- **Operating system.** Current choices include DOS, DOS with Windows, OS/2, MAC, and UNIX. DOS with Windows is the most popular operating system at this time for home office and home business purposes.
- **Processor (CPU).** The equivalent of your computer engine, processor choices for DOS with Windows today include 386, 486, Pentium (586), and Power PC, each being progressively more powerful. Many of the more advanced software packages we've described in this book will run uncomfortably slow on a 386. So if you're buying a new computer, don't consider a 386. If you have one already, both 386 and 486 processors can be speeded up with the addition of co-processors for heavy-duty tasks. Also if you want to upgrade your 486, Intel has OverDrive processors to boost 486 processors into Pentium territory.
- **Disk drives.** We recommend having two floppy disk drives (one 5.25 inches and one 3.5 inches) or a dual floppy drive that accommodates both. You also need a hard disk drive capable of storing a minimum of 200 megabytes (MB) of data. You may also wish to have a CD-ROM drive. If you underestimated the disk space you need, however, you can buy software utilities that will compress the size of files and free up additional space; however, to then access the files, you have to decompress them. Of course, you can also scrap an old hard drive and buy and install a bigger one. The biggest ones now are one gigabyte (ICG)—1,000 MB—important if you store color graphics. Disk drive speed, measured in milliseconds (ms), is also important. Most manufacturers are using drives under 20 ms; 17 is reasonable, and 16 is pretty fast; 11 ms is about as speedy as you can get now.
- **Random Access Memory (RAM).** Absolute minimum memory for today's business software is 4MB, however, we recommend 8MB. You can always add additional megabytes for around $45 to $65 for 1MB modules or $130 to $140 per 4MB modules.
- **Clock speed.** Although a variety of things affect the speed at which your software will run, not all processors operate at the same speed. Each has a clock speed that is measured in megahertz (MHz). The higher the speed, the faster it will run; so consider the faster clock speeds on whatever model of processor you're considering. Aim for at least 33MHz to 66MHz.
- **Ports.** You need at least two serial (RS 232) ports for accessories like an external modem, a mouse, a label printer or business card scanner, and one parallel port for your printer. Within limits, additional ports can be added.
- **Expansion slots.** Vacant expansion slots make it possible for you to expand the capacity of your computer internally so that you can keep pace with technological advances without having to buy an entirely new computer; i.e., adding a voice

- mail card, a fax-modem card, a hard drive on a card, or a sound board. Three or four open slots should be adequate.
- **Footprint.** The size and shape of PCs vary widely from the standard desktop that might be something like 6 inches high by 21 inches wide by 16.5 inches deep, to smaller footprints that are about 4 inches shorter, to slimlines that are a couple of inches shorter, to towers and minitowers that sit on the floor instead of the desktop.
- **Video performance.** The video adapter or video card that usually comes standard with your computer is what links your computer's processor to the monitor. For most Windows users, an accelerator video card is the most appropriate because it provides good performance at a reasonable price. CPU speed and, of course, the monitor you select, also have a major impact on the video quality of your computer.
- **Service.** Everything that runs breaks, so select a computer that has local or on-site service.
- **Warranty.** Get a computer with a reputation for reliability, and one with a twelve-month or longer warranty. To double your warranty up to another twelve months, purchase your equipment with Gold MasterCard, Visa, or American Express. We advise doing this even if you have to pay an additional small percentage of the sales price to cover the dealer's bank charge.
- *Low noise.* Noise is caused by the cooling fan inside the system's unit and if it's too loud, it can become an ongoing subtle source of irritation.
- *Sound capability.*
- *Software or peripherals*, such as a modem or a mouse, that are included in the price.
- *A toll-free hotline to manufacturer.*
- **Understandable and complete documentation** that tells you how to set up and use the computer.
- *Local users' group.*
- *Total cost.* Always get quotes in writing.

Features to Look for: Keyboards

- **Feel.** A comfortable feel is most important and highly personal. Touch varies. Some like it soft; some like it hard. Location, layout, and even sound affect everyone differently.
- **Separate numeric keypad, separate functions keys, and separate cursor control keys** conveniently located for your fingers.
- **Ability to reprogram keys.** If you don't like the location of certain keys, you can switch their function with other keys.
- **Ability to turn the audible keyboard click on or off.**
- **Lighted cap-lock and number-lock keys** so you know when these functions are on or off.

- *Built-in mouse or track ball.*
- **Optional right or left cable exits.**
- **Ergonomically designed keyboards** like the MiniErgo by Marquardt Switches ([315] 655-8050).
- *Spill resistance.* Alps American makes a keyboard with a layer of nonconductive rubber underneath its casing to help protect against spills and dust accumulation ([800] 825-2577).

Features to Look for: Monitors

- **Resolution.** The better the resolution on your monitor, the sharper the image and the easier on your eyes. Most PCs sold today are equipped to support monitors with VGA graphics, which provide at least a decent 640 × 480 resolution. Sharper images require 720 × 400 resolution. Better is Super VGA with 800 × 600, but 1024 × 768 resolution is best for most Windows users, and best on your eyes.
- **Color.** A color monitor is preferred by most people. But at high resolutions (1024 × 768), not all color screens are equal. Some can operate in only 16 colors, others up to 256 colors, and others up to 16 million colors. The key is the amount of Video Ram or VRAM in the video adaptor. To get up to 256 colors or more at higher resolution, plan on getting 1MB of video memory.
- **Size.** As resolution of monitors increases, so does the size. But the larger the monitor, the more dramatically the price increases. A realistic size for a home office is 15 or 17 inches measured on the diagonal.
- **Flicker.** Whether your screen will have a flicker depends on how often the screen is redrawn; this is measured in hertz (Hz). A flicker-free monitor needs what's called a "refresh rate" of no less than 70 to 75Hz.
- **Flatness of the screen.** Although no screen is completely flat, the more curved the screen the more distortion at the edges.
- **Ergonomic and safety features.** Look for monitors with adjustable, tilt and swivel stands, front access controls, and low electromagnetic field emissions that meet Swedish MPRII specifications.

Can You Use a Notebook as Your Main Computer?

Although by far most people depend primarily on a desktop and another large group of home-office workers have both, according to *PC Computing Magazine* everything in your desktop PC will fit in a seven-pound notebook. And some *Home Office Computing* readers report they've opted to use a notebook as their primary computer. Naturally, the decision is highly personal, but here's a summary of the pros and cons:

Notebook versus Desktop

Desktop

Pros

- More for the money
- Graphics and multimedia capability
- Better display
- Bigger, more versatile keyboard
- Technological advances are always one step ahead.
- It's always ready to operate. No bothersome recharging
- Better ergonomics
- Larger memory, faster speed, more expandable, more peripherals

Cons

- If you need to take a computer with you, you'll need to have a second computer.
- Takes up more space, uses more energy, and doesn't have built-in power backup.

Laptop

Pros

- Portability. Goes almost anywhere.
- Can do the job of two computers. You won't need one for home and one for away.
- Size. Fits almost anywhere.
- Batteries serve as a built-in uninterruptible power supply. Your computer won't go down if the lights go off.
- More rugged
- More energy efficient. A laptop consumes ten times less power.
- Models with active matrix color screens are sharper and cause less eyestrain.

Cons

- Costs more for less
- Limited to VGA resolution
- Easier to lose or have stolen

Features to Look for: Notebook Computers

In addition to the features we've discussed for desktop computers, here are issues and features to consider in selecting a notebook computer.

- **Capability.** Both 386 and 486 notebook computers are available. All notebooks come with a hard drive (from 40MB to 120MB, and 200MB on the way at this time), and almost all have a built-in floppy drive.
- **Size.** Around 8.5 / 11 by 2 inches, with some as slim as 1.5 inches.
- **Weight.** 4 to 7 pounds.
- **Keyboard.** Some keyboards require that certain keys share multiple functions. Around 82 keys is a good notebook keyboard. You won't have a separate numeric key pad, as some share it with other keys by pressing the numberlock key.
- **Power source and battery life.** All notebooks can be run off internally rechargeable batteries or from AC power through an external AC adapter. Some

adapters are larger and heavier than others, weighing more than a pound. Batteries, depending on the model, run from less than two hours to three hours or more. There are two types of batteries: NiCad and Nickel Metal Hydride, which is preferable because they hold their charge longer and they don't run down faster if you recharge them before they're fully discharged.

- **Display.** Notebook screens have improved significantly with almost all now having an LCD screen, which is backlit with 32 to 54 shades of gray scales equivalent to VGA resolution, making them much easier to use in all light at all angles than earlier models. Newer active matrix screens boost sharper images at various angles. Color notebooks are available, too, but they weigh more and are about twice as expensive as a color desktop. Although the prices are dropping, the lower-cost models have the less-desirable passive matrix screens that reduce the quality of the color. Also check out the number of colors that can be displayed at once on the screen.
- **Screen size.** Look for notebooks with a 10-inch diagonal screen.
- **Durability.** According to *What to Buy for Business*, notebook computer life is shorter than that of a desktop—more like two to three years than five. But amazingly, they held up quite well to *PC Computing's* challenging cold, heat, jostling, and spilling tests.
- *Built-in trackball or mouse attachment*
- *Internal modem or fax/modem*
- *Ports.* Most laptops have serial and parallel ports for linking to a printer, mouse, scanner, etc.
- *Built-in adapter.* An adapter such as *LapLink* allows you to connect your notebook to your desktop.
- *Docking station.* Allows you to insert your laptop into a desktop unit so you can use it more easily at home with a standard monitor and keyboard.
- *Expansion cards.* The size of a credit card, these PC Cards or PCMCIA slots let you add extra memory, video support, pagers, and so forth.
- *Removable hard disks.* This feature can protect your data from theft and from damage if you must leave your notebook in inclement weather.

Subnotebooks, Palmtops, and Handheld Organizers

Although a notebook computer will fit in a briefcase, we predict the day when we'll have the power of our desktop in the palm of our hand, or at least our purse, if not on our wristwatch. Although that time is not here yet, it's on the way with subnotebooks, palmtops, pocket organizers, and personal digital assistants.

Subnotebooks are lighter and smaller than notebooks, weighing 2 to 4 pounds with some only slightly more than an inch high. The IBM *ThinkPad* squeezes most features of a first-rate notebook into 3.5 pounds, 7.23 × 10 × 1.62 inches. And the newer *PowerBook Duo*s are equivalent to a 486 computer with RAM expandable up to 40 megabytes and up to 320MB hard drive, coming in at just over 4 pounds.

But subnotebooks have their limitations. Although they have normal QWERTY keyboards so you can touch-type, they are compressed, so some people have trouble getting their fingers on the keyboard. And they don't have built-in floppy drives, although they do have lightweight external floppy drives and PC Cards. Some are pen-based portable platforms. Each subcompact makes its own compromises on space, keyboards, screens, battery life, etc.

Palmtops are next on the PC downsizing scale. Smaller and less expensive than subnotebooks, they have even smaller screens, more cramped keyboards, and less full-powered processors. They are definitely not substitutes for a full-fledged computer.

Next on the smallest side are pocket organizers like the Sharp *Wizard* and the Casio *Boss* that will fit into your pocket and purse and enable you to keep track of your calendar, appointments, address book, notes, memos, and planning. Using a PC link, you can transport data to and from your desktop and you can back up data as well as add functions with RAM cards.

And finally there're what're known as PDAs, personal digital assistants, which at this point are more promising than they are perfected. These are electronic pen-based notepads designed to be extensions to laptops or desktops, such as the Apple Newton *Message Pad* and the Sharp *Expert Pad*, which will undoubtedly improve.

In between palmtops and subnotebooks is a new breed of computer like the Zeos *Pocket PC*, only $595, with 1MB RAM and built-in word processor, spreadsheet, contact database, calendar, planner, calculator, and more. Also in a class of its own is the Hewlett-Packard *Omnibook 340*, which is not only a 486 computer that comes with all the above built-in goodies but also has a retractable mouse, a full-sized keyboard, and best of all, the ability to import and use your own favorite Windows or DOS software. It's slim enough to fit in many a purse, weighs less than 3 pounds, and has 9 hours of battery life.

So as you can see, smaller and smaller computers are being developed and are beyond easy categorization. If you want to have a very small computer that can go with you when you leave your home office, our advice would be to compare whatever models you're considering with the criteria we set for desktops and notebooks and come as close as you can, compromising on those features that make the least difference to you and what you need it to do. You certainly have a lot of choices.

Checklist of Features to Look for: Subnotebooks, Palmtops, Pocket Organizers

_____ **Processor 386, 486, other**
_____ **Hard drive**
_____ **Hard drive capacity** ____ **MB**
_____ **Memory (RAM)** ____ **MB**
_____ **Built-in floppy drive**
_____ **Size:** ____ **height** ____ **width** ____ **length**
_____ **Weight** ____

____ **Keyboard:** ____ **size** ____ **number of keys** ____ **QWERTY**
____ **Battery life:** ____ **hours**
____ **AC adapter, size and weight**
____ **Type of batteries: NiCad and Nickel Metal Hydride, other**
____ **Display:** ____ **backlite** ____ **LCD** ____ **gray scale notebook**
____ **Active matrix screens**
____ **Screen size:**
____ **Built-in trackball or mouse attachment**
____ **Modem or fax/modem** ____ **internal** ____ **PC card**
____ **Ports** ____ **serial** ____ **parallel**
____ **Built-in adapter or link to notebook to your desktop**
____ **Expansion or PC card capability**
____ **Built-in software or ability to add your own**
____ **Pen**

Buying a Computer of Any Size

Once upon a time, if you wanted to buy a computer you went to your friendly local computer store, who provided you with whatever support and service you could get, even repair. Today, you have many choices. Growing numbers of computer manufacturers like Dell, Gateway, Zeos, even IBM (low-end computers only), and others are selling their computers directly by mail order. Because they have no local dealers to service and support products, they have to offer a lot of service and support themselves; i.e., one-year warranties that include on-site service (not usually for notebooks) as well as toll-free technical assistance and thirty-day money-back guarantees.

At the same time, your local computer store has seen the growth of consumer electronics outlets and national office supply warehouses like Office Depot, Staples, OfficeMax, and computer superstores like CompUSA and Computer City, and even department stores like the Office Center at Sears, all of which are selling computers. These stores generally don't provide service and support (which are now being taken over directly by the manufacturers), and generally, at this point, most don't offer thirty-day money-back guarantees.

Now add to your options "super channel" computer mail-order catalog companies like PC Connection ([800] 800-0004), Micro Warehouse ([800] 367-1080), PC Compleat ([800] 669-4727), Insight Computer Systems ([800] 998-8036), and USA/Flex ([800] 477-8323). These "super catalogs" often offer lowest price guarantees, thirty-day money-back guarantees, as well as other support services of their own.

Tandy/Radio Shack has its own unique solution. You can select a computer at one of its many store locations and it then is custom made to your desires and shipped from their factory in Texas.

Here are several factors to consider in deciding where you want to buy your computer:

What to Look for: Where to Buy a Computer

- **Price.** Some will meet lowest offers. Still easiest to get lowest prices through mail order, which compete nationwide, whereas dealer prices are lowest in big cities.
- **Delivery time.** Although some mail-order companies have same-day shipment, others take a week for delivery. At a dealership you walk out the door with your computer.
- **Money-back guarantee versus hands on.** Usually money-back guarantees are available only through mail order to compensate for the fact that at a dealer you can see and try out the computer firsthand.
- **Prepurchase information.** Some sources are only "order takers." They know little or nothing about the technicalities of the sophisticated products they are selling. Others, especially the ones you encounter when ordering directly from the manufacturer, are highly trained specialists. Also consider whether you have access to product literature.
- **Availability of accessories.** Try to buy from a source that will carry the supplies and accessories that you may need later; i.e., added memory, cables, extra batteries. Or be sure you've lined up another source.
- **Support.** Manufacturers are offering more direct support. All major mail-order manufacturers have technical support phone lines. Some mail-order dealers do, too. The availability of the support varies. Check out the hours: 24 hours a day or business hours only; 7 days a week or only during the work week. Access time: How long you need to wait on hold. Cost: Is the line toll free? Do you pay for the call, or is it a 900 number? Some manufacturers also offer on-line support through major on-line services like CompuServe and America Online.
- **Warranties and repair.** Most computers come with a one-year warranty. Some offer an extended warranty option. Is service at your site, at the local dealer, or must the equipment be shipped back to the manufacturer? Some local dealers will provide you with a loaner machine while yours is away. What is the turn-around time: same day, next day, two day?
- **Strength and reputation of vendor.** Proceed with caution when getting an incredible deal from an obscure vendor.

How to Keep Your Costs Low, and Other Ideas for Getting a Computer When You Can't Afford One

1. Buy a computer with bundled software, provided the software is what you need.
2. Order proven hardware by mail from reputable mail-order companies that have lowest price offers, but take into account shipping and other charges.
3. Buy a computer that includes peripherals, such as printer and modem, in the purchase price.

4. Buy last year's model, but be sure you will be able to get service, software, and peripheral devices locally.
5. Buy a used computer, after having it checked out. Disk drives are the most likely sources of problems.
6. Watch for ads for special sales and introductory offers or shop for bargains in newsstand magazines like *Computer Shopper.*
7. Comparison-shop. Prices among sources vary.
8. Ask your clients, customers, or employer to buy you a computer or give you one on a lease/purchase basis. Show them how such an arrangement could save them money or otherwise benefit them.
9. Buy or rent a computer or peripherals with colleagues or friends.
10. Buy at computer-show prices. Typically, exhibitors will offer special prices if you buy at the show, and these prices are often good.

Software

Throughout this book we've recommended software for just about every aspect of operating a home office, from more obvious tasks like word processing, bookkeeping, and contact management to more unusual ones like software for learning how to adjust your ergonomic chair or to tell your computer to distinguish between an incoming voice or fax call. Which type of these many kinds you need and which package of the many you'll have to choose from depends entirely on what you need them to do for you and your personal preferences.

Software is very much an "I need something that will help me to . . ." kind of proposition. When Jenna Stacowski started her medical consulting service, for example, the first thing she needed to do was to get proposals out on the desks of as many potential hospital customers as possible. So she started out with a sophisticated word-processing program, choosing Microsoft *Word.* "That's really all I needed for a long time," she says.

Eventually, however, she had several clients, and some were slow in paying her invoices (which she sent out on her letterhead using her word processor). Then she began to think, "I need something to keep track of who owes me what, what's come in, and which expenses I need to bill to which clients." At that point, she decided to get a financial management program (she chose Intuit's *Quicken*) and a program to track and bill her time and expenses. She chose *Buy the Hour* by Austin Computer Resources. Again, she thought, "Now, that's really all I need."

But, after a while, she not only had her current clients to keep in contact with, but a growing list of past clients and a growing pool of potential clients as well, so she thought, "I need something that will enable me to send out a really professional-looking newsletter." She decided to get a desktop publishing package, Microsoft *Publisher.* No sooner had she started creating her newsletter than she realized that getting together a mailing list for all the names and addresses she'd collected on cards and in her billing and word-processing programs was a chore and she thought, "I need something that keeps track of all my contacts, so I can sort which ones I want to send out various types of mailings to." She got a contact manager, Franklin Quest's *Ascend*.

Her story's not over. As you might guess, this is a never-ending story because there can always be one more "I need something that will help me to . . ." The time came when she wanted to add overheads and handouts to go along with her proposals, so she bought a presentation graphics program (Lotus's *Freelance*); then one day she wanted to include sketches of several products in her newsletter and tracked down a program called *Image Star* that would enable her to do that.

Not everyone adds features to their software library one by one, of course. Some people go out and buy everything they think they'll need. Others aren't sure what they'll need, so they get an integrated package like Microsoft *Works*, Lotus *Works*, or *PushButton Works* that performs multiple tasks which they either use indefinitely or eventually replace with more sophisticated packages as they outgrow the limits of certain elements of the integrated package.

Growing in popularity are software "suites" that bundle several separate powerful Windows programs into one package. The three most popular suites are *Microsoft Office*, which includes *Microsoft Word* word processing, *Excel* spreadsheet, and *PowerPoint* presentation graphics; *Lotus Smart* Suite, which includes *AmiPro* word processing, *Lotus 1-2-3* spreadsheet, and *Freelance* graphics; and *Borland Office*, which bundles *WordPerfect*, *Quattro Pro* spreadsheet, and *Paradox* database software.

Clearly there are certain basic things we believe every home office should put their computer to work doing. Below we outline what we consider to be the bare-bones basics. You may or may not think that you need all these programs right now; but chances are, to take full advantage of the benefits your computer offers your business, you will eventually want to get into using them.

The Bare-Bones Home-Office Software Library

- Word processing (Many have basic desktop publishing capabilities)
- Financial management (Your choice: check writing, accounting, or spreadsheet. See chapter 14)
- Contact database (Your choice: mailing list, contact management, information management, time management, or full-fledged database. See chapter 15)
- Communications (Linking you to the on-line world of the information highway. See pages 206–207 in this chapter)
- Tax preparation (with links to your financial management program)

Start with what you need and proceed to build your library as the needs arise. You might wish to do a review of what activities your business requires you to spend the most time doing and what percentage of your time goes to which activities. Then explore software options to help carry out your most time-consuming activities more quickly and easily. You may even want to keep a time log, as shown below:

Time Log*

For one week, keep track of how you spend your time in 15-to-30-minute intervals, using the number codes below. Tally up the time for each category at the end of the week and calculate what percentage of your week goes to each one. Also put a ** by the activities you dislike doing. Software may make them less onerous. Note which activities result in producing actual income and which should have more time devoted to them but are being squeezed out by other more trivial, but pressing, matters. Often software can free income-producing time by streamlining less important activities.

00 Correspondence
01 Writing proposals or reports
02 Talking on the phone
03 Marketing
04 Scheduling meetings and appointments
05 Managing projects
06 Reading for key information
07 Traveling or being on a client's site

08 Bookkeeping
09 Invoicing
10 Collections
11 Filing
12 Planning
13 Doing presentations
14 Gathering information
_____ (Add others)

* You have permission to make a copy of these pages to keep your log.

Date _____

Time	Activity	Code

Total Hours		*Percent of Total*
_____	00 Correspondence	_____
_____	01 Writing proposals or reports	_____
_____	02 Talking on the phone	_____
_____	03 Marketing	_____
_____	04 Scheduling meetings and appointments	_____
_____	05 Managing projects	_____
_____	06 Reading for key information	_____
_____	07 Traveling or being on client's site	_____
_____	08 Bookkeeping	_____
_____	09 Invoicing	_____
_____	10 Collections	_____
_____	11 Filing	_____
_____	12 Planning	_____
_____	13 Doing presentations	_____
_____	14 Gathering information	_____
_____	_____ (Add others)	_____

Total hours worked that week_____
(To calculate the percentage for each category, divide that number by the total; i.e., 6 hours' filing divided by 50 hours worked that week = 12% of the week spent filing.)

After you've got the basics, you can add software as particular needs or problems arise. For example:

- You land an especially large project: project management software could help.

- You send out a lot of packages through UPS and you're tired of writing addresses on multiple sheets and labels: a program like *UPShip* ([800] 927-4276) automates the process for you.

- You can't find your computer files: a file manager like Lotus *Magellan* for DOS or *Eclipse Find* for Windows lets you find any file by name or by a key word in the file.

- You need to link up with your desktop while you're away: a program like *Co-Sessions, PC Anywhere, Remote Control* or *Close-Up* lets you call in to your computer at home and work from it on your notebook.

- You have this idea to add sound to your presentations: you can get a whole CD-ROM sound library like *Sound Library Pro* by Wayzata Technology ([800] 735-7321) that includes 1,200 sound effects or *1000 of the World's Greatest Sound Effects* by Interactive Publishing ([914] 426-0400).

Finding and Buying Software

There is a variety of resources to help you find out if there's a program that meets a need you have and to help you pick which one would do the best job. Many magazines publish lists of the best-selling software, do reviews of new product announcements, and rate software packages. You may want to read reviews of the same packages in several magazines because software reviewers, like movie critics, notice and report on different characteristics. User groups, on-line bulletin boards, and software catalogs like *Datapro* or *Shareware Express* can also be helpful for finding out if there's software that does something you need.

You can shop or browse through specialty software stores like Egghead, superstores like Office Depot, Staples, and OfficeMax, or software mail order catalogs like **Micro Warehouse** ([800] 367-7080), **MacWarehouse** ([800] 255-6227), **The PC Zone** ([800] 258-2088), **DellWare** ([800] 426-5150) or **PowerUp Direct** ([800] 851-2917). Office Depot and Staples have mail-order catalogs now, too. You can also order a variety of computer accessories through these catalogs.

Such catalogs commonly take orders twenty-four hours a day, seven days a week, and some offer overnight delivery and a thirty-day no-risk guarantee, often making mail order one of the cheapest and most efficient ways to buy software.

Software Dispatch has an interesting service that lets you browse through and actually try out and compare software options for Windows and Mac using a CD ROM disk. A QuickTime movie tutorial first explains how to shop, try out, and purchase the software you want. When you're ready to buy, you then call their software dispatch 800 number to purchase a code that allows you to unlock the software and manuals you've been trying out for immediate installation ([800] 937-2828; ext.600).

Sometimes the best way to find the right combination of software is to hire a computer consultant, many of whom are home businesses themselves. A consultant can offer personal, affordable service and advise you as to which packages to select, install them for you, and help you get up and running with them. You can locate computer consultants through the Yellow Pages or contact the

Independent Computer Consultants Association (see Resources at the end of this chapter).

Shareware

Years ago when freelance software writer Andrew Fluegelman couldn't get a software company to buy his software, he engineered an innovative way of selling it. He made it available free. He asked that if people liked the free software, they send him a $25 donation, and thus shareware was born. Many software authors now distribute their products in this way. They are widely available from computer user groups, from bulletin board systems and on-line services like CompuServe, and from catalogs that specialize in this software. The catalogs charge a fee for duplicating and mailing the disk. People who decide to use the software pay the author afterwards for documentation and upgrades.

Examples of well-regarded shareware packages include *Above and Beyond*, a Windows personal information manager available on America Online and CompuServe, *As-Easy-As*, a DOS spreadsheet program from Trius ([508] 794-9377 [800] 468-7478), *Paint Shop Pro*, a Windows graphics conversion and manipulations program ([612] 930-9171), *PrintSwitch*, a Windows utility that lets you change your default printer with just one click available on America Online and CompuServe, and *Time Is Money*, a DOS billing program for consultants who bill by the hour ([407] 767-9278). Disk vendors have large collections of shareware which they sell for $2 to $5 per disk. Two of the best-known vendors are Public Software Library ([800] 242-4775) and Public Brand Software ([800] 426-3475).

Public Domain Software

Public domain software is free. It's been developed by computer enthusiasts who want to share their accomplishments. Alfred Glossbrenner describes public domain software and its availability in his book *How to Get Free Software*.

Features to Look for: Software Checklist

___ **Does it do what you need?**
___ **Reputation (popular proven programs are a sure bet)**
___ **Does it avoid things you dislike?**
___ **Is what it will do worth the money?**
___ **Does it run on your machine?**
___ **Does it run quickly enough on your machine?**
___ **Will it conflict with anything else on your computer?**
___ **Is it easy to learn and use?**
___ **Is the documentation clear?**
___ **Do the package and the manufacturer have a good reputation?**
___ **Is user support provided? How so?**
___ **Toll-free ___ Call at your cost ___ 900 number_____**

Printers

You may have noticed that The Well-Equipped Home Office on page 161 included a laser or ink-jet printer. The reason for this is clear. Laser and laser-quality printers have come down in price so dramatically that no one should sacrifice the professional quality they need as a home-based business. You can get a high-quality ink-jet printer for as low as $300 and a laser for as low as $600.

Working from home still results in enough problems with being taken seriously that it just doesn't make sense to look anything less than the very best— especially when you can look so good, so affordably. So let's talk about how you can have a *Fortune* 500 look without spending a fortune. You have two choices for achieving that top-quality look: a laser or an ink-jet printer.

▪ Laser printers form their images out of tiny dots. The more dots, the higher the resolution and the better the print quality. The higher the resolution, the more your document looks as though it had been typeset at the print shop instead of on your own printer. Lower-cost laser printers, the ones around $600, have 300dpi (dots per inch), while higher-cost home-office lasers, those costing around $900, have 600 dpi.

▪ Ink-jet printers squirt ink directly onto the paper. This means that if you're using paper that absorbs ink, your image may not be quite as sharp; and with nonabsorbent paper, the image can smudge right after printing and later if the paper gets wet. But ink-jet printers run as low as $300 and have almost as good print quality as the 300dpi lasers. (The higher 600dpi resolution is not available in ink jets, at this time.) Where ink-jet printers really shine is when it comes to color. You can get beautiful color documents and overheads with ink-jet printers priced as low as $500! Laser color, of course, is beyond most home office budgets at this point (i.e., $10,000).

For most business purposes, a 300dpi printer is fine, so a laser printer like the Hewlett-Packard *LaserJet 4L* or the Canon *Bubble Jet* ink jet will present a most impressive image for your business. Certain businesses like graphics or desktop publishing, résumé writing, and word-processing services where the quality of the print image is very important will most likely want a 600dpi printer like the Hewlett-Packard *LaserJet 4* or Apple *LaserWriter 360*. For an even cleaner printed image, you can purchase a Postscript option for an additional $1,000 to $1,500. But again, this option is only worthwhile if you're in a business where very high resolution is important.

If space is a consideration, Panasonic offers a side-writer line of laser-quality printers that stand only 14" high and take up only .52 square feet of space. That's about the size of a standard mailing envelope! They're priced under $1,000.

If you're interested in a color printer, thermal wax transfer printers like TekTronics *Phaser* or the Fargo *Primera* (under $1,000) produce startling near-photo finished documents. These are heat and light sensitive, however, so they can fade. You can even get dot matrix color printers that look quite good. These printers, however, will not double as a high-quality black-and-white printer.

They are specialty printers. The ink-jet color printers like the Hewlett-Packard 500C (under $500) or 1200C ($2,300) not only produce excellent color, they will also serve perfectly well as your high-quality black-and-white ink-jet printer.

If you need a printer when you're away from your home office, portable printers that link up to your notebook are available, too. Some like the *Diconix* are ink jets; others, like the IBM *Portable*, are thermal fusion. Although portables cannot do double duty as your primary professional printer, they come in handy on the road or at client sites, weighing as little as 2.5 to just over 8 pounds with battery. They also come with an AC adapter. Some will print on card stock, transparencies, and envelopes. Costs run from just over $300 up to around $1,000 and they cost about 4 to 5 cents per page to operate. These portable printers will most certainly fit into a briefcase. The *Diconix* is only 2.4 × 11.7 × 7.7 inches.

Here are other features you will want to consider in choosing your printer.

Features to Look for: Printers

- **Print method.** Laser, Ink Jet.
- **Print quality.** 300dpi, 600dpi, Postscript option.
- **Price.** Typical ink jets run about half the price of the lower-end lasers. But when considering price, don't forget to factor in the cost of copies (see below). The printers we've been discussing are in the $300 to $900 range, with another $1,000 up for Postscript and some of the color models mentioned.
- **Cost of copies.** Cost per laser copy typically ranges from 2 to 3 cents per page. Most costs quoted are based on 5 percent of the page including a black image. Ink-jet copies range around 5 to 6 cents per page.
- **Speed.** Laser speeds are measured in pages per minute (ppm) with models at the prices we've been discussing ranging from 4 to 10ppm. Our HP Laser Jet4, at 8 pages per minute, doesn't leave us feeling impatient. The typical ink jet will run about half as fast as an entry-level laser. Ink-jet speeds are measured in characters per second (cps). Models range from 60 to 300cps. At 120cps, we were highly impatient. But for color prints, we don't mind the wait. In addition, ink-jet printers normally have two settings: draft and print quality. Draft quality runs faster.
- **Footprint.** Ink jets take up slightly less space than lasers, ranging in size from around 6 to 13 inches high, 13 to 17 inches wide, and 10 to 23 inches deep. If you are tight for space, models do vary in width, height, and depth. The Panasonic *SideWriter* laser is most unusual in that it saves space by sitting upright instead of lying flat like most models.
- **Memory.** Laser printers come with at least 512K of random access memory (RAM). Many have 1 to 2 Megabytes, and some have 4MB or more. The amount of memory affects not only the speed of your printer but also what type of printing you can do. 512K is sufficient for text work and up to half-page graphics (simple newsletters and flyers). For a full page of graphics, you need 1 to 1.5MB (think ads, presentations, and overheads). For Postscript, you need a minimum of 2 to 3MB; 4 to 5MB is better. You can always add memory, but memory upgrades often run more than it would have cost to purchase additional memory initially.

- **Paper handling.** Of course, the more paper a printer holds, the less often you will run out and need to refill it. Ink-jet trays have a standard paper supply of from 100 to 150 sheets. Some have manual feed slots. Lasers have cassettes like copiers that hold from 100 to 250 sheets. Lasers can have manual feed slots, too, which is handy for feeding envelopes, special paper, etc.
- *Dual cassettes.* Some printers have an additional optional paper tray or cassette so you can increase or change the paper supply. For example, you can use one for your letterhead, the other for plain paper.
- *Paper size.* Most laser and ink-jet printers take both letter- and legal-sized paper. A few will accommodate ledger paper.
- **Fonts.** Laser printers include a limited number of built-in fonts. The number varies, but the average is around 14. Postscript can have as many as 35 or more. Some fonts come with bold and italic styles. Few ink jets come with any resident fonts. One problem, however, is that the fonts in your software and the fonts in your printer may not be the same. But if you use Windows, the printing is software driven and you don't have to worry about what fonts come with your printer. You can get a greater variety of fonts by adding font cartridges to your printer or by buying fonts such as *TrueType* on floppy disks. There are other options as well.
- **Toner cartridges.** Some lower-cost printers require toner instead of cartridges, but these are on the wane because cartridges are easier to use. Laser toner cartridges generally print from 3,000 to 6,000 pages, depending on the model. Cartridges can be recycled.
- *Envelope feeders.* Feeding envelopes into printers can be problematical, although just about all lasers can take standard-sized envelopes fed in one-by-one or in a special envelope cassette. But your software will need to be able to transpose the image vertically. If you need to print a lot of envelopes, get a model with an envelope feeder. They run about $300.
- *Color.* Ink jet, thermal heat transfer, dot matrix.
- **Warranties and service.** As is true of computers, the best discount prices on printers are offered by mail-order dealers, computer warehouse stores, and office warehouse stores, although local computer dealers also have special discount offers—so watch for ads. Two-year warranties are common, especially for ink jets. Most warranties cover repairs only if you send the printer back to the dealer's or manufacturer's service depot, often a two-week process. Some dealers will do repairs themselves. Fortunately lasers are remarkably reliable. Most leading manufacturers have customer support service lines with specialists who will walk you through problems.
- **Documentation:** Look for clear and easy-to-understand instructions, especially for explaining how to install drivers and fonts, and for troubleshooting.
- **Manufacturers:** Canon and Hewlett-Packard have dominated the ink-jet market; Hewlett-Packard and Apple lead the laser market. There are many other reputable manufacturers, too.

Scanners

Although certainly not a must for every home office, scanners have begun to appear with increasing frequency at the top of the home office "wish list." Whereas laser printers and faxes were long at the top of wish lists, many people have acquired those items and now suddenly we are hearing that the next thing they want is a scanner.

A scanner makes it possible to get an image from a piece of paper into your computer and incorporate it into a report, proposal, database, or presentation that you're working on in your word processor, desktop publisher, or presentation graphics program.

There are three kinds: The more inexpensive handheld ones (around $100) are usually about 4 inches wide and therefore limit the size of the image you can scan. The more expensive (around $900) but more versatile flat-bed scanners are much like copy machines in size (i.e., 12 × 24 inches) and work similarly. You can place an 8.5-×-11-inch sheet with an image you want scanned on a flat glass plate, and a light-sensitive bar scans in the image. Some models can handle even larger sheets. The third kind of scanner is called a sheet feed and is priced between the handheld and the flat bed at around $350 to $500.

Both flat-bed and handheld scanners are available in color, black-and-white, and gray-scale models. The cheapest ones scan in simple black-and-white dot images and would be adequate for a simple line drawing. If you want to scan in a black-and-white photo, however, you need a scanner that can pick up the many shades of gray a photo represents. And of course, if you want color images you need a color scanner, which varies by model as to the number of colors it can distinguish.

Scanners also vary according to what kind of hardware they require, so be sure whatever scanner you're selecting is one that will operate with your computer. Scanners must also be used with particular software, which is usually included.

Two leading flat-bed scanners at this time are MicroTeks and Hewlett-Packard ScanJets. Logitech ScanMan has been a well-rated handheld.

Copy Machines

When we first started working from home, the smallest copy machines were bigger than most closets and way outside the budget of a fledgling home office. But all told, we undoubtedly spent the equivalent of several years in time traveling to and from copy stores, waiting in line, and groaning over copies flecked with spots from overused and smudged machines. Now, not only can you get a copy machine the size of a briefcase for under $300, but laser printers have become so affordable, fast, and high quality that some people are simply bypassing copiers altogether. And some people are even opting to let their fax do double duty as copier.

But in many situations there is truly no substitute for having your own copier. First, your fax can only meet the most minimal of copy needs, and using your laser printer only makes sense up to a point. It's time-consuming, ties up your printer for other more appropriate use, the cost is higher than with most copiers, and you can't copy things that don't come from your computer.

With the price and size of minicopiers dropping while their features are expanding, now that your time is money, it doesn't take many trips to the copy store to have paid for a copier. For example, let's say your time is worth $25 an hour and it takes you thirty minutes to get to the copy store, wait in line, make your copies, and return home. If you do that only three times a week, you'll pay for the copier in just over ten weeks!

You can get a minicopier for as little as $300 or as much as several thousand, depending on the number of copies you need to make and the features you want. Quality minicopiers in all price ranges make excellent copies, as good as or better than those you get at the copy store. They are surprisingly easy to use, reliable, and require virtually no maintenance. On the average, making your own copies will run you about 4 to 5 cents each, less than most copy stores charge for single or a low volume of copies. Cartridges, however, are not cheap, running around $75 and needing to be replaced about every 1,500 to 4,000 copies depending upon the model of copier.

Popular lines of minicopiers include Canon, Minolta, Sharp, and Xerox. Which one will be best for you generally depends on how many copies you need and the type of documents you're reproducing. The very low volume copiers that cost as little as $300 have minimal features, but if you need to make only a few copies a week and usually require limited numbers of copies for each document, these copiers can serve you adequately. The Canon 310, for example, is one of the smallest copiers (costing around $400) and weighs less than 16 pounds. It is truly portable, coming with a handle so you can use it in various locations or take it to a trade show or project site.

If you need to make over 500 copies a month or even a few copies of many-paged documents, this is still considered low-volume in the copier world but you'll need one of the more sophisticated models. These copiers run around $1,500 to $3,000 and can produce from 800 to 3,500 copies per month, but they are definitely desktop copiers with a home-office-sized footprint. There are many models in between with a variety of features. Here's what to look for:

Features to Look for:
Copiers for under 1,000 Copies a Month

- **Quality of copy.** Produces high-quality copies on plain paper as well as on different weights of paper such as letterhead, card stock, label sheets, and transparencies. Copy quality varies, so take in samples of the types of originals you will be copying and try them out.
- **Recommended maximum volume.** Be sure the model you buy is designed to produce the volume of copies you expect to make each month. Otherwise you could damage the machine. It's true. We did it. Late one night we pushed our machine beyond the call of duty for an early-morning meeting and although it finished the job, it was never the same! Models range from 500 to 3,500 copies.

- **Copy speed.** Quoted speeds are based on continuous copying of 8.5-×-11-inch paper from an original. Good low-volume copiers usually make around 6 to 10 copies per minute. But if you most frequently make just one copy, the speed you're most interested in is the time involved in making the first copy. This can range anywhere from five to twelve seconds.
- **Ease of use.** Make sure the control panel keys and the means of getting the toner into the copier are easy to use. Copiers with toner cartridges are much more convenient than those requiring you to load toner from a bottle. Not all cartridges are as easy to use as others, however. The easiest are single user-replaceable cartridges.
- **Type of cartridge.** Most copier cartridges simply replace the toner. Others involve periodic serving of other elements. Canon, however, has a Single Cartridge System: each cartridge includes not only the toner but also the drum and the development unit, making their copiers virtually service free. Each time you replace the cartridge, you're essentially getting a new copier.
- **Reliability.** Sources of information on reliability are the *User Ratings of Copiers* by Datapro Research Corporation, *Copier Selection Guide with Durability Ratings* by Buyers Laboratory, Inc., and *What to Buy for Business*.
- **Readily available service,** either on-site, which is more expensive, or carry-in.
- **Moving or stationary platen.** The top of lower-priced copiers often moves back and forth while making a copy. The copies are just as good, but the machine requires more space than is immediately apparent.
- *Reduction and enlargement capability.*
- *Paper input tray capacity.* Models range from 50 to 250.
- *Cartridge life.* Generally from 1,500 to 3,000 copies.
- *Manual light and darkness adjustment.*
- *Multiple paper trays* for different sizes of paper.
- *Automatic document feeder.* A rare feature on a desktop copier.

Buying a Used Copier

Be aware of some common buzzwords in selling used copiers. A "refurbished" copier has received a good cleaning and some new paint. A "reconditioned" machine has been newly painted and upgraded internally to match the manufacturers' new products. A "remanufactured" copier has gone back to the factory assembly line and had all worn parts replaced, in addition to getting a new paint job and internal enhancements. You decrease your chances of buying someone else's troubles with a remanufactured copier.

Modems

When you use a modem and communications software, your computer becomes both a library and a telephone to the world.

A modem translates the electronic signals from your computer into electric pulses of sound that can travel across telephone lines to another computer that also uses a modem to reconvert the acoustic signals back into a form it can process.

With a modem, you can gain immediate access to an estimated 95 percent of the information that's been published in the past fifteen years. You can do market research, check the availability of a name for your business, find venture capital, do credit checks, and even develop mailing lists. A modem teamed up with a telephone line can turn your notebook computer into a powerful communications device as well.

With a modem, you can save time and energy by running electronic errands—sending mail, doing banking or shopping, paying bills, getting airline schedules, and making reservations—all without leaving your desk. You can overcome the isolation of working alone by visiting the homes and offices of tens of thousands of people across the country and beyond, while still sitting in your chair. The connections you make on-line can be sources of new business, ways of learning from other people's experiences or mistakes, and an effective means for maintaining contact with clients, colleagues, and customers.

A modem also enables you to transmit information over the telephone lines via your computer even faster than on a fax machine. And the documents or data arrive in a form that can be edited or printed out by all types of computers. For example, you can send a document created on your PC-style computer to someone who can read, change, or print it on a Macintosh computer.

Prices of modems have declined dramatically, with even very high speed modems that can transmit at 9,600 and 14,400 bits per second available for under $200.

Features to Look for: Modems

- **Type.** You have a variety of choices. These include internal, stand-alone, and pocket-digital modems and acoustical modes. Internal modems are cards that are inserted into your computer. Some computers, especially notebooks, come with them already installed. The advantage of internal modems is that they save desk space and cord congestion, plus an internal modem leaves a serial port free for other devices. Stand-alone modems are small, flat boxes that attach to your computer. Pocket modems are small enough to fit in your pocket and are used if you don't have an internal modem in your notebook computer. Acoustical modes, more difficult to find today, still have a use with pay phones and anywhere lacking a modular telephone jack.
- **Speed.** 2,400 bits per second is now considered slow, 9,600 is a standard speed, but 14,400 and even 28,800 are becoming the high-speed standards today.

- **Hayes compatibility.** Hayes is the leading modem manufacturer, and its products create the standard.
- *Error correction.*
- *Data compression.*
- *Fax/voice mail combinations.* Some modems are part of a package like the *Complete Communicator*, which is a fax/modem/voice mail system all in one.

Forty Ways You Can Benefit from Going On-Line

1. Getting and generating sales leads
2. Sending and receiving electronic mail
3. Banking by computer
4. Getting price quotes and ordering products
5. Learning about U.S. government procurement needs
6. Accessing a client's or employer's mainframe computer
7. Getting stock market quotes
8. Reading AP and UPI newswires
9. Reading stories from *The Wall Street Journal, Barron's,* and the Dow Jones News Service
10. Using the *Official Airline Guide*
11. Looking things up in encyclopedias
12. Making travel reservations
13. Buying, selling, exchanging, or financing real estate
14. Bartering for goods and services
15. Checking your personal account with your brokerage firm
16. Using the nation's 4,800 Yellow Pages directories
17. Holding meetings and conferences
18. Researching several thousand databases on almost any subject
19. Obtaining free public domain software
20. Sending telex messages to any of the 1.5 million telex subscribers around the world or fax messages to any fax owner
21. Getting IRS tax publications
22. Reading over 200 newsletters
23. Advertising
24. Calculating your net worth
25. Downloading software programs
26. Incorporating your business
27. Doing market research
28. Checking patents
29. Learning what proposals the government is seeking
30. Looking up 10,000 corporate SEC filings
31. Getting economic and marketing forecasts
32. Learning about foreign trade opportunities
33. Finding employment

34. Getting detailed demographic information
35. Doing credit investigations
36. Discovering investment opportunities
37. Getting medical information
38. Learning about pending congressional legislation
39. Finding venture capital
40. Locating personnel for your business

Resources

Vital (**) and Helpful Peripherals, Accessories, and Utilities

Protecting Your Equipment and Data

■ **Be safe: back up.** You don't have to hassle with backing up all your data on floppy disks or on a cumbersome tape drive. Most people just won't do it. The easiest and surest way to back up your disk drive just in case it should crash is to add a removable hard drive to your computer onto which you can back up your entire drive. For example The DAK Catalog features a Take-It-Anywhere Removable Hard Drive kit with docking bay, expansion card and carrying case [800] 325-0800.

■ **Don't lose files from a goof-up.** So you hit the wrong key. All that work is gone. Not necessarily. Get a file-recovery utility like *Norton Utilities*, *PC Tools* or *MacTools*. It may save you from a disaster. Tools like this come built into DOS 6.2.

■ **Diagnose the problem.** When something's gone wrong with your computer, you may be able to find and correct the problem yourself. Before calling for help, let software like *Norton Disk Doctor* or Delrina's *System Sleuth* search out and correct the problem if they can.

■ **Immunize your computer from getting a virus.** Get virus protection software like *Norton Antivirus* and run all new software through it before loading it into your computer. DOS 6.2 also can do this for you by constantly checking your system for viruses, but it can only detect those known at the time when the software was released. So you need to keep updating your virus checker.

■ **Don't lose it all when the lights go out.** Get a backup power supply, called an uninterruptible power supply (UPS). Basically it's a battery that will keep your computer running when the electricity goes out, for anywhere from five minutes to an hour. It at least gives you the chance to save what you're working on and turn off your system.

■ **Surge protector.** Don't allow a power surge to fry your equipment. Protect it with a surge protector like *The Filtered Strip* SP-700, by Curtis Manufacturing (sold where office supplies are sold or call [800] 955-5544), or *The Clearmax*, a transparent surge protector with noise filtration for six outlets. It shuts the power off automatically when a surge is detected. This device is sold at office-supply stores or you can call Paramax (800) 472-5555. You can also get a whole-house surge suppressor mounted to your breaker panel, as a snap-in circuit breaker or as an electric meter socket adapter. Prices range from $75 to $500.

▪ **Child-proof your computer** with a lock like *LamaLock*, which locks the floppy drive; (800) 880-9980.

▪ **Don't let valuable data go up in smoke.** Keep disks or backup disks safe from fire with the *Fire-Safe Media by Sentry GroupChest*. It will store thirty 5.25-inch disks or sixty 3.5-inch disks in a fireproof, heat-proof, humidity-proof safe that will protect them in temperatures up to 1,550 degrees Fahrenheit for a half hour. Sold where office supplies are sold or call (800) 828-1438.

Handy Helpers

Share your printer. You and your partner or assistant can share a single printer with a card like the one by Western Telematic's PSC-6 (714) 586-9950, which enables two computers to hook into the same printer.

Boost your printing power. Add Postscript capability to your LaserJet with PostScript Cartridge Plus, from Hewlett-Packard.

Traveling with Your Office

Pack your office for the road. Pack your notebook, portable printer, disks and cellular phone in one handy briefcase like the *Galizia CompacCase*, an office in a briefcase ([800] 883-2273). Or pick out one of the Kensington notebook carrying cases ([800] 535-4242) that come in various sizes depending on how much of your office you want to take with you.

Retrieve faxes while you're away. *EchoFax* by Tanji Design attaches to your answering machine and stores all incoming faxes, which you can access by phone and have transmitted to a fax at your location or to your laptop computer. Available from SkyMall ([800] 424-6255).

Make space to work on crowded airplanes. When you're trying to work with your notebook on an airplane, the *SkyDesk*, ([800] 836-0820) is a light-weight plastic copy stand that hooks to the back of the seat in front of you to hold your notes and copy above your notebook. Or Glacier Technologies' *Paper Chaise* is a collapsible travel copyholder for your PC ([800] 842-7345).

Make labels the easy way. Use Avery's *Personal Label Printer* with their *LabelPro* to print out single mailing labels and even put your logo on them. Avery labels, by the way, come in many fluorescent colors! Or make file, disk, and storage unit labels with Brothers *P-Touch*.

Computer in the car. You can plug your notebook or computer or fax machine to your portable phone with IDEA Cellular Data Link from ORA Electronics (818) 772-9977.

Keep Your Equipment Clean and in Working Order

Eliminate cord clutter. Keep the space behind and beneath your desk from looking like a cord jungle with a cord manager like *Rip-Tie* from The Rip-Tie Co. ([800] 348-7600), which neatly bundles cords with velcro strips.

Clean equipment inside and out. Keep all your office equipment looking good and working well with *Dust-Off Office Care Kit* that contains eight items for cleaning your phone, computer, keyboard, monitor, laser printer, and fax (Falcon Safety Products [908] 707-4900). Feed *Scrubex* sheets through your laser printer, copier, or fax and the solvent-coated sheets will pick up residues. (At office supply stores or [708] 627-9600; [800] 331-8000.)

Do It Yourself

Tinker tools. Sometimes documentation on office equipment will tell you to turn a screw or change a knob, or you may be so bold as to replace a chip or install a card or new drive. The *MiniKit* by Jensen Tools should be in your desk drawer for just such times. It's a little zippered-case tool kit filled with twenty tiny home-office electronics-sized screwdrivers, pliers, and the like ([602] 968-6231; [800] 426-1194).

Get copies straight. If you're trying to line up something on your copier that's not the standard 8.5 × 11 inches, the *STRAIT-jacket* can help. It's a nonreproducible grid that static will hold in place on the glass so you can line up your original perfectly and keep it in place. From STRAIT-jacket, (503) 749-1052.

Books

Computer Power for Your Small Business. Nick Sullivan. New York: Random House, 1993.

Computers Simplified. Richard Maran and Eric Feistmantl. Old Tappan, N.J.: Prentice Hall, 1993. An introduction to computers for the totally nontechnical person.

Computers and Visual Stress: How to Enhance Visual Comfort While Using Computers. Edward G. Godnig and John S. Hacunda. Seacoast Information Services, 4446 South County Trail, Inc., Charlestown, RI 02813.

Doing Business on the Internet. Mary J. Cronin. New York: Van Nostrand Reinhold, 1994.

Healthy Computing. Dr. Ronald Harwin and Colin Haynes, American Management Association, AMACOM, P.O. Box 1026, Saranac Lake, NY 12983; (800) 538-4761, (800) 262-9699.

How to Look It Up On-Line. Alfred Glossbrenner. New York: St. Martin's Press, 1987.

Photocopier Maintenance and Repair Made Easy. Eric Kuaimoku, New York: TAB Books, 1993.

Practical Guide to Scanning. UMAX, 3170 Coronado Dr., Santa Clara, CA 95054; (800) 562-0311 (free booklet).

The Office Equipment Advisor. John Derrick. What to Buy for Business: 350 Theodore Fremd Ave., Rye, NY 10580; (800) 247-2185. A 512-page shopper's guide to choosing office equipment; published in 1993.

Windows Shareware 500, The Last Word on the Best Virus-Free Windows Shareware. John Hedtke. Chapel Hill, N.C.: Vantana Press, 1994.

Magazines

Computer Shopper. Ziff-Davis Publishing Co., 1 Park Ave., New York, NY 10016.

Directory of Online Databases. Cuadra Associates, Inc., 2001 Wilshire Blvd., Santa Monica, CA 90403. Published by Elsesvier Science Publications Co., Inc., P.O. Box 882, Madison Square Station, New York, NY 10159.

Home Office Computing. Scholastic, Inc., P.O. Box 2511, Boulder, CO 80302; (800)288-7812. *The* periodical for home-based businesspeople, covering both business and technology.

MacUser. Ziff-Davis Publishing Co. (for full citation, see above, under *Computer Shopper*).

Macworld, the Macintosh Magazine. PCW Communications Inc., 501 2nd St., San Francisco, CA 94107.

PC/Computing. Ziff-Davis Publishing Co. (see above).

PC Magazine. Ziff-Davis Publishing Co. (see above).

PC World. PCW Communications, Inc. (see above).

What to Buy for Business. 350 Theodore Fremd Ave., Rye, NY 10580.

Windows Magazine. CMP Publications, 600 Community Dr., Manhasset, NY 11030.

Catalogs

Mail Order Equipment Catalogs
PC Connection (800) 800-0004
Micro Warehouse (800) 367-7080
PC Compleat (800) 669-4727
Insight Computer Systems (800) 998-8036
USA/Flex (800) 477-8323

Mail Order Software Catalogs
Micro Warehouse (800) 367-7080
MacWarehouse (800) 255-6227
The PC Zone (800) 258-2088
DellWare (800) 426-5150
PowerUp Direct (800) 851-2917
Software Dispatch 20525 Mariani Avenue, Cupertino, CA 95014; (800) 937-2828, x 600

Computer Hardware and Software Directories

Books:

Glossbrenner's Guide to Shareware for Small Businesses. Alfred Glossbrenner. New York: Windcrest/McGraw-Hill, 1992.

How to Get Free Software. Alfred Glossbrenner. New York: St. Martins, 1989.

The Mac Shareware 500. John Hedtke. Chapel Hill, N.C.: Ventana Press, 1993.

The Windows Shareware 500. Ruffin Prevost and Rob Terrell. Chapel Hill, N.C.: Ventana Press, 1993.

Directories Available in the Reference Section of Libraries:

Business Software Directory. Published by Learned Information.

Datapro-McGraw-Hill Guide to IBM Software. Published by Datapro Research Corporation.

Datapro-McGraw-Hill Guide to Apple Software. Published by Datapro Research Corporation.

Directories Available On-Line:

Business Software Database. Produced by Ruth Koolish Information Sources, Inc., contains descriptions of business software packages for microcomputers as well as for mainframe and minicomputers. Available on Dialog and Knowledge Index accessible through CompuServe.

Computer Buyers' Directory. Produced by Ziff-Davis, contains product information on over 90,000 hardware and software products; on Ziffnnet, accessible through CompuServe and Prodigy.

Computer Database Plus. Produced by Ziff-Davis, contains magazine reviews and articles on hardware and software products; on Ziffnnet, accessible through CompuServe and Prodigy.

Microcomputer Abstract. Produced by Learned Information, Inc., contains many types of articles including product announcements and software and hardware reviews. Available on Dialog and Knowledge Index, accessible through CompuServe.

Microcomputer Software and Hardware Guide. Produced by the R. R. Bowker Company, is derived from information received directly from over 3,500 software publishers and over 1,000 hardware manufacturers. Available on Dialog and Knowledge Index, accessible through CompuServe.

On-Line Services

America Online. 8619 Westwood Center Drive, Vienna, VA 22182; (703) 893-6288 or (800) 922-0808.

CompuServe Information Service, Inc. P.O. Box 20212, Columbus, OH 43220; (800) 848-8990, (800) 848-8199 (in Ohio), or (614) 457-8650.

Delphi General Videotex Corporation/DELPHI. 1030 Massachusetts Avenue, Cambridge, MA 82138; (800) 544-4005 or (617) 491-3393.

Dialog Information Services. 3460 Hillview Avenue, Palo Alto, CA 94304; (415) 858-3719, (800) 334-2564, or (800) 387-2689 (in Canada).

GEnie, General Electric Information Services Co. 401 N. Washington St., Rockville, MD 20850; (800) 638-9636 or (301) 340-4000.

Mead Data Central—Nexis and Lexis. P.O. Box 933, Dayton, OH 45401; (800) 227-4908 or (513) 865-6800.

Prodigy Information Service. 445 Hamilton Avenue, White Plains, NY 10601; (800) 776-3449.

Technical Help

Independent Computer Consultants Association, 933 Gardenview Office Parkway, St. Louis, MO 63141; (800) 774-4222.

PART 3

Protecting Your Assets:
Legal, Tax, and Insurance Matters

CHAPTER
NINE
■■■■■■■■■■■■■■■■■■■■■■■■■■■

Zoning, Permits, Regulations,
and Your Legal Decisions

"The law's made to take care o' raskills," wrote George Eliot in *The Mill on the Floss* in 1860. More recently, home-based businesspeople have come to regard laws, and sometimes their interpretation and administration, as the work of rascals. Although home-based businesses usually do not face all the laws and complicated regulations larger businesses must deal with, they nevertheless encounter regulation from all levels of government.

At the city and county level, zoning, business licenses and permits, and fictitious name registration may shape your business actions. State law may require you to obtain a professional or occupational license to pursue your chosen work, collect sales tax for your product or service, and prohibit certain types of businesses from being conducted from your home. The federal government requires licenses of specific types of businesses; also, more recent laws, such as the Americans with Disabilities Act (ADA), may apply to your home business.

In this chapter, we'll also discuss contracts and whether or not it would be beneficial for you to incorporate your business. We'll also talk about how to select and when to consult a lawyer. The terms we'll be using as we describe these legal issues may be different in your state or locality, but the general principles will be similar.

Is It Legal for You to Work at Home?—Zoning
Ordinances, Other Laws, and Restrictions

In too many cities and suburbs, the answer to whether it's legal for you to work at home is no, because zoning ordinances often prohibit you from using your home for business purposes. In a few situations, state or federal laws and home association regulations may also limit the business use of your home.

Although zoning originated in Roman times, current ordinances that restrict the business use of homes arose from a desire to protect neighborhoods from the smokestacks of the Industrial Revolution. Some of today's zoning ordinances were written back in Civil War times. Now, over a century later, yesterday's good intentions often no longer apply.

No matter how outdated an ordinance or regulation may be, however, violating one can be risky business. If you are operating illegally, you may be forced to stop conducting your business, and you will certainly find yourself faced with the discomfort of playing legal hide-and-seek. You may find yourself unable to complain about justifiable problems neighbors are creating, such as noise, for fear they'll retaliate by reporting you. So it's important for you to find out whether it is legal for you to work at home and what you can do about it if it's not.

How to Find Out Whether Zoning Ordinances Permit You to Work at Home

Zoning ordinances are created at the city or county level of government and vary widely from one locality to another. In Sierra Madre, California, for example, home businesses are permitted if you take out a business license. In adjacent Pasadena, however, you must apply for a home occupation permit before you can get a business license. And in nearby Bradbury, home businesses are not permitted at all. You can find out about your situation by answering these three questions:

1. Does your city or county have zoning ordinances? Some areas of the country, like the city of Houston, do not have zoning. To find out about your area, contact your city or county government. To figure out which unit of government is responsible for zoning, use this rule of thumb. If you would call the police in an emergency, you're governed by the city. If you would phone the sheriff, you deal with the county.

Within city or county government, zoning is usually handled by either the Building Inspector or the Planning Department. Otherwise, your area may have a special Zoning Administration you can contact.

2. How is your property zoned? Zoning ordinances divide the city or county into four basic classifications: Residential, Commercial, Industrial, and Agricultural. Each of these areas includes further distinctions, such as Residential–Single-Family Units, and Residential–Multiple-Family Units. Also, the types of activities that can be carried out in each area vary by locality. However, certain general observations can be made.

Most home businesses can be operated in an area zoned for agricultural use. After all, farming was the original "home business."

Many cities prohibit any residential use of buildings in an area zoned for industry. This causes problems for work-at-homers like artists who might want to rent warehouses or other industrial buildings to work and live in. A common exception to this restriction allows a guard to work and sleep on a building's premises in order to provide security. Consequently, some artists arrange to work as watchmen by night and painters or sculptors by day.

Most zoning codes allow buildings in commercially zoned areas to be used for both residential and business purposes. In fact, a familiar part of American tradition has been the neighborhood mom-and-pop shop, with the family living upstairs or in the back.

Residential zoning restrictions present the most problems for people working at home. Many localities either allow no business uses in residential areas or limit the nature and scope of business activities that can be done at home. Some communities allow more latitude in multiple-unit residential areas with apartment buildings and condominiums.

To find out which kind of zone you live in, locate your property on the official maps at the government office responsible for zoning. Chances are you live in a residential area and may be facing a number of possible restrictions.

3. Specifically, what is and is not allowed in your zone? Nine out of ten localities restrict using residences for offices or businesses in some way, according to a study entitled *Home Occupation Ordinances* done by Jo Ann Butler and Judith Getzels in 1985 for the American Planning Association. Some communities distinguish between a business and a profession.

In such cases, businesses generally cannot operate from a home, but recognized professionals like physicians, lawyers, dentists, musicians, artists, architects, and counselors can maintain home offices. What qualifies as a profession, however, may vary from one locality to another. For example, barber or beauty shops are considered professions in some places but not in others. Photography, real-estate brokerage, interior decorating, dance instruction, and roofing have been classified as businesses by some courts, while the giving of singing and music lessons has usually been found to be a profession.

What particular zoning ordinances restrict and allow reflects the tastes of the local personalities responsible for the ordinances. As a result, contradictions between communities abound. For example, some communities prohibit a separate entrance for a home office; others require it. Irksome restrictions may limit the hours you can work and prohibit using your address in advertising, including Yellow Page listings, and using outside buildings, such as garages, for your office. So before adding or remodeling an outside building for use as a home office, it's important to check your community's zoning and building codes.

Despite many variations in zoning codes, the American Planning Association study found some patterns. Following are the most common restrictions on home offices and home businesses (the percentages represent the percent of communities having the particular restriction):

- Restrictions limiting increases in vehicular traffic (46%)
- Restrictions on use or size of outside signs (42%)
- Restrictions on on-street parking (33%)
- Limitations on employees (33%)
- Limitations on the amount of floor space used (20%)
- Restrictions on retail selling times on the premises (13%)

- Prohibitions on outside storage of materials (11%)
- Restrictions on inside storage of materials (8%)

You can look this up yourself by going to the office in city hall or the courthouse that administers zoning. First, locate your home on a zoning map. This will either be mounted on a wall or contained in a book of zoning maps. It may be a large book. You will find the classification for your home indicated on the map. With this in mind, read the zoning ordinance while at city hall, or you can get a copy of the zoning regulations to take with you either free or for a small fee. Read the regulations to determine what specifications apply to the type of zone in which you live. This is public information, and you do not have to answer any questions to obtain it.

What You Can Do If You Aren't Zoned for Business

Many people living in areas that aren't zoned for business just ignore the law. They figure no one will know and there will probably be no problems. Often this is the case, because zoning officials usually don't have the time to go looking for violators. This is simply a fact, not encouragement to ignore zoning laws. There are many ways of solving zoning problems without violating the law. In any case, officials can find out about violations in a variety of ways.

Most commonly, zoning violations are reported by unhappy neighbors who call with complaints of too much noise, traffic congestion, or cars parked in front of their homes. Feuding neighbors might call just for spite, which happened to a man in the Pacific Northwest who was operating a contracting company from his home.

Each morning, four or five men would meet at his home office and he would send them out on their assignments for the day. They met inside, were not noisy, and did not congest parking. Yet the neighbors complained and zoning officials forced the contractor to stop doing business from his home. He then sold his house, moved to another county, and began operating his business from his new home. Pursuing him, his old neighbors checked the zoning regulations, found he lived in another area not zoned for business, and reported him once more. Again he was stopped from doing business.

Obviously, good relations with neighbors are important in avoiding zoning problems. But there are other ways city officials find out about violations. Something as simple as an application for a business license or sales permit can call their attention to violators. A photographer who worked part-time from his apartment discovered this the hard way when he tried to get a loan to buy new equipment. His bank required that he get a business license, which he did. Subsequently, a report of the license went to the zoning department and he was cited for a violation.

Similarly, the owner of a word-processing service discovered she had to pay state sales tax on some of her services. Applying for a sales tax permit meant the city would be notified of her home business, but failure to apply would put her in the position of violating state law. Too often, ignoring zoning ordinances leads to one of these legal double binds. A journalist even found the zoning inspector at his door within days of having a business telephone installed in his home.

Obviously the best strategy is to avoid zoning problems by taking preventive steps. Following are ten ways to prevent problems and to deal with them if they arise.

1. Establish and maintain good relations with neighbors. Find out how your neighbors feel about your working from home. Often neighbors feel safer knowing someone will be in the neighborhood during the day. Some are glad to have your business nearby. When your neighbors are supportive of your work, they can be valuable allies should you need special permits or a variance to work at home.

If they are opposed to your working at home, carefully note their concerns—both those they state explicitly and those you discern from their nonverbal communication. Respond to them positively and nondefensively. Offer assurances and guarantees.

A fear that is often behind neighborhood opposition even when the home business would not create noise and traffic—the two primary concerns neighbors have—is that property values will suffer. The fact is that developers of new upscale homes are now as a matter of course customizing rooms that can be used for home offices. Home offices and higher property values go hand in hand.

Judith Corbett, who successfully obtained a variance after having been cited by Los Angeles's Building and Safety Department, had served her neighbors as the chair of their Neighborhood Watch. As a result, her son was able to get nearly all her neighbors to sign petitions supporting her in her time of need. A man in another city operates a million-dollar mail-order business from his home in an upscale neighborhood. Big semis make deliveries at least once a week. At his peak season, he has eight employees, but no one complains to the zoning

---

What Happens When You're Charged with a Zoning Violation

If authorities find you are in violation of a zoning ordinance, they will send you a notice ordering you to stop. After receiving such a notice you must stop, or file an appeal immediately, because each day you continue can be a separate violation.

If you do not comply with the order, authorities have two alternatives. Typically, they seek an injunction, an order from the civil court prohibiting you from continuing the violation. As in other civil lawsuits, you will be served with a notice of a hearing and have the opportunity to hire a lawyer or defend yourself. Violating an injunction, once it's issued, puts you in contempt of court, punishable by fine or imprisonment.

The authorities can also choose to prosecute the violation of a zoning ordinance as a municipal misdemeanor. This type of proceeding is usually a last resort, however. It begins with issuing a warrant or bill of complaint from the municipal court. If found in violation at the ensuing trial, the offender can be fined and/or imprisoned.

authorities. Why? Every family has had a teenager or stay-at-home mom be employed by him at some time.

2. Know specifically what business activities you can and cannot do at home and adjust your business to meet the restrictions. If retail sales are prohibited on your premises, for example, distribute your wares through sales representatives or mail-order advertising. If employees other than your immediate family are prohibited from working in your home, contract with an outside secretarial service or have your employees work from their homes instead.

3. Rent a private mailing address or office suite to use as your official business address, but before doing this, find out if part of getting a city business license is one or more physical inspections of the business. Also, over twenty states have consumer protection laws that require any business using a post office box address or private receiving service to disclose in all advertising and promotional materials, including order blanks and forms, the complete street address from which business is actually conducted.

4. Contact your local Chamber of Commerce. Chamber staff may know how others have solved similar zoning problems.

5. Consult with an attorney who specializes in zoning matters and who wins most of his or her zoning cases. You may be able to find this out from staff at the zoning office.

6. Apply for a use permit, which will allow you to use your home as a business. You may be able to get a use permit from community officials after an investigation of your business plans and facilities. Use permits usually do not require a public hearing.

7. Apply for a variance. You can ask the local zoning board for a waiver of zoning restrictions in your case. Variances are exceptions granted by a zoning board, a planning board, or an appeals board. Variances are escape valves built into the system. But no one has an inherent right to a variance, and zoning boards do not like granting them. In fact, boards will only consider variances under certain circumstances. Filing fees are charged to initiate the process. These fees may range from hundreds to thousands of dollars, whether your application is approved or not.

You may have a case if you can show that what you are doing is comparable to a permitted occupation. For example, someone tutoring children in how to use computers might be able to show how this new occupation is similar to teaching children to play the piano, which has traditionally been allowed at home.

You also may have a case if you can show that literal enforcement of the ordinance would deprive you of your livelihood and cause a hardship for you. For example, a single parent with three small children at home might be able to show that there is no other way either to provide or to care for the children.

Finally, you may have a case if you can show there would be no harm done to the neighborhood or larger community. Since getting a variance requires a public hearing, such an approach is often your best bet. Poll your neighborhood. Find out how people feel about your working at home. Honor their concerns, get them on your side, and bring them to the hearing. If many neighbors come out to support you, and no one opposes you, it certainly will help.

Public support from people other than your neighbors can also make a difference. For six years after he retired as first violinist of the Boston Symphony, Herman Silberman taught violin in his condominium in San Diego, California. Then the homeowners' association reported his business to zoning authorities and they ordered him to cease and desist from teaching in his home.

Silberman's students, however, effectively used the appeals process and obtained a variance so he could continue offering his lessons. They circulated a petition on his behalf and won over the six-person planning commission.

Learning the history and operations of the planning commission or zoning authority deserves your attention as well. Identify the members and review their voting records to discover what they usually allow and what they deny. Attend zoning board meetings on other cases to see how the hearings are conducted, how the board operates, who is most influential.

In larger communities, board members may represent special political or economic interests. In smaller communities, the people on the zoning boards are generally citizens like yourself. But whatever the size of your community, understanding the board members should help you build the best case for yourself.

Regardless of how well prepared you are, it's wise to consult an attorney. Legal expertise can help you in evaluating your situation and planning your appeal.

8. Get your community's zoning ordinance amended. Since zoning ordinances are often antiquated, you might consider mobilizing other home businesses in your community to get the ordinances amended. Artists in Los Angeles and New York, for example, successfully mobilized to get changes in zoning that allow them to live and work in studios located in industrial areas.

David Hughes of Colorado Springs, Colorado, rallied residents using his computer bulletin board. The result was that nearly two hundred people packed a city council meeting and a more permissive ordinance ended up being passed than the one that had been headed for enactment.

When Ron Miller's wife wanted to start providing translation services in her Melbourne, Florida, home, he checked their zoning and found that the city prohibited home-based businesses. He went to the City Manager, who wrote Ron, "The prohibition has been carefully reviewed by City Council twice in recent years, and both times the Council has voted to make no changes." Ron then went to work. He wrote a draft ordinance for the city council, obtained statistical information, and found that 12 percent of the county's population worked at home. He collected copies of all ordinances regulating home occupations from nearby cities; he wrote thoughtful letters to the council members after each vote. A major story on his battle was printed in a local weekly newspaper. He enlisted the support of the local home business association. In the end, by a 6-to-1 vote, Melbourne voted to allow home-based businesses.

Ways to locate fellow open-collar workers in your area are through civic organizations, professional and trade associations, Yellow Pages, or local newspaper advertising. You can join together to propose an amendment either through the zoning commission or directly to your city council or county legislature.

In drawing up the proposed amendment, enlist the help of a lawyer who believes in your cause.

The box below lists the types of provisions a reasonable zoning code might include. You can use these as guidelines for proposing an ordinance, or for reviewing a proposed ordinance or amendments to an existing code.

9. Get a change in state law. This is based on the fact that states regulate their cities and counties. Vermont is the first state to require its cities to allow home-based businesses and Oregon was the second. Vermont's law is short and to the point:

> Protection of home occupations. No regulation [referring back to local zoning] may infringe upon the right of any resident to use a minor portion of a dwelling for an occupation which is customary in residential areas and which does not change the character thereof. 24 V.S.A. 4406(3).

Reasonable Provisions for Zoning Regulations of Home Offices*

1. The home office or business is clearly secondary to the use of the dwelling as a residence and does not change the residential character of the dwelling or the lot in any visible manner.
2. The work done in the home office or business creates no objectionable odor, noticeable vibration, or offensive noise that increases the level of ambient sound at the property lines.
3. The home office or business does not cause unsightly conditions or waste visible off the property.
4. The home office or business does not cause interference with radio or television reception in the vicinity.
5. The home office or business has no more than two full-time employees who are not residents of the household. Special permits may be granted to allow more employees.
6. The home office or business has no signs visible from the street that are inconsistent with signs allowed elsewhere in the zoning regulations.
7. The home office or business sells no articles at retail on the premises which are not raised or grown on the premises.
8. The home office or business occupies no more than 40 percent of the dwelling.
9. The ordinance should recognize that parking requirements for businesses that serve clients, patients, or customers are different from home offices where the only business visitor is apt to be an occasional overnight courier.
10. The home office or business does not create a volume of passenger or commercial traffic that is inconsistent with the normal level of traffic on the street on which the dwelling is located.
11. Parking of a truck(s) or van(s) should be allowed to the extent they do not interfere with the residential look of the neighborhood.

* Adapted from a model ordinance developed by the National Alliance of Home Businesswomen, an organization that contributed a great deal to the working-from-home movement.

A more detailed bill passed the California Assembly in 1993, only to be vetoed by Governor Pete Wilson. As the numbers of people working from home grow and the restructuring of the economy makes it necessary for people to make it on their own, the political climate will be ripe for similar laws in many states.

10. Home business associations can lobby city planners and home developers to include provisions allowing home-based businesses both in covenants that run with the land in single-family-home developments and in the bylaws and covenants, codes, and restrictions (CC&Rs) of condominiums.

Because working from home is now "in" (according to the January 1 issue of *USA Today*), publicity is likely to be favorable to the home business cause. Find news reporters who will cover zoning-related stories. In larger cities, coverage may be harder to get, so you may need to use imagination to create a story suitable for TV that is more than talking heads. Crowds of people create interest, but what if home-based businesspeople operating with zoning problems themselves are not willing to be recognized or to identify themselves? Why not have them board a bus in a remote location and arrive en masse at city hall wearing disguises—like a mustache, a bandana, or a mask of some sort? If people are not willing to do this, how about using mannequins, dolls, or even signs to indicate witnesses afraid to show their faces? Emphatically make the point that these zoning violators are among a community's most productive citizens who are aching to be able to pay city license taxes in exchange for their legitimacy.

Homeowners' Association Regulations

Sometimes homeowners' and condominium association regulations are included as covenants that run with the land and restrict homes in the area from being used for business purposes. A deed with this kind of restriction can preclude your working from home if challenged by the association. So to ensure your ability to work from home, find out about any such limitations before buying a new home. If one exists, determine whether it can be waived and have your waiver acted upon as a condition of your purchase.

State Laws

A number of states have Industrial Homework laws. These laws were generally passed in the late 1930s to protect women and children from abusive labor practices. The laws are concerned with people employed in manufacturing products, and sometimes certain home businesses are prohibited entirely. For example, some states, such as California, Illinois, Pennsylvania, and New Jersey, prohibit the preparation at home of food and drink for commercial purposes, as well as articles used in serving food and drink. Such prohibitions make catering businesses in which the food is prepared at a home kitchen against the law. Other items that often cannot be manufactured at home include drugs, poisons, bandages, toys, and dolls. Illinois forbids the manufacture of metal springs, while Massachusetts doesn't allow the manufacture of clothing, except for women's hosiery and hats. California says "no" to making clothing for children under the age of ten, as well as to making toys and dolls.

Aside from prohibiting the manufacture of particular items, states with Industrial Homework laws require a potential employer to get a permit for such work; require the workers to get certificates; and require that homeowners permit inspection of their homes. New York specifically excludes clerical work, such as typing, transcribing, and bookkeeping, from the requirements of its law. California has a law requiring talent agents to be licensed, but forbids granting a license if the business is to be conducted "in rooms used for living purposes." No doubt this was intended to curb exploitative "casting couch" situations. In all likelihood, these state laws should not affect you. To find out about such laws in your state, however, consult with your attorney, or if your state has an agency that helps small businesses, contact that agency.

Federal Laws

Under the Fair Labor Standards Act, the federal government requires companies engaged in interstate commerce to provide all employees working at home, including clerical personnel, with "homework handbooks" in which the employee must keep detailed records of hours worked. Some states, such as California and New Jersey, also require the use of homework handbooks by businesses not covered by federal law. Also under federal law, the U.S. Department of Labor may prohibit categories of homework, and, since the 1940s, it has banned the manufacture of women's apparel in workers' homes. The rationale for this ban is to protect workers against minimum-wage violations, abuses of child labor laws, and the harrowing conditions of sweatshops. The Wage and Hour Division of the Department of Labor enforces these regulations.

In addition, some occupations that can be based at home, such as investment advisers and firearm dealers, require federal licensing. Also, if you serve the public in your home office, as a professional practice would do, employ seven or more full- or part-time people, or are engaged in interstate commerce, the Americans with Disabilities Act applies to you.

States with Laws Regulating Home-Based Work

California	Ohio
Connecticut	Pennsylvania
Hawaii	Rhode Island
Illinois	Tennessee
Indiana	Texas
Maryland	Washington
Massachusetts	West Virginia
Michigan	Wisconsin
Missouri	
New Jersey	District of Columbia
New York	Puerto Rico

Business Permits, Registrations, and Licenses: What's Required?

Other than observing the ordinances, laws, and regulations governing business use of the home, operating a home business, on a full- or part-time basis, requires taking the same legal steps as operating a business anywhere else. The permits, registrations, and licenses vary greatly from locality to locality. They also depend on the nature of your business. So use the following checklist as a guide for identifying which legal steps you need to take. Then consult a lawyer or appropriate government agencies if you're not sure how these requirements apply to your business or locale.

Legal Checklist

Depending on your type of business and your state and local requirements you may need to:

Federal

- Obtain employer's ID number with Form SS-4, if you have employees, are a partnership, or are incorporated
- Obtain federal license if required by federal law

State

- Obtain any trademarks, copyrights, patents needed
- Incorporate, form limited-liability company, or file statement of partnership if not a sole proprietor
- Register business name (in some states)
- If needed, obtain seller's permit—also known as Certificate of Authority and Resale Certificate
- Obtain state trademark if needed and available
- Obtain any required state licenses

City Hall or County Courthouse

- Check your zoning
- Obtain a local business license
- Register business name if using a name other than your own or a variation of your name

Should You Incorporate Your Business?

A common question people ask when starting a business is "Do I need to incorporate?" Depending on whom you ask, you will get different answers. Even accountants and attorneys, the experts on this subject, disagree. As a single-person business, your choice is between a sole proprietorship or a corporation. If you're going into business with one or more other people, you can choose among a partnership, a corporation, and possibly a limited-liability company. There are other forms of business organization, but they would be less usual for a home-based business. These are limited partnerships, joint ventures, and professional corporations. In considering each of the main options, take into account:

- The cost in dollars and time to start and maintain each form of business organization
- Your business image and your ability to get work
- The risk to your personal assets and future earnings
- Your goals for the size of your business and whether you want the business to extend beyond your lifetime
- If you need or want financing, the ease of obtaining loans and investors
- How much government regulation you will experience
- How much taxes will cost you

The following section outlines the pros and cons of each of the major choices for a home business.

Sole Proprietorships

As a sole proprietor, you and the business are one and the same. You are the boss. What the business earns is your income; what you incur in business debts is money you owe. If you move to another city, the business moves. If you die, the business ends. Sole proprietorships are by far the most common form of small business, whether home-based or not, because sole proprietorships have a number of advantages. They cost the least amount of money to start because there are fewer legal filings and these usually do not involve drawing up legal documents. All this makes sole proprietorships the easiest type of business to start. It's also the easiest to discontinue and provides you with the greatest freedom from regulation.

However, sole proprietorships are limited to your lifetime, and you will have difficulty raising large amounts of money in the form of capital and loans. Your personal liability is unlimited, and so insuring yourself against at least the major risks of your type of business is vital.

Partnerships

Partnerships enable you to share the work and responsibility of a business with someone else. Parnerships cost less than corporations to form and, because there are few government regulations to contend with, they are also easy to start. Although informational tax returns are required of partnerships, they do not pay income taxes.

But there are some special risks involved in being in a partnership. First, you become legally responsible for the business actions of your partners, even for such things as damages should a partner become involved in an auto accident while doing business for the partnership. The second, the withdrawal or death of a partner, may end a business.

Anyone entering into a partnership should have an attorney draw up a partnership agreement first and obtain partnership insurance as soon as the agreement goes into effect. (For further details on insuring your business, see chapter 11.) These precautions are important because it's as difficult to find a truly suitable partner as it is to find a good mate. Because partners have difficulty sharing authority or have clashing values, partnerships terminate at an even greater rate than marriages, 50 percent of which end in divorce.

Even your best friend can be a disaster as a partner. That's what one person found. The now former friend and partner took charge of the partnership books. He subsequently withdrew most of the profits for himself and left his former friend having to pay taxes on money he never received! The partner discharged his debts by declaring bankruptcy. A partnership agreement did not but might have provided some protection for the wronged partner.

Limited Liability Companies

Originated to meet the legal and tax needs of large corporations engaged in joint ventures, Limited Liability Companies (LLCs) can be used by home-based businesses. To use an LLC, your state must have passed legislation authorizing them; so far, over thirty states have done so. A few states do not allow limited liability companies to be used for some professions and occupations.

Because many states require at least two members, a limited liability company is not a substitute for a sole proprietorship. On the other hand, many states allow corporations to be formed by only one person. An LLC is more like a partnership and can be used where a limited partnership or an "S" corporation won't work or is impractical. (An S corporation, like a partnership, pays no corporate income taxes. Earnings are passed on to shareholders in proportion to their ownership, which is advantageous if the individual tax rate is lower than the corporate tax rate.) For example, some states, like California, don't recognize Subchapter S corporations, which means that even though a corporation may pay no federal tax as an entity, it must fully pay state corporation taxes. The limited-liability company allows income and deductions, as in a partnership or an S corporation, to flow through to its members.

An LLC has the advantages of a corporation in limiting liability, although because of the newness of this form of business organization it's not established whether this protection would be recognized by courts in other states. As with a corporation, insurance is one's best protection against many kinds of losses. Unlike corporations that have unlimited duration, a limited-liability company generally dissolves upon the death or withdrawal of any member. A limited-liability company is formed by filing with the state "articles of organization" and is governed by an operating agreement that is comparable to a partnership agreement.

Corporations

The words *corporation* and *incorporated* suggest strength, stability, and reliability. For a small business, this may mean having an easier time getting the attention of prospective customers and investors. The appearance of substantiality that comes with being incorporated is why even con artists often cover up their schemes as corporations.

In the past, many small businesses used to incorporate in order to take advantage of tax benefits. However, since 1986 the tax advantages of being incorporated have lessened or disappeared. In fact, some corporate tax rates, particularly for personal service corporations, are higher than individual tax rates.

Forming a corporation may limit your liability if something goes wrong, but keep in mind that you are personally responsible for your own acts whether you are incorporated or not. Also most lenders will require the owners of corporations to execute personal guarantees for loans and mortgages. Being incorporated may protect you from personal liability for the acts of your employees. However, insurance is the only meaningful form of protection because if you are sued, whether you win or not, the high cost of defending yourself can put you out of business. Bear in mind, though, that becoming a corporation may raise your insurance costs.

A reason for incorporating that can overshadow all other considerations is preserving your self-employment status for tax purposes. If your work is such that you work for few clients during a year or are in an industry being targeted by the IRS for making employees out of independent contractors, a newer and better reason to incorporate yourself is to preserve your self-employment status and avoid being classified as a common-law employee by the Internal Revenue Service or a state revenue agency. Further, if you work for companies who fear working with you as an independent contractor might make them vulnerable to costly penalties and back taxes if you are reclassified as a common-law employee, your ability to market yourself may depend on being incorporated. Maintaining your status as an independent contractor is discussed in chapter 10.

Being employed by your corporation may enable you to obtain workers' compensation for yourself as a form of disability insurance. A corporation may have advantages for you for sheltering retirement benefits if your net income is high enough. It also offers better opportunities for raising capital if you choose to expand your business. Ownership can be more easily transferred. Because a corporation has a separate legal identity from your own, it can survive beyond your lifetime. If you are only using your home as a launching point for a company you plan to build into a much larger enterprise, it may cost much more to change an ongoing business into a corporation than it costs to incorporate at the outset of your operations. One other reason that prompts some to incorporate is that appearing to be employed, even though the employer is your own corporation, may make it easier to obtain credit or buy a home or a car.

On the other side of the ledger, corporations are much more expensive to start. They involve extensive paperwork and record keeping, are closely regulated, and may be subject to double taxation because some states do not recognize S corporations. This means you may be paying state corporate taxes as well as state and federal individual income taxes.

We believe that when all the factors are taken into consideration, most people—other than persons whose work places them in danger of being classified as common-law employees—are best advised to begin as a sole proprietorship. If you do decide to incorporate, we advise that you get the help of a lawyer experienced in small business start-ups.

Although we recommend getting advice on incorporating from an attorney or accountant, consider this—of the nation's 428,000 attorneys listed in Yellow Pages in the USA, 256,000 filed sole proprietorship returns and 126,000 were covered by partnership returns in 1991. This means that virtually nine out of ten attorneys are not covered by corporations. Accountants similarly choose sole proprietorships and partnerships as their form of business. It's fair to ask professionals advising you if they are incorporated and, if not, why not.

Finally, although it's relatively easy to set up a corporation with an incorporation kit (available in office-supply stores) or by using a service, it's even easier to make costly mistakes in attempting to make the legal and tax decisions involved in incorporating yourself. Companies that provide incorporation services are quite familiar with forming Delaware corporations but may not be so with the corporation laws of other states. Keep in mind before incorporating in Delaware that you will have to register as a foreign corporation in your own state and pay taxes both where you live and work, and in Delaware.

Trademarks

A way of protecting your business identity is with a trademark or service mark. A trademark is a distinctive word, name, symbol, or combination of these used to distinguish a product or service from those of competitors. Historically, trademarks were developed to indicate the origin and authenticity of products. A *service mark* is simply a trademark for services.

Anyone can, as intellectual property lawyer Gerry Elman says, "place a ™ or SM symbol next to any word, words, or logo that one regards as the trademark of his business. One doesn't need to get governmental permission. . . . It's just like staking your claim in the gold rush. But the next step in the gold rush is generally to go to the government office and register the claim one has staked out." Registration provides benefits that include being able to bring suit in a federal court without satisfying the usual jurisdictional requirements as well as the possibility of being awarded attorney's fees and treble damages. You can use the ™ or ˢᴹ symbol as soon as you adopt it, but you must wait to use the "circled R" until your mark is approved for federal registration.

Registering a trademark is different from registering a trade name. A trade name is used to identify a business and the laws and procedures are different. In some states, such as California, you cannot protect an unincorporated company name on a statewide basis, but you can protect a trademark. Trademarks can be registered either with the U.S. Patent and Trademark Office for nationwide protection or with your state government if state law permits.

In the past, you could only get a federal registration of your trademark if you were actually using it in interstate commerce. Now you only need to allege that you intend to use the mark in interstate or foreign commerce. A trademark registered with the federal government can use the "small R in a circle" as a notice that your mark is protected. An additional advantage of registration is that federal law makes it "incontestable" after five years, which does not happen with state trademarks.

For trademark information and applications, you can phone (703) 557-3158 or write the U.S. Patent and Trademark Office, Washington, DC 20231. You can also have questions answered by calling (703) 308-HELP. For copyright information, you can phone the Information Line at (202) 707-3000 or write Copyright Office, Library of Congress, Washington, DC 20559 and ask for General Information Packet Number 118. Patent applications may be obtained from the Superintendent of Documents, Government Printing Office, Washington, D.C. 20402; (202) 783-3238.

Why and When You Need Contracts

Contracts are the job descriptions and pay scales of the self-employed. When you work from home, they are your most important safeguards against problems with customers and clients, and they help ensure that you are taken seriously as a business. Take heed from stories like these.

Artist Mary Kennelsworth was employed by a greeting card company when she decided to do sideline free-lance work at home. Having been employed with an established organization, she didn't realize that potential customers might not take her small business seriously.

"Perhaps it was because I was new at this or because I met customers in the living room with my two-year-old crawling around the floor. Whatever the reason, I did some work for several customers who didn't pay me. When one saw the work I'd done, she told me it wasn't what she had in mind. Another person never even came to pick up the work. When I called him, he said they had decided to have it done by their printer."

Management consultant Eric Paine had a similar experience. "When I first began consulting, I was so eager to get some business I didn't even think about a contract. The company I was talking with wanted to explore what I could do for them, and I was eager to show them. At first, things went very well. I completed the work over a three-month period, during which they seemed satisfied.

"When I submitted the final report with my bill, however, they asked for a few revisions. I made the revisions and resubmitted my bill. I didn't hear anything from them for a couple of months, and when I called they told me they were still reviewing it and might want more revisions. Now it's six months later. I haven't gotten any money and they aren't returning my phone calls."

Certainly Mary and Eric are not without any recourse, but the amount of time and energy spent trying to collect or entering into a lawsuit may be so great that it's not worth the effort. Better to offset such possibilities up front by signing a contract before taking the work.

Whatever your business, be it selling knickknacks, catering, or computer programming, create a standard contract to use with your clients or customers. In it, spell out your business agreement with specifics such as what you will provide, when you will provide it, what it will cost, and when they will pay you.

Contracts can be verbal or written, but written ones are certainly preferable. Psychotherapist Greg Rohan has clients fill out and sign a basic client information form (name, address, phone number, and so on) and at the bottom is a payment contract that reads this way:

"I understand I am to pay for services at the time they are rendered unless I have made other arrangements, and agree to pay for appointments I do not cancel at least 24 hours in advance."

He reviews this statement verbally to be sure the person understands and agrees. Whenever he makes other financial arrangements with clients, he writes these agreements on the form before they sign it. He attributes never having problems with collecting fees to this procedure.

Barbara Bickford has a printed order form that she uses for her word-processing services. On the form she lists the services ordered, the charge for each service, and the date and time she will have it to the customer. She has customers sign the order to confirm their agreement to all these items. Then, unless a company has previously established credit with her, she gets a 50 percent deposit on the work to be done.

Eric Paine now uses a "letter of agreement" for his management-consulting contracts. He meets with his clients to work out the specifics of the consulting he will do and afterward sends them a detailed letter indicating everything they agreed to in the meeting. He sends two copies and asks that one be signed and returned to him.

The best way to develop contract agreements that are customized to your needs is to consult a lawyer. You can also talk with colleagues about the contracts they use, ask your professional or trade association for information, or attend a workshop on contracting. Pro forma contracts are now available on computer software.

Sometimes your clients or suppliers will offer you a contract. When this happens, review the terms carefully. Ask questions about provisions you do not understand. The contract should cover all important points you have discussed. Contract terms must be correct as well as clear and specific; ambiguous language can lead to conflict later on. Usually these contracts are presented as a "standard form," so they appear to be unchangeable. Actually, a contract is always negotiable. Read the fine print and feel free to write in modifications. And bear in mind that any handwritten modifications need to be signed or initialed by both parties.

In most cases, we suggest having a lawyer look over the contracts you negotiate at first. Later, you may feel familiar enough with the way contracts are written to make informed changes on your own.

Selecting a Lawyer

Some people only go to the dentist when they're in agony with a toothache. Then, too often they're faced with extensive, expensive, and time-consuming dental work. So it is with going to a lawyer. In either case, the better approach is to go in for periodic checkups and avoid developing emergencies.

You can call on a lawyer to:

- Help you decide upon and set up the form of business you want to establish (a sole proprietorship, partnership, or corporation).
- Advise you on regulations affecting your business and assist you in filing for necessary licenses, permits, and registrations.
- Advise you on insurance you need and refer you to a good agent.
- Review contracts and other legal documents.
- Help you with collection problems. Sometimes a letter on a lawyer's letterhead is enough to get payment from a debtor.
- Provide you with advice and help you take action to avoid lawsuits.
- Represent you in unavoidable lawsuits.

Whether you need a lawyer right now or not, find one you can trust who understands your business situation. You may actually consult your lawyer infrequently, but when those times come, you'll be a step ahead if that person already knows you and your business.

The best way to find a lawyer is through referrals from others with businesses like yours. If you don't already know such business owners, contact them through professional and trade associations or the Chamber of Commerce. Then talk with the lawyers you've been referred to. Tell them about your business situation and select the lawyer you feel best understands and reflects your business interests.

You can now obtain legal services through prepaid legal plans that cater to businesses. For an annual fee, usually around $200, you may get unlimited telephone consultation with an attorney, the writing of collection letters and letters to government agencies on your behalf, review of contracts and other documents, and provision of partnership agreements and articles of incorporation, all at no additional charge. For more involved legal matters, you can obtain legal representation at greatly reduced rates.

Once you've selected a lawyer, think of that person as an essential part of your business team. Get professional advice to avoid legal problems, just as you would call on an accountant to avoid an audit. Law, like taxes and insurance, is an area where you can use experts to help you keep your business on track.

Resources

Books

American Jurisprudence Pleading and Practice Forms Annotated, published by the Bancroft Whitney imprint of Lawyers Co-op Publishing Company, is a set of books containing thousands of forms. It is updated with pocket supplements and can be found in law libraries. Law libraries are usually located in courthouses. There you will find many other books of forms and documents, some localized and some for legal specialities.

The Contract & Fee-Setting Guide for Consultants & Professionals. Howard L. Shenson. New York: Wiley, 1990.

Forming Corporations and Partnerships. John C. Howell. Blue Ridge Summit, Pa.: Liberty Hall Press, 1991.

Getting Business to Come to You. Paul and Sarah Edwards and Laura Clampitt Douglas. New York: Tarcher/Perigee, 1991 (pages 59–64). This book contains our material on selecting and protecting a business name.

Inc. Yourself. Judith H. McGowan. New York: HarperCollins, 1992.

Nolo Press publishes a line of self-help legal books that are also used by lawyers and judges. Among the titles they publish are: *Everybody's Guide to Small Claims Court, How to Form a Nonprofit Corporation, Patent It Yourself, The Partnership Book,* and *Simple Contracts for Personal Use.* Most of these books are written for national readerships; others for specific states such as California, Florida, New York and Texas. For a free catalog, write Nolo Press, 950 Parker Street, Berkeley, CA 94710; (510) 549-1976. (800) 992-6656.

Small Claims Court, Making Your Way Through the System: A Step-by-Step Guide. Therasa Meeham Rudy, HALT, 1319 F Street NW, Washington, DC 20004; (202) 347-9600.

How to Name a Business and Service. Stephen Elias, Kate McGrath. Berkeley, Calif.: Nolo Press, 1992.

Software

It's Legal (DOS). Parsons Technologies, One Parsons Drive, Hiawatha, IA 52233; (319) 395-9626, (800) 223-6925. Uses an interactive approach to developing documents.

The Desktop Lawyer (DOS and Macintosh). The Open University, P.O. Box 1511, Orlando, FL 32802; (800) 874-0388.

Other Forms of Legal Help

Tele-Lawyer provides advice about small business and consumer matters by phone. You can call a "900" number, use a charge card, or pay by check in advance. In some cases, they make referrals to local low-cost providers of legal help; (800) 835-3529.

Caldwell Legal, USA. P.O. Box 245778, Sacramento, CA 95824; (800) 222-3035. Provides a prepaid legal plan for businesses for $240 a year. Caldwell also has affiliates in British Columbia, Manitoba, and Ontario.

On-line services including *America Online*, *CompuServe*, and the *Internet* have legal forums and resources. While attorneys will not give specific legal advice, the conversation and documents, such as full texts of Supreme Court cases, can be valuable.

CHAPTER
TEN
■■■■■■■■■■■■■■■■■■■■■■■■■■■

Claiming Your Tax Benefits

When you become self-employed, your experience as a taxpayer changes dramatically. As one person reflected, "My biggest shortcoming was in not researching my tax situation. I was totally unprepared for the responsibility of shepherding part of my income to the IRS. Consequently . . . I worried all my hair out."

Whether taxes cost you your hair or turn your hair gray, or you experience delight in leading a more tax-deductible lifestyle as you see formerly nondeductible parts of your cost of living become tax deductions depends on your getting the information you require and acting on it. This chapter will guide you through the primary issues you will need to become aware of as a self-employed person—the benefits, the requirements, and the traps.

At times, we do not present the conventional views you may hear or read, and we advise you to find a tax counsel who truly knows this area of tax law. Some do not. We will provide you with citations for the unconventional information that you may be told is wrong. With this, you can check a tax professional's knowledge or his or her willingness to learn.

Our intent in this chapter is not to make you a tax expert, but to let you know in general what you're entitled to under the law, so that you neither overlook items you should be deducting nor exaggerate your deductions recklessly—in other words, so that you operate from a smart, realistic middle ground.

First, let's consider the tax benefits of working from home. Fundamentally the tax system of the United States recognizes what President Calvin Coolidge said in 1925: "The business of America is business." To be certain, hungry for tax revenue, Congress is eliminating business deductions. Beginning in 1994, the meal and entertainment deduction was reduced to 50 percent; club dues (including airline, athletic, and country clubs), even though you are a member only because of business and use the club only for business, are gone; and the share of the dues you pay a professional or trade association that is used for lobbying is not deductible (and it's up to the association to notify you of what percentage of your dues goes to lobbying).

Nevertheless, business deductions continue. You need to take full advantage of them in order to help offset lost fringe benefits such as health insurance, pension plan, sick leave, and vacations. These are worth between 25 percent to 50 percent of employee wages. That means that if you were earning $30,000 a year as a salaried worker, your fringe benefits were worth between $7,500 and $15,000. You will learn in this chapter that you not only can take many deductions but why you *should* take everything to which you are entitled.

Second, many people struggling to make it on their own, after having been disposed of by downsizing corporations, are directly hurt by the tax policies of government. Over a hundred thousand individuals each year have their business deductions taken away from them by being classified "common-law employees." The Supreme Court of the United States also dealt home-based businesses a painful blow in the *Commissioner of Internal Revenue v. Soliman* case, by interpreting the law so that it took away the home-office deduction from hundreds of thousands of people who work *from* home rather than *at* home. Consider this: If the same standard applied to home-based businesses in the Soliman case were to apply to all businesses, every business that principally serves its public away from its headquarters—taxi companies, ambulance companies, locksmiths, installers of all kinds, mobile everything—would not be able to deduct their offices, garages, storefronts, and warehouses!

You will read things that will make you angry; they make us angry, but they reflect the forces that have an impact upon us. What we can do is treat our tax lives as Judge Learned Hand wrote was expected of us: "Anyone may arrange his affairs so that his taxes shall be as low as possible. He is not bound to choose that pattern which best pays the treasury. There is not even a patriotic duty to increase one's taxes. . . . Nobody owes any public duty to pay more than the law demands; taxes are enforced exactions, not voluntary contributions."

In general, the deductions you can claim when working from home fall into one of two categories: *home-office expenses* and *ordinary business expenses*. You can claim ordinary business expenses whether your office is in a downtown building, a suburban storefront, or in your home. Since the primary tax advantage the home-based worker has over other taxpayers is home-office deductions, let's turn first to how you can qualify for these deductions.

Meeting IRS Criteria for a Home-Office Deduction

As long as you meet the necessary criteria, whether you live and work in a house, an apartment, a condominium, a cooperative, a mobile home, or even a boat, you can deduct the cost of operating and maintaining the part of your home that you use for business. The Internal Revenue Service has two basic criteria your home office must meet in order to qualify as a tax write-off. The first is that *the portion of your home you wish to claim as a business expense must be used exclusively and regularly for business.*

Exclusive Use

"Exclusive use" means that the portion of your home you're claiming as a deduction is used only for business. Your home office may be an entire room you have given over to that purpose or it may be simply an alcove in your living room or a breakfast nook off your kitchen (one, however, that is not used for dining). It need not be separated from the room by a partition, but it must be a separately identifiable space. So for tax purposes, think of your home office— your business space—as an entity separate from the part of your home given over to personal use.

If people must pass through your business area on the way to another room, does your home office fail to meet the exclusive use test? No, according to the case of *Hughes, Jr. v. Commissioner* (T.C. Memo 1981–301).

Currently there are two exceptions to the exclusive-use rule. You may take a deduction for space used to store inventory and for space used as a day-care facility.

As for the first exception, if you're in direct sales of cosmetics, gift baskets, health products, or household cleaning products, for example, and meet the following criteria, you can take a deduction on space used for inventory, even if that space, in a laundry room or basement, for example, is also used for nonbusiness purposes:

- Your business must involve wholesale or retail sale of products.
- The inventory must be kept for use in your business.
- Your home must be the only fixed location of your business.
- You must use the storage space on a regular basis.
- The space you use must be separately identifiable as space suitable for storage.

As for the second exception, if you operate a licensed day-care facility in your living room, you are not excluded from claiming your living room because you also use it in the evening when the children have gone home. You calculate your deduction on the basis of the percentages of both space and time the room is used for day care.

Regular Use

"Regular use" refers to using the business segment of your home on a continuing basis. Let's say you have space set up as a photo lab in a bedroom and you use it exclusively for that purpose once every several months. This would be what the IRS calls "incidental or occasional use" and would not qualify you to take a home-office deduction.

Whereas the exclusive-use test is strict in not allowing mixing personal and business use in a space used for an office—such as its serving as an occasional bedroom for visitors if you have a roll-away bed or having computer games on your computer—the few court cases on "regular use" suggest that the regular-use test is more flexible.

Possible Deductible Home-Office Expenses

- Cleaning a home office
- Condominium association fees
- Household furniture converted to use in the home office
- Household supplies used in the business space
- Mortgage interest (partial)
- Real estate taxes (partial)
- Repair and maintenance of office portion of home
- Security system
- Telephone line used exclusively for business if it is a second telephone line. The basic local service for a first line, including taxes, is not deductible; however, business long-distance calls on the personal line are deductible and services added for business use like call waiting may be deductible.
- Trash collection
- Utilities attributable to business use of home (electricity, gas)

The second criteria your home office must meet in order to qualify as a tax write-off is that *the portion of your home you use exclusively and regularly for business must be either your principal place of business or a place where you meet with customers or clients in the normal course of business.*

Principal Place of Business

After years of conflicting Tax Court and appeals-court decisions, the Supreme Court ruled in January 1993 that for a home office to qualify as a principal place of business, it must be the place where the most important functions of the business are performed. This means where the revenue is generated. In Publication 587, the Internal Revenue Service uses two examples of sales-people: one who makes most of his sales by phone or mail from his home office; the other who spends most of his time with his customers and makes his sales at their offices. The IRS says the first salesperson's home office meets the principal-place-of-business qualification, but the second salesperson's does not.

The Supreme Court also ruled that if it's not clear where the important activities that lead to delivering goods and services take place, then the amounts of time spent in the home office and elsewhere are to be compared, but if it's still not clear where the principal place of business is, the presumption is that the home office does not qualify for a deduction.

Since surveys indicate that four out of five home-based businesses do most of their income-producing work outside their home office, millions of people who have no other office other than their home cannot take a deduction for the cost of having an office. Bills are pending in Congress as we write this to reverse this unfair ruling.

What kind of businesses are likely no longer to qualify for home-office deductions? Presumably disqualified are such popular home-based businesses as auditing services, all kinds of construction work, catering, cleaning services, mobile disk jockeys, errand services, home inspection, interior decorators, makeup artists, meeting and wedding planners, pet sitters, photographers, private investigators, professional organizers, real estate appraisers and salespeople, professional speakers and trainers, as well as many consultants and anyone whose business is based on a truck.

While the Soliman case was about an anesthesiologist with a six-figure income taking a $5,000 home office deduction (it takes that kind of salary to be able to afford to take a case to the Supreme Court), most home businesses can ill afford to lose this deduction. After the Soliman case, some tax professionals and office equipment industry executives said this deduction was not worth much. Is that so? A typical American home averages about 1,600 square feet, is worth $110,000 and, including utilities, insurance, repairs, and property taxes, costs a homeowner about $10,000 a year. A 200-square-foot bedroom (12.5% of the home) used for a home office will result in about a $1,600 home-office deduction, including depreciation. Figuring that our typical homeowner is just getting started and is only in a 15 percent income tax bracket, combined with paying less in self-employment taxes, the home office deduction is worth about $500 a year. Five hundred dollars will pay for a month or two of health insurance, buy a low-cost laser printer, or enable our home-based businessperson to make a modest investment in marketing to get more business. And for many people who spend more on housing or are in a higher tax bracket, the home-office deduction is worth more each year. Renters particularly benefit because, unlike homeowners, who can deduct mortgage interest and property taxes on Schedule A, renters get no such deductions.

There are reasons beyond the dollar savings for taking your home-office deduction. These are:

■ You need to take the home-office deduction in order to begin deducting business mileage on your vehicle as soon as you leave home; otherwise, the mileage deduction doesn't start until you reach your first business location.

■ If you qualify to take a home-office deduction, you do not need to keep a log of your use of your computer if you use it only for business. In fact, using it for nonbusiness purposes risks having your home-office deduction disallowed because that would violate the exclusive-use test. Without the home-office deduction, the computer is considered "listed property," and to deduct it and other equipment, you must answer the question on the back of Form 4562 that asks "Do you have evidence to support the business use/investment claimed?" Answering this "yes" means you need to have kept a log of the business and personal use of your computer.

■ If you qualify to take a home-office deduction and fail to take it, thereby overstating your income for self-employment tax purposes, you are subject to penalties (Revenue Rulings 56–407, 57–538 and 79–396). The idea is that the government does not want you qualifying for higher Social Security benefits than you are entitled to. So unless you claim all allowable deductions in figuring net earnings from self-employment, you may be penalized.

■ When you go to sell your home, you will be responsible for paying tax on the portion of your gain relative to the amount of your home used for business, whether you took the home office tax deduction or not. As stated by IRS

Publication 587, "If you used any part of your home for business, you must adjust the basis of your home for any depreciation you were allowed for its business, even if you did not claim it." If you think about it, if you do not take the home-office deduction, you are paying taxes on the same money twice—once when you don't take the deduction and then again when you sell your home. However, you can usually postpone paying tax on the gain, which we will discuss below.

But is taking the home-office deduction worth the risk of being audited? Many tax advisers advise not taking the home-office deduction for this reason. Taking a home-office deduction does increase one's chances of being audited, but the truth is IRS targets self-employed people anyway. This is because the self-employed are one of the largest groups of nonfilers. In short, you do yourself no favors when you don't take the home-office deduction if you are entitled to it.

What can you do to help prove your home is where you generate most of your income? Have a separate business telephone number, have a sign at your mailbox or door, have clients or customers regularly come to your office, keep a log or have them sign a "guest book," use your home address on your business card, and receive mail there. Be careful the steps you take to prove you have a home office do not conflict with your zoning or homeowner association rules.

A Place for Meeting

Even if your home office is not your *principal* place of business, you are also entitled to deduct home-office expenses if in the normal course of your work you see clients, patients, or customers face-to-face at home. Lawyers, doctors, psychotherapists, and management consultants are examples of people who might maintain outside offices yet also see clients at home. The space used for meeting clients, not for doing paperwork or other activities, is deductible.

Here's another exception. If your home isn't your principal place of business, but you have on your property a separate freestanding structure—a barn, a greenhouse, a workshop, a studio, a detached garage, a cabana, or anything physically detached from your home—and it is used exclusively and regularly for business, you can claim the home-office deduction for the use of that space. If a literary agent has a downtown office where she does most of her business, but has converted a guest house on her property into an office where she works every Monday and Friday, she will be able to take the deduction for her home-office space.

Deducting Home-Office Expenses

When you qualify for a home-office deduction, you can deduct a variety of expenses in addition to your regular business expenses.

Direct expenses for the business portion of your home—such as painting your office or fixing a leak in it—are fully deductible. But you should be aware that the IRS makes a distinction between capital improvements (like adding a room that you use for business, installing customized cabinets in your home

Figure 10-1.

office, or designing space for your computer) and repairs that you'd make in the normal course of maintenance (like fixing a broken window or repainting your office). Repairs are deductible. Capital improvements, however, are depreciated, which means that the deduction must be spread over a period of several years.

Indirect expenses related to the entire home—such as mortgage payments, insurance, utility bills, exterior painting, roof repair, depreciation—are deductible in part. To calculate the part of these expenses you can deduct, divide the square footage of your office space by the total square footage of your home. Thus, if the office measures two hundred square feet and the whole home measures sixteen hundred square feet, your office takes up 12.5 percent of the total space and you can deduct 12.5 percent of your indirect expenses.

(Alternatively, if the rooms in your home are about the same size, you can calculate the deductible portion by dividing the number of rooms used for business by the total number of rooms in your home.) It's a good idea to draw up a floor plan of your home to indicate the portion used for your home office. This will provide documentation of your use of a portion of your home for business even if you no longer live in it when you need the verification.

The amount of home-office expenses you deduct cannot exceed the amount of gross income you've earned from your work at home. So to ensure that you will not be using a home-office deduction to offset the income you've earned from a business, you must calculate the deduction in a particular sequence of steps. This makes the calculation somewhat complicated, but IRS Publication 587 entitled *Business Use of Your Home*, which comes out each year, contains instructions, a worksheet, examples, explanations, and references to other IRS publications for calculating your deduction. If you complete your own tax return, we recommend that before filing you show the result to a tax specialist at least the first time you claim a home-office deduction. Figure 10-2 is an example of a completed Form 8829, using the typical data used in this chapter. Form 8829 must be used by people who report their business income using a Schedule C.

Note that *the home-office deduction can be used to bring the taxes on what you earn at home to zero, but it can't be used as a loss to reduce taxes on the income you earn at a full-time job or from other sources. However, you can carry forward to future years the home-office expenses you were not able to deduct.*

Traps and Pitfalls

◼ If you use your home office for more than one business or business purpose, failure to meet the qualifications for all businesses will disqualify the entire deduction. For example, if you have two businesses, one that meets the Soliman test as a principal place of business and another that does not, the home office loses its deductibility if this is revealed to the IRS.

◼ If you incorporate your business, you lose the home-office deduction. However, Doug Perreault, a Tampa, Florida, CPA, says it is an unsettled "question whether IRC Sec. 280A(c)(6) allows one to have one's corporation reimburse actual costs of the home office. . . . Rent is normally a fixed monthly amount whereas a reimbursement fluctuates from month to month depending on the actual amount."

◼ Finally, if you own your own home and are entitled to a home-office deduction, consider this pitfall. Suppose you paid $80,000 for your home and now plan to sell it for $120,000. Generally, if you purchase another home that costs $120,000 or more, the $40,000 increase in value will not be taxed if you "roll over" your money by buying and occupying the new home within twenty-four months. But let's say you have been entitled to a home-office deduction of 20 percent. When you sell your house, you will need to pay a tax on 20 percent of the increase in value (on $8,000) unless you disqualify your home-office deduction in the year of sale. You can disqualify it by making the use of the room nonexclusive. But be careful. You need to disqualify it by doing more than putting a personal item like a TV set in the office. The IRS has disallowed only the square footage occupied by the personal item, insisting that the rest of the room is still an office, and charged income tax on the portion of the gain attributable to the remainder of the home office. If you think this is inconsistent with the exclusive-use test, you're right.

What do you need to do to truly disqualify your home office? You might completely convert the room to nonoffice use or rent space elsewhere for your office, such as in a professional suite. The process of rolling over the gain can then be continued until you move to a less-expensive home, into rental housing, in with relatives or to a nursing home. Then the tax on the gain must be paid.

If you are fifty-five or older, you are eligible to exclude from your taxable income up to $125,000 of profit you get from the sale of a home you have lived in for three of the last five years. You can do this only once. If you have a home office and want to take full advantage of this deduction, you need to disqualify your use of a home office two years before the year you sell your residence.

Form **8829**	**Expenses for Business Use of Your Home**	OMB No. 1545-1266
Department of the Treasury Internal Revenue Service (5)	▶ File only with Schedule C (Form 1040). Use a separate Form 8829 for each home you used for business during the year. ▶ See separate instructions.	**19**93 Attachment Sequence No. **66**

Name(s) of proprietor(s) *Kelly Martin*	Your social security number 123 45 6789

Part I   Part of Your Home Used for Business

1	Area used regularly and exclusively for business, regularly for day care, or for inventory storage. See instructions	1	*200*
2	Total area of home	2	*1,600*
3	Divide line 1 by line 2. Enter the result as a percentage	3	*12.5* %
	• For day-care facilities not used exclusively for business, also complete lines 4–6.		
	• All others, skip lines 4–6 and enter the amount from line 3 on line 7.		
4	Multiply days used for day care during year by hours used per day . **4** hr.		
5	Total hours available for use during the year (365 days × 24 hours). See instructions **5** 8,760 hr.		
6	Divide line 4 by line 5. Enter the result as a decimal amount **6** .		
7	Business percentage. For day-care facilities not used exclusively for business, multiply line 6 by line 3 (enter the result as a percentage). All others, enter the amount from line 3 ▶	7	*12.5* %

Part II   Figure Your Allowable Deduction

		(a) Direct expenses	(b) Indirect expenses		
8	Enter the amount from Schedule C, line 29, **plus** any net gain or (loss) derived from the business use of your home and shown on Schedule D or Form 4797. If more than one place of business, see instructions			8	*30,000*
	See instructions for columns (a) and (b) before completing lines 9–20.				
9	Casualty losses. See instructions **9**				
10	Deductible mortgage interest. See instructions . **10**		*6,000*		
11	Real estate taxes. See instructions . **11**		*1,300*		
12	Add lines 9, 10, and 11. **12**		*7,300*		
13	Multiply line 12, column (b) by line 7 **13**		*913*		
14	Add line 12, column (a) and line 13.			14	*913*
15	Subtract line 14 from line 8. If zero or less, enter -0- .			15	
16	Excess mortgage interest. See instructions . . **16**				
17	Insurance . **17**		*500*		
18	Repairs and maintenance . **18**	*400*	*1400*		
19	Utilities . **19**		*1,800*		
20	Other expenses. See instructions . **20**		*1,200*		
21	Add lines 16 through 20 **21**		*4,900*		
22	Multiply line 21, column (b) by line 7 **22**		*613*		
23	Carryover of operating expenses from 1992 Form 8829, line 41 . . **23**				
24	Add line 21 in column (a), line 22, and line 23			24	*1,013*
25	Allowable operating expenses. Enter the **smaller** of line 15 or line 24			25	*1,013*
26	Limit on excess casualty losses and depreciation. Subtract line 25 from line 15 .			26	*28,074*
27	Excess casualty losses. See instructions . **27**				
28	Depreciation of your home from Part III below . **28**		*260*		
29	Carryover of excess casualty losses and depreciation from 1992 Form 8829, line 42 **29**				
30	Add lines 27 through 29			30	*260*
31	Allowable excess casualty losses and depreciation. Enter the **smaller** of line 26 or line 30 .			31	*260*
32	Add lines 14, 25, and 31			32	*2,186*
33	Casualty loss portion, if any, from lines 14 and 31. Carry amount to **Form 4684**, Section B .			33	
34	Allowable expenses for business use of your home. Subtract line 33 from line 32. Enter here and on Schedule C, line 30. If your home was used for more than one business, see instructions ▶			34	*2,186*

Part III   Depreciation of Your Home

35	Enter the **smaller** of your home's adjusted basis or its fair market value. See instructions . .	35	*110,000*
36	Value of land included on line 35	36	*30,000*
37	Basis of building. Subtract line 36 from line 35 .	37	*80,000*
38	Business basis of building. Multiply line 37 by line 7 .	38	*10,000*
39	Depreciation percentage. See instructions	39	*2.6* %
40	Depreciation allowable. Multiply line 38 by line 39. Enter here and on line 28 above. See instructions	40	*260*

Part IV   Carryover of Unallowed Expenses to 1994

41	Operating expenses. Subtract line 25 from line 24. If less than zero, enter -0-	41	
42	Excess casualty losses and depreciation. Subtract line 31 from line 30. If less than zero, enter -0- .	42	

For Paperwork Reduction Act Notice, see page 1 of separate instructions.   Cat. No. 13232M   Form **8829** (1993)

Figure 10-2.

The Home-Office Deduction for Salaried and Commissioned Employees

If you are a salaried or commissioned employee of someone else but work from home, you may still be eligible for the home-office deduction. An employee's home-office expenses, like other unreimbursed employee business expenses, are deductible only to the extent that they exceed 2 percent of adjusted gross income. Like anyone claiming a home-office deduction, you must meet the exclusive- and regular-use tests, and your home must be your principal place of business or a client meeting place. In addition, however, the *business use of your home must be required and expected by your employer.* Using your home must be *for your employer's convenience.* To support this claim, get a statement in writing to this effect from your employer.

What does this mean in practical terms? A concert musician needs a practice room thirty hours a week but, because the orchestra does not provide a space for individual practice, he uses a room at home as a studio. The studio qualifies for a home-office deduction. If, on the other hand, you merely take your briefcase home at night and do some work in the evenings, you are not entitled to the deduction.

Deducting Ordinary Business Expenses

Ordinary business deductions include expenses that are necessary for the operation of your business but are not included in the home-office deductions described above. If you are a salaried employee, these are expenses required for your employment but not reimbursed by your employer.

Now let's discuss such business expenses in more detail.

Everyday Expenses

The most common types of expenditures are items or services used in the day-to-day course of your work: the telephone, office supplies, postage and shipping costs, printing and duplicating expenses, advertising and promotion charges, fees for professional services. Not all deductible expenses are quite this obvious, however. A fashion consultant who subscribes to *Vogue* or a painter who buys books on art history can deduct these expenses because it's allowable to deduct the cost of books, magazines, and newspapers related to your work. Furthermore:

If you're a dance instructor, you can deduct the records and tapes you use for your classes.

If you're a psychotherapist, the cost of any personal-growth seminars you attend in order to evaluate their suitability for your clients is deductible. (So are the facial tissues your clients use.)

To a caterer, cookbooks are a business expense.

If you're a restaurant critic, your meals out are deductible.

If you hold sales meetings at your home, the coffee you serve—and the paper cups—are write-offs.

A color or wardrobe consultant can deduct the cost of mirrors in the office.

If you're a journalist, you can deduct the daily newspaper.

A swimming teacher giving lessons at home can claim a portion of the pool expenses.

If you are a professional speaker, you can deduct your audio and video equipment.

Ordinary Business Expenses

Accounting and bookkeeping fees
Advertising expenses used for prizes and contests
Attorney fees
Automobile expenses including
—Auto club membership
—Garage rental
—Loss on sale of auto
Bad debts
Bank service charges
Bankruptcy
Books and periodicals related to business
Business conventions including those on a cruise ship
Business meals (50%)
Capital expenditures (Section 179, Internal Revenue Code)
Career counseling costs
Commissions paid to agents and sales reps
Consultant fees paid to reduce cost of business
Copyright costs
Depreciation
Dues for professional and trade associations
Education expenses for maintaining or improving required skills
Electronic mail services
Financial counseling fees
Furniture and equipment (office)
Gifts (business), but limited to $25 per recipient per year

Health insurance*
Insurance expenses (including portion of homeowners')
Interest on trade or business debts
Legal fees
License fees and taxes
Messenger services
Office furniture and equipment
Office supplies
On-line services used for business
Operating losses in a prior year
Organization expenses of corporation (amortizable over not less than 60 months)
Passport fee for a business trip
Pension/retirement plan contributions
Postage and shipping
Printing and duplicating
Professional association dues
Professional books and journals
Repair and maintenance of business property
Social Security taxes (50%)
Start-up expenses (amortized over 60 months)
Tax preparation of business tax return
Taxes, state and local taxes on business
Theft losses of business property
Travel expenses

* Expired 12/31/93 but may be renewed or covered in health insurance reform legislation

In fact, an entertainment-industry musician can deduct the cost of going to movies, subscribing to cable television, buying records, and attending entertainment-industry seminars. These are all research-related expenses that enable such a musician to keep abreast of the profession and get ideas for future work.

Travel

Whenever you leave home to meet with business contacts, do work-related research at the library, buy office supplies or postage, negotiate a contract, or attend a work-related class or meeting, you are making a business trip. If you happen to stop at the dry cleaner or grocery store en route, the entire trip still counts as business. You will, however, need to keep a log of your business and nonbusiness travel if you also use your car for trips that are just personal.

If you use public transportation such as buses, subways, or taxis (a taxi driver will give you a receipt if asked), record the date, destination, cost, and purpose of each trip in a travel diary. If you mainly travel in your own vehicle, log all business-related mileage. Then deduct the cost in miles (in 1994, the IRS is allowing 29 cents per mile, plus parking and toll fees).

The alternative is to calculate what percentage of your overall car use is devoted to business, and take that percentage of your total automobile expenses (including gasoline, repairs, maintenance, insurance, and depreciation) as your deduction.

Entertainment

Home-based workers can deduct not only restaurant meals, drinks, and tickets to events such as concerts and plays—but also expenses incurred while entertaining business associates at home, such as wages for hired help, the cost of flowers, and the cost of food and drink. However, this deduction is limited to 50 percent of their cost, and there are strict rules for deducting business meals, such as the requirement that the business discussion be directly preceding, during, or directly following consuming the meal or beverage. Besides these typical entertainment expenses, business gifts are also deductible, up to $25 per business associate, the limit since 1962.

The IRS will disallow any expense that you can't substantiate, however, so be sure to keep receipts as well as a record of people in attendance at each event, their business relationship to you, a summary of the business discussion of the event, and the date. In other words, saving a credit card receipt from a restaurant is not enough; you must fill out the reverse side with the names of the people you entertained and a summary of the business discussion, in order for the IRS to accept it as a deduction.

Business Property: To Deduct or Depreciate?

When it comes to the way tax law deals with business property, we're in the arena of depreciation and capital-expense deductions. These are terms of confusion to many people who are innocent of our labyrinthine tax system. Our purpose in the next few paragraphs is to help you think about these things so you can take maximum advantage of them.

If furniture in your home office and the equipment you use in the course of your work can be used for three years or more, you can depreciate the property. To depreciate means that rather than deducting the entire cost of your new printing equipment in a single tax year, you spread the deduction over the life of the equipment. You can also take furniture that was previously for personal use, put it to use in the business portion of your home, and depreciate it.

The decision to depreciate is a strategic one. Suppose you spend $1,500 on a laser printer for your business. If you buy it in a year when your earnings are high, you may want to take the large deduction all at once in order to bring your taxable-income level down. If, on the other hand, you have a year when your earnings are low, you might be better off spreading out the deduction over a period of years. (The IRS, by the way, has guidelines for the amount of time over which you depreciate particular kinds of property.) Also consider that because depreciation expenses lower your gross income, they may lower the amount of self-employment tax you pay too.

Because a computer may be the most expensive item of business equipment you buy, we'll use it as an example of how to deduct business property costing more than $100.

If you use your computer more than 50 percent of the time for business, you have two options for deducting the cost of your computer. You can deduct the cost in the year you purchase the computer, as a Section 179 capital expense, or you can depreciate it over five years. You are allowed up to $17,500 as a Section 179 capital-expense deduction. If you spend more than the maximum amount eligible for a capital-expense deduction, the excess amount can be depreciated. But the amount of property that can be taken as a capital expense cannot exceed the taxable income from a business. In other words, you cannot offset income from a job or other source using the capital-expense deduction.

Your other option is to depreciate your computer. You can use the Modified Accelerated Cost Recovery System (MACRS). Or you can use straight-line depreciation. This method spreads out the time you depreciate your equipment. Automobiles and light trucks must be depreciated over five years and stringent limits are placed on automobile deductions each year.

A word of caution is in order here. If you use your equipment partly for business and partly for personal reasons, you will need to substantiate your deduction with adequate records proving business usage.

Rent, Lease, or Buy?

Virtually anything you can buy today can also be rented or leased. Your choice is a business decision of which the tax consequences may be less important than other considerations. For instance, does leasing enable you to obtain equipment you could not afford to buy? Because leasing is normally equivalent to 100 percent financing, does it let you have more money on hand for working capital? Does leasing allow you to pay for equipment or other items out of your earnings rather than using your savings or a home-equity loan? Of course, you must qualify for a lease, which means you must have good credit, though probably not as flawless for leasing office equipment and furniture as is needed to lease a car. As a general rule, you will need to have been in business for at least a year.

In terms of taxes, when you rent on a daily, weekly, or monthly basis, you are incurring an ordinary business expense; whereas a purchase is subject to being depreciated or, if it qualifies, being a Section 179 capital expense deduction. Because Congress and the IRS are constantly revising the tax code, we suggest you consult with your tax specialist before making a decision about leasing.

A lease can be another name for a rental, in which case it's called an operating lease. It can also be a way to finance a purchase, in which case it's called a capital or finance lease. Ownership remains in the name of a third party (usually a leasing corporation) for the term of the lease. A thousand dollars is the minimum fair market value—the equivalent of the purchase price—for most capital or finance leases. At the end, you can purchase the leased item for an agreed-upon percentage of the purchase price. From then on, it's yours.

How much that agreed-upon percentage is will determine the tax treatment you get. If you only pay 1 percent or 2 percent, it will be considered by the IRS as a purchase, and you need to either take it as a Section 179 capital expense deduction or depreciate it. If you pay 10 percent or more—21 percent to be safe—you should be able to deduct your lease payments as ordinary business expenses.

Leasing has a cash advantage over a purchase on credit because a lease usually requires little or no down payment, while a credit purchase may require 20 to 30 percent down. However, a disadvantage of leasing is that it's much more expensive than buying, since the leasing corporation includes charges to cover its overhead and make a profit.

Technological obsolescence is often a reason cited for leasing. At the end of a lease period, you can give back what may be obsolete equipment that may have little market value. On the other hand, if you're in a business like desktop video, multimedia production, or presentation graphics, in which capability is rapidly improving while costs are declining, you may want to turn over your equipment before the lease is up. If it's a purchase structured like a lease, you could find yourself at the end of a lease with obsolete equipment you can't resell for a reasonable price.

If you do decide to rent or lease, make certain you understand the contract—especially the fine print. Rental and lease agreements are printed so that customers will think the terms are fixed. But remember, everything is negotiable, even the terms of contracts with major corporations like IBM or Xerox. The contracts are written to their advantage, not yours. Elaine Ré, a national authority on negotiating, says that superior power in a negotiation isn't based on the size of the business, but on how attractive or unattractive it is for a party to make or not make a deal. Your contract may mean the difference between a salesperson's meeting a quota or qualifying for a bonus. So you do have some leverage in negotiating your contracts.

Here are some points to negotiate:

- The exact nature of the financing agreement—does it have liens or restrictions?
- The amount of each payment.
- Who is responsible for insurance, maintenance and taxes?—usually the lessee.
- What happens to the leased item at the end of the lease?
- Renewal options.
- Cancellation penalties, if any.
- Disadvantageous terms and conditions.
- Length of the lease period.

Taking into account all the ways leasing might have an impact on the operation of a particular business, you can see there is no stock answer as to whether renting, leasing, or buying is best for everyone.

Start-up Costs

Prior to the time you begin business, the money you spend is considered by the IRS as a capital expense and cannot be deducted in the current tax year as you would the ordinary business expenses described earlier in this chapter. Some of these expenses, however, can be amortized over sixty months, which means that you can realize as deductions a portion of these expenses spread over a period of years. You must file an "election" to amortize these costs, or else they cannot be recovered until you sell or close the business. This is done in conjunction with Form 4562 with an attached statement.

Qualifying for amortization is money you spend investigating and preparing to begin business for: initial office supplies, market surveys and research, consultants, professional services, travel for securing customers, suppliers and distributors, organizing a corporation or partnership, occupational licenses, officially filing your business name with the county or state, and sometimes franchise fees.

When does business begin so that you can deduct money you spend in the current tax year? For a store, it's generally when the doors open; for a partnership or corporation, it's when it begins the activities for which it is organized; for a home-based sole proprietorship, it's certainly when you make a sale but it can begin earlier if you can show you began business activities. So a specialized temporary help service that starts advertising for people to have in its database and sends out notices to prospective customers that it has temps should be able to make the case that it has begun business. It might also be the act of obtaining a business license or registering your assumed business name.

If you claim expenses that should have been amortized as ordinary business expenses and they are disallowed, you lose the ability to amortize them with no deduction until you end the business. So it's a good idea to get professional advice so you can maximize your deductions at this stage and avoid costly mistakes.

Money for Your Retirement

Because no corporate or government job is funding a pension plan for you when you're on your own, one of the important things to do is to put money aside for the years when your earning ability will decline. As a self-employed person, even with a part-time business, you can provide for your own retirement and in the process reduce how much income tax you owe.

You can do this with either a Simplified Employee Pension (also called a SEP-IRA) account or a Keogh or HR-10 plan. A Keogh requires enough paperwork that most people need professional help to have one, but a SEP-IRA is much simpler. You can usually start a SEP simply by completing a Form 5305-SEP, which will be provided by any of the various vendors happy to have you invest your money with them, including banks, savings and loans, insurance companies, brokerage firms, and mutual funds.

Currently, the most you can deduct each year for a contribution to a SEP-IRA plan for yourself is the smaller of either 13.04 percent of your "net earnings from self-employment" up to $150,000 or $19,565. This dollar limit is indexed for inflation and will rise beginning in 1995. Your *net* earnings from self-employment are the amount on which you pay self-employment tax reduced by the amount of the self-employment tax. (This calculation leads to your not being able to reduce the amount of self-employment tax you pay, but it does reduce your federal income tax.) If you have a bad year, you can reduce or skip paying into your SEP. Keep in mind that if you have employees with either of these plans, you will be contributing to their retirement, too.

A variation of a Keogh plan, called a "money purchase plan," has a $30,000-dollar limit because it allows up to a 20 percent deduction of *net* self-employment earnings. For more information on retirement plans for the self-employed, obtain IRS Publication 560. It's also a good idea to get counsel from a financial planner, which is itself a popular home-based business.

Tax Responsibilities of the Self-Employed

Estimated Tax Payments

If you are a sole proprietor, a partnership, or a shareholder in a Subchapter S corporation, you are considered self-employed. Since you don't have an employer deducting taxes from your pay throughout the year, you are responsible for making advance payments of your estimated federal income tax. Estimated tax payments are due quarterly—on April 15, June 15, September 15, and January 15—and are filed on a Form 1040-ES. At the end of the tax year, you will file a final Form 1040 with a Schedule C, which itemizes your business expenses for the whole year.

To avoid underpayment penalties—which are substantial—individuals whose adjusted gross incomes were under $150,000 need to have paid at least 100 percent of their prior year's tax bill. People whose incomes were over $150,000 need to have paid 110 percent of the amount they owed in the prior year.

It's in your interest to make your estimated tax payments during the year. This system also keeps you from owing a large sum of money all at once, which can be overwhelming. If your state of residence has income taxes, as most do, you will have to make estimated tax payments throughout the year for state taxes as well.

Self-Employment Tax

Your estimated tax payments will also include the federal self-employment tax—Social Security and Medicare. If you were employed by someone else, your employer would pay half of your Social Security and Medicare and the other half would come out of your paycheck. Self-employed people must pay the full amount themselves; however, 50 percent of the self-employment tax is deductible on the 1040 form.

What if you are a salaried employee *and* you operate a home-based business as a sideline? In this case, you'll be filing both the usual Form 1040 and a Schedule C for your home-business deductions; you may also have to pay additional self-employment tax. No matter how little your sideline income is, you should be aware that it is subject to tax—although by taking advantage of the home-office deduction, you may find you owe little or no taxes.

Employment Taxes

Home-based workers who employ others must comply with many additional tax requirements. IRS Circular E, *Employer's Tax Guide*, covers the federal regulations, and your state tax agency can inform you of state requirements for employers with regard to income, state unemployment, and workers' compensation taxes.

If you employ your children or grandchildren, their earnings are deductible. Family businesses do not need to pay Social Security or unemployment taxes on minor children, and the children pay no income taxes on the first $3,000 of earned income. To substantiate this claim, keep time records of their work (the records will be more believable to the IRS if a nonrelative keeps them), note the work done, and pay family at the rate you would pay a nonfamily member for the same work.

State and Local Taxes

Depending on where you live, you will face a variety of state and local tax requirements. All but nine states (Alaska, Wyoming, Nevada, Florida, Tennessee, South Dakota, New Hampshire, Texas, and Washington) have state personal-income taxes. But even those may have taxes on business. For example, Florida levies an income tax on corporations. Some cities, like Kansas City, have earnings taxes apart from the state income tax; others have unusual taxes on business. New York, for example, taxes unincorporated businesses.

Requirements for Selling
Taxable Goods and Services

If you sell taxable goods and services from a home-based business, you must pay state sales tax in all but New Hampshire, Delaware, and Oregon, which manage to stay afloat without a sales tax. Handicrafts, antiques, silk flowers, and pet products are all examples of taxable goods; if you operate a repair service, the parts you use may be taxable.

Taxable services are difficult to pinpoint and vary greatly from state to state. In California, for instance, taxable services include printing, audio tape duplication, videotape rental, and some aspects of word-processing services. This is a tricky area; you may think the services you are providing are not taxable, when in fact they are. And since state tax authorities are very serious about collecting their sales taxes, it's important to check with your local agency to find out whether your work falls into a taxable category.

One woman we met ran a graphics business without being aware that her work was subject to sales tax. After five years in business, she was audited—and the amount she owed for five years' worth of sales tax plus penalties and interest was so high that it forced her to close up shop.

Check rates, too. They vary within states because many cities, counties, and special districts collect sales tax; it's been calculated that there are over 10,000 different sales tax rates in the United States.

Making Sure You Qualify for Your Business Deductions

Just because you and your clients consider you to be self-employed does not mean the IRS will agree. As companies rely increasingly on consultants, freelancers, outside services, and independent contractors instead of hiring permanent employees, the IRS is taking a growing interest in assuring that such arrangements are not just a way for both parties to avoid paying conventional taxes.

Should the IRS decide that you are an employee masquerading as an independent contractor, you will find yourself in the worst of all possible worlds. You will receive neither the fringe benefits that accompany employment nor the tax benefits available to the self-employed.

Therefore it's increasingly essential that we take every precaution to set ourselves up in a way that clearly demonstrates that we are independent, self-employed individuals in business for ourselves. In fact, a recent magazine headline proclaimed, "The IRS Wages War on the Self-Employed." Every week 2,000 or more people who may have considered themselves to be self-employed individuals working as independent contractors for their clients are being reclassified as employees.

Some industries are being targeted more aggressively than others, specifically the computer field, construction, entertainment, health care, and travel. In the data-processing industry, for example, a survey showed that because of this problem, three out of four companies had reduced or eliminated contracts with independent engineers, consultants, and other technical people. Some state agencies are taking a more aggressive stance in this area as well; i.e., California, Colorado, Georgia, Illinois, Michigan, Pennsylvania, New York, and Texas.

A video director told us, "I've got one client now who refuses to deal with me on any basis other than as an employee. I submit a time card, and my company invoices separately for equipment rental." As the video director observed, "Since I only work for them occasionally, can you imagine what would happen to our business relationship if every time I completed a project with them, I went down to file for unemployment!"

Whether you're in these industries or these states, if you have only one or two clients, especially if one of your clients is your former employer, you should be aware of what can happen should the IRS decide to reclassify you as an employee. Here's what happens.

When you are reclassified as an employee, the company you've been working with, your client, will be assessed for the back taxes it didn't withhold for you as an "employee" and will be slapped with a 100 percent penalty for not having withheld taxes from your wages—even though you paid them yourself. You, on the other hand, will owe back taxes, because:

- You took off business expenses before calculating how much you would pay in self-employment tax (Social Security and Medicare) and therefore you paid less federal income tax than you would have if you were an employee.
- If you were paying for health insurance, you may have taken the 25 percent deduction you were allowed as a self-employed person. As an employee, this deduction would be disallowed and you would owe the difference.
- As a self-employed person, you may have put money aside in a retirement plan, such as a SEP, and deducted this from your federal income tax. Once you're classified as an employee, you can only deduct the $2,000 allowed for an IRA, so you may be penalized for overcontributing.
- Because of the loss of these deductions, you may have underpaid your estimated taxes and could then be assessed a penalty for underpayment.

You should also know that if you are reclassified by the federal government, they will report it to your state agencies and, if you were reclassified by a state agency, they will report it to the IRS.

Obviously, any self-employed person who for any reason may be vulnerable to being reclassified needs to take specific steps to protect his or her right to remain in business. Here's what you can do. You can make sure that you meet as many as possible of the criteria the IRS looks for in determining whether someone is an employee or self-employed.

The key to this determination is the question of control—who calls the shots with regard to how you work. Following is the text of the twenty questions contained in IRS Publication 937 that serve as guidelines for determining this issue of control. Below each question are specific measures you can take to demonstrate that you are in fact an "independent" businessperson and not an employee. Language from the IRS publication is in italics; it is followed by our recommendations.

*1) **Instructions.** An employee must comply with instructions about when, where, and how to work. Even if no instructions are given, the control factor is present if the employer has the right to control how the work results are achieved.*

Whenever possible take the initiative to be the one who spells out the contract between you and your clients. Have a standard contract that you can modify for each project that is printed on your letterhead and that clearly spells out the terms of your agreement. Focus the agreement on the results or service you agree to produce. You can base your contract on the one contained in *AgreeMentor*, a software program that contains a model contract usable for independent contractors that is as bulletproof as the attorneys who developed it could make it. Then have the result reviewed by your own attorney.

*2) **Training.** An employee may be trained to perform services in a particular manner. Independent contractors ordinarily use their own methods and receive no training from purchasers of their services.*

Take on work that you are clearly already trained to carry out. If prospective work requires additional training, secure your own training from an outside source and pay for it yourself.

*3) **Integration.** An employee's services are usually integrated into the business operations because the services are important to the success or continuation of the business. This shows that the employee is subject to direction and control.*

Outsourced work is increasingly integral to the operations of the company doing the outsourcing. Whole functions like public relations or office management are now outsourced and, of course, there is nothing an independent contractor loves more than to become indispensable to a client's operations. But to protect your independence, make your "outsider" status apparent.

Avoid having office space set aside for you on your client's site. Use your own equipment as much as possible. Do not give out your client's phone number as a place where you can be reached. If you must take calls while on a client's premises, have your calls forwarded from another number rather than giving out your client's number. Hold as many meetings as possible on your own premises or at a third location.

*4) **Service rendered personally.** An employee renders services personally. This shows that the employer is interested in the methods as well as the results.*

As a sole proprietor you will most likely be rendering your services personally, so everything you do to meet other criteria is that much more important. One of the most significant things you can do is incorporate. Although this can be expensive, it establishes a separate business identity for you.

Provide a copy of your certificate of incorporation to your client. Having evidence in your client files is important because IRS and state agencies audit companies, and you may not even know that this is happening. So providing your clients with tangible evidence can make your case for you when you're not there.

Whether you incorporate or not, use a business name distinct from your own.

Have a business telephone line, which, of course, is on your business card and letterhead. Obtain a business license, providing a copy to your clients. If you have a truck or car that you can have your business name on, have it photographed and appear in a brochure or at least provide a snapshot to your clients. Have a separate business bank account in the name of your business into which you deposit payments from clients. The endorsement with your business name is more evidence of your independence.

Never use a résumé; that communicates "employee."

*5) **Hiring assistants.** An employee works for an employer who hires, supervises, and pays workers. An independent contractor can hire, supervise, and pay assistants under a contract that requires him or her to provide materials and labor and to be responsible only for the result.*

Again, as a sole proprietor, you may not hire others to carry out any particular aspect of your contracts (although you can and, when feasible, it is to your advantage to do so). Nonetheless you most likely will use other outside services, such as printers, travel agents, or graphic or secretarial assistance. Keep track of receipts and checks covering such costs related to each project. And although it might help your bottom line, don't be tempted to rely routinely on your client's employees as your support staff. This will also help you avoid the impression of your being an integral part of your client's workforce.

*6) **Continuing relationship.** An employee generally has a continuing relationship with an employer. A continuing relationship may exist even if work is performed at recurring although irregular intervals.*

Of course, we all hope to have a continuing relationship with our best clients and customers. To protect your independent-contractor status, however, make sure that each project is clearly time and/or task defined and that each new project with past clients is rebid, renegotiated, and occurs under a new and separate contract.

*7) **Set hours of work.** An employee usually has set hours of work established by an employer. An independent contractor generally can set his or her own work hours.*

Using a personal organizer or software like *Timeslips*, you can keep track of time spent on projects for various clients to help you demonstrate that your time is divided among your clients and that it varies week by week or month by month according to your own priorities and demands.

*8) **Full-time required.** An employee may be required to work or be available full-time. This indicates control by the employer. An independent contractor can work when and for whom he chooses.*

Always having more than one client simultaneously is one of the best ways to protect your independent-contractor status. Therefore whenever you are working primarily with one particular client, you should make sure to consistently invest both time and money in marketing for additional clients. Document both the time and money you spend marketing and administering your business.

*9) **Work done on premises.** An employee usually works on the premises of an employer, or works on a route or at a location designated by an employer.*

The more work you are able to do in your own home office, the better. This is also now critical to making your home office your principal place of business in order to qualify for a home-office tax deduction as well. Hold client meetings at your home office or at conference facilities that you pay for, and track the hours spent working on each project in your home office to help demonstrate your independence.

*10) **Order or sequence set.** An employee may be required to perform services in the order or sequence set by an employer. This shows that the employee is subject to direction and control.*

Make sure that the contract or letter of agreement you have with your clients spells out what you will do, but does not define the order, sequence, or method by which you will do it.

*11) **Reports.** An employee may be required to submit reports to an employer. This shows that the employer maintains a degree of control.*

Although informal or formal progress reports may be essential to some contracts or to keep clients happy, in negotiating a contract, when possible limit required reporting to a final report to be delivered upon completion of a project or make report preparation a discrete billed activity.

*12) **Payments.** An employee is paid by the hour, week or month. An independent contractor is usually paid by the job or a straight commission.*

Although you may use hourly fees to calculate your final bid or quote, working on a flat fee better safeguards your independent status. This means that carefully tracking the time it takes to complete each project you undertake is vital so that you have a history upon which to estimate accurately flat fees that realistically reflect the amount of time you actually need to complete a new project. Cases, however, have been won when the worker was paid on an hourly basis.

*13) **Expenses.** An employee's business and travel expenses are generally paid for by an employer. This shows that the employee is subject to regulation and control.*

Of course, we all want and sometimes need to pass direct costs on directly to our clients. To safeguard your independent status, build as many expenses as possible into your flat fee rather than billing for them separately. Or charge a per diem to cover travel and expenses instead of billing by the item. This means, of course, that you need to obtain firm quotes on your business expenses, so that you don't end up eating unexpected costs and losing money on a project.

*14) **Tools and materials.** An employee is generally furnished significant tools, materials, and other equipment by an employer.*

Equip your home office with the equipment and tools you need to carry out your work without having to rely on the resources of your clients. Purchase all materials used on a project yourself and build the costs of these materials into your fee structure.

*15) **Investment.** An independent contractor has a significant investment in the facilities he or she uses in performing services for someone else.*

Setting up, equipping, and supplying your home office adequately is an investment that demonstrates your independent status. A separate business telephone line, a separate business bank account, a variety of accounts with vendors and suppliers are all indications of your investment in your own business.

16) **Profit or loss.** *An independent contractor can make a profit or suffer a loss.*

One consequence of getting paid a fixed fee rather than working by the hour is that, indeed, there is the potential of incurring either a profit or loss depending upon whether you have accurately estimated your costs and time.

17) **Works for more than one person or firm.** *An independent contractor is generally free to provide his or her services to two or more persons or firms at the same time.*

Once again, having multiple clients for whom you work at the same time on a schedule at your own discretion is one of your best protections. Just be sure to document time spent working for your various clients especially if you are concerned about being able to meet other criteria. Provide clients with nonconfidential information in a letter or memo about other clients you serve that is kept in a company file.

18) **Offer services to general public.** *An independent contractor makes his or her services available to the general public.*

The more visible you are as an independent business, the more clearly you meet this criterion. The more high profile your marketing efforts, the better; advertising, listings in professional and trade directories, active participation in business organizations as a business, a Yellow Pages listing, or other ongoing advertising all show you are actively offering your services in the marketplace. Be sure to provide evidence of these to your clients for their files.

19) **Right to fire.** *An employee can be fired by an employer. An independent contractor cannot be fired so long as he or she produces a result that meets the specifications of the contract.*

Make sure you have contracts that clearly spell out the terms of your agreement so that, in fact, you cannot be let go until completion of a contract as long as you are meeting the specified terms. Building in a cancellation fee is also a good idea.

20) **Right to quit.** *An employee can quit his or her job at any time without incurring liability. An independent contractor usually agrees to complete a specific job and is responsible for its satisfactory completion or is legally obligated to make good for failure to complete.*

Again, be sure to have a clear contract covering what you will provide and under what circumstances you can cancel a contract. Be scrupulous about meeting contractual obligations.

Be able to demonstrate how you could, or have, called upon others to work under your auspices to carry out aspects of contracts when you have been unable to do so yourself. Be able, in other words, to demonstrate that you have reliable backup to handle overload or emergencies as a business would.

We have described many things you can do to protect your independence. Now let's mention something you are probably best advised to avoid. You're apt to see or hear about IRS Form SS-8. This form is used by companies to get a determination from the IRS as to whether someone is an employee or an independent contractor. SS-8 has three pages of questions and specifies a variety of documents to be submitted with it. The complexity of SS-8 will help you understand why so much effort is needed to make it clear you are a business. Reportedly 90 percent of IRS SS-8 determinations find that someone is an employee. These are not good odds, so what you need to do is to establish yourself so clearly as an independent business that your client company will not be tempted to get an SS-8 determination.

The Hobby Rule

The IRS presumes an enterprise is a hobby (and not eligible for deducting losses to offset income from other sources) if it does not show a profit for three years out of five. So to meet IRS standards, the business needs to be showing a profit by its third year. However, this is a rebuttable presumption.

If you can show a calendar or other records to document that you have put in a substantial amount of time and are serious about making a profit; if your losing money is due to circumstances beyond your control or is normal for the type of business you have chosen; if your activities show a businesslike approach (see "Twelve Money-Saving Ways to Give Your Home Business a *Fortune* 500 Image" on page 65); and, of course, if you are depending on the business for your livelihood (and getting by through borrowing, living off earnings, etc.), you may still be able to claim your business deductions. Be prepared to prove to the IRS that yours is a serious business and not a hobby.

When You Mail Something to the IRS

When you mail a tax return or any important document to the IRS, use certified mail, return receipt requested. This is acceptable proof that you filed the required documents even if the IRS loses them.

Keeping Adequate Tax Records

Clear, complete records of your income, expenses, assets (such as a computer or typewriter), and liabilities (such as loans or notes) enable you to minimize your taxes and to defend yourself in the event you're audited. The IRS does not specify what form your records should take, but you must be able to substantiate any claim you make.

Think of your records as footprints; the written documents—invoices, bank statements, canceled checks, deposit slips, and especially receipts—are the paper trail that your business operation leaves behind. You can either maintain your records yourself, hand over the task to a professional, or use some combination of the two.

Receipts are particularly crucial because they back up your claims for business expenses. Get in the habit of obtaining receipts by paying with a check or credit card (there's automatically a paper record), asking for a receipt, or creating one immediately upon expenditure. Suppose you make a long-distance business call from a pay phone—no receipt. Then create your own, writing down the expense and its business purpose on a piece of paper, in a logbook, or on an appointment calendar.

Some people consider it sufficient to place all their receipts and tax records in one box or envelope. Then they try to sort things out at the end of the year. We discourage this shoe box approach to record keeping.

First, the shoe box gives you no sense of where you stand financially during the year, and it provides no help in calculating your estimated taxes each quarter. You're forced to accomplish all your tax organizing at tax time, taking valuable hours and energy away from your daily business. In addition, it's too easy for some things to miss the box. Keeping track of your expenses as they occur increases the likelihood that you'll claim all your deductions and thereby minimize your taxes.

Whatever record-keeping system you develop, the important thing is finding one that's comfortable and effective enough so you will use it routinely. If you don't want to do it all yourself, get the help you need during the year to keep on top of your financial records.

Getting the Help You Need

Tax law is not only complicated, it's also constantly changing. So unless you're a trained tax expert, we recommend getting professional help in preparing your taxes. When tax time arrives you'll want to continue carrying out your work as productively and enjoyably as possible. You certainly don't need to get bogged down in tax complexities.

In fact, if your tax return is at all complex, having tax help is not only desirable but essential. In one case, the IRS actually leveled a negligence penalty against someone on the grounds that his tax return was too complicated to complete himself.

For tax help, you need someone who keeps up with the continually changing law, IRS code, tax rulings, and cases. The IRS alone issues a new ruling every two hours of each workday. You also need someone who has experience and empathy with home-based businesses in general and your type of business in particular. Too often we've heard tales of home-based workers selecting professionals whose experience has been only with large traditional businesses. As a result, these open-collar workers have received advice that was either inaccurate for their situation or contrary to their best interests.

Although there are other alternatives, including tax attorneys and tax consultants, we believe an accountant or an "enrolled agent" is generally your best choice for tax help. Accountants not only prepare your tax returns at filing time but also can be considered, along with your lawyer, as part of a team of professional advisers to whom you can turn throughout the year. They can set up your record-keeping system, perform certified audits, represent you to the IRS, prepare financial reports or statements, and help you with tax-planning decisions.

Accountants may be one of the more expensive sources of tax help, but in the long run their assistance can save you more than they cost. A Certified Public Accountant, or CPA, has had formal training in accounting, earned a college degree, and passed a tough state certification examination.

Charging about one-third less than a CPA, an enrolled agent can prepare your return and is eligible to represent you before the IRS and the tax court as your tax preparer. These agents have received their "enrolled" status either by passing a two-day examination given by the IRS or by working for the IRS full-time for at least five years.

Accountants who are not certified are called Public Accountants and may or may not be licensed by the state. They are qualified by experience and perhaps have had special training. They generally cannot represent you before the IRS as your tax preparer.

To find a tax professional, ask for recommendations from someone who's successful doing work similar to yours. We think it's a good idea to use someone whose practice is about the same size as your business. You might locate a CPA like that by contacting the American Institute of Certified Public Accountants society in your state for the names of accountants who serve on the Small Business Committee or its equivalent. Then communicate with firms on that list until you find an accountant who understands your tax situation and with whom you're comfortable.

You can locate enrolled agents in the Yellow Pages, or call the National Association of Enrolled Agents referral line at (800) 424-4339 to obtain a list of enrolled agents in your area.

For even less costly tax help, you can go to a tax preparation service. The level of service you receive, however, is also limited. Tax preparation services are often so conservative and routine that they may advise against legitimate deductions.

The following box contains suggestions for questions to ask and things to look for when you interview to find your tax specialist. You may need to interview a number of firms until you find someone right for you. Although the usual guideline is to find a specialist you are comfortable with personally and philosophically, consider finding someone who balances your tendencies: If you are inclined to be creative with your deductions, find a tax preparer who focuses on documentable facts and is a problem-solver. If you are fearful about claiming tax deductions, find a more aggressive professional who makes you feel stretched. But most of all, find someone who is knowledgeable. Tax law is constantly changing—there have been thirteen major changes in tax law since 1980—and you need someone who keeps up. In the process of meeting and interviewing these and others you choose to serve you, you will learn what other people do in presenting themselves effectively and not so effectively that you may be able to apply to how you present yourself to prospective clients.

Considerations When Interviewing a Tax Specialist

- Is the tax preparer full-time or part-time? Tax law is so complicated, staying abreast takes a significant investment of time.
- Is the tax professional available throughout the year or just during tax season?
- How many tax returns does the preparer do each year? Eight hundred returns is about tops for an individual; too few returns is also a warning sign.
- Can the specialist communicate understandably with you about your business?
- How often does the specialist quote the tax code to you rather than figuring out the best solution to your tax situation?
- Does the professional seem too good to be true?
- Does the specialist belong to a professional association?
- What is the specialist's training and experience in preparing tax returns?
- How much will it cost and how is the fee calculated?
- How does the specialist check returns for accuracy?
- What type of continuing-education courses does the person take? Are they relevant to your tax or accounting needs?
- Are you comfortable with how your questions are answered about the home-office deduction or some other subject about which you have some information? How does the information compare and did you gain any insights?
- Look at the books on their shelves. Do they have a tax weekly or monthly newsletter? A loose-leaf service like those from Research Institute of America and Commerce Clearing House? Tax information on CD-ROM?
- Are the specialist's self-employed clients never audited (the tax specialist may be too conservative) or audited too often (exceeding 1 chance in 62 if you're self-employed and make $25,000–$100,000; or 1 chance in 32 if you earn over $100,000—this compares with 1 in 63 for all returns).
- Can the specialist represent you before the IRS if you're audited?
- Has the specialist had experience appearing in IRS appeals?
- Will the specialist pay any penalties and interest resulting from his or her errors, and has this ever happened? Has she ever paid a negligence penalty to the IRS for her own negligence?

Using Your Computer to Do Your Taxes

While we recommend using computer software for your business accounting, the records you create with your software are not sufficient to satisfy the IRS. So paper records are essential. However, tax-preparation software has gotten so easy to use that some home-based businesspeople are using it to calculate their own taxes. Among the best tax-preparation programs are Chipsoft's *Turbo Tax* and *Andrew Tobias' Tax Cut*. The programs must be changed each year to reflect changes in the tax laws, and each February or March, computer magazines review the various revised programs.

Because tax programs have built-in assumptions that may not apply to your unique business situation, we recommend you have your return reviewed by a tax professional.

Remember, accounting programs and tax-preparation programs are not the same. As New York accountant Irvin Feldman explains, "Tax rules and accounting rules are very different. Accounting rules have some logical basis as opposed to tax rules, which are designed simply to raise money and perform some social purpose." This means that there are no software packages that will do both. You must know the possible tax consequences of treating something a particular way before you do it.

What If You're Audited?

The self-employed are unfortunately more apt to be audited than salaried Americans. But need you fear an audit? No one wants one, but wise preparation and action can see you through an audit, and if you don't give the IRS an opportunity to exact more money from you, you'll be a less-desirable target in future years.

The IRS conducts three types of audits:

- Correspondence audits are computer-generated adjustments. These come about because of discrepancies between what you report and other information the IRS has. For example, if you and your spouse are a partnership and someone you do work for reports what it paid you using your Social Security number instead of the partnership's Federal ID number, you will get a deficiency notice from the IRS. You can respond to these by mail, supplying documentation of your position.
- Office examinations. You or your tax specialist is summoned to appear at an IRS office with your records. However, if the matter in dispute is unambiguous, your tax representative may be able to convince the IRS to resolve the matter by mail.
- Field examination. An IRS agent comes to your premises. If you have claimed a home-office deduction, an agent can come to your home, yardstick in hand, to measure the space you have claimed.

The most common are office audits, accounting for over half. Field audits and correspondence audits split the balance of IRS audits.

Some Difficult, or Impossible, Deductions

- You can't rent part of your home to your own corporation or to your employer in order to qualify it as income property eligible for deductions that you ordinarily would not qualify for as a home office.
- You can't claim your family dog as a watchdog because you have inventory stored at home.
- You can't take a home-office deduction for managing your stock portfolio.
- Deductions for landscaping and lawn care are no longer allowed, even if you have clients or customers coming to your home office.

Some items that will invite IRS audits are:

High Schedule C losses from a part-time business.

Farfetched business deductions, like claiming nylons because you must dress up for business meetings.

Payments to family members as employees. Remember to keep records of when family members work and what they do.

Items on the tax form preceded by solid black darts. These items are viewed with particular care by the IRS.

You can head off an audit by providing lots of documentation with your return. Your tax preparer should be able to warn you if an item is likely to raise IRS scrutiny. Then you can include documentation such as notes of explanation and copies of canceled checks to circumvent the difficulty of locating records several years later and, more important, to avoid the time and trouble of an audit.

Besides being able to document all your deductions, here are some tips from experts:

1. Respond to the IRS within the time specified, but your response does not have to be immediate. Take the time to think things through and find the records you need. Make copies; don't send originals. Use certified mail, return receipt requested. That's an excellent idea for filing tax returns, too.

2. Get a copy of either or both the American Business Management Association's *Tax Kit* and Frederick Daly's *Stand Up to the IRS* book. They contain invaluable advice for dealing with an audit.

3. Don't go to a field audit yourself. Have someone—a CPA, an enrolled agent—represent you. If you do appear yourself, don't volunteer any information. Someone on the Working From Home Forum recently told about having his home-office deduction questioned. The part-time business qualified, but the taxpayer overjustified how he deserved the deduction by saying he not only used the office for his own business but also for after-hours work for his employer. The after-hours work did not meet the "convenience of the employer" test, and the whole deduction was disallowed.

4. Never send or bring records that are not related to the matter being questioned. To do so opens up the possibility that other aspects of your finances will be examined. It's not in your interest to arouse an agent's curiosity about items not being questioned or about past years. For all practical purposes, the job of IRS personnel is to collect money, and consequently their position is an adversarial one. It is therefore to your advantage to get the best advice you can from the moment there might be difficulty.

Letting Congress Hear from Us

We estimate that there are some seven million people in the "underground" economy today—people who are engaged in legal business activities but who are not filing or paying income taxes.

We believe that two principal reasons for evading taxes are the complexity of the tax system and the heavy burden of the higher Social Security and Medicare taxes that is imposed on the self-employed.

The laws and interpretations of the IRS relative to home-office deductions, however, may change as a home-office constituency begins to exert its influence on Congress and the executive branch. Squeaky wheels *do* produce reform. We have been told that each letter received by a representative or senator is perceived as equaling the sentiments of 27,000 constituents. Thus it is clearly in your interest to express your views on the tax system and to suggest ways it can be altered to improve the situation of home-based workers.

Resources

Books and Other Printed Information

A Common Sense Guide to Retirement Plans for Self-Employed People and Business Owners. Fidelity Investments, free booklet; (800)544-4774.

The Artist's Tax Guide and Financial Planner. Carla Messman. New York: Lyons & Burford Publishers, 1992.

Kiplinger's Sure Ways To Cut Your Taxes. Kevin McCormally. Washington, D.C.: Kiplinger Books, 1994.

Stand Up to the IRS. Frederick W. Daily. Berkeley, Calif.: Nolo Press, 1993.

Tax Kit. American Business Management Association, P.O. Box 111, West Hyannisport, MA 02672; (800)333-4508. Although written for multilevel marketers, this is a formidable resource in claiming and protecting one's self-employment tax deductions.

Software

AgreeMentor. Jian Tools, 127 Second Street, Los Altos, CA 94022; (415-041-0101; 800-346-5426). Software for independent-contractor agreements.

The following tax programs include Schedule C and supporting forms, along with the ability to calculate depreciation. You may also import financial data from your accounting program—i.e., *Quicken, Managing Your Money* and *CA-Simply Money* as described in chapter 14—directly into your tax program. You can use one of these programs to organize piles of receipts and to get an idea of what forms you will need from among those included with the program. Then you can calculate how much tax you owe and take the results to a tax professional and see how close the program came to the professional's conclusions.

Andrew Tobias' Tax Cut. Meca Software Inc., 55 Walls Drive, Fairfield, CT 06430; 1(800)820-7458; (203)255-1441.

CA-Simply Tax. Computer Associates, 1 Computer Associates Plaza, Islandia, NY 11788; 1(800)225-5224; (516)342-5224.

Personal Tax Edge. Parsons Technology, One Parsons Drive, Hiawatha, IA 52233; (800)223-6925.

TurboTax, MacInTax. ChipSoft Inc., 2650 Elvira Rd., Ste. 100, Tucson, AZ 85706; (800)964-1040.

IRS Materials

The Internal Revenue Service provides assistance in a number of ways. These include:

Tax Forms and Publications:

For IRS Publications and tax forms call (800) TAX FORM. These will be mailed to you. Publications addressed to specific tax topics pertinent to a small business include: *Basis of Assets* (#551), *Business Expenses* (#535), *Business Use of a Car* (#917), *Circular #E, Employers Tax Guide* (#15), *Depreciation* (#534), *Employment Taxes and Information Returns* (#937), *How to Begin Depreciating Property* (#946), *Selling Your Home* (#523), *Taxpayers Starting a Business* (#583), and *Travel, Entertainment, and Gift Expenses* (#463).

Recorded Tapes:

The IRS's Teletax provides prerecorded information on over one hundred topics on tape. You can also find out about the status of your refund by calling (800)829-4477. For a directory of tapes, press 123.

Classes and Workshops

Classes and workshops are offered by the Internal Revenue Service. Call your nearest IRS office for subjects, dates, and locations.

CHAPTER
ELEVEN
■■■■■■■■■■■■■■■■■■■■■■■■■■■

Insurance: What You Need and How to Find It

It was shocking! We began a series of interviews with home-based businesses to find out what types of insurance home-based businesses buy. We expected the answers to be a routine litany of the basic home-office insurance coverage we'd written about since the first edition of *Working From Home*. But were we ever surprised by the answers we got! We uncovered several startling and disturbing realities:

- Over two-thirds of the home businesses we interviewed had *no* business insurance of any kind!
- Most of those without insurance didn't know they needed it!
- Many without insurance mistakenly thought they were automatically covered by other insurance they had!
- Others wanted insurance but couldn't get it!

Who are these uninsured home-business owners? You might think they couldn't be "serious" business owners. But no, many of the people we spoke with are running highly professional, successful businesses. Most are equipped with state-of-the-art computer and home-office technology, with faxes, laser printers, copy machines, and scanners. Some are doing over $100,000 a year in business.

Yet, surprisingly, only one in four of those we talked with had any protection against theft, damage, or other loss of their business equipment. Not only do those without coverage lack endorsements on their homeowners' or apartment dwellers' insurance to cover such losses, some don't even have homeowners' or apartment dwellers' insurance in the first place. In fact, one man whose home office is filled with thousands of dollars' of expensive biofeedback equipment and elaborate proprietary computer systems didn't even know there was such a thing as apartment dwellers' insurance.

And this is not the only area of insurance protection where home offices are going bare. We found one out of six home businesspeople were operating without health insurance; this compares with other recent findings that 22 percent of all self-employed people lack health insurance. Our research also showed that most didn't have insurance covering business uses of their automobiles even when they regularly transported business products and equipment. And only one in ten had disability insurance.

Sometimes these open-collar workers were without business insurance because they judged their risks to be too small to justify the cost of added insurance. Sometimes the cost of available insurance was simply beyond their budgets. This was particularly true in regard to those without health insurance. But often people are going without because they don't realize they aren't covered for business activities as part of their existing insurance policies.

We were equally startled to discover that some people are desperately trying to get insurance but can't seem to obtain what they need. Some have spent months searching, with no results. Some have purchased insurance only to discover that it didn't cover certain key things they needed. One man, for example, purchased business property insurance to find that it didn't include loss from theft or water damage. A computer programmer insured his computer with a special separate policy only to find that the insurance didn't cover loss of the data on his disks, just the cost of the floppy disks themselves. Still others are being turned down for insurance *because* they work from home. This was particularly true regarding disability insurance.

So it seems that we're in the midst of an insurance crisis, partly of our own making and partly due to a lack of awareness by the insurance industry of the needs of home-based business activity. In this chapter we want to clear up the major misconceptions, the myths, and the misunderstandings we've uncovered about insurance for the home office so you can identify what you do need, how you can get it, and when you should have it.

Insurance Myth #1: It Won't Happen to Me
Fact: Bare Bottoms Can and Do Get Burned

Insurance is just one of various approaches you can take to managing the risks that arise from doing business from your home. Preventing the risk in the first place is, of course, the best method. Staying healthy, keeping your property in good repair, securing your home and auto, doing a high-quality job, and maintaining your equipment are a few examples of how we can protect ourselves from risks. Planning to absorb any risk that occurs is another alternative. If you virtually never have business visitors come to your home, for example, or if you never carry business equipment in your car and don't have inventory, you might feel that your needs for the specialized insurance protecting you from these risks would be so low that you might opt to "take your chances."

The Ounce-of-Prevention List

It's so much easier to prevent problems than to defend yourself against them once they've occurred. Here is a list of things you can do to avoid ever having to use your insurance:

1. Keep your home in good repair. Have wiring, plumbing, water heater, air ducts, and chimneys inspected and cleaned regularly.
2. Don't overload your electrical circuits. Of course, have circuit breakers but have circuits upgraded or rerouted if they start going out frequently.
3. Repair cracked sidewalks, banisters, stairs, doorways, eaves, and overhangs.
4. Eliminate potential hazards like icy steps, dogs that tend to bite, slippery rugs or floor surfaces in halls and entryways, file drawers that open into doorways, decorative or art objects that could easily fall over on someone, etc.
5. Install smoke detectors and replace the batteries regularly. You could even consider installing a sprinkler system.
6. Take the steps outlined in chapter 7 to secure and protect your property from burglary and vandalism; i.e., installing outdoor lighting and securing door and window locks.
7. Take steps to protect your computer data and office equipment described in the Resources list in chapter 8; i.e., making sure that you back up data, have a surge protector, provide an uninterruptible power supply, install a virus protector, etc.
8. Have an automobile security system to prevent break-ins. There are many kinds, ranging from low-cost devices that lock your steering wheel to sophisticated tracking systems like Lo-Jack or others with alarms, etc. Even with insurance, you can only replace the equipment you've lost, not the work you had in your briefcase; so preventing a theft is an important goal.
9. Don't accept work that is beyond your capabilities or skills.
10. Live healthfully: exercise regularly, get enough sleep, follow a good diet regimen, reduce stress, and create an ergonomically and ecologically sound environment for yourself (see chapter 7).

In some cases, you can shift the risk to others. For example, suppliers can carry the risk of materials or equipment in transit to you; customers can carry the risk on items you ship to them.

But let's consider a few all-too-real-life examples to illustrate why being insured can not only save you money but can put your mind to rest and in some cases save your business. A computer consultant who specializes in hardware was delivering $20,000 worth of equipment to a client when he was held up at gunpoint and both his car and the shipment of equipment were stolen. Loss of the equipment was not covered under his insurance. He didn't have property insurance that would protect his business equipment off the premises. So he had to pay for the stolen equipment as well as purchase new equipment to provide for his client. The resulting cash flow crunch nearly put him out of business.

Thirty-seven-year-old marriage and family counselor Nadine Barney was stricken with the Epstein-Barr virus after five years of managing a successful counseling practice. She was unable to work, and as a single woman and head of her household she lost her business, her savings, and ultimately her apartment. She lived with her mother while she recovered and after three years was able to rebuild her business. She wishes she'd had disability insurance but admits she had never even thought about it.

In recent years, fires have swept through northern and southern California. Many hundreds of homes were burned to the ground in seconds. We were touched by a story in the *Los Angeles Times* about one woman, an author, who was in her home office proofreading chapters from a book she was writing when the kitten in her lap tensed up and began to act strangely. She looked up and saw a huge cloud of smoke billowing across the canyon. Suddenly a neighbor was yelling for her to get out. She looked at the VCR, the computers, the antiques, and the clothes. She was still clutching the first few chapters of the book she had been working on and, in the end, that's all she took when she jumped into her car as a police officer ordered her to leave.

Having only recently completed our survey on home-office insurance, we had to wonder if she had insurance to cover the business aspects of her loss. If so, did it cover her computer? Did it cover the data? Did it cover the other losses she would experience from the interruption of her business? We don't know. But we do know that, one way or another, the answers to those questions would have made a major difference in her life.

They certainly did for pioneering information broker Sue Rugge, who lost everything in her home and home office in the 1991 Oakland, California, fires including tens of thousands of dollars' of accounts receivable. She thought her homeowner insurance policy would cover her home-office loss. It didn't. That's what publicist George Craighton discovered, too, when a fire swept through the home office he'd carved out in the back of his garage. Fortunately none of his clients sued him for failing to complete his contracts on schedule, but what if they had? This possibility hadn't occurred to him until after the fire.

As we contemplated Sue's and George's situations, and that of others we've talked with or read about whose home offices were destroyed in the Florida hurricane or the L.A. earthquake, we thought about our business. What if these things had happened to us? Our home and the business equipment is covered, but our data isn't. What if this manuscript and our research were destroyed? What if we were injured as our son was and couldn't keyboard for several months? We don't have business-interruption insurance, and at the time we didn't have disability insurance.

How would we live? Where would we start? We had to ask ourselves which risk is cheaper in the long run: taking your chances that it won't happen to you or investing in insurance you hopefully will never need to use? Of course, each of us must answer that question on our own. But here's our conclusion.

Insurance Rule of Thumb #1: Only risk what you can afford to lose.

Insurance Myth #2: I Don't Need That Because . . .
Fact: You're Probably Not Covered

We were amazed at the reasons people gave us for not having insurance. Here are just a few of the most common ones: "I don't need that because my homeowners' insurance already covers that." "I don't need that because I never have anyone come to my house." "I don't need that because I don't use my car for business." "That's covered on my auto insurance." "I don't do anything dangerous." "I'm only doing this part-time." "I'm just a freelance consultant." Do any of these sound familiar to you?

Like the emperor with no clothes, many home-business owners make these assertions with astonishing confidence, certain they are already covered when clearly they were not. It's one thing to decide to take your chances on not being insured, but it's quite another to discover that you needed insurance for a risk you didn't realize you were taking, or worse, to think you're covered when in fact you're not.

The most common misunderstandings concerned business-property insurance, liability insurance, and auto insurance. So let's straighten out the facts about these.

Your homeowners' or apartment dwellers' insurance most likely does not cover your business property—This is the most common misconception we encounter. People often believe they don't need any additional insurance because they think their existing homeowners' or apartment dwellers' insurance would cover any loss or damage to their business equipment, furniture, and supplies in the event of fire, theft, or other catastrophes.

In fact, basic homeowners' or apartment dwellers' policies do protect you from damage or loss to your *personal* property, but they usually explicitly exclude coverage for any *business* uses of your premises. The standard form for homeowners' coverage lists as an exclusion: "business property pertaining to a business being conducted on the residence proper." Also, if your home office is in a separate, detached structure, it and its contents may not be covered.

So, check the restrictions and limits on your policy to make sure you have ample coverage for damage or loss to your business property. You could even find that running a business from your home voids the coverage of your policy altogether or that there are limits as low as $200 on what you can recover in case of loss from fire, burglary, or other damage to "property used or intended for use in a business."

By the time you add up the value of your computer, printer, software, answering machine, filing cabinets, desk, chair, fax and copy machine, you have thousands of dollars' worth of business property to protect. In such circumstances, the limits on your policy could be negligible compensation.

Should you be unable to get homeowners' insurance without such limitations, you can broaden your coverage either by getting an endorsement that raises the amount of coverage to include your business equipment or by buying a separate policy to cover your business equipment. A separate policy may have the advantage of covering "mysterious disappearance" of property, whereas homeowners' policies don't usually allow for this contingency in the event of theft. Also, a separate policy can pay off at the stated value or the replacement cost of an item without figuring in the depreciation factor included in many homeowners' policies.

If you own a computer, you may want to get either an endorsement to your homeowners' policy or a special *"floater"* policy (also called a *rider*) to cover risks unique to computer owners. In the event that a power surge wipes out your $600 software or destroys six months' of work on disk, this kind of policy can be well worth the expense. Another alternative to getting a rider is to get special computer insurance from a company like Safeware, (800)848-3469 or (614) 262-0559, which costs from $50 to $200 a year and also includes protection against fire and theft of hardware, software, and temporary rental items. However, policies covering data loss will be more expensive. For example, their more comprehensive packages called Key and Key Gold with premiums starting at $200 do pay up to $5,000 for data loss and add protection for other office equipment like copiers and telephones.

You can even get a policy that covers portable computers, personal organizers, and personal assistants. The Computer Insurance Agency, Inc., for example, offers a policy that replaces portables should disaster strike while you are on the road. Premiums for such insurance run from $60 to $3,000 with a $50 deductible.

Your homeowners' or apartment dwellers' insurance also doesn't cover liability for accidents or injuries to customers and other business visitors—The standard homeowners' or apartment dwellers' policy protects you from *personal* liability if a guest is injured while visiting your home. But once again, what many people don't realize is that these policies do not protect you if the visitor is coming to your home for any business-related purpose, including delivery of packages related to your business. This means even if you never have clients, customers, or colleagues who come to your home, you may still need to have additional coverage.

The good news, however, is that many homeowners' or apartment dwellers' policies can be broadened to protect you by covering injuries to business visitors from such everyday mishaps as slips and falls, dog bites, and tripping on stairs. This liability coverage for home-business activity is available even if you live in an area not zoned for home-office use. If your business is such that you get the coverage you need by adding an endorsement to your homeowners' policy, you may only pay $20 to $40 a year for the additional coverage. Such endorsements are referred to as an "incidental business option," "incidental office occupancy," and a "business pursuits rider." Typical language for such an endorsement is "The residence premises shall not be considered a business property because an insured occupies a part thereof as an office, school, or studio."

However, if you have employees in your home, work outside your home, are incorporated, or use a name other than your own, incidental office coverage will not be enough. Some companies also take the position that full-time businesses cannot be covered by an extension of a homeowners' policy. In this case, a business owner's policy costing $250 to $500 will probably cover most of your insurance needs, including coverage while you're away from your home. However, many insurance companies may not be willing to insure some home businesses, such as catering, in which liablity risks are perceived as significant. In this case, coverage needs to be sought from companies that specialize in insuring the particular business. In the case of a catering service, a home-based caterer should look for companies that specialize in insuring catering services and restaurants.

Becoming available as we write this edition are new policies from companies like Continental and Aetna that are tailored to the needs of home-based businesses. Continental Insurance's HomeWork option to their homeowners' policy combines a variety of business coverages, such as business property on and off premises, loss of income if your home is damaged and you cannot do business, and various liability coverages for less money than you would pay for individual policies.

Excluded from liability coverage, however, are claims for injuries or damage that result from the actual rendering of services or sale of products. Protection for these kinds of claims requires additional coverage such as malpractice, errors and omissions, or product liability insurance, depending on your particular business. One of the best sources for locating them if you are in a business that exposes you to such risks (i.e. psychotherapy, software design, programming, accounting, etc.) is through your trade or professional association. Note that such professional liability policies can be expensive.

Your existing insurance probably does not cover business losses in your car—Sometimes people are surprised to discover that if they have an automobile accident while on a business trip or if business property is stolen from their car, the damage or loss may not be covered under their existing property insurance policy. We've talked with people who had computers and other more specialized business equipment stolen from their cars, only to find that it was not covered. Freelance photographer Mary Hold, for example, had her camera equipment locked in the trunk of her parked car while she was running an errand on the way home from a shoot. The car was stolen. Mary's equipment, along with the film she'd shot, was not covered under her auto insurance policy because the car was being used for business purposes. She had to bear the entire loss.

Then here's an additional consideration. Let's say you're delivering the food and trimmings for a banquet you're catering and someone rear-ends your van. Will your auto insurance cover the injury? Risk management consultant Fred Carter from San Francisco tells us that the carrier will probably cover *that* particular accident. But, if you've led your carrier to believe you're using the car only for private pleasure or travel to and from work, when a claim occurs that clearly reflects business use, the carrier may not be willing to insure you anymore. At least you may be billed for some additional premium.

So Carter advises that "you should be sure your car is rated as a business auto if it's used to transport equipment to be sold or used in your work or if it is used to transport employees, clients, or customers."

And even if you don't use your car to carry equipment or clients, because you will undoubtedly be traveling for business purposes at some time or another, we advise that you review your insurance with your agent and determine if you need to make adjustments in either your auto or property insurance to cover your business travel. That's what we did and, indeed, our rate did go up somewhat when our car was listed for business, but the increase was minimal.

Without general liability insurance you may be safer at home than away—Insurance broker Toby Haynes of Pasadena, California, considers the risks of liability for home-based entrepreneurs to be greater when they're working away from their offices than when they're working at home. If you do any of your work, for example, in the homes of your customers, you might accidentally knock over and break an heirloom vase. Or suppose you're sponsoring a training program in a conference facility at a hotel and a participant slips and breaks a leg on the polished conference room floor. You would probably be named, along with the hotel, as a defendant in any resulting lawsuit.

Rarely would any of the personal insurance you now have protect you from risks such as these, but general liability insurance will. It costs only several hundred dollars a year. So if you are self-employed and do any part of your work away from home, this coverage is a wise investment, even if you're thinking "I'm not going to injure anyone or damage anything enough to justify the cost of extra insurance." That may be true, but you're not just protecting yourself from your own clumsiness or oversights. In today's litigious environment, you're protecting yourself from situations over which you may have no control, like slick floors or fragile chairs.

General liability can also be obtained by adding an endorsement or rider to your homeowners' policy, a small-business insurance package, or one of the newer home-office packages.

But do exercise caution when you shop for a general liability policy. You need to be certain it will pay for attorneys' fees and other costs of defending yourself in case you are sued. Unfortunately, anybody can sue someone in today's world, but not everyone can afford an adequate defense. Although traditionally defense costs have been covered without limit, some carriers are now setting limits.

Insurance Rule of Thumb #2: Assume you need it unless you can find proof you actually don't.

Insurance Myth #3: I'm Just Doing . . .
Fact: Business by Any Other Name Is Still Business

Part-time, full-time, sideline, moonlighting, teleworking—it doesn't matter. For insurance purposes, any type of business-related activity probably means you are not covered for the necessary insurance protection on some personal policy.

This is particularly true with regard to partnership insurance. Under the law, you are liable for the actions of your business partners. This is true in both formal and informal partnership arrangements. But, of course, none of your insurance, business or personal, covers them, so if you are operating a business in partnership with anyone else or undertaking a joint venture of some type, it is wise to consider having partnership insurance to protect you against suits arising from the actions of your partner.

Business is still business for more common activities as well. For example, if a UPS delivery person delivers a business package to your home, that's still business even if you didn't intend for him to come. If a colleague or customer drops by unexpectedly to discuss business, that's still business even if he wasn't invited. And what if a repairman comes to fix your computer? That's business, too.

Insurance Rule of Thumb #3: Never assume you're covered for business purposes on any personal policy. If you are doing any business in your home, have your existing insurance reviewed by a knowledgeable insurance professional to see what risks involved in your business activities are not covered.

Insurance Myth #4: It Costs Too Much
Fact: Many Types of Home-Office Insurance Can Be Surprisingly Affordable

Attorney Arnold Goldstein states in his book *Starting a Business on a Shoestring* that the average cost of conventional business insurance can run from $8,000 to $10,000 per year. Only rarely would a home-based operation require such an investment. Some types of coverage will cost only a few additional dollars a year.

The same is often true for extending your auto insurance or liability insurance. Covering your vehicle for business use may cost $100 or less a year. And general-liability insurance costs only several hundred dollars a year. Insuring yourself against such risks will become more expensive, however, when you have sufficient inventory, equipment, or other business activity for which an extension on your homeowners' or auto insurance is not feasible. Even then, your cost is apt to be in the hundreds, not the thousands.

A small-business policy provides more extensive coverage than you can get from adding a business endorsement. It will compensate you for your property damage from disasters like fire, theft, vandalism, and lightning but will also cover loss of business data and lost income from such events, which riders do not. It also protects you from lawsuits claiming personal injury or injuries arising form defective goods, or breach of contract.

Discuss with your insurance agent which choice is best for your business, particularly if more than 20 percent of your residence is used for business purposes or when your business activity has a high risk of liability, such as catering or manufacturing handmade toys for children. Also if you have over $3,000 in business inventory on hand, you should consider a small-business policy or separate business-inventory insurance.

Insurance Rule of Thumb #4: Phase in your insurance as you grow, adding additional coverage as your profits increase.

Even though insurance is less costly when you operate a business from your home, getting all the insurance you need ideally can be a considerable expense for a start-up business. This is particularly true if you add in the cost of health and disability insurance. Therefore, we asked financial consultant Dan Silverman of the Silverman Group in Los Angeles to recommend a plan for phasing in your insurance costs as you grow. He recommended the following:

- **Start-up.** If your budget is limited get only the essential coverage at first: property, liability, auto, and medical.
- **Growth and expansion.** As your business grows, increase the limits on the essential coverage and add disability, term life insurance, and basic financial planning.
- **Established and profitable.** Maximize limits on all essential coverage and obtain equity life insurance, retirement planning, and a complete financial plan.

Insurance Myth #5: I Can't Get It
Fact: You Don't Have to Put Up with That

Unfortunately we did find that far too often people working from home run into problems getting insurance once they decide to buy it. We have a gigantic file from the Working From Home Forum on CompuServe filled with messages from people who were trying to no avail to find various types of insurance.

This is particularly true with regard to securing health insurance, disability insurance, and errors and omissions insurance. It seems there are even some companies that will not issue certain types of insurance to someone who is home based. Sometimes a company will issue the insurance but at a prohibitive cost. To make matters worse, we've also heard months can pass sometimes before a company will notify you that they won't cover you.

Warren Whitlock, who sells and services printers, told us that after going out on his own, his health insurance policy rose to $500 a month. Management consultant Sharon Connell hasn't been able to get health coverage at all after leaving her tenured university position. Private investigator and information broker Russell Koogler was unable to renew an errors and omissions policy; most companies balked at issuing him a policy because he works from home. Mercury Auto Insurance denied us auto insurance on the basis that we worked from home! But 20th Century Insurance was happy to insure us.

Despite the frequency of such travails, the insurance agents we spoke with assured us that if you work with a good broker who is sufficiently interested in you and your business, he or she will take the time required to locate policies that will meet your needs. We agree.

Sometimes problems in getting insured arise because working from home is still somewhat unusual. It doesn't fit the normal pattern. That means the agent must make a special effort to work with the insurance company to find out what additional steps need to be taken. In our case, for example, Bruce Norman, vice president of Mercury Insurance, told us that when what people do for a living can't be verified by an employer, they request an additional application be submitted for review and approval. He therefore advises people working from home to allow at least thirty days to process their applications.

If you're having trouble finding any insurance you need, locate a general agent who will take the time and make the effort to produce results for you. Don't settle for anything less. As someone working from your home, you don't have to. Silverman worked on behalf of Sarah for over nine months before he found her a good, affordable disability program—but he did it! So don't give up, and find an agent who won't either.

Your clout as a business consumer is growing. You are part of the fastest-growing segment of American business. According to BIS, a leading company in researching the small-office and home-office market, home business alone is three times the size of the small-business market. And as we mentioned earlier, some companies like Continental and Aetna are realizing this and beginning to tailor policies to meet our needs. So if you encounter problems getting the coverage you need, keep looking because there are companies that will eagerly welcome your business.

Insurance Rule of Thumb #5: The right agent can probably find what you need. Expect results or change agents until you get them.

You'll undoubtedly find there is a wealth of different companies with a wide variety of policies. What is and is not available also varies from state to state. Terminology also differs from company to company, policy to policy, and state to state. Nonetheless these guidelines should serve as a starting point for talking with your agent to find out if you're covered where you need to be!

Assessing Your Insurance Needs

Now that you're familiar with the myths and the facts of insuring your home office, you can fill out the Home Office Insurance Work Sheet below to see if you, too, may unnecessarily be going bare without knowing it. Then discuss the work sheet with your insurance agent.

Note: The average premiums and coverage we describe on the work sheet are purely guidelines and may not be applicable to you. They were developed for us by chartered financial consultant Dan Silverman of the Silverman Group in Beverly Hills, California. He based these figures on a composite of the average home-office worker: a male, age thirty-eight, in good health, married with children, a sole proprietor working from home in a service-related business like computer consulting, public relations, word processing, or desktop publishing with from $5,000 to $7,000 of business property, living in a large metropolitan area. Silverman estimates someone living in a smaller community could pay 30 percent less. Obviously, your rates and premiums will vary depending on your age, type of work, where you live, and so forth.

Home Office Insurance Work Sheet

Indicate in the column below which types of insurance you think you Have Already (H); Don't Need (D); Want But Can't Get (W). Then use this work sheet to review your insurance needs with your lawyer and/or insurance agent.

Status	Type of Insurance	What It Covers Who Needs It	Estimated Average Cost
	Liability	Costs of injuries occurring to business-related visitors while on your property—if you ever have delivery personnel, clients, or customers who come to your home.	$15–$100 per year when added as a rider to homeowners' policy
	Business Property	Protects you from damage or loss to your business property—if you have any equipment in your home office that's used for business purposes.	$100–$150 per year for $5,000–$7,000 of equipment

Status	Type of Insurance	What It Covers / Who Needs It	Estimated Average Cost
	Small-Business	Provides coverage for losses when you have more extensive inventory or equipment than you can protect by adding a business endorsement or rider to your homeowners' insurance. It also covers general liability, business interruption and loss of earnings, errors and omissions and product liability, although these policies can be purchased separately as well.	$250–$500 per year
	Generally Liability	Damages from accidents occurring while you are on someone else's property. Useful if you ever do some portion of your work on someone else's premises.	Included as part of small-business insurance or several hundred dollars a year if purchased separately
	Business Interruption	Protects you against losses arising from not being able to do business due to damage from fire or other disaster causing you to close, relocate, or cut back your business while you recover; i.e., funds for loan payments, payroll, relocation costs.	$100 per $10,000 in coverage or included as part of small-business insurance
	Special Computer	Risks related to your computer hardware, software, and data. Applicable if computer-related losses can't be adequately covered under your property or small-business insurance.	$89 per year for $5,000–$8,000; $109 per year for $8,000–$11,000; $129 per year for $11,000–$14,000
	Malpractice, Errors and Omissions or Product Liability	Insures you against claims or damages that arise out of the services or products you offer. You need to consider this if the work you do could inadvertently inflict an injury or loss on your clients or customers.	Varies by the risks involved. Can run from hundreds to thousands of dollars annually.
	Health	Cost of illness or injury. Everyone needs health insurance.	Premium is based on age, the state of your health, and where you live. (Blue Cross of California Individual Policy) $250 deductible = $161 per month; $500 deductible = $124 per mo; $1,000 deductible = $79/mo; $2000 deductible = $67/mo.

Status	Type of Insurance	What It Covers Who Needs It	Estimated Average Cost
	Disability	Protects you from loss of income when you are unable to work due to illness or injury. Necessary if you would need to have some form of income should illness or injury prevent you from carrying out your work for an extended period of time.	Premium is based on age, income, and condition of your health. Earning $35,000 per year to pay $2000 per month after 90 days = $682 per year; earning $100,000 per year to pay $5000 per month = $1562 per year.
	Workers' Compensation	Compensates you for costs of work-related injuries. Available primarily for employees. State regulations vary. May be called State Disability Insurance.	Provides bare-bones coverage for about $200 per year
	Auto-Related	Loss of business property while in your car and costs of accidents arising while you or someone on your behalf is driving your car for business purposes. Necessary if you use your car for business purposes other than driving to and from work, especially if you transport equipment or merchandise in your car or have someone else driving the car for business purposes.	Average auto policy costs $725 per year plus up to $100 for business coverage
	Partnership	Protects you against suits arising from the actions of any partners in your business when you have partners or do joint ventures.	A $500 fidelity bond

Because, as we have mentioned, certain types of insurance present particular problems or are more of a challenge for home-based business operators to obtain, the following information about specific types of insurance can assist you and your agent in meeting your needs.

Health Insurance

If we were writing this book around the turn of the century, when most people worked from home or very near it, we would not have much to say about health insurance. Few people had it. Blue Cross didn't begin until 1929 when some Dallas schoolteachers started paying a hospital fifty cents a month to prepay for their maternity care if and when they had children. Now as we write this, health care consumes one in every seven dollars of our national economy and is rising.

A national debate about health care reform is reaching a climax. We do not know if a national health care plan will be adopted or when it might take effect if it is. We do know that health reform is happening in some states in an effort to address the problems that have developed over the last several decades. States like Hawaii, Oregon, Vermont, and Florida are in various stages of offering their citizens a "universal" plan, for example.

Chances are, however, that until things change, you will have to find your own coverage and meet the challenge of obtaining a good policy. Nevertheless, a self-employed person or couple has choices. Blue Cross and Blue Shield plans pride themselves on offering policies for individuals, including the self-employed. Other companies serve the self-employed as well. If you cannot find satisfactory and affordable coverage through such companies, there are options, each with its advantages and disadvantages.

Four Fallback Options for Finding Health Insurance When You're Self-Employed

1. Consider joining a health-maintenance organization (HMO) like Kaiser Permanente, or a preferred provider organization (PPO). To locate such organizations in your community and find out which ones accept individual members, contact your local medical society or your city's office of consumer affairs.

2. Check out hospitalization policies available from professional and trade organizations, including trade unions you're eligible to join, college alumni/ae associations, and chambers of commerce—your own or even one in another area.

3. Explore possibilities of getting coverage under the company of an employed spouse.

4. Investigate policies offered by nonprofit organizations that seek to provide affordable health insurance to the self-employed.

Until health insurance becomes easily available to the self-employed, we must fend for ourselves. So whatever options we choose, we need to get the best deal we can and avoid the hazards too many of us now experience. The following lists discuss what to look for in health-care coverage, the principal hazards, and what to do to prevent or deal with them.

What to Look for in a Health Insurance Provider

While selecting health insurance is apt to be a series of trade-offs between what you can afford or are willing to pay and what is desirable, here are some characteristics to seek. A health insurance provider should:

- Cover you if you become sick or injured, without major exclusions, such as limiting coverage to in-hospital care only.
- Offer rates and deductibles you can afford. Of course, the higher the deductible, the less the monthly premium costs. You should request a rate sheet that tells you the rate based on your age and location and how long

that rate will be in effect. If the company requires other information about you in order to give you the rate, that's a company to rule out—take such insurers off your list.

- Guarantee renewability. You want to see words like "guaranteed renewable" or "not cancelable by the company, for any reason except nonpayment of the premium."

- Be underwritten by an insurance carrier that is licensed in your state and has superior ratings by one or more of the insurance rating services.

- Pay benefits based on customary costs, not by a fixed schedule. Rigid limits on what the insurer will pay is how people wind up with medical bills far beyond their deductible.

How to Avoid the Six Most Common Complaints about Health Insurance

These are the most frequent complaints we hear from self-employed people and what you can do about them:

1. The policy excludes entire organ systems from coverage, like reproductive, respiratory, or digestive. As one person on the Working From Home Forum said, "When I got my policy, it had riders attached which exempted any part of my body a doctor had ever looked at with more than a passing glance. Another rider exempted *any* problem of *any* kind having to do with a kidney or anything attached to it! But I had naturally passed a kidney stone about five years ago. I had no surgery or complications, but spent two days in the hospital."

Keep shopping. Don't buy a policy that doesn't protect you.

2. The policy denies claims, delays payment, or only pays part of the charge. This is an all-too-frequent experience: "Eventually they covered a part of the bill, but it has taken a year to collect it. Meanwhile we paid the whole thing out-of-pocket" is an often-heard refrain.

Notorious for this practice are companies whose policies are sold in conjunction with membership in business associations, but this problem happens even with national insurance companies that have good ratings.

To prevent this from happening to you, before you buy a policy, check out the company with your state insurance commission. Many states provide information on a company's history of complaints. California, for instance, publishes comparative listings of justified complaints against insurers, property insurance as well as health and life. These ratings are expressed in terms of complaints per million dollars of premiums and allow comparison with the prior year. They also provide the dollar volume of premiums collected. As a general rule, it's wise to do business with larger companies. Other states calculate the number of consumer complaints received per thousands of policies in force.

Other items to find out about are the company's payment ratio/percentage and what percentage of physicians and health-care providers will accept the company's coverage as payment. Ask these and other questions of the insurance agent or salesperson. Don't let a loose or evasive answer pass; verify critical information by calling the insurance company after the sales representative leaves. This means you won't be a one-appointment sale. Resist any salesperson who pressures you into an instant decision.

If you are having problems getting an insurance company to pay your claim, you can either use the services of a medical claims assistance service, file a complaint with your insurance commission, or in extreme cases, use an attorney. Some insurance carriers make a practice of stalling and stonewalling in the knowledge that many claimants will simply give up. But juries have made significant awards of damages against insurance companies for operating in bad faith, so squeaky wheels can get attention.

3. The policy costs $200 to $500 a month above what a group plan would cost. To get around this, many self-employed people have purchased polices through group plans. Sometimes this results in a decent policy, but often today you can get as good a policy on an individual plan as you can on a group plan.

As a general rule, insurance sold by or provided through associations' packages offers limited benefits. These plans are attractive to small businesses because they typically offer to insure employees at rates 10 to 50 percent or more below health insurance from major carriers. But there are a number of reasons to be wary even if you are willing to compromise by taking the limited benefits.

First, some national associations and chambers of commerce have been sponsoring health insurance plans for decades and doing a satisfactory job. However, some of these plans are not underwritten by an insurance company, but instead by a Multiple Employer Trust or Multiple Employer Welfare Arrangement (MEWA). MEWAs may have inadequate capital, be owned by a foreign corporation that does not meet U.S. standards, and may evade U.S. regulation or be subject to only limited supervision by the Department of Labor under the Employee Retirement Income Security Act (ERISA). After ERISA was passed, some associations were invented as a way of selling insurance. Some offer real membership benefits beyond insurance, others do not. The Government Accounting Office, an investigatory arm of Congress, estimated that between January 1988 and June 1991, underfunded MEWAs left 398,000 beneficiaries with more than $123 million in unpaid claims. Because of increased enforcement by federal and state officials, abuses are waning.

In addition, an association health plan will probably not be regulated by your state's insurance commission. Therefore, you cannot obtain financial information and complaint records on the plan from your state insurance commission. This also means that if the association's plan becomes insolvent, you will not be eligible for benefits from your state guaranty fund—a safety net that covers individuals when insurance companies become unable to pay claims.

Finally, if members of the association make many claims, rates are apt to be increased dramatically, then large numbers of people will drop out as they find better insurance, and the rates go up even higher. If you wish to drop out, too, but have made a claim, you may find replacement insurance even more prohibitively expensive because you will be deemed to have a preexisting condition by other companies.

An alternative to association coverage if you have employees or are a corporation is to lease your employees, including yourself, from an employee leasing company. The leasing company is apt to be eligible for large group rates, but check out the insurance company underwriting the leasing company plan. Employee leasing companies are listed in the Yellow Pages.

4. The insurance company offers a reasonable rate when you sign up but then boosts the rate. Some companies make a practice of providing a "low ball," that is offering an initial rate far below their cost and then doubling, tripling, or even quadrupling your premiums the next year.

To avoid this, assure that your rate is being pooled with a sizable population and that the experience of that entire population will be the basis for new rates. You might experience a 20 percent increase if that's what the trend is, but you'll be pooled with a large-enough population that if you or one of your employees gets ill, it won't substantially affect your rate.

This is another reason to check a company for its complaint history with the state insurance commission. You can also often find out about companies' track records by asking about them on the on-line services and local computer bulletin boards.

5. The company boosts your premium after paying a claim. "The claim was settled, but when the policy came up for renewal they almost doubled the premium" is another all-too-frequent complaint.

If you don't want this to happen to you, avoid a policy that uses an experience rating, because one bad claim and your rates will skyrocket. You want a policy that is based on community rates.

6. You are told your health insurance is no good and find out that the bills are unpaid. Having once served as a trustee in bankruptcy cases, Paul remembers cases where bad health insurance led people to financial ruin. With medical costs being so high, virtually everyone is medically indigent without good health insurance.

You need to invest the time to check out any health insurance carrier—be it a Blue Cross plan, an insurance company, or an HMO. Chances are when you think of stable health insurance, you think of Blue Cross. After all, Blue Cross companies cover nearly two out of every five Americans, but even some Blue Cross companies have had financial problems. West Virginia Blue Cross went under and currently Blue Cross of Illinois is under a credit watch. Another mistaken assumption is that "big is safe." This is not necessarily the case, either. Just a few years ago, major insurance companies like Mutual Benefit Life, Executive Life, Monarch, First Capital, and Fidelity Banker's Life failed.

How to Determine the Financial Stability of an Insurance Company

Most insurance companies have a rating that reflects their financial stability. But even before turning to a rating service, if you haven't heard of a company, you should first determine from your state insurance commission office if the company is licensed to do business in your state. If a company is not licensed to do business in your state, you are at risk. So continue your search. If it is, go on to check its rating.

Five services rate life and health insurance companies. They are the A. M. Best Co., Duff & Phelps, Moody's Investor Services, Standard & Poors, and Weiss Research. The rating systems vary somewhat, but all are now based on letter grades. For your peace of mind, you want to get an insurance company with at least an "A+" from Best, an "AA+" rating from Duff & Phelps, an "Aa3" from

Moody's, an "AA" or above from Standard & Poors, or a "B—" from Weiss. Fewer than one in four or five insurance companies will achieve these ratings. Not all the rating services rate all the companies; this is because, with the exception of Weiss Research, insurance companies pay for being rated. Blue Cross companies are rated by Weiss Research and some are rated by Standard & Poors.

To find out how your insurance company or one you're considering is rated, first ask your agent. Also *Best's Insurance Reports* can be found at most libraries. Duff & Phelps ratings may be found in the *National Underwriter Profiles* described in the resource list. A. M. Best ratings are offered via a 900 number at $2.50 a minute. The number is (900)424-0400. To get the rating, you need to know the company's ID number. You can get it by calling Best at (908)439-2200 or look up the company in a directory found at library reference desks entitled "Best's Agents Guide to Life Insurance Companies."

Weiss Research charges $15 for a verbal report, consisting of a letter grade with brief explanation; $25 for a one-page report mailed to you; and $45 for a complete report on a company. Weiss now also rates property and casualty carriers.

You can also find consolidated ratings in *Insurance Forum*, a monthly newsletter that costs $50 per year. Its annual ratings issue shows the letter ratings by company from all the ratings services except Best. For the ratings issue, send $10 to P.O. Box 245, Ellettsville, IN 47429; (812) 876-6502. *Insurance Forum* also publishes what the publisher, Joseph Belth, calls a "watch list" of companies that fare poorly on four or more of the dozen key ratios that indicate the financial health of insurance companies. These ratios are developed by the National Association of Insurance Commissioners, which collects the information on which the ratios are based from insurance companies.

Quotesmith Corporation offers a price-comparison service on 400 insurance companies and Blue Cross and Blue Shield plans for health insurance, term life, individual and group dental, single-premium-deferred annuities, long-term care, and the Medicare supplement. Information provided includes rates, coverages, and financial stability ratings and is mailed or faxed the same day. Each request is $15 and each product category and deductible amount is an individual request; Quotesmith, 50 North Brockway, Palatine, IL 60067; (800) 556-9393. Quotesmith is also a general agency that sells many of the policies it compares.

The Insurance Rating Service, a division of the Robert S. Warner insurance agency, provides three three-page financial analyses of life insurance companies for $15. Each analysis is based on data from A. M. Best, Standard & Poors, Moody's, and Duff & Phelps. P.O. Box 852, Southport, CT 06490; (800) 497-6561.

Wilkinson Benefit Consultants, Inc., 100 West Road, Ste. 300, Towson, MD 21204; (800) 296-3030, (410)832-7503, provides a hands-on advisory service on health-care coverage. Clients range from self-employed individuals ($270) to larger companies. This company does not sell insurance.

After shopping and checking out your options, you are apt to find you want to be insured with a major company or Blue Cross and Blue Shield that you are apt to pay more for. But what good is insurance coverage if you can't collect on it when you need it or it's not accepted by the hospital when you need care?

If You Now Have a Job That Provides Health Insurance, You May Be Able to Keep It with COBRA

If you are now employed by a company with twenty or more full-time employees, you may be able to maintain your present group health coverage by paying the premium plus 2 percent yourself for up to eighteen months following the end of your employment, whether you quit on your own or were involuntarily terminated. This is thanks to COBRA, which stands for Combined Omnibus Budget Reconciliation Act, which was passed in 1986. At the end of the eighteen-month period, you can convert your COBRA coverage into an individual policy. You must elect to take COBRA within sixty days from the date you leave your employer. At the end of the eighteen months, you may wish to find a lower-priced plan. But if you or a member of your family has had a recent medical problem, you will probably find it to your advantage to stay with the company after COBRA expires, even though an individual policy is apt to cost more and offer fewer benefits. Your state, however, may have a COBRA-like law that extends benefits to you beyond those of the federal law.

Disability Insurance

Statistically, an executive at age thirty has a 48 percent chance of being disabled for ninety days or more before reaching the age of sixty-five. While working at home should lessen the chances of a disabling accident or illness, the possibility of being disabled without income is sufficient motivation to get self-employed people to pay for the protection disability insurance provides. Also known as loss-of-income insurance, it's particularly important to the self-employed, who have no sick leave to draw on in case they do face illness or accident.

There are a number of factors to consider in selecting a disability plan. They include:

1. **How "disabled" you must be to receive benefits.** If a plan defines disabled to mean "totally disabled," you need to be unfit for any kind of work. If you are highly trained, you may consider yourself disabled if you cannot pursue your chosen career. You might not want to work at something you would be "able" to do, such as telephone solicitation. Therefore, a more advantageous definition of disability is "unable to engage in any gainful occupation for which the insured is suited by education, training, or experience."

2. **How long after a disability you must wait before payments begin.** The waiting period may range from seven days to six months. The longer the waiting period, the less you should have to pay for the policy.

3. **How long after disability the payments continue.** Payments may continue for any time from thirteen weeks to throughout one's lifetime. But statistics indicate the average disability lasts for five years.

4. **How much it will cost.** Cost of disability insurance depends on the

factors stated above, the company you choose, and how much the policy will pay you. You can calculate how much coverage you need by adding up your costs of living and subtracting any income from investments, royalty payments, Social Security, or spouse's earnings.

5. **Is the policy both "noncancelable" and "guaranteed renewable"?** Both these terms refer to whether the policy can be terminated after you become sick or make a claim. A policy that is noncancelable and guaranteed renewable can only be canceled if you fail to pay the premiums. The premiums can't be increased so long as you are current in your payments, and the policy must be renewed by the company but not necessarily at the same rate.

Another type of disability insurance is credit disability insurance. It's usually designed to continue loan payments should you become disabled.

The cost of disability coverage can seem high, but that's because with other forms of insurance, claims are paid in one lump sum. Disability payments, should you need them, can stretch out over many years. For several ways you can reduce the cost of disability protection, see Insurance Money Savers on page 286.

Employee-Related Insurance

If you have employees, there are various kinds of insurance you may be required to provide for them. For example, you may need to provide workers' compensation insurance, employee insurance benefit plans, or non-owned auto insurance.

Workers' compensation protects workers should they be injured on the job. Whether this coverage is required for a small business varies widely from state to state. For example, California requires an employer to have workers' compensation coverage if one person comes in to work only a few hours a week, while some states don't require this insurance until an employer has more than ten employees. So if you hire people to help you in your business, check with your insurance agent, your attorney, or the appropriate state agency to find out what's required in your state.

At the same time, you can consult your attorney or agent regarding other benefits you may need to give your employees. There are federal regulations for providing employee benefits like pension plans, retirement plans, group life and health insurance plans, and employee welfare benefits. These regulations may apply to your business, too.

If your employees ever use their own cars while working for you, your family or personal automobile insurance policy will not cover accidents. However, you can get non-owned auto insurance to protect yourself in this situation. This kind of policy covers you against damages that result while employees are driving for any purpose related to your business and is particularly important for businesses with sales representatives or delivery personnel. This insurance is also necessary for a nanny or a child-care helper who drives your car for any purpose connected with her work for you. For other issues relating to employee requirements see chapters 10 and 21.

Life Insurance, Retirement, and Financial Planning

Even though you're working from home, you probably won't want to work full-time forever. Often in the prime of one's career, that time seems far away. Studies show, however, that by the time people reach fifty, more than half of them begin to worry that inflation will reduce their standard of living when they retire, and 40 percent worry about becoming financially dependent on others. So thinking about a financial and retirement plan is another form of insurance open-collar workers should consider, because when you work from home on your own, any plans for your retirement will be entirely up to you.

We were startled to read that consumer health experts are now predicting that anyone who expects to be sixty-five years old by the year 2000 should plan to have from $50,000 to $200,000 in savings just to pay for long-term health care. That's a lot of money to accumulate after you're fifty, and that's for medical care alone. So setting up and following a comprehensive financial and preretirement plan that begins well before the age of fifty is all the more important.

Retirement plans for the self-employed are discussed in chapter 10.

If you are a single parent, the primary breadwinner in a two-career family, or a person supporting anyone other than yourself, life insurance is also a must. Dan Silverman recommends beginning with a basic term insurance policy, which provides benefits if you die during the term of the policy. Then as your revenues grow, he suggests adding equity or whole life insurance in which part of your premium goes toward that insurance and part is set aside as savings that you can cash in or borrow against. Robert Hunter, president of the National Insurance Consumer Organization in Washington, D.C., recommends that for most families with young children the rule of thumb is to purchase insurance equivalent to five times your annual income.

Insurance Money Savers

Property Insurance

Sometimes discounts on insurance rates are available if you protect your home as follows:

1. Fire-smoke alarms or smoke, heat, or ion detectors approved by Underwriter's Laboratory.
2. Dead bolts on exterior doors.

Disability Insurance

1. The longer the period after illness before the insurer begins payments, the lower the premium.
2. Costs can be halved if you cover the possibility of being disabled only up to age sixty-five rather than for your lifetime.

3. Some credit card suppliers like American Express' Corporate Card provide lump sum benefits of $10,000 to $50,000 for small-business owners for an annual tax-deductible fee of $45.

4. Buying yourself a Workers' Compensation Policy if you're incorporated can be a low-cost form of disability insurance for work-related disabilities.

Health Insurance

1. To deduct 100 percent of health insurance costs as a sole proprietorship, employ your spouse, so that your insurance premiums become a business expense. You can then become a dependent on your spouse's policy. If you do this, expect scrutiny and document your spouse's work with time sheets. Because this is a loophole in a changing area of the law, check with your tax professional before proceeding.

2. Some companies write policies that charge lower premiums if you are a nonsmoker and nondrinker and if you exercise regularly.

Auto Insurance

1. If you drive a minimum number of miles, as many do who work from home, you may be able to be placed in a lower-risk category and thereby pay lower premiums.

2. Purchase umbrella insurance to increase your coverage to a million dollars or more.

3. Good Sam, an organization for recreational vehicle enthusiasts, allows anyone to join for about $35 a year and offers special rates on auto insurance from National General Insurance.

Small-Business Insurance

Buying a small-business insurance policy can save you time and money if you would otherwise be buying a variety of individual policies like business property, general liability, business interruption, errors and omissions, and special computer insurance. If, however, you only need one or two of these, you may save by buying just those you need.

Continental Insurance's HomeWork Endorsement, which is linked to the company's auto and homeowner policies, provides comprehensive coverage at a rate well below what individual policies would cost. Coverage includes business personal property coverage up to the full property limits of the policy and $10,000 of coverage for business property off your premises, business income and extra expense coverage if your home is damaged by a covered peril, and business liability protection, among other items.

Keeping Adequate Insurance Records

In the case of loss, it is always the burden of the insured to prove the value of what is lost. Some insurance companies can be very rigid about this, requiring bills of sale and receipts. After a theft or fire, it's difficult to itemize everything that is missing and document what you paid for it. So here are several methods for keeping a current inventory:

■ **Retain receipts of every durable item you purchase.** If you depreciate business property for tax purposes, you'll already have some of these records.

■ **Keep a written inventory.** Organize the inventory room by room. List each item in a room, its date of purchase, its price, and its present value. Insurance companies give away booklets that will help you organize this information.

■ **Keep an inventory of your business equipment** (as well as articles in your home). Videotaping or photographing items close-up will help establish that you owned them; however, a video or photos that make something look in worse condition than it actually is can lead to disputes about its value. You can use a database or specialty software to keep your inventory records.

A good agent can direct you to companies that are reasonable in processing claims, and in the event of a loss, the agent can run interference for you in collecting on your policy. A complete and accurate inventory of your property, however, is needed to make sure you can collect what you're entitled to.

Finding the Professional Help You Need

Insurance is a highly competitive industry. Companies differ in their rates, premium payment plans, and insurance packages, so it's important to find an agent who is willing to investigate all your options until the best ones have been located.

Insurance agents do not charge you for their service; they receive their compensation from the insurance companies for whom they write policies. Therefore we suggest talking to several insurance agents and comparing the different plans they propose. There are independent agents who deal with multiple companies and there are agents employed by a given company who write policies only for it. Often agents specialize in particular kinds of insurance (health, auto, liability, etc.) or they may have considerable experience in writing particular kinds of insurance. So in selecting agents, find out if they have a specialty, and ask what type of insurance they write most frequently. Check out how many companies they represent and what kind of commissions they would get if you bought a particular package they're recommending. Normal commissions would be 15 percent or less. And, of course, be certain that they are licensed in your state.

Agents are listed under "Insurance" in the Yellow Pages, or you can ask your attorney, accountant, or colleagues for a referral. Be sure, however, to find out how familiar the agent is with your particular kind of business and with home business in general. An agent may have been quite well suited to the professional who referred you, but you want to work with someone who understands as much as possible about your field. You can even ask to talk with other clients he or she's served in your field. Find someone who is willing to invest the time to answer your questions, search for the best policies for you, and discuss the pros and cons of the various options. In fact, ask the agents you talk with for a spreadsheet with at least four possible packages. This way you can compare the many features of each policy.

Use the insurance checklist with your lawyer and insurance agent. Discuss your needs in each area. If you work from home for someone else, you can review the list with your employer as well.

Putting together an insurance package that meets your needs within your budget limitations is a challenge for you and the professionals who can help you. Develop a plan that can grow with your business.

Whatever package of policies you get, find out whether there are discounts you can qualify for on your insurance. Sometimes discounts are available if you have fire-smoke alarm systems or smoke, heat, or ion detectors approved by Underwriter's Laboratory. Other discounts are available for having dead bolts on your exterior doors. Also, nonsmokers and people who run as part of a regular exercise program can sometimes get lower rates on health or life insurance policies. (For more information on such health policies, see the Resources list at the end of this chapter.) As someone working from home, you may be able to save money on auto insurance too. If you drive only a minimum number of business miles, you are placed in a lower-risk category for insurance coverage, and it therefore costs you less.

Then remember that insurance is inherently a gamble between you and an insurance company. The insurer is betting that bad things won't happen to you. So don't wipe out your protection against risks by buying from a shaky company. Be sure to check out the financial stability of whatever insurance company you're considering.

And how much insurance do you need? You should insure against what you can't afford to lose, but you don't need to pay for insuring what you can afford to risk.

Once you find the insurance package you need and it is in force, you can work at home knowing you're protected from many of the pitfalls that may occur along the way.

Resources

Books

Don't Get Burned: A Family Fire Safety Guide. Gary and Peggy Glenn. Huntington Beach, Calif.: Aames-Allen Publishing, 1983.

Insuring Your Business. Sean Mooney. New York: Insurance Information Institute Press, 1992.

Health Insurance: Understanding It, and Medicare. Wayne Lackner. Fee Publishing Company, P.O. Box 681H, Kent, OH 44240.

How to Make Insurance Companies Pay Your Claims. William M. Shernoff. Mamaroneck, NY: Hastings House, 1990.

National Underwriter Profiles are three different books charting financial data. One covers health- and accident-insurance companies, including Blue Cross and Blue Shield plans, another life insurers, and the third covers property and casualty insurers. Published annually, includes Duff and Phelps and Standard & Poors ratings. National Underwriter Company, 4347 Newark Street, Hoboken, NJ 07030; (800) 543-0874. Priced somewhat over $40 each.

Taking the Bite Out of Insurance. National Insurance Consumers Organization, 121 N. Payne Street, Alexandria, VA 22314; (703) 549-8050.

Winning the Insurance Game. Ralph Nader and Wesley J. Smith. New York: Knightsbridge Publishing Company, 1990.

Other Printed Information

Buyer's Guide to Insurance. National Insurance Consumers Organization, 121 N. Payne Street, Alexandria, VA 22314; (703) 549-8050. $3.00.

Health Insurance Association of America. 1850 K Street N.W., Washington, DC 20006. Offers consumer booklets.

How to Survive a Catastrophe: A Guide for Business. A free pamphlet from the Insurance Information Institute available through National Consumers Insurance Helpline (800) 942-4242, or send a self-addressed stamped envelope to the Institute at 110 William Street, New York, NY 10038.

Organizations That Are Not Insurance Companies and Attempt to Provide Good-Quality Health Insurance at Affordable Rates:

Co-op America. 2100 M Street N.W., Suite 310, Washington, D.C. 20063; (202) 872-5307, 202 872-5307. Co-op America is a nonprofit organization.

Small Business Service Bureau offers 170 Blue Cross, Blue Shield, and HMO plans in fourteen eastern states; 800-222-5678.

Support Services Alliance. P.O. Box 130, Scoharie, NY 12157; (518) 295-7966, (800) 322-3920. The Alliance offers Blue Cross, Blue Shield, and U.S. Life.

Rating Services

A. M. Best Company. Ambest Road, Oldwick, NJ 08858; (908)439-2200.

Duff & Phelps Credit Rating Company. 55 East Monroe Street, Chicago, IL 60603; (312) 368-3157.

Moody's Investor Services. 99 Church Street, New York, NY 10007; (212) 553-1658.

Standard & Poors Corporation. 25 Broadway, New York, NY 10007; (212) 208-1592.

Weiss Research. P.O. Box 2923, West Palm Beach, FL 33402; (407)684-8100, 800-289-9222.

Software

MedSure. 45 Kellers Farm Road, Easton, CT 06612, (800) 552-3302. Helps you know what information to ask for about insurance policies, shows you how to analyze it, and enables you to print a claim form.

Two programs to help you plan your retirement, **Retire ASAP**, Calypso Software, P.O. Box 3367, Redmond, WA 98073 ([800] 225-8246, [206] 822-7780) and **Retirement Planning Thinkware**, Fidelity Investments, P.O. Box 4200, Crawfordsville, IN 47933-9923; (800) 457-1768.

Telephone Help

National Consumers Insurance Helpline (800)942-4242 is cosponsored by the American Council of Life Insurance, the Insurance Information Institute, and the Health Insurance Association of America. Besides answering general questions about auto, health, and life insurance on a toll-free hotline and sending free brochures, if a question cannot be answered or if the matter involves a dispute with an insurance company, callers are referred to consumer specialists.

PART 4

· ·

Managing Your Home Office

CHAPTER
TWELVE

Getting Organized and Staying That Way

Although the single most frequently mentioned advantage of working from home is the freedom and flexibility to do what you want when you want the way you want, once one lives with the joys of near total freedom, it's not uncommon to hear comments like these.

"My work is taking over the house. There are stacks of paper everywhere and I can't find what I need. I'm not getting as much done as I should and I'm always behind. There's so much to do, I don't know where to start!"

This common refrain has led a few who begin working from home to move back to an office before they drown in overdue projects, missing receipts, and backed-up paperwork. For some, just the fear of such havoc is enough to keep them from thinking they can successfully work from home in the first place. But keep in mind, most of us have had little or no experience at running our lives however we may want to. No matter how much we think we want and are ready to be 100 percent in charge of our lives, when we actually get the opportunity, knowing how and when to do what can be somewhat overwhelming.

Those who have faced the chaos of total freedom, however, and gained experience working from home find that success comes from creating a system for how they will manage their work and home life. With a system tailor-made to your needs, goals, values and preferences, you can get both your work and your home organized and keep them that way. You'll be able to find the things you need in a handy place when you need them. You'll have the time to accomplish your priorities. And you'll be able to enjoy the extra time you've saved by not commuting to work.

If using a system immediately makes you think of clean desks, rigid schedules, and hours of filing, sorting, and cleaning, STOP! Don't confuse having a system with being chained to an inflexible regimen. Rather, think of a system as a way of resolving competing demands on your time and space so that what's most important gets done easily and efficiently.

The routine that people are most familiar with, of course, is the nine-to-five office system. Chances are you've arranged your work and home around this framework for most of your professional life. If so, going to the office organized your day for you. You managed everything else in your life in the time that was left after work and on weekends. This is only one of many possible systems for organizing a workday, however, and it's one many of us want to get away from. Part of the joy of working from home is the freedom to create systems that are more suited to our personal preferences and desires.

There is one stipulation. To work at home successfully without the familiar office routine, you have to become a self-organizer, someone who can create and operate your own systems. In talking with people who work at home, we met some who were natural self-organizers. Organizing their work seemed to come effortlessly. Others we've met have struggled with how to reorganize their lives around their new work schedules and have still come out winners.

In this chapter we want to share with you what these people either knew already or learned along the way. From their experiences, you can glean the essential features of creating your own successful systems.

Becoming a Self-Organizer

As we talked with people about how they organized their work at home, the most obvious self-organizers, regardless of the type of work they did, typically described their routines something like this:

"I don't have trouble working at home because I have a routine I follow every day. I get up at five every morning and run. Then I make long-distance calls from seven to eight. During the rest of the morning I do paperwork. In the afternoon I meet with clients. Every Monday morning I pay the bills and update my records."

"At first I was quite disorganized. Then I realized that if I work just as if I'm at the office, I'm very productive. So now I'm at my desk by nine sharp and I usually quit working by five. If I have lunch I take no more than an hour, but I usually take a short break in the morning and the afternoon."

"I work best with deadlines. Whenever a project is due I count backward from the due date and figure out how much I'll need to accomplish each day. When I've gotten that amount done for the day, I stop."

These more obvious self-organizers are choosing to follow formalized systems similar to those practiced in a traditional office setting. But for those of you who want to break away from formal routines, you'll be glad to know that there are less obvious, but equally successful, self-organizers who do not follow such traditional structures. At first these people sound rather disorganized, typically describing their daily routines something like this:

"I don't like schedules and things like that. I like to roll with the punches and do whatever comes up."

"I don't have any particular schedule. Sometimes I take off the whole afternoon. But then there are times when I work all night too."

"I do the things that need to be done. Some days are very light and I don't do much work. Others are quite busy. A lot depends on how I feel."

When we pushed further about how they decide what to do or when to take time off, we found that, indeed, these seemingly disorganized workers also have organized systems. In fact, their systems are sometimes more complex than the formal ones we're more familiar with. It's not uncommon, for example, for such workers to create a different system for different days of the week or for different aspects of their work. One management consultant and trainer told us:

"People who work in an office may think I'm not organized because they see me with such a variety of schedules. But actually I know exactly what I'm doing. Today, just because it's five o'clock, I don't have to stop working. But tomorrow will be different. Tomorrow I will be training all evening. So to be at a peak, I'll probably take off in the afternoon."

Whether their systems are conventional or unconventional, the self-organizers we spoke with share these characteristics:

1. People who are organized realize they can be in charge of how they do things. After years of too many rules and regulations while growing up, going to school, or working in an office, it's possible to feel you must do things in certain ways whether you want to or not. Too often, the result is that "being organized" takes on a negative connotation. It comes to mean doing things someone else prescribes and may even prompt resentment, rebellion, and a desire to sabotage all efforts at organization.

Self-organizers, however, have discovered that even if it doesn't seem so, they're free to choose how they're going to do things. Also, they are willing to live with the consequences of their choices. Often self-organizers only gain this wisdom after they start working from home. As one man who started a rug-cleaning service told us, "The first three weeks after I quit my job, I goofed off most of the time. Then it dawned on me, I could goof off forever. No one was ever going to tell me I was fired or give me a failing grade. If I kept this up though, I wouldn't be able to pay the rent and I'd have to get another job."

Or as someone who is now telecommuting told us, "I hate to admit it, but I used to try to look busy so I wouldn't get assigned any more work. But after I started working at home, I realized no one was watching me. I was either going to exceed my quota or I wasn't. It was all up to me."

2. Self-organizers keep their priorities in mind and orchestrate their work around these goals. Knowing what's really important to them pervades everything self-organizers do, from the hours they spend working to their choice of tasks. A salesman who started his own sales company expressed his priorities this way: "I want to make this business go. That's the most important thing to me right now. I don't care how many calls I have to make or how many letters I have to send out, I'm going to do it."

A woman who runs a part-time business designing flower arrangements has a different set of priorities, to which she is equally committed. "Being here to nurse my daughter is what's really important to me. I've built my day around her schedule. But I still get my work done."

A graphics designer told us, "Everyone thinks my office is a mess just because you can't see any clear space on the desk. It may not look great, but that's not what's important. When I'm working on a project I need everything at arm's reach."

And a mail-order merchandiser laughed when we asked how he decided what was most important to him. "Knowing how much each item is costing me is what's crucial. Any overage will eat away my profit. You better bet I keep a record of my expenses on a day-by-day basis. I never get behind on that. Knowing what other companies are doing is important too, but if I have to make a choice between keeping my records up and reading the trade journals, there's no doubt which one will have to wait."

3. Self-organizers take responsibility for what happens in their work. Since they realize that they can usually structure their work the way they want, self-organizers have also learned that they're responsible for whatever results they get. If they aren't getting what they want, they realize it's because their approach isn't working. They take responsibility for problems as well as solutions, like the owner of a word-processing service who told us, "My daughter is still interrupting me. I haven't gotten this worked out yet. I'm going to have to do something different."

Or like the consultant who admitted he has a hard time finding things once he's filed them. "It happened again this morning. It took me fifteen minutes to find something I was looking for. So I'm setting up a better filing system."

Or like the bookkeeper who confessed, "I'm always tired in the afternoons, so I make more errors. Now I start a couple of hours earlier in the morning so I can quit around three o'clock."

4. Although self-organizers often don't realize it, they have made a habit of following the basic principles of good systems organization. Natural self-organizers have learned the principles of good systems organization by osmosis. They picked it up from their parents, a teacher, or on the job. The most common way people learn organizing habits is from the way they were taught to clean up their rooms as young children.

Think back to the time you were nine or ten years old, and remember how whoever was rearing you got you to clean your room. Were you effectively taught how to organize your things? Or:

- Did your parents give up on getting you to clean your room and do it themselves?
- Did they condemn and nag you, saying, "What's the matter with you, anyway? Why haven't you cleaned up your room?"
- Did cleaning your room become a dreadful battle of wills between you and your parents?
- Did your room become an embarrassing shambles that was hidden behind closed doors?

Whatever your experience with cleaning up your room, don't be surprised if you use that same approach with yourself when you begin working from home on your own and want to get organized.

If you weren't blessed during childhood with learning the basic skills for creating and using systems, don't despair. There's no need to struggle through the hazards of learning by trial and error. You can use the principles set forth in this and subsequent chapters to design systems that will work for your home office.

Seven Dynamic Principles for Designing a System That Will Work for You

In organizing a home office, you're actually creating a system that will coordinate many different aspects of your professional and personal lives. Your system should include a plan for using your time, managing your money, keeping track of the information you need or the flow of paper through your office, and getting the help you need to keep everything running. Whether you're setting up a system to handle your mail, manage your schedule, or keep track of your files, the basic principles are the same and you will find them throughout all the chapters in this section.

1. Set Goals

To create a workable system you need to know what it's being designed to help you do. Career counselor Ines Beilke discovered this principle when she began her long-awaited sabbatical. "At the college where I work, I have a very tight schedule. My sabbatical was going to be my chance to do so many things I'd been wanting to do. Two months later, working at home without the schedule I'd been used to, I almost panicked because I'd gotten nothing done."

Ines found that the only way she could get back on track was to remind herself of the goals she had set for the year: to complete a project she had undertaken and to spend time relaxing and going camping with her husband. She told us, "I kept reminding myself every day of what I wanted to accomplish with the time I had. Then I could make a plan to be sure I got it done."

In creating a system for managing both your household and your office, we recommend that, like Ines, you define your goals for both your work life and your personal life. Ask yourself questions like these:

What does success mean to me?

What are the five most important things in my life?

What do I want to accomplish in my work?

What is important to me about my home? My family? My friends?

Make a list of goals you have for your career, your personal development, your relationships, your children, your home. Be specific. Precisely how much money do you want to make? How large do you want your business to be? What skills do you want to develop? What do you want to provide for your children, or for yourself in terms of your own personal development? When do you want to have achieved these goals? What do you want to accomplish this year? Next year?

2. Turn Goals into Tasks

The more specific you are about what you need to do to achieve your goals, the easier it will be to create a system to help you carry out the tasks that will enable you to do it. Once Ines set her personal and professional goals, for example, she realized that to reach them she would have to start turning down requests to do other things people were asking her to do. Instead, she had to set dates for the camping trips she and her husband wanted to take. She had to call and arrange appointments with each of the people she wanted to contact for the project she was doing, and so forth.

In designing a system for your office, identify the specific tasks you will need to do in order to achieve each of your goals. Ask yourself questions like these:

What will I need to do to get this accomplished?

How much money will it take?

How much time will I need?

When do these things need to be done?

Watkins Distributor Sharon Hayes keeps track of her goals by keeping a diary. She says, "I set goals in the diary and spend a few minutes each day going back to these goals and keeping track of what I've done to reach them. I also keep a daily log of how much time I spend on various tasks and decide *ahead of time* how much time I should be spending on each one. Then I reward myself when I made headway on my goals."

3. Set Priorities

The principle of setting priorities is expressed by the familiar adage, "First things first." It involves putting the tasks you have to do in logical order.

If, for example, you have to run errands, make phone calls, do paperwork, and hold a meeting, decide which of these activities needs to be done first, second, third, and so on. If you have ten phone calls to make and only half an hour to make them before you must leave for a meeting, order the calls in terms of importance and make the most essential calls first.

Or when you're organizing your filing cabinet and have ten different types of records to keep track of, decide which ones are most important and which you will use most often. Then place them so they will be accessible in order of importance and frequency of use, saving the lower and more-difficult-to-reach drawers for the infrequently used and least-important files.

Or when you have a series of errands to run, save both time and gasoline by ordering the errands in terms of their location in relation to one another. We organize our business and personal errands, for example, into what we call our "standard errand routes." We do errands along an "eastern route," going to the gas station first because it's nearest, then to the printer, and last to the grocery store so perishable items won't spoil. At a different time, we do errands along the "western route," going first to the bank because it closes early, then to the dry cleaner, which is near the bank, and finally to the post office, which is on the way home.

Five Proven Steps to Better Goal-Setting

Ken Blanchard, author of the popular *One Minute Manager*, says you set goals so you'll know when you're doing something right. After all, you can't know if you're on course if you don't know where you're headed.

1. Begin by visualizing or imagining in full detail the result you want as if it's already occurred.
2. Then, to state your goal, describe the situation you desire using an action verb in the present (not the future) tense. For example, "I earn $50,000 a year." "I deposit $10,000 a month into my bank account." "I speak to three associations each month and receive my full fee. They are pleased with my performance and invite me back." "I complete twenty pages of reports each day." Write it down.
3. Add a definite date by which you intend to accomplish this goal. For example, "By December 31 of this year, I will have closed six accounts." "By next Friday at 5 P.M. I will have made twenty calls." Best-selling author Harvey MacKay puts it this way: "A goal is a dream with a deadline."
4. Write out a list of the steps you will need to take to accomplish this goal and decide when you will perform each of them. Put them on your calendar.
5. Post your goals where you will see them regularly and review them daily. **Do at least one task related to achieving your goals every day.**

4. Put Like Things Together

Putting like things together could be called the "combining principle." It's not a new idea, either. We've all heard it expressed as "killing two birds with one stone." It's a matter of figuring out what similar things could be done together.

Whether you're planning your day, organizing your files, or setting up a way to handle your mail, put similar tasks together. For example, when you have to go out of the house for a business meeting or to make a bank deposit, do all other activities that need to be done outside the house on the same trip. You can go to the post office and the print shop while you're out, or you can arrange your outing to correspond to the time you have to pick up a child from school.

Other examples of using this principle at work would be keeping all files and materials related to financial record keeping in one place, and setting aside time to do all your paperwork at one time during the day rather than scattering it throughout various times. When you pay bills, you could combine that task with checking your bank statement. Likewise, you can set up one time to place whatever phone calls you need to make for the day and keep all the files you use in conjunction with your calls close to your phone.

5. Create Routines

Quite contrary to the popular belief that following routines is dreary, routines actually bring your system to life. A routine is only dreary when it becomes an end in itself rather than a vehicle for taking you toward your goals.

By structuring your activities into regular routines, you save the time and energy spent making hundreds of little decisions every day and trying to remember today what you decided yesterday. So once you've discovered when, where, and how best to do something, turn it into a routine and you'll find you can operate more easily day in and day out according to your goals.

In setting up our routines, for example, we've found that it's easier to reach people by phone first thing in the morning, so now we have a regular routine of making phone calls from 8:00 A.M. to 9:30 A.M. On the other hand, if we do errands during prime business hours, we miss important calls, so now we have a regular routine of doing errands after 4:00 P.M.

In setting up routines, however, be sure they match your style of working. If you like precise schedules, make yours very exact: "I'll do this every morning at 9:00 A.M." If you prefer more flexibility, make yours less specific: "First thing every morning I'll decide which things to do," or "I'll do my filing sometime during the first week of each month."

Once you've adopted a routine, set up ways to remind yourself of it. Use calendars, timers, tickler systems, "to-do" lists, posters, index cards, or computer programs to help you remember specifics of the routines you've set up. For example, if you have a routine for closing out the end of each week on Friday afternoon, you might keep a checklist posted on your file cabinet to remind you of each of the tasks you need to complete before the afternoon is over. Finally, make your routine a habit by doing it the same way repeatedly until it becomes second nature.

6. Remain Flexible

Although you will need to follow your routines consistently to make a system work, you will soon find yourself wavering from a system that is too rigid. Life is simply too unpredictable for any system to operate flawlessly without at least occasional changes. So allow yourself leeway for emergencies and unanticipated events. But then resume your routines the next time around.

7. Evaluate the Results

At least once a month take a look at the system you've designed and see if it's working. Are you achieving your goals? Can you see daily progress? Are you feeling satisfied with your business and your lifestyle?

Fourteen Signs That Indicate You Need a Better System

1. Feeling as though you never have enough space. (In her book *Getting Organized*, Stephanie Winston claims that 80 percent of overcrowding is the result of disorganization.)
2. Never having enough time for what most needs doing.
3. Finding too much paper lying around and working its way into the rest of your home.
4. Not having any time away from work.
5. Not finding what you need when you need it.

6. Being late for appointments or deadlines.
7. Doubting your ability to manage your work.
8. Feeling things are getting out of hand.
9. Discovering overdue bills.
10. Not knowing your bank balance.
11. Failing to return phone calls because you feel embarrassed that it's been so long since the person called you.
12. Feeling that you have to do everything yourself.
13. Procrastinating.
14. Not getting important things done because of endless interruptions.

Evaluating, however, is not a time for criticizing and condemning yourself. It's a time for acknowledging what's working and what needs attention. We like to take time at the end of each period to review our accomplishments, and the insights we've gained.

In reviewing your efforts, pay attention to whether you're following your system. If you're not, it wasn't designed well enough to meet your needs. A good system is easy to use and should make life simpler, not more complicated. Finally, decide whether or not it's helping you to get the results you want. If it isn't, adjust and revise your system until you can achieve your goals with ease by following it.

Customizing Your System

Below we've identified fourteen decisions you should make to set up a comprehensive home-office system that's tailored to your unique preferences and work demands. There's no one right answer, but most people run into trouble if they haven't addressed the issue each of the following questions raises. So decide:

1. **How many hours will you work each day and each week?** If the nature of your work is such that you cannot set a precise figure, define clearly how you will decide on the amount of time you'll spend working from week to week or day to day.

2. **Which hours of the day will you work?** As we'll discuss in the next chapter, unless your work demands it, there is no reason to limit yourself to typical hours. You can work at hours better suited to your circumstances.

3. **How many breaks do you plan to take each day** and when will you take them? Some people like to break for five minutes each hour. Others prefer taking longer breaks after working for several hours. Still others break when they come to a stopping point in their work.

4. **When will you do household chores?** Some people like to take a break for household chores and find that the change of pace allows them to come back to the office refreshed and ready to work. Others find that if they stop to do a

household chore, the next thing they know the whole morning has slipped away.

5. **When will you eat lunch and will you snack while working?** Having the kitchen only steps away often becomes a problem for people who work at home. Consciously deciding how you will handle this should make it easier to keep your weight and concentration in bounds.

6. **When and how will you dress?** Some people find that to work effectively they need to get dressed as if they were going to the office. Others relish the freedom to stay in a robe all day.

7. **Will you watch TV during daytime hours?** If so, how much and when? Some people find it's easy to get hooked on game shows or soap operas. In fact, some people claim they work best while watching TV. Others can't work well with the television on but get hooked nonetheless. Even if you wouldn't be caught dead watching a soap, the variety available on daytime TV today can lure you with movies, sports, and news.

8. **Under what circumstances will you take off a day, afternoon, or a morning?** Sick leave and days off take on a new perspective when you work at home. If you're self-employed, establish your own leave policies, consistent with the nature of your business. If you're employed at home, you'll be on your own to coordinate your work with the established leave policies.

9. **When do you decide to get someone to help you with your work?** Many work-at-homers try to do everything themselves. Some can. Others end up saving money by spending it to hire help.

10. **If you have children, when will you be available to them?** Most people find they cannot allow children to have unlimited access to them during working periods. So you will need to make age-appropriate arrangements for their care and set boundaries regarding when you will and won't be available to them.

11. **What information do you need to keep track of?** Usually, in-house office procedures include policies for records you need to keep. Working at home, however, you will probably have to establish your own record-keeping procedures.

12. **How will you manage your money?** If you're self-employed you will need to establish a system for managing the financial aspects of your business. Even if you're working at home on a salary, you'll have to arrange a procedure for managing your home-office tax records.

13. **What interruptions are you willing to allow?** There will be phone calls. There may be people coming to the door to repair things, sell things, or make deliveries. Neighbors may want to visit. It's easier to have a policy than simply to respond to each interruption as it occurs.

14. **Do the decisions you make in answering these questions apply to every workday or are there exceptions?** This will depend on your work style and the nature of your tasks. A psychotherapist may not allow any

interruptions during client hours but may be more flexible while doing paper-work. While working on a deadline, a writer or manufacturer may need to keep very strict hours, but the same person can be much more flexible in slower periods.

Unless you address these questions and incorporate them into your system, you will probably be faced with answering them afresh every day. That can be a tiresome and sometimes disastrous situation. For a closer look at the major issues we've raised, read the chapters that follow. They contain ideas and suggestions that will help you make the best decisions for creating a system that's right for you.

Resources

Books

Creating. Robert Fritz. New York: Ballantine, 1991.

Everyday Zen, Love and Work. Charlotte Joko Beck. San Francisco, Calif.: HarperCollins, 1989.

In the Spirit of Business. Robert Roskind. Berkeley, Calif.: Celestial Arts, 1992.

Lifegoals: Setting and Achieving Goals to Chart the Course of Your Life. Amy E. Dean. Santa Monica, Calif.: Hay House, 1991.

Making It on Your Own: Surviving and Thriving on the Ups and Downs of Being Your Own Boss. Sarah and Paul Edwards. New York: Tarcher/Perigee, 1991.

The Path of Least Resistance. Robert Fritz. New York: Ballantine Books, 1989.

True Success: A New Philosophy of Excellence. Tom Morris. New York: Grosset/Putnam, 1994.

Unlimit Your Life: Setting and Getting Goals. Dr. James Fadiman. Berkeley, Calif.: Celestial Arts, 1994.

Tapes

How to Stay Up No Matter What Goes Down. Sarah Edwards, P.O. Box 5091, Santa Monica, CA 90409; (800) 842-5906.

The Goals Program. Zig Ziglar. Carrollton, Tex.: The Zig Ziglar Corporation.

The Psychology of Achievement. Brian Tracy. Chicago: Nightingale-Conant; (800) 323-5552.

Seminars

Technologies for Creating. Courses for learning how to become the creative force in your own life. For courses near you, contact Technologies for Creating, P.O. Box 116, Williamsville, VT 05362; (800) 848-9700 or (802) 348-7176.

CHAPTER
THIRTEEN
....

Managing Time: Working on Purpose

Overwhelmingly, people working from home find they have a greater sense of control over how they use their time. They have fewer interruptions and more flexibility to work in ways that are most productive for them. On the other hand, some also encounter difficulties managing their time, difficulties that they either didn't have at the office or had to a lesser degree. Primarily, we find that three-quarters of the people who have trouble with time report difficulty getting down to work, while the other quarter have trouble getting away from work. We hear problems like these:

"I have a hard time getting started. By the time I've eaten breakfast and read the paper, done my exercises, gotten dressed and put things away, half the morning is gone."

"I can't stick to business. It's too easy to think of something else I need to do when I get tangled up in a tough problem. The plants always need watering, the trash always needs emptying, there are always errands that need to be run instead."

"It's not infrequent to start the morning with a clear day ahead of me, no appointments, no place I have to be, just a whole day to get my work done. Then something will happen. The dog will get sick. The plumbing will break. And there goes the day."

"My problem is just the opposite. I'm always working—morning, noon, and night. The other day I overheard my son asking my wife, 'Why doesn't Daddy ever do anything but work?' That got me to thinking, but I don't seem to be able to get away from it. It's always there waiting to be done."

For those who are already working from home, these problems may sound all too familiar. In this chapter we want to address each of them, and provide

Diagnosing Your Time-Management Problems

Place a check by the problems you encounter most frequently:
☐ Getting started and sticking to business
☐ Organizing your workday
☐ Procrastinating
☐ Being interrupted
☐ Getting away from work
☐ Overworking

specific recommendations about what you can do to take charge of your time and avoid the problems you're most likely to encounter. You can begin by using the checklist above.

Getting Down to Work and Sticking to Business

It's so easy and enjoyable to sleep in on rainy mornings, spend extra time over the newspaper, take the day off, reorganize a closet or polish the silver, run errands, take your toddler to the park, sign up for a midday tennis class, or work in the yard during the cool morning hours.

The opportunity to partake in these kinds of activities at times of your choosing may be precisely what attracted you to working from home. The question is, with no boss in the office next door and all these opportunities to do something else, can you get to work and stick to business on a regular basis?

Yes. Fortunately, it is possible to have the best of both worlds. You can combine the many activities in your personal life with effective and efficient work habits. But it takes a new way of working. It may require new skills, some fresh attitudes about work, and a few new tricks of the trade. You'll need to set up a work schedule, arrange ways to cue yourself to get started, and master the art of working efficiently.

Five Ways to Set Up a Successful Work Schedule

We've found that only about 10 percent of people who work at home follow the same schedule they had at the office; most people take advantage of the rich opportunity working from home provides by devising their own unique work schedules. The quality of your life can change with a creative schedule, so open your mind to all the possibilities. Don't limit yourself to the old ideas of what makes up a workday.

Here is a variety of ways you can approach designing your schedule.

1. Establish your schedule around the demands of your work. Let the work itself serve to get and keep you going. This may happen naturally or you may have to make it happen by organizing what might seem like an atypical workday.

When psychotherapist Greg Rohan first opened his practice, he found his clients preferred appointments in the late afternoons and evenings, after traditional working hours.

"Since I was home anyway, I began setting up appointments throughout the entire day, a few in the morning, a few in the afternoon, and a few in the evening. I was very disorganized and I wasted most of the time in between. I finally decided to limit all my appointments to between 2:00 P.M. and 9:00 P.M. This way everybody's happy. I'm free in the mornings and very efficient from one o'clock on."

Data-entry clerk Helen Gillis begins her day when her supervisor calls to transmit her workload for the day. "I never have any trouble getting to work, because Marge calls at 8:30 A.M. sharp. So whether I'm dressed yet or not, I'm at my terminal and ready to work through to my first break."

Lynne Frances found that her cleaning service is its own built-in alarm clock. "I have crews at my apartment every morning at the same time. From that point on there are all sorts of demands, people coming in, deadlines, phone calls. The business is a built-in motivator."

Janet and Carl Jeninski, who operate a bed-and-breakfast inn at their home, worked out a more unusual arrangement. When they're at home, they feel as though they work twenty-four hours a day. "We put in eighty-hour weeks. Our work is our life and we love working side by side. But we need time away too, so we work three weeks a month and take the fourth week off at a cabin we own with several other people. We hire someone to come live in our home and manage the inn while we're gone."

2. Establish your schedule around those times of the day you work best. Everyone feels more alert and energized at certain times of the day. During these high-energy periods, it's easier to get to work and produce a higher-quality job. Our high-energy periods come at different times of the day. Paul is a morning person. He's up at dawn and ready to work. By midafternoon, he's running down. He does his prime work during the mornings and saves the afternoons for errands and other less-demanding activities.

On the other hand, Sarah doesn't usually get going until midmorning. For years when she worked for the federal government, she would sit at her desk at 8:00 A.M. nursing a cup of coffee to keep her eyes open until around 10:00 A.M. By 3:00 P.M. she was raring to go, but the workday was winding down. So now she usually reads and does less-demanding activities in the morning and saves her prime work activities for the afternoon or evening.

Thor Thorensen, vice president of Advanced Computer Techniques Corporation, has a highly unusual pattern that makes having his office at home ideal for him. "I prefer working from late afternoon to two in the morning. When I was working at other companies, I had to work from eight to five like everybody else. Now I can pick my hours." And since he picks them, he finds it easy to stick to them.

3. Establish your work schedule around the other priorities in your life. Raising a family, exercising, painting, or some other activity that's important to you can serve as an effective way to structure your workday and make those things you value a regular part of your lifestyle.

Twila Carnes, for example, who works from home on-line with a computer, has established a schedule that allows her to devote sufficient time to other priorities. A single parent, she logs on to the computer at midnight, works until seven in the morning, gets her kids up and off to school after breakfast, and goes to sleep until around three in the afternoon when they come home. "With this schedule, I get to be a full-time mother and still earn a living. That means a lot to me."

Artist Gary Eckart is a marathon runner. He spends up to fifty hours a week training for the races he competes in on weekends. "I schedule my work around training runs. My morning run starts the day. When I get back I begin working at the drawing board. After my afternoon run, I come back and start filling and shipping orders."

One common pattern among people who work from home is to work long hours four days a week so they are free to pursue their personal interests over a long weekend. Engineering job-shopper Kevin Maher loves to ski. He gladly works from nine to nine Monday through Thursday so he can go to the mountains over the weekends. "I'm motivated to get everything done before Thursday night. If I leave early Friday morning, I can beat the crowds to the slopes."

4. *Organize your schedule around particular work tasks.* Landscape designer Joseph Turner teaches Monday, Wednesday, and Friday at a university. His time on campus defines the schedule for those days, and he limits everything involved in his teaching to those three days. Tuesdays and Thursdays he works with customers and completes their landscape designs. He finds that by separating these two aspects of his work into different days, he stays focused on the tasks he needs to do for each.

Potter June Wright throws her pots in the morning and markets her wares in the afternoon. "I organize my whole day around these two tasks. I get up, fire up the kiln, and don't even get dressed. Until lunch I'm the artist. At lunch I close down the studio, get dressed, and become the businesswoman. I make calls, deliver work I've done, and arrange for shows I want to enter."

5. *Set up an arbitrary schedule.* Establishing any schedule is always better than having no schedule. Whatever schedule you initially set up will help you define the one you'll ultimately want to adopt. Once you begin to adhere to an arbitrary schedule, you'll notice the times you have difficulty working and can then begin tailor-making a more compatible one.

Using Rituals to Make Sure You Get Started

Even with an established and workable schedule, many people still find they need to prompt themselves to get started at the appointed time.

Working from home, you don't have the forced rituals of shave, shower, and dress that millions of office workers experience between 6:00 A.M. and 7:00 A.M. daily as they get themselves off to work. Some commuters have to resort to a full ashtray of cigarettes, a pot of strong coffee, or a shot of vodka to get going. Usually open-collar workers don't have to go to such extremes, but without the pressure of having to arrive at the office on time, they still have to find a way to be sure they get out of bed and into their work.

Of course, for Greg Rohan, Lynne Frances, and Helen Gillis, the work they do provides those cues. Greg's clients ring the doorbell; Lynne's cleaning crews arrive at the kitchen door; Helen's phone rings with work from her supervisor.

If you can arrange to have your business cue you, this is a surefire work starter. Since this is often not possible, however, people create a variety of rituals they use to give themselves the message "It's time to work." Here are some:

- Hearing the closing music of "Good Morning America" or the "Today Show"
- Getting into your work clothes
- Simply walking into your home office
- Turning on the answering machine or calling to switch on the answering service
- Pouring a thermos of coffee to take into the office
- Starting when your spouse leaves for work or when your kids leave for school
- Setting a clock radio to go off at the selected hour
- Hiring a reminder service to call when it's time to start
- Walking or driving around the block and starting to work when you get back
- Starting each day by making long-distance calls before 8:00 A.M.

Seven Tips for Getting Started

1. **Take action:**
   Sit down at your desk.
   Clear the desk.
   Turn on the computer.
   Get out the pertinent files.
   Sharpen your pencil.
   Make up or review a "to do" list.
   Dial the first phone number you need to call.
2. **Begin with the most interesting thing** you have to do.
3. **Start asking questions:**
   At the end of the day, what do I hope to have accomplished?
   What tasks am I most concerned about getting done?
   What needs to be done next?
   What will happen if I don't get this done?
4. **Set a deadline** for yourself or tell someone else you will have completed a project by a certain time.
5. **Bribe yourself.** "If I get such-and-such done today, I can . . ."
6. **Make a game out of your work.** "Let's see how many of these I can finish before noon," or "Can I make three calls in ten minutes?"
7. **Use positive aphorisms with yourself.** "This is the first day of the rest of my life." "The early bird gets the worm." "The sooner I start, the sooner I'll be done."

These rituals can help you get to the desk, the drawing board, or the computer terminal. Once you get there, however, if you're still faced with the horror of the blank page, the overflowing in-box, or the empty computer screen, you may still need an action plan for really starting to work.

If you're still having trouble getting started in the morning, try this tip from business consultant Dan Shafer. "Leave something half done when you quit for the day. That runs counter to your upbringing, right? Like fingers scraping a chalkboard? But it works. As a writer, I've used this trick dozens of times. I just leave off in the middle of a sentence and I know exactly where to start in the morning."

Sticking to Business and Working Efficiently

Once you get started, your work can develop a momentum that keeps you going all day. But sometimes it can be as difficult to keep working as it is to get started in the first place. Household distractions and interruptions, poor work habits, lack of planning, or procrastination can thwart your efforts to stick to business. Before we consider these problems, however, let's take a new look at what it means to "stick to business."

Traditionally, it meant sitting at your desk riveted to work tasks without interruption and looking busy even if you weren't. Actually, once people start working at home with no one looking over their shoulders, they're often surprised to find they work better when they don't "stick to business" in such a traditional way. This is how writer Marcia Seligson describes the way she gets her work done:

"When I'm writing intensively I don't sit at the typewriter without moving for six hours. I typically write for half an hour, and then I'll start thinking about something I'm developing and get up and wander around the house, make a cup of coffee, or water a plant. It's part of my thinking process, wandering and pacing around for ten minutes or so and then going back to the typewriter."

Publisher and magician Mike Caveney describes a similar process for using time-out from his office while ideas gestate in his mind. "When I'm working on something, I might go mow the lawn, but I'm thinking about what I was working on."

When graphics designer Nancy Rabbitt started her home business, she was relieved by the change she was able to make in how she keeps herself working. "I discovered that when I'm stuck or my mind isn't sharp, I can go on to something else. We've been taught to sit there and struggle with a work problem. But you go nowhere when you do that. It takes longer if you try to force a solution. And to handle the responsibilities of my business, I have to go on and come back to the problem later when I'm ready."

From reactions like these, we've identified a more flexible work pattern among successful home-office workers which confirms our own experience. Since we began working at home in a more flexible way, we've become more creative and the quality of our work is immeasurably better. We've given birth to some of our best ideas while jogging, reading, or driving somewhere.

Although the flexible pattern we're describing is not the way we're used to thinking about work, management consultant and psychologist Tom Drucker argues that "if they have the choice, most people will work this way. The truth is, most people do. At the office they just have to look like they aren't."

Still, flexible work patterns like those we've described strike fear in the hearts of many supervisors and some workers. Although they may allow that such flexibility might be fine for artists or professionals, they doubt it would be efficient for most office workers. Their fear is, "Will the work get done?" Many home-office workers we've talked to argue that it does.

One telecommuter who does data entry at home told us she had tried working both ways, and "when I take a break at least every hour and go do something totally different, I actually get more done in the same amount of time than if I work straight through to a midmorning or midafternoon break."

Freed from having to stick to business in the strict sense, people generally can find shortcuts to get the work done more efficiently. The secret to doing this, however, lies in being able to make the distinction between breaks and distractions, between shortcuts and diversions. Supervisors can't make these distinctions, because to an onlooker they often appear the same. But *you* can tell the difference, and when working from home you will probably have to.

A classic research conclusion known as the "Hawthorne Effect" has shown that people are more productive when there are changes in their work environment. You can improve your efficiency by occasionally moving around while you work, changing the room arrangement or decor of your home office, or working in a different place for a while. If your work allows you to move around while you work, you can do certain tasks by a pool, in the living room, on the porch, in a restaurant, or at the park. A portable phone, portable dictating unit, portable computer, or portable typewriter are all tools that make it possible to effect a change of scenery.

Steps for Maximizing Your Efficiency

1. Plan the workday.
2. Safeguard your work from unwanted distractions and interruptions.
3. Recognize and sidestep procrastination.
4. Set reasonable work goals.
5. Praise yourself frequently for your work.
6. Reward yourself for a job well done.
7. Take frequent, regular breaks.
8. Schedule work so it won't conflict with your favorite extracurricular activities.
9. Arrange for a change of scenery.

Planning Your Day

Planning your workday at home is not much different from planning a day at an outside office, with one important exception. Since your home and office are so closely interwoven, we recommend planning your entire day at one time—work, household responsibilities, social activities, and so on. Otherwise it's too easy for them to interfere with one another.

Time management experts claim that the best approach to planning your day is to use a time-planning system of some kind. There are many systems available at stationery stores or through the mail. They range in price from under $20 to over $100. Three popular systems are the *Day Runner*, the *Day-Timer*, and *Franklin Planners*. Alternatively, you can use an electronic personal organizer such as Sharp's *Wizard*, Casio's *B.O.S.S.*, or Psion's *Organizer*, each costing several hundred dollars. With the *Wizard* system, you can buy add-on program cards that will give you a dictionary, thesaurus, language translator, or time/expense manager.

A third option is to manage your day on your computer using calendar and appointment software like *Ascend*, by Franklin Quest, *Lotus Organizer*, or Microsoft's *Personal Calendar*, personal information management software like *Info-Select* (MicroLogic) or *PackRat* (Polaris), or contact management software like *Act* (Symantec) or *Sharkware* (CogniTech Corporation).

Calendar and appointment software also enable you to set priorities, create "to do" lists, and outline and track goals. Many programs also have the ability to print out your schedule on one of the popular paper systems like *Day Runner*, *Franklin Planners*, or *DayTimer*, so you can manage your calendar on your computer and then carry a printed version with you when you're out of the office. Personal information managers are a step up from calendar and appointment programs in that they let you create more extensive records and search for them by key words. Contact management software provides even more extensive functions that let you track not only appointments but also client records and sales calls. (Personal information managers and contact managers are described in chapter 15.)

In selecting time-management tools, make sure that the one you choose is more than a simple monthly calendar and address book. Time management involves much more than just entering phone numbers and appointments. A time-management system should include a calendar for the year, month, and week, a daily planner, a place for setting goals, building and prioritizing "to do" lists, and planning projects. If you are using a paper system, it should allow you to add, subtract, and rearrange pages to suit your needs.

We will introduce you to the elements of a time system that we believe are essential for working successfully at home.

The Basic Requirements for a Home-Office Time-Management System

1. All in One. Unless you have employees to help you manage your schedule, we strongly advise against trying to manage yourself using multiple systems; i.e., one calendar at your desk, one you carry with you, a one-year planner on the wall, a monthly planner in your computer, a daily pocket planner, etc. Such a system not only wastes time but also risks the inevitable missed appointment or double scheduling. So while it may take you a while to find just the right system for your needs, we urge you to seek out ONE system that will work and use it and only it.

2. Portability. Whatever system you work out for yourself, make sure it enables you to take it with you if you work even periodically away from your home office. Since the average home business is only "at" home sixteen hours a week, this means most people need a portable system. Certainly there are people who use one master calendar and planner at their office only, but they are invariably the people who have to get back to you to schedule something when they're away from the office. Again, this is time-consuming, but even more important, it often results in missing out or not following through on important opportunities. Between laptop computers, subnotebooks, *Day Runners*, personal organizers like the *Wizard*, and the new personal digital assistants now being introduced, there's no need to have to get back to someone in order to schedule an appointment.

3. Long and Short Range. Your time-management system should have yearly, monthly, weekly, and daily planning capability all in one. By using a computer, of course, you can enter an appointment once and it can appear on all four such calendars.

4. Multipurpose Daily Planning. By working from home you are most likely carrying out all the functions that many people would perform in a larger office. Your daily planner should have more than just one "to do" list and an hourly appointment schedule. It should have a place to sort, itemize, schedule, and organize the following types of activities you may need to carry out each day and display them on one page:

- Appointments and meetings by time of day
- Correspondence, billing, invoicing, and filing tasks you must do
- Phone calls you need to place
- Major projects you want to accomplish that day
- Errands you need to run and odd jobs you should do
- Plans you need to make and things you should read or write

Such a daily planner prevents you from feeling like one frustrated woman who told us, "I have so many 'to do' lists I need a list of my lists." A daily planner like our specially designed *Time Manager* (figure 13-1) saves you the hassle of having multiple "to do" lists. You can even design or customize such a form for yourself using form-generating software like *PerForm Pro* (Delrina).

5. "Thought of Everything." Your time system should provide you with a place to record or jot down future tasks, ideas, and thoughts that are not time specific. We call this the "Thought of Everything" list. The *Day Runner* has a "Memory" section to serve this purpose. Ascend Software calls it the *Master Task List*. This is the place where you put everything there is no other place for. It's the place of last resort, where you put something instead of resorting to making

DAY:			DATE:	

APPOINTMENTS • MEETINGS	Time/$		MAJOR PROJECTS FOR TODAY	
8				
9				
10				
11				
12				
1				
2				
3				
4				
5				

CORRESPONDENCE • BILLS • BILLING

ERRANDS • ODD JOBS

THINGS TO PLAN • READ • WRITE

PHONE CALLS

THOUGHT OF EVERYTHING?

Automobile • Transportation
Business Supplies • Equipment
Family • Friends
Finance
Food
Grooming
Health • Fitness
Home Maintenance • Repair
Inspiration
Leisure • Fun
Marketing • Prospecting
Organizational Work

©1983 Paul & Sarah Edwards

Figure 13-1. Time Manager

notes on the back of envelopes or paper napkins, or instead of having multiple sticky notes pasted all over your desk, computer, and walls. You could use the back of your daily planner or the notes section for this purpose if you're using a paper system. If you're using an electronic organizer, you can put such items in the "memo" section. With free-form personal information manager software like *InfoSelect*, you can store such information of any length or any form.

Time Management Software

Calendar and Appointment Software

Purpose: To automate your appointment calendar and address book, notepad and "to-do" list.

For whom: Home businesses with intensive daily schedules like therapists, facialists, electricians, errand services, medical claims processors, and pet-sitters.

Examples:

Ascend. Franklin Quest, 2550 So. Decker Lane Blvd., Ste. 2C, Salt Lake City, UT 84119; (800) 877-1814.

Lotus Organizer. Lotus Development Corporation, 55 Cambridge Parkway, Cambridge, MA 02142; (800) 635-6887, (617) 577-8500.

Personal Calendar. Microsoft Corporation, 1 Microsoft Way, Redmond, WA 98052; (800) 426-9400, (206) 882-8080.

Farside Computer Calendar. Delrina, 11810 115th Avenue, N.E., Kirkland, WA 98034; (206) 820-7007.

CalendarWise. Blue Cannon Software, P.O. Box 7641, Charlotte, NC 28241; (800) 779-0850, (704) 398-0850.

Calendar Creator Plus. Misco and PowerUp Corp., P.O. Box 7600, San Mateo, CA 94403; (800) 851-2917, (415) 345-5575.

Sidekick. Borland International, 1800 Green Hills Rd., P.O. Box 66001, Scotts Valley, CA 95066; (800) 331-0877, (408) 438-8400.

A Surefire Daily Planning Process

Now here's a step-by-step process for putting the system to work on a daily basis. Each day:

1. **Use your daily planner to build one "to-do" list.** Find time either at the end of the day or first thing in the morning to fill out your daily planner, listing all the tasks you need to do in each category: appointments, correspondence, phone calls, major projects, errands, reading.

   To be sure you're including everything, go through the day in your mind, review your appointment calendar, go over your list of things to do in the future on the "Thought of Everything" list, check deadlines in your current project files, and review upcoming-event or tickler files you have.

2. **Screen your items**. Once you have identified the things you need to do, go through a screening process to be sure they need to be done. Ask yourself these kinds of questions: Does this have to be done today? What will happen if it isn't? Can someone else do it? Is this task worth the time required to do it? If not, could I do a scaled-down version that will take less time?

3. **Assign all tasks an "A" or "B" priority**. "A" priorities are tasks that should be done today. "B" priorities are those that might well be done today, but are not crucial.

4. **Identify your top three "A" items** and rank them first, second, and third. The top three "A" items are those tasks you feel are most important to get done before the end of the day. They will take priority during the day.

5. **Plan to do your top three "A" items first**. Block out your day around these three tasks and indicate on the planner the times during the day you will spend on completing them. Leave larger blocks of time for creative work. When possible, schedule these creative tasks to coincide with your peak energy periods.

6. **Plan to do the remaining "A" tasks next**. You can save time by doing the "A" tasks in each category together: making all "A" phone calls at the same time, running all "A" errands together, and so on.

7. **Plan to move to the "B" tasks after you've finished all the "A" items**, again saving time by doing those in the same category together when possible.

8. **Check off the items as you complete them**.

9. **Carry over to the next day tasks you didn't have time to do**. List the tasks you didn't get done on the daily planner for the next day. If you carry tasks over more than a week, consider whether you should drop them.

Magic Timesavers

Once you begin working on the tasks for the day, whatever you're doing—whether it's writing a letter or attending a meeting—your goal should be to "work smarter, not harder." Here are some timesavers to build into your daily routine.

Set up an organized information system for keeping track of names, addresses, phone numbers, and files. The number-one timewaster is not being able to find the information you need when you need it. A simple-to-use filing system that keeps this information at your fingertips will save you more than a two-week vacation. You'll find many ideas for creating such a system in chapter 15.

Use technology to save time. Technologically advanced equipment that will enable you to speed up daily tasks include a Touch-Tone telephone with a redial button and the ability to program frequently called numbers, a fax, a computer, a high-speed printer, a photocopier, electronic mail services like CompuServe and MCI Mail, an electronic postage scale, a postage meter, an electric stapler, a letter-opening machine, a letter folder, and dictation equipment if you have a secretary or use a secretarial service. Computer software mentioned throughout this section can help you save time.

---

14 Technology Time Savers

Home-office technology can streamline many of the most time-consuming administrative tasks we must perform routinely in running a home office. Here are a few examples from our book *Making Money With Your Personal Computer at Home*:

1. Use integrated software like *Microsoft Works* or *Lotus Works* that does multiple tasks all in one or use software suites like *Lotus SmartSuite* or *Microsoft Office* that integrate several stand-alone Windows programs.

2. Use templates for standardized documents like letters, fax forms, newsletters, invoices, proposals, cards, catalogs with software like *AmiPro*, *Microsoft Word*, *Microsoft Publisher*, *WinVoice*, and *PageMaker*.

---

3. Use the outlining feature of a word-processing program that lets you move entire sections of text around by moving the title associated with that section.

4. Use spellchecker, grammar checker, dictionary, and electronic thesaurus software that come with many software packages.

5. Scan names, addresses, and phone numbers directly from business cards into your computer using a card scanner like *CardGrabber* by Pacific Crest ([800] 870-3391).

6. Use software like *Intellect* by Clearwave Communications that lists all the messages you receive on your voice mail or answering machine (both voice and fax) while you are away; (303) 223-3873. Incoming messages and notes you take can then be transferred to your contact-management or personal-organizer software if you desire.

7. Use an automatic addressing and envelope-printing feature that comes with many word-processing programs.

8. Fax documents instead of mailing them. Place orders by fax. Get a fax board installed in your computer so you can fax directly from your file without printing out your documents and you can turn incoming faxes into text files for editing and updating.

9. Use a label printer like Avery's Label Printer ([909] 869-7711; [800] 462-8379) or the Envelope Toaster addressing system by Address Ease ([215] 641-1837; [800] Toast-It) to quickly print out single-address labels.

10. Invest in an envelope feeder to speed up printing out envelopes, letterhead, or other special papers.

11. Use special preprinted papers from companies like Paper Direct (800/APapers) to produce attractive customized flyers, business cards, presentation folders, brochures, and newsletters quickly.

12. Save time writing checks by hand by printing out your checks directly from financial-management software like *Quicken*.

13. Put your signature on disk. Save yourself the time and drudgery of signing your name again and again on correspondence. Have your signature scanned into any Windows software program using Orbits *Scanned Signature Service* ([708] 520-3300), or turn your signature into a laser printer font for use with Windows using *WriteType* Personal Handwriting Font Software ([800] 925-8840).

14. To avoid waiting in post office lines, get a digital postage scale like Pelouze that calculates your rates automatically or use a postage meter. Also keep on hand a supply of stamps in various denominations, along with Express Mail and Federal Express envelopes and certified and registered mail forms. Also pre inked and customized rubber stamps for marking first-class, priority, and fourth-class mail as well as your return address can also save time and create a more professional image.

Learn to say "no." A simple "no" can save you hours of time. Evaluate the request for your time from clients, family, and friends. You may find that many requests are in keeping with your goals, while others are clearly at odds with them. Although saying "no" may be difficult at first, with practice you will find it easier to draw the line tactfully and protect your time.

Make use of idle time. Take advantage of idle moments, the times you're waiting for a call, an appointment, or a printout. Read the journal articles you've highlighted, change the ribbon you've been meaning to replace, or slip out to put on dinner during these downtimes.

Build a time cushion into your plans. In estimating how long it will take to do something, include not only the time it takes to do the actual work but also allow time for getting ready, setting up, driving to and from where you're going, and putting it all away. Then add in some leeway for the inevitable delays in getting the job done.

Make quick decisions on small matters. Decisions take energy. If the stakes are not high you can afford to make snap decisions. When deciding things like which brand of paper clips to buy, save your energy and act impulsively.

Do two things at once. Plan a project or listen to an informational tape while shaving, driving, or cooking dinner. Scan periodicals at night while watching TV.

Keep a list of fill-in jobs or five-minute tasks. When you're between projects and waiting on hold, there are myriad minitasks you can do: jot down the agenda for a meeting, write a note, clip an article, sort incoming mail, proofread a letter.

This is not to say you should be working every minute of every day. Breaks and idle time throughout each day and week are important to refresh your mind and spirit.

Now let's talk about specific timesavers for handling those tasks that are notorious for consuming—and too often wasting—much of our time.

Reading. There is more information in even a highly specialized field than any one person can keep up with. To cut the time you spend reading without losing out on vital information, skim tables of contents, directories, and headlines and read only pertinent material. Learn to read more quickly by taking a speed-reading course. Use a clipping service that will clip pertinent articles for you, or subscribe to specialty newsletters or digests that summarize developments in your field.

Meetings. Before scheduling a meeting, ask yourself if the matter could be handled by phone or by mail. Speakerphones and call-conferencing capabilities are making phone meetings easier and more cost-effective. Newer technology, however, like Polycom's *SoundStation* ([800] 451-0995), is making phone meetings even more desirable. Their flat speakerphone sits on your desk or conference table, and its three built-in microphones pick up conversations from a full 360-degree radius. You can have a free-flowing, hands-free conversation without clipped words, echoes, and "howling" effects that have made using speakerphones so irritating. Also Shur Brothers offers a ceiling- or wall-mounted microphone for its ST audio-conferencing systems.

Although these systems now run over $1,000, we can expect to see prices drop;

and even now, they certainly can save time and money if your business would otherwise involve frequent cross-continental air travel to meet personally with clients or potential clients. And video conferencing is standing in the wings for home offices as well. Although video phones have yet to catch on, they undoubtedly will. Intel's *ProShare Personal Conferencing* software already makes it possible to meet face-to-face on computer via telephone for meetings and to work jointly on documents or designs. For more information, call (800) 538-3373.

To keep meetings efficient in person or by phone or computer, limit their length. If you don't complete your agenda within the allotted time, you can schedule another meeting or follow up by phone or mail. Time limits force people to say what they have to say and hear what they have to hear quickly, with fewer diversions into nonessential details.

If you have meetings away from home, schedule them, whenever possible, so you will not be traveling in rush-hour traffic. When you have business that relates to more than one person, arrange joint meetings, if feasible.

For formal meetings, plan to use an agenda, have a leader who keeps the meeting on track, and generally restrict meeting time to decision making rather than actually working on projects. Have a system of referring such work to individuals or subgroups to do outside the meeting. For more casual meetings, begin by agreeing on what you want to accomplish. When conversation strays from the goals, bring it back politely.

Learn to use body language to signal the end of a meeting or appointment. Shut your notebook, pick up your papers, rise and begin moving toward the door, using closing comments like "I'm glad we could meet," "We got a lot done," and "I'll look forward to hearing from you soon."

Correspondence. Set up an efficient routine for processing your mail. To cut time spent on correspondence, use postcards, response checklists on which people can quickly indicate their answers, and small letterheads for outgoing mail. Write your own responses to inquiries on the bottom of the original request and return it to the sender. Use stick-on notes, standardized forms, and form letters, and keep all correspondence materials together in a convenient location.

Use the phone instead of writing a letter when a call will accomplish the same thing in less time. Fax, or use electronic mail, instead of using regular mail whenever you can. Ask for information you need in a hurry to be faxed to you.

To create customized forms for fast action, use *FormFlow* or *PerForm* by Delrina Technology and *JetForm* by ECAP Systems for DOS. Other software programs, such as *401 Great Letters for Windows* from Microbase Information Systems and *Letters* from Nine to Five Software for Macintosh, contain preformatted standard letters as well as other forms for a variety of business purposes. These can be adapted to your needs and can save you the time of having to struggle with what to say. *To the Letter* by Diana Booher is a large handbook of sample letters for the busy executive, and *Letters That Sell* by Edward D. Werz provides ninety ready-to-use letters to help you sell your products, services, and ideas. Also to make sending out form letters a snap, computerize your mailing list. In chapter 15, you'll find a variety of suggestions for how to use your computer to make handling correspondence more efficient.

You can even save time buying stamps by phone or mail. You can order them by phone from 1-800-STAMPS24 and charge them to MasterCard or Visa. To order stamps by mail, use the order forms you can pick up at post offices.

Errands. Keep time spent on errands to a minimum by doing as many things as possible in one trip. Do errands during your low-energy periods. Avoid rush-hour traffic and go when you are least likely to encounter lines and crowds. For example, avoid the post office while the twelve to two o'clock lunch crowd is there. Take other work with you to do while you're waiting in lines you cannot avoid.

Call ahead to make sure the person or material you need is ready and available before you take the time to drive by. If you're spending too much time on errands, schedule biweekly or monthly trips for supplies or consider finding an office-supply store that will deliver goods to you.

Phone calls. Keep names and phone numbers current and within arm's reach so you won't have to spend time looking for the numbers you want to call. Use the auto-dialer feature available on most phones. It holds frequently called numbers in its memory with one-number codes. All you need to do is punch one number to put a call through. Or use the address-book feature of your time-management or contact-management software to dial your phone number for you. You can call up the names, addresses, and phone numbers of business contacts in your computer immediately even while you're working in another file and keep a record of your conversations.

Keep phone conversations in bounds by having a set time of day for making and returning calls. Use an answering machine or service to protect yourself from untimely interruptions. In fact, you can use an answering machine to screen your calls, only picking up those that are high priority and returning all others at a designated time.

Limit time on the phone by telling callers you only have a few minutes. Rather than discussing points in detail over the phone, ask for or send written materials to be reviewed later. Arrange to call back after you or your caller has had time to think over ideas brought up.

Learn to use closing comments like "Thank you for calling" and "I'll get back to you soon" to bring the conversation to an end.

Projects. To manage large projects efficiently, break them down into smaller tasks and list them in the order in which they need to be completed. Assign deadlines to each task and set up a Project File that will serve as the clearing-house for the entire project. On the inside cover of the Project File, write the following information, in pencil:

Names, phone numbers, and addresses of all people involved

Tasks to be completed

Schedule and deadline for each task

Dates and locations for project meetings

All correspondence, proposals, and contracts

Keep all correspondence and material related to the project in this file. As work progresses, check off the tasks you complete and note any modifications in your project schedule. To track project tasks most efficiently consider using project-management software. In the planning stage, this software enables you to set goals for the project and divide the work into smaller tasks. It helps you identify the resources you will use, determine the costs involved, track your progress, and evaluate your results. Popular project-management programs include *Harvard Project Manager, Microsoft Project, CA-Super Project, Time Line*, and *MacProject Pro.*

Staying Cool, Calm, and Collected

Planning your work ahead of time is clearly the best way to avoid the panic of getting behind schedule or becoming overwhelmed with too much to do. Knowing what you have on hand and what you have to do also helps you say "no" to projects and activities that you can't realistically handle.

It's not uncommon for new open-collar workers, eager for business or the opportunity to prove their worth on the job, to leap into every opportunity that comes along. In reality, taking on more than you can do, and do well, sets you up for failure.

The first time Joyce Green started a word-processing service she actually put herself out of business by agreeing to do more than she could. She took on the typing of several doctoral theses simultaneously, thinking this would launch her business. Instead, her son became ill and she ended up being unable to deliver. Trying to juggle the typing and the care of her son put her further and further behind. Two months later her customers were furious and demanded their deposits back. They took their business elsewhere and spread the bad word about Joyce on campus. Their deposits, of course, had been spent, and she had to borrow the money to repay them. "I ended up going back to another job. But this time it's different. What I learned from that horrible experience is to take on only what I know I can do. Now I refer business out when I'm busy. I also try to stay ahead of schedule because I know there will always be some unexpected interruption."

Writer and editor Nancy Shaw works with her husband, Jim, from their oceanfront town house. She keeps her sanity with her demanding schedule by planning all her meals for the week on the weekend. She gets the groceries in on Saturday and cooks most of the main courses on Sunday. "This way I can relax during the week and just concentrate on the work I need to do. When we're ready to eat, I just go to the freezer, and everything is ready."

In the midst of deadlines, delays, competing priorities, unforeseen emergencies, and demands from family, customers, and friends, even a well-organized day can get pretty hectic. It's on just such days that you realize that you don't actually manage time, you manage yourself.

With the pressures of the day, you can lose precious time stewing, floundering, and storming around the office. There are moments when chaos reigns despite the best-laid plans. So we've collected a list of things you can do to keep your wits about you and stay in the right frame of mind in the midst of it all.

1. **Take a deep breath**. In the pressure of a stressful situation, most people start holding their breath or breathing more shallowly. This leaves them with less oxygen to think clearly, and signals to the body that it's under stress. The adrenaline starts pumping, the heart beating, the palms sweating. By taking a slow, deep breath, you bring oxygen into your system and fool your body into thinking it can relax. Immediately you begin to feel more relaxed and at ease.

2. **Count to ten**. This old adage still serves us well. When your mind starts racing and there are more problems than you can handle at once, slowly counting to ten will give you a few moments to recover your perspective.

3. **Use aphorisms**. Studies of highly successful executives show that they have slogans or jingles they repeat to themselves to get through rough situations. In other words, they give themselves pep talks with sayings like these: "Hang in there, Charlie." "You can do it." "Inch by inch everything's a cinch." "When the going gets tough, the tough get going."

Psychologist Shad Helmstetter calls these aphorisms "self-talk," and his book *Self-Talk Solutions* is filled with many useful things you can say to yourself to get through the most challenging of times.

4. **Project the best**. Instead of worrying about what you fear might happen in the future, use the techniques of Olympic athletes and concentrate on what you *want* to have happen. Actually visualize things going precisely the way you want them to go.

5. **Look for the learning experience**. Instead of worrying about mistakes you've made, think of what you can learn from them. The road to success is lined with mistakes. So rather than chewing yourself out for getting in such a mess, be your own fan club. Congratulate yourself for getting one step closer to success, and cheer yourself on.

6. **Take a five-minute break**. Take a walk, get a hug, play with your dog, or throw a private tantrum. Then ask yourself, "What's the best thing to do right now?"

7. **Slow down and take one step at a time**. Just because things are happening at a breakneck pace around you doesn't mean you have to be caught up in the same whirlwind. Concentrate on doing one thing at a time.

8. **Remind yourself, ". . . and this too shall pass."** Nothing lasts forever. You've been through tough times before and you're still here. Tomorrow is a new day.

Taking Charge of Interruptions and Distractions

Even the most carefully laid plans are vulnerable to interruptions and distractions. Like financial consultant Michael Fey, most people find this is even true when they are working at home: "There are interruptions you can't even contemplate."

The most common interruptions and distractions you are likely to encounter fall into three categories: being distracted by household responsibilities, by other family members, and by your own lack of focus. Let's take a look at each of these and some of the things you can do to tackle them.

Escaping from Household Responsibilities

The Problem: When you're working from home, the various aspects of your life can become so interconnected that it can sometimes be hard to tell whether you're working or you're busy doing other activities.

Errands and household responsibilities become part of the workday. They can be insidious, monopolizing the best part of your day before you know it. Writer Marcia Seligson recounts what often happens: "You could spend half a day, every day, doing trivia—the laundry, the errands, taking the car in. You can spend days paying the bills, arguing with the phone company."

Certainly all the trivia Marcia refers to is work. And it needs to be done. Therefore, while you are doing it, you feel productive. Career consultant Marilyn Miller describes this feeling: "Originally I had problems focusing, because whether I was doing household duties or whether I was doing my work, I kept telling myself, 'It's okay, you're working.' "

Many of the business errands you run are the type that someone else would have done at the office—getting supplies, taking out the mail, delivering a package, and so forth. Now, when you have to do them yourself, they fit in naturally with stopping to get a birthday card and dropping off the dry cleaning.

Also, when you were working away from home, all the household responsibilities weren't there staring at you. You didn't know about the broken pipe until you got home. Somehow you squeezed in all the major responsibilities and just let the rest go. And that's what you will have to do when you work from home. It's just harder, because everything is there in front of you.

The Solutions: Your daily planning process and priority system should help, but the best safeguard is your attitude and determination. You will need to cultivate the attitude that even though you are at home, you are at work. You'll need to train yourself to operate as if you were at an outside office.

Calligrapher Jean Hilman handled her problem this way: "When I first started working at home, I'd tidy up the house before I got to work, but I would always find one more thing to do. Finally I decided that come 9:00 A.M., wherever things were, that's the way they would stay until my work was done. After all, that's the way it was when I had a job."

Marilyn Miller found she had to get over the old rule "You always answer a ringing phone" and turn over her personal line to the answering service. Obviously you don't have to answer your personal phone while you're working. You wouldn't be answering it if you were away at an office.

Simply closing the office door is helpful to many people. Some take coffee and other things they'll need into their office first thing in the morning so they don't have to go out later amid the many household items that need attention. Others are comfortable doing housework during a break or during their natural downtime.

Getting Solid Family Support

The Problem: Since your family is probably used to having you generally accessible when you're at home, discovering they can't talk to you during large blocks of time can be quite an adjustment. "I had to learn to pretend he wasn't here," one wife reported about her spouse. "That took a while, but now I only interrupt him during those times I would have called him at the office anyway."

And what a surprise for a child of any age to discover that Mommy's home, but can't be seen. "I really didn't need to talk to her," one sixteen-year-old told us, "but I kept interrupting her just to see if I could. Now I'm used to it and I only bother her if I need to."

The Solutions: Work out a clear plan with your family and get their support. Let them know when you will be working and what your expectations of them are during that time. The plan should define the following:

1. **How everyone will know when you are working** and when you aren't. How you'll signal your family that this is work time.

2. **When you are not to be interrupted,** the particular hours or activities.

3. **What other expectations you have:**
   Any areas of the house that must be kept neat.
   The sound level you expect in the house while you are working.
   Who is responsible for taking care of household events while you are working.
   Whether you expect anyone else, such as a spouse or an older child, to be responsible for making sure you aren't interrupted.
   Whether you want anyone to answer your business phone.
   Whether you have any particular expectations for them when you have business visitors.

4. **How any young children will be cared for** while you are working.

In setting up your plan, remember, you want to *work* at home, not become a police officer. And when someone is opposed to doing something you expect them to do, problems will usually develop. So most people find that in order to get the support they need, everyone involved needs to be consulted before an operations plan is decided on.

Expect a lot of testing in the beginning. At one time or another, everyone will forget the plan. Everybody will push and explore the limits. Even you will probably forget sometimes. But most people find that if you simply keep your expectations to yourself, the plan will go out the window. "I wasn't able to work at home because of the kids," an entertainer told us. "If I had set and kept the limits in the beginning it might have been different."

Be prepared to discuss exceptions. What emergencies will you want to know about? What type of problems should you be interrupted for even if you're working? What household events will you be willing to handle?

Often family members find it helpful to have cues or signals that remind them when you are not to be interrupted. Marketing consultant Robbie Bogue finds that getting dressed in professional work attire is one way he can signal his family that he's at work. At the end of the workday, he changes into "comfy" clothes, signalling that now he's "at home." Here are some other signals people use:

- Posting a schedule on the office door
- Closing your office door

- Hanging up a Do Not Disturb sign
- Posting an Out sign on the door, meaning "Don't interrupt," or an In sign, meaning "It's okay to come in"

You will probably find you'll have fewer interruptions if you let people know exactly when you are available. When family members hear a vague "Later" or "When I'm done," too often they just make further interruptions to see if "later" has arrived. So if it's "not now," let people know exactly "when."

Some people post the time of their next break on the door. One consultant arranged for family members to knock once when they needed something, and he would come out at the first opportunity.

For small children, a speech therapist suggested a tactic she used with her children. She drew a picture of a clock showing what the face of the clock would look like when she was free to see them; i.e., "when the little hand is here and the big hand is here." Or you could buy one of the plastic Will Return signs retail stores use from an office-supply store and do the same thing. A truly innovative and highly effective solution is to create your own traffic light system. Buy a small three-canister track-lighting strip and mount it on the door frame. Put a green bulb in the top canister, a yellow bulb in the middle one, and a red bulb in the bottom one. Having the green light on signals "Come on in"; the yellow light says, "Knock" or "Ask before entering"; the red says, "Don't bother me unless this is an emergency." Of course, you need to make clear to your children what constitutes an emergency.

Many parents of small children find that the child is fine entertaining herself around the home until the moment the parent gets on the phone. A parent on a business call seems to attract interruptions the way a bear is drawn to honey. Here are several clever ways parents tell us they deal with telephone interruptions when there's no other adult around to handle the child's need for attention.

One parent keeps what she calls a "phone box." It's a box of interesting toys or intriguing objects the child has never seen. So, when her son starts whining or begging for attention while she's on the phone she pulls out the "phone box" and appeases him with some irresistible distraction.

Of course, a cellular phone (with a mute button) can be a helpful tool as well for getting the glass of water the youngster must suddenly have the minute she sees her mom on the phone or going into the living room to see the new Lego creation that just has to be viewed now that Dad's on the phone.

Finally, many parents create "twin" offices for their young children: a small desk with mock (or actual, depending on the age) computer and telephone, paper, pencils, and pens. So kids can "play" work right alongside Mom and Dad. To guard against kids' deciding to "play work" on Mom or Dad's real computer, you can get a disk lock like *Lama Lock* ([800]880-9980) that prevents the child from booting up the computer. Of course, this means you can't leave your computer on with open files unattended. However, as a safeguard, you can use the file-protect feature of many software programs when you need to leave your desk temporarily; i.e., for lunch, a break, to run an errand, etc.

Most importantly, when the family follows your plan, let them know how much you appreciate not being interrupted. Be sure you don't make the mistake one advertising executive made: "Every time my ten-year-old would come to the door and interrupt me, I'd talk to him about what he wanted and how he shouldn't be interrupting me. We'd have an out-and-out argument. A friend pointed out to me that he got more attention by interrupting me than he got if he waited until I was free."

Giving a lot of attention to someone who interrupts, even if it's negative, will only encourage more interruptions. So when you're interrupted, keep your responses short and sweet and give family members more attention before and after business hours.

Most families find that by sticking with it, through what is usually a bumpy beginning, they can eventually evolve a creative and individualized plan that will work for them. For more ideas, see chapters 19 and 20.

Keeping Focused on Your Work

The Problem: Many people interrupt themselves. A phone call reminds them of someone else they should call. The dog barking in the backyard reminds them they need to put out the trash. Hearing the kids squabbling, a parent wants to get involved.

The Solutions: Set up your environment to help you stay focused on the job at hand. Put temptation out of sight. Close the door. Soundproof your office in one of the ways suggested in chapter 7. Close off the TV room. Close the kitchen door. Put away books or magazines.

Psychology Today once described a surgeon who was concentrating so intently on his work that he was unaware the ceiling had collapsed around him. When he finished he asked the nurse, "What's all this plaster doing on the operating room floor?" This story highlights how effective the power of concentration can be.

The ability to maintain deep concentration can safeguard you from almost any interruption. Working with psychologist Frederick Robinson's ideas about concentration, we've identified four simple principles for developing improved attention and concentration.

1. **Cultivate a zest for the work you are doing.** Become involved in mastering it, taking it to its limits, finding a new or better way of doing it. Become fascinated with the possibilities. Make the work come alive. See it in relation to the big picture, the difference it makes in the world, in the lives of others. There's nobility in all work; discover the nobility in yours.

2. **Keep thinking about your immediate goal.** Sift out everything that doesn't relate to your goal. At other times, seek to find a relationship between everything and your goal. This is how people can be watching TV or reading an article and suddenly find a way to do their job better.

3. **Take it easy. Don't push.** The most economical use of your mental and physical energy is also generally the most effective.

4. **Let your subconscious work for you.** Grapple with whatever you're focusing on. Really get in there and wrestle with it. Then take a break. Often ideas and solutions will appear to come from nowhere. This is the key to how people are able to take productive breaks while mowing the grass or running an errand.

Put an End to Junk Mail

Opening, perusing, and tossing out stacks of unwanted junk-mail solicitations can eat into your ability to work productively. How much junk mail do you have to sort through every day? If it's more than you want, you can cut off your junk mail at its source. The nation's largest credit bureaus sell names and addresses of consumers to direct-mail marketers, and they have all agreed jointly to delete names of consumers who do not want their names and addresses to be sold by direct-marketing agencies. You can request that your name be removed by writing to any of the following:

The Direct Marketing Association
Mail Preference Service
P.O. Box 9008
Farmingdale, NY 11735

TRW Target Marketing Division
Mail Preference Service
901 N International Parkway, Ste. 191
Richardson, TX 74081

Equifax Options
P.O. Box 740123
Atlanta, GA 30374-0123

Trans Union Corporation
Consumer Relations Department
TransMark Division
555 W. Adams
Chicago, IL 60606

A simple letter will do, i.e.: "Please have our names and addresses deleted from your members' direct-mail lists."

For additional information about ending junk mail, you can call The Direct Marketing Association at (212) 768-7277.

End Unwanted Telephone Solicitations

Responding to unwanted phone solicitations can eat into your ability to work productively. How many times a day are you interrupted by a call from someone wanting to sell you siding or carpet cleaning? Well, you don't have to take it anymore. The Telephone Consumer Protection Act provides us with the right to notify solicitors that we don't want to get their calls. Here are several sources for getting rid of the calls you don't want:

■ The Center for the Study of Commercialism has a step-by-step guide on using the Telephone Consumer Protection Act to stop unwanted calls. Send $3 to 1875 Connecticut Ave. N.W., Ste. 300, Washington, DC 20009.
■ Add yourself to the Private Citizens' list of consumers who don't want calls from telemarketers by calling (800) Cut-JUNK.
■ To find out about the Prefone Filter Company's filter for telemarketing messages, call (800) NO-2-JUNK.

- Get your name removed from telemarketers' lists by writing to the Direct Marketing Association, Telephone Preference Service, P.O. Box 9014, Farmingdale, NY 11735. A simple letter asking for your name to be removed from lists of their telemarketing members will do the job.

If disruptions continue to be the bane of your workday, despite all efforts to control them, there are several last-ditch approaches you can try. Consider relocating your office to a different area of the house. If your work allows you to move around, work somewhere else during certain periods. Public libraries are a good place to go. College campuses, hotels, or restaurants are other possibilities.

Consider changing your office hours too, perhaps working after the children are asleep or early in the morning before other activities have started. Rearrange your schedule, putting tasks at different times of the day.

Finally, learn how to tolerate the interruptions you can't avoid. Set up reminders or cues to get back to work easily after you've been interrupted. Leave yourself a short note about where you left off. Mark the page or the file you're on. Leave your work as it was, so you can step right back into it when you return.

Preventing Procrastination

With all the freedom you have working from home, it's a snap to procrastinate. You can easily put off or never get to something you want to avoid. But procrastination arises from a number of causes, and recognizing the reasons can keep you from succumbing to it.

Perfectionism

In the face of impossibly high standards, we're all likely to put off what we fear can't be accomplished. Therefore, to avoid procrastinating, think *performance*, not absolute *perfection*. Set manageable, concrete goals to be achieved at specified times.

Fear

In their book *Procrastination: Why You Do It, What to Do about It*, Jane Burka and Lenora Yuen say the major cause of procrastination is fear of something, whether it's fear of success, fear of failure, or fear of change. Finding out what you fear, and then deciding whether it's realistic, or how you could handle things if your worst fears came true, can free you to go ahead with the task.

Large, Overwhelming Tasks

When what you're doing seems so large and complex you don't know where to start, procrastination is often the result. In a situation like this, break the work into small chunks that will take you no more than ten to thirty minutes each. Take one small step at a time.

Unpleasant Tasks

If you hate doing something, you're likely to procrastinate about tackling it. When possible, delegate or hire someone to do the tasks that are most distasteful to you. If you must do them yourself, think about how good you'll feel when the task you've been avoiding is done. Bribe yourself with the promise of a reward when you finish, and keep your promise. You might offer yourself small rewards for doing each part of a larger task. Also use the tactic of doing unpleasant tasks first to get them out of the way and free the rest of your day.

Creating Pressure to Perform

Some people motivate themselves by creating the pressure of a crisis atmosphere. They procrastinate until the last minute and then dramatically complete the work. Since this strategy actually helps them get the work done, they're often confirmed procrastinators. The emotional expense, however, is great and detracts from the kind of consistent, concentrated effort a successful business needs. So instead, motivate yourself by working at a reasonable pace to finish one step at a time rather than working yourself into a panic to do it all in one last-ditch effort.

Waiting for the Right Moment

People get entrenched in procrastinating by telling themselves they can't start something until something else has happened. Their thought is, "I'll do this as soon as . . ." (For example: "I'll clean out that storeroom as soon as my son moves out.") The way out of this trap is to do it now. Now is not only the right moment, it's the only moment. Tomorrow has a way of never coming, so start today.

A Useful Warning

Sometimes procrastination is a warning signal, a way to tell yourself this is not the right thing to do or that it is a waste of time and doesn't need doing. A potter we talked with, for example, kept putting off delivering a particular pot she had sold. All she needed to do was to take a picture of it for her portfolio and deliver it. After much delay, she realized that if she sold this pot, she would not be able to duplicate its unique and unusual finish. Once she realized this, she knew she did not want to sell it and called immediately to work out a new agreement with her customer.

When, for whatever reason, you find that you continue to avoid important tasks, identify what you're doing instead, and cut off your escape routes.

If you chronically procrastinate and find you can't cut off the escape routes, ask yourself these three questions:

1. **Under what circumstances would I be motivated to do what needs to be done?** Listen carefully to your answer. Don't censor it. Think

about what's stopping you from going on with what you need to do. If you're honest with yourself, you may recognize you're not willing to work as long or hard as it takes to get the job done. You may not have scheduled enough free time for yourself. You may not be willing to do some of the tasks your work entails. In any case, now you have to face the truth because you are the boss. But you can't fire yourself. You have to learn to live—and work—with yourself. So you may have to compromise or strike a bargain with yourself about such things as setting up a different schedule, getting additional help, or allowing more free time.

2. **Do I enjoy my work?** If the honest answer is "no," it's no wonder you are having difficulty getting yourself to do the tasks involved. When you work at home, it is particularly important that you enjoy what you do at least most of the time. If you don't, seriously consider finding different work. As magician and publisher Mike Caveney says, money alone is often not motivation enough to get you to work when you're on your own. "I can't think of anyone who works harder than we do. At midnight or eleven o'clock we'll knock off and watch the news. If we were to do it just for the money, it wouldn't work. You have to love it."

3. **Am I depressed?** If you chronically can't get yourself going, your procrastination may be a sign that you are depressed. Working at home alone, day in and day out, you can be more vulnerable to depression and it can grow on you gradually. Depression can arise from not having enough personal contact, enough excitement and stimulation, or enough structure for doing things. You can also become depressed from too much contact, too much stimulation, and a schedule that is too rigid or overloaded.

The isolation, unexpected interruptions, uncertain financial conditions, loss of regular routines—all these changes people face when they work at home— can lead to depression. In fact, depression could be an occupational hazard of working at home unless you take preventive action. To combat the situation:

- Keep moving. Even though you may not feel like it, stay active. Physical exercise for twenty or more minutes daily is a good way to keep your spirits up.
- Make daily contact with people.
- Set up and follow a schedule that is neither too tight nor too loose.

Whether feeling depressed is related to working at home or other events in your life, if it continues or worsens despite your efforts, contact someone for professional help. It is important that depressions not deepen or continue for weeks on end.

How Do You Avoid Your Work?

☐ Socializing on the phone
☐ Visiting with friends and neighbors
☐ Daydreaming, planning a glorious future
☐ Worrying, but not acting
☐ Working on other, less-important projects
☐ Getting sick
☐ Watching TV
☐ Starting later, stopping earlier
☐ Cleaning out all the file cabinets
☐ Taking longer, more frequent breaks

Closing the Door on Work

If you have more work to do than you can possibly get done in a regular workday (and who doesn't?), how do you put it aside if it's always there with you? At an outside office, you can close the door and go home, but some people who work at home find that's not enough when the door is right down the hall next to the bedroom.

Short of moving the office out of your house, there are several things you can do to get away from the work around you.

Separate Your Office Space

When you have an office space or work area that's as remote as possible from the rest of the house, it's usually easier to "close the door"—literally—the way you would when working away from home. Psychotherapist Richard Nadeau has his counseling practice in a separate wing of his home. "When my last client leaves, I put away the coffee cups, empty the ashtrays, and close the door to that portion of the house. I don't go back in again until the next day when I begin to prepare for my first client."

Graphics designer Mary Stoddard has to walk across an outdoor courtyard to get to her studio in the garage. Lauren Brubaker has his recording studio in the basement so that "downstairs I'm at work, upstairs I'm not."

Whatever you do, if you have a tendency to overwork, *make sure you don't put your office in your bedroom!* Any other room in the house will be easier to get away from!

Set Up an End-of-the-Workday Ritual

Michael Warner, who operates his company, InfoSource, from home, has created a unique ritual to close his workday. "At the end of the day I walk to the garage, open and close the car door, walk in the front door and shout, 'Hello, dear, I'm home.' It gives me the feeling that I don't have to go back into the office until I 'leave' for work the next morning."

Here are some other rituals people use:

- Taking a walk around the block
- Running errands
- Taking an exercise class at the end of the day
- Taking a shower and changing clothes
- Picking the kids up from the baby-sitter or from school
- Having a snack while watching the five o'clock news

Set a Firm Schedule

If possible, set up a fixed "closing hour" and do not compromise except for emergencies. This is usually easier to do when you're salaried than when you're self-employed. In our work, for example, we give many evening speeches and seminars. We have early-morning meetings with our editors. We give all-day seminars too. If we weren't careful in planning our week, we would end up working morning, noon, and night.

For situations like ours when you're working at different times of the day during the week, we've developed two general rules:

1. **Set aside either the morning, afternoon, or evening** of each day as "free" time during which you do not work. As you fill in your appointment calendar, block off either the morning, afternoon, or evening of a day by putting a big "X" over the one free period.

We realize, of course, that some days will be more hectic than others, but to make this system work, we've found we have to be fairly rigid about this rule. When we have X'd out an evening of a fully scheduled day and someone wants us to meet that night, unless it's crucial we have to say, "No, that evening is already filled." And it is. It's filled with time off.

2. **Allow at least one full "free" day per week.** Usually this is Saturday and/or Sunday; however, it can be any day of the week. A family we know operates a swapmeet booth every weekend, and takes Monday and Tuesday off. A professional dog handler works at shows on weekends and teaches evening classes during the week. His free day is Friday, and during the rest of the week he doesn't go to work until one in the afternoon.

Put Nonwork Events on Your Calendar in Advance

There is another simple step you can take to close the door on work when you need to. Use your calendar to prepare yourself to take time off. Most people reserve their appointment calendars for work-related activities or special social occasions. Personal or family activities are usually fit in around business. Writing these activities on your calendar helps give them equal time.

Get Out of the House

When work is home and home is work, people sometimes find they have to get away from the house to get really away from work. They come to feel the way graphics designer Nancy Rabbitt does: "When you commute to work, coming home is like a retreat, a refuge. But when you work at home, it's no longer a refuge. To relax and refresh myself I have to go someplace else, get away for an evening or go off for a weekend."

Getting away isn't always easy, however. Have you ever thought of planning an evening at the theater or taking a short trip, but then waited to see if you'd be free or if you'd feel like it when the time came? What happened? Too often, when the time came, you were too busy or too tired to go.

Genevieve Marcus and Bob Smith, who run an educational foundation from their home, have found that to get away from work they have to make reservations in advance. When they see an event that looks interesting, they buy the tickets right away. If they want to spend a weekend at a vacation resort, they pay for the tickets and the hotel room in advance.

"Then we have to go. We have to drop what we're doing," Genevieve explains. "Right before it's time to go, I always wish I hadn't bought the tickets. I never feel like going. But since I've paid for them, I go and I always end up having a wonderful time. When I get back, I'm glad I got away."

Protect Your Free Time

Home-business owners frequently complain that clients, knowing they're at home, call or even drop by any time of day or night. When this is your situation, you'll have to create ways to protect yourself from business intrusions into your free time.

Nancy Rabbitt found a double solution to this problem. Although she had fixed business hours, she kept getting calls in the early morning or having the doorbell ring while she was still in the bathtub. "I now have an answering service, which I keep on before and after business hours. When customers call, they're told the hours they can reach me and asked to leave a message. I also have a box on the front door so if someone comes by before I'm open for business, they can leave off whatever work they're bringing. Or in the evening, they can pick up their work after I'm closed."

If you are one of those people who can't stand to hear a phone ring without picking it up, a phone with a button for turning off the ring may help you turn a deaf ear.

When All Else Fails

Perhaps you're a person who simply can't stop working, a "workaholic." If many of the signs of overworking apply to you, an office at home may aggravate the situation. You don't have to move your office out of the house, however, to escape from overwork. You can get to the root of the problem.

People who overwork often link their self-worth and sense of well-being to whether or not they are being productive. They feel bad if they aren't always doing something. They fear the worst will happen if they let up.

Behavioral scientists have found that the constant drive to work is usually traceable to very basic concepts and beliefs about ourselves and about life. These convictions are related to what we unconsciously believe we must do to survive, to be loved, to succeed, to be worthy as a person.

Often overworkers have gotten the idea they must overwork from their parents, or even grandparents, who were living in more difficult economic times than those today.

One woman we know traced her belief that she had to be working all the time to her immigrant grandparents' struggle to survive and rise above poverty. She recalls her grandmother working from dawn to dusk seven days a week. She remembers every family member being sent to work, and how her mother continued this tradition years after they were all affluent.

Similarly, one man recognized how his tendency to overwork arose from growing up in the Depression. His father never lost his job, but those around him did. The father worked long hours during that time and ever after. For years to come, the father would recount how being caught with an idle moment could have cost him his job and the family's livelihood.

In addition to the experiences in our past, societal conditioning also invites us

---

Signs of Overworking

1. Do your spouse, children, or friends nag and complain that you need to spend more time with them? Do frustrated children, friends, and other loved ones feel last on the list for your time? Do they sulk, badger, or act up for your attention?
2. Do you have many business associates but few friends? Are you always too busy to get together with people? Do you hear yourself saying things like "I can't make it," or "Sorry I had to miss it"?
3. Do you work even in nonworking situations? Do you "work" your social gatherings, and talk shop wherever you go?
4. Do you work at your play? Is all your recreation as much work as being on the job, because you play to win every point and improve your previous performance, and you refuse to take losing lightly?
5. Do you feel uncomfortable if you're in a situation where you can't be productive, growing nervous as you wait in a grocery line or for a red light to change?
6. Do you think of nongoal-directed fun as frivolous? Do you feel that "doing nothing" is being lazy, and do you consider those who don't work as hard as you do unmotivated?
7. Do you let the clock run your life? Do you look at the clock often, wanting to cram as much as possible into every minute, or are you frequently late because you had to get just one more thing done before you left?
8. Do you take everything so seriously that you miss or resent humorous comments in a work situation?

---

to overwork and rewards us for doing so. Many men have been conditioned to believe that their value lies in how much money they can make or how high up the corporate ladder they can climb—both of which often seem to depend on putting in overly long and difficult hours.

In recent years, many women have found themselves in this trap too, feeling they can't get ahead unless they overwork as much as so many men do. Women also get caught in the "Superwoman" syndrome, working full-time and trying to be the perfect mother, lover, and housewife all at once.

If you're self-employed, concern about your economic security can drive you to think that you must keep working all the time or you'll never make it. Sometimes family and friends unintentionally intensify such concerns because of their own fears. Not wanting you to fail or suffer needlessly, parents may subtly suggest that you take another job. Worried about mounting bills, spouses can thoughtlessly comment that you should have kept your job.

Usually overworkers are not aware of such patterns, beliefs, and conditioning, but once recognized for what they are, these factors can be changed. The overworker can develop new values that support a healthier, more balanced, and even a more productive and secure life. If you overwork, here are several steps you can take:

1. Change your ideas about success. There's a difference between hard work and overwork. Success today does not require working yourself into the grave. In fact, success can be easy. A consistent, steady effort proves more successful than a stress-filled obsession. Reassure yourself of your ability to achieve your goals or get reassurance from others who will support you. When sales trainer Harriet Brayton left her job, she was so frightened about whether she could make it on her own that she at first couldn't even sleep. She kept thinking of work she could be doing. She turned to her father for reassurance. "For a while I was calling him every day. A successful businessman himself, he kept telling me, 'Harriet, relax, you're doing fine. Just keep going.' And that's what I would say to others. It works. I'm doing fine now and I still take time to play."

2. Have a talk with yourself about the therapeutic effects of relaxing. Convince yourself that you're entitled to relax and that there's more to life than work. In fact, you owe it to yourself. Your life will not only be just as good when you stop working so much, it will actually be better. Studies like the one by Dr. Charles Garfield of the University of California, San Francisco, School of Medicine, show that workaholics not only have more heart attacks and other illnesses, but actually don't get as much accomplished! You may be surprised to discover that you get more done and have more energy after you begin to take more time off.

If this is hard for you to believe, read about others who used to feel as you do. Writer Norman Cousins is a good example. He has written about how, after a near-fatal disease, he learned to change from an inveterate overworker to someone who could relax and enjoy life while he still had it.

3. Find out what drives you to overwork and give yourself permission to stop. Below we have listed what psychologist Taibi Kahler has identified as the four most common messages people use to drive themselves and the messages they need to hear to stop.

4. Explore how you became so driven. Try to discover how you got the idea you have to work so much. If you overwork, look back into your roots to find out what experiences or social pressures influenced you to overwork. Use the Five-Step Change Process (see p. 338) to recognize what you believe about overworking, why it's important to you, and how you can develop new, healthier, and more rewarding ways to accomplish what you want to do.

5. Set up minibreaks. Set aside five to fifteen minutes a day to "do nothing." Spend that time doing anything that you enjoy but don't have to do. It's surprising what people call "doing nothing." For example:

- Working in the garden
- Watching TV
- Taking a walk
- Sitting in the sun
- Playing ball with the kids
- Brushing the dog
- Taking a nap
- Reading a magazine

At first you may find these five to fifteen minutes uncomfortable, but make yourself take them. Don't expect "doing nothing" to feel good at first. You're going against your conditioning and years of habit. It takes a while to shed the discomfort and develop new habits. To help the process along when you are

---

How to Escape What's Driving You

Driving Message	New Beliefs
Be Perfect	You can learn from making mistakes. Mistakes take you closer to success. No one is perfect.
Try Hard	Do your best and you'll do a good job. Doing well doesn't have to be hard. You don't have to struggle to succeed. Success can come effortlessly.
Hurry Up	You can go at your own pace. You'll get more done when you go at a reasonable and steady rate. Slow down. Take a breath. Take one step at a time and you'll reach your goals.
Please Others	You can't please everyone all the time. You have to take care of yourself before you can take care of others. It's okay to say "no."

feeling uncomfortable, take notice of the old beliefs your feelings stem from and mentally replace them with the new beliefs that will free you from overworking.

At first you will probably have to schedule your leisure time by formally putting these five- to fifteen-minute work breaks into your day. Set a goal of taking one break at ten o'clock in the morning and one at three o'clock in the afternoon, for example.

6. Set aside part of each day for leisure. If you are now working most of the waking day, build up to enjoying a portion of every day off. For example, graduate from minibreaks to setting aside a whole hour once a week for leisure time in the evenings. Then adding one or two hours a week as free time begins to feel more comfortable. Eventually, you will be able to limit your work to eight or ten hours a day.

7. Avoid invitations to work on something else. When you start taking time off, some people may see that you're free, for a change, and try to put you back to work—finally you're available to do some of the things they've been waiting for you to do! Tell them these "free times" are health breaks that will keep you alive longer, and send them on their way.

8. Raise your prices. If the cause of your overwork is too much business, consider raising your prices. This is a better alternative than hiring an employee or turning work down because you earn more from your own efforts. You want to give existing clients plenty of notice, perhaps even extend your current prices for a period of time.

A Five-Step Change Process*

Step 1. Ask yourself, "What *positive intention* do I have for working so much and driving myself so hard?" What are you hoping to get? What are you hoping to avoid? Here are a few sample answers:

To make enough money to relax someday
To be somebody
To keep from going under
To avoid hassles in the family

Step 2. Ask yourself if you would be willing to consider other ways of achieving your positive intention besides overworking.

Step 3. Then, using your creative abilities, think of three *other* ways you could achieve your positive intention.

Step 4. Ask yourself if you are willing to use these three new ways instead of overworking.

Step 5. Check to see that you have no doubts about using the new alternatives. If you do, go back to Step 3 and come up with some other ways that will overcome your doubts.

* From neurolinguistic programming techniques developed by Richard Bandleo and John Grinder.

Refuse to let anything interfere with the time you've blocked off for leisure, and avoid the trap of working at your play. Do leisure activities because you enjoy them, not because they will produce some work objective for you. Your leisure time is for doing things that are gratifying in and of themselves. Play golf, for example, because it feels good, not because you can talk over a business deal. If you play golf with a prospective client, that's probably not leisure. If you jog to improve your time, you are probably working at it and not playing. So you'll need to include another way of relaxing.

Finally, as time-management consultant Dr. Terry Paulson advises, spoil yourself when you relax. See that baseball game you've been itching to go to. Listen to your favorite album or radio talk show. Buy yourself that science fiction thriller you've been meaning to read. And read it. Or, in the good doctor's words, "Pamper yourself . . . there are no replacements."

Resources

Books

Feeling Good: The New Mood Therapy. Clinically Proven Drug Free Treatment for Depression. David Burns. New York: Avon, 1980.

The How-to-Be Book: A Table with Exercises to Take the Stress Out of Your Life. Thomas Thiss. Minneapolis: Deaconess Press, 1994.

If You Haven't Got the Time to Do It Right, When Will You Find the Time to Do It Over? Jeffrey J. Meyer. New York: Simon & Schuster, 1990.

Letters That Sell. Edwards D. Werz. Chicago: Contemporary Books, 1987.

Making It on Your Own: Surviving and Thriving on the Ups and Downs of Being Your Own Boss. Sarah and Paul Edwards. New York: Tarcher/Putnam, 1991.

The Now Habit: A Strategic Program for Overcoming Procrastination and Enjoying Guilt-Free Play. Neil Fiore. Los Angeles: Tarcher/Perigee, 1989.

Timelock: How Life Got So Hectic and What You Can Do About It. Ralph Keyes. New York: Ballantine, 1991.

To the Letter. Diana Booker. Lexington, Mass.: Lexington Books, 1988.

Transitions—Making Sense of Life's Changes: Strategies for Coping with Difficult People and Confusing Times in Your Life. William Bridges. Reading, Mass.: Addison-Wesley, 1980.

When Good Enough Is Never Enough: Escaping the Perfection Trap. Steven J. Hendlin. Los Angeles: Tarcher/Putnam, 1992.

What You Can Change and What You Can't: The Complete Guide to Successful Self-Improvement. Martin E. T. Seligman. New York: Knopf, 1994.

What to Say When You Talk to Yourself. Shad Helmstetter. Scottsdale, Ariz.: Grindle Press, 1986.

Work a 4-Hour Day, Achieving Business Efficiency on Your Own Terms. Arthur K. Robertson and William Proctor. New York: William Morrow, 1994.

Tapes

Believe and Achieve. Clement Stone's New Success Formula. Los Angeles: Renaissance Tapes.

How to Master Your Time. Brian Tracy. Chicago: Nightingale Conant; (800) 323-5552.

How to Stay Up No Matter What Goes Down. Sarah Edwards, Here's How, P.O. Box 5091, Santa Monica, CA 90409.

Time-Management Systems

Day Runner. Harper House, 2750 West Moore Ave., Fullerton, CA 92633; (800) 232-9786.

Day Timer. Day-Timer Concepts, One Willow Lane, East Texas, PA 18046; (800) 317-9152.

The Franklin Planner. Franklin Quest, P.O. Box 31406, Salt Lake City, UT 84131; (800) 544-1776.

Time Management Software

Anytime. Individual Software. 5870 Stoneridge Drive, #1, Pleasanton, CA 94588; (800) 331-3313.

Ascend. Franklin Quest, 2550 South Decker Lane Blvd., Ste. 2C, Salt Lake City, UT 84119; (800) 877-1814.

Calendar Creator Plus. Misco and Power-Up Corp., P.O. Box 7600, San Mateo, CA 94403; (800) 851-2917.

Delrina Daily Planner and **Farside Calendar.** Delrina, 11810 115th Avenue, N.E., Kirkland, WA 98034; (206) 820-7707.

Lotus Organizer. Lotus Development Company, 55 Cambridge Parkway, Cambridge, MA 02142; (800) 635-6887.

Personal Calendar. Microsoft Corporation, 1 Microsoft Way, Redmon, WA 98052; (800) 426-9400.

Sharkware. CogniTech Corporation, P.O. Box 500129, Atlanta, GA 31150; (404) 518-4577.

CHAPTER
FOURTEEN
∎∎∎∎∎∎∎∎∎∎∎∎∎∎∎∎∎∎∎∎∎∎∎∎∎∎∎

Managing Money: Financing and
Cash-Flow Management

If you're like the majority of the people who work from home, whether you're salaried or self-employed, you have neither the time nor the inclination to spend hours doing complicated record keeping. Fortunately there's usually no need to get complicated, but you do have to spend a little time setting up a system for managing the records you need to keep in order to track the money you're making. Otherwise, it's all too easy for your income to slip through the cracks.

Picture this: A check bounces and your credit is marred. It's tax season and you're buried beneath a mound of receipts trying to figure out just how much you spent on supplies and equipment. You're at a party and overhear how you lost out on a way to make your money work for you by earning higher interest rates. With an effective money management system you can avoid these and other problems of money mismanagement, which is the number one reason for small-business failures.

Unfortunately, many financial record-keeping systems for small businesses are scaled-down versions of those used in large organizations. They require too much time, too much energy, or too much money for a one-person home office. At the same time, systems for managing household money matters aren't adequate for home-business needs, either.

Faced with choosing between two extremes, some home-office people adopt the bookkeeping systems designed for larger businesses. Others, seeking to avoid the hassles of complex systems, fly by the seat of their pants, hoping everything will work out in the end. For too many, both of these strategies produce disappointing results. People frequently tell us:

"I've tried several times to use a formal record-keeping system, but it takes so much time that I get behind after a few weeks. Then for the rest of the year I just try to keep up with what's necessary. The receipts and everything, they're all in a box in the corner of my office. I guess until I can hire someone to do it for me, I'm doomed to trying to straighten it all out at tax time."

To avoid this dilemma, a money management system for a home office should meet four criteria:

1. **It should be simple and easy** enough for you to use in the time you have. In fact, it should be so simple that it's as easy or easier to use than not to use.

2. **It needs to have a fail-safe mechanism** so that if you fall behind, there is a way of picking up again without undue effort.

3. **It needs to be easily expandable** into other larger systems if and when your business needs grow.

4. **It has to do the job for you.**

What You Need to Keep Track Of

The specific financial information you need to keep track of depends on whether you're salaried or self-employed and on the type of business you're in. Here is a checklist of the typical kinds of information you may need to manage. Review it and check off the items that apply to you:

- **Banking transactions:** making deposits as well as keeping track of and balancing your savings or checking accounts.

- **Bills:** paying and keeping track of your personal and business-related expenses.

- **Time and expenses:** keeping a record of time and costs you need to bill to your customers, clients, or employer.

- **Billing or invoicing:** keeping records of money people owe you and sending statements to get paid for services or products you've provided.

- **Inventories:** keeping track of products you have on hand.

- **Sales records:** keeping track of the products you've sold and any sales tax you've collected.

Easy-to-Use Record-Keeping Systems

As with time management systems, there is a variety of ready-made money management aids available at stationery, office-supply, and software stores to help you keep track of the information you need. When you're salaried or affiliated with a sales organization, the company may have a system of its own for you to follow. If so, you'll need to incorporate it into a comprehensive system that addresses all aspects of your personal and business finances.

The right system will enable you to:

- Know how you're doing financially: whether you're making a profit; how far ahead or behind you are each month.

- Keep track of how you are spending your money so you can adjust what you spend in accordance with your goals.

- Determine which of your business activities are the most profitable.

- Be prepared, save time, and avoid stress when you do your taxes, when you seek loans and investors, when you want to sell your business, or any time you need to prepare financial statements, profit-and-loss statements, or balance sheets.

- Provide your tax preparer with everything needed to complete your federal and state returns in minimum time, therefore saving you money.

- Minimize your taxes by enabling you to take the legal deductions to which you are entitled.

- If you're self-employed, estimate your quarterly state and federal tax payments so you can put aside enough to pay what you owe.

- Provide adequate records should you be audited by the IRS or state agencies.

- Have everything in one place so you know where to find it when you need it.

In this chapter we provide you with a framework to set up a system that will meet these criteria and provide some guidelines for getting additional help when you need it.

Is Your Money Management System Working?

1. Do you know your bank balance?
2. Are your bills paid on time—without late charges?
3. Are your tax materials already in order when tax time comes?
4. Do you get invoices out within the week?
5. Can you locate a receipt, order, or payment record you need in less than five minutes?
6. Do you know exactly what you're spending your money on?
7. Do you have the money you expect to have on hand when you need it?

Basic Money Management

We find the easiest way to handle your money is to use a personal computer. With the proper software, you can write checks, reconcile your bank accounts, do budgeting and basic bookkeeping, and produce needed financial reports. There are hundreds of financial software programs; we recommend, however, selecting one that meets the level of complexity your business demands, is easy to learn and use, and will enable you to transfer your financial records to more sophisticated software when your business growth demands it. Using these criteria, we recommend the following:

Level 1. One- or two-person business with no employees. Our choice at this level is a check-writing program like MECA's *Managing Your Money* or *Quicken*, by Intuit software. These programs are extremely easy to use and make keeping track of cash transactions (checks, money orders, and currency) as simple as writing a check.

While professionals agree that a double-entry bookkeeping system is more accurate and reliable, most single-person home offices find that a check-writing program works well. If you have someone else doing your record-keeping, however, be certain not to rely on a check-writing program. A double-entry bookkeeping system in this case is a must. *In the Black*, by MicroRim, is a program worth considering because, although it's a double-entry system, you don't have to know how to do double-entry bookkeeping; the software does the double-entry functions for you.

Level 2. Fewer than five employees, or a need for billing or inventory capabilities. If your business has fewer than five employees or you need to do regular billing or keep track of inventory, we recommend a program like Microsoft *Profit, M.Y.O.B.,* by Teleware, Peachtree's *Accounting for Windows*, and *Quickbooks* by Intuit. In addition to check writing and basic financial management, these programs enable you to do payroll and invoicing, pay your bills, and control your inventory. Of course, this greater capability requires greater effort on your part to learn the program.

Level 3. More than five employees and a need for accounts receivable and accounts payable capabilities. If you employ more than five people and your business involves a significant volume of credit purchases or sales, you will benefit from using a software program such as NEBS's *One Write Plus* or *DacEasy*. *One Write Plus* is based on the popular paper system of the same name and enables a home business to track significant volumes of open accounts payable and accounts receivable. It does everything the above programs do and in addition provides a powerful general ledger capability.

Some people are also using their computers and modems to pay their bills electronically using a service called *CheckFree*. This service eliminates having to lick stamps and seal envelopes when paying your bills. You don't need to sign checks and you can schedule automatic payments on dates you choose. Currently, this service costs $9 a month for up to twenty checks a month. You can use *CheckFree* in conjunction with many money management programs like *Quicken*.

Electronic Spreadsheets

In addition to basic money management software, many home businesses also like to use spreadsheet software to forecast and manipulate financial information. These programs offer vastly more flexibility than is possible with pencil and paper. When you change an entry on an electronic spreadsheet, the software alters all the other affected figures automatically to reflect that change so you can easily:

- Do financial modeling—play "what if" with numbers
- Do tax planning
- Plan alternative budgets
- Project monthly sales, cash flow, profit and loss
- Do financial problem-solving
- Track and plan your project schedules
- Track your productivity
- Evaluate a stock portfolio

Recording Time and Expenses

Software may also be the simplest, quickest, and most accurate way to make records of your time and expenses. *TimeSlips*, by TimeSlips Corporation, for example, enables you to track every minute you spend working on a project for up to 30,000 clients or jobs. With such a program, you can either:

- Record the time yourself by keeping track and then logging in the exact hours each day when you start and stop working on a particular project. The program will then tally the number and minutes spent on that project.
- Let the program track the time for you. If you're working on the computer or nearby on the telephone, you can simply push a few keys and the program will begin tracking your time.

Time and expenses software calculates the total hours you spend on a project and can automatically prepare your invoice according to whatever hourly or per diem rate you have specified. *TimeSlips* has many other features as well. You can arrange to have multiple billing schedules so one kind of work can be charged at one fee while another can be billed at a different fee. You can also record expenses billable to a certain project and add them to your invoice.

If you prefer paper-and-pencil recording, you can, of course, use your appointment calendar or daily planner to record time and expenses information. Or you might prefer recording it in a personal organizer that travels everywhere with you like a Sharp *Wizard*. If you do keep paper records, use a pen, not a pencil for your entries, because pencil entries are not acceptable in an IRS audit. Erasures are not acceptable, either. So make corrections by crossing out the erroneous entry with a single line so it is still visible. You can use similar systems for recording and calculating business mileage and travel expenses you won't be billing to anyone but need to use in calculating your business deductions for tax purposes.

Several long-distance services offer a free or nominally charged service which allows you to code all your outgoing calls for easy categorization later on. AT&T's program, for example, is called *Call Manager*, a free service; however, it's only for business lines and the calls, of course, must be made using AT&T. Once the service is initiated, you enter any number from 1 to 9999 after a call you want coded. For example, if you're a consultant, punch "22" before you call a client whom you are billing on a time basis. When the bill comes, all the "22" calls will be grouped together and totaled for you, giving you the basis for billing your client.

If you're using a residential line for outgoing calls or want to record incoming calls, you can get a device called *CallCost* that stores information about outgoing and incoming calls, including the duration of each call and the number dialed. Periodically, you can upload this information into your computer using software that comes with *CallCost*. *CallCost* ([800]-245-9933) also lets you assign account codes anytime during an incoming or outgoing call as well as preassign an account code to a group of numbers.

Financial Management Software

Check-Writing Software
Purpose: Most home-based businesses can use one of these easy-to-learn programs to carry out most of their financial management tasks. You can pay bills, write checks, keep your bank balance, record and track income, and create financial reports.

For: One- or two-person service businesses with no employees and little inventory.

Examples:
Managing Your Money, MECA
Microsoft Money
Quicken, Intuit

General Ledger Accounting Software
Purpose: Makes double-entry bookkeeping and accrual-based accounting somewhat easier because it automates various accounting functions for keeping a general ledger. Accountants will often advise business clients to use a general ledger system like these because these programs meet what is known as "generally accepted accounting standards." They reduce posting errors and, if you use an accountant for year-end work, your information will not need to be reentered into such a system by the accounting office.

For: Home businesses that have employee payroll, considerable inventory, or wish to use the accrual method of accounting.

Examples:
DacEasy Instant Accounting, DacEasy
In the Black, MicroRim
Microsoft Profit
M.Y.O.B., Teleware
One-Write Plus, MECA
Pacioli 2000, M-USA Business Systems
Peachtree Accounting, Peachtree
QuickBooks, Intuit

Spreadsheet Accounting Systems
Purpose: Provide access to more powerful financial analysis including forecasting, modeling, projecting.

For: Either cash- or accrual-based accounting for all types of businesses that prefer working with spreadsheet software.

Examples:
Lotus 1-2-3, Lotus Works, and *Improv for Windows*, Lotus Development Corporation
Microsoft Works & Excel, Microsoft
Quattro Pro, Borland

Time and Expense Software
Purpose: Tracks the time you spend on each job or client.

For: Any business that bills by the hour and needs to track time allotted to each project or client.

Examples:
Timeslips, Timeslips Corporation
Buy the Hour, Austin Computer Resources

Invoicing
Purpose: To create professional invoices easily

For: All businesses that must submit bills to clients.

Examples:
- Dedicated time-tracking and invoicing software like *Timeslips* and *WinVoice* (Good Software)
- Invoicing software designed to work with money management or accounting software like *Quicken*'s invoicing package *QuickInvoice.*
- Word-processing programs like *Microsoft Word* or Lotus's *AmiPro* that provide you with templates or design capability to create your own invoices.
- Professional form-design programs like *PerForm Pro Plus* (Delrina) or *WindFORM* (Graphics Development International) that contain invoicing templates and ways to design your own forms.
- Add-on programs like *Form-To-Go* (Intex Solutions, Inc.) which provide templates you can use with a spreadsheet.
- Accounting programs that include invoicing like *M.Y.O.B., One-Write Plus*, and *QuickBooks.*

Features to Look for: Financial Management Software

The more sophisticated a program, the more features and flexibility it has, but generally the more complex and costly it will be. Select a package that has the features that best match your current and projected needs.

- Check register
- Check writing
- Memorizes recurring transactions
- Schedules future transactions
- Reconciles account
- Link to credit-card statements
- Bill-paying reminders
- Interface to CheckFree
- Prints checks to laser, ink-jet and dot matrix printers
- Prints out check register
- Preset budget categories
- Adds categories
- Splits transactions among categories
- Number of redefined reports and charts
- Views supporting data of reports and charts

- Financial planning
- Portfolio management
- Debt-management planning
- Estimates tax liability
- Data readable by or transportable to tax software
- Generates invoices
- Calculates payroll deductions
- Customized reports
- Calculator/calendar
- Contact manager
- Tasks minder
- Help with accounting principles
- Ease of use
- Tutorial
- Clarity and simplicity of documentation
- Unlimited free support
- Toll-free support

Tax Preparation Software

Purpose: Enables you to prepare your taxes electronically. Financial records can be entered manually or imported directly from your bookkeeping or financial management software.

For: All businesses because it cuts short the time you must spend completing your taxes.

Examples:
Andrew Tobias's Tax Cut, MECA
Turbo Tax, Chipsoft
TaxCut Multimedia, MECA CD-ROM tax program

Features to Look for: Tax Software

- Capability and memory required
- Edition for your state
- IRS forms included and excluded
- Ability to import data from your financial package

Leaving a Paper Trail

The Internal Revenue Service still requires a paper backup of all financial transactions. Computer records alone, because they can be altered, will not do. So to make yourself an easy-to-keep *paper* trail, we recommend using partitioned accordion files to keep records of paid bills, and receipts for cash and charge card payments of expenses.

Simply place labels on the partitions of the accordion file to correspond to the categories of tax deductions you take—for example, advertising, automobile, dues, publications, entertainment, and so forth. We keep our accordion files in a room right by our entryway. Then, filing receipts, along with taking messages off the answering machine located nearby, is part of our ritual when coming home. Receipts don't get lost or accumulate for filing at some other time. Another place to keep your accordion file is near the computer with your bookkeeping software. In that way, it will be handy when you enter cash and credit card expenses into your computer records.

Managing Cash Flow

If you are self-employed, having a system for managing your cash flow is a matter of survival. Cash flow is to your livelihood what breath is to life. If the cash doesn't keep flowing, your business doesn't keep going.

We recommend a system that enables you to minimize what others owe you, utilize your cash on hand for maximum benefit, and hold on to what you have.

Collecting the Money You're Owed

For ideal cash management, you should collect on services or products at the time you deliver them. Do this whenever you can. You may be able to do so more often than you think. When Sarah was in private practice, for example, she expected her clients to pay at the end of each session. Only on rare occasions did they request other arrangements. Since this was the way she was used to operating, she continued this policy when selling advertising time on a Los Angeles radio show we were pilot testing. Not a single advertiser objected, yet to her surprise, a radio consultant told her one year later, "No one ever pays for radio time up front."

Of course, there may be times when you will need, and want, to extend credit. But remember, credit is always a privilege. You owe it to yourself to check out if your client is credit-worthy. If you're working with a well-established company, you may be able to check their credit quite easily. Diane Sobotik has worked with *Fortune* 500 companies for years. She finds the easiest route to doing a credit check is to simply call the accounting office and ask them for credit references. She finds most companies have a sheet all typed out that lists their regular vendors. You can call and check their payment history.

When this is not possible, you can and should ask clients desiring thirty-day payment to complete a credit application—just as you are asked to do to obtain credit from those whose products and services you buy. On your credit application you ask for and then check out their references, including bank references. Standard credit application forms are available on software such as *PerForm Pro Plus*, by Delrina, *B-Tools*, by Star Software, and *Winning Forms*, by Random House and request such information as:

- Type of business
- Years in business
- Dun & Bradstreet rating
- Names, addresses and phone numbers of partners and corporate officers
- Person to contact regarding purchase orders and invoice payments
- Bank references
- Confirmation of accuracy
- Release of authority to verify
- Policy statements
- Trade references

In addition, depending upon who your clients are, you may be able to obtain credit information through several on-line sources, including:

1) Dunn & Bradstreet (available through NewsNet, 945 Haverford Road, Bryn Mawr, PA 19010; [800]345-1301) provides three types of reports on over nine million public and private U.S. companies:

—The Business Information Report provides information on a firm's operation, profitability, and stability.

—The Payment Analysis Report compares the company's payment habits over two years.

—The Family Tree Service shows corporate ties among a company and its parents, branches, divisions, and subsidiaries.

2) TRW Business Credit Profiles (available through CompuServe, P.O. Box 20212, Columbus, OH 43220, [800]848-8990; Dialog, 3460 Hillview Avenue, Palo Alto, CA 94304, [800]334-2564, and NewsNet [800] 345-1301) offers credit and business information on more than 13 million companies. The information available includes credit histories, tax liens, judgments, and bankruptcies.

Another resource for checking credit is the National Association of Credit Managers (NACM), which has local offices throughout the U.S. offering seminars on credit collection principles and information on obtaining credit reports. In addition, some companies are joining credit exchange groups, where companies operating in the same industry or related industries get together on a monthly basis to discuss credit concerns. This can be especially helpful in industries where customers may be playing one supplier against another. If you experience chronic collection problems with major clients, you might consider joining or starting such a group.

Even once you've decided to extend credit, there is a variety of steps you can take to make sure the money you're owed comes in as quickly as possible:

Get deposits, retainers, or partial or progress payments.

Get payment up front for expenses or arrange to charge expenses to your client's account. Here's how consultant Molly McClelland handles this. When asked to travel for her clients, she says, "If you'd like me to make the travel arrangements, I'll be happy to take care if it. Whom in your office should I have my travel agent contact for a credit card number?" She says it works like a charm.

Take bank cards instead of extending credit. (See below for how to do this). With new clients, information researcher Janet Gotkin uses what she calls her credit card–cleared check policy. She bills clients she's never worked with before through American Express or, if they prefer, she offers the option of their sending a check and waiting for the check to clear before proceeding.

Use a check guarantee service. Telecredit is one of the largest in the country. They charge a small percentage for each check and have a monthly minimum, but you do not have to process all your checks through the service.

Use a factor. Factors are specialized privately owned finance companies that purchase accounts receivable. The factor offers some combination of the following services: immediate cash on accounts receivable, maintains ledgers and bookkeeping duties on accounts receivable, collects accounts receivable, assumes the losses that may arise, furnishes loan funds to its clients on a seasonal or term basis, and offers advisory services. One consultant uses a factor because expenses on behalf of his clients can get steep and particularly his large clients stretch out their payments. He couldn't find a bank to handle his receivables, but by using a factor, he gets paid in a timely fashion. He pays 4 percent in exchange for getting his money forty-five to sixty days earlier and he builds a service charge into his contracts to cover the cost of the money.

Whenever extending credit, have clear terms for when you must receive payment. Offer discounts of 2 to 5 percent for receipt of payment within 20 days from the date of the invoice. Some companies are known for taking 90 to 120 days to make payment, so negotiate payment terms of 30 days as part of your sale.

Include a delinquent interest or financing charge on overdue accounts as part of your payment agreement. In most jurisdictions it is illegal to charge such fees without written consent, but charging such delinquent fees can be important in offsetting the expenses that may be incurred in collecting on such accounts. So include information about these fees in all your contracts or as part of the credit application.

Bill immediately upon delivery of a service or product, instead of waiting until the end of the month. A thirty-day period usually begins from the date a customer receives your invoice.

Act promptly on overdue accounts. Don't let them slip by. The longer the account is overdue, the less likely it is to be paid. The first day a client is past due, get on the phone, refer to your contract, and ask for your money. Link any ongoing or future service to payment. Do not continue working for someone whose account is overdue.

Business writer André Sharp has established a fee schedule that helps him avoid cash flow problems. First, he asks for 50 percent of his fee in advance. The balance is due upon delivery of a project. He requires that individuals and clients he doesn't know or whose dependability he is uncertain about pay all major expenses in advance. With new clients he always makes and keeps a copy of the check payment as further proof that there is a contract. These policies help his immediate cash flow, cover his expenses, and convey a high level of professionalism.

What to Do When the Check Is Not in the Mail

Up until the time you've collected what you're owed, you've given your product or service away . . . and that's exactly how it feels when you end up having a hassle collecting the money you've earned. To inspire timely payments and avoid hassles, private investigator Bob Taylor adds a light touch by using a stamp on his statements that reads, "If you pay us, then we can pay them, and they can pay you." His favorite stamp, though, is a little angel in a praying position with the caption "PLEASE."

For those times, however, when even all your best efforts fail to produce the check, Leonard Sklar recommends the following ten tips in his book *The Check Is Not in the Mail:*

1. Call the person who owes you money instead of sending another letter or bill.

2. Ask for payment in full, no matter how large the bill.

3. Create a sense of urgency that your bill must be paid NOW.

4. Follow up on overdue accounts immediately! The longer the account goes uncollected, the greater chance you won't receive payment at all.

5. Pin down the debtor. Ask for exactly what you want and when you want it by. Don't be vague and don't let him or her be vague.

6. Offer payment options. "Would you rather take care of this by check or cash?"

7. Blame a third party for your insistence that you receive payment now: "My accountant is insisting that I get this completed."

8. To make sure that you have a way to counter possible stalls, excuses, and evasions, role-play with a colleague what you're going to say before you place a collections call.

9. Develop and give your clients and customers a very clear and comprehensive payment policy that spells out exactly how and when bills are to be paid.

10. Don't do business with individuals, companies, or organizations that have poor credit records.

If all else fails, do not hesitate to engage a collection agency or take your case to small-claims court. Small-claims courts routinely handle such cases. Sometimes just filing the case will spur payment; other times you will need to wait until you get a favorable judgment. Should you have trouble collecting on your judgment, you can get help from a company like Lutz Asset Research. For $125 this company will locate judgment debtor bank accounts. They claim to find 50 percent of their accounts if provided with a valid current address. For information call (800) 999-CASH.

Obtaining MasterCard and Visa Merchant Accounts

Sales go up when customers can pay you with a credit card. According to credit card industry experts, a business can expect to increase its sales between 10 and 50 percent. Whether the increase is closer to 10 or 50 percent depends on the type of business, with mail-order operations particularly benefiting. Not only will your sales go up, but installment sales are possible with your billing someone's credit card over a period of months or your collecting all your money at once while the customer decides to pay his balance over time.

Yet there can be few tasks more difficult for a home-based business than obtaining a merchant account. This is because most banks discriminate against home-based as well as some specific types of businesses where there have been chargeback problems. Nevertheless, home-based businesses do manage to be able to offer their customers the ability to use their charge cards. Here are four basic avenues for securing a merchant account.

Financial Institutions

Banks. Even though banks as a general rule are not granting home businesses merchant accounts for taking Visa and MasterCard, do try your own bank, particularly since they know you as a customer. If your bank denies you a merchant account, try small independent banks, particularly ones that have their merchant accounts processed by an out-of-state bank instead of doing it themselves or using a larger local bank. Banks in smaller communities are more apt to work with home-based businesses.

Find out in advance what the bank's criteria are for granting merchant accounts. This information should be available in writing. Typically this includes but is not limited to:

- Your type of business. Mail-order and telephone-order businesses have a difficult time.
- How long you have been in business
- Your credit history both as a business and personally
- Your record with previous merchant accounts
- Your current banking relationships.

The bank will want to know about your business's financing, track record, and sales projections. You may need to show a business plan and will probably be well served to offer it and your marketing materials even if it is not requested.

Structure a presentation to meet the criteria established by the bank. Make as much effort as you would if you were pitching your services to a new client or applying for a loan. The key to convincing a banker to grant you a merchant account, says former banker John Witmer, is "to convince the banker that you are 1) professional, 2) serious, 3) knowledgeable, 4) persevering, and 5) profitable. Anything you do or say that contributes to that image will help you and anything you say that suggests otherwise is probably fatal."

In talking with bankers, you're more apt to display the self-confidence that produces respect if you keep in mind that you are giving the bank business rather than pleading for relief. Also be prepared to offer establishing a reserve account, which may range in size from a few hundred to several thousand dollars. This account or guarantee of assets would back up any refunds or other defaults that make banks extremely cautious in granting merchant accounts. Whether applying to a bank or another source of merchant accounts, be careful not to omit items from the application or fail to disclose what you will be selling. Merchant account issuers will terminate accounts once disqualifying information becomes known.

Savings and Loans, Thrifts, and Credit Unions. Most people think of banks as THE only financial institutions granting merchant accounts to businesses. However, savings and loans, thrifts, and even credit unions are increasingly offering merchant accounts. You may find these institutions more willing to work with you.

Remember, as Larry Schwartz and Pearl Sax, founders of the National Association of Credit Card Merchants, remind us, these institutions "need reassurance that handling your business will be both safe and profitable." It almost goes without saying that a presentation of your business, your financial ability, and yourself must make your banker feel absolute confidence in you. Home-business owner Ed Verry inspired this confidence by using what he calls the Security Deposit Method. First he pointed out that his business is not prone to large individual sales or the type of customers and products that cause credit card fraud. Then he offered to use the electronic card-verification machines on every credit card sale. (The bank sold him this machine for cost, $250.) But finally, and most importantly, he offered to place an appropriate amount of dollars in a one-year CD account as a security deposit for the bank. He signed a common agreement form that he wouldn't withdraw the money for a specified period of time. He says, "This offer worked wonders for me!"

Business Organizations

Trade Associations. Trade associations sometimes provide access to Visa and MasterCard accounts as a member service. Examples of organizations that may be helpful are the Retail Merchants Association and Direct Marketing Association and others specifically related to your particular industry. To find trade associations in your field, use *Gale's Encyclopedia of Associations*, available at the reference desk in most libraries.

Local Business Organizations. Chambers of commerce and local merchant associations sometimes help their members secure merchant accounts through a bank affiliated with the Chamber or the association. These can be the least-costly merchant accounts with discounts as low as 2 to 3 percent on relatively small volumes.

Independent Selling Organizations

Perhaps the most likely way to get a merchant account is to work through a bank agent or independent selling organization (ISO), which is a company that acts as an intermediary between small businesses and banks. You will undoubtedly pay more using an ISO because these companies derive their income from fees and surcharges added to what you would normally pay if you were able to deal directly with a bank.

While obtaining a merchant account is apt to be easier through an ISO, this can also be risky because unethical people have falsely represented themselves as ISOs and taken the money of eager merchants. To determine if the ISO company you are talking with is "legit," ask for the bank with which the ISO is affiliated and contact the bank to verify the status of the ISO with the bank. You can also check with your local Better Business Bureau.

Here are some typical costs and charges you may be quoted when going through an ISO:

- Application fees ranging between $95 and $325. These may or may not be refundable. Usually they are not, but find out under what circumstances all or part of the fee may be refundable.

- Point-of-sale terminal lease or purchase. ISOs typically charge from $425 to $1,700 for a terminal, which if purchased through a bank would cost about $300. Leasing typically runs between $18 and $80 a month. Some ISOs are offering software that can be used in place of a sales terminal, priced as low as $150. Leases typically are noncancelable.

- Service fees from about 2 to 7 percent, compared with 2 to 5 percent from a bank. When you are quoted a low fee, look for other charges that tend to make up for the lower service fee.

- Per-transaction charge of $.20 to $.25

- Monthly statement fee of $5 to $10

- Minimum monthly fee

- Voice authorization fee

As you can see, fees vary considerably among ISOs, so it pays to be a comparison shopper. Read the contract carefully for hidden charges and requirements. You may also be required to use a check verification service provided by the ISO for an additional fee. One final warning: The salespeople for ISOs may be so eager to sign you up that they may inaccurately fill out your application with regard to items that would not be approved if reported accurately. If such a falsehood is detected later by the bank, your merchant account may be terminated and your name placed on a terminated merchant list that bars you from getting another merchant account in the future.

Subjects that are sometimes filled in inaccurately include whether the salesperson has personally inspected your premises and the percentage of your sales that are by mail order and telephone. So be sure to check your completed application for accuracy. A list of independent selling organizations or agents for ISOs that have told us or have been reported by members of the Working From Home Forum that they accept home businesses for merchant accounts is given in the Resources list at the end of this chapter.

Options Other than Visa and MasterCard

Certainly people are likely to have a Visa or MasterCard. In 1992 these were the market shares for each of the principal cards: Visa—46 percent; MasterCard—26 percent; American Express—20 percent; Discover—7 percent. But an American Express merchant account is easier for a home business to get than Visa and MasterCard. You can contact American Express at (800)528-5200. Discover Card is reportedly as difficult to get as Visa and MasterCard; however, if you want to try it, their number is (800)347-2683.

One avenue to avoid is running your charges through another company's merchant account. This is called "factoring" and will get you and the holder of the merchant account in trouble.

If you are taking orders over an 800 number, another avenue you might want to consider is allowing your clients and customers to charge their purchases to their checking accounts. According to a newsletter of the National Association of Credit Card Merchants, 64 percent of all noncash payments are made by check, a total of $583 billion a year. To put that number into perspective, only 26 percent of noncash payments are made by credit card. The Credit Card Merchants Association offers a service called *Checks by Phone* to help reach the reported seventy million people who don't have a credit card and others who can't use theirs because it is "maxed out."

Checks by Phone enables you to accept orders for products or services as well as receive payments by phone, fax, or through your modem. You simply obtain a checking or savings account number from your customer and transmit the information to a processing center by fax or modem. You or your bank receives a check by mail. Processing fees, about $1 to $1.25 per transaction, cost you less than charge card transactions. Another benefit of Checks by Phone is it eliminates the need for COD deliveries, one out of two of which are rejected by recipients. A number of companies offer Checks by Phone service, including the National Association of Credit Card Merchants ([407]737-8700) and Telecom Support Systems ([215]935-5887). One caution: While people are ready to use a charge card to pay for something, since charging by check is new, customers may need to be convinced to give out their checking- or savings-account number to pay by phone.

Combating Credit Discrimination

We regularly hear a loan company's radio commercial in Los Angeles that proclaims the company will lend money even if "you're unemployed, self-employed, or have bad credit." To us being self-employed means we're self-sufficient, but putting "self-employed" on a credit application often puts us automatically into the nether lands of creditworthiness. What can we do to counter this?

1. You can either incorporate or register and use an assumed business name. When you fill out an application that instructs you to list your employer, you list your company. A descriptive name for your business can be a help in marketing, too.

2. Have two phone numbers: one for business, one personal. When filling out an application that asks for business and residential phone numbers, be sure to list both numbers even if you use only one of your numbers for incoming calls. With distinctive ringing, you can have two numbers on only one phone line.

3. Answer your phone with your company name so when you are called to

verify employment, the caller reaches your company. This enables you to believably answer that you are employed by your company. Someone who operates as a corporation *is* an employee of his or her corporation.

4. If you have use for an office suite or a miniwarehouse, rent one. It may also serve as your business address. This is particularly helpful if your residence is in an area zoned only for residences.

5. If allowed by your zoning, put a sign with your business name at your mailbox. If a banker, supplier, or prospective customer makes an on-site inspection, their first impression may be "This is a business." When they enter your home office, make it look as professional as possible and certainly remove personal items, such as toys and laundry, from view.

Maximizing Your Cash on Hand

Let your money make money for you while you have it. Don't just let it sit in a noninterest-bearing account. Here's why. Let's say you let $1,000 sit in a noninterest-bearing account. Five years later the buying power of your $1,000 will have shrunk to only $837 if inflation remains at even a minimal 3.5 percent. But if you invest that same money at 5 percent instead, in five years, you will have the buying power of $1,077. So here are some steps you can take to make the most of your money while you've got it.

Deposit money immediately. CPA Barry Schimel, author of *100 Ways to Prosper in Today's Economy*, suggests making deposits as often as once a day.

If your balance is large enough, an interest-bearing checking account will make money for you.

Avoid bank fees. Avoid banks with ATM charges. Keep a high-enough monthly minimum balance to avoid monthly fees. If you have both your personal and business accounts at the same bank, arrange to use what's called "relationship banking"—that is, linked accounts, which allows you to save on fees and some minimum-balance requirements if you have more than one account in the same bank. Compare account fees, minimum-balance requirements, and interest-bearing accounts among banks. Also pay attention to whether the bank charges apply based on an "average balance" or a "low balance."

Use cash management services provided by a bank if your business volume is large enough, i.e., $100,000 a year. A lock box, for example, is a program in which you have your customers mail their payments to a box maintained by the bank. The box is located so that in most cases payment is received the next day, and it is immediately deposited by the bank into your account.

Deposit surplus cash on hand in interest-bearing certificates and money-market funds.

Invest excess cash. Arrange to have excess cash transferred to funds with a higher yield. Some banks will also automatically transfer money back if your account drops below a certain level.

You might consider placing short-term savings in money market mutual funds or tax-free investment funds. Tax-free funds are especially worth considering if you fall into one of the new top tax brackets. For longer-term savings, you might consider bonds. Talk with a financial advisor about what is best for you.

Grow your business. Depending on interest rates, you may be able to bring in more money by investing in your business than by investing your money elsewhere. If a new voice mail system or a part-time assistant will generate more or better-paying clients, you could come out ahead by putting your money to work in your business.

Holding On to What You Have

Cash-flow problems arise because you need to spend money to make money and, of course, to live, while you're providing your services or products. To minimize your problems, you'll want your business to pay for itself as it goes. To do this, we recommend that whenever possible:

- Arrange for thirty, sixty, or ninety days of interest-free credit from suppliers.
- Use low-rate, no-fee credit cards for your personal and business transactions.
- Rent or lease equipment rather than tying up your capital by owning it.
- Make timely but not immediate payment of bills.
- Keep costs down. Don't overstock on supplies.

Getting and Making the Most of Credit Cards

For small and home-based businesses credit cards can be among the only sources of credit. And credit cards provide you with 30 to 60 days' free use of your money. Therefore, we encourage home-based business owners to have and use at least one business credit card to help maximize their cash flow and to finance marketing and other costs of business expansion.

Unfortunately, however, it seems that thanks to credit cards, most Americans are living beyond their incomes. Americans have run up credit card bills of more than $231 billion. At the end of 1991, credit card balances stood at a record high, over $900 for every man, woman, and child in the USA! So whereas wise use of credit cards is to your advantage, we don't advocate that you bury your business in overloaded credit cards.

The best credit card policy is to limit charge cards to financing activities and investments that will pay for themselves in increased productivity or additional business. Even then, paying off your balance each month is the most cost-effective use of your cards. But of course, we can't always get that fast a return on our business expenses, so here are several other ideas for keeping credit card costs down.

Vitality magazine reports that credit cards with favorable rates are often available even to people with slightly blemished credit reports. To gain a share of the market, *Vitality* says, some companies are overlooking the minor credit problems of applicants. So look for low-rate cards.

Low credit card rates won't save you much money if the issuer uses the "two-cycle method." Most issuers compute their financial charges based on the average daily balance in the prior month. This is referred to as ADB. But some issuers are charging interest based on your average balance over the last two months, so if you pay only the minimum balance each month you could end up paying twice on the same charge. Card issuers must disclose their computation method on applications, cardholder agreements, and monthly statements. So check out your existing cards and any future ones you consider.

Credit card minimum purchase requirements are prohibited under the standard contract merchants must sign with the issuing bank and Visa or MasterCard. So if a retailer refuses to accept your card, send a letter of complaint to your issuing bank. If that doesn't resolve the issue, write to the credit card company.

Minimum balance payments can cost the max. For example if you charge $500 on your card and pay only the minimum each month at 18 percent, the item will cost you almost $800 and take six years to pay off. If you pay $50 a month, you'll save almost $250 in interest and be debt-free in only eleven months!

Low-Rate, No-Fee Credit Cards

Of course, when you're able to spend less by paying cash, you need to balance your cash flow needs with the need to keep your costs down. But you can keep the cost of using credit cards down by using low-rate, no-fee credit cards. Here're two ways to find one:

- BankCard Holders of America will send you a list of fifty banks across the USA that offer credit cards with low interest rates and no annual fees or both. For a copy, send a $4 check or money order to BankCard Holders of America, 524 Branch Dr., Salem, VA; (703) 389-5445. The list is updated quarterly.
- CardTrak, a newsletter tracking bank credit cards, provides monthly surveys of low-rate, no-annual-fee, and Gold cards for $5 a month. Write CardTrak, Box 1700, Frederick, MD 21702; (800) 344-7714.

Keep in mind that cards with low interest rates may have high annual fees. If you pay off your balance every month, look for no-fee cards.

Eight Steps to Restoring Your Good Credit

Robin Leonard, author of *Money Troubles: Legal Strategies to Cope with Your Debts*, points out that most creditors are just as interested in positive as they are in negative credit information. Creditors are looking for evidence and positive indications that a person is capable of repaying his or her debts. Leonard claims, for example, that most major credit companies will ignore a negative credit history if you can demonstrate two or three years of consistently responsible credit behavior. So here are the steps she recommends taking to repair a damaged credit rating:

1. *Secure a stable source of income.* Of course, usually creditors are looking for a steady employment history, so when you're on your own, you have to create a record of steady income from your own business. If your business is struggling due to lack of funds to adequately market yourself, you may have to take a full- or part-time job or work temporarily to secure a steady income.

2. *Create a budget* that you can and will live within. Think of living on this budget as a temporary condition, until your business is generating greater income.

3. *Open a passbook savings account* at a local bank and begin saving as much as you can as quickly as you can.

4. *Once you have $500 to $1,000 saved, apply for what is known as a savings passbook loan* or a loan that is secured by your savings. Your goal in applying for this loan is to demonstrate that you can pay it back.

5. *Pay back this loan over a six- to nine-month period* so there will be time for the loan to appear on your credit report. Make sure that your bank reports this type of loan to credit agencies. If it doesn't, go elsewhere.

6. *Obtain a secured credit card.* Some banks automatically offer their savings account holders such a card. These cards give you a credit limit somewhat lower than the amount in your savings account. *CardTrak* newsletter does a monthly survey of secured credit cards. Ken and Doria Dolan's *Straight-alk on Your Money* newsletter recommends Community Bank of Parker ([303] 841-0970) and Orchard Bank's "Program Two" ([800] 688-6830) as secured cards with a good history.

7. *Use this credit card sparingly* and only if you're sure you can and will pay off the entire bill when it comes, because interest on these cards can be around 22 percent.

8. *Apply selectively for other cards* as soon as your credit will justify it. Department stores and gas companies are often more liberal than the major credit card companies, so start there. Get only one or two such cards and charge minimal purchases that you can easily repay. Leonard suggests you might even run a revolving balance for a few months to prove that you can handle the interest charges and meet a regular repayment schedule.

For other information on rebuilding your credit, you can contact the National Foundation of Consumer Credit. They will refer you to credit counselors in your area. (See Resources at the end of this chapter.)

Debtors Anonymous holds meetings throughout the country. To find out about meetings near you, write Debtors Anonymous, General Services Board, P.O. Box 20322, New York, NY 10025.

Protect Yourself from Income Fluctuations

The most difficult time to manage your money is when there's too little to manage. There are several things you can do to protect yourself from the woes of feast or famine, peaks and valleys.

Paying Bills to Maximize Your Cash Flow

Here's a simple but effective manual system developed by Ray Martin, president of Microcomputer Applications, Inc., of Austin, Texas:

1. Check the day's incoming bills and invoices for accuracy and discounts offered for quick payment.
2. Determine the best date to make payment of each bill so that you will neither be overdue nor early in making payment. Then write a check.
3. Place the check in its envelope; stamp and seal it.
4. Code the envelope in the lower right corner with the necessary mailing date. Allow three days for local delivery, seven days for cross-country mail.
5. File the envelopes in chronological order.
6. Each day, mail those bills earmarked for that date.

---

1. Keep a reserve of cash on hand. Bruce Michels, president of Management Advisory Services Consulting Group, advises small businesses to have $2 of current assets on hand for every $1 of current expenses. Accountant Michael Russo says your cash cushion should depend on your own comfort zone. While some need a $10,000 reserve to feel secure, others require more. Still others need considerably less. Find your level of security and operate within it.

2. Market constantly. Set aside at least 20 percent of your time each week for marketing activities and do this all year long, even when you have business. Don't slack off your selling effort when cash flow is great. There is always a lag time between marketing efforts and marketing results, so keep selling every week.

3. Track your income and expenses. Project your expenses and anticipated income at the beginning of each month. Post all due dates. You'll find that establishing this habit will prove invaluable. You'll always know exactly where you stand and you'll be alerted when you need to take action either by deferring costs or accelerating your marketing effort. You'll also know the moment someone is late with payments.

4. Plan to make the most of slow times. Most businesses go through periods of time that are slower than others. For example, holiday seasons are great for party planners and gift-related businesses but not so good for business consultants or training professionals. Anticipate these periods and devise special marketing efforts to attract business during these periods. For example, private-practice consultant Gene Call, who teaches professionals how to market their services, finds holiday times are slow for him so he runs a year-end promotion. Anyone signing up for his January training program in December gets a juicy discount.

Word processor Evalyn McGraw finds Augusts are routinely slow so she builds up cash reserves in June and July and plans her vacation for August.

Before she leaves, however, she sets her late-August marketing plan in motion so that when she comes back there will be business coming in.

5. *Create various income sources.* Another way Evalyn manages her cash flow is to offer several adjunct services. In addition to straight word processing she provides editing and indexing services. She also teaches university extension program writing courses at a local university. So if one area of her business is slow she can rely on other areas. She finds they are rarely all slow at once.

You'll notice, however, that Evalyn is not offering a variety of scattered services that dissipate her efforts or confuse the public about what business she's in. She isn't selling real estate and offering fitness training simultaneously. All her services are related and, in some cases, ancillaries to word processing.

6. *Continually upgrade your skills and improve your business.* Grow with your business. Don't get caught in the rut of offering the same services and products year in and year out. To spark sales add new lines, offer more advanced techniques. And you shouldn't wait for sales to wane. Every change you make in your business provides an opportunity for promotions and gives you a good excuse to contact present and past clients about what you're doing now.

7. *Network, network, network.* Make regular contact with colleagues, clients, and associates part of your ongoing weekly marketing. Participate in professional, trade, and civic organizations so you'll be abreast of new market trends and the latest breakthroughs; this will also help you generate referrals and find out who needs you right now. Don't overlook regular congenial contact with your competitors. They may be overloaded just when you're slumping. Offer to help them with business they can't handle on a subcontract basis. More and more independents are forming consortiums to take on large projects and refer work to members. Consider joining or forming a consortium of people you are comfortable working with.

8. *Remember, you're in charge.* Sometimes it may seem as though your cash flow has nothing whatsoever to do with your efforts. You may feel you are being tossed about at the whim of fluctuations in the economy, the seasons, or your market's fickle passions. In actuality, if you *take* charge, you'll *be* in charge. You aren't dependent on the wishes of a single boss who can fire you on a moment's notice. All your clients would have to fire you before you'd be out of business. You're ingenious, talented, and creative or you wouldn't be in business in the first place. There is always some way for you to serve others and thereby keep the cash flowing in. If you start feeling out of control, just focus on that reality.

Tips for Good Money Management

1. Keep business and personal finances separate. Have two bank accounts—one for business, the other for personal expenses. Have separate bank cards. Keep records and receipts for business and personal expenses separate.
2. Have one place where you keep all of your financial materials, records, equipment, and supplies.
3. Establish a time each day, week, month, and quarter to take care of needed financial transactions.
   - Banking transactions
   - Bill paying
   - Invoicing
   - Tallying monthly and quarterly summaries
   - Filing tax and other necessary reports
4. Establish the habit of filing expense and income receipts immediately after getting them.
5. Keep inventory records as you add to or take from your supply.

When to Get Help

With the tools and ideas suggested in this chapter, you can probably manage your own record keeping while your business is small. Depending on your experience and the size and nature of your business, however, you may want to get the advice of an accountant in setting up your system. Also, you will periodically want to evaluate how well your system is working.

Less-expensive alternatives to CPAs are franchised "business counselors" from companies like General Business Services and Marcoin. They advise small businesspeople on a quarterly basis for much less money than the typical CPA charges. They help prepare and analyze financials and do tax planning and tax returns.

If your business expands or is already too large for this system, you will need to set up a more sophisticated system and get additional assistance. You can hire a full- or part-time bookkeeper or use a bookkeeping service. Finally, since many record-keeping tasks involve filing and sorting, you may be able to hire a full- or part-time secretary or file clerk whose duties would include various record-keeping tasks.

Here are some signs that it's time to go beyond a do-it-yourself system:

- When you would make more money by paying someone to keep your records than the money you save by doing it yourself.
- When you are operating under government or other contracts that require you to use a double-entry bookkeeping system.
- When you need to spend more than thirty minutes a day doing financial management tasks.

Even when you have help in keeping your records, you will need to be responsible for providing the receipts, reviewing and evaluating the records regularly, and making financial plans and projections for your business. So you will still need to establish daily, weekly, monthly, and quarterly routines for carrying out these tasks.

Resources

Books

Basic Accounting for the Small Business. Clive G. Cornish. Bellingham, Wash.: Self Council Press, 1992.

Financial Freedom in 8 Minutes a Day. Ron and Mary Hulnick. Emmeaus, N.Y.: Rodale, 1994.

Money Troubles: Legal Strategies to Cope With Your Debts. Robin Leonard. Berkeley: Nolo Press, 1993.

Personal Finance for Dummies. Eric Tyson. San Mateo, Calif.: IDG Books, 1994.

Save Your Business a Bundle. Daniel Kehrer. New York: Simon & Schuster, 1994.

Small-Time Operator. Bernard Kamoroff. Laytonville, Calif.: Bell Springs, 1993.

The Smart Money Financial Planner. Ken and Daria Dolan. New York: Berkeley, 1992.

Straight Talk on Money: Ken and Daria Dolan's Guide to Family Money Management. Ken and Daria Dolan. New York: Simon & Schuster, 1993.

The Check Is Not in the Mail. Leonard Sklar. San Mateo, Calif.: Baroque Publishing, 1990.

Newsletters

Ken and Daria Dolan's Smart Money on Your Money. Phillips Publishing, Inc., 7811 Montrose Rd., Potomac, MD 20854; (301) 424-3700. A newsletter filled with money tips of all kinds.

CardTrak. Ram Research, P.O. Box 1770, College Estates, Frederick, MD 21702; (800) 344-7714. Information on credit cards, including secured cards, and where low rates can be obtained.

Debt Management

Consumer Credit Consulting Service, National Referral Line. 8611 2d Avenue, Ste. 100, Silver Springs, MD 20910; (800) 338-2227. Provides information and referrals to credit counselors in your area.

Credit Information

National Association of Credit Management (NACM). 8815 Centre Park, Ste. 200, Columbia, MD 21045; (410) 740-5560. Offers seminars on credit collection principles and information on obtaining credit reports.

Independent Selling Organizations (ISO)

Companies that serve as an intermediary for obtaining MasterCard and Visa merchant status in alphabetical order:

Cardservice International has forty-two offices and hundreds of agents throughout the country. Contact: An agent who has provided good service to CompuServe Working From Home Forum members is Tom McSherry (313) 278-3350. Some offices of Cardservice will require an on-site visit. Charges vary between 2.5 to 3.5 percent, plus 30 cents a transaction. Terminal and printer lease is $69 a month, which you own after forty-eight months. Application fees range from $95 to $350.

Merchant Card Services. 1036 S. Riverside Ave., Ste. 239, Rialto, CA 92376; (909) 874-1836. An agency that works with multiple systems. Contact: Tim Mahan functions as an agent for a variety of companies, including: Card-Service, United Merchant Services, Electronic Merchant Systems, and Mercury Bancard Systems. He specializes in companies making mail-order and telephone sales.

Merchant Services, Inc. 231 Quincy Street, Rapid City, SD 57701; (800) 888-4457 or (605) 341-6461. Contact: Deb Marlow. Functions as an agent. Comes to your home for an on-site interview; has a variable application fee ranging from $175 for a retail account to $350 for a mail-order or telephone-order application fee. Rates are under 3 percent for a "card slap" account to 3 to 4 percent for mail-order and telephone-order sales. Statement fees average $8.50. A reserve account of two months of receipts is required for a company engaging in sales by mail order, plus there is an additional 5 percent hold back.

Teleflora Creditline. Contact: Bob Gerver. DataBlue Associates, P.O. Box 293, East Longmeadow, MA 01028-0293. Voice phone—(413) 736-8831. Teleflora limits merchant accounts to bulletin board system operations and shareware producers and requires businesses to have been in business for at least six months. Teleflora's costs are $125 for an application fee and $475 for a terminal and printer, which may be paid off at the rate of $17.95 a month. Alternatively, software is also available. There is a $.25 transaction fee charged on each transaction, rates of 2.55 percent (2.25% if you will accept your payments in the form of bimonthly checks instead of electronic deposit), and a two-dollar monthly-statement fee.

CHAPTER
FIFTEEN
■ ■

Managing Information and Other Stuff:
Getting Rid of Clutter

One signature of the nineties is that we're being overwhelmed with information. Compare the amount of mail we receive with what our parents did; the size of the newspapers, the number of magazines, newsletters, even the number of media that bring information to us—cable TV, fax, audiotext, videotext, videotapes, and more.

As Gertrude Stein has pointed out, "Everyone gets so much information all day long that they lose their common sense." In today's home office, that's not all we lose. We also lose out. Chances are that if you're reading this book, you have at least one pile of unread or unfiled magazines, newspapers, mail, business cards, or telephone notes somewhere in your house. And more likely than not, you suffer routinely from one of the most common symptoms of this information avalanche: that nagging question "Now where did I put that?"

How often this frustrating question interrupts the flow of work! Not being able to find needed information is probably the single most common form of home-office inefficiency. And it's not a minor problem. Think of the missed opportunities when you can't find a business card you need, the lost hours spent searching for correspondence you should refer to, the embarrassing moments when you lose the address for a meeting you're already late for, or fail to return an important call because you can't remember where you wrote the phone number.

Even those with the latest high-tech equipment suffer from this office malady. Forgetting what they named a file or on which disk or directory they put it is as aggravating as misplacing a memo or file folder.

So no matter how small your home-office operation, it's helpful to have a system for processing and organizing the array of information you need at your fingertips. You need a way to easily process your mail, handle phone messages, and store phone numbers, addresses, business cards, and mailing lists. You need a system for recording upcoming events and keeping track of subject matter of interest to you as well as key information relating your clients and projects. And sometimes you have to track this information in both paper and computer files. You also need a way to conveniently store reference materials you want to keep from magazines, books, and tapes.

Five Requirements for Having the Information You Need at Your Fingertips

Since you probably don't have anyone to delegate these administrative tasks to and you're undoubtedly operating in limited space, your system for managing these details needs to be simple, easy to use, and compact. Having an effective system requires:

- Knowing what information you need to have access to.
- Having a proper place to keep the information you need.
- Setting up a regular and convenient time for putting information where it belongs.
- Establishing a familiar routine for processing, storing, and using information.
- Using equipment and supplies that make storing and locating your information easy.

Much of the information you receive in your home office isn't of sufficient value for you to devote precious time and space to addressing and storing it. Such "information noise" just clogs up your office and interferes with your ability to access the information you want and need quickly. Therefore, we suggest that you use the checklist below to identify the type of information you need to have on hand to do your work successfully. With this plan, you will have a place for everything and will be able to find everything in its place when you need it.

This chapter will address how with a minimum of time and energy you can manage the wide range of information needed by most home offices. We also provide guidelines for what to keep, where to keep it, when to throw it away, and when to get help keeping everything in order.

Computerizing Your Information

By 1993, over 50 percent of all home offices were computerized. One of the key factors driving this technological surge is the need to organize and process the rush of information that flows through even the smallest of successful home businesses. We strongly recommend that you computerize as much of the infor-

Identifying the Information You Absolutely Need
A Work Sheet

Check off each type of information you need to work effectively. As you read through this chapter, develop a plan for when and where you will address and store it.

Type of Information	Paper	Computer	Where	When
_____ Customer or client records	_____	_____	_____	_____
_____ Financial and tax information	_____	_____	_____	_____
_____ Project or task material	_____	_____	_____	_____
_____ Business cards	_____	_____	_____	_____
_____ Information on key subjects	_____	_____	_____	_____
_____ Upcoming events and activities	_____	_____	_____	_____
_____ A tickler system	_____	_____	_____	_____
_____ Computer disks	_____	_____	_____	_____
_____ Newspapers	_____	_____	_____	_____
_____ Magazines	_____	_____	_____	_____
_____ Tapes	_____	_____	_____	_____
_____ Books	_____	_____	_____	_____
_____ Mail	_____	_____	_____	_____
_____ Phone messages	_____	_____	_____	_____

mation you use in your home office as possible. Although the completely paperless office is still only peeking over the horizon, with proper backup, a majority of your correspondence, record keeping, contact management, billing, marketing, and other business records can often be stored on your computer. In addition to the money management software we mentioned in chapter 14, here are several other types of software that can help you organize and store the information you need to access quickly and easily.

Word-Processing and Desktop Publishing Software

With any sophisticated word-processing program such as *Microsoft Word, Ami Pro*, and *Word Perfect*, you can create and store correspondence, reports, manuscripts, and other types of written material. The mail merge capability of these programs enables you to quickly personalize and address your correspondence to your entire mailing list right down to individually printed labels or envelopes.

With desktop publishing software like *Microsoft Publisher, Publish*, and *Quark*, you can also create and design very sophisticated documents like newsletters, postcards, ad layouts, manuals, marketing materials, and forms of all kinds.

Both word-processing and desktop publishing software programs often contain "templates" that serve as models you can use again and again to create such things as invoices, newsletters, price lists, and other page layouts.

Information Management Software

Each day you're in business puts you in contact with many people and ideas that you want to keep track of and find at your convenience. This ever-growing base of names and facts is among your most valuable resources, your lifeline to success. Unfortunately, many people find themselves too busy and too disorganized to take advantage of the contacts and information they have. For example, you might meet twenty or thirty interested contacts at a show or exhibit, and while some of them will bring you business from that first contact, a much larger number could become clients at some later time—if you continue to maintain contact with them. Or, say you regularly read several magazines and clip articles of interest to your business. Although you can remember the most recent articles, you usually don't recall important facts and statistics from earlier issues. But if you don't have a full-time secretary or sales and marketing staff, it's easy for business cards, brochures, notes you make, and articles you clip to become strewn throughout your filing system, Rolodex cards, appointment books, business card holders, and other repositories of names, addresses, and phone numbers.

There are three computer solutions to this problem. You can use either mailing list software, contact and personal information management software, or even a full-fledged database management program. The choice depends on your needs, the complexity of information you want to keep, and your computer savvy and ability to learn to use sophisticated software. Here's an overview of the three categories of software:

Mailing List Software. These programs are actually simplified database programs that are preformatted to record basic mailing and contact information like name, address, city, state, and phone number. If you primarily want to reach your contacts by mail, a mail list manager like *My Address Book Plus, My Advanced Mail List, Call or Write,* or Avery's *LabelPro* can be the simplest way to manage your contact lists. Some programs like *My Advanced Mail List* also include a built-in word processor and mail-merge capability that enables you to write brief letters to send to all the names on your mailing list, then print out the letter along with mailing labels complete with Zip + 4 bar code. It will also sort first-class and third-class mail to save you money with bulk mailings.

Contact and Personal Information Managers. No single type of software is better suited for cutting clutter than contact management or personal information managers. With such programs, you can enter the valuable bits and pieces of information that contribute to clutter and get lost after being written on the backs of envelopes and business cards, stick-on notes, telephone message slips, or anything else that was handy when you got an idea or heard some item of information you wanted to keep.

- Contact management software, also a specialized database program, allows you to set up and maintain extensive records of your business contacts. Contact management software combines mailing list management and mail-merge capabilities with other capabilities such as computerized calendar and appointment logs, notepads, automatic phone dialing, and record keeping of calls, alarms that alert you to when to follow up with a contact, daily to-do lists with priority settings, and even faxing capabilities.

■ Personal information management software enables you to locate, analyze, and cross-reference *words*. These words may be ideas, leads for future business, facts and quotes you want to have available for proposals and speeches, as well as business information such as inventory, sales, billings, and personnel records—any kind of information. The strength of this category of software is that, unlike database management software, many of these programs free you from the constraints of formatting information in specified ways using mandatory fields with fixed lengths. Instead, you can enter your information freely, in whatever format or length you choose.

Some of the most noted programs are listed below.

Contact and Personal Information Management Software

Contact Management Software
Purpose: Combines calendar and appointment functions of daily planning with other tasks like mailing list management, clients' files and follow-up contact records, including a built-in alarm that will alert you to needed action.

For Whom: Sales-intensive businesses such as manufacturers' reps, executive search firms, advertising specialists, event planners, professional practice managers, mail-order companies.

Examples:
Act! and *1st Act.* Symantec Corporation, 10201 Torre Avenue, Cupertino, CA 95014; (800) 441-7234, (408) 253-9600. *Home Office Computing Magazine* Best Buy 1994.
BizBase. Creagh Computer Systems, 16855 W. Bernardo Dr., Ste. 201, San Diego, CA 92212; (800) 833-8892.
Goldmine. Elan Software Corporation, 17383 Sunset Blvd., Pacific Palisades, CA 90272; (318) 454-6800.
The Maximer and *Maximizer Light.* Modatech Systems, Inc., 1681 Chestnut Street, Ste. 500, Vancouver, BC, Canada V6J4M6; (604) 736-9666.
TeleMagic. Remote Control International, 5928 Pascal Court, Ste. 150, Carlsbad, CA 92008; (800) 992-9952, (619) 431-4000.
Sharkware. CogniTech Corporation, P.O. Box 500129, Atlanta, GA 31150; (404) 518-4577.

Personal Information Managers
Purpose: Calendar and information-tracking programs that let you make records of information in addition to time, date, address, and phone numbers such as lengthy notes, personal profiles, client records, references, lists, ideas—all of which can be searched by key word(s).

For Whom: Information-intensive businesses that involve a considerable collection of data like public relations specialists, information brokers, private investigators, consultants.

Examples:
Ascend. Franklin Quest, 2550 South Decker Lane Blvd., Ste. 2C, Salt Lake City, UT 84119; (800) 877-1814, (801) 975-9992.
InfoSelect. MicroLogic Corp., 1351 Ocean Avenue, Emeryville, CA 94608; (800) 342-5930, (510) 652-5464.
Lotus Organizer. Lotus Development Corporation; (800) 635-6887.
PackRat. Polaris Software, Inc., 17150 Via Del Campo, Ste. 307, San Diego, CA 92127; (800) 722-5728, (619) 674-6500.

Database Management Software. The third way to manage information is to use a full-fledged database program. Actually, mailing lists and contact and information management are all specialized database programs that provide a predefined structure for keeping track of specific kinds of information, making them simpler to learn and use. With a full-fledged database management program, nothing is predefined. You can set up the database any way you want to track whatever information (data, text, or dates, etc.) in whatever customized ways you want and change them readily when you wish.

Today's powerful database programs have become much easier to learn and use; so if you find preset versions of mailing list and contact management software too limiting, you can tailor the software to your particular needs. Popular database programs include *AlphaFour* (Alpha Software), *File-Maker Pro* (Claris), *DataEase Express* (DataEase International), *FoxPro Access* (Microsoft), and *Microsoft Access* and *Paradox* (Borland).

Database management programs also have more specialized sorting and searching functions so you can call up complex clusters and patterns of information. Some "relational" databases can even join files so that changes you make in one will automatically make the appropriate adjustments in others. "Free form" databases like *InfoSelect* (Micro Logic), *NoteBook* (Pro/Term) and *askSam* (AskSam Systems) enable you to put whatever information you want onto a black screen; when you want to retrieve it, you simply request key terms you entered. Such programs are best for keeping track of pieces of information like summaries of news articles, notes to yourself or from meetings, etc., instead of tracking names and addresses of contacts.

Integrated Software

If you have intermittent needs for a variety of software programs, you may benefit from using what is called an "integrated" software package—that is, one program that does several of these tasks all in one. *Microsoft Works* or *Lotus Works,* for example, contain a word processor, a spreadsheet, and a database program along with other modules. All these modules have similar command structures

Features to Look for: Contact Managers, Personal Information Managers, Free-Form Databases, Mailing List Card Files

The more sophisticated a program, the more features and flexibility it has—but generally the more complex and costly it will be. Select a package that has the features that best match your current and projected needs.

- Capability and memory needed to operate quickly
- Degree of flexibility in what data can be kept other than name, address and phone
- Import and export files from other programs
- Link to word processing and mail merge to print labels and envelopes
- Contact history with date and time stamp
- Follow-up reminders
- Follow-up alarm
- Yearly, monthly, weekly, and daily view
- Calendars

- Address-book and calendar print-outs
- To-do list, drop, and drop to future dates
- Phone dialer
- Expense tracking
- Scheduling
- Ability to search multiple fields
- Ability to define contact groups
- Memo, notepad, daily journals
- Ease of use
- Tutorial
- Clarity and simplicity of documentation
- Unlimited free support
- Toll-free support

---

so you can learn to use them more quickly. You also can move simply and easily from one module to another and transport information and data easily among the various applications.

In MicroRim's *In the Black* you have both a powerful contact management database and financial management system. So instead of having a separate database program in which you keep records about all your client contacts and another program for handling all your financial transactions, these two functions are coordinated in one package. You only enter the information once and it's available for making notes on a phone conversation or recording an invoice.

Make Sure Your Software Is Compatible

Even if you don't use integrated software, in order to manage your information most effectively, the software programs you select should be compatible so you have maximum flexibility to transfer information from one program to another. For example, it is useful to be able to import the information in your financial package into your tax software; or the text you develop in your word-processing program into your desktop publishing program; or charts developed in your spreadsheet into your financial package, your desktop published newsletter, or an overhead presentation.

Compatibility and porting are certainly one strong advantage of using a

Macintosh, or moving to the Windows or OS2 environment in which all software written for that environment is compatible. This need also accounts for why software suites have become so popular (see chapter 8).

Creating Paper and Electronic Filing Systems

Even though you manage and store much of your key information on computer, you will invariably still have plenty of paper coming in and going out of your office. So you need an effective filing system for keeping track of all the paper, and, of course, you need a system for organizing your electronic files as well. It's just as easy to clutter up a disk as to clutter up a desk. And it's just as easy to "misplace" a computer file as it is to misplace a manila folder.

If you've been working at home for any length of time, you undoubtedly already have a filing system. The question is whether the system you have works for you. Remember, the primary purpose of a filing system is retrieval, not storage. If you won't need to use a piece of information again, there's no reason to file it. So if you can't find your desk for all the piles of paper you have carefully stacked around in descending order of importance, you have a filing system. It's just not a system that helps you find everything you need when you need it. If you hear yourself saying "I know I have that somewhere, but I'll have to look for it," take that as a sign that your system is not working.

To work effectively, any filing system, whether in your computer, on your walls, or in a filing cabinet, should enable you to find the information you've stored in a minute or two. Also, it should be easy to weed out and keep current. To create a system that meets these criteria, we recommend that you group the many types of information you use into clear and simple categories that correspond to the various aspects of your work. In other words, organize your files by function and, to the extent possible, use the same major functional categories and titles for both your computer files and your paper files.

Here are several functional categories of files that most home offices will need. You can create specific directories and designate specific file drawers or even whole file cabinets for each of these functional areas. Use this as a checklist to which you can add special functions specific to your business:

__ Client and customer files
__ Project files
__ Business card files
__ Subject files
__ An upcoming file
__ A tickler system

Client or Customer Files

If you provide a service or sell products to key accounts, create a file for each of your clients or customers in your contact management, database, or personal information management software where you can record name, address, phone number, other contact names, sales history, notes, and other pertinent information. Then, if needed, create a corresponding section of your filing cabinet and paper file for each client where you can store written materials they send you such as brochures, annual reports, drafts they want you to look at, etc. Keep these files in alphabetical order by last name or company name.

As your clientele grows, you can subdivide your client files if you wish into "past" and "current" clients, or "active" and "inactive" clients. Or you can subdivide them by industry or type of work; i.e., "banking clients" and "ad agencies," or "transcription clients" and "training clients."

Tips for Organizing Your Computer Files

1. **Create directories and/or disks with the same names as your paper files.** For example, if you have a Projects section in your file cabinet, create a corresponding Projects directory or disk. Keep your computer and paper records related to each other.

2. **Label files with the same names you use on your paper files** to help you find information more easily. To further help you identify the contents of files, use file manager programs to write and view file descriptions.

3. **Back up the contents of your hard disk on floppy disks** or some other storage medium, such as streaming tape or a removeable hard drive, to avoid costly errors. Just in case of error, have a program like the *Norton Utilities* that will restore many mistakenly erased files.

4. **Erase unnecessary backup files daily and purge inactive files monthly** to keep your disk uncluttered.

5. **Use file compression and archiving utilities** to expand the amount of space available on your disks. Phil Katz's *Zipware* and *LHARC* from Japan are either in the public domain or are considered shareware. StuffIt is an archiving program for the Macintosh.

6. **Optimize your hard disk** by using software like the *Norton Utilities* to keep a hard disk operating at top speed.

7. **Use a utility that enables you to find your files,** no matter where they are on the disk by name or key words in case you have forgotten the name of a file or can't locate it, like *Personal Assistant* by Reference Point Software (801) 224-6611.

8. **Use batch files** to do routine and repetitive tasks automatically.

9. **Use macro commands** to use a few keystrokes to perform complex and repetitive operations. Macro-making capability is included in many software programs like Macintosh's *System 7* or as a separate utility like *ProKey* for Windows.

10. **Use disk organization programs** like *Norton Commander* or *Lotus Magellan* to simplify moving, deleting, copying, and renaming files.

11. **Keep disks you use frequently within arm's reach** of your computer. The cardboard or plastic holders that disks are packaged in can be used for storage and kept in desk drawers or on shelves. Special disk storage units, however, are available in multiple sizes, shapes, and designs (see p. 381).

Project Files

Create a directory and file cabinet space for your project files. Then create a separate file for every major project you're working on. For example, if you were writing an article on child abuse, you might create a word processing directory entitled "Child Abuse Article." In this, you would store your query letters, content outline, interview notes, and so forth, along with the actual article itself. Your corresponding paper file would also be entitled "Child Abuse Article" and into this file you would put correspondence received from magazine publishers, the contract made when you sold the article, brochures from clinics you interviewed, etc.

Should certain projects become voluminous, you can subdivide your project files. For example, if you begin writing many articles on child abuse, you can create a subdirectory and a special section in your project file drawer for all these articles and name them by magazine, date, or emphasis.

We recommend that you file paper Project Files in alphabetical order. On the inside cover of each file, you can record pertinent information related to that project—the names, addresses, and telephone numbers of contact people, your deadlines, meeting dates, work schedule, and so on. Or, if you're using contact or information management software, you can keep much of this key information in a file.

Business Card Files

The most effective way to store business card information is in your computer using contact management or database management software. But until recently, that meant taking the time to input the data from the many stacks of business cards that have been collected over time. Now, however, there is a quick and easy way to get business cards into your computer. Pacific Crest Technologies has created CARDGRABBER, a business card management system that scans a business card, then stores the name, title, company, address, phone, fax, and other information as well as an image of the card in a Windows-based address book that users can easily search, customize, sort, and print. (See figure 15-1.)

Figure 15-1.

CARDGRABBER is a Walkman-sized gizmo weighing less than a pound, which makes it easily portable to trade shows or networking activities. It's a scanner with special optical character recognition software and artificial intelligence that you can connect to any desktop or notebook using a cable to the parallel port. The system requires Windows 3.1 or higher, a 386 or higher processor, and a minimum of 2 MB RAM (4 MB RAM recommended). It costs about $349 and is available at major computer and office superstores and computer dealers.

If you still want to keep the paper version of business cards on hand, there are lots of filing systems for business cards, names, addresses, and phone numbers. We recommend using a system that enables you to file business cards and other names and addresses in one place. The system you select should be easy to update so you can add to, change, and remove names in alphabetical order. Here are several popular systems:

1. *Rolodex* **filing system.** This is the familiar system of cards on which names, addresses, and phone numbers are noted and attached to the center of a circular column so that you can flip to the one you're seeking. The uncovered versions are easier to use. Color-coated cards are available to easily identify certain clients, suppliers, or other key people. Adhesive dots can be placed on the upper right-hand corner of cards to highlight most frequently used or high-priority numbers.

2. **Metal business-card holders.** Business cards fit into a metal tray that is separated alphabetically. Keeping spare cards in the back of the file enables you to write out a name and address when you have no business card for a client or customer.

3. **Calling-card files.** In this system, business cards slip into soft plastic wallet-like inserts bound in a ten-by-fourteen-inch plastic notebook.

4. **Stapling cards to file folder jackets.** Instead of placing a business card into a filing system, you can staple it to the inside cover of a Project or Client File. This can be an efficient way to keep numbers or addresses you will only be using in conjunction with information in the file.

Subject Files

Create paper and computer files to keep information on subjects of interest to you. Personal information managers (PIMs) are great for this purpose. If you like to collect favorite quotes to include in articles or proposals, for example, record them in your PIM. Or perhaps you like to collect great jokes to use in presentations. Again you can collect and store them in your PIM. Anecdotal stories, statistics, great ideas—essentially anything you would jot down on a napkin or sticky pad and then either lose or have cluttering up your desk space—all can be included using personal information management software.

Designate space for Subject Files in your filing cabinet as well for such things as magazine and newspaper clippings on subjects of interest, product brochures, warranties, etc. Keep these files in alphabetical order. For example, if you will be buying a copy machine in the future, for example, create a Subject File titled "Copiers" for articles you have clipped, brochures on different brands, or notes you've taken when talking with a salesperson. When you have purchased the copier, clean out the file of materials you no longer need, and relabel it with the trade name of your copier, for example, "Canon Copier." Now you have a place for your instruction manual, warranty information, and supply order forms.

An Upcoming File

This is one type of subject file everyone should have. Use a file folder labeled "Upcoming" to keep announcements, confirmation letters, convention programs you plan to attend, and so forth. Before you file anything, mark the date of the event in the right-hand corner of the first page with a bright-colored marker. File the material in chronological order, with the nearest event at the front of the file.

By using an Upcoming File you avoid having to create a new file for each event you will be attending. Keeping the file in a desk drawer or somewhere near your phone makes information about upcoming events readily accessible. When you need to look up details or locations for these events, you can simply reach for your file.

Clean this file out periodically, discarding material on events that have passed.

A Tickler System

When you have more activities that need to be acted upon by a certain date than can be managed in an Upcoming File, you need a tickler system. Today's sophisticated appointment and calendar software and contact management software is ideal for alerting you to when certain activities need to be done and for making sure you follow through on commitments and plans you've made. Some of these programs simply fill in prescheduled activities on your calendar or "to do" list. Others have a beeper alarm that will actually call your attention to an action on the appropriate day.

You can also set up a paper tickler file for paying bills or following up on various announcements and materials you've received in the mail. You can buy one at a stationery store; they're called "Everyday Files" or "Desktop Files." Or you can create your own.

To set up such a paper system, label one manila file folder for each day of the month (1–31). Have one extra folder labeled "Next Month" or, for a more extensive system, one for each month of the year (January–December). Then, throughout the workday, you can put materials in the file for whatever day in the future you want to act upon them, whether they're checks to be mailed, letters to be answered, phone messages to be returned, or monthly reports to be filled out.

Whatever combinations you work out for your filing system, follow these simple rules for filing most efficiently.

Filing Rules of Thumb

1. **File each folder, card, or record in one, and only one, designated place.**

2. **"If a file is out, use it or lose it."** Every file or record should be in one of two places: in use on your desk or stored in its designated space. Put files away immediately after use. Don't leave them lying around to get to later.

3. **File material immediately.** Whenever you have new information for your files, add it at the time you get it. Don't create "file piles." When you receive mail, read articles, or take phone notes that you want to save, file the pertinent material as soon as you finish reviewing it. If you come home from a meeting with business cards, notes, or flyers you want to keep, file them when you arrive—at the same time you store your receipts for any expenses you've incurred.

4. **Put the most recent materials in the front of the file folders.**

5. **Remove all paper clips before filing materials.** They fall off and get stuck inside the files. If papers belong together, staple them together.

6. **Don't overstuff files.** Keep three or four inches of extra space in file drawers so they will be easy to use and the files won't get damaged. When files get overly crowded, clear them of outdated material.

7. **Label all file folders.** Use a file name that is broad enough to cover all the materials you will want to put in the folder.

8. **To keep from misfiling your folders** when you return them, either remove the papers you need and leave the folder itself tilted up, or tilt up the file behind the one you remove, leaving the drawer open as a reminder to return the file.

9. **Separate "active" files from "storage" files.** Active files are those you use on a regular basis. They should be kept in an area near your work space. Storage files are those you need to keep for legal or tax purposes, but which you no longer use. Keep these in cardboard file boxes in more remote storage areas (see figure 15-2).

10. **When filing accumulates, catch up during "down times,"** while watching TV, or talking casually on the phone.

11. **Don't let file folders grow beyond three-quarters of an inch.** Finding a single paper in a thick file takes too long. Break large files into subfiles.

12. **Reduce legal and large documents to letter size for easier filing.**

Using the Walls as Information Organizers

You can turn your walls into calendars, project planners, and information organizers by using:

Blackboards or whiteboards. Columns and lines for permanent headings can be drawn with indelible markers, paint, or tape. Different colors of chalk or markers can be used to highlight different types of information.

Plexiglass panels, plate glass, or see-through plastic. Clear panels of these materials can be mounted on the wall and held in place by a wood molding. Use grease pencils, crayons, or felt-tip markers of various colors and wipe them off easily with a moist cloth.

Movie screens or clear white walls. Using an overhead projector, clear plastic transparencies, and felt-tip pens, you can easily project and work with information displayed on walls and screens.

Newsprint. Sheets of blank newsprint from pads or rolls can be used to outline material you're working on and can then be hung on the walls for easy reference.

Bulletin boards or cork squares. Information can be tacked or pinned on commercial bulletin boards.

Planning boards. Commercial planning boards are sold as wall units made of magnetic material that can be written on with felt-tip markers and wiped off (see figure 15-2).

Storing Newsletters, Magazines, Books, Tapes, and Disks

The best system for storing newsletters, magazines, books, tapes, and disks depends on how many you have. One or two tapes can be kept in a drawer. A few newsletters can be kept in a Subject File. A few books can be placed on a worktable or credenza between bookends. But, like file folders, once you get more than a few of these items, they can begin to stack up. So here are some tips for keeping them in order:

Newsletters. Using a three-hole punch, file newsletters in standard-size ring binders, keeping the most recent ones in the front. Some newsletters come prepunched.

Magazines. Instead of stashing magazines in corners or under the bed, keep them in chronological order on bookshelves or in cabinets. For ease of access, standing them on end is preferable to stacking them. You can buy open-style magazine files to keep them standing upright (see figure 15-2).

Books. Books can be kept on shelves in closets or cabinets or, more commonly, on bookshelves. Although there is a wide variety of styles to purchase, we made our first bookcase from three pieces of lumber and some bricks. You can arrange books on shelves in alphabetical order either by subject or by author, but always place the most frequently used books on the shelves that are easiest to reach.

To keep bookshelves from becoming disheveled, you can use a Lucite documentation holder that keeps softcover computer and software documentation, directories, booklets, and equipment manuals erect and orderly on a shelf or bookcase while within sight and easy reach (SoftCover-Case, [800] 214-0528). Also, an acrylic answering machine stand can consolidate and streamline desk space by enabling your telephone to sit on top of your answering machine without hindering the use of either instrument (Signature, [909] 943-2021).

Tapes. Special plastic trays are available for storing your tapes, or they can be placed in shallow drawers, wood cabinets, or cardboard boxes. The biggest problem with storing tapes is that they are usually labeled on the front rather than on the spine, which makes locating the one you're looking for a time-consuming process. To avoid this problem, you can label them on the side yourself, with adhesive labels, and then organize them as you would books, in alphabetical order by subject or author.

Disks. There is a wide variety of holders for both 3½-inch and 5¼-inch computer disks as well as CD-ROM disks (see figure 15-2). We recommend keeping software disks and backup copies of software in separate holders from the disks you use to back up your hard drive. Label your data disks by software or, when the data requires more than one disk, use the same names for the disks as for the directories they are backing up.

Eliminate Newspaper and Magazine Piles with Edited-Just-for-You News

If you're tired of having stacks of newspapers and magazines piled around your home office that you're going to get to someday, you can cut your reading time dramatically and shrink or eliminate those piles by using *Journalist* by PED Software Corporation. With *Journalist*, a $129 program for Microsoft Windows, subscribers of CompuServe Information Service or Prodigy can design their own newspaper and have their PC publish it every day automatically.

Your personalized daily newspaper will be based on what it knows you want to read about. You lay out the paper on the screen the way you like, using a mouse; then tell the program which type of news you want each day—i.e., national, world, health, science, business, etc. The program then "clips" articles tailored to your interest from the major news wire services available through CompuServe or Prodigy. You can also give it key words to search. For information, call (800) 548-2203.

Figure 15-2. Storing Information

Disk storage units

Magazine shelf organizers

Cardboard storage files

Wall-unit organizers

A Daily Routine for Handling Mail

For most at-home workers, the mail brings the biggest influx of information into the home office each day. While some of it is vital business information, some may be personal or for other family members, and much is junk mail you would just as soon not receive. Whatever it is, you have to do something with the mail once it arrives at the door.

The first step is to designate one area where you process all mail, personal and business, incoming and outgoing. Often your desk is the best location. It's usually near both the phone and your files. Sometimes, as in our case, another location is more suitable. Our mail usually includes orders that need to be shipped out, so we have a storage room with a large table that we use for processing all of our mail.

Keep all the materials you need for handling both incoming and outgoing mail within arm's reach of the area you've selected. For example, we keep our mailing materials in the cabinets above the table where we handle the mail. These are the materials we find it useful to have nearby:

Manila folders	Postage scale
Stamps	Postage affixer
Mailing labels	Packing material
Envelopes	Postcards
Letter opener	Wastebasket
Filing labels	Marking pens
Stapler	Tape

If it isn't convenient to have these materials near your work space, you can keep them elsewhere in a drawer-organizer tray, and then bring out the tray when you're ready to deal with the mail.

Set aside about forty-five minutes each day to process the mail. Many people like to handle the mail immediately after it arrives. If your mail arrives at an odd time for you, however, as ours does (2:00 P.M.), you may wish to handle it at a more suitable hour. Some people prefer to process the mail first thing in the morning, feeling it's a good way to get the day under way. Others like to do it during what they call the "after-lunch lull." Still others prefer to close the day with the mail.

Which part of the day you set aside for handling mail is less important than doing it at some regular time and not letting it pile up from one day to the next. Avoid the temptation to scatter different pieces of mail hither, thither, and yon. Keeping it in one place and doing it at one time each day will make it much easier to manage. One exception to this is people whose work keeps them out of town or out of the office most of the week. They may prefer to set aside an "administrative day" once a week for processing all mail and other paperwork.

Use the Sort/Act System

Whenever possible, follow the "handle it one time" principle of mail management. Using the system we're about to describe, you can handle every piece of mail once, and trash it or stash it in its proper place within forty-five minutes.

Open the mail, sort it into the following four action piles, and handle it in one of these ways:

1. Throw it away. The wastebasket is our best friend in sorting the mail. We usually throw away three-fourths of our mail, tossing out advertisements and announcements that aren't of interest. In fact, we don't even open mail we know will not be of interest to us.

2. Act on it. Whenever possible, take immediate action. Fill out forms, send any requested material, ship out orders, make out a needed check, call to make a reservation, read correspondence or short newsletters. If the necessary action will take more than a few minutes, however, put the mail into a pile to be filed in the proper place for handling at a later time.

3. Refer it to others. Sort out mail for other family members or employees who are to handle it. Designate some place where this mail will be put on a regular basis. We put our son's mail on the ledge by the stairway to his room, for example.

4. File it. Any piece of mail you have not thrown out should be placed in its proper location by the end of the forty-five-minute period. It should be in one of three places:

- **In the appropriate file.** Put materials that require no further action in the Subject, Client, Chron, or Project files discussed earlier in this chapter. Materials that need further action should be placed in the Upcoming, Project, or Tickler files and flagged for when they need attention. If you wish, you can take this time to add these items to your daily planner or "Thought of Everything" list (see chapter 13).

- **In an area set aside for reading material.** Find a place to put magazines, newsletters, and journals you want to read. Places people frequently use include a bookshelf, a nightstand, or a magazine rack in the TV room or bathroom.

- **In your financial record-keeping system** (see chapter 14).

Some people prefer to create a special place or file for personal mail they want to handle after business hours. We often put our personal mail on the nightstand, for example, since we prefer to read and write personal letters at our leisure.

If you have more mail than you can finish filing in forty-five minutes, you can set up a tray or box on top of your filing cabinet for materials to be filed later. Generally speaking, we don't recommend this, because it's too easy for this kind of "file pile" to get so backed up that it's out of control.

Unless you have someone else coming in to do it, leftover filing is too often something that just never gets done. Then you're always having to scramble through the "file pile" to find missing information and may even overlook vital data that's become buried in the pile.

Profile: Simplicity Works, Lee A. Larcomb, Lumber Company

"I don't like in-baskets and out-baskets or anything else that sits on my desk. I have a hanging-file folder labeled "Accounts Payable." During the week, as mail comes in, I pull out the bills, both business and personal, and put them in the folder. Every week on Sunday morning while I'm watching David Brinkley, I pay all the bills in the folder. If something is not due for a couple of weeks or more, I leave it in the folder. I deal with junk mail immediately . . . it usually ends up in the round file (the wastebasket). Magazines are read as soon as possible each week. If there's an article I like or want to keep, I tear it out and throw away the rest. My rule is keep junk off the desk, do a routine every day, get tough with junk mail and clutter. Just looking at it clogs my mind."

Managing Phone Messages

Set up an area on or near your desk where you handle phone calls. If you're right-handed, place your phone on the left of your work space. This will leave your right hand free for writing while you're talking on the phone. Using a headset will enable you to enter information into your computer while you're talking. Keep the following within arm's reach in your phone area:

▪ **A telephone message pad or computer and software for writing down messages.** The pink tear-off pads we're all so familiar with are designed for multi-employee offices in which a secretary takes messages for several people. There is no place or need for "pink slips" in the home office.

Instead, we recommend entering phone messages in your time-management software by day or by contact or use a spiral-bound steno pad for recording phone notes. Using either method, you won't have hundreds of little slips cluttering the desk and forever getting misplaced. You will always know exactly where all your messages are. Who called, when they called, who needs calling back, their phone numbers, directions to where you are meeting them—this will always be easy to find. In short, all the information you receive over the phone will be in one place.

If you use a notebook, put the date you begin using a particular pad on the front cover of the pad. When it is full, record the date of the last day's messages on the cover also. The pad can then be stored as a permanent record. Be sure to write the date beside the messages as you take them each day.

▪ **Stick-on notes** for writing down information you want to take with you or put into a Tickler File. Avoid the temptation, however, of replacing your time-planning system with little pieces of paper hanging all over your home and office. Besides creating a mess, they're too easy to overlook on the day you most need to see them. Keep as much detail as possible in your personal organizer software or paper system.

▪ **Pen and pencil with eraser.** Although this seems obvious, how many times do you end up saying, "Just a minute, let me find a pen"? We've found the only solution to this is to have a pen that does not leave the phone area. There are pens you can attach to your phone with a little cord, special desk pens with a stand, and, of course, pen and pencil holders you can use next to your phone.

▪ **Business cards, addresses, and phone numbers.** Keep whatever filing system you have selected for storing this information near your phone for easy access.

Calls, of course, can come at any time of day or night, but some people find it easier to manage an office at home if they set aside a time of day for placing and returning phone calls. Often they work alone and don't want the phone to infringe on their business at hand or, for that matter, on their personal lives.

Home-Office Organizing Shortcuts

1. Use a letter opener.
2. Have a large wastebasket near the area where you process your mail.
3. Use memory-resident calculators on your computer so you can make quick calculations no matter what files you're working on.
4. Use a typewriter instead of your computer for filling out forms and simple response–postcards.
5. If you send out lots of mail each day, use a ceramic wheel or automatic stamp applicator.
6. Use card extenders to turn business cards instantly into *Rolodex* cards.
7. Plastic silverware trays keep pens, pencils, Post-It pads, paper clips, rubber bands, scissors, stapler, and Magic Markers organized in your desk drawer.
8. Try plastic stacking trays to keep various types of stationery and documents you use too frequently to keep in a filing cabinet at your fingertips without cluttering your desk.

Writer Kitty Freidman, for example, finds that phone calls disrupt her train of thought, so she places the calls she needs to make first thing in the morning before she starts writing. Then she turns on the answering machine and writes until the end of the day when she takes the messages off the machine and returns her calls.

You are more likely to reach people if you call before 9:00 A.M. meetings, at 11:45 A.M. before people leave for lunch, and in the late afternoon, between 4:00 P.M. and 5:00 P.M.

When working on the phone, record notes and messages on your telephone answering pad or directly into your contact management or personal information management software. At the end of a phone call, you may want to set up a Project File or Client File relating to the call. If you need to follow up on a call, use the information in your notes to put the data into your Upcoming or Tickler system.

What to Keep and What to Throw Away

Deciding whether to keep a piece of paper, a file, a letter, or an announcement can consume undue time and energy. Some people have a tendency to keep everything, "to be on the safe side." Others, not wanting to bother with the decision, throw things away too hastily. We've found the following guidelines useful in making the right decision.

1. **Keep materials you will use in relation to current projects or clients.** When a project is finished or a client or customer is no longer active, cull the file of extraneous material and retire the file to storage.

2. **Review files at least once a year.** If you haven't used a file in the last year, ask yourself whether you have a good reason to keep it.

3. **Keep materials related to work you still do,** if reconstructing them would require a lot of effort. If you currently have no use for the materials but expect you could use portions of them in future work, retire the materials to storage files.

4. **Keep irreplaceable materials.** If they are related to work you still do, materials that are not available elsewhere should be retained if reconstructing them would be difficult, expensive, or time-consuming.

5. **Some documents should be kept permanently.** Keep legal documents, warranties for the life of a product, securities, licenses, capital assets, insurance policies, all tax returns, home improvement contracts, and so forth.

6. **Keep tax records for six years after you've filed the return.** Records supporting a return filed April 16, 1994, should be kept until April 16, 2000. After filing your return each year, you can retire the material to storage files, discarding materials over six years old. Real-estate records and those relating to stocks must be stored indefinitely since records must be kept "as long as they are important for any tax law." Keep the tax returns themselves permanently. Tip: If you do not have a copy of any of your tax returns, you can obtain a copy from the IRS by writing to request Form 4506 entitled "Request for Copy of Tax Form."

7. **When in doubt** about keeping something, ask yourself these questions:
   - What will I use it for?
   - When will I need it?
   - Under what circumstances might I need it?
   - What would happen if I didn't have it?
   - Would I pay to rent extra space to store it?

Generally, we agree with what Stephanie Winston says in her book *Getting Organized*: If you haven't used something in the past year, and it has no sentimental or monetary value, but "it might come in handy someday"—toss it!

Neat, Convenient and Attractive Storage Systems

Despite all the paper, disks, books, files, magazines, and sundry other equipment and supplies an office brings into your home, you don't need to lose the "homey" look and feel you want your home to have. With manufacturers and retailers taking a growing interest in meeting our needs, even storage units and systems are being customized for the home office. Browsing through a Crate and Barrel or Hold Everything store or catalog, you'll find an array of attractive alternatives to gray steel and wire that could be perfect for keeping your home office organized. Here's a sampling:

1. Various-sized handwoven natural rattan baskets for holding newspapers and magazines, or shelf baskets for collecting similar materials like print cartridge refills or booklets in one place on a shelf.
2. Rolling hanging file trolleys in natural wood or forest green that glide from desk side or tuck neatly under a desk or table when not in use.
3. A folding pine bookcase that can divide an office, sit against a wall, or be folded up and put in a closet if need be.
4. A CD ROM tower or flat disk case that fans out when the lid is opened.
5. Plastic stacking media tubs with divided wells, for keeping disks dust-free and in order.
6. Computer "screenies," corkboard, or wood frames for posting notes and reminders around your computer monitor.
7. Wood wall-storage units for books, shelf baskets, disk tubs, paper supplies, and small equipment.
8. Wicker and wood storage bins that can substitute perfectly for steel filing cabinets. In fact, in many cases they will work better for you because you can pull out a file drawer basket and using the side handles take it anywhere in your home office to file, update a file, or work on a project. They're available in double stacks of four or eight baskets.
9. Hanging file boxes of paper-covered cardboard that can hang in your filing cabinet or be taken out, closed with Velcro and carried anywhere.
10. Acrylic magazine butlers for organizing and displaying your magazines and journals.

And if you have lots of forms or paper to keep stacked and sorted, KwikFile F/S Open-Shelf Forms Cabinets can keep them neat and in order along any wall ([800] 368-1057). Or if you have more space in the middle of the room than you have around the walls, you might try Fold'r-Hold'r from Expotacular Ind., Ltd. It's a desk-side filing stand for active files you want nearby that holds the equivalent of up to forty-eight inches of conventional file-drawer space at your fingertips rather than out of reach.

Are You Ready for Audio or Video Teleconferencing?

1. Am I using my speakerphone more often and finding it more irritating day by day?
2. Am I constantly traveling to nonpaying meetings away from my home office?
3. Do I often need to get together with people from other cities to work on joint projects?
4. Am I losing time and money faxing and overnight mailing the same documents back and forth again and again?
5. Am I missing opportunities because I can't get together more often to work with colleagues, clients, or potential clients?

The more questions you answer "yes," the more likely you should begin thinking about teleconferencing.

When You Need Someone to Help

As your work expands, the first person you hire will probably be someone to help with your information management tasks. When is the right time to get this help?

One general answer we frequently hear is "As soon as you can afford it." Certainly, having someone else to take over many of those office housekeeping tasks makes life easier and frees you for more creative and profitable uses of your time.

A more direct answer to the question, however, is to think about getting help when you are spending more than forty-five minutes a day processing information. Finally, if you find that you're simply not able to keep your records up to date, investing in the expense of getting someone to help may be the best use of your resources.

Once you do get help, we recommend that you set up a system you can use yourself when you need to, and evaluate its effectiveness regularly. Someone else can handle the files, the mail, and the phone calls, but ultimately you need to be able to step in at any time and handle these things efficiently, because information is the lifeblood of any office.

Resources

The Complete Book of Contemporary Business Letters. A book and disk from Round Lake Publishing, 31 Bailey Avenue, Ridgefield, CT 06877; (203) 431-9696.

Getting Organized. See full citation in chapter 7.

If You Haven't Got the Time to Do It Right, When Will You Find the Time to Do It Over? Jeff Mayer. New York: Simon & Schuster, 1990.

Information Anxiety. Richard Saul Wurman. New York: Bantam, 1990.

Mastering the Information Age. Michael McCarthy. Los Angeles: Jeremy P. Tarcher, Inc., 1990.

Organized to Be Your Best. Susan Silver. See full citation in chapter 7.

Organizing Your Home Office for Success. Lisa Kanarek. New York: Plume, 1993.

Records Control and Storage Handbook, with Retention Schedules. Order from Bankers Box, 2607 N. 25th Ave., Fankling Park, IL 60131.

Winning the Fight between You and Your Desk. Jeff Mayer. New York: HarperBusiness, 1994.

C H A P T E R
S I X T E E N

■■■■■■■■■■■■■■■■■■■■■■■■■■■■■

Cleaning Up: Sixty-Second Housecleaning

When the house is a mess . . . you certainly are not in touch with the very
best in you.

—Pam Young and Peggy Jones

What a pleasant feeling to walk into a model house—no dust, no muss. But then
model houses don't feel quite right, do they? They lack the sense of being lived
in that makes a house feel like home. If there's one thing a home office is, it's
lived in. And along with that lived-in feeling comes the muss and the mess.

Now that you're working from home, unless you hire a cleaning service,
keeping your home both livable and workable falls to you. But who has time to
keep things up the way the woman of the house once did when she was a full-
time homemaker? We certainly don't. You probably don't either. And if you
take the time, you probably feel as though you're stealing it from yourself or
your work. Let's face it, the demands of our schedules today simply leave very
little time for cleaning.

The Housekeeping Crisis

A recent survey from *USA Today* confirms what most of us know—housework
is the first thing to go when we run out of time. And when you're working on
your own at home, is there ever a day when you don't run out of time?

The majority of American households now consist of two-career couples,
singles, or single parents; and that means most of us are pressed for time.
Certainly deciding to work from home frees you to spend your time more as you
wish, but cleaning rarely comes out at the top of the list. We have found that
successful home-based self-employed individuals work an average of sixty-one
hours a week. That doesn't leave much "free" time. Even if, by working from

home, you're able to save the twenty or more minutes a day you once spent commuting, who wants to spend that extra time *cleaning*?

So what does happen to that "free" time? Surveys show most Americans spend a full weekend day (about thirteen hours) trying to take care of housework, grocery shopping, errands, etc. But at what a price! When we cram cleaning chores into the little free time we save for weekends, we have even less leisure time. So we start off the workweek as stressed-out and tired as we were when we closed the door on work at the end of the week. In a very real way, cleaning as the part-time job we've known it to be in the past no longer works for most households. But does that mean we have to choose between being dead tired or dirty?

We say NO! We say there's another way. It's taken us years to find it. And we had to try just about everything else before we did! First we tried the most obvious solution—hiring someone else to do it. In fact, a survey of the Mother's Home Business Network showed that 39 percent of their membership listed having a maid as their most commonly cited need!

But like many others who work from home, we found that having someone come in to clean was disruptive whether they came during the day or at night. During the day, we couldn't take calls while they were vacuuming. And the clatter in the kitchen could be heard in the background. At night we were either out or wanted to have a quiet evening at home.

In addition, cleaning services can be expensive. The average professional cleaning service we interviewed ran $300 per month. Freelance individuals cost somewhat less. Of course, if you decide to hire someone to clean, you may be able to deduct part of your cleaning costs as a business expense. Still, in paying out that much money, we kept thinking of all the other great things we'd rather do with that $300 each month. Think of the equipment $3,600 a year would buy—a new computer, laser printer, a scanner, a copy machine—and there would still be money left over. Or how about the marketing $300 would pay for, or the fun we could have with it? We could take the whole family to Hawaii for a week with that money! So like four out of five of the successful entrepreneurs we interviewed about this, we decided we'd rather spend that money on our business or ourselves than on cleaning up.

So, other than bringing in a service to do occasional large-scale tasks such as cleaning windows, carpets, and venetian blinds and a seasonal housecleaning, we decided to stick with the do-it-yourself method. Besides, we read it's good exercise!

First we tried setting aside a special time each week to clean our home and office. That lasted about a month. Then we tried a schedule for spreading the work out over the week; i.e., vacuuming on Monday night, dusting on Tuesday, etc. That lasted about a week. We also tried agreeing to do the cleaning randomly in our spare time. That lasted a long time. But no housework got done. We didn't have any *spare* time.

Ultimately we fell into what we call the chronic *crisis method* of housekeeping—that is, you put up with tolerably marginal levels of the mess until important "company" is coming. Then you drop everything and rush around like competitors in a supermarket contest who are trying to see how many groceries they can get in their cart in three minutes. Instead of throwing things in a cart, however, you're throwing things out of sight—paper, books, toys, mail, etc.—as fast as you can stash it somewhere before the doorbell rings. By the time your guests arrive, of course, you're exhausted. And either you vow never to have anyone come over again or you promise never again to let things get so out of hand—another promise that lasts about a month.

We even tried out some of the clever ideas in the "I-hate-housekeeping"-type books. You know, the ones with ideas like using a cleaning apron or a cleaning caddy to carry all your supplies and stuff around from room to room. None of those worked for us because they didn't deal with the real issue. The real issue is that we, like most self-employed individuals, have too many more important things we want to do than to clean. The truth is, we don't want to take the time to clean. So we certainly don't want to take time to create clever cleaning caddies.

Nonetheless we were getting fed up with the dirt and the periodic crises when we hit a turning point. We had just returned from a sixty-city media tour—the crowning glory of seven years of struggling to write and then promote the first edition of this book. You can just imagine how easily we came to rely, over that four-month tour, on returning at the end of each long day's work to an immaculately clean and luxuriously neat hotel room. The bathrooms were always *sparkling*. The beds were always freshly made—with *perfect corners*. And any dirty dishes were whisked away in moments. Dirty clothing and shoes disappeared at night to reappear laundered and shined. It was heaven! We felt like King and Queen for the Day!

But eventually we were home again, and guess what? We'd arise in the morning to get dressed for the day, and no one had cleaned up the bathroom! It didn't sparkle. We'd go into the kitchen for something to eat, and no one had cleaned off the countertops! They didn't shine. We'd come in late at night to drop into bed, and no one had made it up fresh and crisp!

The contrast was a shock! We realized for the first time on a gut level how wonderful it feels to enjoy a *really* clean home. Suddenly it was no longer something your parents tell you to do. It was no longer a social expectation, an outdated role demanded of women, a badge of "superwomanhood," a sign of the sensitive male, or a distasteful duty that proves you're an enlightened New Age couple. No, instead, we realized at the gut level that a really clean, neat place to live and work is a treat, a compliment, a privilege, a reward. It says, "You're important. You're special. You deserve to be honored and treated like royalty."

And we missed that feeling! We wanted it back. We wanted to feel like King and Queen for the Day every day. We deserve it. We work hard. We do good work. And so do you. But the question still remains, Where do you find the time? Our schedules hadn't changed. We still had very little time to devote to cleaning.

But we're firm believers that when you set a goal, when you're determined to have something in your life, the next thing you know a solution arises. And that's what happened. We developed a new perspective on housework and cleaning, and the result is a system that makes it possible for us to keep our home and office clean, neat, and tidy in only seconds a day. We call it Sixty-Second Housecleaning. It's easy. It works, and we think you'll like it too.

We can keep our work and living space neat and clean enough in only seconds a day by doing seven things differently from the way housekeeping is usually done. And fortunately, because we work from home, we can make these changes. They probably wouldn't work for someone who is employed outside the home five-plus days a week. Here's a summary of the seven steps to Sixty-Second Housecleaning, followed by more details on how to put this method to work for you.

7 Steps to Sixty-Second Housecleaning

1. Adopt a new attitude toward cleaning.
2. Think in terms of preventing messes instead of cleaning them up.
3. Clean as you go through the day instead of waiting until you have a block of time.
4. Put your cleaning supplies "on a diet" and keep them near the multiple places throughout the house that need cleaning.
5. Let technology do the work for you.
6. Get everyone to pitch in.
7. Make strategic use of professional cleaning services.

The Sixty-Second Housecleaning Method

Adopting a New Attitude Toward Cleaning

First throw out all your old ideas about what you *have to do* and *should do*. Instead start thinking about what you *want done* and how you can do it most efficiently.

It's time we acknowledge that times have changed. Housekeeping was once a full-time career for most women. Today it's no longer necessarily a woman's responsibility alone, and whatever gets done must be squeezed in around full-time careers and perhaps a family too. A clean house is no longer an appropriate measure of how good a person you are—and that goes for both men and women. We believe housekeeping needs to be redefined to mean maintaining an environment to your liking, one you can live and work in comfortably and successfully. And the truth is that means different things to different people.

Nonetheless two-thirds of women answering a *Good Housekeeping* poll reported they're not happy with the way their homes are kept because they can no longer maintain the housekeeping standards they grew up with. Let's give ourselves a break and stop measuring ourselves by those old standards. It's time for us to set new standards. Let's think about how we want our homes and offices to be. Do we really need to pass the "white glove test"? Just what is "clean"?

For some people "clean" means there isn't a lot of "stuff" around. For others, it means an absence of dust or dirt. Take notice of what bothers you and what makes you feel good. If it bothers you, you deserve to take care of it for your own benefit. So do it. If it doesn't bother you—as long as it's not detracting in any way from the success of your business—let it go and get on with what does matter in your life.

We also need to alter our expectations about how much time we need to spend cleaning. An R. H. Bruskin survey shows that people spend about fourteen weekend hours on chores—six and a half more hours than they want to spend. Still one-third of people we surveyed think they spend too little time. In actuality, we only need to spend as much time as it takes to do what we want done. So start setting your own standards, and you'll find that it's much easier to motivate yourself to make the time to meet them.

Thinking in Terms of Preventing Messes Instead of Cleaning Them Up

Half of housecleaning is unnecessary because a lot of the messes we have to clean up never needed to happen in the first place. For example:

---

18 Messes You Can Prevent

1. Dirt that doesn't get through the door doesn't need to be cleaned up. Good-quality mats at the door and covered or elevated entryways keep dirt, mud, and water out.
2. Well-insulated doors and weatherproofed windows let in less dust.
3. Using liquid soap dispensers instead of bars of soap prevents soap scum buildup on sinks.
4. Deep sinks prevent splattering.
5. Brushed brass plating on faucets doesn't show spots that must be polished.
6. A shower stall or tub wiped down immediately stays clean.
7. Mildew doesn't grow as much in well-lighted bathrooms with plenty of circulation.
8. Dishes cleaned off at the moment they're used don't get food caked onto them.
9. With today's fabrics, laundry folded when it comes out of the dryer usually doesn't need ironing.
10. Clothes hung up at the moment you take them off don't get piled up to be put away.
11. Magazines and papers read or skimmed, clipped, and filed when they arrive don't accumulate into a major catch-up project.
12. Receipts filed when you return from shopping don't pile up for sorting.
13. Semigloss latex enamel paint and vinyl wallpaper don't spot, and they clean easily.
14. Fabrics treated to resist stains are easier to clean and need cleaning less often.
15. Neutral colors for all surfaces are easier to clean than dark or white ones.
16. Tile with dark grout saves hours of bleaching and scrubbing.
17. Streamlined furniture and fixtures don't collect dust and dirt like ornate ones, and they can be cleaned more quickly.

18. Plenty of storage units, drawers, racks, cabinets, and closets prevents messes by making sure there's a place to put everything away in, on, or under.

For more tips on messes that don't need to happen, see *Make Your House Do the Housework*. Don Aslett and Laura Aslett Simons.

In other words, as is true of running your office, a little effort *now* can save lots of effort *later*. You can cut the time required to clean your home and office in half by avoiding some of the biggest messes in the first place. You won't need to clean the stove if you wipe up spills as they occur. You will rarely need to clean the refrigerator if you clean up spills and stains when they happen. You'll rarely need to scour pots and pans if you wash them the moment you empty them.

If you like using your time to clean—and some people do—then you can enjoy the luxury of being as messy as you like; however, we hate doing most cleaning tasks so much that we'd much prefer to take a moment to prevent a mess so we can avoid doing the time-consuming tasks of cleaning it up. We have what we call our *Backup Barometer*. If things start to pile up or look crummy, we jump in to clean up before it turns into a major project that we'll have to struggle and sacrifice time to do.

Cleaning as You Go through the Day, Sixty Seconds at a Time

Don't wait until you can set aside a block of time to clean. Face it, chances are you don't have a day or a morning to set aside for cleaning every week. Realistically, who has big blocks of time to devote to housework? And anyway, if you miss a "block" one week, next week's block has to be even bigger. You probably don't have any "spare" time to squeeze it into either. But cleaning as you go throughout the day literally takes only seconds, and nearly anyone can spare just a minute here and there.

Most repetitive cleaning tasks can be done by following the "sixty-second rule." It's true. We've actually timed them. For example, to clean your whole master bathroom might take an hour. But, let's say that while you're brushing your teeth, you notice that the mirror needs cleaning; it will take only sixty seconds to clean it. Or if you notice that the bookshelf is dusty; it will take only sixty seconds to dust it. If you notice that the bedroom floor is getting dirty; it takes only sixty seconds to vacuum it.

Actually this "do it when you see it" approach is the heart of our Sixty-Second Housecleaning Method. See it; do it; get on with your life. Because you work from home, this is much easier to do. Some tasks like washing the kitchen or bathroom floor will take longer. But there's a big difference between five minutes and all Saturday morning. In other words, you don't have to clean all at once. Do what you can do when you notice it, and you'll be amazed at how much easier cleaning becomes. Your home and office may never be sparkling all at once using this method; but they will be generally clean all the time with less time and effort on your part.

Bare-Bones Cleaning Supplies for Sixty-Second Cleaning

1. Turn a shelf, cabinet, or drawer into a Sixty-Second Mini–Cleaning Center in each of these key locations in the home:

   - Kitchen
   - Each bathroom
   - Laundry area
   - Office

2. Have these basic supplies for each Sixty-Second Mini–Cleaning Center:

   - A glass cleaner
   - An all-purpose cleaner
   - A dust remover/furniture polish
   - Paper towels and/or cloth

3. For bath areas only add:

   - A toilet bowl cleaner and brush
   - A tub and tile cleaner (Some toilet bowl cleaners do double duty as excellent tile and tub cleaners!)
   - A shower caddy stocked with tub/shower cleaning items such as:

     —Tub and tile cleaner
     —Sponge
     —Squeegee for wiping down shower doors
     —Mildew remover (in humid locales)

4. Additional supplies/equipment for each Sixty-Second Center could include:

   - A hand-held or mini vacuum to clean floors and countertops
   - A box of disposable plastic gloves
   - A double-sided sponge: one smooth surface, one rough
   - Trash bag liners
   - A full-powered vacuum sweeper on each floor or in each wing of your home/office.

Warning for the Housekeeping Perfectionists

If the sight of a dusty shelf, a few crumbs under the breakfast table, a crooked picture frame, or fingerprints on the mirror drive you up the wall, you can still do sixty-second housecleaning, but you will need to firmly limit yourself to doing only sixty seconds worth of cleaning at any one time and then get back immediately to whatever task was at hand when you noticed something needed cleaning. Also you may have to limit yourself to no more than ten sixty-second cleaning chores a day and let others go until tomorrow. Otherwise you could find yourself cleaning your way through every day and never getting down to business. If you can't do these two things, don't use this method. You are someone who needs to hire a weekly cleaning service or to set aside a block of time each day or week to keep everything spick and span so you can be free to work without distracting housework staring you in your critical eye.

Putting Your Cleaning Supplies on a Diet and Keeping Them Nearby in Multiple Places throughout the House

The sixty-second approach works best if all the supplies you need to clean are virtually within arm's reach. Having to traipse back and forth to a central cabinet where you keep your cleaning supplies and then having to rummage through an assortment of bottles, cans, sprays, polishes, waxes, and other cleansers is another hurdle that makes cleaning too time-consuming.

Instead we recommend limiting your supplies to the bare essentials and keeping a set of them in a convenient place in every major cleaning area of your home or office. Most people have four times as many types of cleaning supplies as they need. All this excess cleaning material just clutters your cabinets, wastes your time and squanders your money. If you cut down to the essentials, you can have them all in multiple places and still get more from less.

Letting Technology Clean for You

As with running your office, the right appliances will do some of the worst cleaning tasks for you, and we believe they're worth the investment. It's surprising how some people can equip their offices with the latest office technology, but their cleaning appliances may still be no more advanced than the ones their parents used. Perhaps that's because office equipment is tax deductible. However, if you're using the Sixty-Second Housecleaning Method in your home/office, the cleaning appliances and supplies that you keep and use in your work space are also deductible as a business expense.

So when replacing appliances or doing remodeling, opt for timesavers whenever you can. Consider built-in wall vacuums, no-wax flooring, an automatic vacuum sweeper, a frost-free refrigerator, trash compactor, built-in appliances, and self-cleaning ovens. Even a built-in soap dispenser and drinking fountain on the kitchen sink counter can be a super cleaning saver when you have children. While some may consider such things to be luxuries—and they are usually somewhat more expensive than more time-consuming models—now that you're working from home, your time is money, but not when you're using it to clean things up.

Sixty-Second-Cleaning Secrets

Premoistened and Reusable Towels—Virtually every surface in your home and office from countertops to monitor screens, telephones to disk holders gets dusty and dirty, smudged and smeared. An easy way to avoid lugging out spray bottles, paper towels, and dust rags is to keep a supply of premoistened or reusable towels on hand everywhere you might use them. For example, Read/Right has premoistened pads called Klean & Dry for cleaning monitor screens. We keep a supply in our desk drawers. For other surfaces, we use moist towelettes, the ones that are actually for washing your hands and face while away from home. But they're great for quickly cleaning desktops (other than wood), telephone handsets, countertops, bathroom sinks. Pull one out, wipe, and toss! And because they're actually for use on hands and faces, they don't leave your hands covered with harsh, smelly chemicals. We like Wet Ones by L&F Products best. They're the moistest and come in a pop-out plastic bottle for under sink or counter or a travel pack that fits easily in a desk drawer. Nice'n Clean comes in individual packets.

Handi Wipes also are useful for instant cleaning or dusting. They're actually reusable paper towels. You can use them for anything you'd use a paper towel for, but they're stronger than a paper towel. You use them, wash them out, and use them again. We keep them around for instant dusting.

Unfortunately, dust doesn't settle on only the easy-to-reach surfaces. It has a way of getting into the nooks and crannies of electronic equipment where towels can't clean. But *Dust-Off* can. This air-spray canister enables you to clean out the hardest-to-reach areas, and it can even be transformed into a minivacuum. *Dust-Off* is made by Falcon and is often sold in the photography departments of retail stores for about $5.

Getting Everyone Else to Pitch In

Housemessing is always a joint venture. Why not housecleaning? Get everyone in your household (and your employees, too) onto the Sixty-Second House-cleaning Method. Here are some ideas for how to do that:

- Don't slip into letting cleaning become any one person's responsibility.
- Sit down together and talk about by whom and how it will be done.
- Discuss each person's idea of how the home and office should be.
- Determine which tasks are most important to each person.
- Discuss how you all can assist one another in making sure that those things that are most important to everyone get done.

- Present the idea of Sixty-Second Housecleaning. Find out if everyone would be willing to use it by comparing this method to alternative ones (see Housecleaning Methods: Pros and Cons, below).

- Set an example as someone who eagerly and cheerfully keeps things up the way you want them.

Housecleaning Methods: Sample Pros and Cons Checklist

No Particular Method

Pros
- You don't have to make any decisions.
- You don't become enslaved to any method.
- You have ultimate flexibility.

Cons
- Cleaning usually falls to one person who feels resentful.
- Housework often doesn't get done.
- House only sporadically clean.

Regular Schedule

Pros
- House clean all at one time.
- You don't have to think about cleaning at other times.
- Get housework over with all at once.

Cons
- Hard to keep to a schedule.
- Often fall behind.
- Can't find blocks of time to do everything at once.

Hire Someone

Pros
- Saves you time.
- Saves you energy.
- You don't have to do cleaning tasks you don't like doing.

Cons
- Disrupts the workday.
- Increases overhead.
- Funds can be used for more profitable things.

Sixty-Second Method

Pros
- You don't have to set aside blocks of time you don't have.
- House always reasonably clean.
- Much easier to motivate yourself.

Cons
- House never clean all at once.
- You are still doing the cleaning yourself.
- Have to create a new habit.

Children in particular need to understand why housekeeping is important. They need a reason. "Because I said so" is not enough. They also need to know, especially in this day and age, that it's not "mother's job." They need to be shown how much more enjoyable it is to live somewhere where you can find things when you want them. They need to see how inconvenient and unpleasant it is for more and more of your space to become uninhabitable and unusable because it's all taken up with clutter.

Having a sense of responsibility arises from feeling a sense of ownership and participation. It's hard to feel responsible for that which you're *required* to do. Slaves, for example, rarely feel responsible. They may feel obligated, but only until they're free to do as they choose. Therefore, if you don't want to become the "cleaning cop," involving others in making decisions about what and how things will be cleaned up and asking them to decide what they will make a commitment to do is crucial. Once a commitment is made, it's important to expect that it be kept or renegotiated.

The Ten-Minute Cleanup

Publicist Kim Freilich, owner of Kim from LA, uses a variation of the Sixty-Second Housecleaning Method. If she needs to get down to work, but the state of the house is driving her crazy, she sets a timer and gives herself ten minutes to clean up everything she possibly can. She says she's amazed at how much she can get done. It becomes like a game of beat the clock to see how much she can do before the buzzer rings.

We think this is a great idea, too, for getting the whole family involved in quick cleanups. Everyone could fan out to a different area and see who can get the most done before the buzzer goes off. Prizes or treats can be given out to all!

Making Strategic Use of Cleaning Services

Certain cleaning tasks are large scale by nature, and these are the ones that we recommend saving for a cleaning service. They take considerable time, energy, and even some specialized skill. We and about 20 percent of the home businesses we interviewed hire a service to come in periodically for a thorough general cleaning and specialized tasks like cleaning windows, carpets, blinds, and drapes. We use such services quarterly, but we also spoke to people who have someone come in for such tasks monthly or even every other week. You can farm these tasks out to specialized services or you can use one service that provides them all.

Resources

How to Get Kids to Help at Home. Elva Anson. New York: Ballantine, 1991.
Make Your House Do the Housework. Don Aslett and Laura Aslett Simons. New York: Writer's Digest, 1986.

PART 5

Managing Yourself and Others

CHAPTER
SEVENTEEN

■■■■■■■■■■■■■■■■■■■■■■■■■■■■

Avoiding Loneliness

"Isolated? Me? Impossible!" says Nick Sullivan, a senior editor working from home via modem for *Home Office Computing* magazine. "When I work I work. When I socialize I socialize. Whether I work at home or at the office, it doesn't make much difference. I couldn't isolate myself if I tried. I live in the world."

This expresses the amazement most successful open-collar workers experience when they are asked, as they frequently are, don't you feel isolated? Frankly, most people who work from home don't feel isolated once their business or job at home is under way and functioning. Their world is full of clients, customers, neighbors, family, friends, suppliers, business associates, and colleagues.

Although sometimes there's an adjustment period during which you feel cut off from former office mates, working from home does not mean you will be isolated and lonely unless you are a hermit. It does mean you have to be active and take the initiative to be involved in the world around you. Should you begin to feel isolated and lonely, here are three steps to getting yourself back in the swing of things again.

Three Steps to Getting Back into the Action

1. Admit you're missing some type of contact. Admitting you're feeling isolated seems to be the first step to avoiding it. Since people usually start working from home for some important reason, sometimes they don't like to consider that it might not be satisfying to them. Bookkeeper Paulene Smith, for example, left her job because she wanted to be at home with her new baby. "I wanted everything to go well and certainly didn't want to think I'd made the wrong decision. But finally I had to admit to myself I really did miss the old gang at the office. I had to acknowledge that working on my own involved some special problems I hadn't expected."

2. Recognize what you're missing. After admitting you're missing something, the next step in avoiding isolation is recognizing exactly what you miss. Isolation means different things to different people. For freelance programmer George Broady, not having people around wasn't the problem. "It isn't really people I miss. I work better by myself. What I miss is not knowing what's going on. I don't like feeling out of it."

Marriage and family counselor Sharry Cox agrees that "isolation" means more than being alone. "I'm with clients all day, so it took me a while to figure out that it wasn't really contact with people I was missing. I get plenty of that. I miss seeing a friendly face that understands the challenges of the work I'm doing."

In a *Success* magazine article, Robert S. Wieder described how office gossip and the grapevine make a variety of subtle but important contributions to working happily and effectively. It isn't always easy to recognize these intangible but vital benefits of being part of an office culture. Here's a list of things you may miss.

- The inside information. The vital tips. The scuttlebutt about what's going on.
- Esprit de corps. Exciting news or a lighthearted conversation giving you the feeling of being part of a group.
- Some helpful social pressure, a little incentive, to keep your mind on business and your hands off the potato chips.
- Some help or moral support in the midst of an emergency.
- Immediate feedback on your work.
- A way to test out a new idea.
- A pat on the shoulder, an understanding look, a word of encouragement.
- Someone to complain to about how awful things are or brag to about a job well done.
- A candid evaluation of how you're doing or a warning when you're about to make a mistake.
- A chance to build self-confidence in your work by telling someone about what you're planning.
- The sense of belonging that comes from being part of an organization.
- The sense of importance that comes from having a formal title and a needed role in the organization.

3. Take action to get involved in activities that provide what you're missing. Once you know which benefits you're missing, you can set about finding the best way to replace them. A next-door neighbor can provide a friendly "hello" and possibly even a good ear for the joys and tribulations of your day. But only a respected colleague can give you feedback on what you're doing, share news in the field, or recognize and praise a brilliant effort.

You'll have to take action to replace the particular elements of office interaction you're missing. To stay in touch, you'll have to take the time and invest the energy to set up opportunities for the interchanges you miss. Sharry Cox expresses what so many people who work at home discover: "Unless I work at it, I get out of touch with what's going on in my field. I start missing opportunities, learning the hard way what I could easily learn from someone else. Unless I make the effort myself, unless I dial a phone number or drive to a meeting, I lose contact with the people I've known."

In other words, whatever you're missing from contact at the office, chances are *it* won't find *you*. You'll have to find or create it yourself. Here are steps you can take to create the interaction you need.

Nine Ways to Keep in Contact with Peers and Colleagues

1. Join and participate regularly in community organizations and professional, technical, or trade associations. Most fields have a national professional association, and many have local chapters. If there is not a local chapter in your area, consider forming one. Many Chambers of Commerce are now welcoming home businesses and self-employed individuals. Some even have home-business counsels or special-interest groups that meet separately from the monthly Chamber meeting. In addition, the number of home businesses has grown so dramatically over the past few years that independent Home Business Associations are forming spontaneously in communities all over the country. A list of such associations is available on the Working From Home Forum on CompuServe.

When you join one or more such trade and professional organizations, of course, attend the meetings regularly, but in addition, participate actively in the organizations' leadership structure. Volunteer to serve on a committee (membership, hospitality, and fund-raising are good ones to become active with) or run for an office. Make presentations and attend local, state, and national conferences.

2. Read and listen. Specialty publications now number in the thousands and serve needs in almost every area of interest. Newsletters, professional and trade journals, and magazines spur creative ideas and keep you aware of what's happening. Audiocassette tapes are now available from many sources on almost any subject. You can even subscribe to a tape library program. Two such programs are included in the Resources list at the end of this chapter. Workshops and conferences frequently come in tape format now, too. If your work involves driving, listening to these kinds of tapes is a great way to make the best use of your time.

3. Attend workshops, seminars, and courses in your field, or explore new and related fields. Once you've attended a few of these programs, you will be on mailing lists for many others and receive announcements of the workshops in your area of interest. Begin by contacting the continuing-education department at your local college or university as well as your professional, technical, or trade association for workshops they may be sponsoring. Also, look through specialty or trade newsletters and magazines for workshops advertised in your area of interest.

4. Use the telephone. Stay in touch by phone with the people you've known. Call to say "hello," to get an opinion or reaction, or just to share some news. People are flattered when you think of them and enjoy being consulted. Use phone contact to discover what others are doing and when or where you might get together.

Call or write the interesting people you hear or read about. If you want contact with them, ask how you can get involved in what they're doing. We have met several of our most valued colleagues because they took the time to call us after reading about something we had done. We've met other important colleagues because we called when we read about them.

5. Take an electronic coffee break. If you don't have a computer, the ability it gives you to keep in touch with others easily is a good reason for getting one. Asking a colleague a question, sharing a victory, or commiserating about a disappointment isn't a matter of walking to the next office, but it's easier than driving somewhere in your car. It's as easy as using your computer to reach out and be in touch with other people who work from home, not only all over the United States and Canada but increasingly in Europe, Asia, and South America. Using communications software and a modem, people are using on-line services, such as CompuServe, Prodigy, and GEnie as well as local and company-maintained bulletin-board systems to relate to other people.

Commercial artist Diane Wessling Blake, vice-president of MicroGraphic Images, stays in touch with fourteen other home-based employees in the organization through a bulletin-board system operated from the home of the company's president.

"Everyone in our company works from home. It's ideal for me because I've always worked better alone, but I stay in touch with people by going out to teach classes and consult. Inside the company, we never feel isolated because with the bulletin-board system we can contact others whenever we need to."

Visitors to the Working From Home Forum we started in 1983 on the CompuServe Information Service can get involved in three different activities:

- A bulletin board that serves as a message center through which people converse.
- Libraries of information and software for specific businesses, such as desktop publishing, information brokering, mail order, and word processing, as well as on general matters such as telecommuting, accounting, taxes, legal issues, and office management.
- "Electronic conference rooms" in which you can communicate in real time with other people, attend meetings, or just take an electronic coffee break to chat with someone else. Recently, private investigators have been meeting on a weekly basis.

Here's what some of the members of the Working From Home Forum say about how computer networking has affected their lives:

Ray Jassin, who operates a service managing law libraries in the New York area, said, "I can't say enough about how much I've gotten out of both the serious discussions and the fooling around that we do. I've made new friends."

Linda Stern, a writer in North Carolina: "I've gotten very specific advice—

such as whether and what kind of home copier to buy—and more general career guidance as well. I also get inspiration—there are a lot of energetic, interesting people hanging around out there."

David Palmer of Tucson: "Obviously lots of writers (I'm one, too) use CompuServe and the Working From Home Forum as an information resource and a national networking system. A less obvious, but perhaps more valuable use is as a sort of social sanity check. When deadline pressure mounts and nothing wants to come together right, I find that I can 'hide' on CompuServe for a while and relieve some of the pressure. Browsing the messages and maybe helping somebody else solve a problem can be great therapy for someone who has spent too many hours in 'work mode' and not enough in 'wander mode.' "

What you'll discover on-line is a shrewd realism that's based on the experiences of people who are making it on their own each and every day, solving problems like getting health insurance or merchant accounts from MasterCard and Visa or coming up with ideas for projecting a professional image. Expertise in countless areas is only moments away. Just how specialized the help can be is illustrated by one request we feared might go unanswered. Someone had left a message asking about how he could get information for a client on *Pursung* horses. But within hours, an answer awaited him. Every day people reach out to share their moments of joy as well. Be it celebrating the birth of a child or closing a big contract, those in need receive support that would do any businessperson proud.

To participate in the Working From Home Forum, join CompuServe by purchasing a starter kit from a book or computer store. There are no dues for joining the forum. The only cost you incur is for your connect-time to CompuServe. Once you log on to CompuServe, enter GO WORK at any prompt.

6. Schedule breakfast, lunch, or dinner meetings with peers. Even though this may mean breaking up your workday, set a goal to meet regularly with peers you want to stay in touch with. These business meetings may be partially tax deductible. To personalize the meal and save money, you may want to host your colleagues at home.

7. Invite others to visit your home office and arrange to visit their offices. You can invite colleagues over to see a new piece of equipment, to sit in on some work, or to talk over a new idea.

Rather than fearing competition from sharing with people in your own field, consider the experience of a group of Pasadena, California, housewives who came together to support one another becoming writers when their children left home. Over a period of twenty years, their weekly Tuesday lunches, in which they critique one another's manuscripts and talk over story ideas and the ins and outs of publishing, have enabled them to produce hundreds of published books, despite the fact they all write books for children, juveniles, and young adults.

When Jane Minogue, a telecommuting technical writer for CompuCorp, found that telephone contact didn't provide enough feedback and interaction, she invited several other telecommuting writers to come over occasionally so they could discuss projects and share ideas. "We've really enjoyed these meetings. They've helped a lot," she says.

8. Join or set up a networking group to meet with on a regular basis. *Networking* is a widely used term referring to the informal relationships that develop among people through which they make contacts, get information, referrals, leads, and various other forms of support. Certainly much "networking" gets done through professional, trade, and civic organizations, but as this concept has grown in popularity, groups are forming all across the country for the sole and exclusive purpose of networking.

Networking groups come together as study groups, "leads" clubs where you trade referrals and business contacts, or support groups where you can share horror and success stories and get moral support. In talking with people who are working successfully on their own from home, we have found that invariably they have joined or created some type of networking group for themselves.

Today there is a number of formal networking groups with chapters throughout the United States. These groups are primarily "leads" clubs, in that their primary goal is to do business with one another and provide mutual referrals and business leads. Normally these groups meet once a week, early in the morning so as not to interfere with the workday. They are composed of only one member from any one type of business (one desktop publisher, one chiropractor, one bookkeeper, etc.), so there is no internal competition. Another type of networking organization you can find in many communities is women's referral services, which are networks of women business owners who meet regularly to support and refer business to one another.

In the Resources list at the end of this chapter, there is information about several formal networking organizations. If none of these organizations has a chapter in your community, you may be able to set one up. For example, management consultant Ivan Misner founded what has now become Business Network International so he could relate to other businesspeople who could refer business to one another without the system of levying fines that other networking groups he belonged to used. Beginning with that first chapter, he now has over one hundred chapters nationwide. If there isn't a chapter in your location, Ivan will help you begin one; it can become a sideline business for you.

Alternatively many people form a more informal support group of their own. Author and publisher Peggy Glenn tells the interesting tale of how she created a network for herself when she began her first home business, a typing service:

"Although I wanted to work by myself, when I began typing at home, I did run up against feeling isolated. There was nobody to turn to when I was having a really bad day, nobody to say, 'Come on, let's go have some coffee.' I was two weeks into my business and one of my customers sent me roses! Who was I going to tell? My husband was at work. My kids were at school. None of my neighbors were home. There was nobody to talk to.

"So I got brave and called a few other people who also ran typing businesses at home and invited them to lunch, dutch treat. Six or seven of them came, and right then and there was the birth of what has become a great network.

"We support one another. We help with overload. There is somebody to call on a bad day, somebody to call on a good day, somebody you can learn from if you've just received a job that is something you've never done, somebody to refer others to if you don't want to take the job."

When we moved to the Los Angeles area and first set up our home business, we felt isolated in such a large metropolis. But we felt certain there were lots of interesting people nearby, whom for some reason we weren't getting to know. So we decided to start a Friday night Community Network. Every second Friday night of the month we hosted an open-house potluck dinner. We invited everyone we met whom we thought we'd like to know better—our neighbors, our suppliers, and so forth. We asked them to come, bring a dish and a drink—and their friends.

It worked! Each month about twenty people came to eat and talk. Midway through the evening, we had people introduce themselves, explain what they did, and the type of contacts they wanted to make.

Through this network, we made both business contacts and new friendships with people who work at home. We've met a potter, a cartoonist, a word processor, a manufacturer of silk hats, a typesetter, and many more. The people who came also made valuable contacts and friendships. Realizing how much they miss the stimulation of working in a clinic, for example, several health practitioners who work alone at home met at one of our meetings and formed HealthNet, a network for health professionals in private practice.

In a similar vein, Sarah has long had what she calls a "peer mentor" group, a very small group of personal friends who are also self-employed with whom she meets every other week for mutual moral support. They give to one another the kind of interaction an employed person might get from a combination of the camaraderie of sharing meals with fellow workers and the help and counsel of valued mentors. Mobile notary Mary Malloy has formed such a group for herself. She calls her group of peers a "spirit team." Home-business consultant Katrina Newby organized a "brainstorm" group.

9. Affiliate or form other joint business relationships. Drawing on the contacts you make, set up joint projects with people in your field. Think of ways you can collaborate with them. Do a program together. Write an article. Share the workload.

Two human resource development consultants we know, for example, have an interest in future trends in their field, so they've developed a program they offer several times a year at professional conferences. They've also written joint articles for professional journals on future trends.

We've known several artists who regularly share a booth at art fairs. Two other home-based entrepreneurs, Michelle Whitman of High Tech Humor and Debbie Grosshandler of Bit's and P.C.'s, were able to launch their businesses by jointly renting a booth at an important trade show. These joint ventures not only keep costs down but also provide some much needed moral support and involvement with others for those who are working alone.

Formal partnerships can provide similar benefits. Many husbands and wives, such as ourselves, find that working at home together prevents them from having problems with isolation. Sue Rugge, founder of Information on Demand, credits an early partnership with Georgia Finnigan for the initial success of her business. "Although I enjoyed being president and hundred-percent owner of my company, I doubt if I ever would have made it if I hadn't started as a partnership."

Programmer Lucy Ewell and psychologist Elizabeth Scott came together to do what they couldn't have done alone, and started a software firm to develop computer games for girls. Barbara Elman began her word-processing service with a partner. She says of her initial partner, "He gave me the idea and the confidence that I could do it."

In many ways, a business partnership is like a marriage. You may spend more time with a partner than you do with your spouse. Unfortunately, the divorce rate among partners is even higher than among married couples. So pick a business partner with the same care you would take to pick a mate.

Short of a full-fledged partnership is the buddy system, or what Carol Hyatt calls a "planned partnership," in which you and your informal partner agree to meet at least once a week to help each other achieve your goals. In her book *The Woman's Selling Game*, Hyatt describes how the buddy system can work:

> The partner you select can be a friend or not, and preferably should come from the same area of expertise as yours so you can understand each other's problems and provide useful mutual assistance. He or she should be someone whose judgment you respect and who respects yours, so there will be productive interplay. The two of you should contract to meet formally and at regular intervals.
>
> Your first meeting may be to define your goals and discuss their reality, with subsequent meetings devoted to reviewing your progress toward these goals. When you miss the fact that you've strayed from your purpose, been vague about strategy or laissez faire about precious time, it's your partner's job to spot what's happening and give you the feedback and constructive advice by which you can work through what you want. You, of course, will do the same in return.

Although planning and participating in such activities does cost valuable time and money, they are worthwhile investments in yourself and your work. Besides preventing the problems of burnout and isolation, they also keep you fresh and competitive within today's ever-changing marketplace.

Networking to Make New Contacts

Establishing relationships, meeting people in a crowd, approaching business contacts you've never met before—these are all important skills for people working on their own.

Networking to make contact quickly and easily with people you don't know involves more than the customary "Hello-how-are-you?" handshake and exchange of business cards. Whether you're meeting people at a cocktail party or through a computer terminal, networking involves making contact with them in ways that enable you to assist one another in achieving your goals.

Here are several tips for becoming a master networker.

First, step into the role of host. Adele Scheele, author of *Skills for Success*, suggests that successful networkers approach life as a "host" instead of as a "guest." Guests wait to be introduced. They feel ill at ease until someone makes them feel welcome. Hosts, on the other hand, assume responsibility for making sure everyone knows who everyone else is and for helping people feel welcome and at ease.

Second, tell everyone you meet who you are, what you're doing, and what you want to do. As consultant William Slavin has discovered, "I never know who my next client might be, so I treat everyone as a prospective client." Likewise, you never know who might be a future resource, friend, or colleague.

Third, make yourself and what you are seeking clear. Too frequently people introduce themselves like this:

"Hello, I'm Ralph Carnes. I'm the senior technical writer for MicroProductions."

After hearing this kind of introduction, do you know enough about what Ralph does to engage in a conversation? Do you have any idea how you might be able to work with him? It's easy to spend a whole evening introducing yourself this way and wondering why you aren't making any valuable contacts.

But what if Ralph introduced himself this way:

"Hello, I'm Ralph Carnes. I work for MicroProductions, writing instructions for how to use the business software they produce for personal computers. Instead of driving to the company every day, I've just started working from my home. I enjoy it but I'm hoping to meet other people around this area who are interested in computers."

This type of introduction helps people know whether you share common interests and whether you can be of help to one another. Introducing yourself this way is a matter of putting together two needs: what people should know to understand what you do, and what contacts you want to make.

Fourth, be interested in other people. The more you listen to what others are saying and ask questions about their lives and their work, the better you will know how you could be valuable contacts for one another.

Fifth, offer to give people the very thing you want. If you're looking for someone to help with your office overload on occasion, offer to provide backup for them. If you're seeking someone to share a booth with you, offer to share one with those you meet.

Finally, plan a follow-up meeting with people you become acquainted with. When you discover others who share a mutual interest, exchange business cards. Write notes on the back of their cards about where you met them and what your joint interests are. Don't wait for them to call you. Make follow-up calls yourself and propose getting together in person to find out more about what they do.

In summary, staying in touch with others is as important to people working from home as it is for the regular office worker. At the office, it takes relatively little time and energy. For those of us who work at home, it's something we have to plan for and work at throughout our careers. Yes, it does take concentrated effort to stay in contact, but there are ways to do it. You just have to use them.

Resources

Books

Great Connections, Small Talk and Networking for Businesspeople. Anne Baber and Lynne Waymon. Manassas Park, Va.: Impact Publications, 1992.

A Guide to Peer Mentoring: Forming a Home Business Support Group. Here's How, P.O. Box 5091, Santa Monica, CA 90409 ($9.95).

Is Your Net-Working? How to Receive Everything You Want by Giving to Everyone You Know. Ann Boe. New York: John Wiley & Sons, 1989.

Available through Career Network, 435 S. Sierra, Ste. 116, Solana Beach, CA 92075.

Power Schmoozing, The New Rules for Business and Social Success. Terri Mandrell. Los Angeles: First House Press, 1992.

Skills for Success. Adele M. Scheele. New York: Ballantine, 1967.

The World's Best Known Marketing Secret. Ivan R. Misner. Austin, TX: Bard Productions, 1994.

Networking Groups

Leads Club. P.O. Box 24, Carlsbad, CA 92008; (619) 434-3761. (800) 783-3761.

National Association of Women Business Owners. 1337 K St. N.W., Ste. 637, Washington, D.C. 20005; (301) 608-2590.

Business Network International. 1341 Ancona Dr., La Verne, CA 91750; (800) 825-8286.

Directories

Encyclopedia of Associations. Detroit: Gale Research Company (see full citation in chapter 3).

Sources of Audiotape Programs

Nightingale Conant Audiocassette Library. The Human Resources Company, 7300 N. Lehigh Ave., Chicago, IL 60648; (800) 323-5552. Call or write for a catalog.

Personal Progress Library. A membership club that enables members to rent and return a wide selection of business and personal development tapes. 19310 Vanowen St., Reseda, CA 91335; (818) 700-0818. (800) 748-6245.

Success Motivation Cassettes. P.O. Box 2510, Waco, TX 76702.

On-line Information

Working From Home Forum on CompuServe Information Service, 5000 Arlington Centre Blvd., P.O. Box 20212, Columbus, OH 43220.

CHAPTER
EIGHTEEN
■■■■■■■■■■■■■■■■■■■■■■■■■■■

Staying Out of the Refrigerator and
Away from Other Temptations

At first, working at home can seem like Paradise Island. Life's greatest pleasures are at your fingertips. You can literally eat, drink, and be merry at will. Your refrigerator and kitchen cabinets are only steps away. Cocktails are there for your making. The bed is there for your taking.

You have the freedom to eat your favorite foods whenever you're hungry, to have sex in the afternoon, to share a beer with a neighbor at a moment's notice, or to watch a favorite midday TV show.

Like tourists on a holiday, many people working from home start out living it up, indulging in whatever they want, but by the end of a few weeks, they're a little tired of it all. Then they set up routines, time schedules, and effective boundaries to keep their pleasures in bounds.

Sometimes, however, without the structure of a separate office, even experienced open-collar workers indulge to excess. According to them, the enjoyable fantasy of sipping wine and munching culinary delights while working by the pool can become the ugly reality of unwanted pounds and foggy-headed afternoons. In fact, one question we're sometimes asked is "How do you stay out of the refrigerator?" Some people do find this a problem, and when they do, we hear complaints like these:

"I've gained thirty pounds in the six months I've been working at home."

"When I have to work late into the night to get a big order out, I can eat two bags of potato chips without even knowing it."

"I'm having my 'afternoon' drink earlier and earlier in the day."

"A beer with lunch can become a six-pack by dinner."

"Our last baby wasn't planned. She came along about nine months after I began working at home."

In this chapter we will talk about what happens when excesses get out of control and what you can do to prevent such a situation. We will not talk, however, about chronic eating disorders or drug or alcohol addiction. Conceivably someone could engage in and conceal a serious addiction more easily at home, but any such problems are beyond the scope of this chapter and must be solved by seeking professional help.

Avoiding Excesses

Whether it's smoking, eating, drinking, sex, or watching TV, overindulgence is generally related to the stress of having too much or too little happening in one's life. People overindulge most often when they are pressured, overworked, anxious, bored, don't like what they are doing, or are in dire need of contact with other people.

There's medical evidence, for example, that eating causes the brain to release substances called endorphins, some of which act as relaxers on the mind and body. Also, psychologists have found that repetitive, nonpurposeful activity like chain-smoking, finger tapping, drinking, and chewing fingernails, gum, food, or rubber bands helps discharge pent-up frustration and discomfort. So chances are that frequent trips to the refrigerator, munching away on snack food, or reaching for a drink starts out as a way to make you feel better and help you get through the day.

Once someone begins to rely on a particular indulgence to deal with stress, what follows makes it difficult to stop. First, the eating, drinking, smoking, or whatever you're doing to excess becomes a habit. You end up doing it automatically, reaching for a cigarette or candy bar without even thinking about it, raiding the refrigerator without having made a conscious decision to stroll into the kitchen.

To further complicate the situation, many of these activities, like smoking, drinking alcohol, taking drugs, and eating salty or sugary food, produce a chemical reaction in your body that causes you to crave more. So as you indulge

---

The Top Ten Bad Habits

 1. Snacking
 2. Sleeping late
 3. Procrastinating
 4. Talking on the phone
 5. Watching TV
 6. Getting sloppy; staying in nightclothes all day
 7. Taking too long to read the newspaper
 8. Drinking while working
 9. Spending too much time visiting neighbors
10. Working too much

---

to excess, your body begins to demand greater amounts of what you're indulging in. Then instead of feeling better, you start to feel as if you "can't go on without it."

These factors combine to make breaking out of habitual excesses a challenging task. For this reason, the easiest way to avoid problems with excesses is to prevent them from happening in the first place or to catch the problem as early as possible.

Awareness Is the First Step

Take notice right away when you start to exceed a normal or familiar pattern. Most people do notice the difference. "I'm snacking more." "I'm having my after-work drink earlier in the day." "I've eaten a whole bag of potato chips! I don't usually do that."

Act Immediately

Before divergences from your regular pattern develop into a new habit, take steps to deal with the situation. Recognize what you have too much or too little of in your life that is causing stress, and find a different way to handle it. Here is how people working at home have managed to avoid the stressful situations that lead to excesses.

Six Ways to Avoid Overindulging While Working

1. Work at a relaxed and reasonable pace. The best protection against raiding the refrigerator or grabbing another drink is to take good care of yourself. Don't overwork. Take breaks. Learn to relax.

Barbara Bickford found that "the only way I could be sure I wouldn't turn to the junk-food snacks every night was to put an end to working all day and into the night. By taking on so much business that I had to work late, I was really abusing myself. Occasionally, yes, it's okay. But I was doing it as a matter of course. Eating was my way of buying myself off so I wouldn't complain about letting my work consume me."

Don't let your home office become as stressful a place to be as the worst of traditional offices. Take advantage of the fact that you have more flexibility about when and how you work. Use the time you would have spent commuting to relax in one way or another and structure your day to keep the pressures from building up. It can be good for your health. When nationally known speaker and seminar leader Lee Shapiro, known as "The Hugging Judge," went "from the courtroom to the living room," he found his blood pressure went down.

2. Develop what psychologist William Glasser calls "positive" addictions. Glasser uses this term to refer to activities like jogging, swimming, and knitting, which people enjoy and find helpful in handling everyday stress. Glasser found that people who regularly engage in such an activity actually feel as though they are "addicted" to it. They miss the activity when something interferes with doing it at their regular times. They crave it and feel depressed and out of sorts when they're deprived of it. Unlike an addiction such as smoking, drinking, overeating, or taking drugs, however, these activities actually improve your health.

Engineering consultant Jeff Knoghton found himself drinking more when he first started working at home. "I was used to having a drink to unwind when I got home from work. Once I was at home all day, whenever I felt pressure building up, I'd grab a can of beer. Then I started jogging for twenty minutes every morning. I heard it helped you become less tense." If it's a really bad day, he runs again in the early evening. "It just relaxes me, keeps me loose. It's better than beer, because it clears my mind rather than fuzzing it up."

3. Be sure you have enough contact with people you enjoy. An office with other people provides stimulation, company, and someone to share problems with. Working at home can be lonely at first. But the loneliness doesn't have to lead to overindulgence. Instead of heading for the kitchen, reaching for another drink, or turning on the tube, you can head for the telephone. Call someone. Go visit a neighbor. Invite someone to come over. However busy you are, make time in your workday for some kind of interpersonal contact.

4. Treat yourself with something special each day. Plan something you can look forward to as a refresher after work, or once or twice during the day. In this chapter you'll find a list of treats we and others have developed. Build your own list.

5. If you want to snack, set some guidelines. Deepak Chopra, physician and author of the book *Ageless Body, Timeless Mind,* suggests several such guidelines. He advises eating only if you're actually hungry. Sometimes the urge for a snack is actually a desire for something else, such as taking a break or doing something different. If you are actually hungry, he proposes that you stop whatever else you are doing, sit down away from work with your food, take a moment of silence before you eat, and then eat with the intention of enjoyment.

Psychologist Dr. Nancy Bonus, founder of the Bonus Plan, has developed a nondiet weight-loss program that distinguishes between physical hunger and habit or emotional hunger and suggests eating only when your body actually needs fuel. She also advises eating exactly what you want to eat and enjoying it fully by taking very small bites, chewing them thoroughly, savoring the flavor, and pausing between bites. Then she recommends that as soon as you feel slightly full, you *stop eating* immediately and return to work feeling completely satisfied.

6. Keep whatever you want to avoid as far away from your office as possible. Data entry clerk Helen Willis told us, "I don't keep salty or sugary snacks in the house anymore because they just make me want to eat more. So I have lots of nuts and bananas and dried fruit around now. They're much more satisfying."

This is one of the pluses of working from home. Unlike office vending machines, your kitchen cabinets can be filled with whatever you choose. Here

Treats Instead of Sweets:
Positive Ways to Reward Yourself

- Go outside. Walk through your neighborhood or visit your favorite outdoor spot. Notice the grass, trees, wind, sun, clouds, the sounds of birds, barking dogs, and children playing, the faces of strangers and friends.
- Buy yourself some flowers or pick a bouquet from your own garden.
- Take a stimulating shower or a relaxing bath, go to the spa or sauna, soak in a candlelight milk bath with music playing in the background.
- Do something handy around the house. Fix what's broken, build something new, work in the garden.
- Buy yourself a present, something you might not otherwise purchase for yourself but wish someone else would.
- Have a party.
- Enjoy your favorite sport. Take time out for a game of tennis, badminton, golf, or handball, or join a softball or bowling team.
- Curl up in your favorite spot and read an enthralling book or a magazine of your choice.
- Keep a journal in which you write down your thoughts, your feelings, and your goals; make a list of your accomplishments, describe what you've discovered about yourself and your work.
- Serve your favorite meal on your best dishes and invite someone special to join you.
- Take a class you've always wanted to take: photography, modern art, yoga, programming.
- Sit in the sun, take a nap.
- Make a change in your day-to-day life. Rearrange the furniture, get a new hairstyle, go on a vacation.
- Do something childishly carefree. Romp with the dog, turn a cartwheel, buy a balloon, play a video game.
- Dial up a bulletin board on your computer and talk to the world through your fingertips.
- Go to a funny or suspenseful movie, take in a concert, a play, a ball game, a museum, the zoo.

---

are a few more "out of sight, out of mind" tricks people who work at home use to keep themselves from overindulging:

"To avoid walking in and out of the kitchen all day for a cup of coffee, where I invariably grab a cookie to eat along with it, I've set up a coffeemaker in my office. I keep all the supplies—the cups, even the bottled water—on a small cabinet in the office closet."

"I close the kitchen door and think of it as a restaurant. It's only open between noon and one and after five o'clock."

"I don't allow smoking in my house. That way I have to take a break and go outside to smoke. This keeps my habit under control."

"We set up a little icebox and hot plate in the office, which is behind the garage. We 'bring' our lunch to work every day and usually don't go into the house while we're working."

"I work at the computer most of the day. I put the computer on a stand that doesn't have enough space to set down coffee cups, glasses, or food. To eat or drink anything, I have to get up and go somewhere else."

Guidelines for Snacking

1. Don't snack mindlessly. Snack consciously and only when hungry.
2. Take a break from whatever else you are doing. Go somewhere other than your office.
3. Select exactly the food you want to eat when you snack.
4. Sit down with your food and spend a moment silently relaxing before eating.
5. Eat with the intention of enjoyment.
6. Take small bites. Chew your food thoroughly. Savor the flavor. Pause between bites.
7. Stop eating when you feel slightly full and satisfied.

Breaking Old Habits and Creating New Ones

But what do you do if you've already developed a bad habit? And what if it's a habit you've had a long time? Again, awareness is the first step, and then comes corrective action. You must find another way to deal with the circumstances that led you to develop the habit in the first place, different ways of handling the stresses of your work. Then you have to replace your old habit with a new one. Here are five suggestions for breaking undesirable habits:

1. **Anticipate when you are likely to indulge in your habit.** Know the actions leading up to an occurrence. Do you snack or smoke at particular times of the day or in conjunction with particular activities?

2. **Create a new and competing habit to take the place of the old one.** For example, if you have a habit of going to the kitchen for a snack between projects or clients, establish a new habit by making phone calls or taking a walk instead.

3. **Interrupt the sequence of the habit or disrupt its pattern.** If you are used to smoking while you sit at your desk talking on the phone, for example, stand up while you talk on the phone. Clear away all the ashtrays. Keep your cigarettes away in another room, so you'll have to go through several involved steps to get to them.

4. **Set up cues or "anchors" that help you remember to change your**

habit. Put a No Eating Between Meals sign on your refrigerator. Set the alarm for scheduled snack breaks.

5. **Think about how terrific you'll feel when you no longer have this habit.** Begin imagining yourself as a person without such a habit. Think of yourself as a nonsmoker, for example, or as someone who doesn't snack.

Ending Addictions and Compulsions

If you have a particularly stubborn habit of overindulging, you may be suffering from an addiction or a compulsion—you feel enslaved. Recent findings from the emerging field of psychoneuralimmunology suggest that addictions (whether physical or mental, acquired or inherited) are the result of a fundamental distortion in the biological system. This research indicates that these distortions can be corrected by using your mind and your environment to return yourself to a natural state of health.

You'll find a variety of books and programs available to help you apply the methods from this new field cited in the Resources list at the end of this chapter.

Resources

Books

Ageless Body, Timeless Mind. Deepak Chopra. New York: Harmony Books, 1993.

8 Steps to a Healthy Heart. Robert Kowalski. New York: Warner, 1992.

Learned Optimism . . . and How to Acquire It. Martin Seligman. New York: Knopf, 1991.

Making It on Your Own: How to Survive and Thrive on the Ups and Downs of Being Your Own Boss. (This includes the Emotional Road Map.) Paul and Sarah Edwards. New York: Tarcher/Perigee, 1991.

The New Fit or Fat. Covert Bailey. New York: Houghton Mifflin, 1991.

Perfect Health: The Complete Mind/Body Guide. Deepak Chopra. New York: Harmony Books, 1990.

Positive Addiction. William Glasser. New York: Harper & Row, 1976.

The Power of Optimism. Alan Loy McGinnis. New York: Harper & Row, 1990.

The Relaxation Response. Herbert Benson. New York: Avon, 1975.

The Six Pillars of Self-Esteem. Nathaniel Branden. New York: Bantam, 1994.

Take Control of Your Life. Sharon Faelton, David Diamond, and the Editors of *Prevention* magazine. Emmaus, Pa.: Rodale Press, 1990.

Self-Study Programs

The Bonus Plan: Non-Diet Weight Loss Home Study Course. A video, audio and workbook program from Dr. Nancy Bonus. The Bonus Plan, P.O. Box 505, Chatham, NJ 07928; (800) 760-5490.

Sante (for Your Health). An all-in-one weight-control, diet-planning and exercise software program including recipes. Hopkins Technology, 421 Hazel Lane, Hopkins, MN 55343; (612) 931-9376. (800) 397-9211.

Self-Help Organizations

Alcoholics Anonymous. 475 Riverside Drive, New York, NY 10115; (212) 870-3400.

Gamblers Anonymous. 3255 Wilshire Blvd, Ste. 610, Los Angeles, CA 90010; (213) 386-8789.

Narcotics Anonymous. 16155 Wyandotte, Van Nuys, CA 91406; (818) 780-3951.

Overeaters Anonymous. P.O. Box 92870, Los Angeles, CA 90501; (310) 618-8835.

SmokEnders. 4455 E. Camelback Rd., Ste. D-155, Phoenix, AZ 85018; (800) 828-4357.

Tapes

The Art of Meditation: Creating Inner Peace. Jonathan Faust. Kripalu; (800) 967-7279.

Morning and Evening Meditations. Louise Hay, Hay House, (800) 654-5126.

Classes

Transcendental meditation. Classes available in many states. Call (515) 472-0108 for classes near you.

CHAPTER
NINETEEN
■■■■■■■■■■■■■■■■■■■■■■■■■■■■

Staying in Love and
Saving Your Relationship

"How do I know that if I start working at home I won't end up getting divorced?"

"I'd like to work at home, but how do you two stand being around each other so much?"

"What happened to your relationship when you started working at home? Was there an adjustment period? Did you fight all the time?"

Hundreds of people have asked us questions like these after a speech or at breaks during a seminar. We answer that when you're married, working from home is like opening a birthday present. It may be just what you wanted or it may not suit you.

Our files are filled with stories of couples who, like us, discovered that the best part of working from home is the extra time they have to be together. It's hard to build a relationship on weekends and in the few hours that remain when people get home from an exhausting day at the office. At the very least, working from home gives couples a better chance of building a good life together. Occasionally, however, it doesn't work. Instead of things getting better, they go downhill.

For better or worse, you can count on undergoing some changes in your life and your relationship when you begin working from home. And, as with any degree of change, there will usually be a period of adjustment. The question is how the adjustments will affect your relationship. We agree with Peggy Glenn, who had a new husband and three kids when she quit her job to start a home typing service:

"If a person decides to work at home to salvage a dead marriage or revive a dying one, I think it will kill the marriage altogether. But if the relationship is strong and there is trust between the husband and wife, then they'll get through the change, and working from home will strengthen the relationship."

In this chapter we want to share the principles we and other couples have found for staying in love when you work from home. Although there are many differences in how couples go about it, there do seem to be several key ingredients.

First it's important to get off to the right start. Then it helps to be prepared for the inevitable adjustments you will encounter, to realize they are normal, and to know some positive steps you can take to resolve the conflicts that arise. Finally, it's important to recognize the early warning signs of trouble and know what you can do when things aren't getting better.

Getting Off to the Right Start

Couples begin working from home for many different reasons. Sometimes it's by choice, sometimes it isn't. Sometimes it's an opportunity, sometimes it's a necessity. Whatever the situation, you'll get off to a better start if you both agree that the best course of action is to work at home.

It's virtually impossible to work happily at home without the cooperation and support of your spouse, so a joint decision will most certainly work better than issuing an edict or even simply making an announcement that you've decided to work at home. Even if you already have an office at home, it's not too late to sit down and talk about whether it's working out.

Be honest about how you feel about using your home as an office and encourage your spouse to be honest too. Discuss your concerns openly. If you're worried that your spouse will never leave the office, say so. If you're concerned that the children will be neglected, say so. The potential problems you identify can help you develop a practical plan to guard against them.

Specific Steps You Can Take

Make the decision to work at home a joint one.
Express your reasons for wanting to work at home.
Discuss your concerns openly and encourage your spouse to do so as well.
Thank your spouse for each concern he or she brings up.
Respond honestly to each other's concerns.
Take each concern seriously and get the facts about it.
Think of possible solutions and develop a plan for how to avoid potential problems.
Test out your solutions. See if they work. Revise them when they don't work to your or your mate's satisfaction.

One woman told us she felt silly bringing up her real concern. She was afraid that if her husband worked at home, the house would always be a mess and she would become a servant cleaning up after him. Fortunately, she did talk it over with him and they decided to hire a cleaning service.

It's ignoring "silly" concerns like these that get us into the worst problems. This very problem did precipitate one of the few marital casualties we know of. The wife who worked in an outside office couldn't stand coming home every day to a messy house. She'd tidy it up in the morning, and when she got home, exhausted from a day's work, she'd find another mess awaiting her. Failing to resolve this incompatibility ultimately contributed to their divorce.

So when your spouse brings up an objection, thank him or her on the spot for sharing it with you. That's just one more problem you can avoid. Once the objection has come up, you can start talking about the facts of the situation and work out various plans for ensuring it won't be a difficulty.

Avoid the temptation to discount the concern by saying "Oh, that won't be a problem. You don't have to worry about that." Even if it seems as though there would be no problem with a particular concern, explain your reasoning, describe in detail why it won't be a difficulty, even create hypothetical situations to show that indeed there is no need for concern. You may discover something you overlooked.

A radio announcer we talked with, for example, didn't think he'd mind having his mother use his office as a guest room when she came to stay on weekends. His wife wasn't sure. "Since she didn't think it would work, I decided to test it out. Although I wasn't yet working full-time at home, one weekend when my mother came up I had just put my equipment and a number of important files in my home office—that is, the guest room. My wife was right. We had to figure out some other solution before it would work for me to move everything home. Even though it required some construction, we decided to set up a basement studio for my office."

Facing Inevitable Changes

The inevitable changes that take place when you start working from home can strain your relationship. The situation doesn't have to become painful, however. The initial stress can be a sign of new and better things to come. But you must be alert and responsive to difficulties that arise while they are still manageable.

Here are some of the healthy reactions a couple can expect. They don't always feel good, but they are a normal part of the process of changing your lifestyle.

Conflicts with New Identities

The decision to work at home is almost always part of a larger decision to change your life, which changes your identity. People who begin working at home are at turning points in their lives.

Assuming a new identity is a major adjustment in itself. Add working from home and the many accompanying changes in daily routine and you can see why people going through so many adjustments may not be easy to live with. You can understand why they may be unsure of themselves, edgy, worried, or struggling to put up a good front.

Even when spouses want to be supportive, and actually think they are helping, they may not welcome all aspects of their mate's new identity. One woman, whose husband quit his job to become a professional entertainer, described the experience this way: "I didn't marry an entertainer. I married a lawyer. I don't know him anymore. He's a different person."

She wasn't so sure she liked this new person. She also wasn't totally sure who she was now, either. Among other roles in life, she had been a lawyer's wife. Now she was supposed to be an entertainer's wife. "He expects me to come to late-night shows and sit with a lot of other entertainers and their wives while he performs. I'm not sure this is something I want to do."

When she started her typing service, Peggy Glenn's identity changed from being someone's secretary in a nine-to-five job to being an entrepreneur and businesswoman. "It was very, very difficult for my husband. Not only was he unsure about the money I would make in this new business—and we needed the money from my work—he was also unsure about this new change in me. All of a sudden I was someone who was in demand by other people. My customers knew him as 'Peggy's husband.' That was kind of hard on his ego."

Disputes over Duties and Responsibilities

Working from home usually means changes in household routines. Many arguments and conflicts can arise over day-to-day arrangements about:

Cleaning. Living and working at home twenty-four hours a day means more mess and more wear and tear. Who does the extra work to keep the house in order? When does it have to be cleaned up or repaired? Do children now have to be neater because customers are coming to the house? If so, who gets the children to clean up? If the packaging department of your business is on the dining room table, how long can it stay like that, and who puts everything away—the person who made the mess or the person who wants it cleaned up?

Meals. Working at home usually means at least one extra meal there. So you need to discuss who plans it, who buys it, who fixes it, who cleans it up. If you have been fixing the meals, for example, will you still have time to fix them all, or to fix the same kinds of meals, now that you're working at home?

Space. Working at home can place certain limitations on what your family can do there or even on other things you want to do. If your family room is now your office, where does everyone go to relax? Can they have company while you are working? Can your spouse walk around the house in a bathing suit during business hours? You'll need to consider issues like whether your family can play the stereo or talk on the phone whenever they want, or if such activity infringes on your office space.

Children. Children need a lot of attention. They can be a distraction and an interruption that makes work next to impossible. A decision has to be made about who handles this. Does the one working at home take on more of these responsibilities than before? Who keeps the children quiet or out of your office?

Time. Once your office is at home, you need to determine who gets to spend time with you and when. If you're away at the office all day, you clearly can't take the kids to the park after school. And of course you can't make love before lunch. But what about now? What will you say when someone you love asks, "Couldn't you just take a minute for . . .?"

Money. Working from home is likely to mean a change in your income. If you've quit your job to start a business, the amount of money you're bringing in could go down at first. What gets cut—theater tickets, your tennis lessons, your spouse's night class? If you've taken a second job or started a new career at home, it could mean your income will go up. In that case, who decides what the additional money is used for?

Adjusting to New Roles

When people decide to work from home, the nature of their role in the marriage often changes. Sometimes they like and welcome the new role; sometimes the new role is thrust upon them without their consent. Let's consider some of the adjustments individuals and couples can encounter.

A man moving his work home. In our society, while a woman's place is no longer necessarily at home, a man's place is still at the office. As columnist Jim Sanderson wrote, the "Image of the Stay-at-Home Kind of Man" can create some humorous but uncomfortable situations. He found that his wife's friends, the neighbors, and repair personnel who came over either thought he was ill, implied he was lazy, or believed he'd married a "rich dame."

In addition to contending with the perceptions of others, a man moving his office home often finds himself confronted with household or child-rearing responsibilities he's not used to handling. Also, he may have difficulty adjusting to working without the support services he's been accustomed to getting at the office. He may feel angry or depressed about having to do everything himself, from buying paper clips to making copies. On the other hand, he might feel grateful for the independence and new responsibilities.

A woman starting or returning to work. When a woman who has been a homemaker decides to start working from home, she will have less time for household chores. Housework, meals, laundry, and possibly even children will not get her full attention. A husband who may be supportive of his wife's new work style may still not like the inconvenience of doing things for himself that she once did for him. He may have to start packing for his business trips, preparing his own lunches, or shopping for his own shirts. He may even have to forgo some of the conveniences he's become accustomed to, like freshly ironed and folded shirts.

The homemaker turned open-collar worker may also have difficulty getting family, friends, or neighbors to take her new role seriously. After all, she's still at home. Everyone may expect her somehow to do everything she has always done. In fact, polls still show homemakers who decide to launch a career do not get much additional help with household chores. They simply add to their existing responsibilities as wives and mothers.

If the woman who begins working at home tries to keep up with everything, she can get caught in the "Superwoman syndrome," trying to be all things to all people, which is a good way to become irritable, overstressed, burned out, or even sick.

PERSONAL PROFILE: Michael Fey, Financial Consultant

When Michael Fey decided to leave his hectic downtown job and work from his suburban home, his wife decided for the first time in their marriage to work outside the home.

"With my being at home and her starting to work away from home, we had a real shift in role responsibilities. Since I was there, I found myself handling certain domestic tasks." Now, before he sits down at his desk in the morning, he finds himself doing things he never had to do before: getting the house organized, getting the kids off to school, and monitoring their squabbles.

"It's been a real education. I would say it's been an advantage. The kids have gotten to know me better. My wife is glad that part of the responsibility for child-rearing has shifted to me. It's less of a burden on her and frees her to do what she wants. She's also glad because the kids do need to get to know me now. In a couple of years they'll be grown and gone."

Although Michael hadn't expected the changes that took place after he started working at home, he says, and his wife agrees, "We're happier as a couple."

The homemaker. The wife who is a homemaker may feel her husband's presence is an intrusion into her domain: "I married him for better or worse, but not for lunch!" She may feel pressure to become not only a wife and mother but also a receptionist and secretary. On the other hand, she may be eager to have her husband home, thinking he can take on more responsibilities around the house and that they can spend more time together. But will he have the time to take on these new roles? If he's like most at-home workers, he will actually work more, not fewer, hours.

Two-career couples. Wherever they work, at home or away, two-career couples face unique challenges and strains on their relationship.

When one spouse works at home and the other works away, it's easy to fall into "the grass is always greener" syndrome. The spouse who works away from home may be jealous of the one who's been home all day. Those at home may seem to have more free time and less pressure. After all, they haven't had to contend with traffic or wait for the train in the rain. Those working in an outside office may even feel disappointed to find the house a mess when they get home. They're likely to wonder why, with all that time at home, their partner wasn't able to get more done.

From the other point of view, the ones who work at home may feel burdened by household interruptions and responsibilities and jealous of their partner's freedom to get out in the business world and socialize with others during the day. Those who've been working at home all day long may be itching to get out in the evening, while their partner is looking forward to getting home to rest and relax.

When both partners work at home, they may have difficulties drawing lines between their roles as workers and their roles as spouses. It's hard to tell your spouse, "No, I can't talk now, I'm in the middle of a project." It's equally hard to resist the temptation to start sharing the events of your business day when you're excited, devastated, or just eager to talk.

PERSONAL PROFILE: Tom Drucker, Management Consultant and Marcia Seligson, Author

Even when he was an executive for Xerox, Tom was attracted to the idea of working from home. Now that he is self-employed, he feels working at home is a way for him to spend more time with his wife. Instead of trying to play catch-up each night about the events of the day, he enjoys "sharing the day with her while it's happening."

As a writer who had worked at home alone, Marcia likes having Tom home while she's working. "I enjoy his company and it breaks the solitude of writing." At first, however, they were so thrilled to have each other there that they would eagerly interrupt work to talk about what was happening.

"On the job it was easy to create a boundary around myself," Tom recalls. "I had people screen my calls. If I was interrupted I could say, in a straightforward manner, 'Don't interrupt me now.' But when my wife comes in and says she'd like me to read this letter, I'm less likely to say those things. I'm just like everyone else, I'd rather go do something I enjoy than struggle with some difficult task I'm working on."

Aware of the problem, Tom and Marcia have learned how to respect each other's work space. They've begun telling each other when they don't want to be interrupted, and Marcia finds "we're getting better at it now. We save our news for lunch breaks together."

Couples working at home are also susceptible to each other's moods. Usually your spouse is the only one there to talk with about the feelings and events of the day. When one of you is down, it may pull the other down too. When one of you is hassled, the other may pick up the frazzled feelings. When you are angry about something that's happening with work, you may take it out on your partner and disrupt his or her work as well. Or, in order to keep peace in the house, partners may try to hide negative feelings from each other and find there is no place to let off steam.

Partners who both work at home generally feel like getting away from each other once in a while, just as translator Bill Grimes and his partner, Isabel Leonard, do. "We tend to go our separate directions on weekends and evenings. If we didn't, we'd get pretty sick of each other." Bill and Isabel's reaction is a perfectly natural feeling for any two partners to have, but sometimes mates feel guilty about it, or hurt if their partner is the one who wants to get away.

Resolving Conflicts

While these adjustments are normal reactions to the changes that come with working from home, they can produce conflicts that need to be resolved so both your business and your relationship can be successful. Here are a few rules of thumb we and other couples have found useful in resolving conflicts before they become ongoing problems.

Remind yourself the conflict is temporary. It helps to remember that this is a transition period. Your life won't be like this forever. So make an effort to be understanding and patient with both yourself and your spouse while you work out the initial conflicts. It's only for a while.

Approach problems as opportunities. Since adjustments and conflicts are an inevitable and normal part of striving to create a new life for yourselves, each of them is truly an opportunity to take another step toward that new life. So regard problems as obstacles to be removed on the way to reaching your goal.

Remember, you love each other. When your relationship is an important, indispensable element of your life, it's worth practicing restraint to protect it from the corrosive effects of thoughtless arguments. Although you may feel upset at the moment, remind yourself that this is the person you love. This is someone you respect. This person is probably the most important individual in your life.

The many small things married people get upset about are truly insignificant in the shadow of the love they can have between them. Don't overlook what's bothering you or simply put up with it in the name of love, but reach out to your spouse. Try to understand his or her position. Maybe if you can help your partner through the adjustment, he or she will be able to help you. As you discuss conflicts, keep the basic love you have between you in the forefront of your mind and concentrate on how important your relationship is.

Since it's often difficult to keep a positive perspective in the midst of a heated argument, here are a few things you can do to short-circuit flaring tempers. First, when you notice that communications are going from bad to worse, take a break. Go for a walk. Take a deep breath. Remind yourself that the opposite of love isn't hate; it's indifference. And anger is only part of the full range of feelings you have for your mate. Taking a moment to think of the loving feelings will make all the difference in the world in resolving the conflict.

Solve problems so everybody wins. Sometimes in the midst of a conflict, the people involved think someone has to win and someone has to lose. Or they think someone has to be right and someone has to be wrong. In sports events and lawsuits this may be true, but, fortunately, solving problems with your spouse isn't a contest or a trial. It's possible for everybody to win.

Actually, if you approach a conflict as a win/lose contest when you're working at home, nobody will win. The "winner" has to eat, sleep, live, and work with the "loser" every day. Once you've done that, you realize you haven't won much. So whenever you feel that someone must win and someone must lose, know you are on the wrong track. Usually you haven't defined the problem correctly. For example, if there is only one spare room in the house and both spouses want to use it exclusively, it may look like a win/lose situation. Actually the problem is not who gets to use the room. The problem is that there are two people who each need space to do something that's important to them. When you've solved that problem, everyone has won.

When you define a problem in this way, there are almost always options for solving the problem so everyone wins. It's amazing what two creative minds can come up with when seeking a solution that will benefit them both.

Make clear agreements. Making assumptions is the surest route to frustration, disappointment, and unnecessary conflict. When you work from home, the familiar assumptions people make about how things are done at an office no longer fully apply, nor do the assumptions people normally make about how things are done at home. Getting clear agreements about who is willing to do what is crucial, whether they concern how you want your partner to act when the business phone rings, or who will fix lunch.

Thirteen Ways to Keep Romance Alive When You Work at Home

1. Remember, love keeps you together. Don't dissolve it with acid remarks. Keep the bond strong with small kindnesses.
2. Enjoy each other's enjoyment.
3. Keep the positive regard you have for each other in the forefront of your interactions.
4. Compliment each other liberally every day for your individual accomplishments, contributions, and talents.
5. Solve problems when they are small. Don't let them build up.
6. Commit yourselves to solving problems so you both win, instead of defining problems so that one of you must win and the other must lose, or one of you must be right and the other wrong.
7. Work out clearly stated agreements. Don't assume. State what you need and ask for what you want from each other.
8. When you say "no," explain what you're willing to do instead, and when you're told "no," find out what the other person would be willing to do.
9. Close the door on work at the end of the day. Have nonbusiness time. In particular, separate the bedroom from business. Don't take business to bed and don't go to bed mad.
10. Don't hoard negative feelings. Express them when they develop so you don't have an overflow of bad feelings to unload on each other in an explosive argument.
11. Get out of the house together regularly to do things you enjoy. Take mini-vacations for an afternoon or weekend.
12. Follow the advice of Kahlil Gibran: "Let there be space in your 'togetherness.' " Have and pursue your own interests.
13. Take time out to celebrate and don't let a day go by without at least ten hugs.

It's easy to overlook telling your spouse what you expect and then proceed to get angry when he or she doesn't act accordingly. It's also easy to declare what you want and assume it will be done without further discussion. And when you're worried that your partner won't want to do something, it's awfully tempting to use coercion, manipulation, threats, shame, guilt, or pressure tactics to get your way.

Unfortunately, agreements made under such circumstances are either not kept or are kept halfheartedly or grudgingly. Sometimes they're actually sabotaged. Although it's easy to blame the other person for not being supportive, you will nonetheless have to take responsibility for instigating such behavior and will come to regret the day you extracted an agreement under duress.

Agreements that clearly define what each of you will and will not do can make working from home easier and more enjoyable. Here are a few tips for making clear agreements:

- Express precisely what you want and what you expect.
- Make it clear whether you will meet your spouse's expectations or whether you won't.
- Don't say "yes" when you mean "no."
- Accept "no" from each other as okay. A "no" is clearly better than a "yes" the person will not follow through on.

Communicate, communicate, communicate. Besides talking, listen openmindedly to your spouse's feelings and concerns.

As Peggy Glenn discovered in starting her typing service at home with a new husband and three children, "Communication is the key. If you communicate, you can overcome most of the problems."

You might use the time you once spent commuting to and from the office to listen to each other, not necessarily about problems, but about yourselves, your lives, and your dreams. Chances are that this kind of honest and open communication will strengthen your determination to succeed and keep your romance alive.

Laugh a lot. Laughter is the sugar that can sweeten the bitterest moments in periods of adjustment. It can save the day. Be willing to step back to look at yourselves, to see some of the humor in your behavior and your situation. If laughing amid the pressures of life doesn't come easily to you, make a habit of going to funny movies together, going out with lighthearted people, and watching TV comedies.

A Communication Handbook

Since you may well be seeing a lot more of those you live with and since good communication is so vital to assuring that you enjoy being around each other, here is a short course in good communication skills that can go a long way to prevent tensions from building and to reduce them when they do.

General Principles

1. Be nonjudgmental. A climate of trust is vital if people are to enjoy living and working together. So keep an open, accepting mind toward each other's ideas, opinions, and experiences. Never rain on each other's parade. While it may be appropriate and can be helpful to share information and your concerns, avoid put-downs and judgments.

2. Be empathic. Try to see each other's points of view. Put yourself in each other's shoes. Do your best to understand the other person's motivation and reasoning as you listen and learn about one another.

3. Make feelings okay. Often the most difficult aspects of being on your own are not the situations you encounter but the feelings you have about these situations. Those you live with can be more supportive of one another if it's permissible to express the whole range of feelings family members are having. Everything from anger and frustration to elation and fear should be acceptable. In fact, family members can be most valuable by helping each other identify and clarify their feelings. Once clarified, feelings can become the basis for constructive action.

Listening

Often the most valuable role we can provide for each other is simply that of listener. Having someone spend the time to truly listen can help us to clarify values, express feelings, and explore the appropriate available options and solutions. In fact, it's been estimated that the average adult gains 90 percent of his or her information from listening.

"Listening," according to the *Random House Dictionary*, "is to give attention, to attend closely, for the purpose of hearing." For purposes of being supportive of each other, we would expand that definition somewhat. Listening in a way that is supportive means giving attention and attending closely to what someone is saying for the purpose of "understanding."

Here are some guidelines for becoming a good listener:

1. Be attentive and interested. Don't be distracted by your own ideas and thoughts or by the activities going on around you. Have a desire to listen and understand. If you cannot listen fully, say so and find a time when you can.

2. Put yourself in the other person's place to identify what he or she is saying (the content), how he or she is feeling (the emotions involved), and what the situation means to him or her (the values involved).

3. *As you listen, feed back what you are hearing* by restating what you understand to be the most important thoughts and feelings; i.e., "What I hear you saying is . . ."

4. *Do not interrupt, offer advice or suggestions,* or bring up similar feelings and problems you have experienced yourself.

5. *Don't argue,* either verbally or nonverbally, with the person talking or with yourself.

6. *Listen "between the lines"* for not only what is said but also what isn't being said. Listen for the underlying "music" as well as the words.

7. *Don't antagonize* the speaker with hasty judgments or comments about what you're hearing.

8. *Show your support* with appropriate nods, smiles, supportive comments and encouragements.

Problem-Solving and Decision Making

The goal of problem-solving is for family members to assist one another in solving their own problems. Surprisingly enough, giving advice and suggestions are often not helpful problem-solving tools, yet they are the most likely ways we try to help our friends and colleagues. Here are *7 Steps to More Effective Problem-Solving:*

1. *Get an agreement.* Make sure whomever you're talking with actually wants you to help them solve the problem. *Just because they start to complain or discuss a problem does not mean that they actually want you to start helping them solve it.* They could simply want someone to listen or they may need an "Ain't It Awful" session (see page 437). So if someone gets into a problem without specifically asking for help in problem-solving, ask him or her directly, "Can I help? Shall we have a problem-solving session or what would be useful?"

2. *Don't own the problem.* Do not take responsibility for the other person's problem. Your goal is to assist the person in solving his or her own problem. Don't start giving "advice" or suggestions. If you have some initial ideas, write them down and bring them up at Step #7.

Instead of taking the problem on yourself, help the person define the problem. Sometimes the initial problem is not the primary one, or the person isn't really clear about what the problem is, so begin by asking the person to describe the problem. Then, start asking "open-ended" questions (the most useful ones usually begin with "how" or "what") in order to:

- Clarify feelings. Listen for how the person feels about the situation and help him or her sort out feelings.
- Gather information. Find out as much as you can about the situation.

Then, based on the information presented, feed back as clearly as you can your understanding of just what the problem is until you get a statement that sums up the problem in a way that the persons involved agree with.

3. Determine the desired outcome. Query the person to identify the ultimate outcome he or she wishes from the situation at hand. Help him or her go beyond shortsighted immediate desires like restitution, retaliation, or revenge and get to the ultimate goals.

4. Brainstorm alternatives. By asking opened-ended questions, identify what actions the person has already taken or is considering taking. Then you can use a brainstorming process to generate new options.

5. Evaluate alternatives. Focus the conversation on what can be done in the "here and now" and discuss the pros and cons of various solutions. Then help the person prioritize his or her best choices.

6. Predict consequences and reach a decision. Discuss options so that the person with the problem can identify the best possible outcomes and select one to act upon.

7. Develop an action plan and follow up on the outcome. Help the person list the things that must be done to carry out the decision he or she has reached. If it's not working, you can offer to go through these steps together again so the person can arrive at a new decision.

Asking for and Receiving Feedback

You may at times want to ask for feedback from those you live with about your ideas, thoughts, plans, or behavior. Remember, at such times, that feedback is only useful if it's honest. So if you ask for feedback, you must be willing to accept whatever you hear graciously or you will probably not get honest feedback in the future. So if you want to hear positive reactions and compliments only, admit it to yourself and ask for positive feedback only. Otherwise here's a process you can use:

1. Listen carefully. Put your mouth on hold until you have gotten all reactions. Do not argue, disagree, or enlighten the others as to "how it is."

2. Keep in mind as you listen that in giving you their feedback, those you live with are trying to be helpful. Do not take what you hear personally. It need not be the last word. You don't have to use or agree with feedback. But you may benefit if you accept, weigh, and appreciate the motivation for and energy spent in providing it.

3. Ask clarifying questions; i.e., "Why do you say that?" "Would you say that if . . .?" "What if I changed this . . .?"

4. Thank those who offer their feedback. Tell them you appreciate their feedback and will weigh it carefully.

5. If you don't find the feedback helpful, feel free to discard it, but you need not point this out to the people who have been so kind as to give it to you. Before you discard feedback, however, consider that although you don't agree, your clients or customers may. So you might want to solicit further feedback from others.

6. If you did find the feedback helpful, report back later on the value it has had for you. Such reports will make everyone feel good and reinforce the value of helping one another.

Giving Feedback

The general rule of thumb on giving feedback is "Don't give it unless it's wanted." Before giving feedback to anyone in your household, we advise asking if he or she would be interested in hearing your feedback. Then, if so, follow these guidelines:

1. Don't give "advice" and opinions. Raise facts, observations, concerns, and reactions. Provide the reasons for your comments.

2. Try to balance positive with negative feedback. Point out what you think works as well as what you think doesn't, what you like and appreciate as well as what you dislike.

3. When possible, provide the alternatives or changes that would correct or eliminate the negative aspects you identify.

4. Accept that your feedback may or may not be useful and don't expect people to use it unless they find it helpful. You may even be right with your concerns or reactions, but if the person is not disposed to hear and use it, just drop it.

Celebrating Victories (Wins)

Success can be lonely in a harried, busy, and often frustrating world. So one of the most rewarding roles household members can offer for one another is to be a mutual admiration society, serving as cheerleaders, dedicated fans, and an applauding audience. Home is a great place to share your "wins."

So make your home a place where everyone can brag and toot his or her own horn unabashedly. To do this means you all have to genuinely enjoy one another's success and be glad for one another's victories. This means that whenever any good news, big or little, is shared everyone should:

1. Avoid negative comparisons. As you hear the wonderful things your loved ones are reporting, resist the temptation to start thinking about how you're not doing as well as they are. Instead say to yourself, "That's for me!"

2. Momentarily set aside any problems or negative feelings you may be having so you can enjoy others' success. Put your concerns on hold while you celebrate with them. If you find you simply cannot do that, tell those involved that you want to celebrate with them, but first you've got to get some support for the pressing concerns you're facing.

3. Think of little gifts or tokens you can give to one another to recognize one another's talents, importance, and contribution. It might be something like clipping a cartoon you know someone will value, picking up a book you know they would enjoy reading, or just sharing a thought you had during the week about their life.

Ain't It Awful Sessions (War Stories)

Sometimes we all need a chance to complain and ventilate our feelings about the things that bother us. We also need a place to share our *War Stories*, the disappointing, dreadful, discouraging things we have faced and are weathering. Of course, we can't, or at least we shouldn't, do this with our clients and customers. And often family and relatives would rather not hear about difficulties, especially when we express them with the vehemence and the detail that we feel. Nevertheless, home can be a place for us to let off steam, especially if we do it in a way that doesn't tax others' patience.

BUT . . . there is nothing worse than listening to someone complain on and on endlessly about all the details of his or her problems. Nothing will make home a more unpleasant place—more quickly. Habitual complaining makes us feel like screaming "Enough already!" "Give me a break!" or "Get a life!" So we advise using the following "Ain't It Awful" process to meet each other's legitimate needs for complaining without killing the morale around the house.

1. If you want to "bitch," ask those who are around if they will indulge you with a five-minute "Ain't It Awful" session. (If you really have a "biggy" you might ask for ten minutes.)

2. If they agree, set a timer or have someone look at his or her watch and then proceed to complain and complain until you feel empty. Tell about all the awful things that have happened to you. As a matter of fact, exaggerate the situation, give yourself permission to blow it all out of proportion if you wish.

3. Those listening should be uniformly sympathetic, moaning and groaning at each added assault, adding on a chorus of "Oh, no. That's awful!" Since we've all been through hassles of some kind and we can summon the feelings about our own frustrations, it's possible to to do this authentically.

4. When the time runs out, cease complaining and thank those who were listening for their support. If everyone has really gotten into the spirit of this process, you may all be laughing your heads off before the "Ain't It Awful" session ends.

If someone begins complaining without asking for such a session and it starts to become tedious, whoever notices it first should comment that it sounds like the person needs an "Ain't It Awful" session. Suggest you devote five to ten minutes for out-and-out complaining. Sometimes a household may want to have a group "Ain't It Awful" session where everyone joins in with his or her complaints.

Crisis Management

At some time or another, most of us in any household will be confronted with a crisis. And where better to turn at such times than to those we live with? If we respond appropriately to one another at such times, we can help one another to connect with our own inner resources and carry on with confidence and courage.

In other words, usually the crisis itself is not so much about the events that have occurred as it is about our reactions to them. In fact, one way to define a crisis is "a time in which our normal coping or adaptive mechanisms are no longer functioning." Here's how you can help each other at such times:

1. Begin with feelings; move to facts. Usually we're quite emotional during a crisis even if we don't show it. It can be difficult to move right into talking rationally about what happened and what can be done. It's easier and wiser to start with the person's existing state of mind and listen to his or her feelings before asking questions about the facts. Usually the person will calm down when he or she begins talking and you can start asking questions about what happened. But if someone continues to be extremely upset, asking very simple questions will help him or her connect with the *here and now*, questions like, "Did you drive home?" "How long have you been here?" "Can I get you a glass of water?"

2. Evaluate the current situation. Once the person is calmer, find out as much as you can about the situation that precipitated the problem. Explore what it is about this situation that is different from the many other challenges he or she has handled in the past.

3. Help the person define the problem (as described above for problem solving).

4. Explore alternative ways for coping with the crisis and less catastrophic ways of viewing whatever has happened.

5. Lend appropriate support to the person in taking whatever action is needed. Sometimes those we live with can help by volunteering to accompany the person in crisis somewhere, consulting with him or her on a particular action, or taking over some simple routine tasks like picking a child up at the sitter's or calling to cancel a dental appointment.

We hope these guidelines will assist you in enjoying the rewards and benefits of living and working together. We are indebted to Joan Sturkie and Valerie Gibson, whose ideas we adapted for a good number of these guidelines. They are the authors of *The Peer Counselor's Pocket Book*.

What to Do If It Isn't Getting Better

On occasion, the changes and adjustments of working from home seem to precipitate more serious problems than those we've been discussing. The tension and bad feelings build until there is certainly nothing to laugh about and the situation feels intolerable. What happens in a situation like this? What goes wrong? Has working from home destroyed the marriage?

Yes and no. Whether it's a new baby, a new job, or a new house, any new element introduced into a relationship can aggravate existing problems or bring them to the surface. Working from home is like this too.

It's easier to avoid problems when you don't see each other very much. When someone is at the office for most of every day, it's simpler to push the difficulties away. Working at home, couples usually see more of each other. This proximity, and the strain of adjusting to the changes involved, can stir up and bring out problems that were kept beneath the surface before.

In a relationship that's suffering from underlying problems, it's difficult to get in touch with the basic loving feelings that brought a couple together. Every little concern becomes a battleground. Even the smallest differences can become unsolvable, because the real problem is not being addressed. In situations like these, it's important to heal the relationship itself before a couple attempts to solve the more peripheral problems of working from home.

If you're concerned about whether the conflicts you're having are normal adjustments to the changes of working from home, or whether these changes are bringing up more general problems, review the five early-warning signals that follow:

1. Your spouse begins blaming all the problems the two of you are having on your work.
2. Your spouse starts to feel jealous of your work.
3. You start using your work as a way to escape talking with your spouse.
4. You start using your work as a way to avoid sex.
5. You talk about everything but what's really on your mind.

If you notice these warning signs either before or after you begin working from home, we suggest you communicate with your spouse about them. Then, if the problems persist or go from bad to worse, get professional help to improve your relationship.

There's no need to settle for less than the relationship and lifestyle you want for yourself. You deserve it and so does your partner. Don't wait until things have deteriorated to a hopeless state. Act now. You can use the resources listed at the end of this chapter or contact the following organizations for help.

There are many courses on building relationships. Marriage Encounter programs, for example, are offered across the country. You can usually locate them through local churches and synagogues. Otherwise, find out about programs in your area by writing to: International Marriage Encounter, 955 Lake Drive, Saint Paul, MN 55120.

The American Association for Marriage and Family Therapy, 1717 K St., NW, #407, Washington, D.C. 20006, can put you in touch with trained professionals in your community who help couples solve problems.

If your partner won't seek help with you, go yourself. Sometimes all it takes is one person's having the courage to take the first step and lead the way.

Resources

Books

Embracing Each Other. Hal Stone and Sidra Winkelman. San Rafael, Calif.: New World Library, 1989.

Love Is the Answer. Gerald Jampolski and Diane Cirincioni. New York: Bantam Books, 1990.

On the Family. John Bradshaw. Pompano Beach, Fla.: Health Communications, 1987.

Parent Effectiveness Training. Thomas Gordon. New York: Peter Wyden, 1970.

The Peer Counselor's Pocket Book. Joan Sturkie and Valerie Gibson. San Jose, Calif.: Resource Publications, 1989.

The Working Parents' Survival Guide. Sally Wendkos Olds. Rocklin, Calif.: Prima Publication & Communication, 1989.

Tapes

Creating Positive Relationships. Gerald Jampolski and Diane Cirincioni. Chicago: Nightingale Conant; 7300 North Lehigh Avenue, Chicago, IL 60648; (800) 323-5552.

Relationship Series. Hal Stone and Sidra Winkelman. Delos Publishing, 5451 Laurel Canyon Blvd., North Hollywood, CA 91607.

CHAPTER
TWENTY
■■■■■■■■■■■■■■■■■■■■■■■■■■■■

What to Do about Children

Many parents first begin to think about working from home as a way of pursuing both parenthood and a career. This is hardly surprising since studies show that two-thirds of children under age six will have working mothers by 1995, and juggling family and career is already the number one source of stress for women. Studies also show that 40 percent of men and 80 percent of women with children would stay home to raise their families if they could. And nearly half of all children with working parents say they wish their parents were at home.

Certainly bringing work home holds the potential of making juggling these demands easier for both mothers and fathers and yet often parents and others who want to work from home worry about whether they'll be productive enough, working with children in the house. In this chapter we want to affirm that working from home does indeed offer many rewards for parents. At the same time, we want to realistically address what parents can expect, the difficulties they face, and the practical steps they can take to avoid problems and take full advantage of the benefits.

It Can Be Worth the Effort

Our son Jon was eight years old when we moved our offices home. Having both worked long hours away from the house since shortly after he was born, we felt pleasure hearing him come in the door after school and call out, "Hi! I'm home!" We'd take a break to make him a snack and find out the highlights of his day.

Our being in the house so much was a real treat for him too. Until we started working at home, he had only seen us at night and on weekends. From the time he was tiny, we had asked the baby-sitter to be sure he took a nap in the late

441

afternoon so he could stay up late with us when we got home. So, at first, having us there in the afternoon was like a continual holiday for Jon.

We liked knowing we were more available to him, too. Although at times he had trouble knowing when he could or couldn't interrupt us, we were all surprised to discover that he was often too busy with his own things to pay much attention to us. Jon has graduated from college now and is living in Northern California. We often think that if we hadn't decided to work from home, we would be looking back on his childhood regretting how much we'd missed.

When financial consultant Michael Fey moved his office home, he found, just as we had, that being with his teenage children was surprisingly rewarding. "Being at home in the morning, helping the kids get off to school, being involved in their squabbles, it's been a real education! My kids know me better now. They may not like me any better, though, because I'm a real parent. I'm putting down certain prescriptions, not leaving it up to Mom. It's changed their image of what a father is. Daddy isn't just somebody who goes off to fight traffic and bring home a barrel of cash for everybody else to spend."

Both men and women who work at home describe this close involvement with their children as a real advantage. And indications are that it's also a benefit for the children. Often the adult world of work is so removed from the lives of children that it's literally a life apart. Alvin Toffler expressed this separation in his book *The Third Wave.* "Most children today have only the foggiest notion of what their parents do or how they live while at work." He tells a poignant story to illustrate his point.

An executive decides to bring his son to his office one day and take him out to lunch. The boy sees the plushy carpeted office, the indirect lighting, the elegant reception room. He sees the fancy expense-account restaurant with its obsequious waiters and exorbitant prices. Finally, picturing his home and unable to restrain himself, the boy blurts out: "Daddy, how come you're so rich and we're so poor?"

In contrast, when parents work at home a child not only gets to know them better but also experiences their world of work. Management trainers Linda and Bill Belisle have even involved their children in their home business. "Our kids know what it's like to be in business. They've grown up with it. We all work together, and when we have deadlines to meet, the kids pitch in and help. We think it's good preparation for them to succeed in life."

But while the rewards are potentially rich for most parents and children, it is also true that working with kids around is not always easy. Ken and Stephanie Wilson work from home and are the parents of two young sons. They agree that "it's just wonderful for the boys to have both parents here, but it's a real adjustment. It's a real test of living up to what we want as parents and professionals."

Noise, interruptions, and privacy are usually issues parents have to face, as well as knowing what's reasonable to expect of your children and yourself under the circumstances.

Children have an adjustment too. We remember at least one occasion when Jon, feeling frustrated with our ever-present business conversation, asked angrily, "Is this a home or a business?" So let's talk about the different reactions you can anticipate from your children, what you can say to them, and how to make practical, age-appropriate arrangements for their care.

What You Can Expect

Children's reactions to your being at home will vary greatly, depending upon the ages of your children, their personalities, your family, and the nature of your work. In most situations, children are glad to have a parent there more often, but probably will not fully comprehend what it means to have a parent working from home. To them, you are Mom or Dad, and that's it. They probably don't know you as lawyer, doctor, bookkeeper, or whatever else you happen to be. So if you want to make working at home with children both enjoyable and productive, you'll have to introduce them to the career aspects of yourself and show them how to relate to you now that you're more than a mom or dad at home.

Whatever their ages, kids will be kids. Don't expect your children to act like grown-ups just because you're working at home. Don't expect them, for example, to be quiet. Remember, by nature children are not quiet, and to be so for more than short periods of time is unhealthy for their development. Constantly trying to hush them will be a losing battle for you in the short run and not good for them in the long run.

A good rule of thumb, applying to children of all ages, is to "child-proof" your home office rather than trying to "office-proof" your children. In other words, let your kids be kids. Let them engage in normal activities, but set up your office and your schedule so that having "normal" children around will not disrupt your work. Here are some examples of how people have "child-proofed" their work while letting their kids be kids:

Programmer William Keen solved his dilemma this way. "I put the business phone and a desk down in the basement because it just doesn't make any sense to try to keep two dogs and three kids quiet when I have a phone call. By putting the desk and phone at the far end of the basement, under the master bedroom, I get very little noise. Even when the TV is going full blast, I don't hear it."

Artist Gary Eckart managed the problem another way. "I set my workshop up in an RV on the side of the house, because cutting stained glass just isn't compatible with having a toddler around. There's too much risk. If even once she crawled into my studio and got cut or put a piece of glass in her mouth . . . well, I couldn't take that chance."

Word-processor operator Barbara Bickford found the solution not in *where* but *when* she worked. "I make my calls and do all my deliveries while the kids are at school. I take my three-year-old to day care in the morning. When they're at home, home is home; when they're gone, it's an office."

If you have sensitive equipment or materials you don't want children to disrupt or damage, we suggest not allowing them to play in your office while you work because they will then think of it as a play area they can use even when you are not there to supervise them. Judy Wunderlich, who runs a temporary agency for graphic artists in Schaumburg, Illinois, found a creative way of solving this dilemma. As her two young children are under five, she needs to have them in sight while she works, but doesn't want them playing around her computer equipment. So she divided her basement in half with a three-foot-high divider. Her office is in the back half; the kids' playroom is in the front. She can see and hear them and they can see and hear her, but the office is still off limits.

So the first step is setting up your work to accommodate the reality of children in the house. Then remember that you can fully expect your children to behave responsibly and appropriately for their age and level of development. They do not need you all the time and can grow and develop very well while you're working undisturbed at home.

Let's take a look at what you can expect at each age level and how you can get work done whatever ages your children are. Since the age groups we discuss are based on typical stages of childhood development, assess your own children's personalities and rates of development so you can adjust these expectations to your family.

Children Under Twelve

Newborn to six years old. With mothers of newborn babies going back to work earlier than ever before and 56 percent of all mothers going back before their children are six years old, working from home becomes increasingly appealing to parents eager to find ways of avoiding the risks of day care, not to mention the high costs of child-care services.

Research shows that day care poses both physical and mental health risks for children under six, and surveys show that more than 75 percent of mothers are unsatisfied with child care for which they pay from $38–$109 weekly. One of the most common misconceptions new mothers have, however, is that working from home will be a replacement for child care. Often it is not a replacement but it does open up many more flexible and rewarding options for combining motherhood and career. About 50 percent of parents working at home say they can do work while caring for infants and toddlers but since they need constant supervision, want and demand your attention, and try to be part of everything going on around them, the other half of parents who work at home find this unsatisfactory.

When working parents care for toddlers and preschoolers at home, the typical result is that little work gets done and/or the parents end up expecting the young children to behave in ways beyond their abilities. This usually leads to a flood of yelling and unpleasantness. It can also result in emotional or behavioral problems in the children.

Barbara Elman was operating a word-processing service bureau when she became pregnant with her first child. Her story is similar to that of many women who begin working at home with infants and toddlers. During the first six months, she found she could work fine while the baby was right there with her. "Then my daughter became mobile. She started crawling and moving around and needing more attention. I couldn't sit and nurse her anymore while I was proofing, because she wanted to play with the keys and everything else in sight. I couldn't work when she was around. It was difficult then and it's impossible now that she's two-and-a-half."

Experiences like Barbara's have led most people in this situation to the same conclusion. If they want to work without interruption for longer than fifteen minutes, they either need to work at night while the children are sleeping or to get some form of supplementary child care for children under six or seven years.

If you do hire someone to help you with your children and they or others want to know why someone else is caring for them when you're at home, it's important to explain that you are working just as someone does who goes out to the job each day. When consultant Mary Smolinski started to work from home her son was fifteen months old, and she worked only part-time. "I hired a high-school student to watch him while I worked in my office. As he grew, he learned that when Mommy's office door was closed that meant he had to get permission from the sitter before knocking and getting my permission to enter because Mommy was busy. Now he's nine and I no longer need a sitter, but the closed door still means I'm busy. He knows I'm there when he really needs me (maybe to congratulate him on his latest super-fantastic Lego design). But he still has to knock and ask first."

As an added safeguard, now that there's no sitter, Mary also leaves her telephone intercom on in the background so she can hear what's happening in the house.

Keeping an Eye and Ear on Young Children While You Work

Often parents want to see and hear what's going on with their young children while they're working at home, but they don't want the kids playing underfoot or around their equipment. Here are six solutions:

1. Separate your office area from children's play area with shutters that you can open or close depending upon how focused you need to be and the child-care arrangements you've made.
2. Replace your regular office door with a Dutch door, so when you want to supervise what's going on in the household you can leave the top open and still not have pets or kids running in. When needed, of course, you can close the door fully.
3. Use a baby monitor or telephone intercom like Sony's *Baby Call*, (800) 222-7669, the AT&T *Wireless Intercom System*, (800) 229-2901, or Lloyd's Room-to-Room Communicator DAK, (800) 888-7808 to alert you to any problems you need to attend to. Keep the base unit in your office and add as many remote units as you wish to monitor or communicate with various other rooms of the house.
4. Divide a basement, attic, or family room into two rooms with a half wall so you can work in one room while the kids play within sight in the other.
5. Use a portable child-door divider which you can put up or take down as needed to make office or unsafe work space inaccessible to children without their being out of site or sound. Such folding gates are plastic or wood, and they come in various heights and extend to various widths.
6. Use two-line cordless phones so you can pick up business calls while you're in other parts of the house with your children, can follow them around if need be, or get to them quickly while you're talking on the phone.

Seven to twelve years old. Once children are over six, they are usually in school for a good part of the day, which leaves parents with considerably more flexibility as far as scheduling uninterrupted work time goes. Parents can arrange their schedules so they are not working while the children are home, or are doing tasks that require less concentration and can more easily withstand interruptions.

PERSONAL PROFILE: Ken and Stephanie Wilson, Writer and Landscape Designer

Ken and Stephanie Wilson have two boys, ages seven and ten. Stephanie began working from home as a landscape designer. Ken left his job at a major utility company to begin consulting and writing from home.

The Wilsons have located their offices so they are less likely to be disturbed by their children's activities, but they believe that children should have free access to their parents. Therefore, the Wilsons take a flexible approach to interruptions.

As Ken explains, "I don't want to make a rule 'No, you can't come in and see me.' I don't want limits on their coming in and saying 'Hey, Dad, what's this or what's that?' That's why I'm here. I'm glad they're coming in to see me. It means we're relating."

The Wilsons have avoided making rigid rules by letting their boys know in the beginning that an office at home is serious business, and by having frequent family meetings to talk about everyone's feelings. They agree that "it has worked out reasonably well, but it hasn't just happened. It does take effort."

Children over six also require less direct supervision, so it becomes feasible to work in your office while they are playing in their rooms or in the backyard. Another advantage is that children this age often play in the homes of friends, although their friends are just as likely to come over to your house.

Ideally, you would have another adult available for children seven to twelve years of age when you need to work without any interruptions for periods of over an hour or so. This is especially useful if there is more than one child in the family and bickering is likely. However, you can often handle the needs of children this age on short, intermittent breaks and teach them to wait for those break times.

You can usually expect children from seven to twelve years old not to interrupt you when:

- There is some other person over twelve in the house whom they can ask for help.
- You let them know the home office has become your room and they need permission to be there.
- You tell them specifically when you will be available, and you are only unavailable for about an hour at a time.

- They understand that they can and should interrupt you for emergencies. (Beware, though, that what is an emergency to you and what is an emergency to an eight-year-old can be quite different, so you will need to spell out what you mean.)

Children of this age will probably do a considerable amount of testing in relation to these expectations. At first, they may push to find out if you mean what you say and exactly what the limits are. This will be particularly true when you have been with them full-time before you began working at home. But if you are both loving and firm, they can usually adjust to your expectations after a few weeks.

In the first few weeks after we began working at home, we told our son not to interrupt us if we were in a session with a client and had the door closed, but he did anyway. We explained that clients came on the hour, and asked him to wait to talk with us until the break between each hour. We would be free once the client had gone out the front door.

Whenever he disrupted a session unnecessarily, one of us would simply say, "I'm in a session now, Jon. I will be done at—," and then we would close the door. Later, on the break, we'd be sure to check out what he wanted. It didn't take long for him to understand he could get his needs met without interrupting us.

Over twelve years old. Children over twelve should be able to carry out agreements not to interrupt your work for specified periods as long as they know:

- When you do not want to be interrupted.
- What emergencies you *do* want to be interrupted for.
- When they will be able to have your attention to deal with their needs. (We've found this is important not so much because teenagers need your time but because they want to know that you are there.)

In fact, with children who are ten to twelve years old, you may find that involving them in some aspects of your work is rewarding for you both. Teenagers in particular have many more talents and abilities than our society provides them with outlets for. They may well be our greatest untapped natural resource. We often had our son help with mailings, newsletters, or big projects of various kinds. We suggest, however, that such help be strictly on a voluntary basis, if not for a set wage; you will get more willing and productive participation that way.

Sandee and Al Burger started an extermination business in their home when their two children were toddlers. Sandee says, "The family and the business grew together." When the children were old enough, they got fifty cents to sharpen pencils and do other office tasks. In high school, they worked for the business on weekends. The Burgers' daughter, now an adult, has taken a full-time job with the company, which long ago outgrew their home.

Who Cares for Our Children When We Can't Do It Ourselves?

55% of American Parents Get Help Caring For Their Children

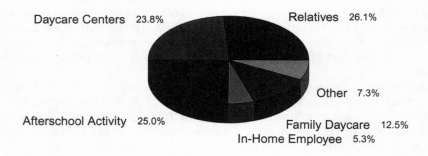

Daycare Centers 23.8%

Relatives 26.1%

Other 7.3%

Afterschool Activity 25.0%

Family Daycare 12.5%

In-Home Employee 5.3%

1990 National Child Care Survey

Figure 20-1.

Child-Care Options

The type of care you arrange for your children is a highly personal decision. What suits some people will not suit others. So for working parents, having a wide variety of creative and flexible child-care options is one of the real advantages of working from home. You are no longer limited to only those arrangements that can provide care from 7:00 A.M. to 7:00 P.M. while you commute to work in a downtown office.

For example, Barbara Elman finds that, in order to be productive, she must hire someone to take care of her daughter part of the day while she's working. Like so many women, Barbara originally wanted to work at home so she could take care of her daughter herself and was hesitant at first about making other arrangements. But she discovered that trying to run a business and parent a toddler was too much to expect of herself, so she decided to explore the different kinds of support she could get. Now she urges women to give themselves permission to find child care that will best fit their needs.

In deciding which options are best for you, review the following pros and cons of each and consider your situation, the nature of your work, the ages of your children, and the help available in your home.

Call on another adult in the family. The advantages of having a spouse or relatives care for your children are that these adults know and are known by the children, and are aware of how you want the children to be treated. Often, too, there's no extra cost involved. The disadvantages are that spouses and relatives may not always be available when you need them; they also may resent your asking them to help on a regular basis; and even if they don't say so, relatives may expect to be paid.

If you do plan to use a spouse or relatives, be sure to let them know what you expect of them, and find out if they are actually willing to meet your expectations. You don't want help that's given out of duty, obligation, coercion, or guilt. Chances are these motivations will just lead to resentment and unreliable support for you, as well as possible negative experiences for your children.

Use a sibling over twelve years of age. The advantages of using older siblings are that they are usually close by; their help is free or they'll be earning spending money you might give them anyway; and by helping you, they have the opportunity to contribute to the family. The disadvantages are that they may not want to watch their younger siblings; they may not watch them very well; and they may sometimes even mistreat them. Another drawback is that older brothers and sisters are usually only available at certain times of the day. Also, sometimes younger siblings resent being "parented" by an older sibling, so they become disobedient and create more squabbles for you to police.

If you do use an older sibling, be certain to talk this over with all your children to get their agreement and support. If they really hate the arrangement, it's better—for your own benefit—to respect their wishes and use siblings only in special situations.

We strongly advise against using children under twelve years of age to supervise a younger sibling, because they generally cannot get younger children to respect and obey them. One way you can measure whether a child is effective enough to watch younger children is to observe whether the child can get dogs or other trainable pets to obey him or her. Also, watch the child interacting with younger children from day to day. See if he or she demonstrates the skill and judgment that caring for a younger child requires.

Hire a baby-sitter, nanny, or au pair to come into your home. There are several options for having a caregiver come into your home and care for your child. You can hire a baby-sitter, someone who by nature and experience is good at caring for children. Usually they have no particular training, background, or licensing. They may be high-school or college students or elderly individuals in need of extra income. They may come into your home daily or live in. Most often you can find them through school placement offices, churches, or personal referrals.

Alternatively you can hire a professional nanny. A nanny has completed a professional training program and has studied child development, health education, safety, nutrition, and more. She will most likely have a repertoire of stories, songs, and games for children of various ages. She will come having had extensive supervision in a variety of other child-care settings.

So you can see, a baby-sitter may have baby-sitting experience, a love of children, and a caring nature, which can make for a terrific helper as long as he or she is willing to learn. In most cases, however, a baby-sitter is likely to need more supervision and training from you than a nanny. But as you might expect, a nanny will cost considerably more. If you can find a nanny through word-of-mouth from other families with nannies or through child-development programs at nearby colleges, your cost will be less than if you must go through a nanny agency (fees could run from $400 to $2,000). An agency can be worth the expense, however, if you don't have the time to locate and screen applicants. Nanny agencies can be expected to screen for training, health, driving and criminal records, family background, employment histories, and references. But do check references yourself anyway. To locate referral agencies, you can contact the National Association of Childcare Resource and Referral Agencies in Rochester, Minnesota, or for referrals to schools of professional nannies, you can contact the American Council of Nanny Schools, (517) 686-9417, or the International Nanny Association, (512) 454-6462.

Another option is to hire an au pair. Au pairs are typically Western European women between the ages of eighteen and twenty-five who come to live in the U.S. with an American family for a year to care for the children. In return, the au pair must be provided with room and board, $100 a week, airfare, medical insurance, and a $300 educational allowance. There are now eight agencies that place au pairs who have met federal guidelines and carefully screen and match au pairs with appropriate families.

Although the cost is lower than hiring a nanny or baby-sitter, the au pair can only stay legally for one year, and they are usually young women away from their families in a new country. So arrange to interview several applicants and make sure the agency will provide a replacement if your first choice doesn't work out. Here are several of the top au pair agencies recommended by *Parents* magazine:

- Au Pair in America. 102 Greenwich Avenue, Greenwich, CT 06830; (800) 727-2437.
- EurAuPair. 250 N. Coast Hwy., Laguna Beach, CA 92651; (800) 333-3804.
- AuPairCare. 1 Post Street, Ste. 700, San Francisco, CA 94104; (800) 4-Au-Pair.
- E. F. Au Pair. 1 Memorial Drive, Cambridge, MA 02142; (800) 333-6056.

There are pros and cons of having some type of caregiver come into your home. The advantage is that you now have someone whose explicit job is to take care of your children while you work. You can also hire a person who clearly wants to work and who is available at the specific times you need child care. Having someone come to your home saves you the time of taking the children elsewhere and also provides you with the opportunity to oversee what the sitter is doing.

The disadvantages are that you have an added expense, and since the children are still there at the house, noise and interruptions may continue to be a problem. Because you can probably still overhear some activities, you may have difficulty not going out to see what's happening when disturbances arise. To overcome this problem, some parents take their children out to the home of a private baby-sitter or family day-care home.

Take your child to a child-care program. Although some parents are fearful of taking their children to child-care programs, many people highly recommend them. The advantages are that licensed child-care programs are generally reliable; they're open every day because they are businesses; and since the children are not at home, you can work with total privacy. The disadvantages are that the child may not get the individual attention you'd like; the hours may not be as flexible as you want; and you'll have to make other arrangements when your child is sick.

There are many good child-care programs, including day-care centers, day-care homes, preschools, and after-school programs. Call your county offices for a list of licensed programs in your area. Then visit several of them while children are there. Talk with the operators and teachers and ask how they handle the various situations you're concerned about in child care.

Find out, for example, what the children will be doing during the time they are there. Will they be learning and playing, or only playing? How many children are in the program, what are their ages, and how many adults are present? How is discipline handled? Talk to other parents who have children in the programs you are considering. Find out how pleased these parents are and whether they have any complaints. And be sure to investigate the provider's credentials.

Join a child-care co-op or trade baby-sitting services. In a child-care co-op, you join with other parents and take turns providing care for your children. Sometimes parents provide all the care by themselves and sometimes they only supplement the work of professionals who are hired to provide the care. The latter arrangement is called a "parent participation" nursery.

The advantages of co-op programs are that they usually cost less than other options; you get to participate in the care of your child; and other parents often become close friends. The disadvantages are that participating in a co-op means contributing time that may take you away from work; you also have to invest time in organizing the co-op and energy in caring for other people's children.

When selecting a co-op program, shop for one that understands and appreciates the needs of working parents. This is particularly important if you are a working single parent and will have to contribute all the time yourself. If you cannot find a satisfactory child-care co-op arrangement in your area, do what many parents have done—initiate a co-op by getting together with other working parents in your neighborhood.

On a more informal basis, some parents also trade the task of baby-sitting with friends or neighbors. Although this is more often done on a backup basis

---

Seven Child-Care Options

1. Call on other adults in the family: spouse, aunts, uncles, brothers, sisters, grand-parents.
2. Have siblings over twelve years of age watch younger children.
3. Have a baby-sitter or nanny come into your home.
4. Take the children to a private baby-sitter.
5. Place the children in a child-care program:
   A day-care center.
   A day-care home.
   A nursery school.
6. Join a child-care co-op.
7. Trade baby-sitting with a friend.

---

when other child-care arrangements aren't available, writer Libby Crowe finds this option works well for her.

Libby started working at home with the birth of her child. At first, working at home with the baby made everything easier. "I worked while she napped or played nearby," Libby remembers. "Now that she's a toddler, she naps less and is less willing to do her own thing." So Libby has worked out a variety of more informal arrangements. "I trade kid-watching with a friend who has a child near the same age as mine, and let my mom help out as often as she will. Occasionally I use day-care services."

Finding someone to help out on the spot may not provide the kind of security you need to run your business reliably, however, so a more formal baby-sitting co-op might be more to your liking. A baby-sitting co-op doesn't have a separate facility like a co-op nursery where parents take turns working in the nursery. As Patricia McManus spells out in her book *The Babysitting Co-op Guidebook*, a baby-sitting co-op works on a point system. A family who needs a sitter calls another member of the co-op and asks for baby-sitting time. The family that receives the help is charged points for each hour of sitting service. The family that baby-sits is given points for future baby-sitting they need. Points are recorded by the co-op's bookkeeper, a position that rotates monthly throughout the membership. The bookkeeper gets paid with a few extra baby-sitting points, too.

For further information on finding or establishing a co-op nursery or baby-sitting co-op, refer to *A Parent's Guide to Child Care and Baby-sitting* and *The Babysitting Co-op Guidebook* by Patricia McManus (see Resources).

Selecting Someone to Care for Your Child in Your Home

Having someone come into your home while you are working from home can be an ideal child-care solution. Because often you will be on the premises, you'll be in a good position to make sure that the caregiver you hire is indeed giving the kind of care you want and expect. Here are several things you can do to make sure you find the right person the first time around:

1. Decide what you're looking for in a caregiver: personal traits, background, experience, and so forth. Also decide what you will want him or her to do; i.e., meal preparation for the children, driving, reading, teaching, etc. One major decision, of course, is whether you'll be seeking a live-in caregiver or plan to have him or her come and go each day.

Prepare a list of questions you will ask all the candidates you interview designed to ascertain if they have the qualities and experience you're looking for. Be sure to ask the same questions of everyone, so you can adequately compare one to another.

2. Get references and check out each and every one thoroughly. Because people are often hesitant to give negative references, ask open-ended questions that will give you as much information as possible from which to form your own opinion. Ask, for example, what different tasks the caregiver did and which ones he or she was best at. Inquire about what the parents liked most about the caregiver. What did they wish he or she had done differently? Why is the caregiver no longer working there? Before you end the conversation, make sure to ask directly if the former employer would hire the person again.

3. Observe the interaction between the caregiver and your child. We didn't do this at first, and the first woman we hired turned out to be very cold and distant with our son. It didn't take long for us to discover this and replace her, but, of course, the experience was disruptive and stressful. The second woman we hired was a wonderful caregiver who was with Jon for many years. However, he adopted aspects of her personality that we would just as soon have preferred he ignored. So also make sure that the person you hire is someone whose habits and personality you won't mind your child adopting.

4. Make sure you put applicants at ease during the interview so they will be forthcoming in talking about themselves. Ask open-ended questions like "Tell me about your child-care experience." "How did you choose to do child care?" "What do you like about it?" "How do you know when a child is doing well?" After the candidates are talking openly and easily, you can ask the more detailed questions you have prepared. Be sure to ask them what they would do to discipline a child and when they think discipline is necessary. Also ask them to describe a child-care situation that gave them trouble and what they did about it. Be sure to watch facial expressions and body language as well as to listen carefully to the content of their answers.

5. Make all your needs and expectations explicitly clear in writing: days of the week, hours, activities, days off, sick leave, what meals they will be preparing, what activities they will be driving to and from and when, etc. Since you will probably be working at home at least part of the time, make sure you have a clear understanding with the caregiver about when you can be interrupted. And once your caregiver is on the job, avoid the temptation to run out and get involved whenever you hear your child crying or some other commotion in the house. In other words, let your caregiver do his or her job.

Also reach an agreement as to when you will be out of the office and what procedures are to be followed if for some reason you are unable to return at the agreed time for the caregiver to leave.

6. Make it legal. Hiring a full- or even part-time caregiver makes him or her an employee, so you must comply with all state and federal hiring practices (see chapter 21). Even if you or your spouse never expects to be nominated for attorney general, be sure you're taking all the necessary legal steps.

Selecting a Day-Care Center or Family Day-Care Home

We have a bias toward licensed family day care, because it's a home environment more nearly like being in your home office. Of course, you must make a personal visit to any child-care home or center you are considering, but here are several things to look for provided from the "Parent's Guide to Choosing Quality Child Care," by the National Association of Pediatric Nurse Associates and Practitioners.

■ Know the licensing requirements in your state and be sure the facility you're considering meets them.
■ Find out if the caregivers are educated in child psychology and child development and/or early-childhood education.
■ Determine that the ratio of children to staff is appropriate for your child's age group. Here's their recommendations:

Infant to 18 months	4:1
18 months to 2 years	5:1
2–3 years	8:1
3–4 years	10:1
5–6 years	15:1
7 years and older	20:1

■ Be sure there is ample square footage of space per child indoors and for outside play areas. (For day-care centers thirty-five square feet is recommended indoors; seventy-five for outdoors.) Family day-care requirements vary by state.
■ Determine that the facility and equipment are kept clean and disinfected.
■ Make sure caregivers are careful about personal hygiene.
■ Ask whether there are appropriate facilities and procedures to take care of sick children.
■ Determine whether the activities program includes all the elements to foster child growth and development.
■ Be sure that your involvement in your child's activities and progress is welcomed.
■ Find out that corporal punishment, humiliation, or ridicule are never employed as disciplinary measures.
■ Determine that safety precautions and security procedures are strictly observed. For us this would include assurance that there is ample protection of smaller children from abuse, extortion, or harm from older children.

A great deal about the climate and atmosphere of a facility can be ascertained by visiting for several hours. Are children generally happy, busy, and engaged? Are they learning values and good behavior? Is there time for rest, meals, and liquids? Is the food healthy? Is there room and flexibility for each child to express his or her own needs and personality without disrupting others?

The National Association for Family Day Care Providers (see Resources list) offers accreditation to day-care providers who meet their state's requirements and have been providing care in their own homes for eighteen months. It publishes an annual *National Directory of Family Day Care Providers.*

Whatever child-care option they choose, most people working at home with children under twelve find that the cost of the care is less than the cost of lost productivity and the stress of trying to parent and work at the same time. Then, too, the financial burden can be partially relieved by taking a tax credit for child- and dependent-care expenses if you have the proper receipts and the provider's Social Security or tax I.D. number.

Claiming Your Child-Care Tax Credit

If you decide to hire help to take care of your children while you work, you are entitled to claim a tax credit for a portion of your child-care costs. A tax credit is more valuable than a tax deduction because you can take a tax credit right off your final tax liability instead of deducting it from your taxable income. For example, if you owe $10,000 in taxes, you can subtract the percentage of child care credit you are entitled to receive directly from that $10,000.

How much you can take for a child-care allowance depends upon your adjusted gross income. It ranges from a 30 percent credit for an adjusted gross income up to $10,000 to a 20 percent credit for an adjusted gross income of $28,000 and more. There is a maximum of $2,400 you can deduct for one child or $4,800 for two or more children.

The following table shows the actual IRS percentage you can claim up to the maximum.

How Much of a Tax Credit You Can Get for Child-Care Costs

Adjusted Gross Income	Percentage of Cost Credited
Up to $10,000	30%
$10,001–$12,000	29%
$12,001–$14,000	28%
$14,001–$16,000	27%
$16,001–$18,000	26%
$18,001–$20,000	25%
$20,001–$22,000	24%
$22,001–$24,000	23%
$24,001–$26,000	22%
$26,001–$28,000	21%
$28,000 and Up	20%

Also if one parent is employed, some companies have dependent-care assistance plans that allow the family to put away up to $5,000 for day-care expenses; this money is deducted from your paycheck before taxes are applied.

Introducing the Idea of Working at Home to Your Children

Whatever ages your children happen to be, when you decide to work at home they will have some reactions to this new way of life. At the very least, they will be curious and have their own ideas about what your being at home will mean. Sometimes these ideas will be unrealistic. For example, children are likely to think you will be as available to them as you have been on weekends or during your other free times at home.

So when you decide to set up a home office, remember to give your children as much information as you can about:

- When and where you will be working.
- When you will and will not be available.
- Who, if anyone, will be available to them while you are working.
- Exactly what you will expect from them now that you are working at home.
- Who might be coming to the house to see you.

Develop a plan with your children like the one discussed in chapter 13 under "Taking Charge of Interruptions and Distractions" to provide all the above information. Be firm in carrying out the plan you agree upon, but give your children the opportunity to ask questions about the plan, your work, and what you will be doing each day. Be sure that you do set aside times when you are not working and are fully available to be parents. Make sure your children know when those times are. If problems (crying, frequent interruptions, and so on) develop, talk with your children before you decide to punish them. Search for the underlying need a child may be expressing, and for underlying feelings of fear or anger about changes in your relationship. Offer support and information. Some questions children may be troubled about in connection with your working at home include:

- Am I still important?
- How much can I get away with?
- Are you still available to me when I need you?
- Who is going to be in charge?

Some messages that help children adjust to parents working at home are:

- You and your needs are still important to me.
- My work is important to our family and to the world.
- You can think and solve problems yourself (for children over three).

- There is time for you to get what you need from me. (Specify when, and follow through.)
- It's okay for us to be mad, sad, glad, or scared and to express our feelings to each other.
- We can solve problems so we are both happy.

Listen to your children's needs and expect them to listen to your demand for time and space to work. With children over four years old, invite them to propose solutions that will satisfy both their concerns and yours. Propose such solutions yourself.

Books that are helpful in understanding how to listen to children's feelings and still communicate your needs to them appear in the Resources list at the end of this chapter.

Personal Profile: Nancy and Mark Porter, Importers and Manufacturers

When Nancy and Mark Porter started their home business, the Susquehanna Hat Company, their oldest child had just started school and their youngest was about six months old.

At first they did their best to care for the children themselves. "We worked around the kids' schedule," Nancy remembers. They found, however, that "if you're really going to go for a business, you have to have child care." So as soon as the Porters were making enough money, Nancy found the name of a child-care home from a friend. "I liked the lady. She had a fenced yard, wasn't too expensive, had a boy the same age as mine, and was right across the street from where my older son went to school. It was the biggest relief to have 9:00 A.M. to 2:00 P.M. free for work every day."

Now seven and three years old, the Porter boys are both in "parent participation" schools. The schools require the Porters to contribute forty hours a year working in the classrooms. Sometimes Nancy dreads putting in the hours, but after she gets there she realizes "it's not so bad." For added convenience, they take turns driving the kids to and from school with a friend whose children are in the same schools. They're happy with these arrangements.

Although they are still working in the same home, Nancy and Mark are now divorced, so child care is even more important. Nancy explains, "If you find a school that's aware of your situation as a single parent, the people at the school become like co-parents. It's a nice personal support system that helps a lot now that we're divorced. And being involved in your children's education strengthens your relationship with them."

Are they still working from home? Yes. Although Mark doesn't live at the house anymore, he comes over every day to work. He finds, "It's good for the children to see me every day and provides them with more continuity than if we weren't working together at the house."

And how do the children feel about having the business at home? Of sharing his bedroom with the hat-storage space, their three-year-old says emphatically, "I like it." He loves to carry the hats back and forth.

Making Sure You Don't Expose Your Kids to Too Many Adult Concerns

The seven biggest stressors for children, according to *Family Circle* magazine, are: separation from parents, parents who are too busy to listen to their concerns, school and homework pressures, anxiety and nightmares brought on by watching violent TV or movies, illness and pain, anxiety about parents possibly divorcing, and death of a relative, family friend, or pet.

Perusing this list should comfort those of us who work from home that we should be better able to help our children through these concerns if we're home and available to them more often. But although working from home is a real plus for parents who want to be there more often for their children—and for kids, most of whom certainly need more from their parents these days—by working from home we also bring business problems and concerns into the family household. So it's important that we don't inadvertently expose our kids to too many additional stresses from the adult world of work. Here are several signs *Child* magazine identifies to alert us that our youngsters could be feeling overburdened by too many adult concerns:

1. Repeated questions about how much everything costs.
2. Frequent questions about whether parents are getting divorced.
3. Anxious habits like hair twisting or thumb sucking while you're addressing work issues or arguing with your spouse.

Of course, we can't avoid having some work-related pressures and concerns, especially while we're building a business or career at home. But arranging for supplemental child care during especially stressful and tense deadlines or projects, and during peak work periods, can help keep tensions from spilling into your children's lives. So can making sure you get out regularly to meet with a support group of peers with whom you can let off steam, express concerns, and get complaints off your mind.

Although it's certainly okay to let kids know you are having a stressful workday, don't be tempted to talk over your work concerns with your children, even teenagers. If children express concerns about or interest in work problems that arise, feel free to explain them briefly but also let them know that these kinds of things are part of being your own boss and that you'll be handling them. It's important to convey a sense of confidence even at times when you don't know exactly how you will handle problems and then to make sure you get whatever help you need.

Handling Special Problems

A variety of problems can arise when a family tries to combine work with having children in the house. Here are several of the most common problems and some of the things you can do about them.

Getting Off on the Wrong Foot

Sometimes a problem can develop and become entrenched in the family before people know it. Then they not only have the initial problem to handle but also a bad habit to break.

If, for example, you start out allowing children to interrupt you whenever they want, you set a precedent. You will probably then have more difficulty convincing them not to interrupt you than if the problem had been handled the first time it happened. Sometimes, breaking out of bad habits like this one takes a bold approach.

When Peggy Glenn started her secretarial service, she discovered that her three teenage children expected more from her now that she was at home. They rebelled against the hurried meals and extra chores that they had put up with when she was working away from home. No, not by arguing. Instead, they began leaving everything around the house for her to do. Because she was at home all day, they thought she should handle all the things a full-time mother would.

To put an end to this habit, she proposed two alternatives, either of which would have been acceptable to her: all five members of the family could do an equal share of the work, or they could get a housekeeper and everyone would pay a proportionate share of the cost, based on individual income.

"All of us had some income," Peggy remembers. "My oldest daughter had a job. The youngest was baby-sitting, and my son had his paper route. Not wanting to part with their money, they thought at first they would rather do a proportional share of the work. But when I didn't do anything more than my share, they soon decided it would be better to hire the housekeeper. Then an interesting thing suddenly happened. They no longer left the messes they had been making."

Resentments

At times, children or parents may feel resentful about a working-from-home situation. Children may resent having to pick up their things because of clients; not being able to make noise at certain times; having strangers in the house and being expected to be polite to them. Parents may resent interruptions; kids who seem uncooperative; and the pressure of having to do two jobs at home: working and parenting.

Most of these resentments are a normal part of life. Remember, if you weren't working from home, you and your family would be resenting other inconveniences, like driving on the freeway, getting up early, never having enough time together, and so on. The best way to handle resentments like these is to express them and get on with living and working from home.

Resentments that build up, however, are probably a sign that you need to make some changes. If you hear *frequent* complaining and whining about why you're always working or why your family can't be "normal" like everybody else's, it's a clue that work may be intruding too much on family life. If you're frequently doing the complaining, cursing, and yelling, it could be a sign that the family is intruding on your work.

Don't overlook these symptoms. Instead, sit down and talk about the basic problem with your children and see if you can come up with some practical solutions, like locating the office somewhere else in the house or changing your work schedule.

Acting Out

Occasionally children will use the fact that you are working at home to act out their personal difficulties. For example, if you and a child have a bad relationship or the child is lonely, your working at home may be a chance for him or her to communicate the problem to you by doing things that will clearly get your attention, like being belligerent to business guests or damaging your business property.

Acting out is definitely a sign of a problem that needs to be solved. Talking it out can help sometimes. It may be especially helpful, now that you're home, to follow through on any solutions and keep a more watchful eye on the child. But if your efforts are not working, your pediatrician, family practitioner, or religious adviser should be able to refer you to someone who can help. Some counseling resources are listed in the Resources list at the end of this chapter.

Constant Interruptions

It's not uncommon for people to tell us that even after a few weeks of "testing," a child is still interrupting their work more than they would like. This can occur for a number of reasons. If it happens to you, consider the following possibilities.

First, you may not have arranged for the level of care the child needs. For example, you just can't expect a four-year-old to entertain himself or herself alone for more than a short period. A television set will not substitute for a babysitter. Unless someone else is there with the child, you will continue to be interrupted. Sometimes, six- or seven-year-olds are "young" for their age and require more supervision than you initially thought. Making other child-care arrangements can solve this problem, too.

There are other possibilities. You may not be letting your children know when you will be available. Perhaps you're not giving them enough time once you stop working. Occasionally children will keep interrupting you because of personal problems they are having with your working at home. Talking with them about their feelings and arranging to spend nonworking time with children should help when this kind of problem is at the root of the interruptions. Usually, however, continued interruptions occur because parents have not been clear and firm enough. They give double messages like, "I told you not to interrupt me. Now what do you want?" And after responding to the child they say, "Now don't interrupt me again." With children, actions always speak louder than words. In this case, the words say, "Don't interrupt," but the actions are saying, "It's okay."

Thinking they are being firm, some parents get angry at the child and spend a lot of time and energy dealing with each interruption. Teachers and army sergeants have both learned this lesson the hard way: negative attention is better than no attention at all. Briefly notifying children that you are working, telling them when you will be available, and closing the door as if you expected the child to act accordingly is the best approach.

Consistency is important, too. Behavioral research shows that being firm 80 percent of the time, but lax the other 20 percent, only increases the chances of repeated interruptions. From the child's perspective, perhaps *this* time will be one of the exceptions. For a variety of specific suggestions for dealing with interruptions from children, see chapter 13, p. 325.

Inability to Say "No"

Some parents find it very difficult to say "no" to their kids. If you are one of those people and you want to keep working at home, you will either have to get someone else to manage your children or learn to say "no" and mean it. Otherwise you will probably end up yelling and screaming and wondering why your children still don't do what you want them to.

You can learn to say "no" without sounding harsh or cruel, by practicing with pets or store clerks. When you can use your voice firmly enough to get the pets to obey you or the clerks to accept "no" for an answer, you're well on your way to being able to make your children obey without screaming and physical punishment.

Guilt

"When I'm at work, I feel guilty that I'm not with my kids, and when I'm with my kids, I feel guilty that I'm not working." This is a dilemma many parents face. Certainly, working at home can help ease the discomfort of feeling that you should be in two places at once, but sometimes it intensifies a parent's guilt feelings instead.

As one woman told us, "When my daughter comes to the door and says, 'Mommy, please don't work anymore,' I could just cry." Of course, feeling this way splits her energy between her work and her daughter. The result is that she doesn't get to enjoy either one. With feelings like these, it's very hard to send a firm, clear, and consistent message to your children about the importance of not interrupting your work. So instead of getting their cooperation, you end up getting even more interruptions and feeling even more torn.

But what can a parent do to combat guilt feelings like these? Recognize that pursuing your career effectively is actually important to your children's futures. We don't feel guilty about working because we've realized that the best thing we can do for our son is to love him and care for him while pursuing fulfilling lives for ourselves. This way of acting shows him that it's wonderful to be alive and to grow up. It says that having children is a joy, that you can love and care for them and live your own life to the fullest, too. For us, working at home has made this all possible.

When It Doesn't Work

If your needs, the needs of your family, and the needs of your business just don't match up, working at home can be more pain than pleasure, and finding another office location is the best solution. Single parent and publicist Kathy Hubbell encountered such a problem. When she opened her public relations firm, she decided to work at home so she could be closer to her children, both of whom were in grade school.

"I never dealt very successfully with my guilt about my not being there when they got home from school," Kathy explains. "I've never particularly liked being a single parent. It usually means one provider, but no parent. So I thought working at home would provide a more cohesive way of life and I wouldn't feel so split."

She felt the kids did benefit from her being at home, but found her own tensions only increased. "It was really difficult for the kids to understand that when I was in my home office, I was at work and couldn't be disturbed. They were so glad to have me home, they'd just launch in and talk away about their day."

The constant interruptions angered her, but she was torn because she felt they deserved her time after not having had it for so long. For her own sanity, she moved her office out of the house. She felt better, but the kids felt worse than ever. She finally found the solution when she placed an ad in a college newspaper for a male student to come serve as a big brother to the kids and adopted family member, in exchange for room and board. When Doug Hagan joined their household, "the kids stopped fighting, chores were getting done, the whole atmosphere changed, and I began to relax about what I'd find when I came home from work."

Does she still like it better having her office away from home? "No, since Doug is here, home has become a better place to be. I want to be here again."

Kathy Hubbell's story illustrates an important point about working at home with children around. It seemed impossible, yet she finally found a solution that made it feasible and even preferable.

When you work from home and live with children, there will almost certainly be adjustments to make and problems of one kind or another to resolve. Yet with firmness and love and time to share feelings, you're just as likely to find solutions that will make working from home rewarding for all of you.

Resources

Books

Normally, knowing how busy those of us who work from home are, we pick a very few titles we believe to be the best resources on a given topic. For this chapter, however, parents have such a wide range of needs that we have selected more resources than usual and provided some notes as to when this particular book would be helpful.

Of course, the age of your child is one factor in seeking the most helpful books, so we've tried to provide books that will be helpful with children at various ages. In addition, it seems that parents either have difficulties that arise from being too strict and rigid, which leads to one set of problems, or they have difficulty being too unstructured and laissez-faire, which leads to a different set of problems, so we've tried to suggest books to provide guidance for each extreme.

Discipline That Works. Thomas Gordon. New York: Random House, 1989. We find this book is most helpful when the heavy-handed discipline you think should work starts producing an increasingly angry, rebellious, sullen, and resentful reaction. It outlines how you can discipline children while also gaining their confidence, respect, and cooperation.

Growing a Business/Raising a Family. Jan and Charlie Fletcher, eds. Seattle: NextStep Publications, 1988. This book addresses issues directly related to running a business and raising a family at the same time.

How to Discipline Your Six-to-Twelve-Year-Old ... Without Losing Your Mind. Jerry Wyckoff and Barbara C. Unell. New York: Doubleday, 1991. Includes many helpful lists of traits to be expected at each age.

In Praise of Single Parents: Mothers and Fathers Embracing the Challenge. Shoshana Alexander. New York: Houghton Mifflin Company, 1994. Practical, firsthand experiences of single parents and how they cope with the demands of raising their children on their own.

101 Things You Can Do for Our Children's Future. Richard Luv. New York: Anchor/Doubleday, 1994. This is an amazing book outlining 101 things we can do to create the world we want so much to create for our children and be the parents we so much want to be. Helps parents keep their lives in perspective. And discusses how we as parents can get support for our needs, too. Includes guidelines for selecting child care and setting up neighborhood co-op nurseries.

Parent Effectiveness Training. Thomas Gordon. See full citation in chapter 19. This is an excellent book for learning how to listen so that children will openly express what they really think and feel. It also teaches parents how to express their own needs so children will be more apt to listen than to tune out. Finally it provides guidelines for doing family problem-solving.

The Preschool Years. Ellen Galinsky and Judy David. New York: Ballantine, 1991. Galinsky and Davis offer a variety of ways to discipline preschoolers including specific language to elicit acceptable behaviors, keeping in mind that the average two- to four-year-old is pressured to change his or her behavior every six to eight minutes.

TA for Tots. Alvyn M. and Margaret Freed. Torrance, Calif.: Jalmar Press, 1991.

TA for Kids (and Parents Too). Alvyn M. and Margaret Freed. Torrance, Calif.: Jalmar Press, 1983.

TA for Teens. Alvyn M. and Margaret Freed. Torrance, Calif.: Jalmar Press, 1988. These three books are useful in helping children understand their own thoughts and feelings, the choices they have for how to express themselves, and a way to make sense of their reactions to parents, teachers, and peers. They provide the same basic information written specifically for each age group.

Teaching Children Self-Discipline at Home and School. Thomas Gordon. New York: Random House, 1989. New ways for parents to build self-control, self-esteem and self-reliance.

Parenting for the 21st Century. Carol Ann Ryser, Elaine Akin, Michael Ryser,

International Learning Centers, 5308 115th St., Kansas City, MO 64137; (816) 763-9165. This book is a short but excellent guide to understanding what behaviors are normal and problematic in children as well as the parenting skills needed for each stage of a child's development from birth through adolescence. There are guidelines for how parents can handle their own needs and feelings appropriately and still parent effectively.

Playful Parenting. Mark and Denise Weston. New York: Tarcher/Perigee, 1993. A wonderful guide for using constructive activities, humor, and fun to solve behavior problems and discipline.

You Can Say NO to Your Teenager. Jeanette Shalov, Irwin Solinger, Jules Sports, Phyllis Steinbrecher, and Douglas W. Thorpe. New York: Addison-Wesley, 1992. Five adolescent psychologists and counselors provide advice for handling recalcitrant teens that helps you understand why teenagers act the way they do and how you can reassert yourself without making matters worse.

Child Care Referral and Information Agencies

The National Association for Family Child Care, 725 15th Street, N.W., Ste. 505, Washington, DC 20005; (800) 359-3817 or (202) 347-3356. This association offers accreditation to day-care providers who meet their states' requirements and have been providing care in their own homes for eighteen months. It publishes an annual *National Directory of Family Day Care Providers.*

The National Association of Childcare Resource and Referral Agencies, in Rochester, Minn.; (507) 287-2020. (800) 462-1660.

The American Council of Nanny Schools, (517) 686-9417.

The International Nanny Association, (512) 454-6462.

Au Pair in America, 102 Greenwich Avenue, Greenwich, CT 06830; (800) 727-2437.

EurAuPair, 250 N. Coast Hwy., Laguna Beach, CA 92651; (800) 333-3804.

AuPairCare, 1 Post Street, Suite 700, San Francisco, CA 94104; (800) 4-Au-Pair.

E. F. Au Pair, 1 Memorial Drive, Cambridge, MA 02142.

Child Care Campaign, 330 7th Avenue, New York, NY 10001; (212) 239-0138. Publishes an information guide, *Care for Your Child: Making the Right Choice,* which you can obtain by sending a self-addressed stamped envelope.

NAPNAP Child Care Guide, by the National Association of Pediatric Nurse Associates and Practitioners. A free booklet provided by Lysol Products, P.O. Box 460, Westbury, NY 11592.

Child-Care Co-ops

A Parent's Guide to Child Care and Baby-sitting. Warm Lines, 492 Waltham Street, West Newton, MA 02165. A guide for establishing co-op, day-care, and baby-sitting clubs.

The Babysitting Co-op Guidebook. Patricia McManus, 915 N Fourth Street, Philadelphia, PA 19123.

Magazines

MOTHERS Resource Guide. P.O. 38, Milwaukee, WI 53172; (414) 762-8303. Published quarterly, this guide lists hundreds of support groups, publications, and resources to help mothers.

Hiring Child Care Kit

Nolo's Law Form Kit: Hiring Child Care & Household Help. Nolo Press Self-Help Law Books and Software, 950 Parker Street, Berkeley, CA 94710; (800) 992-6656.

CHAPTER
TWENTY-ONE
■■■■■■■■■■■■■■■■■■■■■■■■■■■■

Getting Help When You Need It

Most home businesses are one-person or husband-and-wife teams; however, many of us have come from salaried employment where we've been used to having a host of supportive office staff to rely upon. Some of us yearn to replace that support once we're on our own, while others of us are so self-sufficient and self-reliant we'd rather do everything ourselves. And although often the computer and other home-office equipment can do the work of one to two office personnel, in this age of information overload, even the jack-of-all-trades can become burdened by having to do everything without some additional help.

Certainly putting other people's efforts to work for you when you need help can extend your time, your money, and your peace of mind. So in working on our own, we each must somehow find a workable balance between being totally self-reliant or overdependent on the energies of others. Most people who work from home successfully ultimately do call upon the skills and talents of a variety of other people to help them get their work done. They build a network of local suppliers who can provide business supplies and services. They build a team of professionals who can be relied upon to handle legal, tax, insurance, and banking needs. They find support staff and personnel to help carry out the day-to-day operations of their work.

In this chapter we talk about how to identify the help you need, where to find it, and how to make the most of it.

When It's Time to Get Help

We recommend getting help from other people in four situations:

- When you don't have the skills and expertise yourself to do a job.
- When it will cost you more to do the job yourself than to hire someone else to do it.

- When the job can't be done by one person.
- When you hate doing a task, but it must be done.

Particularly at first, you may prefer to do most of the things that need to be done in your business yourself. Certainly the more you can do, the easier it will be to get under way. As a matter of fact, the desire to handle every facet of an enterprise is considered to be an attribute of successful entrepreneurs.

Here are some of the tasks that people working at home often dislike, can't do alone, or find more cost-effective to have done for them. Review the list for the ones that apply to your situation.

Accounting	Office management
Advertising	Printing
Answering the phone	Public relations
Assembly	Research
Bookkeeping	Shipping
Cleaning	Tax preparation
Delivery	Typesetting
Filing	Typing
Marketing	

There are usually some necessary tasks that you don't have the skills to carry out. Some of these skills, like typing, selling, and marketing, you can and probably should learn.

If you don't type, you may be tempted to hire a secretary or a service to do all your typing for you. Resist this temptation. Jeffery Lant, who trains others in how to establish a consultant practice, believes typing is a basic entrepreneurial skill that saves time and aggravation. We agree. You can still use a secretary or service when you want to. But costs mount up when you have to send every little note to a secretarial service and you lose out when you have to wait until Monday to get out an emergency letter.

Of course, the ability to type is essential to doing even rudimentary word processing, desktop publishing, and other computer keyboarding. In fact, in this day and age, a fast keyboard response can be as important as being able to think on your feet. And fortunately, with a personal computer, learning to type is easy because there are software programs like *Mavis Bacon Teaches Typing* you can use to teach yourself quickly and painlessly.

Other skills, like graphic design or accounting, may not be feasible for you to acquire. It's in these situations that you should hire the expertise you need. Studies, like the one done by Thorne Riddell, show that successful business owners recognize when they need professional assistance and get it.

When you first begin working on your own, you will probably have free time to do the majority of things involved in your business. Later, some of those things may no longer be cost-effective to do yourself. Writing and pasting-up a newsletter, for example, can be a good use of your time when you don't have much business. Once your workday is filled with business, paying someone else to do these tasks could actually cost you less.

You may also start out being able to handle all the business you can generate, but a sudden burst of seasonal activity or one big order may be more than you can handle alone. At this point, your choice is to hire help or turn away business. You may find yourself forced to act like Van Von Middlesworth, who has a sideline business producing hand-painted toy soldiers. For shows and special orders he has no problem producing what he needs, but when a large chain wanted a thousand soldiers during the Christmas season, he had to hire help to fill the order.

Finally, when there are tasks that you clearly dislike, neglect, or resist, it's very likely you can find others who are willing to do them. Finding someone else to assist you under these circumstances will undoubtedly make your life and your work pleasanter and have a positive effect on your enthusiasm. The time to get help with these tasks is when you see that help will free you to generate the business you need to cover the added expenses involved.

Six Sources for Getting the Help You Need

Working at home can present various roadblocks to getting the full range of help you need. Money certainly is one, since most people start working from home on a limited budget. Space is frequently another. The typical household can take only so much equipment and very few employees before it begins overflowing. Finally, finding the right people to do the work under home-office circumstances can also become a problem. But none of these obstacles is insurmountable. Here are six workable alternatives to doing everything yourself.

Using Business Services

The service section of our economy is growing rapidly. With the increasing number of services available for small businesses, you will be able to purchase many of the services you need without hiring any employees.

Printing services are available in most neighborhoods. In addition to standard printing and duplicating, many of these shops offer artwork, layout, typesetting, proofreading, and design. You can also use secretarial services, bookkeeping services, answering services, messenger services, cleaning services, and research services, to mention just a few. Many of these services are home businesses themselves.

In our neighborhood, we have been able to create a network of small home businesses with whom we trade. Our artist, cartoonist, audio technician, and typesetter all operate home businesses in our area. It's like having our own organization, without the cost of an office building for the workers or the ongoing overhead of employing them.

By purchasing services, you pay only for what you need when you need it. And since businesses that don't provide a good service won't be able to stay in business, they're likely to want to please and stand behind their work.

Because these businesses have overhead to support, you will pay more per hour or per task than if you hired your own employee. You may also have to wait until a service can get to your work. Then sometimes, just when you need them most, they're too busy to help. The service will improve, however, if you become a regular customer. And the better a customer you become, the more willing they will be to extend themselves and help you out in emergencies.

You can locate services through your local business Yellow Pages, the Chamber of Commerce, or networking groups. Once you find a service, try it out for a while. Then, if you're satisfied, keep using the same service so they'll pay special attention to you.

Hiring and Contracting for the Help You Need

When you need someone to come in and work with you shoulder to shoulder, hiring help is usually going to be the answer, and here are several different ways you can go about doing it.

Full-time employees. If you hire the right full-time employee, you have a loyal and hardworking person you can count on day in and day out to get the job done for you. Such employees are worth their weight in gold and may be the answer to ensuring that you'll have the help you need.

However, the primary reasons most people choose to work from home are to keep their overhead low and to simplify their working life. Hiring employees may deprive you of some of these benefits. There are the direct payroll costs to consider, and unless you have enough work for a full-time person, you may find the employee with nothing to do and yourself manufacturing something to keep him or her busy.

The decision as to when to add full-time personnel, therefore, is one of timing and personal goals. If you hire prematurely, you threaten your financial peace of mind because, remember, the hired help gets paid first! On the other hand, if you postpone hiring needed help, you may lose business. And sometimes that's a choice we must make. There are people who would prefer to stay smaller than add the responsibility and pressure of "meeting payroll."

One consultant told us, "At first I enjoyed having my own secretary. It made me feel like an executive, but paying her monthly salary really put me behind the eight ball. I had to support someone else before I could support myself! Finally I decided to let her go and hire a secretarial service. It felt like someone had taken a weight off my shoulders."

In addition, you have to provide work space, equipment, and supplies for your employee. Unless you plan to rent separate space, this means you will have another person coming into your home every day. In some areas this can present a problem with zoning. Certain municipalities allow home businesses, but prohibit having employees on the property.

Finally, as C.P.A. Bernard Kamoroff points out in his book *The Small-Time Operator*, "Hiring employees will just about double the amount of your paperwork." When you become an employer, you must keep separate payroll records, withhold federal income and Social Security taxes, withhold state income and possibly state disability taxes, prepare quarterly and year-end payroll tax returns, pay the employee's portion of Social Security taxes and unemployment taxes, usually purchase workers' compensation insurance, and prepare year-end earnings statements for each employee.

You will also need to familiarize yourself with state and federal regulations

Legal Checklist for Hiring an Employee

State and federal regulations for hiring employees vary according to the number of employees and/or the nature of your business. This checklist of issues to address is from *The Hiring and Firing Book: The Complete Legal Guide for Employers*, by Steven Mitchell, which provides detailed information about each of these issues. When hiring an employee, you can also check with state agencies and your attorney to determine how and when these government laws and regulations apply to you.

Hiring and Firing Practices
These and other laws define what you can and cannot do in advertising, setting job requirements and job descriptions, screening and selecting job applicants, making a job offer, and terminating an employee:

- Americans with Disabilities Act
- The Civil Rights Act
- Immigration Reform and Control Act
- Fair Debt Credit and Reporting Act
- Wage and Hour Regulations

Benefits, Financial Considerations, and On-the-Job Policies
The following laws and regulations affect your day-to-day operating practices including such things as holidays, vacations, wages and salaries, overtime, privacy, draws and advances, personal liability, and privacy:

- Social Security Tax and Federal Income Tax Withholding
- Federal Unemployment Taxes
- State Withholding
- State Disability Insurance
- State Unemployment Insurance
- Workers' Compensation Insurance
- Employee Benefit Plans (ERISA)
- Federal and Health Insurance Requirements
- Employee Safety and Health Regulations
- Fair Labor Standards Act (FLSA)
- Older Workers' Benefit Protection Act
- The Sherman Anti-Trust Act

regarding such things as minimum-wage laws, fair-employment practices, employee benefits including health insurance and unemployment insurance, and the federal disability act. (For a checklist of these issues, see the box above.) The cost of these requirements has been estimated to add 30 percent to the salary you pay an employee.

Once you set up a system for managing the complexities of having one or more employees, these administrative details will be much less formidable than they seem at first. Handling the excess paperwork is a task you can even pay others to do. Or you can always get a payroll service to manage many of the formalities involved in having employees, although you will still be legally responsible for your employees.

Our advice is to consider some of the other alternatives we'll be discussing before you decide to hire. Then when full-time employees are your best answer, consult your attorney and your accountant for help in setting up the easiest and most workable arrangements for handling the responsibilities of being an employer.

Part-time employees. Although hiring part-time employees may pose some of the same problems as full-time workers do, many home-based businesses opt for part-timers, either to save costs or because several part-time employees can do a variety of specialized tasks that no one person could do alone.

Career consultant Marilyn Miller, for example, has three part-time employees. A secretary works three days a week typing, filing, and returning phone calls. A training assistant accompanies Marilyn to seminars and workshops to manage all the on-site logistical arrangements. And she has a research assistant who does library work for her. None of these employees can do the jobs of the others.

Hiring part-time employees also helps meet short-term high-volume demands. For example, Paul and Gretchen Fava rented a warehouse and hired seventy part-time workers to achieve the high buildup of inventory needed to fill orders for their hand-painted Christmas decorations. After reaching the inventory level they wanted, they returned to the renovated guest house

Employee Fringe Benefits and Personnel Policies

When you have employees, you need to determine the fringe benefits you will offer and establish policies for managing them. Common fringe benefits that employees may expect are listed below:

- Health insurance
- Disability income insurance
- Life insurance
- Paid holidays
- Vacations
- Sick leave
- A retirement plan

Written personnel policies covering the following issues are also advisable:

- Working hours
- Lunch hour
- Job description
- Breaks
- Absences from work
- Probationary period
- Termination
- Payroll schedule
- Confidentiality
- Tardiness

behind their home where they maintain their inventory with the help of only a handful of part-time college students.

Independent contractors. Many people prefer to hire independent contractors for specific tasks and pay on a fee-for-service basis. Independent contractors are self-employed individuals who usually work for more than one client. An independent researcher, for example, will work on projects for various clients and charge individually for each task.

As Bob Baxter's business, Pet Organics, grew from twenty-four accounts to five hundred, he decided to expand by using independent contractors. Instead of mixing, bottling, and preparing to ship his natural flea treatments in his garage, he now contracts with someone to produce, bottle, and ship the products for him. Instead of calling on only those retail stores he could visit himself, he has contracted with independent salespeople to represent his line to retailers.

Rather than hire an administrative assistant, consultant Thomas Kerr has contracted with someone who provides a range of administrative services for him and several other clients. Kerr describes the primary advantage he finds in contracting. "I prefer this arrangement because I can call on the assistance when I need it, which is maybe once or twice a quarter when I have a special project to get out."

As these examples illustrate, using contractors can help you control costs. Also, contractors generally provide their own facilities, supplies, and equipment. Another advantage is that using contractors provides you with the flexibility to find the best services possible for the specific task. Being small-business operators themselves, independent contractors may have a keen understanding of your needs as a small business too. They face many of the same issues you do and may, in fact, work at home.

Since an independent contractor is not an employee, you do not have to withhold taxes, pay employment taxes, or file payroll tax returns for this kind of help. When you pay an independent contractor over $600 a year, you do, however, have to file IRS Form 1099 with the Internal Revenue Service and send a copy to the individual.

A word of caution. Do not think that you can simply employ someone and call him or her an "independent contractor." The IRS position is that if the person is an employee, the label you give that employee doesn't matter. In other words, to the Internal Revenue Service, an employee by any other name is still an employee. To help you understand exactly who is and who isn't an employee, the IRS puts out a free publication, *Circular E-Employer's Tax Guide*. We have summarized these points on pages 253–258 in chapter 10.

The disadvantage of using independent contractors is that *your* work may not be their first priority. They may not be available when you want them. There may be delays in getting your work done while they work for others. Also, independent contractors only become knowledgeable about your business needs if you use them frequently. They may fail to produce work done the way you want it, but unless you have a contract that covers this possibility, you may have little practical recourse other than to go elsewhere.

Technical writer David Treweek learned this the hard way. He hired two freelance writers to assist him in completing a large contract. Coordination with their busy schedules was difficult, then one writer got bogged down in personal problems that nearly resulted in a business disaster. The writer submitted incompleted work directly to the client and charged Treweek for the work that hadn't been done. Only some fast talking saved the contract. He fired the writer and will be more careful in the future to screen those he subcontracts with. So if you are planning to hire independent contractors, get and check out references and spell out procedures, deadlines, and work to be done in clear written agreements. Also consider using contractors for small, less-important jobs before trusting them with larger and more vital work.

Temporary-help agencies. For certain short-term assistance, you can hire help through a temporary service. Temporary services are primarily limited to secretarial and office management personnel. On the other hand, these agencies have the advantage of being able to provide you with reliable help quickly, without your spending the time and money to locate and select someone. The agency handles all financial arrangements with the employee and bills you for the service. The agency also stands behind the work. The cost is usually somewhat higher than using an independent contractor, and you cannot depend upon getting the same person again.

Employee leasing companies. One way to have employees while saving yourself the paperwork and legal responsibility of being an employer is to lease employees from a staffing company. Doctors and dentists have been using these services for years. You maintain substantial control over the employee, except that if the worker assigned you must be fired, you send the employee back to the staffing company instead of releasing the person yourself. For managing all the legal and administrative responsibilities of your staff, you pay the leasing company a fee over and above the cost of the employees' earnings and benefits each month.

Where to Find Help

To find employees, independent contractors, and employment services, you can use:

■ *Telephone Yellow Pages*. Various kinds of employment services are listed under "Employment." Independent contractors are listed by field—for example, word-processing services. They usually have one-line listings under their own names.

■ *College placement offices*. Students seeking part-time work or contracting out their services are often listed with these offices.

■ *Referrals from associates*. Associates are good sources of information about independent contractors they have been satisfied with. Part-time employees of associates may also be looking for additional work.

■ *Chambers of Commerce*. Temporary services, contract staff firms, and independent contractors in your area may be members of the local chamber. Also, other members may have used services they can recommend.

■ *Networking groups*. Networking groups are formal and informal meetings of independent businesspeople who come together weekly for the purpose of referring business to one another. In chapter 17 we recommend that home-based business owners join at least one such networking group for marketing and affiliation purposes. Finding reliable support services is another excellent reason for participating in such a group. As you get to know the individuals in your group, you may find that using their services can be a highly reliable source of support.

■ *Classified ads in local newspapers or specialty newsletters.* Often neighborhood papers or trade papers are more helpful in locating the people or services you need than are larger metropolitan papers. Read the ads under "Business Services" and "Positions Wanted." Sometimes local papers even feature articles on local independent businesses.

You can also place ads for the assistance you want, but screen applicants by phone or mail and check their references before giving them your address or having them come to your home. Usually you can make arrangements to have applicants forward information through the newspaper.

■ *Community, business, and computer bulletin boards.* Read the bulletin boards at banks, community centers, grocery stores, laundromats, print shops, and libraries. Often home businesses and independent contractors will post their cards or flyers in these places. Also scan computer bulletin boards like Compu-Serve.

Bartering or Exchanging Arrangements

Barter is a cashless exchange of services that some home businesspeople find useful for getting the assistance or the products they need. You offer your services to someone who needs them in exchange for their services to you. Barbara Elman, publisher of *Word Processing News*, has a barter arrangement with her answering service. They answer her phone; she does their mailing labels each month on her word processor.

Barter obviously reduces your costs or enables you to have assistance you could otherwise not afford. However, it may be difficult to find the appropriate person to trade services or products with. Barter clubs enable you to overcome this problem. They keep a credit balance for you, so if you offer a service to one member, you get credit to receive services from any other member. These clubs often require a considerable start-up fee, though, and may or may not have the business services you need in your area.

To barter for services on your own, take the initiative and ask people who offer the work you need whether they are willing to barter. You may be surprised at how many people will consider it.

Marilyn Miller, for example, was surprised to discover that she could barter to have color slides made for her management-training presentations. When she realized she would need slides of higher quality than those she was presently using, to accompany a planned fee increase, she decided to approach an audio/video service about training its staff in exchange for a set of top-quality four-color slides. They said "yes!" So go ahead and ask. You may be surprised at the response.

Another home-business owner has arranged a unique exchange with her printer. She shopped around until she found a printer who would give a good price. Then when she has printing done, she asks the printer to invoice the client directly but mark up his price by a 15 percent referral fee. The cumulated 15 percent fees are applied to future printing jobs she has done.

In addition to individually arranged barter agreements, there are over five hundred barter exchange networks in the U.S. offering virtually every possible personal and business service. Most barter networks charge a fee to join and a commission on each transaction, which is split between the two parties. Some networks also charge a monthly fee. The advantage of such an exchange is that you can collect barter credits so you don't need to locate someone who needs your service in order to take advantage of theirs. As a designer, for example, you might provide design services for an ad agency in the network and then use your barter credit to have your printing done by a printer who belongs to the network.

When bartering, make a clear agreement as to the value of the services you are exchanging and evaluate the trustworthiness and experience of those you barter with, just as you would when purchasing the service. As with all contracts, you're best protected against misunderstanding by putting the agreement in writing.

The IRS considers business services received through bartering as income, and business services you provide through bartering as deductible business expenses. So keep records of your exchanges, and make sure the values you claim represent actual market rates.

Affiliating with Others

Affiliating with others whose skills support and supplement yours can be another way to find the help you need. There are at least three different ways you can affiliate.

Calling on customers and clients. Explore the possibilities of using or buying the services of companies for whom you are working. These companies may be glad to see you purchase services like word processing or duplicating to help offset their overhead costs. They may even be willing to let you use company services without charge, or as part of the fee they're paying you.

Sharing expenses or efforts. Pooling expenses with colleagues or competitors can provide you with help you might not otherwise be able to afford. Two women we interviewed share a secretary, each employing her part-time. Other home businesses are using what's called co-op advertising, in which several of them share the costs of advertising their related products and services.

Peggy Glenn found she could call on her competitors to take overload work from her typing service and, in turn, she gladly provided backup for them. Lynne Frances found she could share certain expenses with an owner of another cleaning service, and they assist each other when short on cleaning crews.

Joint ventures. By entering into joint ventures with others who have skills or expertise you need, you can accomplish much that would be impossible to do yourself. In a joint venture, you affiliate with others to provide a service or produce a product, and then share together in any profits. No one individual has to make a large cash investment. Each invests primarily his or her own time and talents. But everyone involved benefits when the venture is successful.

A professional development consultant we know arranges joint ventures on all the training films he produces. He writes the material and joins with others who produce the film and still others who market it. They all share an agreed-upon percentage of the profits on the finished films.

Since partners are often investing their time without payment or at a reduced fee, a joint venture usually becomes a side venture. Locating dedicated and honest partners is therefore crucial. You have to rely on their conduct and efforts for the success of your project. Legally, joint ventures are partnerships. This means you will be liable for anything your partners do in relation to the project. Having a written contract or partnership agreement is a necessary safeguard.

The best way to locate people interested in sharing expenses or joint-venturing is through professional or trade associations in your field, networking, and relationships with competitors or other businesses that complement yours.

Getting Assistance from Family Members

Using family members to do jobs that need to be done provides an opportunity for them to share in your work and is a way for you to limit your expenses. You can ask for volunteers or you can offer wages.

Hiring your children has a tax advantage too. When you hire your children to work for you, their salaries are a deductible business expense, while their earnings are taxed at a much lower rate than yours. In fact, there is no tax for earnings below a certain amount each year.

The disadvantage is that family members can be unreliable workers. Sometimes they don't want to help or may be too busy doing other things to follow through for you. Other times family squabbles spill over into work activities, and vice versa. So when you hire a family member or ask your family for free assistance, we recommend that it be strictly a voluntary matter rather than something you expect, coerce, or finagle someone into doing.

Calling on Employers or Contractors

If you are salaried, working on a commission, or under a contract, explore the services your employer or contractor can provide for you. At-home workers are still a relatively new phenomenon. Companies are not always aware of their needs. So express your needs and ask for support.

If you are working with a franchise or are in direct sales, explore with the franchiser or the direct-selling organization what additional support services they can furnish you with. Different companies offer different levels of assistance. Many provide extensive training, promotional materials, and displays. If you are working under a contract, contractors are often more than happy to let you use their facilities and support services when doing so helps reduce the expense of the contract or improves the quality of the project.

Making the Most of the Help You Get

Whatever type of help you use, there are several guidelines you can follow to ensure a top-quality job.

Clearly define what you want done. First, before you even decide on the type of help you want, define precisely what you need someone to do. We suggest writing or sketching it out. Sometimes you have to do some research to find out what you actually need.

Producing the covers for some tape albums we created was a good example. Originally we thought it would be a simple process. But before we hired a printer, we decided to talk with several to find out what it would involve. There turned out to be many different ways of doing it, and having reviewed the choices we were in a much better position to hire a printer with experience in the process we preferred.

Find the right people. Finding the right people is usually a matter of looking carefully at past experience and present capabilities. Getting referrals from a satisfied customer in your field is probably the best way. When that isn't possible, getting—*and checking*—references or looking at examples of past work can help provide the information you need.

In talking with prospective help, raise the problems and concerns you have in relation to the work you're hiring for. If you're under a tight deadline, for example, express your concern that it be done in time. If you need the worker to take certain precautions when dealing with customers, explain what they are. Then listen and watch the person respond. Does he have solutions? Is she confident about handling the situations you present?

Don't assume the help you get knows what you want. We discovered the hard way that just because people are good at what they do doesn't mean they know how to do what you want. Be specific. Draw sketches. Write out a list. Bring in samples. Define the end product with care and monitor the progress. Have checkpoints to look at, or talk with workers about the progress they're making. Consider hiring someone for a small job and reviewing the work before hiring that person for larger or more important projects.

Hiring a typesetter to set copy for a flyer is a good example of this process. Writing out the correctly spelled text is only the beginning. Don't leave the typesetter with the job of deciding on layout, size, and style of type unless you're willing to take potluck. Specify your preferences. If you do not know enough to be specific, ask for the typesetter's recommendations and a sample of what the piece would look like. Then ask to see the way the copy will look before it is finalized.

Set deadlines. Set deadlines for when the work is to be completed and get the worker's agreement that it will be completed by that time. To be on the safe side, call or talk with the person along the way to see if things are on schedule. The more notice you have of problems, the easier it is to revise your plans.

Get an understanding about what will be done if work isn't satisfactory. The best policy, of course, is to expect the person will stand behind the work and redo it if it isn't right. You do not have to accept less than the quality you wanted, providing you were clear about what you were expecting in the first place.

Also identify who will pay for costs incurred from mistakes. After one costly error, private practice consultant Gene Call now negotiates with all the designers he uses to ensure that if the mailings they design for him don't meet U.S. Postal Service requirements, the designers will be liable for the resulting cost. Added postage on 100,000 mailings, because the piece was oversize, is an expensive error. And more than once a designer has had to pay the extra bill.

Treat the people you hire like people. We've found that when we are considerate, thoughtful, and understanding of the people we hire, they go out of their way to do a better job. Greeting those who work for you, complimenting them when they're helpful, and listening to the concerns they raise are part of the honey that sweetens any business relationship. One sympathetic word that shows you understand the pressures or difficulties can win you work that goes above and beyond the call of duty.

Pay on time. The best way to have people begin dragging their feet or doing less than their best on your job is to delay or overlook payment you owe. Pay immediately in accordance with whatever arrangements you have established.

Reward good work. Reward good work with praise, repeat business, and referrals. Under whatever arrangements people work for you, they generally appreciate recognition for a job well done. Giving it to them is a way of increasing their desire to please you again and again.

With the variety of possible arrangements you can make for getting help, you should be able to find whatever support you need while working from home. Whenever you want assistance, you can review the options we've discussed for getting the help you need, and then use the strategies given to make the most of the help you get.

Resources

Books

Small-Time Operator. See full citation under chapter 14.
The Hiring and Firing Book: The Complete Legal Guide for Employers. Steven Mitchell, Legal Strategies, Inc., 1795 Harvard Avenue, Merrick, NY 11566; (516) 377-3940. (800) ALL-BOOKS.
Selling Through Independent Reps. Harold Novick (see chapter 23 for full citation).

Newsletters and Periodicals

Barter News. P.O. Box 3024, Mission Viejo, CA 92690; (714) 831-0607.
Internal Revenue Service (see chapter 3 for full citation): **Employers Tax Guide**, Circular E.

Trade Associations

The International Reciprocal Trade Association. 101 Channel Terrace, Falls Church, VA; (703) 237-1828. For information on how bartering can benefit your business and to identify barter exchanges in your area, send a self-addressed, stamped envelope.

PART 6

Getting Business and Growing

CHAPTER
TWENTY-TWO
■■■■■■■■■■■■■■■■■■■■■■■■■■■■

Pricing: Determining What to Charge

On our way to teach a marketing seminar, we stopped at this out-of-the-way service station/general store/post office where an ol' boy in bib overalls asked us what we were doing all dressed up in three-piece suits. When we told him we'd stopped to get a soda on our way to give a marketing seminar he said, "Boys, I'm gonna tell you all you need to know about marketing in three sentences. You got to know what your stuff costs. You got to know what you can sell it for. And you got to learn to live on the difference.

—TIM ROONEY, MARKETING CONSULTANT

"What shall I charge?" This is one of the most common questions prospective home-based business owners ask at our seminars. If you've ever read anything about pricing or attended a seminar on pricing, you've undoubtedly discovered the question is not so much "What shall I charge?" as "How do I determine what to charge?"

Although you'll encounter a wide variety of "formulas" set forth confidently by business experts, in reality there is no simple answer to what to charge. Even veteran businesspeople often find themselves wondering if they're missing sales by charging too much, or if they could get away with charging even more. That's why the range of advice novice entrepreneurs receive about pricing is often enough to make their heads spin. Here are a few examples of the type of advice we've been given:

"Set your price so low that they can't refuse."
"Never discount your prices."
"Charge the going rate."
"Charge just below the going rate."
"Charge just above the going rate."

"Add up your direct costs, overhead, and profit and that's your price."

"Find out what everyone else charges and position yourself in the middle."

Does this sound familiar? Now add to this conflicting advice what Sonny Blain found out—there may not *be* a "going rate." When Sonny set out to research what to charge for hypercard programming he found programmers who were charging as little as $30 an hour and others who were charging over $100 an hour, and almost every amount in between. So how *do* you know what to charge? The answer is that you don't *know* what to charge, you *discover* what to charge.

Pricing, like marketing, is an experiment. It's like cooking without a recipe. You're balancing many sensitive factors and adjusting the combinations until you get one that suits the palates of your customers. Like diners choosing a restaurant, some customers want a no-frills cafeteria while others prefer only an elite tearoom or a trendy bistro.

In this chapter we want to provide you with a guide to various elements you can consider in determining your own ideal pricing recipe. You'll learn from the experience of many successful home-based businesses how to avoid the most common mistakes open-collar workers make in pricing their services, and discover how taking the time and energy to find the right price can be a key to your success.

Begin with Some Basic Research

Occasionally, the price of a particular home-based product or your service is driven, like the price of hamburgers or gasoline, pretty much by the marketplace. Clothing merchandising consultant Martina Polaski's specialty is such a business. "All the manufacturers pay the same thing for what I do. It's the rock-bottom price. They know what they can get it for and that's that." Under such circumstances, pricing is a matter of finding out how you can run your business successfully at the prevailing price.

Most home-based ventures, however, tend to be more personalized and customized by nature. This means you probably won't be unduly constrained by what someone else is charging. More likely you'll have a great deal of flexibility, as we described above. Therefore, to find the right price, you need to begin by doing some investigation to determine the following:

1. How much is your product or your service really worth in concrete terms? Value, like beauty, is in the mind of the beholder. It's highly subjective. The value people place on what you offer will vary according to their needs and their perceptions of what your product or service will do for them. So the more concrete you can make the value of your work, the easier it will be to determine your price, and then get it.

Here are several ways to concretize the value of what you offer. Can someone get this product or service elsewhere? How much are they paying now? What would they have to pay someone else? Does your product or service save or produce money for your customer? For example, if you're supplying dried-flower gift baskets to local hospitals, the hospitals save the costs of having them shipped in from out of the area. Or, if hiring you to design a direct-mail campaign will generate $25,000 of income for your client, you could be a bargain at $5,000.

When the benefits of your business are more intangible in nature, think in terms of how much they are worth relative to other things people buy. For example, people might spend $50 for an entertaining evening at the theater. Paying $50 to attend your evening workshop on real-estate investing, however, could be profitable and might even be entertaining. Parents might pay $65 or more for a pair of sports shoes for their junior highschooler, but paying you that for two tutoring sessions could help their child catch up in math.

2. What will people actually pay? No matter how much a product or service may be worth, if people won't pay that much for it, it won't sell. A good example of this problem is Carol Hartager's beautiful hand-painted greeting cards. Since they could each easily be framed as a work of art, she thought $10 was a fair retail price. Greeting-card store buyers didn't agree. They thought $10 was too much. When Carol placed them on consignment in a local store, she discovered that the customers thought so too. They didn't sell until she had reduced the price to $3.

So perception of value can be as important as the actual value. If the customer perceives the price as too high, you'll end up without work or with a garage full of inventory. At the other extreme, if buyers perceive something as too cheap, they either won't buy it or they'll worry about what the "catch" is. Many new entrepreneurs are surprised to discover they can actually sell more by charging more. A book, for example, that wasn't selling at $19.95 sold briskly when repackaged as a workbook at $99.95; a particular software package sold much better at $69.95 than it did at $30.00.

So don't rely on your own perceptions of what people will pay. Your perceptions are limited by your particular upbringing and experience, and may be outdated or at least different from those of your market. Find out what your clients and customers are accustomed to paying and match your price to their expectations.

Shirley Glickman learned this the hard way. As a teacher, she knew what public school systems paid for outside consultants. So when she left her teaching job to conduct values-clarification workshops for corporate training departments, she set her fees based on her experience in the school system—and had a lot of trouble closing sales! Prospective clients seemed interested until she mentioned her fee. Then their interest cooled. She feared her price was too high. By asking around at professional associations for trainers, however, she was amazed to discover that companies were used to paying almost double her fee for outside consultants. With such cut-rate fees, they weren't taking her seriously. When she raised her prices to what was expected, she closed sales.

Underpricing is one of the most frequent mistakes home-based businesses make. So as desktop publisher Matt McCaffrey advises, "Don't sell yourself short—I landed a typesetting contract recently at a rate 35 percent above the prevailing wage in my area because I valued my time appropriately and was firm in my requirements."

Programmer Kristi Wachter agrees. She says, "I still feel weird telling people I'm charging $75 an hour when this little voice in my head keeps reminding me of all the jobs I've worked on at a salary of $5 an hour. But companies are used to paying this kind of money for the consulting help they need. And remember, they're paying for all the time you've put in to develop the expertise you have. You are not an employee any longer, you're supporting yourself. No one's paying for your coffee breaks, benefits, or anything else."

Marketing consultant John Elmer, writing for *Marketing News*, takes a three-pronged approach to marketing. Elmer points out that each aspect of pricing serves a different purpose:

1. Calculating your costs simply sets a baseline that enables you to determine if you can offer a product or service profitably.

2. Ascertaining what your competition is charging orients you to what your marketplace has been paying and will consider to be a fair price.

3. Determining what your customers or clients would "expect" to pay for what you're offering helps you avoid turning off your buyer with a price that's too high to be "worth it" or too low to be "worth anything." It can tell you when you can raise your prices or explain why sales have not been as brisk as you expected.

Elmer suggests using a research technique called PSM (Pricing Sensitivity Measurement) to gather the data you would need to let your marketplace set your prices. Using the PSM method, you have prospective buyers read a product description accompanied with pictures, samples, or diagrams. You then present them with a pricing scale starting with $0 up to fifteen to thirty possible prices. Prospective buyers use the scale to indicate at which point they would consider the product or service to be too "expensive" for them to buy on the one end and too "cheap" to be considered of high enough quality on the other end.

The result is a price range in which people will perceive value without "sticker shock."

3. *Are you charging enough to make this worth your while?* You can make a million dollars but if it costs you more than a million to make a million, you've lost money. As graphics designer Todd Minor found out, making money can be deceptive. He had two major contracts his first year in business that produced over a quarter of a million dollars. Things seemed to be rolling along. But by year's end, he was in debt. In his eagerness to be the low bidder on these contracts, he had unknowingly run his company into a hole.

So in setting your prices, make sure you'll have more coming in than you have going out. That means charging a price that covers your direct and indirect costs with some to spare. In fact, a commonly used pricing formula is:

$$\textit{direct costs} + \textit{overhead} + \textit{profit} = \textit{price}$$

Direct costs refers to costs you incur as a direct result of producing your product or providing your service. For example, if you are doing word processing, the paper you print the job out on is a direct cost. If you provide a mobile computer-repair service, the cost of driving to your customer's office is a direct cost. So is the cost of any parts you replace for them. If you are doing public relations, costs of telephone calls you make to book a client on out-of-town talk shows is a direct cost as is the cost of printing and mailing media kits on their behalf. And so is the time you spend on these projects!

Yes, your time is a direct cost. For purposes of doing business, you have to factor in the cost of your time as if you were an employee of your business. For the single-person service business, your time is all you have to sell. You can't make any more money than you can bill out. For example, as a psychotherapist, you only have so many hours a week in which to see clients. As a trainer, you only have so many days a month on which you can train people. Even if your business is manufacturing a product, your time is a labor cost.

To determine what to charge for your time, consider what you would have to pay if you had to hire someone with your background and experience to do what you do. Or if you are doing the same thing as you did on your last job, calculate your salary *including the fringe benefits* into your current rates. Many new home-based business owners underprice themselves by leaving out the value of their time or by forgetting to include the cost of their fringe benefits when calculating their fees. Also remember you can't possibly bill out every hour of the business week. Some portion of your time must be spent marketing and administering your business. So you have to set the cost of your billable time high enough to compensate you for your time that isn't billable.

Overhead refers to all the costs of being in and doing business that are not directly attributable to a specific product or service, whether or not you have any business. For example, the cost of your computer equipment, your software, utilities, office supplies, an 800 number, advertising and marketing costs, tax preparer's and attorney's fees, even bank charges and other administrative costs, are all overhead costs. Everything you must spend to stay in business counts as overhead.

At first, of course, you may not know what your overhead is, but you can estimate those costs you are aware of. Also you can go to the library to consult books such as *Annual Statement Studies* by Robert Morris Associates, Dun & Bradstreet's *Industry Norms and Key Business Ratios*, Prentice Hall's *Almanac of Business and Industry Financial Ratios*, and *Business Profitability Data* from Weybridge Publishing Company for a review of industry norms. In doing interviews for our book *Best Home Businesses for the 90s*, we discovered that most home businesses do not know precisely what their overhead is, and that average overhead ranged roughly from 20 to 30 percent of income. Standard for larger businesses is from two and a half to three and a half times the wage rate, but home businesses can usually beat that. Some tell us they multiply their hourly wage by 2.6.

Sometimes people have difficulty distinguishing between overhead and direct costs. The simplest explanation we've found is that overhead relates to costs you have when you're in business, whether you have any customers or clients or not. Direct costs, however, are costs that you incur the moment you start to provide a product or service to a client or customer.

Examples of Direct Costs:

Your salary
Consultant fees
Travel and transportation costs
Telephone calls on the project
Copies made for the project
Materials used for the project
Postage used for the project
Outside services
Special supplies required

Examples of Overhead:

Office supplies and equipment
Marketing costs
Basic business telephone service
Utilities
Business taxes
Vacation, holidays and sick
   leave
Pension fund and retirement
Health insurance

Profit is any money that's left over after you pay all your direct and indirect expenses. Many business experts advise adding 15 to 20 percent or more to your price over and above all your costs. This is considered your reward for the risk you take to be in business or as an allowance for development. Many home-based businesspeople, however, do not include profit in calculating their prices. Often this is because they aren't aware they could be adding in profit or because they fear that to survive they must cut their prices to a bare minimum. Others, however, feel that being self-employed is more a benefit than a risk. They reason that if they have charged adequately for their time, they're being compensated sufficiently. Viewed this way, profit is more like a tip. It's what you get because you haven't paid yourself enough.

You can use costing or spreadsheet software to experiment with various scenarios until you find your best possible price. Of course, you won't know how much you can really charge until you actually take your product or service out into the marketplace. The feedback you get there will guide you as to the changes you need to make. You may be able to charge more than you imagined, or you may find that you have to adjust your costs so you can lower your price.

Ultimately, the important thing in setting your price is that one way or another you are earning enough to provide yourself with a comfortable enough lifestyle to make running your business well worth the effort. If you can't command such a price, then you should rethink your business choice.

4. Can I make more money doing a little for a lot or a lot for a little? And how much volume do you want? Often pricing requires that you face directly just how you want to structure your business, how much you want to work, and what type of role you want to play in your business. If you want to make $65,000 a year as a psychotherapist, for example, you could see twenty people a week for $65 each. Or you could see thirteen people a week for $100 each. Or you could have five groups of about twelve people each, who pay $25 apiece each week. Which would be easier and more cost effective: getting sixty people who would pay $25 each, or finding thirteen people who will pay $100 a week?

If you are a public speaker and want to make $100,000 a year, you could give just one speech a week if you charged about $2,000 a speech. Whereas if you could only get $1,000 a speech you would have to give two speeches a week in order to make your goal. How much effort will it take you to book that many speeches? How much will it cost?

If you have a pool-cleaning service and charge $50 a month, you can serve sixty clients yourself and make $3,000 a month. Or you can hire, train, and supervise three employees and pay them $25 a client. Then, by keeping your fee the same, you could serve 180 clients and make $4,500 a month. Which work style and lifestyle would suit you better—the challenge of supervising three employees for a possible additional $1,500 per month, or the quiet satisfaction of working for yourself?

Fee Setting Work Sheet or Spreadsheet

Use this sheet to gather the information you need in order to set your fees.

Yearly salary: enter your amount

Yearly salary you want to earn	_____
Days per week you wish to work	_____
Billable hours worked per day	_____
Days worked per year	_____

Expenses: enter your amount

Operating overhead	Monthly	Yearly
Marketing	_____	_____
Travel	_____	_____
Legal costs	_____	_____
Insurance	_____	_____
Postage	_____	_____
Repairs	_____	_____
Supplies	_____	_____
Taxes and licenses	_____	_____
Travel costs	_____	_____
Telephone	_____	_____
Utilities	_____	_____
Other	_____	_____
Total expenses	_____	

Desired profit %	_____

Calculations:
Salary + Expenses + Profit ÷ days or hours worked =

Daily rate	_____
Hourly rate	_____

Pricing Products versus Pricing Services

Although many of the principles are the same whether you're pricing a product or a service, some factors involved in pricing a product differ from those involved in pricing a service. Many service businesses, for example, have very few costs of doing business, but when you sell a product, it invariably involves paying for your product up front and keeping an inventory on hand. On the other hand, products hold the potential for *passive income*—that is, income that comes to you whether you're working or not. In providing a service, your income is directly wed to how many hours you can work. If you're ill or take a vacation, there's no income. And unless you add employees and the added costs they bring, you can only reasonably work some fixed number of hours a week. Products, of course, can be selling while you sleep. All these factors have implications for setting your prices.

A Handy Formula for Pricing a Product

In pricing a product, you'll need to attend to manufacturing costs, setting wholesale versus retail prices, and providing for markups and discounts. The following is a formula many home-based businesses use to set an initial price for their products:

total material costs + overhead + minimum profit + retail margin = retail price

The reactions you get from this initial price can allow you to make the adjustments you need to find the optimum price you can command. For additional information on pricing a product, we recommend reading *Homemade Money*, by Barbara Brabec, listed at the end of this chapter in the Resources list.

Pricing Your Service

In setting fees for your service, you'll need to consider whether you want to charge by the hour, the day, the project, the piece, or the head. Whichever alternative you use, here are several formulas home-based consultants and service businesses have used to set their fees. Experiment with those that would be most appropriate for your industry.

1. Find out what other consultants in the field are charging or what your potential clients are now paying or expecting to pay and price your services accordingly. For example, if you are a copywriter and other copywriters in the area are charging between $60 and $75 an hour, you might test pricing your services at $65 an hour.

2. Figure what you were or would be making per hour as an employee and multiply this figure by two or three to cover your fringe benefits, overhead, expenses, and profit. As a word processor making $10 an hour on your job (about $21,000 a year), for example, in starting your own business, you could

multiply your previous hourly wage by 2.5 and test out charging $25 per hour. That is, by the way, within the range we've found to be the national norm.

3. Identify what you would like to earn annually, divide by about 2,000 hours per year, and then multiply this figure by two or three since you won't be able to bill for all 2,000 hours. For example, if you are a seminar leader and want to make $100,000 a year, divide $100,000 by 2,000 ($50), multiply by three, and you would charge $150 per hour or a rate of about $900 a day. If you worked a little over two days a week, you'd hit your goal.

4. Quote prices on the lower end of the range others are charging and keep raising your prices until you get resistance. This is what Sandra Kurtzig calls the "flinch method" of pricing. In her book *CEO: Building a $400 Million Company from the Ground Up* she says, "We'd sit across from a customer and tell him the software cost $35,000. If he didn't flinch, we'd add, 'And the financial package is $20,000.' Still no flinch, 'Per module.' And if he still hadn't flinched, we'd say, 'And the updates are $10,000.' Still no flinch: 'Per year.' The second we detected a flinch, we backed down one level."

Publisher Hal Schuster puts it this way: Your fair price is the price point at which you can maintain sufficient business. Raise your prices slowly at intervals until you find a manageable point in your workload. Then stop raising them. Then if you are consistently attracting more business than you can handle, you can raise them again.

Calculating Your Billable Days

In a service business not every workday will be billable, and many home businesses are surprised to learn just how few billable days there are in a year. Yet the number of days you can actually bill will influence how much you'll need to charge. Of course, the number of days you can bill depends on many things like how actively you market, how much time is required to run your business, and what type of work you do. But here's a way to estimate the number of billable days you might want to project in pricing your services:
From 365 days:

1. Subtract weekends: 365−104=261
2. Subtract 2 days a month for running your business: 261−24=237
3. Subtract 4 days a month for marketing: 237−48=189
4. Subtract 13 days for holidays, vacation and sick days: 189−13=176

In setting his price, programmer Mark Kleinschmidt uses this formula. He determines how much he wants his annual income to be, multiplies by 2.6, and divides by the estimated number of billable hours.

Flat Fee versus Hourly Wage

Many service businesses charge by the hour. And, on the face of it, that seems fair. Sometimes, however, customers and clients become nervous as they imagine the sound of your clock ticking. They have very little idea of what's actually involved in your work and envision their bill mounting out of control. You certainly *never* want clients to be shocked when they receive their bills. So here are several ways to avoid the time-clock jitters:

1. Make a bid that reflects your estimate of the number of hours you think the work will take and call the clients before proceeding beyond that estimate. If you come in under the estimate, they'll be pleasantly surprised. If you run over, you're giving them a chance to remain in charge of their cost before proceeding.
2. Establish a flat price to provide price stability in your client's mind but in your contract make it "subject to any change in orders." This will protect you from unexpected demands they make as the work proceeds that would put you in the hole because they would take more of your time or add to your costs.
3. Set a fixed price, but designate a specific allowable percentage of overage. That is, 100 hours at x number of dollars with a possible variance not to exceed 15 percent. Or offer a fixed cost plus expenses not to exceed a specified amount.
4. Establish an assessment stage for a project during which you are paid either a flat fee or an hourly rate to define the scope of the work to be done. Essentially under such an arrangement you are being paid to prepare a proposal that will outline the scope of the work, the detailed costs involved, and the work to be accomplished. Be sure to get a clear up-front agreement in writing that specifies what you will deliver by when.

These strategies are designed to protect both you and the client and avoid fee disputes. Some people find, for example, that a flat fee is an invitation for the client to ask for more and more to be done under that one charge. So having all fee agreements spelled out *in writing* is essential. Writer Chris Adamec find that no matter how much she wants to do a particular project, she needs to make her offer *in writing* and never begins doing any work on the project until she has received an acceptance *in writing*.

Other problems can arise, however, if you have underestimated what you can do for the price you've quoted. Technical writer Raj Khera never bills by the word or the page because in his field, the shorter the better. To convey this point to clients, he sometimes paraphrases a quote from Abraham Lincoln, saying, "It takes me two weeks to prepare a twenty-minute speech, but if you want a two-hour speech, I'm ready now." He's done eighty-page projects for $7,000, 270-page projects for $25,000 and 8-page brochures for $2,000. Each was for a fixed fee and he made good money, but how much depended on how on target he was in estimating his costs. The more experience he's gained, the more accurately he's able to estimate the time and costs involved and the more money he makes.

Programmer Ron Thompson uses a popular approach to making estimates that he calls the "fudge factor." When a client asks him how long it will take to complete a project, he figures the high side of how long he actually thinks it will take, doubles that estimate, and then tacks on a 100 percent safety factor. As often as not that "fudged" number is pretty close to what it actually takes. Programmer Mark Kleinschmidt has found he needs to multiply his estimates by three. Project management consultant Philip Dyer finds that his projects usually run 100 percent more than the "reasonable" estimate.

Promotions specialist Rick Wallace uses an interesting approach for making appealing estimates without selling himself short. He gives a tentative quote of an hourly fee with an estimated time of completion immediately but makes it clear the estimate is tentative until he can see the actual work. After seeing the work to be done, he sends a one-way fax using a standard form he's created, confirming his initial quote. If he needs to charge more than the estimate, he gives the client a chance to change his mind before proceeding. He explains the difference and offers the client a choice: he'll do the more limited work for the original price or quotes a new price for the more extensive work. This method helps educate the client as to the cost of various aspects of his work.

Often clients may have little knowledge of the value of your services or the various aspects of how you work, so any way you can demonstrate why prices vary or need to be what they are can be helpful. Here's an example of just how helpful such information can be. Judith Wunderlich, who runs a specialized temporary-help agency, lets the freelancers she places set their own prices so when a client calls for help she quotes a range of prices from let's say $20 to $30 an hour. Human nature being what it is, most people jump at the $20 price at first. But Wunderlich doesn't stop there. She faxes copies of blind résumés and samples to the client with the hourly rate of each person clearly marked. When clients can "see" what they'll get, she finds they usually pick the middle range over the lower ones.

One final thought about making pricing estimates. Gerald Weinberg, author of *The Secrets of Consulting*, sums up our philosophy: Price your work so that you'll be glad if you get the business or if you don't. The last thing you want to do is get the business and then think, "Oh, my gosh, now I've got to do *all* that work for that little money!"

For details on pricing a service, we recommend *How to Set Your Fees and Get Them*, by Kate Kelly, and *Selling Your Services*, by Robert Bly. Both these books are listed in the Resources at the end of the chapter.

Various Pricing Strategies: Pros and Cons

What to charge is a popular topic on the Working From Home Forum we manage on CompuServe Information Service. Here is a variety of strategies people have shared for setting fees.

Value Added

Steve Singer owns a small business-forms company in the Chicago area. He advises considering three factors in setting your prices: (1) How available your product or service is: the more common the service or product, the less you can charge; (2) the value you add to what is normally provided: the more you've added, the more you can charge; and (3) the prevailing price range in the industry. He points out that you need to walk the tightrope of being neither too high nor too low. Being too low hurts your credibility. But being too high invites competition. Singer has found that the more value you add, the more you will sell, and the less price will be a factor in the final sale.

Private investigator Alan Kaplan adds value by listening to the major complaints of his clients against his industry and then gives them something nobody else is giving that removes those complaints. He has noted, for example, that clients don't like the risk and uncertainty of an open-ended contract, or even a capped contract, with no guarantee of results. So for one type of client, he sets a fixed fee with a guarantee that if he isn't successful, the client will get his money back. He admits it's a risky strategy, but he's betting he's as good as he wants his clients to believe he is. And he does have a fallback strategy. If he finds the case is much more complex than anticipated, he can cut his losses and bail out by giving the client his money back.

Top of the Line

George Hoeing discovered quite by accident that the more he raised his prices, the more he could sell of his Tribal line of designer workout clothing for body builders. Whenever he put his outfits on sale, his sales dropped. Puzzled, he began experimenting with raising his prices. And, sure enough, the more he charged, the more people bought. With top-of-the-line pricing, people considered his sportswear all the more valuable. Programmer Tim Berry finds that the best time to charge top-of-the-line prices is when you are consciously trying to create a buyer perception of high quality à la designer jeans, BMWs, and fancy resort hotels. If you go top of the line, however, you have to maintain a top-of-the-line image and have entrée into circles with top-of-the-line budgets. And of course you have to have something special. You may have heard the Depression-era story about the man who was standing on the corner with a tray of apples marked $500 each. When asked if he had sold any, he said, "Not yet. But when I do, I'm going to make a *killing*!"

Percentage of Results

Sometimes when you're introducing a new service, you'll meet with skepticism and resistance. One way to overcome this resistance is to set your fee based on a fixed percentage of the results you will achieve for your client. This has been referred to as "impact pricing." People whose business is doing telephone audits, for example, could charge a percentage of the savings the audit produces. Or a sales trainer could charge a percentage of the increase in gross sales revenues for a specified number of months after his training program. Or a safety engineer might contract for a percentage of the money saved after his safety program is initiated. A variation of this would be to bill for your direct costs up to a specified amount in addition to some percentage of the results you produce. Be sure when using a percentage-of-results strategy, however, that you have a clear written agreement as to specifically how and when the results will be documented, measured, and validated.

The Bargain Basement Special

You've heard the old joke, "I may be losing money on every sale, but I'll make it up in volume." Well, of course, losing 10 cents on every sale means losing $100 on every 1,000 sales and $1,000,000 on 10 million. Discounting your service can be such a trap, especially for a home-based business, because even though you may have lower overhead as a result of working from home, your volume is usually limited. Home businesses usually can't handle sufficient volume to make only pennies on every sale.

Yet often out of eagerness to get in initial customers, a desperate new entrepreneur will be tempted to price him- or herself as a bargain basement special. He or she thinks: "After all, work does beget work and therefore it's important to get work whatever the price. Which would I prefer: sitting on the porch reading a novel or being underpaid for working?"

Should you be tempted to try pricing yourself as a bargain, keep this in mind: Once you set your price, your clientele will beget clientele from the same economic stratum. It is difficult to change upward once you have set your prices. When you raise your prices, your business will show slow or no growth because you've priced yourself beyond the budgets of your old customers and will need to start from scratch building a new clientele who can pay your new price.

Stanton Kramer is the person who first pointed out this phenomenon to us, and he should know. He's changed customer bases three times on the way to getting to the price range he wants to be in. Interior designer Lillian Hamilton also discovered this phenomenon, but to help bridge the price gap as she raises her prices, she continues to serve previous customers at the original price for a full year. She calls this her "preferred client" price and let's them know it's a courtesy she offers to her valued customers.

If you decide to start out pricing yourself on the "low" side, remember that you'll never know how much more you could actually have charged. It's the reverse of buying something, knowing for sure you'll find it at a lower price sometime in the future. Setting prices is like fording a river; you never step in the same water twice. The important thing is that you feel sufficiently compensated each step along the way. If you're feeling resentful and taken advantage of, you need to raise your prices.

A Start-Up Price

Rather than entering the market as a bargain basement special, you might consider this approach to establishing a novice-business rate: Determine what established businesses in your field are charging. Calculate what you would be paid if you were doing this same work on a salary. Then pick the difference between the two and make that your start-up price. Let your clients and customers know that this is an "introductory" price.

Staying in Budget Without Cutting Your Rate

Many business experts will advise you: *Never* cut your rate. In radio, the saying is "Never go off the rate card." Obviously, you won't present a very substantial professional image if you quote a price and then agree to do the work for less when you meet price resistance. The solution is to offer a range of services or products and to break down the price of your service by type of activity. Then you can essentially cut and paste a customized price that fits your client's budget.

For example, career coach Marilyn Miller offers private consultations, one-day seminars, a six-week workshop, a two-tape audio program ($29.95), and a six-cassette album at $69.95. With this menu of products and services she can meet her range of clients at a price point each can live with. You can do the same with your services. Consider having such price distinctions as a full-day rate and a half-day rate; a rate that includes a final report and one that does not; an in-town price and an out-of-town price; a price for rush service (twenty-four hours or overnight); a price that includes workbooks and one that does not; a price for working from typed copy and another for working from handwritten copy; a price for short-term work and another for long-term projects; a paid-in-full up-front price and a thirty-day credit price.

In other words, give your clients a range of options that in essence says: You can have it fast, you can have it cheap, or you can have it great, but you can't have all three. This "price-options" approach gives you lots of room to negotiate your price, and any reductions you make can be directly related to the effort it demands of you and the value your client receives. So you are always compensated fully for what you provide.

Working on Retainer

Working on a retainer can be quite desirable for a home business because it comes close to duplicating the regularity and security of a paycheck. With the retainer, you agree to be on call for a specified number of hours for an agreed-upon monthly fee. Normally the retainer is paid in full or on a periodic payment schedule (i.e., monthly, quarterly, or annually) with each payment made in advance of the work to be done. In other words, the retainer operates like a "draw." The clients prepay to have your time available to them as needed up to a certain amount. If they don't use all the time, they lose it. Usually the retainer involves a quantity discount that is offset by the security of knowing you will have a steady income.

When working on a retainer, however, it's vital to have a contract or letter agreement that clearly spells out your fee structure and what work is to be done over what period of time. Otherwise, you may find yourself being called upon to work far more hours than your monthly fee can cover, or a client may stretch the contracted number of hours out over a longer period so that your quantity discount is no longer profitable. With a clear agreement, should the workload drop below a specified level, you can simply bill at a higher rate. Should your client complain, you can point to your agreement.

Ken Sobel, owner of For Your Information, Inc., a marketing research company servicing *Fortune* 500 packaged-goods manufacturers, typically works on a retainer. His clients might pay for $20,000 of work over a twelve-month period, and to make his retainer more attractive Sobel provides $25,000 worth of service (that is, a 20% discount). To qualify for this discount, however, Sobel's clients must agree to two things: (1) they must commit to pay the full $20,000 regardless of the amount of work they actually use and (2) they must commit to pay in advance of the work.

Sobel requires that the first $10,000 be paid at the time his services begin and the second $10,000 after six months or when he's logged $12,500 of services, whichever comes first. He reports that so far none of his four retainer clients have ever had unused time at the end of the year. If they have used up the retainer value before the year runs out, however, they can pay on a project-by-project basis with no discount or open a new retainer at the special rate.

When working on retainer you can become very comfortable, but keep in mind that clients often think of such consulting services as a temporary expenditure, not an on-going commitment. So don't get too dependent. You may be wise to anticipate a natural attrition rate for retainer clients. As you do a good job for them, their need for your services may be progressively reduced and they may start looking forward to freeing up the funds they're now investing in your services. Usually you can sense this time approaching and can take appropriate action such as:

1. Look and listen carefully for additional types of work you could offer that the client may be unaware of needing and get them excited about the benefits of proceeding to provide new services.
2. Offer a smaller retainer with less of a discount or offer an annual subscription or maintenance fee as a way to continue providing some more minimal level of services.
3. Begin preparing to accept and line up new business. Remember, satisfied customers make excellent referral sources and may even return for repeat business at any time in the future if you leave on good terms and keep up regular communication. So always accept inevitable cutbacks or terminations with grace and goodwill. And always continue your marketing activities no matter how busy you get so that you will have a stream of new clients waiting in the wings when you need them.

Adjusting Your Pricing Strategy to Your Changing Business Situation

As you can see from the above pricing strategies, there are three factors that affect what you can charge: your image of yourself, your reputation, and the market for what you have to offer. Each of these factors is subject to change over the lifetime of your business. Therefore, anticipate the need for adjusting your pricing strategy to different stages of your business.

Novice businesspeople, for example, may enter a field at a moderate price and raise it gradually as their reputation and self-assurance grow. But let's consider a less-obvious evolution. If you're introducing a new product or service and discover that the response to it is strong, you may be able to charge a premium price right from the beginning because you have no competition. When others notice your dramatic success, however, they may well jump into the field and undercut your price. Then you may face having to adjust your price down in order to remain competitive.

Coleen Sager encountered such a dilemma as the developer of one of the first customer-service training programs in the country. She found companies were eager for her information and the dramatic increases it could mean in their bottom lines. Her seminars and video programs sold briskly at a premium price. Over the years, however, many other trainers, seeing her success, added a customer-service training program to their offerings at much lower rates. Ultimately, her products and programs cost much more than everyone else's.

Of course, she still had her reputation as one of the leading authorities, but eventually cost sensitivity won out in the marketplace and her sales began to decline. So Coleen was presented with a monumental challenge. Obviously she couldn't just cut the price of her existing programs without damage to her reputation and stature. The situation called for an innovative new pricing program. And that's exactly what she initiated.

Instead of promoting her three-day seminars, Coleen began marketing herself as a corporate speaker. Because of her reputation, she could command top speaking fees and still save her clients money. By bringing her in to speak they could get the best for less. They got her most important information in a condensed form for less than the cost of the lower-priced multiple-day seminars on the market. When the speech went well, she could then work out customized follow-up seminars.

Another stage of business involves retraining long-term clients. We've already mentioned making provisions for guaranteeing some period of price stability for preferred clients. Another way to price for retention is to add on value to existing services when you raise prices, or retain your existing price but add on charges for additional services.

Raising Your Fees

Even though we all would enjoy bringing in additional income without increasing our workload, most of us hate to raise prices. We fear our clients will decide to cut back on what they buy from us, or even worse, will take their business elsewhere. Nonetheless we know that periodically we owe it to ourselves to raise our rates. When that time comes, it need not be a traumatic moment. Planning ahead can help. Here are several rules of thumb for making raising your rates easier and even routine.

1. Begin by letting your existing clients or wholesalers know well in advance when you will be raising your fees.

2. Provide information about why you need to raise your prices. Relate rate increases to increases in service or to economic conditions your clients may or may not be aware of.

3. If you wish, you could provide a grace period for existing clients and customers. Typically Sarah carried existing clients at the previous year's fees. No one ever complained because when their fees did go up the next year, they were still paying less than newer clients, so they still felt fortunate.

4. Alternatively, you might offer a temporary incentive for your long-term customers; i.e., "I'm raising my prices, but for the next month we'll include the shipping for free."

5. Build anticipated fee increases into the contract, so no one will be surprised when contract renewal comes and your fees are higher. Or include information about fee increases along with all fee information. That's what Chip Morgan, president of Chip Morgan Broadcast Engineering, does. Morgan believes that we should all plan to raise our prices annually, because, after all, we are one year more experienced and our cost of doing business usually goes up each year. So, here's how he does it. He tells his clients up front that he raises his fees each year when quoting them this year's fees. In this way, no one is surprised when the fee goes up in the new year. "They expect it anyway," he says. This makes the anticipated increase clear from the start.

6. Announce price increases matter-of-factly and with confidence. Do not be defensive or uncomfortable about your decision. Such negativity sparks precisely the type of reaction you most want to avoid.

7. With long-standing clients, be open to considering exceptions but always attach them to a specific deadline at which time your new prices will go into effect.

8. Do not be overly concerned if a few clients do decide to go elsewhere. Sometimes a fee increase simply catalyzes a decision that was already imminent. But, of course, don't let them leave without making an effort to find out if they are dissatisfied and how you could continue serving them.

What to Do When Told Your Price Is Too High

When you're told that your price is too high, marketing consultant Laura Douglas advises simply asking "In what way is it too high?" Then ask, "What price did you have in mind?" You do this not in order to lower your price, but to get a better idea of what the people you're talking to really want done. Remember, you can always offer reduced services for what they want to pay.

Keep in mind, too, that people usually have no idea how much time is actually involved, much less the expertise required to do what you will be doing. Douglas suggests preparing a small graph that illustrates how much more it would cost the company to do the job in-house. Include factors such as how much more time it would take an inexperienced person, and other costs they may not think of. Such comparisons provide your prospective clients with a more realistic idea of what they need, and their response provides you with a better means of knowing if and how you could help them.

Developing the Confidence to Get Your Price

Many of the problems people have in pricing their products arise from limiting attitudes and beliefs they have about money. Often, we are not even aware that we have these attitudes and beliefs. Many arose during our childhoods from the assumptions our families held about money, and they can interfere with our charging what we are actually worth.

Speech and diction coach Saundra Keen, for example, was barely surviving on the fees she charged for her private consultations. Even though as an actress Saundra had studied with the top speech coaches for many years and had crafted a beautiful voice for herself, she believed that no one would want to pay very much for her coaching because she didn't have a college degree in speech communications. With our help, her self-esteem grew, and she began to notice that her clients were improving dramatically. She finally realized that actual results were the bottom line of her value, not academic degrees.

She remembered that throughout her childhood her father had always told her that if she ever wanted to make any money, she would have to go to college. Little did she know that, once she'd decided to pursue her acting career directly from high school, her father's old admonition about making money would prevent her from earning a decent living twenty years later.

Saundra decided to raise her prices but still was fearful that no one would book an appointment once they heard what she was asking. You can imagine her surprise when she finally worked up the courage to state her new price and the response was "That's very reasonable."

In reality, close examination of one's attitudes about money shows that they are often self-fulfilling prophecies. Those who believe in themselves and their product and expect people to pay for it gladly are infinitely more successful than those who expect to have difficulty earning a living. Examples of common negative beliefs that prevent people from setting prices that enable their businesses to flourish include:

- People hate to part with their money.
- Making money is hard.
- You have to work your fingers to the bone to make even a meager living.
- Rich people are dishonest. They rip other people off.
- Anyone can do what I do, so how can I charge very much for it?
- The work I do is so much fun, I really shouldn't charge anything.

Have you ever noticed, however, that when someone really wants something, he or she will pay almost any price for it? They can't get the money out of their pockets fast enough. Or have you ever noticed that truly successful people almost always love what they do and talk about it as something they would do even for free? Also think about how many of the most successful people achieve the success they do because they enable others to enjoy life more. And can anyone else ever really do exactly what you do?

To identify other limiting attitudes and beliefs about money that may stand in the way of your setting a price that will enable your business to thrive, we suggest making the following statement out loud. Say it several times and notice your internal reactions.

> People will gladly pay me well for the work I love doing.

If you have a negative reaction to believing any portion of this statement, think about what you believe instead. How did you come to hold these beliefs? What would convince you to believe this statement? In being able to agree fully with each aspect of this statement, you'll find setting and getting prices you want to be much easier.

A Simple Step-by-Step Pricing Guide

Although, as you can see, there is no one pricing formula that will work for everyone, we offer the following process for determining what approach might work best for you at a given time.

1. Work out several possible pricing strategies from those mentioned in this chapter.
2. Test each alternative with several prospective clients.
3. Select the alternative that gets the best response.
4. Remember, pricing is an experimental process, so continue fine-tuning until you're satisfied with the results.
5. Keep track of your income and expenses and evaluate your pricing every quarter. Make changes when the numbers or any of the following indicate the need to adjust:

- Many complaints about your price.
- Many other complaints that may be dissatisfaction with your price in disguise.
- A downturn in sales or the fact that people lose interest after hearing the price.
- People saying, "Boy, that's a bargain."
- Your prices have been the same for a long period of time.
- You're turning away business because you don't have time to do it.
- Sales are fine but profits are low.
- You feel resentful about working so hard for so little return.

Pricing is like the pulse of your business. When it's working, you're working. And that means that life's working!

Resources

Financial Freedom in 8 Minutes a Day. Ron and Mary Hulnick (see chapter 14 for full citation).

Getting to Yes: Negotiating without Giving In. Roger Fisher and William Ury. New York: Penguin, 1981.

Homemade Money. (See chapter 3 for full citation.) Information on pricing products.

How to Set Your Fees and Get Them. Kate Kelly, Visibility Enterprises, 11 Rockwood Drive, Larchmont, NY, 10538; (800) 784-0602.

Money Is My Friend. Phil Laut. New York: Ivy Books, 1989.

MoneyLove. Jerry Gillies. New York: Warner, 1978.

The Contract and Fee-Setting Guide for Consultants and Professionals. Howard Shenson. (See Chapter 9 for full citation.)

Selling Your Services. Robert Bly. New York: Henry Holt, 1991.

CHAPTER
TWENTY-THREE
■■■■■■■■■■■■■■■■■■■■■■■■■■■■

Successfully Marketing Your Home Business

If you're working from home in your own business now, you already know that unless you bring in some business you won't be working from home for long. Without customers or clients, you'll soon be back out looking for a job. For many people, the fear that they won't have enough business prevents them from even pursuing their desire to go out on their own. For those who do proceed, getting business remains their number-one concern. Year after year, the *Home Office Computing* annual reader survey reports that issues related to getting business make up the bulk of the top-ten concerns of home-based businesses. And no wonder because, ultimately, the only difference that truly matters between those who succeed and those who don't is that those who make it have enough business to keep going.

Because marketing is such a concern to people who are working independently from home, we have written an entire book (with marketing expert Laura Clampitt Douglas) on how to market yourself as a home-based business, *Getting Business to Come to You*. We named it that because that's what we must do if we are to survive and thrive on our own. We can't spend most of our time out marketing. To succeed we have to set up our marketing so that it develops a momentum of its own and business starts coming to us, leaving us free to concentrate on the business we get!

The biggest hurdle most people face in getting enough business is that they know little or nothing about how to go about letting people know what they can do in a way that those who need it will buy it. Actually this is not surprising because most of us don't learn anything about marketing in school or even on the job unless we happen to have worked in this field. But since few home businesses can afford to hire a professional to do their marketing, most of us must fend for ourselves.

The problem of marketing ourselves is compounded by the fact that most of what's taught and written about marketing is designed for larger businesses, and unfortunately many home businesses flounder trying to use the marketing methods best suited for bigger operations. So we have to experiment and improvise. Sometimes what we try works; sometimes it doesn't.

Fortunately, however, with the right information, marketing a home-based business need not be complex or expensive. In fact, there are highly successful marketing methods for every home business and every personality type. We have interviewed owners of several thousand successful home businesses, and most of them have told us they get their business by "word of mouth." In other words, they have become so well established that almost all their business comes from referrals. Prospective clients and customers are calling them, and that's exactly what we all want. Remember, though, that few of them started out with the phone ringing. What we set out to learn from these successful businesspeople is what they did to create the word-of-mouth momentum that brings in a steady flow of business.

In *Getting Business to Come to You* we outline the thirty-five marketing methods many successful home businesspeople told us they use to get their businesses going. Some of the methods, like direct mail and advertising, are used by larger businesses, but we tell you how to tailor them to the budget and scope that will work for a home business. Other methods, like gatekeeping and sampling, are used in ways that are especially suited to home businesses. Our goal in writing *Getting Business to Come to You* was to give you all the tools, skills and how-to's to actually use these methods. A summary of these thirty-five low- or no-cost ways to get business follows.

Some people like Elio Samame have told us our book has helped them make their businesses a success. Elio came to the United States from Peru with less than $500 and a dream. He came to America to be a fitness trainer and to start his own gym. He began working from home. Every day he tried one marketing idea from our book. His operation grew from a home-based business to a gym, and then he had to move into a larger gym. That's the power of effective marketing. Others have had similar results, and you can too.

There are several mistakes, however, that we continue to notice home businesspeople making again and again that thwart even their best marketing efforts. Despite investing considerable time and money in marketing, too many people are disappointed with the results they get. Inadvertently they are sabotaging the time, money, and effort they are putting into their marketing. In this chapter we want to identify these common marketing traps and the simple steps we can all take to avoid them.

Don't Leave Your Success to Chance: Develop a Marketing Mindset

The greatest mistake someone can make in marketing is thinking that because you have a good product or service, people will buy it. For example, most people think that Christopher Columbus or Leif Ericson discovered America. But 2,000 years before Ericson, Basques, Phoenicians, Druid priests, Libyans, and Egyp-

Principal Marketing Methods
for Home-Based Businesses*

Word-of-Mouth
1. Networking
2. Mentors and gatekeepers
3. Volunteerism
4. Sponsorships
5. Charitable donations

6. Referrals
7. Business name
8. Letterhead and business card
9. Product packaging
10. Point-of-sale display

Public Relations
11. Writing articles
12. Letters to the editor
13. News releases
14. Speeches and seminars

15. Publicity:
    Newspaper
    Magazine
    Radio and TV
    Business and trade publications

Direct Marketing
16. Sampling
17. Incentives
18. Discount pricing
19. Contests and giveaways
20. Newsletters

21. Circulars and flyers
22. Trade shows and exhibits
23. Sales seminars
24. Demonstrations
25. Direct mail

Inventive Advertising
26. Classified ads
27. Business directories
28. Yellow Page advertising
29. Bulletin boards and tear pad
30. Your own radio show

31. Your own TV show
32. Online networking
33. Fax
34. Direct response ads
35. Card decks

* From *Getting Business to Come to You*, Paul and Sarah Edwards and Laura Clampitt Douglas (New York: Tarcher/Perigee, 1991).

tians may have visited our shores. Instead of becoming famous for discovering America, Columbus achieved his fame by *marketing* his discovery of America!

Like Columbus, you will need to get your name associated with whatever field you've chosen. Your job is to let everyone who needs your product or service know about it, and to do so in a way that convinces them to buy it *now*.

That means developing a marketing mindset, habitually thinking about how others will find out about you and making a commitment that your business deserves the time, energy, and even the investment of some money to make sure people have the opportunity to use your products and services. Without such an investment of time, energy, and money, the world will lose out on the benefits of your talents and abilities.

So the first step in making sure you have ample business is to view yourself and what you're doing as important enough to invest in promoting and to realize that, in fact, this is something that you can learn to do successfully—even if you don't think so at the moment. Many, if not most, people who go out on their own are initially reticent about marketing, but those who are successful discover they can not only do it, but can actually enjoy it. That's what this chapter is designed to help you do.

Don't Waste Your Time: Test the Waters

"I've been marketing my service for six months, and I'm just not getting any business. What can I do?" writes a woman in desperation. She has been trying to launch an out-of-town service in which she would run the offices of professionals who are on the road most of each week. This sounds like such an excellent idea and, in fact, we have talked with several people who have tried it. So far, however, we have yet to meet anyone who has made a go of this business. Evidently the people who would need such a service either don't think they need it or are not willing to pay for it. As of yet, no one has positioned this business in a way that people will buy it.

This illustrates the first thing you can do to make sure you'll have plenty of business. Be certain that there are enough people who need and will pay for what you are setting out to offer. All the effective marketing in the world will not sell something to people who are convinced they don't need it or are simply unwilling to pay for it. So before you even start marketing yourself, do some homework to find out what you can offer that people need and will pay for.

Seven Ways to Find Out if People Need and Will Pay for What You Want to Offer

1. Talk to the competition. Find out if there are others doing something similar and how successful they are. Talking with such people can provide a wealth of information. Don't be shy about approaching them. They may soon be your colleagues, and if you approach them as such instead of thinking of them as the enemy, they will probably be willing to talk with you. Find out as much as you can about what they offer and what they don't. How long have they been in business? What do they like best about their business? What do they like least? Ask their opinion about whether this is a good business to be in, what they specialize in, and if they ever need backup or someone to handle their overload. Find out if they would recommend this business to someone else.

You may find a few people who just won't want to share, but if generally speaking most people are open and forthcoming, the business is probably a pretty good one. If most people are tight-mouthed and unfriendly, that's not a good sign.

And if there is no one doing what you want to do, explore further. It could mean that there's an unmet need, or it could mean there is no need. So you'll need to check it out.

2. Talk directly to people who would need or are using something like what you can offer. Often conversations with potential clients or customers will tell you exactly what you need to do to succeed. Here are the kind of questions you can ask.

Questions to Ask Potential Clients

- *Have you ever used this type of product or service?*
- *If not, why not?* They may not have known about it. They may have heard it wasn't useful or that it cost too much. Continue exploring their answers with questions like *Would you be interested in finding out more about it? What would make it useful for you? What would you want to pay for it?*
- *If you have used something similar, were you happy with it?* Listen to what they liked and didn't like. Each comment can tell you possible things you will need to say to market yourself to others.
- *Would you do it again?* Investigate further. Find out why or why not. Think about how what you offer could be different, better, more useful.
- *Are you using one now?* Find out if they are satisfied and why they are or aren't.
- *What would make it more appealing to you?* Find out if there are any circumstances under which they would be interested. This information will help you better define what you can do profitably.
- *What do you expect to pay?* Finding out what people would expect to pay can help you set your price, but in addition, it can help you identify what you will have to do to get the price you need to charge.

---

3. Get feedback on a prototype or sample of the product or service you have in mind. Showing people what they would get and finding out how they respond can provide you with a wealth of information. If you have a product, make up a sample and show it around using some of the following methods. If you have a service, you can also provide a sample in the form of a seminar, an article, a free demonstration, etc.

Listen carefully to all their reactions. Again, people will tell you exactly what you would have to do to meet their needs. Often they will tell you these things by complaining about what they don't like or telling you why this wouldn't work. Follow up on such comments. Always ask them what *would* make it appealing to them.

4. Participate in a trade show, expo, or swap meet and take orders. Having a booth at a show where your potential clients and customers will be walking by can provide you with a wealth of information about what they will or will not be interested in.

5. Advertise a preproduction offer. If you are starting a newsletter, developing a software program, preparing to offer a training seminar, or creating a product of some kind, you can place a strategic ad or do a select direct mailing to find out what kind of response you get. If the response is not adequate to proceed, you can return the limited orders you did receive with a message that you are no longer offering the product.

6. Use questionnaires and surveys. You can ask potential clients and customers to complete a survey or questionnaire providing you with their reactions to your business concept. You can mail such a questionnaire, but your response will be better if you have people fill it out in person, at a trade show perhaps or at a speech or seminar you conduct. In such situations you can give a prize or gift of some kind to those who will complete the survey. Or you can use the completed forms in a drawing for a valued prize.

7. Hold a focus group. Identify and then invite seven to ten people whom you would define as needing your service to join you for a discussion that can provide you with the information you need. To provide an incentive for their coming, you might offer a free one-hour workshop or demonstration followed by an hour-long discussion. This is what we recommended to the woman who wanted to run an out-of-town service. We felt she could get to the bottom of the resistance she'd been encountering by holding such a group and asking them questions like:

- Have you ever heard of an out-of-town service?
- Have you ever used one?
- If not, why not?
- If so, what was your experience?
- Would you use one again?
- What needs do you have while you're out of town?
- How are you meeting those needs now?
- How satisfied are you with what you're doing now?
- What additional help could you use?
- What complaints do you have about trying to run your business from the road?
- How much would you expect to pay for such help?
- Had you heard of my business before I contacted you?
- How would you most likely hear about a service like mine?
- Where would you turn if you were trying to find help while out of town?

Finally, we suggested that she tell them toward the close of the evening that she had not been getting the positive reactions she had expected from her marketing and ask them why they think this might be and what they would suggest.

For more ideas on do-it-yourself market research see the Resources list.

Don't Try to Market More than One Business at Once: Focus

An Indiana couple was described as follows by the *Los Angeles Times*: "They teach jobless people the printing business on nineteenth-century, hand-fed platen presses. They market and sell coffee from small-scale farmers in Nicaragua, baskets from Africa, and corn dolls from Appalachia. They recycle tons of garbage from the local neighborhood, take in boarders, run a direct-mail operation that posts newsletters for about 30 nonprofit organizations and they sell bumper stickers."

Wow! At first glance you might think, "Oh, what an enterprising couple!" But consider this: they made $6,100 last year. How sad. So much energy, so much effort, so many good intentions, so little return. This is an extreme example of an all-too-common mistake—marketing more than one business at a time. Depending on whether you count the various craft sales as separate businesses, this couple operates between six and eight different businesses. That means they are making less than $1,000 a year from each business! And what kind of life can you lead on $6,100 a year?

The saddest part of this story is that if this couple were to focus all their time, money, and energy on any one of these businesses, they probably could earn triple the income, if not more, than they are realizing now. Yes, we know, it's very tempting to think "Well, now that I'm on my own I can do all the things I've wanted to do. Some of this and some of that." And it's easy to want to try doing several different things "just in case any one thing doesn't work out, there will be other things to fall back on." But actually failing to focus on one business at a time has just the opposite effect.

Instead of providing us with greater security, trying to run more than one business at once makes marketing yourself successfully much more difficult. First, marketing a business takes considerable time and effort as well as some financial investment. Spreading your limited time, money, and energy over two or three businesses (let alone six to eight) means that no one business is likely to get the full investment it needs to actually take off.

In many ways, starting a home business is like having a baby. Just think about it: Have you ever known any woman who was doing more than one thing in the delivery room? Well, so it is with a home business. Bringing a new business into the world demands that we focus 100 percent of whatever energy and attention we have on that end.

Second, consider this. How would you respond if you were to meet someone who introduced himself as a real estate broker and then in the next breath told you that he also has a cleaning service and sells a line of sports equipment. Most people's reaction would be to feel confused and skeptical. They would wonder, "Is this person serious about all these businesses?" "Could he be doing very well at any one of them?" Think about it, would you want to rely on this person to sell your home? Would you want to refer one of your own clients to him to clean their office? Or would you want to do business with someone who seems to be more focused?

So while it's very tempting to try to "cover all the bases" by having several things going at once, we strongly urge you to make a commitment to just one business at a time. Once you get that one business under way and going strong, then you can consider if you have the time and energy to launch a second one. Even then, however, you will need to be careful not to confuse your potential clients about what business you're in.

A wedding makeup artist who attended one of our seminars learned this the hard way and is eager to tell others that our advice to focus is wise. She had established a wedding makeup service, and things were going so well she decided to add a line of cosmetics. To launch this new aspect of her business, she took a booth at a wedding show. To her dismay several of her clients came up asking in alarm, "Aren't you doing makeup anymore?" Others commented in a puzzled tone, "I thought you did makeup." She spent the whole show assuring people that she was still primarily a wedding makeup artist, but she was just . . .

Having learned her lesson well, she didn't drop her idea of adding a cosmetic line. Instead, she continues to market herself as a wedding makeup artist; then she sells cosmetics to her clients in hopes of keeping them as clients after their weddings.

Don't Try to Be All Things to All People: Niche

Consider these two introductions. Which one helps you understand what this person does for a living? Which one would you be more likely to remember, to use or to refer to?

■ "I'm a facialist. Everyone has skin and everyone could look better if he or she takes good care of it. So, anyone, man or woman, of any age, can benefit from having a facial."

■ "You know how as you age, you start to notice changes in your skin. Well, with the proper care much of this can be prevented. I'm a facialist and I specialize in working with people who are starting to notice changes in their skin and want to preserve a more youthful appearance."

If you're like most people, you're more likely to take note of the second introduction. Most of us want to work with a specialist, someone we believe really knows how to solve a particular problem or need we have. Yet when we go out on our own, too often we're so panicked about making sure we have enough business that we try to be all things to all people. Saying "I can work with anyone" not only makes us sound desperate, it does nothing to help distinguish us from all the other people who do something similar to what we do. There are many facialists, many photographers, many medical transcriptionists, many desktop publishers, many business consultants, and so on. It's much more difficult to market yourself to anyone and everyone, and equally difficult to market yourself as part of an undifferentiated pool of others who do generally the same thing you do.

It is much easier to market yourself as a specialist serving a special niche; i.e., as a facialist who works with aging skin, a photographer who specializes in weddings, a medical transcriptionist who works with doctors who speak English as a second language, a business consultant who works with family businesses that are passing their business from one generation to the next. In other words, if you want to stand out from the competition, if you want to charge a decent fee, then you must be more than a general "worker" someone would hire as an employee or get from a "temp" agency. As a specialist, you become more memorable. People are more apt to think of you when they need what you offer or meet someone else who does. And they are more likely to pay you what you're worth.

In addition, as a specialist, you are less of a threat to your competition. As a specialist you can refer business to them and they to you. So identify what group you are best suited to serve based on your experience, interests, contacts, and expertise and specialize.

How to Carve Out Your Niche

Actually there are many ways to define your niche. You can specialize, for example, in WHO you serve, WHAT you offer, WHERE you do it, WHEN you do it or HOW you do it. For example:

WHO you serve—A computer consultant could work only with women. A PR firm could specialize in environmentally conscious companies. A caterer could provide parties and weddings for the Polish community. A desktop publisher could work only with ad agencies.

WHAT—A computer consultant could work only with Macs. A PR firm could specialize in only doing publicity book tours for authors. A caterer could specialize in health food that tastes sinful. A desktop publisher could specialize in newsletters or résumés only.

WHERE—A computer consultant could be Eastside Computing. A PR firm could specialize in getting PR in foreign countries. A caterer could specialize in outdoor events. A desktop publisher could be a Mobile DTP and work on the client's site.

WHEN—A computer consultant could specialize in after-hours calls when everyone else is closed. A PR firm could specialize in damage control helping companies manage media response to a scandal, tragedy, or accident. A caterer could feature rescuing clients facing a last-minute dinner party; e.g., Spur-of-the-Moment Parties. A desktop publisher could specialize in fast turnaround; e.g., Same Day DTP.

HOW—A computer consultant could use only particular software; a PR firm could feature doing PR by fax alone. A caterer could prepare meals on his or her clients' premises. A DTP could specialize in producing only high-quality color work.

Clever Home Business Niches

Here are a few examples of cleverly niched home businesses:

- An insurance agent who specializes in writing policies for race horses, jockeys, and other stable personnel.
- An actress who specializes in conducting drama-based sexual harassment training programs.

- A psychotherapist, married to a veterinarian, who specializes in pet bereavement counseling.
- A ex-chef who designs and remodels kitchens.
- A one-time tennis pro who started a scholarship matching service specializing in tennis scholarships.
- A nurse who provides medical background material for litigation support to lawyers.
- A chiropractor who started a specialized temporary-help agency supplying backup personnel for chiropractic offices.
- A handyman who specializes in working for single women who don't have a man around the house to fix things.
- A social worker in private practice who specializes in managing the health care of elderly parents whose adult children are not able to do it.

Don't Rely on Passive Methods That Work for Big Business: Initiate

"I just spent all the money I have on a display ad in this great magazine. I even put in an extra phone line to be sure I could take all the calls I thought I'd get and I hired someone to come in during the day to answer the phone. But I'm not getting any calls. The only call I got today was from someone who wanted to sell me radio advertising!"

This comment was from the owner of a referral service. We'll call him Tim. But we hear similar complaints all too often. Because many of us know so little about marketing and we often really don't like doing it anyway, it's easy to gravitate toward what we call passive marketing methods like advertising and direct mail. After all, aren't these the advertising medium of corporate America and if it works for them, why not for us? And these are relatively nonthreatening ways to market. You take out an ad or you send out a mailing and wait for the phone to ring.

Although there are circumstances in which these more passive methods do work, more often than not, passive advertising methods do not work well for home businesses unless they are coupled with personal initiatives. Usually we don't have the budget to pursue these methods long enough and on a large-enough scale to get sufficient results. And more often than not, the kind of products and services home businesses offer are not the type that people will buy from an ad or a mailing. People are much more likely to buy services from home businesses like facialists, wedding photographers, medical transcriptionists, pet-sitters, and business consultants, for example, based on referrals or a personal contact than from a flyer they get in the mail.

Usually the best ways to get business involve personal initiative. Methods that work particularly well focus on creating visibility and building relationships. Then direct mail and advertising can be used to follow up on the contacts you've made. In other words, use personal initiative to build relationships and to let those who need you get to know you and your business. Then, you can use mailings and even advertising to keep yourself and your business in mind so that when the moment comes when someone needs you, he or she will think of you immediately.

We call this "top of the mind" marketing. And it works. For example, the referral service we mentioned above would be better served by networking or speaking at various business and professional meetings and then following up each month by sending those potential clients who expressed an interest a snappy newsletter featuring the services available.

Here are seven of the best methods for building relationships and creating visibility:

1. Networking: Leveraging Your Contacts, New and Old

Networking is the most popular way to start and build a home-based personal or professional service business. Networking refers to using face-to-face contact to establish relationships that can lead to business. Professional-practice consultant Gene Call of Los Angeles calls networking "word-of-mouth marketing" because it's based on talking with people about what you do and listening to find out how you might serve them.

Once a business is established, "word of mouth" comes to mean getting referrals from satisfied customers who talk about you, but until a business is self-sustaining, "word of mouth" means moving *your* mouth, telling people about your business, speaking with everyone you already know (family, friends, vendors, and colleagues), and making a determined effort to meet and talk with lots of new people, too.

Family and friends are the oldest networks of all. They have launched many businesses as have members of civic and professional organizations. Now, electronic networks are available, too. Membership in professional and trade associations is another way to find out what others are doing, what's working, what isn't, and where there are holes in the market that you might be able to fill. You can also join associations and groups where your potential buyers might gather.

Today there are networking organizations, business guilds, and "leads clubs" whose sole purpose is to generate business leads for their members. These groups usually meet at mealtimes, and membership is usually limited to one person in a given type of business. For example, as the only member of her women's network and her breakfast leads club to offer executive secretarial services, Dorothy Baranski was able to build her business from these two sources.

Telecommuting consultant Gil Gordon summarizes how networking has worked for him: "Everything in business, whether it's getting an article published or finding a distributor, is a result of networking. I keep in contact with old friends, past co-workers, sales reps who used to call on me. I've joined a couple of carefully chosen small associations or discussion groups composed of the people I need to meet for my business and I'm fortunate enough to know a couple of people who pride themselves on being "matchmakers." They love to get people with common interests together. I can't stress this enough. Just as in job-hunting, your friends and contacts are your best assets."

Despite the fact that most successful home-based businesses are built on word-of-mouth marketing, we've found that networking is still overlooked and sometimes even consciously avoided by some. Yet networking gives you a chance to show personally that you are interested in meeting your prospective clients' needs. It gives you the opportunity to find out what they need and show how you can serve them better. In the process, prospects also have a chance to discover that they like you, and almost everyone likes to do business with someone they like—particularly when dealing with a service business.

To make the most of your networking activity, however, be sure you get out regularly, go to activities where your potential clients or referral sources gather, make a point of meeting new people everywhere you go, and follow up later on the contacts you make. Marketing consultant Robbie Bogue finds that getting dressed in professional attire at the beginning of the workday makes it easier for him to actually get out to luncheon and evening networking events because he's already dressed and ready to go when the time comes. He also recommends that once you get to an event, don't stand around with appetizers and drinks in your hands or you won't get much networking done.

2. Direct Solicitation

Talking personally to people who need what you offer is the quickest and most reliable form of getting business. Of course, the dreaded words *cold calling* can send a shiver down the spine of even experienced salespeople. But we've been surprised to find that many home-based businesses have successfully marketed their businesses by placing informal, personal exploratory calls to acquaint themselves with the needs of the people in their market niche.

When David Goodfellow decided to provide and sell mailing list services to small businesses, he got started by going through the Yellow Pages and calling small companies in his community to determine whether they needed his services. He started with "A" and never got past "K." He generated a steady flow of business from the first half of the alphabet!

Bob Garsson did direct solicitation for years and found that the first call of the day was the toughest one. He says, "I could find hundreds of excuses not to make that first call, but once I got that one out of the way, I could go strong the rest of the day."

To warm up his calls, a financial consultant we interviewed looks at name-plates on the desks of the businesses he visits. Or he calls the company and tells the secretary, "I'm supposed to mail something to a man I met at your company and I can't remember his name. He was about thirty-five and his name was something like—" The operator offers twenty names, while he takes notes to call them back.

Since a sale usually isn't made until after the fifth call, the key to selling by phone (or to any other form of selling) is to keep at it. You can figure that every "no" you hear brings you that much closer to a "yes."

To help overcome your dread of direct solicitation, think about your calls as relationship building, because after all, that's what they are. You are introducing yourself to people who could use what you have to offer, getting acquainted with them, and finding out about their needs. What's the worst thing that can happen? They don't need you now. Okay, but they may in the future. Or they may run into someone who does. And you'll be foremost in their mind!

3. Sampling

Sampling means letting people experience a sample of your work as a means of getting them to buy. Debbie Fields and Famous Amos both launched their cookie businesses by letting people sample their cookies. Famous Amos told us that when he opened his first store, he carried fresh hot cookies everywhere he went. Debbie Fields started her business at home and told us that the first day she opened a shop, no one came in. There she was with trays piled high with cookies and no customers. In a moment of desperation, she carried a tray of piping hot, freshly baked chocolate chip cookies down the sidewalk, giving away samples. The story goes that people followed her back to the store the way children followed the Pied Piper.

The effectiveness of sampling is not limited, however, just to gourmet delicacies. Gene Call, Helen Berman, and Linda Jagoda all used sampling to launch their businesses. They offered a free introductory seminar to give people a sample of what they would get if they signed up for a series of seminars. The way Ted Laux began his book-indexing service with a TRS Model I computer is another excellent example of how to use sampling to get business. Laux looked through bookstores for books that didn't have an adequate index. To demonstrate how much more effective these books would be had the publishers used his services, he indexed the books and sent copies to the publishers. Several liked the results and he was in business. His indexing software gave him his unique advantage, and the sample became his platform for showing off just what he could do.

Participating in trade shows is an excellent way to get customers to sample your product or service. It's not unusual for such shows to attract from 20,000 to 100,000 people. And, at many of them, you can not only generate leads but actually sell products and services.

A moonlighting artist launched a new line of greeting cards at one trade show. She booked over $10,000 worth of orders from gift shops. An independent publisher attended the American Bookseller's Association convention with her newly published book on word processing and got orders from stores across the nation.

In addition to exhibiting at a trade show, you can speak or conduct a seminar there. If you speak, show promoters will sometimes give you free booth space in lieu of a presenter's fee. If your reputation warrants, you can sometimes be paid a presenter's fee and also get free booth space. You can also sell your books or products from the back of the room after your presentation.

Speaking at a trade show workshop, speech pathologist Dr. Roger Burgraff sold over $2,000 worth of books on communications to a group of health professionals. Marketing specialist Carol Dysart sells business opportunity packages during her trade show presentations. One sales trainer offers to do free sessions for exhibitors on how to work a trade show. These exhibitors often become his new customers.

Besides attracting customers, trade shows are good avenues for reaching retailers, wholesalers, reps, and buyers. And exhibiting is also a good way to test a new product, build your mailing list, and do informal market surveys.

If you haven't exhibited at a show before, attend some in your field first. Talk to exhibitors about how worthwhile exhibiting has been. At the same time, ask if any exhibitors are interested in carrying your product or sharing future booth space.

Consult the Resources list at the end of this chapter to locate trade show information. Think about the various platforms you could use to show off your products or service.

4. Pricing Incentives

The way you price your service can be a route to quick business. When Arlene Daily started her business promoting restaurants on the radio she used a discount pricing strategy. She offered restaurant owners the opportunity to come on her show and promote their restaurants at a price they couldn't refuse. She gave lots of service for the price. She prepared their commercials. She featured them in live personal interviews and invited listeners to meet her at the restaurants for various publicity activities.

This approach enabled her to break even immediately and, since she now had satisfied advertisers, selling to new ones at a higher price was much easier. For more information about pricing strategies, see chapter 22.

A photographer offered an apparently absurd service to advertising agencies: a huge (30″×40″) color print in an hour for $150. Obviously, if two customers took him up on it, one customer would get his color print on time and the other would get his print two hours later. But the photographer knew that the chances were that no one would order a rush color print of that size. However, the psychological impact was powerful. The idea was not to sell huge color prints fast but to instill in the minds of art directors that here was a photographer who could deliver photographic services unmatched by any other photographer.

5. Publicity

Author and business expert Jack Lander claims that, square inch for square inch, free publicity is more effective than paid advertising. We agree. Here are a few examples of just how powerful publicity can be.

When Shell and Judy Norris began Class Reunions, Inc., they thought that managing college and high school reunions would be a part-time venture. Because of the novelty of their business, however, the *Wall Street Journal* wrote an article about them. It began a landslide of publicity that has kept them busy full-time ever since.

When Dan Cassidy started his computerized scholarship-matching service he had very little money for marketing so he arranged to appear as a guest on a local radio station. He got a hundred calls from that first appearance and now successfully markets his business primarily by making free guest appearances on radio and TV.

Sally Van Swearingen also built her business using publicity. Sally is a wedding makeup artist. To get visibility for her business, she sent news releases to the local media talking about the kind of makeup brides must have now that most weddings are videotaped. The release resulted in many articles in local newspapers and magazines and ultimately a recurring spot on a local morning TV show. Her business grew so fast, she now has her own salons in multiple locations in Los Angeles.

You've heard the saying "Success attracts success." Publicity operates on that principle, too. It assumes that if you create enough momentum around yourself and your business and then provide a good-quality service or product, your business will grow. Another way of thinking about it is that people are attracted to a bright, shiny, fast-moving object, something that stands out in a crowd.

To take advantage of free publicity, however, you have to qualify for it by making yourself and your business newsworthy. Then you have to invest some time and energy in contacting local newspapers, magazines, and radio and TV stations, or hire a publicist or public relations firm to do this for you.

Public relations consultant Michael Baybeck suggests regularly setting aside a specific amount of time, preferably five hours a week, for "PR" efforts. He also advises treating PR like an investment account in which you send out one news release a month, make five PR-oriented phone calls a week, and have at least one PR lunch a month.

Becoming newsworthy. To make yourself "newsworthy," you have to have something to say or offer that is different and of interest to others. The fact that Susan Smith is starting a mailing-list service on Tenth Street isn't particularly newsworthy. But if Susan's new business opens by announcing the results of a survey she conducted showing how retailers can cut the mailing cost of sales circulars in half, that could be newsworthy. Armed with this survey she'll have a much better chance of getting news coverage.

At times, becoming newsworthy is a matter of taking advantage of a moment's opportunity. Joseph Cossman, author of the book *How I Made a Million Dollars in Mail Order*, and an expert at self-promotion, once found a mallard duck in his swimming pool. He called the local newspaper and TV station, who covered the story. The newspaper syndicated the report nationally and each time it appeared Cossman was identified as the author of the book *How I Made a Million Dollars in Mail Order*. Not bad publicity for just one phone call.

News releases. Effective publicity is not just a matter of getting your message out, however. That message has to reach your market. Sending a news release to selected publications can result in a product review or announcement of your business in the particular trade and professional publications, newsletters, magazines, or newspapers that you know your customers will be reading.

A news release is usually a one- to two-page statement of some news-worthy event. It announces a new product, releases the results of a survey, or reports on an upcoming promotional event such as an all-day art exhibit at a local shopping center or a free evening seminar on how to save the most money under a new tax law. Editors and producers expect news releases to appear in a standard format. See the Resources list at the end of this chapter for further information on publicity.

Interviews. News releases or calls to local radio, TV, and print media can lead to appearances on radio or TV talk shows or to feature or news articles about you and your business.

A good example is Charlotte Hartman, who designs beautiful custom-made bridal dresses. To attract more business for the upcoming spring season, she scheduled a February fashion show at a nearby shopping mall. After reading an article about how more marrying couples are opting for elaborate weddings, she began calling local radio and TV stations to suggest a story on new trends in wedding gowns.

Her strategy paid off. She appeared as a guest on several radio and TV programs and, of course, talked about her upcoming fashion show. Before her PR event, she sent press releases to local papers and got news coverage of the show, complete with photographs.

Cable TV opportunities. An easy way to get TV exposure is to volunteer your product or service for a TV benefit auction. Producing your own TV shows by taking advantage of "local origination" or "public access" programming will bring you high local visibility and give you valuable on-camera experience.

Acting and media coach Judy Kerr generates business with her cable show, "Judy Kerr's Acting Class." Hair stylist Ed Salazar builds his reputation and clientele with his beauty and style show, "30 Minutes with Salazar." Financial consultant James Irwin has developed a following in the business community with his "Business in the News." To find out about cable TV possibilities in your area, contact your local cable station.

Writing articles. With over 6,000 business and trade publications available today, you can probably find a way to have an article you've written published in a magazine or newsletter that your customers read. This builds your credibility and establishes you as an expert in your field.

To get an article published, send it to publications that your customers respect and read, or send a query letter proposing an article you could write. Remember to include a picture of yourself and a brief biographical sketch along with your name, address, and telephone number to be included at the close of the article.

You can sometimes get paid for your articles, or you may be able to trade articles for advertising space. But no matter what arrangement you make with the publishers, always make sure they will include a brief description of you, and your name, address, and telephone number.

Teaching courses and seminars. Adult education is growing at a rate of 35 percent per year. Teaching adult education classes is another way to enhance your reputation, meet prospective clients, and make business contacts. You'll find opportunities to teach courses in college continuing-education programs, adult education organizations, churches, YW-YMCAs, and even department stores and hotels.

When management consultant Marilyn Miller wanted to expand her business into the gift-buying industry, she offered to do a seminar for the industry's annual convention. Her topic, leadership skills, turned out to be popular. Several hundred managers attended. Many asked for her card at the conclusion of her presentation, and, by following up on their interest, Miller landed several consulting contracts. You may be surprised at some of the paying business opportunities that arise from offering seminars.

Books, workbooks, and anthologies. Writing a book or pamphlet, developing a workbook, or contributing a chapter to an anthology will not only increase your credibility but can also become an ongoing source of income. You can sell your books at seminars, use them as promotional items, give them away as incentives for people to buy your product or service, or use them to help you get appearances on radio and TV programs.

Writing a book saved Patricia Massie and Pauline Link's fledgling catering service, Adam and Eve. When business tapered off, they decided to write a book on how to cater a party and use it to get appearances on local talk shows. It worked, and it gave them the exposure they needed for the phone to start ringing again.

Getting a book or workbook published doesn't have to be an arduous affair. You can publish a small, simply bound version yourself using desktop publishing software and following the ideas presented in *The Self-Publishing Manual*, by Don Poynter. Or you can send an outline and two chapters of your book ideas to established publishers. Another alternative is using book packagers who, for a fee, will sell your book to established publishers.

Ideas for Free or Low-Cost Publicity

Producing brochures and flyers
Posting on-line notices and listings
Networking at social events
Giving speeches
Writing articles
Getting articles written about you
Sending personal letters and notes
Mailing announcement cards
Placing periodic telephone calls
Making slide presentations
Submitting unsolicited proposals
Joining professional and trade
   organizations
Exhibiting at trade shows and
   conferences
Guesting on radio and TV talk shows

Sending out news releases
Placing yourself in directory listings
Carrying your product with you
Wearing a symbol
Bartering
Donating and volunteering
Writing a newsletter
Teaching classes
Giving away samples
Offering discount coupons
Contacting past customers
Putting up signs and posters
Joining others in promotions
Being active in civic clubs and churches
Placing classified ads
Hosting your own cable talk show

If you don't have time to write a book, but could squeeze in time for a chapter (that's only about 3,000 words, or twelve double-spaced typewritten pages), you can reap the benefits of a book by contributing a chapter to an anthology.

For example, Dottie Walters, who heads Royal Publishing from her home in Glendora, California, publishes several anthologies every year, each on a different theme, from sales power and effective communication to stress management. A different person contributes each chapter, which includes a full-page biography and picture, along with the address and telephone number of the author. Authors buy copies of the anthology wholesale and sell it retail. The best part of this arrangement is that while you're promoting yourself with the anthology, every other author using it is promoting you, too.

Since insurance specialist Wayne Cotton contributed to one of Walters's anthologies, he has used it to increase enrollment at his high-priced business seminars. He gives the book away free to each registrant. The "gift with purchase" concept can be used to build any business. Estée Lauder, the famous cosmetics mogul, built her entire business on this promotional concept.

Speaking. You can also promote your services or product by speaking before civic, trade, or professional groups. There are more than 9,000 daily speaking opportunities in the United States. Speaking on subjects related to your business is a particularly useful sales tool in such personal-service businesses as real estate, child care, consulting, or counseling, where people like to feel they have a trusted relationship with the professional.

Consultant Bill Slavin finds that speaking and leading seminars provide him with the high profile he needs to attract business. "You never know for sure who will be a client in the future," he says. "So I've found that you have to treat everyone you meet as a potential client. You can convert the acquaintances you have made at speeches or seminars into clients with a follow-up call and an appointment. But be sure you focus the follow-through conversations on your business or they will think of you as a speaker or seminar leader instead of as a business."

Making impressive visual aids and handouts to accompany speeches, seminars, and proposals is easy with desktop presentation software. Use this software to create 35mm slides, overhead transparencies for speeches, and charts for proposals. Leading programs are *Harvard Graphics*, *Freelance Graphics*, and *PowerPoint*. You can print what you create on your printer, a plotter or, using a modem, you can transmit your work over a phone line to a service that produces color slides, overhead transparencies, or color prints for you. Services generally ship your order back to you within twenty-four hours by air courier.

Actually, in a small business virtually every contact you have with others is free promotion—for good or for bad. So it's important to convey the right image of yourself and your business in all your interactions. Pay attention to:

- Appearance
- Voice
- What you say
- What you write
- How you dress

6. Using Gatekeepers

Another method used by successful home-based businesses is to build relationships with one or more key influencers in your field who provide you with all or most of your business. These people are your "gatekeepers." Woodworker Robert Livingston used this approach when he started a cabinet-making business as a way to support his work in the theater. He obtains his business from just a few key architects who refer their clients to him. Graphics designer Tom Dower gets all the business he needs from his publicist wife, Kim Freilich. Janell Besell's husband is an anesthesiologist, so when she opened her billing service his office became her first client. Through referrals to his colleagues her business has grown rapidly.

At first glance you may think these individuals are unusually lucky to be so well connected. Actually, if you begin thinking about those you know who hold your work in high regard and value your talents, you'll undoubtedly find that you, too, have key connections. If you don't already have them, you can probably get them by volunteering your skills for charity or civic activities that will attract such supporters to you.

To identify gatekeepers for your business, think of all the businesses and professionals and anyone else who comes in regular contact with your potential clients and customers at the precise time they need your products or services. These are your gatekeepers. Make a list of them. Then, set about identifying as many such individuals as possible. If you are a mobile disk jockey, for example, and you specialize in providing music for nonprofit fund-raising events, your gatekeepers would include planners, florists, caterers, hotels, and tuxedo rental stores, among others. So you would make yourself known to as many such sources as possible.

In establishing relationships with gatekeepers, provide them with samples of what you do and be sure to approach them as colleagues with whom you can work mutually to help each other's business to grow. Talk about how you can help them; don't just ask them to help you.

7. Service: Giving More Than the Competition

Nothing sells like service. If your results are "extra-ordinary," if your service is outstanding, people will quickly take notice and want to tell everyone they know. Suddenly you have the equivalent of a volunteer sales force. When Nathan Pritikin started his first Pritikin treatment program, he didn't even intend to go into business. He wanted to demonstrate the dramatic restorative effects of diet and exercise on seriously ill individuals. His results were so dramatic, however, that he found he had opened a floodgate of new clients.

Charlotte Mitchell's business is literally based on going the extra mile. As Notary on Wheels and Fingerprinting on Wheels she goes where her clients need her. Medical transcriptionist Vickie Fite believes her success is the result of the following business philosophy: "I go the extra mile for people. I work harder than I would for an employer." And home-based marketing consultant Linda Jagoda puts it this way: "Treat your clients, no matter what size, to royal service. Your smallest customer can bring you one of your biggest clients later on."

Norm Dominquez's success also demonstrates that service beyond what's expected is a low-cost but effective means of marketing. Dominquez operates Unicom Paging, Inc., a mobile communications service in Phoenix, Arizona, and says of his marketing approach, "The name of the game is service. Phoenix is highly competitive. So I focus on the smaller companies who need only fifteen to sixteen pagers, and we provide an incentive to our customers too, so they'll want to refer us to other people. Besides our seven-day-a-week, twenty-four-hour service, our incentive offer is eight months of free service credited to their account. We also have a philosophy of trust. I don't do extensive credit checks and I don't get burned any more than the norm."

Don't Market in Barren Fields: Target

Georgina creates elegant, trendy, custom-designed women's clothing, but she was disillusioned. "I've been networking like crazy for months. I went to five meetings this week alone. But I'm not getting any business." When Georgina expressed these frustrations to us, we wanted to know where she had been networking and why she'd chosen these groups. She told us she was attending meetings of small-business owners because she'd noticed how plain and dowdy their wardrobes usually were. "They really need me!" she exclaimed.

In fact, the response Georgina was getting said otherwise. The women she was meeting may need her, but from what she told us, they didn't know it. Evidently the women Georgina has been networking with were not particularly image conscious. At their luncheon tables, they talked excitedly about new equipment, hiring practices, and investment opportunities. Beautiful, sophisticated clothing was apparently low on their list of priorities, if it appeared at all. Georgina had been networking in barren fields.

For your marketing efforts to pay off, you have to market in fertile ground. You have to target your marketing to places and media that reach people who are actually experiencing a need for what you offer. In Georgina's case, we suggested that she network with groups of professional speakers, ad agency executives, or public relations specialists—people in professions in which image and appearance are vital to success. Or she could network with beauty salon operators, wedding consultants, or fitness trainers—professionals who come into daily contact with people to whom image is obviously a high priority.

Charles was also marketing in barren fields. He was trying to start a scholarship-matching service. "This is a lot harder than I thought it would be," he told us. "I've been advertising in a newspaper every weekend for the last four months, and I've had very few calls. I'm not giving up, though. I'll give it a year, and if the advertising doesn't work by then I'll have to look at doing some other business."

While there are many parents who need to find scholarship funds for their college-bound children, how likely would they be to look in the newspaper for help in finding such scholarships? Most parents would be more likely to contact a school counselor, a college testing service, teachers, or maybe a parents' magazine or a school newspaper. If they see an ad in the newspaper, they might be concerned about not knowing anything about the company offering the service or they might worry about being taken in by scams.

In other words, Charles needs to start marketing in more fertile ground. He could give speeches for parents of high-school students. He could network with school counselors—or even try a classified ad in a parents' magazine. Instead of advertising all year in one newspaper, Charles could sample a variety of marketing activities until he finds the fertile ground where his business can take root.

Don't Bet It All on One Horse: Experiment

Most certainly Charles shouldn't put all his marketing bets on only one possible source of business. If you remember, that's the same thing Tim did in trying to get his referral service off the ground (p. 510). Not only were they marketing in barren fields, they had blown their budget on their first best guess as to where to market.

Unfortunately, there's no cut-and-dried formula for making sure you find the most fertile ground the first time around. Marketing starts as an experiment. You try some of this and some of that, sampling several targeted activities simultaneously on a small scale, experimenting until you find the several most fertile fields.

In addition, if you make a habit of using several methods simultaneously, those who need what you offer will keep running into your name, your face, and your message repeatedly in multiple contexts. That results in what we call "top of the mind" marketing, marketing that makes sure your name comes to mind when the moment comes that someone does need your product or service. You will be more likely to be the one who comes to mind if your clients and customers regularly read, hear, or see something about you.

We've found that if you select about five different methods and do them each regularly, you'll multiply the impact of everything you do. Marketing is contagious. It spreads like dandelions. Each activity you undertake in fertile ground will seed the others. The person you meet networking at a professional association, for example, might say, "Oh, I know who you are. I saw your article in the journal." Or when someone receives your newsletter, they might say, "Yeah, that's the person I met at the trade show demonstration!"

By specializing and then marketing yourself in a variety of ways, you can position yourself as a preeminent specialist in your field. In order to know which combination of methods will work for you, of course, you will need to be sure to track your results and then let results be your guide. The best way to track your results is to make a policy of asking each person who calls or contacts you how he or she heard about you and then recording the answers in your contact management or money management software, so you can print out a report regularly of where your business is coming from and then compare these results with how much money you're spending on each marketing activity.

Helen Berman is a good example of how multiple marketing activities generate success. She wanted to become a consultant and sales trainer in the publishing industry, but the competition was tough. There was already a number of well-known consultants serving that industry. How was she to break in?

She was sure that the cost of what she calls "push marketing"—that is, trying to get through to the thousands of her potential customers by telephone—would be too high. If she called a list of people who didn't know her, she was going to have to call a lot of people before she'd be able to make even one sale. So instead, she chose to use what she calls "pull marketing"—building a high profile for herself with interested and qualified individuals. Then when she calls, these individuals already know who she is and the same calls will lead to a higher ratio of sales.

To implement her strategy, she contacted the meeting planners for upcoming conferences in her field and proposed that she offer a seminar on her particular sales expertise. She got several bookings. Simultaneously, she began calling the trade magazines in the field to talk about writing a sales column for them. Soon she was writing a column for *Folio*, the leading trade magazine in the field. With this credibility and name recognition she now gets business from both her calls and her mailings. She's also writing a book and creating her own seminars, which are not only profitable in their own right but also provide a source of funds for a direct-mail campaign.

Here's another example. When aspiring director David Beaird came to Los Angeles to make movies, everyone told him Hollywood didn't need another director. And indeed he found the studio doors closed tight. Having taught acting classes in Chicago he decided to find another way in. He rented a theater and began teaching classes. Soon he put on a play he'd written and invited the press and industry representatives to come. The momentum was building, and, based on the response to his play, he was able to attract backing for a low-budget film. Although the film was never commercially distributed, it received critical acclaim at the Cannes Film Festival and that led to further financial backing. After his second low-budget film, he reached his "critical mass" and was placed on the list of directors of a major studio.

Private-practice consultant Gene Call is another outstanding example. Southern California–based Call offers seminars that help professionals learn how to market their private practices. He began his business with a background in marketing and sales, as do many of the premier marketers we've met. For him, getting business is an art and a passion. When business is slow, he views the downturn not as a problem but as a challenge that gets him charged up, an intriguing puzzle to be solved with new, fresh, and more creative approaches.

An avid networker, he built a mailing list of prospective clients and invited them to a free preview evening. Fourteen professionals came to his first preview. From this small group he filled his first day-long workshop. Through clever, well-designed direct-mail pieces and further networking, his previews grew. Now more than sixty people attend his five-week program every month. He holds events for graduates and offers advanced classes and private consultations. Even his answering machine message is a master sales tool, communicating the benefits of More Business for Professionals, the name of his consulting business.

Linda Jagoda of Scottsdale, Arizona, has used multiple methods to market her own marketing firm and is now grossing half a million dollars a year from her 2,500-square-foot home. She too is an avid networker and started her business by giving seminars to attract clients. In addition, she uses a half-page ad in the Yellow Pages from which she got General Telephone as a client, advertises in four print publications, and makes frequent use of direct mail. She says, "Consistent marketing saves you when times are the toughest. It causes people to call you out of the blue. You never know what new business the next week is going to bring."

Don't Wait: Follow Through

Marjorie came up during a break to tell us how uncomfortable she felt about marketing and to share a disappointing story. She was trying to sell advertising specialties. Several months before, she'd met someone at a conference who seemed quite interested in her service, but only that week she'd learned he had placed a large order with her competition. "He told me he'd call as soon as their budget was approved," she lamented. "He asked for my card. It was only a couple of months ago. I don't understand what went wrong."

Obviously this woman had done everything right, up to a point. After all, she had sold her contact on placing an order, and he did. Unfortunately he placed it with someone else. She did the work; the competitor got the order. She had come face-to-face with the old saying "Out of sight, out of mind." To make sure a contact actually does call you when the moment comes that they need you, you have to follow through and keep in touch.

Follow-through is part two of "top of the mind marketing." Do give out your card, but more importantly, get cards from the contacts you make and call them back to arrange for a follow-up conversation within the week. Then send something appropriate every week or so. Nothing is colder than a long-forgotten contact, no matter how eager the person seems at the time you first talk. You have to follow through.

Of course, we get busy. We forget. We don't want to be bothersome. So we tend to just wait for them to call. "After all, they said they would call when they're ready." But don't leave business to chance. Think of how many other people may be contacting them while you're waiting. Think of Marjorie. Take action to keep your name ever-present in the minds of prospective clients.

Create a contact database using mailing lists, contact management, or personal information management software like *Act, Ascend, Lotus Organizer, Maximizer, Packrat,* or *Sharkware.* Then, set aside a specific time period each week to make follow-up contacts. Look through your database (or card file, if you prefer) for names of contacts you haven't spoken with recently. Call them or send them something—a clipping, a thank-you note, a newsletter, a novelty. Then once a month, or at least once a quarter, send a mailing to everyone on your contact list: past, present, and potential clients and referral sources. Consider holding a party or open house occasionally. Here are several ways to follow up and keep in touch:

Direct mail. Experience proves that following up mailings with a personal phone call does improve response. A similar result can be obtained with a triple mailing—all different pieces. The first mailing might entertain. Send an amusing clipping from *The Wall Street Journal*, for example, and include your logo but no name or address. The second, mailed a week later, might further pique the recipient's curiosity with an elegant solution to a problem that he or she may be having. No name and no address on this mailer, either, but do include your logo. Finally, send a third mailer, which has your name and address and logo on it, and includes a brochure that lists your services. This campaign can be tricky because you have to know what kind of solution to offer. But if you know the problems people on your mailing list are having and target those, you can get results, especially since they already know who you are.

Newsletters. Newsletters filled with informational tidbits of interest to your clients and customers can be great as ongoing follow-up with networking contacts. Whereas brochures are often tossed out, newsletters are more often read and even filed away, particularly in businesses for which there is a dearth of published information.

Personal letters and thank-you notes. Sales trainer Steve Maier advocates writing personal letters to prospective clients. He told us, "I could never isolate a job I got because the client was attracted by a brochure I sent out. I've discovered that a brochure is something you use to ensure that your name is in someone's file after you've talked to them."

So instead of mailing out brochures to attract business, Maier focuses on personal mailings. "I write letters to the people I want to talk to, trying to provide value in the letter, addressing to the extent possible the particular problems they have and offering ways they might solve their special problems."

Maier's strategy works. He has found that the simple thank-you notes he writes to follow up contacts he makes generate enough business to pay his $5,000 annual printing bill.

While you cannot depend on networking to produce immediate prosperity, compared with other business-getting methods, the investment is smaller and the return, surer. So if you want to get more business, get your mouth moving and have a good time while you're at it!

Don't Try to Be What You're Not: Tailor

"I just don't have a sales personality. And, I really don't like marketing. But you're saying I have to do more of it. I'm good at what I do; I just want a chance to do it!"

This is a frequent lament from the growing number of gifted and talented professionals, artists, and specialists who are going out on their own in today's service and information economy. They aren't particularly interested in running a business. They aren't entrepreneurs in the classic sense of loving business enterprise per se. They want to create a job for themselves doing what they do best and the more they hear about the importance of marketing, the more frustrated they feel.

Well, we have good news for everyone who doesn't like to market. You don't need to have a sales and marketing personality to get plenty of business. You do not need to be a natural-born entrepreneur. There are marketing methods suited to every personality, and the most successful home businesses are those that find methods that are tailored to their personalities so that marketing becomes an integral part of what they do naturally and comfortably.

We have met and interviewed plenty of successful home-business owners who are shy and introverted people, yet they are successfully marketing themselves using methods that are suited to their personalities. We have met and interviewed others who are highly technical problem-solvers and yet they have been able to market themselves successfully by calling upon those very strengths. They tailor their marketing to their personality and to their business.

So whatever your personality, no matter how you feel about marketing now, know that you can find methods that will make marketing second nature to you. If speaking before groups leaves you shuddering and stuttering, you don't need to feel inadequate. If you'd rather have a root canal than call a stranger on the phone, don't try to get yourself to do it. You'll just put it off, dread it, and find a million other things to do before you pick up the phone. Start with methods that actually appeal to you. Get in contact with the excitement and pride you feel about your work and identify your most natural way to share with people whom you'd like to work with. Once you find that, do it and do it and do it some more.

If you would like help identifying what marketing methods you are suited to do well, you'll find information in the Resources list about *The Business Generator,* a tool we developed with psychologist Dr. Jessica Schairer to help you identify your personal marketing style and match it with marketing methods that can work for your business. *The Business Generator* also helps you know how much marketing you need to do each day, week, or month, and to be sure you actually do it!

Keeping up your marketing efforts month after month, year after year, will make the difference. Once you identify the strategies that produce the most results, continue them even after your business is thriving. If you sometimes generate more business than you can handle, you can subcontract the work to others and still make a profit. Or you can refer it to reliable colleagues with or without a referral fee.

Ultimately, your happy, satisfied customers become your greatest source of new business. Marketing consultant Cork Platts reminds us that "referrals are golden. Do something special for each customer or client and they'll remember you to everyone else who needs you." In business, as in all of life, what goes around comes around.

If you don't waste your time, if you focus, niche, target, experiment, follow through, and tailor your marketing efforts, and if you do these things regularly and service your clients and customers well, you will find that when you go into your home office every Monday morning, there will be ample business waiting there for you. And as you sit down to get started doing it, you will know that all the effort you've invested in your goals and dreams has been worth it. You'll be living them! You owe that to yourself!

Materials and Supplies to Help You Market in Style

The more easily you can let everyone you meet see, touch, or learn more about what you do, the more quickly you will become known for what you do and the more people will think of you when they need what you offer or meet someone else who does. Therefore, the more professionally, cost-effectively and time-efficiently you can show off your business, the better. Fortunately, today, there is a wide range of materials and supplies to help you market yourself more easily and effectively. Here are a few examples:

1. **Predesigned four-color materials** you can use to create one attractive, coordinated professional visual image for your home business. With your computer, desktop publishing or word processing software, templates, and printer, you just add the text and you have:

   - Letterhead
   - Business cards
   - Stationery
   - Postcards
   - Brochures

   - News releases
   - Overhead transparencies
   - Presentation folders
   - Laser signs
   - Portfolios

2. **Tabletop presentation binders** that hold your presentations in clear plastic pouches and open up into a tabletop stand so you can flip the pages of your presentation one by one for everyone to see as you talk. It snaps closed into a carrying case.

3. **A portable light stand** for making tabletop overhead presentations without lugging around an overhead projector. The light table, called LightFolio, fits neatly into an over-the-shoulder carrying case that folds out into a presentation stand. (Available from Sky Mall, [800] 424-6255.)

4. **Acrylic display stands, easels and literature holders** in which to place your business cards, brochures, or flyers at expos or other locations where your customers will see them. Similar stands are available for collecting business cards from others for promotional drawings at expos or conferences.

5. **Flip pads you can hang anywhere** without a stand, easel, or tape. Called *Static Images*, these sheets by Avery Dennison adhere to any surface and can be erased by using special marking pens.

6. **White dry erase wallboards** for formal presentations or taking notes at impromptu meetings.

7. **A three-fold paper folder** for quickly folding brochures and flyers. It folds 500 sheets in twenty minutes.

8. **An envelope sealer** quickly opens the flap, moistens, and seals your mailings at a pace of up to thirty-five envelopes a minute!

9. **Presentation protectors** for covering overheads, samples, or other materials you want to show to lots of people and let them examine without damaging them. Simply slip your materials into these see-through protector covers and place them in a three-ring binder if you wish.

10. **Business card accessories.** Laminators that will instantly turn your card into magnets or luggage tags for premiums and giveaways. A special stapler called *Card-It* that will instantly create "die cuts" so you can attach your card to any piece of paper, brochure, or folder without having to use paper clips or staples.

These practical materials for marketing yourself more effectively are available from companies like the ones listed in the Resources at the end of this chapter. Call or write them for their catalogs or names of dealers near you.

Resources

Books

Big Marketing Ideas for Small Service Businesses. Tom and Marilyn Ross. Buena Vista, Colo.: Accelerated Business Images, 1991.

Bulletproof News Releases. Kay Borden. Marietta, GA: Franklin-Sarrett Publishers, 1994.

Do It Yourself Marketing Research. George Breen and A. B. Blankenship. New York: McGraw-Hill, 1989.

Getting Business to Come to You. Paul and Sarah Edwards and Laura Clampitt Douglas. New York: Tarcher/Perigee, 1991.

Getting the Most from Your Yellow Pages Advertising. Barry Maher. New York: AMACOM, 1988.

Getting Publicity. Tana Fletcher and Julia Rockler. North Vancouver, British Columbia: Self-Counsel Press, 1990.

The Great Marketing Turnaround. Stan Rapp and Tom Collins. New York: Plume, 1992. (Also authors of **MaxiMarketing.**)

Guerrilla Marketing: Secrets for Making Big Profits from Your Small Business. Jay Conrad Levinson. Boston: Houghton Mifflin, 1993. (Also author of **Guerrilla Selling** and other books.)

How to Get Clients. Jeff and Marc Slutsky. New York: Warner, 1991. (Also authors of **Street Smart Marketing.**)

How to Get Your Point Across in 30 Seconds—or Less. Milo O. Frank. New York: Simon & Schuster, 1986.

I Can See You Naked: America's Best Book on Making Presentations. Ron Hoff. Kansas City: Andrews and McMeel, 1992.

Letters That Sell. Edward W. Werz. Chicago: Contemporary Books, Inc., 1987.

Look Before You Leap: Market Research Made Easy. Don Doman, Dell Dennison, Margaret Doman. Bellingham, Wash.: Self-Counsel Press, 1993.

Positioning: The Battle for Your Mind. Al Reis and Jack Trout. New York: Warner, 1986. (Also authors of: **Marketing Warfare** and **Bottom Up Marketing.**)

Power Talking: 50 Ways to Say What You Mean and Get What You Want. George Walther. New York: Putnam, 1991. (Also author of **Phone Power.**)

Sales Magic, Revolutionary New Sales Techniques that Will Double Your Sales Volume. Kerry Johnson. New York: Morrow, 1994.

The World's Best Known Marketing Secret. Ivan Misner. (For full citation, see Chapter Resources for chapter 17.)

The Sales Script Book. Donald J. Moine, Ph.D., and Gerhard Gschwandtner, Personal Selling Power, P.O. Box 5467, Fredericksburg, VA 22405, 1986.

Secrets of Successful Speakers. Lilly Walters. New York: McGraw-Hill, 1993.

Selling Through Independent Reps. Harold J. Novick. New York: Amacom, 1994.

Selling Your Services. Robert W. Bly. New York: Henry Holt, 1991. (Also author of **The Copywriter's Handbook.**)

Speak and Grow Rich. Dottie Walters and Lillet Walters. Englewood Cliffs,

N.J.: Prentice Hall, 1989. How to get booked for speeches at seminars, conferences, banquets, and more, for fee or free.

The Unabashed Self-Promoter's Guide: What Every Man, Woman, Child, and Organization in America Needs to Know about Getting Ahead. Jeffrey Lant, Jeffrey Lant Associates, 50 Follen St., Ste. 507, Cambridge, MA 02138.

Words That Sell. Richard Bayan. Chicago: Contemporary Books, 1987.

Ziglar on Selling. Zig Ziglar. New York: Ballantine, 1991. (Also author of **Zig Ziglar's Secrets of Closing the Sale.**)

Newsletter

Win-Win Marketing. 662 Crestview Drive, San Jose, CA 95117 ([408] 247-0122).

Tapes

Word-of-Mouth Marketing, a complete training program with a consultation by the trainer. Gene Call, Business for Professionals, 1821 Wilshire Blvd., Santa Monica, CA 90403; (800) 794-7858.

Complete Home-Business Marketing System

Paul & Sarah Edwards' Business Generator. Includes the Edwards's book **Getting Business to Come to You,** a seventy-five minute video, **Top of the Mind Marketing,** and **The Marketing Partner,** a sixty-four-page workbook and guide for developing and following through on a marketing plan tailored to your personality and your business. Here's How, P.O. Box 5091, Santa Monica, CA 90409.

Computer Solutions

BizFile. CompuServe Information Service, 5000 Arlington Centre Blvd., P.O. Box 20212, Columbus, OH 43220; (800) 848-8199 or (614) 457-0802.

Databased Marketing. Herman Holtz. New York: John Wiley & Sons, 1992.

Desktop Marketing With the Macintosh. Tracy Emerick and Stacy Gasteiger. New York: Brady Books, 1992.

Making Money With Your Computer at Home. Paul and Sarah Edwards. New York: Tarcher/Perigee, 1993.

Software

401 Great Letters. Microbase, Inc., 3923 South McClintock Drive, Suite 401, Tempe, AZ 85282; (602) 897-7800. (800) 897-3637.

IdeaFisher. Idea Fisher System, Inc., 2222 Martin Street, Ste. 110, Irvine, CA 92715; (800)289-4332 or (714)474-8111.

Directories

Directories are generally published annually, cost a great deal more than books, and you can often find them at the reference desk in libraries. Increasingly, directory information is becoming available in on-line databases.

Broadcasting Yearbook. Reed Reference Publishing, 121 Chanlon Rd., New Providence, NJ 07974. (800) 521-8110.

Directories in Print. Julie E. Towell, ed., Gale Research, Inc., 835 Penobscot Building, Detroit, MI 48226; (313) 961-2242. (800) 877-4253.

Encyclopedia of Associations. Gale Research Company, Book Tower, Detroit, MI 48226 (available in libraries and on Dialog Information Service).

National Directory of Addresses and Telephone Numbers. Detroit: Omnigraphics, Inc. Annual. (800) 234-1340.

Standard Rate and Data Service, Inc. 3002 Glenview Road, Wilmette, IL 60091; (708) 256-6067 (produces eleven directories). (800) 323-4588.

Trade Shows and Professional Exhibits Directory. Gale Research Co., Book Tower, Detroit, MI 48226; (313) 961-2242. (800) 877-4253.

Marketing Supplies and Materials

Avery Dennison Consumer Service Center. 20955 Pathfinder Rd., Diamond Bar, CA 91765; (800) 232-8379.

Ideal Art. P.O. Box 291500, Nashville, TN 37229; (800) 433-2278.

Paper Direct. 205 Chubb Ave., Lyndhurst, NJ 07071; (800) A-PAPERS.

Queblo Images. 131 Heartland Blvd., Brentwood, NY 11717; (800) 523-9080.

CHAPTER
TWENTY-FOUR
■■■■■■■■■■■■■■■■■■■■■■■■■■■

Moving On: What to Do When Your Business Outgrows Your Home

Sooner or later, the day comes when you think about whether it's time to move the office away from home. Perhaps your business has grown so much it's bursting at the seams, and working from home feels more like living at the office. Or maybe you've had an intriguing job offer or promotion possibility that promises to take you back to a corporate skyscraper. Whatever the reason, many people who work at home eventually face the question of whether they should move on.

For some, the decision is easy because working from home is only a stepping-stone on the road to another goal. Computer consultant Bill Slavin explains that his dream had always been to build a big organization, so "as soon as it was financially feasible, I moved my business to a downtown office."

In contrast to Slavin, there are those for whom working from home is a cherished way of life they refuse to give up. They share the sentiments expressed by mime and typesetter Tina Lenert when she declared, in unequivocal terms, "I wouldn't want to work any other way." Tina and others who feel this strongly about their home offices will do whatever must be done to keep working from home, even if it means moving to a larger house or restricting the growth of their businesses.

Then there are those who realize that they will be able to make significantly more money with less effort if they keep their business at home. Loan broker Robert Roboti found, for example, that by moving his office back home he was able to reduce his overhead to the point that he can keep an additional $10,000 of income each month. Telemarketing expert George Walther discovered that moving his business out of his home required that he generate two to three times as much work just to sustain the same income. As you might imagine, although Robert and George were initially eager to move out, once they did both decided to return home and stay there.

For most people, however, deciding whether to stay or move out is less clear-cut. When faced with the choice, the great majority of people who work from home feel torn between opportunities to grow and expand on the one hand, and the convenience, comfort, financial benefits, and flexibility they get from working at home on the other. Medical transcriptionist Georgia Hahn, for example, sought our advice about her situation because she had the opportunity of taking on a large account that would require hiring several staff members, and she feared this would mean moving her business out of her house.

"I've become very spoiled having the business here at home. I make enough money to live comfortably and I've been with my kids since they were little. They're in school now and I'm a successful businesswoman. I've had the best of both worlds, but now I have to make a painful decision. What's it going to be, my easygoing life or a bigger business?"

Fortunately, moving on doesn't have to be the either/or decision Georgia fears. For us, working from home started as an island of relief from high-stress careers that has turned into a satisfying lifestyle. And there's no need to move out just because the business is growing. We have a spectrum of options to choose from if we want to expand without leaving home.

In this chapter, we'll talk about how you'll know when it's time to move on, and the full range of options you have. We'll also share some of the creative solutions others have found for preserving the benefits of working from home while taking advantage of promising career and business opportunities.

When to Move Out

When Gerald and Sandy McDevitt consulted with the Small Business Administration about their home business, they asked, "How will we know when it's time to move out?" The representative simply told them, "You'll know," and we would agree. When it's time for a change, the signs will be impossible to ignore.

As the McDevitts discovered, the issue is usually a matter of space. Two years ago accountant Sandy McDevitt was having difficulty using the software she had purchased for her computer. There were too many commands to recall. In her frustration she had an idea: what if there were a template she could lay over a computer keyboard that would display all the commands she needed to remember in using various software?

With part-time assistance from her husband, Gerald, a computer analyst for the U.S. Navy, Sandy turned this idea into a home business called Creative Computer Products. The object was to produce "keyboard templates" for the major lines of personal computers.

Sandy and Gerald ran the whole operation from their family room and kitchen, taking orders by mail or phone and then packing and shipping them out. For shipping, they rented a mailbox and had daily UPS pickup. Then, by the time they began getting twenty-five to thirty orders a day, several things happened that made it clear they had outgrown their home.

First, the mailbox service told them they had too much volume for it to handle. At about the same time, the McDevitts ran out of storage space at home, and the family room and kitchen started overflowing with materials. There wasn't enough space for eating, let alone working.

So Sandy and Gerald rented a space they thought would be large enough to meet their needs and moved most everything out of the house. A year later, they had to rent a second space the same size as the first one, and now they still don't have enough room. Their printing press remains in the garage, where they produce all their in-house literature, and they have a fifteen-foot camera on order but no place to put it. The next step came later that year when the McDevitts bought a building of their own and consolidated the whole business in one place.

Aside from outgrowing the confines of a home, the quest for a different business image is the next most common reason for a change. In the early days of our consulting business, our firm, Public Affairs Assistance, won a major federal contract. Although we could do most of the work at home, the officials would not allow overhead expenses for a home office. Besides, we needed a place for the contract officers to preview the materials we were developing. The basement office we had in our first home was next to the laundry room and just wouldn't convey the right image.

Since we wanted to keep as much of our work at home as possible, we considered several options short of moving the office out. The final answer was to rent a professional suite temporarily, but there were other possibilities we could have chosen. In fact, here are twelve solutions we and other people have found for these dilemmas. Some may be totally inappropriate for your situation, but others should be catalysts that will help you resolve the issue of how to grow while working from home.

How to Keep the Benefits of Working From Home

1. Rent a professional suite. If you find you need a place where you can create a highly official business image, hold conferences, or get more extensive office services, consider renting a professional suite from an organization like Head-quarters Suites. Such suites are part of a complex that includes small offices, central conference facilities, and a full range of secretarial services available to anyone subleasing space from the complex.

When we rented a suite while working on the federal contract, we had a small office, a separate phone, and a receptionist at the complex to take our messages. The conference room there was useful for making presentations and holding meetings with the contract administrators. The cost of such suites varies by community but is generally less than renting a separate outside office and hiring the equivalent office services.

2. Rent private office space. Renting an office doesn't necessarily mean you have to say good-bye to working from home. Some people have rented a second office for certain activities (receiving mail or phone calls, working on large equipment, holding meetings) while still maintaining a home office where they can do creative or detail work. And you need not rent such space full-time. You can rent space part-time or by the day. In renting part-time space, you arrange for the hours you need the space each week and pay a flat monthly fee which can include some additional services like mailing, addressing, answering service, name on building directory, etc. Such rental arrangements are usually advertised in the Yellow Pages as "Business Identity Programs" under Office Rentals.

Hypnotherapist Nancy Bonus holds her weight-loss group meetings in office space she sublets from a private clinic, paying only for the hours her group uses the space each week. She sees individual clients and does all the management of her business at home. Bob Weil runs his part-time picture-framing business from his apartment but rents workshop time on Saturdays from a large picture-framing company. Marjorie Dahl does image consulting from her home, helping men and women "dress for success." However, when she holds workshops or brings together several clients to look over a number of garments, she rents a hotel suite.

Many homes simply can't accommodate the additional equipment and furniture involved in hiring staff. When necessary, entrepreneurs often rent space for their employees and continue to work at home themselves, either full- or part-time.

Writer Collin Gribbons, for example, who publishes eight newsletters and magazines for Canadian labor unions, needed a secretary and wasn't comfortable with having one come to his home. His work was generating a seemingly endless parade of air-express trucks, and his loud daisy-wheel printer was clattering away hour after hour, so he had begun to worry that his business would bother his neighbors. His solution was to rent outside office space where his secretary now works full-time.

Having an office doesn't preclude his working from home; it just provides another option. Collin says he still works at home, using his computer and modem to link up to his outside office. "I can always send material to the office by phone when I don't want to go in, but a lot of the more office-oriented tasks, like courier pickups and telephone messages, are now handled away from home."

3. Contract work with other businesses. Instead of moving his business to a warehouse, Bob Baxter hired a company to bottle and package his pet health-care products, jobs he once handled in his garage. When developing a large marketing program for a customer, consultant James McClaren subcontracted with several small businesses rather than renting office space and hiring employees for the duration of the contract. Using a free-lance writer, a packager, and an office-services company, he got the program done without leaving home.

4. Move to a bigger home. Whether you buy, lease, or build, a new and larger place to live may provide the added or specialized space you need to continue working from home. Husband-and-wife team Theresa Arnerich and Tom Morrell operated a seminar firm from their condominium, but space was tight. Their shipping department was in the garage, and the one office they shared also doubled as a bedroom for Tom's daughter when she visited on weekends. Theresa threatened to find an outside office, but they decided to build a new house instead. It would be tailor-made to working from home.

Theresa says, "I'm actually glad we worked from the condo for a while, because we found out what we needed before building. We learned, for example, that we want the offices on a separate level, away from the kitchen and other household activities. We want to be able to close the space off from social events and from household maintenance personnel who come in. We also want the offices near the bedroom so we can work late and make early morning calls without having to go across the whole house." For Theresa, the best part about the new house will be the luxury of having an office she can call her very own.

5. Hire employees who will work from their homes. Some companies, like MicroGraphic Images (software) and Escrow Overload (temporary escrow employees), have expanded by adding personnel who work from their own homes.

Commercial artist Diane Wessling Blake of MicroGraphic Images says, "By having our employees work at home, we can expand as rapidly as we need to and keep our costs to a minimum. In a fast-growing industry like ours, this is very important." The founders and chief executive officers of these companies all still work from home, too.

6. Rent storage or warehouse space. When potter June Wright had the chance of filling an order for over two thousand goblets to be used at a special benefit, she knew she'd have to hire helpers. She also knew they wouldn't all fit in her studio behind the house, so she found a warehouse to rent and hired ten students, part-time, for one month.

This arrangement worked so well that if she can get more orders on such a grand scale, she wants to keep it up. She would continue running the business and creating pots from her own home, but would have a supervisor overseeing operations at the warehouse.

7. Add on to your home. There are many options for adding on or converting unused areas of an existing house into extra business space. Many of these options are described in chapter 6.

We added on to two different houses in order to work from home. We bought our first house so we could move from a two-bedroom apartment and start working at home, but it didn't have a suitable place for Sarah to see psychotherapy clients. So we enclosed a side porch, providing a separate entrance and complete privacy for her clients.

Then when we first moved from our home in Kansas City to California, we tried sharing one office in part of our living room. It didn't work. Each of us needed to have our own private office space, so once again we added on. This time we built a second story.

8. Rent an adjacent apartment or buy a second condo. When lawyer Mark Cane passed his bar exam, he worked from his apartment but rented an office from a group of lawyers in a professional building where he could meet with clients. The cost of prime commercial space was high, however, and his overhead was consuming most of his income. When the studio apartment next to his became vacant, he talked to the landlord about renting it for his law office. He explained that his work was very quiet and would not disturb other tenants. The landlord agreed to the idea, and Mark's net income rose in his first month at the new location.

9. Buy a duplex or apartment building. Although this may seem like a rather extreme solution, it can be a successful one. Lynne Frances started Rainbow Cleaning Service from her apartment. She ran the business from a bedroom that also served as sitting room and office.

"I enjoyed it until the business just got too big," she recalls. "I had to hire a secretary, and then the number of my cleaning crew employees kept increasing until finally I had worked my way up to twenty. Of course, they were all coming to the apartment for work assignments. Even then it wasn't such a nuisance until it got up to twenty-eight. Then if I'd have one of my kids or my folks come to visit, it was just people around at all hours of the day and night."

After five years of this, she decided enough was enough and rented an outside office. She was running the service from this office when we met her, but she wasn't happy. "People just don't realize what a great way of life it is to work from your home. To move out is a terrible shock!" She had forgotten what a chore it was to have to get dressed up in the morning and rush off in a car to be at the office before the first crew arrived. "And," she told us, "it seems I never get anything done at home now that I have an outside office. When I get home at night the dishes are waiting in the sink, the bed's unmade, and the trash is overflowing."

The next time we saw Lynne, she had reached what was for her the ideal compromise: she had bought an apartment building. She lived in one unit and ran the cleaning service from another. "Now," she says with satisfaction, "I've got it all."

10. Negotiate to keep a job at home. A tempting job offer or promotion can lure you back to the office, but if you're ambivalent, consider negotiating to take the position while working at least part-time at home. Develop a plan that demonstrates how this would benefit the company and increase your productivity without jeopardizing vital communication with the office. Suggest perhaps two days in the office and three at home, or propose a schedule for regular meetings in the office.

11. Limit your business growth. Sometimes staying at home means making a hard decision. What is more important to you—a larger business or the particular work style that only a home office can provide? A surprising number of people are opting to limit their businesses to ones that can be contained within the walls of their homes. Some people we've met have scaled their businesses back in order to return to a home office after moving out of their homes.

Perhaps this is not so surprising after all when you consider a Robert Half International poll which showed that two out of three men and women said they would be willing to reduce their salaries an average of 15 percent in order to gain more family and personal time.

When collections negotiator Patricia Lineman's business grew to ten employees, she finally realized she had to move to an outside office. She found, however, that she didn't like the added pressure, inconvenience, and responsibility of supervising others. She discovered she wasn't a manager at heart, so she consciously decided to cut back her business, close her office, and return to the more comfortable lifestyle of being a one-person home-based business working one-to-one with her clients. She's making less money, but enjoying it and her life a lot more.

But moving home and limiting growth doesn't have to result in less income. Technical writer David Treweek found he actually could make money by limiting his growth. He discovered that in order to provide salaries, desks, and equipment for two writers in rented outside office space he had to double his gross income to retain 20 to 23 percent profit. Instead, he chose to make more by doing less business.

12. Raise your prices; refer or franchise additional business. Raising your prices can enable you to continue your income growth without adding clients, personnel, or space. Or instead, consider referring business you can no longer accommodate to a competitor for a referral fee. When you consider that marketing costs can run 40 percent in many businesses, a referral fee is not unreasonable. Licensing or offering a franchise to others to carry out your business in other geographical locations is another way of expanding financially without necessarily expanding your space.

TIP: Make Sure People Can Still Find You

If you do set up a new office outside your home and decide to change your phone number, lawyer Gerry Elman advises that you pay to keep the old number and have it automatically forwarded to your new one. Also, he suggests, if your expansion plans involve a change in the name of your business, pay for a second telephone listing with your old name so that when people look under your old business name, they'll find you there.

A Future of New Options

Establishing the right work arrangement at home is often like raising a family— you have to keep making adjustments for new developments, some of which can be foreseen and some of which can't. If, like many we've met with, your intention is to continue pursuing your career to the fullest and to do so from the luxury of your own home, combining a little determination with a little ingenuity should enable you to find a way to do both.

With the desire to work from home growing at such an accelerating pace and the cost and size of sophisticated office equipment shrinking every year, we're beginning to see new housing and community developments that open new options for those who want to pursue thriving careers from home.

So often when people talk about the "electronic cottage" of the future, science-fiction movies come to mind, with images of chrome and steel modules, hermetically sealed and controlled by a master computer. Consider the possibility that the electronic cottage will not look like that at all. In our opinion, the electronic cottages of the future will look more like Rohn and Jeri Engh's wood cabin on their farm in isolated Osceola, Wisconsin, where they produce a newsletter for photographers; or like Doug Hansen's second-floor apartment in West Hollywood where he writes screenplays for a living; or like Vicki McLane's ranch-style house in a Kansas City, Missouri, suburb where she works for Hallmark Cards.

Gradual updating of zoning ordinances and continuing telecommunications advances will make it increasingly possible for you to live and work in almost any location of your choice.

New living arrangements like "Hoffices," part of a real estate development in Oak Creek, Wisconsin, "Workman's Mill" in Frederick, Maryland, and Shopkeeper Homes in La Jolla, California (see fig. 24-1), allow families to conduct business from first-floor offices and shops while living in pleasant condos above. In the future we may see the emergence of rural housing developments linked electronically to urban metropolises. Perhaps ultimately our home offices will be staffed by robotic employees who will tend to both our home and office needs.

Before laughing too hard about such possibilities, consider a few of these "famous last words" compiled by the editors of *Science* magazine:

"What can be more palpably absurd than the prospect held out of locomotives traveling twice as fast as stagecoaches?" (*The Quarterly Review*, 1825)

"The ordinary 'horseless carriage' is at present a luxury for the wealthy; and although its price will probably fall in the near future, it will never, of course, come into as common use as the bicycle." (*The Literary Digest*, 1889)

". . . as a means of rapid transit, aerial navigation could not begin to compete with the railroad." William Baxter, Jr. (*Popular Science*, 1901)

"While theoretically and technically television may be feasible, commercially and financially, I consider it an impossibility, a development of which we need not waste time dreaming." (Scientist and inventor Lee De Forest, 1926)

So who knows what lies ahead? Much of it will be in or beyond the realm of our imagination today. Perhaps orbiting space stations will be among the home offices of tomorrow. As an open-collar worker, you could find yourself ideally prepared for the new frontier of living and traveling in space.

Whatever lies ahead, in the meantime you can enjoy a comfortable, reward-

Figure 24-1. Shopkeeper homes like these in La Jolla, California, are an example of a new living arrangement the future may bring as more people work from home.

ing, and productive life by working from home. And in moments of frustration, when the cat has eaten the corner of your latest report, you haven't seen another human being in four days, or your two-year-old has just hung up the phone in the middle of a business call, take heart.

Remember why you decided to work from home. Consider the overhead you're saving. Reflect on what you can do in the time that used to be wasted commuting. Think of the tax benefits of working from home. Remind yourself how it feels to be there watching your children grow. Recognize how much more control you have, not only of business but of your life in general. Remember, most of all, that working from home is a ticket to realizing a new American dream for personal and professional success, a way to have your cake and eat it too! Someone's going to do it; it might as well be you!

Resources

Books

The Franchise Advantage: Make It Work for You. Donald D. Boroian and Patrick J. Boroian. Chicago: Prism Creative Group, Ltd., 1987.
The Franchise Option. William Ginalski and DeBanks Henward III. Washington, D.C.: International Franchise Association, 1987.
Franchising. Robert Justis and Richard Judd. Cincinnati: Southwest Publishing Co., 1989.
Franchising: A Planning and Sales Compliance Guide. Norman Axelrad and Louis Rudnick. Chicago: Commerce Clearing House, 1987.

Associations

International Franchise Association. 1350 New York Avenue, N.W., 900, Washington, D.C. 20005; (202) 628-8000.

APPENDIX

∙∙∙∙∙∙∙∙∙∙∙∙∙∙∙∙∙∙∙∙∙∙∙∙∙∙∙∙∙

Home Businesses from A to Z

* = businesses covered in *Best Home Businesses for the 90s*
† = businesses covered in *Making Money with Your Computer at Home*
Some businesses are covered in both.

†Abstracting service
Accounting service
Advertising
  Agency
  Brokering
Aerial photography
Aerobics classes
Affixing company logos
  to baseball caps
Alarm service
Animal show judging
†Answering/voice mail
  service
Antique
  Locating service
  Repair
  Refinishing
  Restoration
Apartment finders
Appliance
  Refinishing
  Repair
Appraising
  Personal collections
  Precious metals
Architectural
  Designer
  Model maker
Art
  Instruction
  Repairs

Show promoting
Studio
†*Association
  management service
†Astrology charting
  service
Athletic equipment
  repair
Auctioneer—real
  estate
*Auditing services
Audio/video
  Consultant
  Editing
  Engineering
  Production
Auto
  Brokering
  *Detailing
  Upholstery cleaning
Baby-sitting
  Agency
  Referral service
  †Backup service
Badge- and Button-
  making
Balloon
  Decoration
  Bouquet delivery
  service
Bartering service

Basement
  Cleaning
  Finishing
  Waterproofing
Bed and breakfast
  inn
Bicycle
  Custom construction
  Repair
*Bill auditing
†Billing and invoicing
  service
Book
  Indexing service
  Packager
Booking agency
  Entertainers
  Models
†Bookkeeping service
Breakfast-in-bed service
Bridal
  Consulting
  Makeup service
Broadcast consulting
  engineer
Bronze work
Building design
Building inspection
  service
Building restoration and
  preservation

Business broker
Business cards—
   customized
   (holograms, "pop-
   outs," photographs)
Business consultant for
   small and start-up
   businesses
*Business network
   organizer
†*Business plan writer
Business services for
   small communities
Button sales
Cabinet making
Cake decorating
Calligraphy
Camp consultant
Caning repair
Car pool service
Career counseling
Carpet and Rugs
   Cleaning
   Dyeing
Catering
Ceiling repair
Certificate hand lettering
Chartering services
   Airplanes
   Yachts
Chess instruction
Chimney sweeping
Claims adjuster
Cleaning services
   Aquariums
   Ceilings
   Floors
   Ships
   Signs from store
      windows
   Venetian blinds
†Clip art service
†Clipping service
Closet
   Design
   Organizing
Clothing alterations
Clothing rental
   Bridal gowns
   Maternity outfits
Clown for parties,
   promotions
Coin-operated equipment
   maintenance
   Dry cleaning

Laundries
   TV
*†Collection agency
Color consulting
Computer
   Animation
   Backup service
   †Bulletin boards
      service
   †*Consulting
   Debugging
   Graphics
   †*Programming
   †Repair
   Room installation
   †Sales and service
   †Training
   †*Tutoring
Concierge services
Condiminium
   management service
†Construction
   estimating
Consultant broker
Contest organizer
Copying services
   Audiotapes
   Computer disks
   Photocopies
   Videotapes
†*Copywriter
Costume rental
†Coupon newspaper
   publishing
†Creativity consultant
Dancing instruction
Data
   †Conversion service
   Entry overload
   Processing service
Databased entry and
   maintenance
†Databased marketing
   service
Dating service
Day care
   Adults
   *Children
Debt negotiation service
Debugging software
Deed investigator
Delivery services
   Candy
   Flowers
   Parcels

Dental practice
   management
   consulting
†*Desktop publishing
   services
†*Desktop video services
†Diet counseling and
   planning service
†Disk copying service
Discount contracting
Disk formatting service
*Disk jockey service
Dispatcher
Dog grooming
Doll
   Clothing making
   House building
   Repair
†Drafting service
Dressmaking
Duplication service
   *Audiotapes
   †Computer media
   *Videotapes
Economics research
*Editorial services
Educational
   Consulting
   Record-keeping service
Electric hair removal
Embroidery
†Employee manual
   development
*Employee training
Employment application
   checking
Employment agency
Enameling repair
Energy consulting
Entertainment
   Belly dancing
   Children's parties
   Magic
   Mime
   Musician
   Singing
Environmental
   consultant
   Pollution control
   Recycling
   Toxic waste
*Errand service
Escort service
Escrow temporary agency
Etiquette consultant

Event clearinghouse
Executive director services
*Executive search service
Exercise and physical fitness instruction
†Expert brokering service
*Export agent
Eyesight trainer
*Facialist/skin-care specialist
Family historian
Fashion consultant
†Fax-on-demand services
Film-processing service
Financial
  Consulting
  †Information service
  †Management service
  Planning
Fishing and hunting information
*Fitness trainer
Flower arranging services
Food
  Crafting
  Mail-order sales
  Service management
  Special-diet delivery
†Form design service
Fountain pen repair
Free classified advertising newspaper
Fund-raising
Furniture
  Custom made
  Repair
  Stripping
Garage door service
Garden care
Generating sales leads
Genealogy research service
Gift
  *Basket service
  Buying service
  Wrapping service
Glass
  Etching
  Repair
Goldsmith
Gold handicapping service
Gourmet cooking school

Government
  Bid notification service
  Form-filling service
  Lobbyist
  Procurement consultant
Grant writing
Graphic designer
Greeting card
  Artist
  Writer
Gunsmith
Hair salon
Handicraft making
Handwriting analyst
*Hauling service
Health enhancement product sales
Herb growing
Home
  Delivery beauty service
  Historian
  *Inspector
  Repair service
  Security analysis service
  Security patrol service
Horseback riding instruction
Hospital utilization authorization service
House
  *Cleaning service
  Painter
  Portrait painting
  Sitting
Housing consultant
How are you today calling service
*Image consultant
Importer
Independent insurance adjuster
†Indexing service
Indoor environmental tester
†*Information search and retrieval service
*In-home health care
Instructional design
Insurance agent
Insurance inspection and audits
*Interior decorator

Interpreting service
Interviewer—print, radio, or TV
Inventor
†Inventory control services for businesses
Inventory household effects
Investment
  Advisor referral service
  Counseling
Janitorial service
Jewelry
  Appraisal
  Design
  Making
  Repair
Job placement and referral service
Kit building
Knitting
  By hand or machine
  Instruction
  Selling supplies
Lactation consultant
Landscape
  Contractor
  Design
Language instruction
Laser cartridge remanufacturing
Laundry services
Law
  †Library management
  Office management consultant
Lawn care service
Lawyers' aide/freelance paralegal
*Leak detection service
Lecturing/public speaking
†Legal-transcript digesting
†Legal transcription service
Letter writing
Lighting consultant
Library management
Limited-edition book sales
Limousine service
Lingerie sales
Liquidated goods broker
List broker

Literary agent
Leatherwork
Loan
  Broker
  Packager
Locksmithing
Lost pet location service
Mail forwarding service
*Mail-order business
†*Mailing list services
  Compilation and rental
  Maintenance
Mailing service
  Hand addressing
  Presorting
Makeup artist/consultant
*Management consultant
Manicurist to go
Mantel repair
*Manufacturer's agent
Manufacturing specialty
  products
Manuscript editing
†Market mapping service
Marketing
  Consultant
  Research
Marriage broker/
  matchmaker
Massage
  Instruction
  To go
Mechanic to go
Mediator
Medical
  †*Billing service
  *Claims assistance
  Management
    consultant
  Records review
  †*Transcription service
†*Meeting and event
  planning
Memory training
Messenger service
Miniature items for
  collectors
Mobile communications
  service
Mobile services—see list
Model making
Monitoring TV, radio
Monogramming
†Mortgage auditing
  service

†Multimedia production
  service
Murals
Music
  Arranging and
    composition
  Instruction
  Instrument repair
*900 number-audiotext
  service
Name creating consultant
Nameplate
  Engraving
  Making
Needlepoint
  Instruction
  Supplies sales
*†Newsletter publishing
New Age crafts
  Channeling
  Numerology
  Psychic reading
Nursery of rare and
  unusual plants
Nurses' registry
Nutrition
  Analysis
  Consulting
Office automation
  consultant
Office lunch service
Order fulfillment service
Out-of-town business
  service
Package design and
  development
Paging service
Paralegal
Parent guidance
  instruction
Parking consulting
Parking lot maintenance
Party
  Entertainment
  Planning
  Production
Patio construction
†Payroll preparation
  service
†People tracing service
Personal services broker
Personnel consulting
Pest control service
Pets
  Breeding

Identification service
*Sitting
Portraits
Training
Photography
  Blow-up service
  Color correction,
    retouching, restoring
  Unique local landmarks
Picture framing
Plant
  Care
  Interior plant design
  Doctor
  Rent-a-plant service
Plastics
  Laminating
  Recycling
Political campaign
  management
Postmark service
Portfolio preparation
  service
Potter
Power wash service
Presentation support
Pricing and estimating
  consulting and
  service
Printing—quick
Printing broker
*Private investigator
Process server
*Professional organizer
*Professional practice
  consultant
†Professional practice
  management
*Proofreading services
†Property management
  service
†Proposal and grant
  writer
Public opinion
  Analysis
  Polling and surveys
†*Public relations service
Publicity service
†Publishing
  Books
  Catalogs
  Directories
  Guides
  Newsletters
  Small lots

Purchasing agent service
Quilting
  Making
  Selling by catalog
Rare book finding service
Reading service
Real estate
  *Appraisal
  †Brochure service
  Sales
Record searching service
Recording studio
Record-keeping service
†*Referral service
  Tradespeople
  Roommates
Relocation consulting
*Reminder service
Remote facility
  management
Rental services
  Books
  Office equipment
  Pictures
  Robots
*Repair service
  Appliances
  Mobile homes
  Shavers
  Snow blowers
  Umbrellas
  Watches
Repossession service
Research analysis
Research service
Restaurant consultant
*Restoration services
  Photographs
  Furniture
†*Résumé writing service
Retirement counseling
†*Reunion planning
Reupholstering
Reweaving
Roof inspector
*Rubber stamp business
Safety consulting
Sales training
†Scanning service
Script preparation service
Scriptwriter
Secondhand products
  broker
Second medical opinion
  referral service

*Security consultant
†Self-publishing
Selling
  Ideas to businesses
  Odd lots of
    merchandise
  Old currency and stock
Seminar
  Leader
  Producer
  Promoter
Septic tank pumping
Sewing and tailoring
Sewing machine repair
Sharpening services
  Ice skates
  Knives
  Lawn mowers
  Saws
Shopping services
Show promoter for
  consumers or trade
Sightseeing guide service
†*Sign-making service
Singing telegram service
Skylight installation
Small-business
  convenience services
Software
  †Publishing
  Writer
  †Location service
Songwriting for special
  occasions
Sound studio
Specialty retail shop
Speakers bureau
Speech
  Instruction
  Writer
†Sports league statistics
Square dance
  Calling
  Instruction
Statue repair
Stock market analysis
Stock portfolio
  management
Store-opening service
Stuffed animal vending
Swimming pool/spa
  maintenance service
Tax preparation
Taxidermy
†*Technical writer

Telephone repair service
Telephone sales
†*Temporary help service
Tennis instruction
Terrace
  Design
  Repair
Textile design
Tool repair
*Tour operator
Toymaking
Trade association
  operation
Trade show exhibit
  builder
Training broker
Transcribing
  †*Court reporter notes
  Radio and TV
    programs
*Transcript digestive
  service
Translation service
Travel agency
Tree service
Tropical fish care
Trophy
  Engraving
  Making
†T-shirt design service
Tutoring
  Academic
  Achievement tests
Typesetting
Upholstery
  Cleaning
  Installation and repair
Urban planning
†Used computer broker
Vending machine
  Operation
  Repair
Venture capital broker
Video
  Buying service
  Editing
  Production
  Transfer service
Videography
Vinyl repairing service
Visiting service
Wake-up service
Wardrobe consulting
Washing services
Water treatment service

Weaving—using a
    computer
*Wedding makeup artist
*Wedding consultant
Weight loss instruction
Welding and soldering
Window-washing service

†*Word processing/
    secretarial service
Writing
    Company newsletters
    Computer
      documentation
    Trade publications

Yacht broker
Yellow page brokering
Yoga instructor
Zipper repair

INDEX